GLOBAL ISSUES

2020 Edition

Sara Miller McCune founded SAGE Publishing in 1965 to support the dissemination of usable knowledge and educate a global community. SAGE publishes more than 1000 journals and over 800 new books each year, spanning a wide range of subject areas. Our growing selection of library products includes archives, data, case studies and video. SAGE remains majority owned by our founder and after her lifetime will become owned by a charitable trust that secures the company's continued independence.

Los Angeles | London | New Delhi | Singapore | Washington DC | Melbourne

GLOBAL ISSUES

SELECTIONS FROM *CQ RESEARCHER*

iStock.com

2020 EDITION

FOR INFORMATION:

CQ Press

An Imprint of SAGE Publications, Inc.

2455 Teller Road

Thousand Oaks, California 91320

E-mail: order@sagepub.com

SAGE Publications Ltd.

1 Oliver's Yard

55 City Road

London EC1Y 1SP

United Kingdom

SAGE Publications India Pvt. Ltd.

B 1/I 1 Mohan Cooperative Industrial Area

Mathura Road, New Delhi 110 044

India

SAGE Publications Asia-Pacific Pte. Ltd.

18 Cross Street #10-10/11/12

China Square Central

Singapore 048423

Printed in the United States of America

ISBN: 978-1-5443-7447-5

This book is printed on acid-free paper.

Acquisitions Editor: Anna Villarruel

Editorial Assistant: Lauren Younker

Production Editor: Andrew Olson

Typesetter: Hurix Digital

Proofreader: Sally M. Scott

Cover Designer: Anupama Krishnan

Marketing Manager: Jennifer Jones

SUSTAINABLE FORESTRY INITIATIVE

Certified Chain of Custody

Promoting Sustainable Forestry

www.sfiprogram.org

SFI-01028

19 20 21 22 23 10 9 8 7 6 5 4 3 2 1

Contents

ANNOTATED CONTENTS vii

PREFACE xiii

CONTRIBUTORS xv

CONFLICT, SECURITY, AND TERRORISM

1. **The Israeli–Palestinian Conflict** 1
   Background 10
   Current Situation 17
   Outlook 22
   Notes 23
   Bibliography 27

2. **Saudi Arabia's Uncertain Future** 31
   Background 39
   Current Situation 47
   Outlook 50
   Notes 51
   Bibliography 56

3. **Turmoil in Central America** 59
   Background 66
   Current Situation 74
   Outlook 77
   Notes 77
   Bibliography 82

4. **The 5G Revolution** 85
   Background 87

Current Situation 92
Outlook 95
Notes 96
Bibliography 98
The Next Step 99

INTERNATIONAL POLITICAL ECONOMY

5. **Africa in Transition** 103
   Background 110
   Current Situation 117
   Outlook 121
   Notes 122
   Bibliography 126

6. **India Today** 129
   Background 136
   Current Situation 144
   Outlook 148
   Notes 148
   Bibliography 151

7. **The Future of Cash** 153
   Background 161
   Current Situation 168
   Outlook 171
   Notes 172

Bibliography 177
The Next Step 178

8. **European Union at a Crossroads** **181**
Background 189
Current Situation 197
Outlook 200
Notes 201
Bibliography 204
The Next Step 205

9. **U.S. Foreign Policy in Transition** **209**
Background 217
Current Situation 226
Outlook 230
Notes 230
Bibliography 235
The Next Step 236

RELIGIOUS AND HUMAN RIGHTS

10. **Future of Puerto Rico** **239**
Background 247
Current Situation 254
Outlook 258
Notes 258
Bibliography 261

11. **Global Tourism Controversies** **265**
Background 272
Current Situation 280
Outlook 283
Notes 283
Bibliography 286

12. **Global Population Pressures** **289**
Background 297
Current Situation 304

Outlook 307
Notes 307
Bibliography 311

13. **Algorithms and Artificial Intelligence** **313**
Background 321
Current Situation 327
Outlook 329
Notes 331
Bibliography 335

ENVIRONMENTAL ISSUES

14. **Climate Change and National Security** **337**
Background 345
Current Situation 352
Outlook 356
Notes 356
Bibliography 360

15. **Global Fishing Controversies** **363**
Background 370
Current Situation 378
Outlook 381
Notes 382
Bibliography 386
The Next Step 387

16. **Extreme Weather** **389**
Background 397
Current Situation 404
Outlook 408
Notes 409
Bibliography 415
The Next Step 417

Annotated Contents

CONFLICT, SECURITY, AND TERRORISM
The Israeli–Palestinian Conflict

The long-sought goal of an Arab-Israeli peace settlement is looking more distant than ever. President Trump's decision in December 2017 to formally recognize Jerusalem as Israel's capital and relocate the U.S. Embassy there infuriated Palestinian leaders while heartening conservative Israeli Prime Minister Benjamin Netanyahu. Trump defended his decision as a recognition of reality and has vowed to work toward a settlement in the region. But Jerusalem is hallowed ground for both Arabs and Israelis, and critics say Trump has moved so far in Israel's favor that the United States can no longer be a neutral broker between the two sides. Both Netanyahu, under investigation for alleged corruption, and aging Palestinian leader Mahmoud Abbas, widely accused of stifling Arab democratic rights, have uncertain political futures. Frustrated with the dimming outlook for peace, more than a quarter of Palestinians favor armed struggle.

Saudi Arabia's Uncertain Future

U.S.-Saudi relations are warming after years of conflict with the Obama administration. Citing mutual opposition to the Sunni kingdom's Shiite arch-enemy, Iran, President Trump and the Saudi king struck a $350 billion arms deal in 2017 aimed at fighting terrorism and creating American jobs. But critics warn that Trump's unflinching support for the kingdom could pull the United States into one of the regional proxy conflicts between the Saudis and Iran. Meanwhile, the Saudis are seeking U.S. investors for high-tech and renewable energy ventures to help diversify the oil-dependent economy. They also are considering selling part of the massive, state-owned Aramco oil company to outside investors, which would open a window on the kingdom's secretive finances. To lure international support and investments, a new, 32-year-old crown prince is pushing social and economic reforms in the religiously conservative society. But human rights groups say the Saudis oppress dissidents at home and continue to fund extremist groups that share their hatred of Iran.

Turmoil in Central America

Anti-government protests have erupted in four Central American countries, aimed at leaders of a region long plagued by political corruption, gang violence, drug smuggling, poverty and weak law enforcement. Homicide rates in the Northern Triangle—Guatemala, Honduras and El Salvador—are among the world's highest, and the increasingly authoritarian regime of President Daniel Ortega threatens stability in Nicaragua. The demonstrations are part of a fledgling anti-corruption movement in which protesters, prosecutors and investigative commissions have recommended that dozens of officials be jailed. But strongmen such as Ortega and Guatemalan President Jimmy Morales are pushing back, triggering even more dissent. Tens of thousands of Central Americans—many of them unaccompanied minors—have in recent years tried to flee to the United States, prompting the Obama and Trump administrations to crack down on undocumented immigration along the U.S. southern border. Meanwhile, the United States has become increasingly concerned about China's growing political influence in Central America.

The 5G Revolution

5G, the fifth generation of cellular technology, promises to transform societies around the world by vastly expanding the number of devices connected in cyberspace and increasing the speed at which those devices communicate, experts say. But as the United States competes with China and other countries for dominance in developing 5G technology, new concerns are emerging about how to prevent cyberthieves and hostile foreign governments from stealing consumers' data or hacking and disabling critical infrastructure. Trump administration officials see Chinese technology giant Huawei, for example, as a

potential security threat to 5G systems globally. The U.S. telecom industry and federal regulators promise 5G networks will be safe from cyberattack, but critics note that the administration already has repealed an Obama-era requirement designed to protect those networks. Other experts worry that the new technology—still years away for most Americans—will leave behind minority, low-income and rural customers, saying telecom companies will prioritize areas where they get the best return on 5G investments.

INTERNATIONAL POLITICAL ECONOMY
Africa in Transition

Strong economic growth, driven by resource-rich Angola, Nigeria and South Africa, has helped sub-Saharan Africa shed its image as a war-torn region plagued by famine, disease and political volatility. In recent years, amid a surge in Chinese investment, a new "Africa Rising" narrative portrayed the region's 46 countries as making impressive economic progress, with a growing middle class and rising democratic aspirations. That narrative became less persuasive, however, after world commodity prices began to fall in 2014. In addition, some autocrats, while professing democratic ideals, have been suppressing human rights and clinging to power. Like the rest of the world, African countries face the long-term consequences of climate change, which could erode economic progress and the quality of life on the continent. And automated manufacturing technologies such as robotics pose a challenge to the labor force. Analysts say the next several years will pose a crucial test: Can African economies innovate quickly enough to deal with increasing urbanization, rapid population growth and a big gap between the rich and the poor?

India Today

India has the world's fastest growing economy, a status experts believe will continue for at least the next three years and possibly longer. Since taking power in 2014, Prime Minister Narendra Modi has overhauled the country's tax structure, modernized bankruptcy laws and cracked down on corruption. With globalization, India's economy has produced more than 100 billionaires, and the middle class has expanded significantly. But major challenges confront Modi as he seeks another five-year term in 2019: The sprawling nation of 1.3 billion people remains riven by differences in income, education, religion, language and caste. Income disparity is rising, and one in five Indians lives in extreme poverty. In foreign affairs, India-Pakistan relations remain tense, and India worries that China, its economically and militarily stronger neighbor to the north, is undermining New Delhi's influence in South Asia. How India performs economically in the future will help determine not only the fate of its impoverished masses but also the country's place as a regional and global power.

The Future of Cash

While cash continues to circulate widely in the United States, many consumers, as well as many business experts, believe paper money will soon become antiquated. Advocates of a cashless society point to countries such as Sweden and to some Chinese cities where mobile payment applications are supplanting paper currency. In the United States, digital payment systems are helping to change consumer habits, and some businesses have stopped accepting cash. Advocates of a cashless society argue that credit and debit cards and digital payment methods are efficient and transparent and inhibit financial crimes. Because cash is anonymous and largely untraceable, it can facilitate illicit activities such as tax evasion and money laundering. Critics of the cashless trend raise concerns regarding privacy, security and equality. They argue that cash lacks the fees associated with cards or electronic money transfers and that cashless businesses discriminate against people who must, or choose to, rely on cash. In the face of this criticism, some businesses that went cashless are reversing course.

European Union at a Crossroads

Amid the United Kingdom's Brexit crisis and a surge in populism throughout Europe, the 28-nation European Union (EU) is facing renewed questions about its future. Nationalist-populist governments rule in Italy, Hungary, Poland and Greece, and populist parties are posing stiff challenges in France and Germany, the EU's most powerful members. A slowing economy and worsening relations with the Trump administration, which calls the EU a foe on trade, present additional challenges to the Union. But many political analysts believe the EU remains strong, noting that the U.K.'s expected departure from the federation has chastened foes of European integration and led them to drop their drives for Brexit-style secessions in other countries. The EU also has drastically cut illegal migration from Africa and the Mideast—a major source of populists' anger. Nevertheless, many experts said 2019's elections for the EU's Parliament would be crucial. They predicted a strong showing for populists, who would be in a position to keep the EU from becoming more powerful.

US Foreign Policy in Transition

After more than 70 years as the standard-bearer of multilateral engagement and constructive diplomacy, the United States is undergoing a dramatic foreign policy shift that has led some to question whether the nation is giving up its global authority. Departing from the approach of previous presidents, who tended to cooperate with allies through multilateral agreements to promote democracy, free trade and environmental protection, President Trump is championing an "America First" policy aimed at protecting U.S. jobs and interests. Preferring to rely on his instincts and personal rapport rather than professional diplomats, he has ended U.S. participation in several major international treaties, praised authoritarian leaders and waged a trade war against key economic partners. Trump's supporters say he is using America's economic and political might to its advantage and trying to prod uncooperative allies—particularly in Europe—to do more to protect their own security interests. But critics say Trump's conduct has isolated the United States internationally and undermined the nation's claim to moral leadership.

RELIGIOUS AND HUMAN RIGHTS
Future of Puerto Rico

Puerto Rico is still reeling from two devastating hurricanes in September 2017 and an 11-year recession, which have renewed a bitter debate over the U.S. territory's political status. Hurricanes Irma and Maria damaged or destroyed nearly 500,000 homes and battered the antiquated electric system, leaving millions without power or shelter and badly hurting the already weak economy. Four months later, 40 percent of Puerto Ricans still lacked electricity, and recovery was stymied by what critics call mismanagement of the government-owned utility and the Trump administration's indifference. Meanwhile, Puerto Rico declared bankruptcy before the storms after saying it could not make payments on its $73 billion public debt. In Maria's aftermath, more than 100,000 Puerto Ricans have migrated to Florida or elsewhere, and demographers say the island could lose 14 percent of its population by the end of 2019, further weakening its economy. The struggles have revived debate about whether Puerto Rico should become the 51st state. Advocates say statehood would reinvigorate the island's economy, but opponents say Puerto Rico should focus on economic and political reforms instead.

Global Tourism Controversies

Global tourism is growing rapidly, propelled by rising prosperity, cheap airfares and the ease of online booking. But many destinations, from the canals of Venice to Arizona's Grand Canyon, are struggling to accommodate hordes of visitors. In Amsterdam and Barcelona, residents are blaming "overtourism" for congestion, pollution and escalating rents, and U.S. national park superintendents say crowds and vehicles are damaging precious sites such as Yellowstone and Yosemite. But the travel industry and many government officials say curbing tourism would harm the economy. The industry accounts for some 118 million jobs worldwide and a significant percentage of economic activity in many places. To deal with tourism's pressures, some destinations are limiting the number of visitors, while others are fining drunken behavior, raising tourist taxes, restricting short-term vacation rentals or steering visitors to less crowded sites. Meanwhile, critics say "sustainable tourism," a niche aimed at protecting a locality's environment and cultural heritage, can have negative consequences by spawning development that changes a destination's character.

Global Population Pressures

The world's population, currently 7.6 billion, is expected to peak later this century at 11.2 billion, and possibly much more, before slowly declining. Countries such as Japan and Germany already are seeing declines, but others, such as Niger and India, are projected to explode in population in coming years. Some experts downplay the potential effects of a rising global count, but many say strains on natural resources will be intense, leading to conflicts over land, water, food and energy, and sparking mass migrations from poorer to wealthier regions. Yet experts differ on how best to manage the world's population pressures. Some say that with greater access to contraception, women in developing countries will choose to have fewer children. Others say a better approach is to conserve precious natural resources by reducing personal consumption. Meanwhile, the Trump administration, following through on a campaign promise, has cut off U.S. funding for international family planning programs, triggering an outcry from some aid organizations.

Algorithms and Artificial Intelligence

Algorithms increasingly shape modern life, helping Wall Street to decide stock trades, Netflix to recommend movies and judges to dispense justice. But critics say algorithms—the seemingly inscrutable computational tools that help give artificial intelligence (AI) the ability to "think" and "learn"—can lead to skewed results and sometimes social harm. AI might help mortgage companies decide whom to lend to, but qualified borrowers can be rejected if the underlying algorithms are faulty. Companies might use AI to screen job applicants, but skilled talent can be turned away if the algorithms reflect racial or gender bias. Moreover, the use of algorithms is raising difficult questions about who—if anyone—is liable when AI results in injury. The technology is even stirring fears of an AI apocalypse in which computers become so powerful and autonomous that they threaten humankind. Some experts want the federal government to strictly regulate AI to ensure it is not misused, but critics fear more rules would stifle the technology.

ENVIRONMENTAL ISSUES
Climate Change and National Security

U.S. military officials increasingly view climate change as a "threat multiplier," a factor that can aggravate poverty, political instability and social tensions. That, in turn, could foster terrorism and other forms of global violence while impairing America's military effectiveness. Rising seas, due mainly to Arctic ice melting, already threaten Naval Station Norfolk in Virginia, the world's largest naval base; dozens of other coastal installations also are at risk. Meanwhile, drought in some regions and record rainfall in others have forced millions of people to migrate across borders, adding to tensions in northern Africa, the Middle East and Southeast Asia. Defense Secretary James Mattis said climate change is affecting the stability of areas where U.S. troops are operating. President Trump, who has labeled climate change a "hoax," now says he has an "open mind" on the issue. Some politicians and economists argue that the real danger to U.S. security lies in the erosion of jobs, trade and industrial productivity caused by the costs of unnecessary federal environmental regulations.

Global Fishing Controversies

Scientists warn that industrial-scale fishing is depleting the world's stocks of tuna, cod and other sea life, making it harder for small-scale fishermen in developing countries to eke out a living and raising alarms that overfishing threatens entire species. At the same time, the ocean-warming effects of climate change are driving some species, such as lobster, to cooler waters, upending long-established commercial fishing patterns. Studies have found that one-third of species are overfished—up from 10 percent in 1974—often by trawlers outfitted with high-tech fish-finding tools such as sonar and drones and equipped with gear that can haul in thousands of fish at a time. Diminishing stocks have led to calls for a ban on fishing on the high seas and the establishment of protected zones off coastlines. But fishing industry representatives argue that the migratory habits of fish would make bans ineffective, and they warn that restrictions could put thousands of commercial fishers out of work.

Extreme Weather

Climate scientists say that rising global temperatures caused by greenhouse gas emissions are making some extreme weather events increasingly likely and severe. They predict that heat waves, wildfires, hurricanes and other weather-related disasters will continue to set records and send damage costs soaring, even as countries around the world pledge to reduce emissions in response to global warming. Climate change skeptics, including President Trump and some conservatives, say fears that carbon emissions are making severe weather more frequent and more destructive are largely groundless, and administration officials are taking steps to minimize the role that climate science plays in setting government policies. Recent trends in extreme weather have led many experts to ask whether initiatives such as the financially troubled National Flood Insurance Program should continue to subsidize repeated rebuilding in disaster-prone areas. Some experts believe people living in such areas should be encouraged to leave. Others disagree, saying people have the right to live where they choose.

Preface

In this pivotal era of international policymaking, scholars, students, practitioners and journalists seek answers to such critical questions as: Are cashless payment policies discriminatory? Is a European army a realistic prospect? Is the United States relinquishing its global supremacy? Students must first understand the facts and contexts of these and other global issues if they are to analyze and articulate well-reasoned positions.

The 2020 edition of *Global Issues* provides comprehensive and unbiased coverage of today's most pressing global problems. This edition is a compilation of 16 recent reports from *CQ Researcher*, a weekly policy brief that unpacks difficult concepts and provides balanced coverage of competing perspectives. Each article analyzes past, present and possible political maneuvering, is designed to promote in-depth discussion and further research and helps readers formulate their own positions on crucial international issues.

This collection is organized into four subject areas that span a range of important international policy concerns: conflict, security and terrorism; international political economy; religious and human rights; and environmental issues. *Global Issues* is a valuable supplement for courses on world affairs in political science, geography, economics and sociology. Citizens, journalists and business and government leaders also turn to it to become better informed on key issues, actors and policy positions.

CQ RESEARCHER

CQ Researcher was founded in 1923 as *Editorial Research Reports* and was sold primarily to newspapers as a research tool. The magazine was renamed and redesigned in 1991 as *CQ Researcher*. Today, students are its primary audience. While still used by hundreds of journalists and newspapers, many of which reprint portions of the reports, *Researcher*'s main subscribers are now high school, college and public libraries. In 2002, *Researcher* won the American Bar Association's coveted Silver Gavel Award for magazine excellence for a series of nine reports on civil liberties and other legal issues.

Researcher writers—all highly experienced journalists—sometimes compare the experience of writing a *Researcher* report to drafting a college term paper. Indeed, there are many similarities. Each report is as long as many term papers—about 10,000 words—and is written by one person without any significant outside help. One of the key differences is that the writers interview leading experts, scholars and government officials for each issue.

Like students, writers begin the creative process by choosing a topic. Working with *Researcher*'s editors, the writer identifies a controversial subject that has important public policy implications. After a topic is selected, the writer embarks on one to two weeks of intense research. Newspaper and magazine articles are clipped or downloaded, books are ordered and information is gathered from a wide variety of sources, including interest groups, universities and the government. Once the writers are well informed, they develop a detailed outline and begin the interview process. Each report requires a minimum of ten to fifteen interviews with academics, officials, lobbyists and people working in the field. Only after all interviews are completed does the writing begin.

CHAPTER FORMAT

Each issue of *CQ Researcher*, and therefore each selection in this book, is structured in the same way. A selection begins with an introductory overview, which is briefly explored in greater detail in the rest of the report.

The second section chronicles the most important and current debates in the field. It is structured around a number of key issues questions, such as "Should the high seas be closed to fishing?" and "Does climate change pose a global economic threat?" This section is the core of each selection. The questions raised are often highly controversial and usually the object of much argument among scholars and practitioners. Hence, the answers provided are never conclusive, but rather detail the range of opinion within the field.

Following those issue questions is the "Background" section, which provides a history of the issue being examined. This retrospective includes important legislative and executive actions and court decisions to inform readers on how current policy evolved.

Next, the "Current Situation" section examines important contemporary policy issues, legislation under consideration and action being taken. Each selection ends with an "Outlook" section that gives a sense of what new regulations, court rulings and possible policy initiatives might be put into place in the next five to ten years.

Each report contains features that augment the main text: sidebars that examine issues related to the topic, a pro/con debate by two outside experts, a chronology of key dates and events and an annotated bibliography that details the major sources used by the writer.

ACKNOWLEDGMENTS

We wish to thank many people for helping to make this collection a reality. Thomas J. Billitteri, managing editor of *CQ Researcher*, gave us his enthusiastic support and cooperation as we developed this edition. He and his talented editors and writers have amassed a first-class collection of *Researcher* articles, and we are fortunate to have access to this rich cache. We also thankfully acknowledge the advice and feedback from current readers and are gratified by their satisfaction with the book.

Some readers may be learning about *CQ Researcher* for the first time. We expect that many readers will want regular access to this excellent weekly research tool. For subscription information or a no-obligation free trial of *Researcher*, please contact CQ Press at www.cqpress.com or toll-free at 1-866-4CQ-PRESS (1-866-427-7737).

We hope that you will be pleased by the 2020 edition of *Global Issues*. We welcome your feedback and suggestions for future editions. Please direct comments to Anna Villarruel, Sponsoring Editor for International Relations, Comparative Politics, and Public Administration, CQ Press, an imprint of SAGE, 2600 Virginia Avenue, NW, Suite 600, Washington, DC 20037; or send e-mail to *Anna.Villarruel@sagepub.com*.

—*The Editors of CQ Press*

Contributors

Sarah Glazer is a London-based freelancer who contributes regularly to *CQ Researcher*. Her articles on health, education and social-policy issues also have appeared in *The New York Times* and *The Washington Post*. Her recent *CQ Researcher* reports include "Privacy and the Internet" and "Decriminalizing Prostitution." She graduated from the University of Chicago with a B.A. in American history.

Karen Foerstel is a freelance writer in Lancaster, Pa., who has worked for the Congressional Quarterly *Weekly Report* and *Daily Monitor*, *The New York Post* and *Roll Call*, a Capitol Hill newspaper. She has written two books on women in Congress, *Climbing the Hill: Gender Conflict in Congress* and *The Biographical Dictionary of Women in Congress*.

Kerry Dooley Young is a freelance writer based in Washington, D.C. She earlier worked for *Congressional Quarterly, CQ Roll* and *Bloomberg News*. She has traveled widely in Latin America.

Kristin Jensen is a freelance journalist in the Washington, D.C., area. She spent more than 22 years at *Bloomberg News*, where she covered government, politics and health care from Washington and Zurich.

Sean Lyngaas is a freelance journalist who has reported from West Africa for *The New York Times*, *The Washington Post*, the BBC and other news media. He was previously a cybersecurity reporter for FCW in Washington, D.C. He holds an M.A. from The Fletcher School of Law and Diplomacy, and a B.A. from Duke University.

Jonathan Broder is a Washington-based reporter and editor. He was a senior writer for *Newsweek*, a senior editor at *Congressional Quarterly* and served as a foreign correspondent in the Middle East, South Asia and the Far East for the *Chicago Tribune*. Broder's writing also has appeared in *The New York Times Magazine*, *The Washington Post*, *Smithsonian* and the *World Policy Journal*, among other publications. He previously reported for *CQ Researcher* on financial services deregulation and on India.

Hannah H. Kim is an independent business journalist and book ghostwriter. She is from Los Angeles and is a graduate of the Iowa Writers' Workshop.

Bill Wanlund is a freelance writer in the Washington, D.C., area. He is a former Foreign Service officer, with service in Europe, Asia, Africa and South America. He holds a journalism degree from George Washington University and has written for *CQ Researcher* on abortion, intelligence reform, the marijuana industry and climate change as a national security concern.

Barbara Mantel is a freelance writer in New York City. She has been a Kiplinger Fellow and has won several journalism awards, including the National Press Club's Best Consumer Journalism Award and the Front Page Award. She was a correspondent for NPR and the founding senior editor and producer for public radio's "Science Friday." She holds a B.A. in history and economics from the University of Virginia and an M.A. in economics from Northwestern University.

Susan Straight is a freelance writer in the Washington, D.C., area. She was a longtime book editor at *National Geographic*. She edits the Association of Science-Technology Centers' *Dimensions* magazine and has written more than 200 articles for *The Washington Post*. She holds a B.A. in English from the College of William & Mary and an M.A. in media and public affairs from George Washington University.

Patrick Marshall, a freelance policy and technology writer in Seattle, is a technology columnist for *The Seattle Times* and *Government Computer News*. He has a bachelor's degree in anthropology from the University of California, Santa Cruz, and a master's degree in international studies from the Fletcher School of Law and Diplomacy at Tufts University.

Charles P. Wallace was a foreign correspondent for 35 years, working for United Press International, the *Los Angeles Times* and *Time* magazine on virtually every continent. He won the Business Journalist of the Year award in 1999 for economic reporting on Europe. He previously reported for *SAGE Business Researcher* on the European Union.

Stephen Ornes is a freelance science and medical writer in Nashville, Tenn., whose articles have appeared in Scientific American, Discover, New Scientist, Science News for Students, Cancer Today, Physics World and other publications. His book, Math Art: Truth, Beauty, and Equations (Sterling Publishing), was published in April.

Global Issues,
2020 Edition

1

The Israeli–Palestinian Conflict

Sarah Glazer

President Trump meets with Israeli Prime Minister Benjamin Netanyahu in the Oval Office on March 5, 2018. Netanyahu faces possible bribery and corruption charges that could force a change in his government—although not necessarily one more favorable to a Palestinian state. Trump has said he hopes to broker an "ultimate deal" for Israeli-Palestinian peace based on a new U.S. plan.

From *CQ Researcher,*
April 13, 2018

President Trump upended nearly 70 years of American policy in early December 2017, when he recognized Jerusalem as Israel's capital and announced the United States would move its embassy from Tel Aviv to Jerusalem in mid-May 2018.[1]

The announcement infuriated the Palestinians, heartened the Israelis, and sparked a heated debate over its potential to prevent the revival of moribund Israeli-Palestinian peace talks and its impact on the United States' role as Mideast peacemaker.

Trump defended his decision as "a long overdue step to advance the peace process" and said it would be "folly" to keep pursuing what he termed the same old failed strategies. But critics said Trump has put the United States decisively on Israel's side against the Palestinians and likely killed the U.S. role as a neutral broker in any peace talks.[2]

The uproar comes at a crucial time in the Mideast, with experts fearing that the hopes of achieving an independent Palestinian state alongside Israel—the so-called two-state solution—are slipping away. With negotiations having accomplished little since 2008, when the two sides nearly achieved a breakthrough, Palestinian frustration has been growing. In late March 2018, Palestinian activists began protests on the border with Israel to protest Trump's Jerusalem decision and an Israeli blockade of the Gaza Strip—the thin band of Palestinian territory on the Mediterranean Sea—as well as to commemorate the suffering of Palestinians.[3]

The weekly protests, which continued into November, were frequently violent, with Palestinian protestors lobbing grenades and burning tires across the fence at Israel troops and Israeli soldiers retaliating with tear gas and gun fire. By mid-November, more than 170 Palestinians, many unarmed, had been killed under fire from Israeli army soldiers.[4]

Israel responded forcefully over the ensuing months with air strikes against installations of Hamas, the militant Palestinian group that rules the Gaza Strip, while Hamas sent rockets into Israel. On November 13, after two days of the heaviest fighting since the 2014 war, Israel and Gaza's Hamas rulers reached a cease-fire.[5]

However, the cease-fire is politically unpopular in Israel, dividing the conservative coalition government of Prime Minister Benjamin Netanyahu. Hardright, hawkish ministers who favor a militaristic response instead of a cease-fire threatened defection and are expected to challenge Netanyahu in the next election. That internal dissent presaged the possible collapse of Netanyahu's coalition and calls for early elections by his right-wing rivals. However, Netanyahu publicly opposed early elections November 18, saying they could bring an Intifada-level disaster, and appeared to have averted an abrupt dissolution of his government.[6]

While the cease-fire was holding in the days immediately following the agreement, the truce did not address the underlying issues that led to the conflict and is far from a long-term peace accord.[7]

For most Israelis, whether on the right or left, "it's not enough to have a few months of quiet; all understand there needs to be a different solution," said Noa Landau, diplomatic correspondent for the Israeli daily *Haaretz*, explaining public dissatisfaction with the cease-fire. Whether it's a military operation or a cease-fire, she said, "if it's short-term it's not a solution."[8]

For many Mideast observers, the challenges involved in reaching a longer-term peace accord are daunting. Mahmoud Abbas, head of the Palestinian Authority, and Israeli Prime Minister Benjamin Netanyahu "do not share mutual trust or intimacy, the gap between their positions is deep and both face domestic challenges from extremists at home," wrote Elie Podeh, a lecturer in Islamic and Middle Eastern studies at The Hebrew University of Jerusalem.[9]

Negotiations have long foundered on five crucial issues identified in the historic Oslo Accords of 1993, an agreement that was expected at the time to lead to a Palestinian state:

- Jerusalem's status;
- the borders of Israel and a Palestinian state;
- the arrangements for refugees;
- Jewish settlements; and
- security.

With Palestinians demanding full control over the West Bank, the Gaza Strip, and East Jerusalem—lands captured by the Israelis in the 1967 Six-Day War—talks have revolved around whether Israel would give up all or most of this territory so the Palestinians could form their own state. In exchange, the Palestinians would have promised to cease attacking Israel—a compromise commonly dubbed "land for peace."[10]

One obstacle to peace, but one that is still reversible, according to veteran American negotiators, is the growth of Jewish settlements in the West Bank and East Jerusalem, populated by religious Jews claiming a return to their historic homeland as well as Israelis seeking apartments in a crowded housing market.

As the impasse continues, both sides feel besieged. Israelis have long had to endure suicide bombings, rocket attacks from the Gaza Strip, and hostility from Palestinians (who are predominately Muslim) and neighboring Arab countries that oppose a Jewish state in the biblical land of Palestine. Jerusalem, revered home to three of the world's great faiths—Judaism, Christianity, and Islam—contains some of the world's most hallowed religious sites, including for Jews the Western Wall and for Muslims the Dome of the Rock, known in Arabic as Haram al-Sharif.

The Palestinian side, meanwhile, is struggling with intense poverty. Those Palestinians who live in Israeli occupied territories reside primarily in the Gaza Strip; the West Bank, a Delaware-sized territory bordering northeast Israel; and East Jerusalem. The Israelis have walled off most of these territories for security reasons and tightly control the movement of people and goods into and out of the West Bank and Gaza.

The Palestinian economy in Gaza is in shambles and relies on international aid to survive. In Gaza, conditions are "disastrous," according to spokesman Christopher Gunness of the United Nations Relief and Works Agency

Enemies at Close Quarters in an Ancient Tinderbox

Ground zero in the Israeli-Palestinian conflict is three slices of land nestled between the Mediterranean Sea and Jordan: the West Bank and Gaza Strip, populated mostly by Palestinians, and the state of Israel. Both sides claim Jerusalem as their capital. Israel captured East Jerusalem in 1967, and some peace plans have called for it to become the capital of a Palestinian state and West Jerusalem the Israeli capital. As peace talks have faltered through the years, the economic divide between Israelis and Palestinians has grown. Israel's per capita gross domestic product is $36,200, compared to $4,300 in the West Bank and Gaza Strip.

Israel

Area: 8,019 square miles (slightly smaller than New Jersey)

Population: 8.3 million (July 2017 est., includes the Golan Heights and East Jerusalem)

Religion: Jewish 74.7%, Muslim 17.7%, Christian 2%, Druze 1.6%, unspecified 4% (2016 est.)

Per capita GDP: $36,200 (2017 est.)

Unemployment rate: 4.3% (2017 est.)

West Bank

Area: 2,263 square miles (slightly bigger than Delaware)

Population: 2.7 million (July 2017 est.)

Religion: Muslim 80-85%, Jewish 12-14%, Christian 1-2.5%, unspecified less than 1% (2012 est.)

Per capita GDP: $4,300 (2014 est.)

Unemployment rate: 26.7% (2017 est.)

Gaza Strip

Area: 139 square miles (about twice the size of Washington, D.C.)

Population: 1.8 million (July 2017 est.)

Religion: Muslim 98.0-99.0%, Christian less than 1%, unspecified less than 1% (2012 est.)

Per capita GDP: $4,300 (2014 est.)

Unemployment rate: 26.7% (2017 est.)

Source: The World Factbook, Central Intelligence Agency, https://tinyurl.com/2h2e3k

Support for Two-State Solution Wanes

Fewer than half of Palestinians and Israeli Jews support the creation of a Palestinian state alongside Israel—a change from June 2016, when slim majorities still favored a two-state solution to the Arab-Israeli conflict. Nevertheless, both groups prefer a two-state approach over others, such as a single state with equal rights for Palestinians and Israelis or a single state with only partial rights for either group.

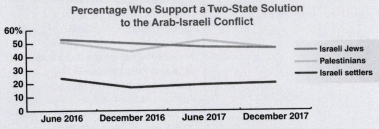

Percentage Who Support a Two-State Solution to the Arab-Israeli Conflict

— Israeli Jews
— Palestinians
— Israeli settlers

Note: Israeli Jews reside inside Israel; Israeli settlers are Jews living in the West Bank; Palestinians live in the West Bank, Gaza Strip and East Jerusalem.

Source: "Palestinian-Israeli Pulse," Tami Steinmetz Center for Peace Research, Tel Aviv University and the Palestinian Center for Policy and Survey Research, Jan. 25, 2018, https://tinyurl.com/ycx6hflg

for Palestine Refugees (UNRWA). Nearly 80 percent of residents depend on humanitarian aid. Ninety-five percent of the water is undrinkable, electricity supplies are dwindling, and the public health system is largely dysfunctional, "thanks to over a decade of blockade" by Israel and Egypt, Gunness said.[11]

Compounding Palestinian troubles are internal divisions. The Palestinian Authority (PA)—the governmental body established in 1994 to oversee majority-Palestinian areas in Gaza and the West Bank—has been feuding with the militant Islamist group Hamas since Hamas won parliamentary elections in Gaza in 2006. The two sides fought a brief war in 2007, which Hamas won. Hamas has been the de facto government in Gaza ever since then and is using the territory to attack Israel.

Given all these troubles, fewer than half of Israeli Jews and Palestinians favor a two-state solution, according to recent surveys, mainly because they do not see that approach as politically feasible. Nevertheless, a two-state solution still garners more support from both groups than the other options discussed most frequently, such as a binational state with equal rights for Palestinians and Israelis, one state in which equal rights are denied to either Palestinians or Israelis, or a single state in which the other side is expelled from the entire territory of historic Palestine.[12]

On both Israeli and Palestinian sides, today's leaders are politically vulnerable, contributing to the public's skepticism of a peaceful resolution. Abbas, the 83-year-old president of the Palestinian Authority, is in declining health. He has been accused of suppressing free speech and has not faced voters since winning a four-year term in 2005. Many Israelis, members of the Trump administration, and Mideast experts do not think Abbas is a viable negotiating partner because of his political weaknesses.[13]

Conservative Israeli Prime Minister Netanyahu faces possible indictment on bribery and corruption charges as well as elections that could force a change in government—although not necessarily one more favorable to a Palestinian state.[14]

"If Netanyahu is knocked out, a more right-wing government" could well be the result, Tel Aviv political analyst Dahlia Scheindlin predicted in April. In November, even as Netanyahu faced criticism from his hard-right coalition partners and the defection of one of them from the coalition, *Haaretz* diplomatic correspondent Landau predicted, "Chances are we'll see the exact same government after this round" of elections.[15]

Netanyahu's coalition government depends on right-wing parties that explicitly reject a two-state solution. Netanyahu told his cabinet last year he was prepared to give the Palestinians only "a state minus," where Israel would retain some territory captured in 1967 and control Palestinian air space for security reasons.[16]

Such a limited state would differ little from the status quo, according to Rashid Khalidi, a professor of modern Arab studies at Columbia University. For decades, "an imposed reality of one state" has existed over the territory in which Israelis and Palestinians live, with Israel already enjoying total military control, Khalidi said.[17]

Trump said he hopes to break through the obstacles by brokering an "ultimate deal" based on a new U.S. peace plan, whose release was promised [spring 2018] but has yet to surface. Since November [2017], a Trump-appointed team has been drafting the proposal. The team consists of the president's top negotiator, Jason D. Greenblatt, a former chief legal officer for Trump's real estate company; David M. Friedman, ambassador to Israel, Trump's bankruptcy lawyer, and a strong supporter of Jewish settlements; and Jared Kushner, the president's 37-year-old son-in-law and senior adviser. The plan's final details have not been released.[18]

Many observers say any Trump peace plan will be dead on arrival because of Palestinian anger at the Trump administration, while others speculate the administration will delay the plan's release or not release it at all. Some experts predicted that Netanyahu would push to delay release of the peace plan until after Israel's elections, because any Israeli concessions in the plan could be used by his hard-right rivals in the election to paint him as too soft on Hamas.[19]

Despite talk of impending elections that could over-turn the government, the Trump administration remains committed to releasing the peace plan within the next two months, a White House official told the Israeli newspaper *Haaretz* on November 15, 2018.[20]

The Palestinians were further angered by Trump's decision in March to appoint John Bolton, a former U.S. ambassador to the United Nations, who opposes creation of a Palestinian state, as his national security adviser; Palestinians condemned him as a "war-monger."[21]

In an interview three weeks before his appointment to the post, Bolton told *CQ Researcher* he favors a solution far outside the usual choices: Return Gaza to Egypt and split the West Bank between Israel and neighboring Jordan. Bolton said a Palestinian state is not economically viable and that Palestinians should instead be integrated into working economies in Egypt and Jordan. His solution, he said, would improve Palestinians' "prospects dramatically."

Since Trump's Jerusalem announcement, Abbas has refused to meet with administration officials. Abbas declared the United States could no longer broker peace as an impartial party. But at the United Nations in February, Abbas appeared to leave the door open for the United States to participate in multilateral peace talks that he proposed.[22]

Many advocates of a two-state solution saw Trump's statement on Jerusalem as unwisely forgoing a bargaining chip: getting the Palestinians to recognize West Jerusalem as Israel's capital in exchange for Israel recognizing East Jerusalem as Palestinian.

But Trump said he is merely recognizing "reality," because Israel's government already resides in Jerusalem. He added, "Israel is a sovereign nation with the right like every other sovereign nation to determine its own capital."[23]

In August, Trump said that as a result of his moving the American embassy to Jerusalem and recognizing the city as Israel's capital, the Palestinians "will get something very good" in the peace plan because it's now "their turn."[24]

Trump's defenders also pointed to a carefully worded sentence in his initial announcement of the embassy move that "we are not taking a position [on] the specific boundaries of Israeli sovereignty in Jerusalem, or the resolution of contested borders." Some pro-Trump analysts saw that as leaving open the possibility for East Jerusalem to become the Palestinian capital—a concession long sought by the Palestinians.

But in an unscripted moment with reporters in January, Trump said he had taken Jerusalem "off the table."[25]

That statement more accurately reflects Trump's pro-Israel intentions to hand over all of Jerusalem to Israel and effectively removed the United States as an impartial broker, say many advocates of a two-state solution. "It's a shift in the American position to, 'We are siding with Israel'" and is the "death certificate" for America's role as peacemaker, says Daniel Seidemann, founder of Terrestrial Jerusalem, a liberal, pro-peace group that tracks developments in the city that could affect peace negotiations.

Amid the controversies, here are some of the questions being debated by Israelis, Palestinians, and Americans:

Is a two-state solution still viable?

A joint Israeli-Palestinian poll released in June found a slow but steady decline in support for a two-state solution among both Palestinians and Israeli Jews over the past 10 years. From a long-standing majority in favor as recently as June 2017 among Palestinians, support has fallen to 43 percent for both groups.[26]

The main reason, according to pollsters, is declining public confidence in its feasibility. The growth of Jewish settlements on land that Palestinians want for their state is one factor. For Palestinians, President Trump's Jerusalem announcement is another, said the Palestinian Center for Policy and Survey Research, a polling organization in the West Bank city of Ramallah that conducted the survey with Israeli researchers.[27]

Nevertheless, the pollsters argue that this hardening of attitudes is reversible. The pollsters tested whether adding new conditions to the standard peace package would change the minds of those opposed to a two-state solution. For example, about 40 percent of Israeli Jews and Palestinians changed their minds to favor a two-state approach if a peace agreement were to promise that the new Palestinian state would be democratic, a December poll revealed.[28]

"The less democratic the Palestinian Authority becomes, the less excited Palestinians are to live under a state governed by the PA," says analyst Scheindlin, who helped design the survey, pointing to recent PA crackdowns on the free press. In Israel, "people are really concerned [that] if it's not a democracy . . ., revolutions and anger and violence will spill into Israel."

A stumbling block right now is the leadership on both sides. Palestinian leader Abbas, viewed by many as autocratic, does not control the Hamas-ruled Gaza Strip despite recent attempts at reconciliation. Young Palestinian adults told Khalil Shikaki, director of the Palestinian Center for Policy and Survey Research, they are so convinced a future Palestinian state would be corrupt and authoritarian that "they believe they have a better chance of obtaining equal rights in a future one-state solution," as part of Israel, he says.

While still possible, a two-state agreement is unlikely under the divided Palestinian leadership and an Israeli government that permits settlements in occupied territories to grow, says Khaled Elgindy, a former adviser to the Palestinian leadership during the 2004-09 peace negotiations and a fellow at the Brookings Institution's Center for Middle East Policy in Washington. "If I were advising the Palestinian leadership, I'd say, 'Fix your own house first'" by holding elections or bringing Hamas into the political process.

Two-state advocates see Prime Minister Netanyahu's government as another obstacle because of its commitment to building settlements, which the Palestinians and some legal scholars view as illegal, and Netanyahu's support for a "state minus" for Palestinians—a state without full government authority, particularly in the area of security.

Columbia University's Khalidi criticized the "state minus" concept, noting Netanyahu would deprive a Palestinian state of the fertile Jordan Valley on strategic grounds. "It matters little whether this travesty is called a one-state or two-state 'solution,'" he wrote, because the state would be too small and weak to be viable.[29]

But former Netanyahu adviser Dore Gold says that if a Palestinian "self-governing entity" is created, Israel "must hold on to the powers and territory which are vital for its security in an unstable Middle East," including the air space over the West Bank.

Gold, president of the Jerusalem Center for Public Affairs, an Israeli think tank that specializes in foreign affairs, stresses Israel's vulnerability in a Mideast where its Arab neighbors are acquiring state-of-the art weaponry.

Mideast experts debate whether the growth of Jewish settlements has closed off the possibility of two states. The settlements now so permeate the 60 percent of the West Bank controlled by Israel that the map is "honeycombed" with them and it is hard to see how the Palestinians could carve a country out of the territory, says Scheindlin.

Seidemann of Terrestrial Jerusalem estimates that 163,000 Israeli settlers now live on the Palestinian side of what many agree would be the new borders between Israel and a Palestinian state. "If Israel has the will and capacity to relocate those settlers, the two-state solution is alive; if we don't, it's dead," he says.

David Makovsky, who was on U.S. Secretary of State John Kerry's negotiating team in 2013-14, says Kerry proposed to let Israel keep some large West Bank settlements and to compensate the Palestinians with land swaps. Kerry proposed to evacuate mainly settlements outside Israel's security barrier, encompassing about 70,000 people. However, that number has since grown to about 97,000, estimates Makovsky, a distinguished fellow at the Washington Institute for Near East Policy, a research group that studies Middle East policy. "I do think there is a tipping point" where two states become impossible, says Makovsky. "I don't think we're there yet, but we could be getting closer to it."

Supporting a different vision of a single state is former Palestinian negotiator Diana Buttu, a lawyer in the Israeli coastal city of Haifa. She envisions a country similar to post-apartheid South Africa, with no religious identity and all citizens enjoying equal rights. Such a state, she says, could bring people together "who've suffered under the weight of history."

However, neither side has endorsed a single-state approach.[30] One state is "not a solution; it's a bloodbath," says Jonathan Rynhold, a professor of political studies at Bar-Ilan University in Ramat Gan, Israel. "Israelis will oppress Palestinians or Palestinians will kill Israelis. It's not going to be Switzerland," says Rynhold, who fears that one state may be the direction in which Israel is drifting if it does nothing to limit settlements.

Dennis Ross, a U.S. Middle East negotiator under Democratic and Republican administrations and now a distinguished fellow at the Washington Institute for Near East Policy, agrees. A single binational country would negate not just Palestinian national aspirations but also Israel's identity as a Jewish state. "If you look at the rest of the Mideast where you have more than one identity, you have ongoing conflict," he says. "These two identities are only going to be satisfied with two states."

Has Trump's recognition of Jerusalem as Israel's capital removed the United States as an impartial broker in peace talks?

Both the Palestinian Authority leadership and numerous supporters of a two-state solution say President Trump's Jerusalem move so favored Israel that the United States can no longer present itself as an impartial peace broker.

In a televised speech just after the announcement, Palestinian Authority President Abbas called Jerusalem the "eternal capital of the state of Palestine" and condemned Trump's "deplorable" move as a proclamation that the United States was "abandoning the role of sponsor of [the] peace process."[31]

Former Palestinian adviser Elgindy wrote that Washington's credibility as a peace broker was already

Children play in the Shatila refugee camp, in southern Beirut, the Lebanese capital, on June 25, 2017. The camp was set up in 1949 for Palestinian refugees after Israel's successful War for Independence that year. The United Nations today counts 5 million Palestinians as refugees. Nearly one-third live in city-like refugee "camps" in Jordan, Lebanon, Syria, the Gaza Strip, and the West Bank, including East Jerusalem.

strained by nearly 25 years of failed talks, but that Trump's decision could be the last straw.[32]

In Israel, by contrast, Trump's announcement was warmly welcomed by Prime Minister Netanyahu and his supporters. "What Trump did is introduce an important correction in how people think about Jerusalem without determining what the borders will be between any future Palestinian entity and the state of Israel," says Gold, a former Israeli ambassador to the United Nations. That correction was needed, he says, because international bodies such as UNESCO, the United Nations' world heritage organization, have taken to referring to Jerusalem's holiest site only by its Muslim name, Haram al-Sharif, without recognizing it also is the site of the Second Jewish Temple, destroyed in A.D. 70.[33]

Israel's position is that Jerusalem should be united under Israeli sovereignty. Gold says that is necessary to protect ancient sites from fundamentalist Islamists' destruction.

A number of former U.S. negotiators say Trump's Jerusalem announcement was misguided but add that the United States has never been totally impartial. Rather, America's closeness to the Israelis and the U.S. government's perceived ability to influence them is what has made the United States a uniquely indispensable

A Palestinian woman talks with Israeli security guards in the village of Hizma, near Jerusalem's Old City, on May 26, 2016. The Palestinian village borders four Israeli settlements and is cut off from Jerusalem by a wall built by Israel in 2005.

force in peace negotiations, says Aaron David Miller, who advised Democratic and Republican secretaries of state on peace negotiations.

"If we didn't have a relationship with Israel that was close, then I doubt that our phone would be ringing," says Miller.

Other factors are far more crucial for a successful negotiation, according to Miller: an American president willing to apply both "the honey and vinegar" to close the gaps between the two sides, as well as Israeli and Palestinian leaders "who are masters of their politics, not prisoners of their constituencies and ideologies. Right now you don't have that" in either the Trump administration or the Mideast, says Miller, vice president and Middle East program director at the Woodrow Wilson International Center for Scholars, a nonpartisan policy forum in Washington.

Some analysts welcomed Abbas's proposal to create a multilateral negotiating team of countries and organizations. Possible candidates mentioned by Abbas are the permanent members of the U.N. Security Council, which includes the United States, and the so-called Middle East Quartet consisting of the United Nations, United States, European Union, and Russia. His proposal implied the United States could participate in, but not lead, the peace process.[34]

The days when the United States could monopolize the mediator role are over, especially for the current administration, according to Daniel C. Kurtzer, former ambassador to Israel under President George W. Bush. "If the Trump administration believes they can go back to the old business of shutting everyone else out and putting forward a plan the Palestinians are likely to reject, as we're reading in newspapers, they're not understanding reality," said Kurtzer, a professor of Middle East policy studies at Princeton University. "A multilateral peace process is very hard to manage, but given the Trump administration's policies, it may be the only alternative available to us."

Other former diplomats who participated in peace negotiations under both Republican and Democratic administrations say multiple brokers will not work. Elliott Abrams, who supervised U.S. policy in the Middle East for the White House under Bush, says international peace conferences have been tried before—at Madrid in 1991, co-sponsored by the United States and Soviet Union, and in Annapolis, Maryland, in 2007, involving the Arab League, the United Nations, and others. Neither produced a final accord. "An international conference is not going to achieve a peace agreement," he says.

Even if negotiations are presented as multilateral, the United States would still play the crucial brokering role, predicts former U.S. negotiator Ross. The Palestinians can propose a multilateral approach "if they need a face-saver," he says, but "if it was so easy for others to play a role, they would have done it by now."

Some say the issue of a broker is moot because "there is no real peace process to steward now," according to Elgindy. "Unless you change the dynamics outside the room, talks can't go anywhere," he says, citing settlement-building and Hamas–Palestinian Authority conflicts as stumbling blocks.

Some Palestinians are so disillusioned with the peace process that they consider the question of the United States' role irrelevant. "I don't think there are going to be future negotiations. They've been stalled for well over a decade; there is no appetite any longer for it to be continued," says former Palestinian negotiator Buttu, charging that previous negotiations were "a fig leaf for Israel's expansion of settlements, construction of checkpoints, for home demolitions."

THE ISRAELI–PALESTINIAN CONFLICT   **9**

Is the Palestinian cause still the primary concern of Arab countries?

The Palestinian issue has "probably never been the primary concern of the Arabs; what's always been their primary concern has been their security and their survival," and that is especially true today, says former negotiator Ross. "That probably does leave the Palestinians more alone than ever. They can't count on the Arabs being of much support either material or political; the level of support they get is more in the category of slogans."

Some experts suggest that changing regional dynamics could mean Arab countries will be more likely to support U.S. or Israeli peace efforts over Palestinian objections—or at least step out of the way.

Ongoing military conflicts have demonstrated that issues besides Israel have taken on new urgency for countries such as Egypt and Saudi Arabia with Sunni majorities. These Sunni nations face a growing threat from an expansionary, Shiite-dominated Iran, whose forces are fighting in Syria to support the Bashar al-Assad regime and are backing other forces hostile to Sunni countries.

(Sunnis and Shiites are sects with differing beliefs within Islam. Sunnis are the largest sect, making up about 85 percent of Muslims, while Shiites are the second largest sect.)

In an example of Iran's assertiveness in February, Israel intercepted in its airspace what it said was an Iranian drone launched from Syria. Israel then attacked the Iranian command center inside Syria.[35]

Israeli government, military, and diplomatic experts see an opportunity for their nation to ally with Sunni countries as they face off against a common enemy—Iran—in the Syrian proxy war just across their border. "I think there's been a sea change in the views of many key Arab states towards the state of Israel," said former Netanyahu adviser Gold. "Iran has been in a mode of expansionism on overdrive: You've got Iranian revolutionary guards training forces in Yemen; in Iraq, where Shia militias are under Iranian command; in Syria and in Lebanon."

"The important pragmatic Sunni states are more ready to do business with Israel because they understand that Israel is not the main problem of the Middle East,"

compared with 10 years ago when "nobody was ready even to speak with us," says Brigadier General (reserves) Udi Dekel, who has held senior positions in the Israeli military and is now managing director of the Institute for National Security Studies, a Tel Aviv think tank. That, in Dekel's view, creates an opportunity for Arab states to help peacemaking efforts by telling the Palestinians, "Please play a positive game with Israel."

At a White House meeting with President Trump on March 5, Netanyahu said, "Israel has never been closer to the Arabs, the Arabs have never been closer to Israel, and we need to use that to broaden our talks with the Palestinians."[36]

While acknowledging these changes, former Palestinian adviser Elgindy says the Israeli government tends to overstate this convergence of interests with Arab states. Arab governments "still have to toe the line at the U.N. and talk the talk" in favor of the Palestinians for their domestic constituencies, he says.

Arab governments, other experts say, have long played a double game—forging secret alliances with Israel out of self-interest while stoking rage about the Palestinians' plight to curry the favor of their citizens. "The Arab governments have spent the last 70-plus years trying to persuade the public that the Palestinian issue was the center of their concerns," says former Ambassador Kurtzer. "It's very hard today to turn that off."

Rage over the Palestinians' treatment is often cited as an ingredient in popular uprisings such as the Arab Spring, a series of anti-government uprisings in the Middle East that began in 2010 in Tunisia. "A lot of what fueled the rise of these movements is, they don't see justice in Palestine," says lawyer Buttu. "If Arab states want to address things holistically, they need to turn their attention back to Palestine." The Palestinian cause, she says, has helped fuel the growth of the Islamic State and conflicts in Yemen, Syria, and Iraq.

But Ross disagrees with such a linkage. "It's very clear that if you solve this [Palestinian-Israeli conflict], you're not stopping one barrel bomb in Syria," he said.[37]

The big unanswered question is whether the apparent shift among Arab countries will help peace prospects in the Israeli-Palestinian arena, says Miller at the Wilson Center. It could mean that Arab countries will step away from their role as Palestinian advocates, putting less pressure on Israel to compromise with the Palestinians.

Relatives of a Palestinian who was killed by Israeli soldiers during protests on the Gaza-Israel border mourn at his funeral in Gaza on April 9, 2018. Tensions rose in late March as Hamas called for mass protests on the Gaza Strip border at the start of Passover, with Hamas claiming that at least 15 Palestinians were killed and more than 1,400 wounded on March 30.

Or, Ross says, it could mean they will take a more active role in the peace process, either as intermediaries or as allies seeking Israel's support in the military arena against common enemies.

BACKGROUND

The Zionist Movement

In 1897, Viennese journalist Theodor Herzl undertook a campaign for Jews to migrate to Palestine, convening the first Zionist Congress in the Swiss town of Basel. As a highly assimilated Jew witnessing the vicious anti-Semitism that had erupted in Paris and Vienna in the 1890s, Herzl had become convinced that even an assimilated Jew could never be accepted as an equal citizen in Europe.

Jewish survival, the Zionists argued, depended on establishing a Jewish state in Zion, the biblical name for the land of Israel. At the time, Palestine and other Arab lands were under the rule of the Turkish Ottoman Empire based in Istanbul; no nation of "Palestine" existed, but rather three districts ruled by the Ottomans.[38]

During World War I, the Ottoman Empire collapsed, and Britain and France divided up its Arab possessions, with Palestine going to the British.[39]

Zionist leaders lobbied the British to endorse their national project. In 1917, the British issued the landmark 67-word Balfour Declaration, written by Foreign Secretary Arthur James Balfour.

"His Majesty's Government view with favor the establishment in Palestine of a national home for the Jewish People and will use their best endeavors to facilitate the achievement of this object, it being clearly understood that nothing shall be done which may prejudice the civil and religious rights of existing non-Jewish communities in Palestine or the rights and political status enjoyed by Jews in any other country."[40]

With those words, the writer Arthur Koestler quipped, "one nation solemnly promised to a second nation the country of a third."[41] To this day, Palestinians see the declaration as a betrayal of Palestinians' rights to their homeland.

Jewish immigration to Palestine rose between the two world wars as anti-Semitism intensified throughout Europe. Some Jews managed to immigrate later during the Holocaust, as Adolf Hitler's Nazi regime pursued a policy of genocide in which nearly 6 million European Jews were killed.[42]

In 1936, when Jews constituted a third of the population in Palestine, Palestinians began a three-year revolt against British rule and the growing Zionist presence. British forces crushed the uprising.

When the revolt ended, Britain issued a "white paper" in May 1939 calling for an independent Palestinian state under majority Arab rule in 10 years and limiting Jewish immigration. The policy remained in effect until the end of World War II.[43]

But after the war, the British were forced to change their policy. The Haganah, the primary Jewish militia, defied the British and smuggled shiploads of Jewish refugees into Palestine. After Jewish militias undertook an anti-British campaign, Britain in 1947 turned the Palestine issue over to the United Nations.

A U.N. commission recommended splitting the region into Jewish and Arab states, with Jews inhabiting 55 percent of the territory and Arabs 44 percent. Jerusalem would be under international rule.[44] The Palestinians and Arab nations opposed the plan, but on November 29, 1947, the U.N. General Assembly voted for partition.

Both Jews and Arabs saw the partition plan as a precursor to Jewish statehood. Fighting broke out immediately between Palestinian and Jewish residents, ending in the defeat of Palestinian forces.[45]

CHRONOLOGY

1800s-1930s *Zionist movement seeks a Jewish state in Palestine.*

1897 Viennese journalist Theodor Herzl convenes first Zionist congress in Switzerland.

1917 Britain, which gained control of Palestine after the Ottoman Empire collapsed, promises to help achieve a Jewish homeland in Palestine.

1939 Britain reverses policy, promising a majority-Arab state in Palestine. As the Nazis escalate their attacks on Jews, Jewish militia smuggles Jewish refugees into Palestine.

1940s-1960s *United Nations proposes Jewish and Palestinian states.*

1947 United Nations approves partition of British-occupied Palestine into Jewish and Arab states. Palestinian Arabs reject the plan but are defeated in civil war with Jewish militia.

1948 Zionist leaders declare Israeli statehood; Arab states invade Israel but lose. More than 700,000 Palestinians flee Israel.

1949 Armistices divide Jerusalem into Israeli and Jordanian sectors and make the West Bank part of Jordan.

1967 In Six-Day War, Israelis conquer Jordanian section of Jerusalem, the West Bank, Sinai Desert, and Gaza Strip.

1968 Israeli government endorses settlers moving into occupied territory in West Bank.

1970s-1993 *Negotiations follow new rounds of conflict.*

1973 Syria and Egypt launch surprise attack on Israel on Yom Kippur holy day; Israel eventually repels them.

1978 Camp David Accords result in peace treaty between Egypt and Israel.

1987 Palestinians in West Bank begin six-year uprising (first intifada) against Israeli occupation.

1993 At White House, Israeli Prime Minister Yitzhak Rabin and Yasser Arafat, leader of the Palestine Liberation Organization, a group fighting for an independent state, sign Oslo Accords designed to lead to a two-state solution.

1995-Present *Prospects for a two-state solution dim.*

1995 Israeli extremist assassinates Rabin in retaliation for signing Oslo Accords.

2000 Israeli-Palestinian negotiations at Camp David in Maryland fail. . . . Second intifada begins in Israel.

2005 Second intifada ends. . . . Israel withdraws from Gaza Strip, relocates Jewish settlers.

2006 Hamas, an Islamist group that rejects Israel's legitimacy, wins parliamentary elections in Gaza; ruling Fatah party refuses to cede power, provoking civil war. Hamas wins and rules Gaza.

2008 Israeli Prime Minister Ehud Olmert and Palestinian Authority leader Mahmoud Abbas nearly reach two-state deal.

2009 Olmert's successor, Benjamin Netanyahu, refuses to impose a moratorium on Jewish settlements in the West Bank.

2013 President Barack Obama visits Israel and West Bank, leading to talks under Secretary of State John Kerry.

2014 Kerry's peace effort collapses. . . . Responding to Gaza rockets, Israeli operation kills more than 2,000 Palestinians.

2016 United Nations condemns Jewish settlements.

2017 President Trump recognizes Jerusalem as Israel's capital; U.N. General Assembly criticizes the decision.

2018 Israeli police recommend Netanyahu indictment for bribery (February). . . . U.S. embassy opens in Jerusalem, sparking violent protests (May). . . . U.N. blames Israel for Gaza protesters' deaths (June). . . . Cease-fire reached between Israel and Gaza after heaviest fighting in four years (Nov. 13). . . . Netanyahu's government threatened as hawkish coalition partners threaten defection (November).

Israel Orders Demolition of "Illegal" Palestinian Homes

"The first hammer blow feels like you're hitting yourself."

Azzam Afifi, a Palestinian father of three who has lived in East Jerusalem's Old City his entire life, was forced to do the unthinkable. After Israeli municipal officials ordered him to raze his house for being illegally constructed, he demolished it himself with a sledgehammer to avoid paying the city a fee to do it.

"The first hammer blow feels like you're hitting yourself. It's not easy to demolish your dream," Afifi said in the 2014 documentary "Jerusalem: Hitting Home," about Palestinian families forced to raze their homes deemed illegal by Israeli authorities.[1]

More than 9,000 Palestinians have lost their homes in East Jerusalem since 2000, according to the Land Research Center, a Palestinian research and advocacy group based in Jerusalem.[2] Israel captured Palestinian-dominated East Jerusalem in the Six-Day War in 1967 and annexed it.

Israeli government planning policies make it "virtually impossible" for a Palestinian to obtain a building permit and construct a home legally, said the United Nations Office for the Coordination of Humanitarian Affairs, which responds to humanitarian emergencies and natural disasters. At least one-third of Palestinian homes in East Jerusalem lack a valid building permit, putting 100,000 people at risk of displacement, it said.[3]

Demolitions of Palestinians' homes and commercial/agricultural buildings rose from an annual average of 84 between 2011 and 2015 to 203 in 2016 before falling slightly to 173 in 2017, according to Ir Amim, a liberal advocacy group in Jerusalem pushing for a peace agreement that would divide the city between Israel and a Palestinian state.[4]

Many Palestinians forced out of their East Jerusalem homes will move to "slums," where the municipality provides few city services, says Betty Herschman, director of international relations and advocacy at Ir Amim. These neglected neighborhoods are typified by large, unsafe apartment buildings separated from the city center by a security barrier that Israel erected 15 years ago in response to suicide bombings.

Jerusalem Mayor Nir Barkat's office told *CQ Researcher* in March that "the city does not discriminate based on race, religion or gender." It added, "The municipality receives a disproportionately low number of building permit applications in predominantly Arab neighborhoods." Just 14 percent of all applications were in Arab neighborhoods from 2010 to 2016, according to the mayor's office, which said that 99 percent of those applications were approved in 2016.

That small number of applications is no surprise, according to Ir Amim: Although Palestinians make up about 37 percent of Jerusalem's total population, zoning plans have set aside only 9 percent of the entire city—and 15 percent of East Jerusalem—for Palestinian residences.[5] As a result, large swathes of East Jerusalem in which Palestinians live lack an approved zoning plan to allow building, and many residents do not bother to apply for permits they believe are nearly impossible to get, says Ir Amim.

An Independent Israel

After Israel declared its independence on May 14, 1948, Egyptian, Syrian, Iraqi, and Jordanian armies immediately invaded. By the end of the conflict in March 1949, which Israelis call the War of Independence, Israel remained an independent nation. President Harry S. Truman had immediately recognized Israel in 1948, a move seen as vital to assuring international legitimacy, although the Arab world unanimously rejected the Jewish state. Approximately 750,000 Palestinians fled after Israel's victory, most to Lebanon and Syria. Some 200,000 fled to Gaza. Palestinians call this displacement from their homes the *Nakba* (catastrophe).

The combatants signed armistices in 1949. These agreements effectively created Israel's first borders—the

The battle over zoning and home demolitions in Jerusalem is one front in the long-running Israeli-Palestinian conflict. The United Nations says the annexation is illegal and refuses to recognize Jerusalem as the Israeli capital. President Trump, in December 2017, broke with long-standing U.S. policy by officially recognizing Jerusalem as Israel's capital and announcing plans to move the U.S. embassy to the city, saying it is a "long-overdue step to advance the peace process."[6] The embassy opened in May 2018.

Since the 1967 war, the Palestinian population in Jerusalem has risen from 70,000 to more than 300,000 out of Jerusalem's total population of 890,000.[7]

"Demographic anxiety" drives Israel's policies as it seeks to ensure a large Jewish majority in Jerusalem, Ir Amim's Herschman says.

"The birth of a Jewish child is a *simcha* (a celebration). The birth of a Palestinian child is a demographic problem," says Daniel Seidmann, a Jerusalem-based lawyer, in describing the government's view. Seidmann, who has represented Palestinian and Israeli residents before city planning boards, is the founder of Terrestrial Jerusalem, a nonprofit group tracking city developments that could affect peace negotiations.

City officials say the demolitions are needed to enforce zoning rules. David Cohen, an adviser to Jerusalem's mayor, added that the demolitions also protect the city's archaeological sites and green, or open, spaces from illegal construction. When Palestinians build on these sites, much damage is done to the civic fabric, he said. "Residents should understand that quality of life means many different things," said Cohen, in explaining city demolition orders issued to Palestinians.[8]

Dore Gold, former director-general of Israel's Ministry of Foreign Affairs, says the government has "permitted and even encouraged Palestinian construction in East Jerusalem." The problem, he says, is that "we are in need of much more housing for both Jews and Palestinians. . . . You can get a building permit if you're a Palestinian Arab, just as much as if you're an Israeli Jew."

Yet the governments of Israeli Prime Minister Benjamin Netanyahu and Mayor Barkat have approved plans since 2009 for 10,000 housing units in Israeli neighborhoods and Jewish settlements in East Jerusalem. By contrast, zoning plans approved for Palestinian neighborhoods envision housing units only in the hundreds.[9]

—*Sarah Glazer*

[1] "Jerusalem: Hitting Home," Al Jazeera World, 2014, https://tinyurl.com/y8r4on94. To view the film, see https://tinyurl.com/yb5z8f28.

[2] "Statistical Report on Home Demolitions in East Jerusalem during (2000-2017)," Land Research Center, January 2018, https://tinyurl.com/ydxjbann; "LRC: Israel Demolished 5,000 Homes in Jerusalem," Al Jazeera, March 14, 2018, https://tinyurl.com/y7wju8qt.

[3] "High Numbers of Demolitions," United Nations Office for the Coordination of Humanitarian Affairs, Jan. 15, 2018, https://tinyurl.com/y8gpzord.

[4] Oren Haber, "The poor man's lamb in Beit Hanina," *Times of Israel*, Feb. 9, 2017, https://tinyurl.com/y9sy833f.

[5] Aviv Tatarsky and Efran Cohen-Bar, "Deliberately Planned," Ir Amim, February 2017, https://tinyurl.com/y9lvp9ss.

[6] "Statement by President Trump on Jerusalem," The White House, Dec. 6, 2017, https://tinyurl.com/yb8yrkxx.

[7] "Israel Population 2018," World Population Review, https://tinyurl.com/ycj2qbc5; Isabel Kershner, "50 Years after War, East Jerusalem Palestinians Confront a Life Divided," *New York Times*, June 25, 2017, https://tinyurl.com/ya6l2j32.

[8] "Jerusalem: Hitting Home," *op. cit.*; Mershiha Gadzo, "Silwan demolitions: 'They're Destroying Jerusalem,'" Al Jazeera, Oct. 9, 2017, https://tinyurl.com/y09atca3.

[9] "Amendment to Basic Law: Jerusalem Approved but in Modified Form," Ir Amim, Jan. 2, 2018, https://tinyurl.com/y8cwfybk.

so-called Green Line, including the division of Jerusalem between Israel and Jordan, leaving only 22 percent of the original Palestinian lands outside the new borders of Israel. The area on the west bank of the Jordan River was annexed by Jordan and renamed the West Bank.[46]

In Arab countries, Israel's victory was followed by anti-Jewish violence. More than 800,000 Jews eventually fled those countries, most heading for Israel.

The 1948 borders held until 1967, when the Six-Day War redrew Israel's map. Jordan lost the West Bank and East Jerusalem. Israel seized the Golan Heights from Syria and took the Sinai and Gaza from Egypt.

After the victory, Israel was a majority Jewish country of 2.7 million ruling 1.4 million Palestinians in the West Bank and Gaza Strip. The government decided to occupy those territories, at least temporarily. Some

Jewish Refugees from Arab Lands Get New Attention

"The Palestinians have to recognize there are two sets of refugees."

Joseph Esses, who was born in 1919 in the Syrian city of Aleppo, had fond memories of growing up Jewish next to his Muslim neighbors. But Arab attitudes toward Jews took a fateful turn after 1948, when the state of Israel was founded.

One evening after that historic event, Esses was walking home from his clothing shop when three Muslim men cornered him on the street. Beating him with fists, rocks, and sticks, they taunted him, "You want a country? Here is your country!"

Esses recalled witnessing numerous atrocities against the Jewish community in Aleppo—the killings of friends and relatives in broad daylight and hangings for the "crime" of being a Jew. After being in and out of jail for two years and enduring torture, Esses escaped to Lebanon in 1950 and found his way to Canada, leaving behind all his family heirlooms and property.[1]

After 1948, 856,000 Jews were forced to leave the Middle Eastern countries where their families had lived for generations. Most of this migration occurred rapidly: 90 percent of the Jews who fled Iraq, Syria, Libya, and Yemen had departed by 1951. About 650,000 ended up as refugees in Israel; another 200,000 went to the United States, Canada, or Europe.[2]

The forces pushing Jews from their homelands included discriminatory laws—stripping them of citizenship, confiscating their property, and barring them from specified jobs—as well as anti-Jewish riots.

Within a few years, thriving Jewish communities in Iraq, Syria, Egypt, Algeria, Libya, and Yemen had virtually disappeared. Today, outside of Israel, only 4,500 Jews remain in the Middle East, almost all in Morocco and Tunisia.[3]

In *Uprooted: How 3000 Years of Jewish Civilization in the Arab World Vanished Overnight*, British writer Lyn Julius, the daughter of Iraqi Jewish refugees who fled to the United Kingdom in 1950, chronicles this story. More Jews than Palestinians were forced from their homelands after 1948, and about as many Middle Eastern Jews ended up as refugees in Israel as the number of Palestinians displaced from that land, she wrote.[4]

"The Palestinians have to recognize there are two sets of refugees—not just them," says Julius, who thinks recognition of this fact and compensation for Middle Eastern Jews, known as Mizrahi Jews, should be on the agenda of any future peace negotiations. "This hopefully would lead to a recognition that a wrong was done to people on both sides and would lead to a kind of reconciliation."

President Bill Clinton took a step in this direction in July 2000, immediately after the Camp David peace talks, when in an Israeli television interview he suggested creating an international fund to compensate Jews from Arab countries who became refugees in Israel. During the Camp David summit, "the Palestinians said they thought these people should be eligible for compensation," Clinton told the interviewer. In 2014, U.S. Secretary of State John

Israelis began planning to settle the areas, claiming them as the biblical Jewish homeland of Judea and Samaria—a claim that settlers make to this day.

In September 1967, a top Israeli government lawyer concluded that settling the occupied areas would violate international law, which forbids the settlement of militarily occupied land. But the legality of the settlements remains highly contested, with the Israeli government maintaining that the territory involved is "disputed," not occupied, and therefore settlements are

legal, according to Bar-Ilan University's Rynhold. "Israel has a legal case, but most of the world doesn't accept it," he says.

International opinion opposed the occupation from the beginning. In 1967, the U.N. Security Council approved a resolution setting out the parameters for a negotiated peace settlement between Israel and Arab states, including the "withdrawal of Israel armed forces" from territories it had occupied and a "just settlement of the refugee problem."[47]

Kerry proposed compensation for Jews from Arab countries ahead of a peace agreement between Israel and the Palestinians.[5] However, no such international fund has been established.

Recently, in Egypt, Tunisia, and other Arab countries, interest has grown in Jewish culture. Exemplifying this trend are a popular Egyptian TV series, "The Jewish Neighborhood"; the emergence of films and novels in Arabic featuring Jewish characters; Jewish cultural festivals; and the restoration of abandoned synagogues.[6]

Palestinian scholar Najat Abdulhaq, who is based in Berlin and teaches at the University of Erlangen–Nuremberg, traces this growing interest among young people to the 2010-11 Arab Spring protests and the questioning of their governments' official line. "Literature, culture and films are intellectual spaces where we can discuss taboos" about Jews and can go beyond the Israeli-Palestinian conflict, she said during a recent talk in London. Curious about shuttered synagogues and nostalgic for the once-cosmopolitan, inclusive societies portrayed in films, young people are seeking a reappraisal of the role that Jews played in their societies, she said.[7]

Julius said she is skeptical of a real rapprochement, suggesting the trend toward restoring Jewish synagogues is driven by Arab countries' desire to attract Western tourism—garnering favorable public relations "without the inconvenience of live Jews."[8]

In her book, Julius argued that anti-Semitism in Arab countries predated the Israeli-Arab conflict. Bigotry against non-Muslims has a long tradition in the Middle East, she wrote.[9] "Even minorities who've got no Israel of their own have been persecuted," Julius says. "You only have to look at the plight" of Christian groups and Kurdish Yazidis.

For many years, the Israeli government described the migration of Mizrahi Jews as the product of a long-held desire to return to the Jewish homeland. But Julius says that most arrived out of desperation. Wealthier families went to the United States, Europe, or Canada. In the early years, Mizrahis were typically housed in tent camps and faced discrimination in a society dominated by European Jewry.

Only recently has Israel recognized the plight of the Mizrahis. In 2010, the Israeli Knesset (parliament) passed a law declaring that compensation to Jewish refugees from Arab lands for property losses should be part of any future peace negotiations.[10]

—*Sarah Glazer*

[1] Michelle Devorah Kahn, "Tales of a Convicted Jew's Escape from Syria," *National Post*, Dec. 1, 2014, https://tinyurl.com/y844m8yk.

[2] Lyn Julius, *Uprooted: How 3000 Years of Jewish Civilization in the Arab World Vanished Overnight* (2018), pp. 120, x-xxiii, 5.

[3] *Ibid.*, pp. 132, 5, 264.

[4] *Ibid.*, p. x. An estimated 711,000 Palestinian Arabs, who had left what became Israel after the 1948 war, were recognized by the United Nations as refugees in 1950. See "General Progress Report and Supplementary Report of the United Nations Conciliation Commission for Palestine, Covering the Period from 11 December 1949 to 23 October 1950," United Nations Conciliation Commission, Oct. 23, 1950, https://tinyurl.com/y7zd2fby.

[5] Alan Baker, ed., *Israel's Rights as a Nation-State in International Diplomacy* (2011), p. 61, https://tinyurl.com/y9qt3m8m; Julius, *op. cit.*, pp. 267-69.

[6] "Rethinking and Reclaiming History: Emerging Arab Interest in Jewish Heritage," SOAS University of London, Jan. 30, 2018, https://tinyurl.com/y82lg6sz.

[7] *Ibid.*

[8] Julius, *op. cit.*, p. 234.

[9] *Ibid.*, p. 87.

[10] *Ibid.*, p. 270.

The Palestinians are not mentioned in the resolution, nor does it require that the Palestinians be given any territory, although they are alluded to as the "refugee problem." The Palestine Liberation Organization (PLO), founded in 1964 and labeled by critics as a terrorist organization, opposed the resolution at the time. However, it later agreed the resolution should be one of the bases for the Oslo Accords it signed in 1993.[48]

The U.N. today counts 5 million Palestinians as refugees, including all descendants of the original 750,000 refugees. Nearly one-third live in refugee "camps"—which look more like cities than camps—in Jordan, Lebanon, Syria, the Gaza Strip, and the West Bank, including East Jerusalem.[49]

Early Peace Process

Egypt and Syria launched a surprise attack on Israel on October 6, 1973, coinciding with Yom Kippur, the holiest day on the Jewish religious calendar. The attackers were trying to regain territory lost in 1967, and Egypt advanced

Israeli security forces on Sept. 26, 2017, attend the funeral of an Israeli border guard killed in a Palestinian attack on a Jewish settlement in the occupied West Bank. Israelis say Palestinian attacks must halt if peace talks are to succeed, but Palestinians cite the growth of Jewish settlements in the West Bank and East Jerusalem as an obstacle to peace.

swiftly into the Sinai. But Israel counterattacked and routed the Arab armies. The United States helped negotiate an end to the war, marking the beginning of long-term American participation in peace efforts.

In 1978 at Camp David, hosted by President Jimmy Carter, Egypt and Israel held direct talks leading to the 1979 Egypt-Israel peace treaty, Israel's first with any of its neighbors. Under the treaty, Israel returned the Sinai Peninsula to Egypt in 1982 in exchange for Egypt's promise to maintain "normal and friendly relations" with Israel.[50]

Israelis continued building settlements, with the Jewish population growing to 11,000 in the West Bank and Gaza by the mid-1970s. Israel's 1977 election marked a historic shift to the right when the conservative Likud party, which maintained that these territories were part of Israel, won.

In 1987, Palestinians in the occupied territories began to rebel, confronting Israeli troops with stones and barricades. During the ensuing four years of conflict, known as the first intifada (uprising), and the seven years that followed, Israeli forces killed an estimated 1,376 Palestinians, and Palestinians killed 185 Israeli civilians and soldiers.

Israeli and Palestinian negotiators began meeting secretly in Oslo, Norway, in 1991, leading to the Oslo Declaration of Principles of 1993. PLO Chairman Yasser Arafat and Israeli Prime Minister Yitzhak Rabin signed the agreement on the White House lawn on September 13, 1993, under the gaze of President Bill Clinton. The agreement called for mutual recognition by Israel and the PLO, complete Israeli withdrawal from Gaza, and a phased withdrawal from the West Bank. Palestinians would elect an interim government, the Palestinian Authority, to rule territory that Israel evacuated.[51]

Talks were to begin in five years to settle five major issues: borders, settlements, security, refugees, and Jerusalem's status. However, a series of events—including the continued expansion of settlements and growing Israeli opposition to an independent Palestinian state because of the intifada—contributed to a breakdown in the peace process.[52]

In 1995, an Israeli extremist assassinated Rabin in Tel Aviv. In the wake of a breakdown of talks in 2000, armed Palestinian groups began the second intifada.

In response to the second intifada and to suicide bombings throughout Israel, Israel began to construct a wall between itself and parts of the West Bank. The insurgency ended in 2005 after Arafat's death and the election of Mahmoud Abbas as Palestinian Authority president.[53]

In 2005, Israel unilaterally withdrew its troops from the Gaza Strip and evacuated more than 8,000 settlers. Hamas won parliamentary elections, but the Palestinian Authority rejected the results, as did Israel and the United States, calling Hamas a terrorist organization. Hamas, an offshoot of the Muslim Brotherhood, called for the destruction of Israel and the establishment of an Islamic state. It also opposed the Oslo Accords' two-state solution. Fatah—the Palestinian nationalist political party—and much of the international community called for a boycott of Hamas' government until it accepted previous Palestinian commitments to recognize Israel and renounce violence.[54] Increasingly violent clashes led to a civil war in Gaza that Hamas won in 2007, splitting the Palestinian population into two political spheres.

Before Israel's Gaza withdrawal, the George W. Bush administration (2001-09) had undertaken a so-called road map to peace, which sought to establish an independent Palestinian state by 2005, preceded by an end to Palestinian violence and a cessation of all Israeli settlements built since

March 2001.[55] But that plan died after Israeli Prime Minister Ariel Sharon called for additional measures banning Palestinian violence.[56]

Starting in December 2006 and continuing until mid-2008, Abbas and Israeli Prime Minister Ehud Olmert met 36 times, and both have said they got closer to a peace agreement than any effort since then. Olmert said he offered a near-total withdrawal from the West Bank, keeping only 6.3 percent for settlements and compensating the Palestinians with equivalent land swaps, and a Jewish withdrawal from Arab neighborhoods of East Jerusalem with holy sites under international control.[57]

As talks were drawing to a conclusion, however, Olmert became enmeshed in a corruption scandal for which he later went to prison. Abbas was unwilling to sign a deal because he would be closing a negotiation with a lame-duck leader, according to Palestinian negotiators. "I feel he [Olmert] was assassinated politically as Rabin was assassinated materially. I feel if we had continued four to five months, we could have concluded the issues," said Abbas.[58]

The Obama Years

President Barack Obama's visit to Israel in 2013 culminated in a major pledge of friendship—a memorandum of understanding, signed in September 2016, in which the United States promised $38 billion in military aid to Israel over 10 years.[59]

Secretary of State Kerry began peace talks in July 2013. But nine months later, in April 2014, they broke down. Some participants blamed Kerry for fostering misunderstandings between the parties.[60]

In December 2016, Kerry pinned the blame largely on Netanyahu, whose government he called "the most right-wing in Israeli history." He warned that growing settlements were pushing Israel toward a "separate but unequal" nation. "If the choice is one-state, Israel can either be Jewish or democratic; it cannot be both—and it won't ever really be at peace," Kerry said.[61]

Kerry defended the Obama administration's last act regarding Israel. On December 23, 2016, the U.N. Security Council passed Resolution 2334 condemning Israeli settlements as a "flagrant violation" of international law. The United States, departing from its long-held stance backing Israel, abstained, permitting the resolution to pass in a 14–0 vote.[62]

Israel warmly welcomed Trump's election as U.S. president. Naftali Bennett, leader of the right-wing Jewish Home party, which opposes a two-state solution, proclaimed Trump's victory the end of the Palestinian state.

In February 2017, Trump met with Netanyahu at the White House for the first time, but the president baffled experts with a statement that either overturned decades of U.S. support for two states or was simply ill-informed. "I'm looking at two-state and one-state, and I like the one that both parties like," Trump said.[63]

Trump's unorthodox statements have kept experts guessing about his intentions.

CURRENT SITUATION
Israeli Politics

The future of Israel's leadership remains uncertain. Prime Minister Netanyahu was left with a razor-thin one-seat majority for his ruling coalition following the November 14 resignation of his defense minister protesting a new cease-fire with Hamas in Gaza. The resignation cast doubt on the survival of Netanyahu's government and had been expected to push the country toward an election months earlier than expected—possibly to March 2019 instead of a year from now. (Elections must be held by November 5, 2019.) The defection of Defense Minister Avigdor Lieberman and his ultranationalist party, Yisrael Beitenu, left Netanyahu with only 61 seats for his coalition out of 120 in the Israeli parliament.

Most political commentators viewed Lieberman's resignation as the opening salvo in the next election campaign, where Lieberman, a defense hawk, is expected to challenge Netanyahu and paint him as too soft on Gaza, along with other right-wing rivals. Lieberman has called the recent cease-fire a "surrender to terror."[64]

Theoretically, Netanyahu could rule until the next elections, scheduled for November 2019. But with the threatened resignation of another cabinet minister the same week, Minister of Education Naftali Bennett, and the possible departure of Bennett's right-wing Jewish Home party from the coalition, Netanyahu's government appeared to be teetering on collapse.[65] Other cabinet members crucial to Netanyahu's coalition joined Bennett in calling for early elections.[66]

However, the situation appeared to be turning in Netanyahu's favor by November 19. A few days before, Bennett had joined the criticism of the cease-fire and threatened to resign if Netanyahu didn't give him the post of defense minister; however, Netanyahu didn't grant that demand and assumed the defense portfolio for himself November 18 following the resignation of Defense Minister Lieberman. On November 19 Bennett announced that he was dropping his demand for the post and would not withdraw his party from the coalition after all. That left only one coalition partner, Finance Minister Moshe Kahlon of the hawkish party Kulanu, calling for an early election.[67]

The government crisis erupted in the wake of a new cease-fire negotiated November 13 with Palestinians' Hamas rulers in Gaza, after two days of heavy fighting. Netanyahu's likely conservative campaign rivals, including Lieberman and Bennett, are expected to tap into the public's anger over the unpopular cease-fire, which was brokered by Egypt, following other cease-fire attempts over the previous five months that failed to last.[68]

Residents of Israeli towns on the southern border with Gaza, which had been battered by rockets from Hamas, protested in the streets following announcement of the truce, while residents of Gaza celebrated the truce as a victory.[69]

Over two days of fighting beginning November 11, set off when an Israeli undercover operation in the Gaza Strip had its cover blown, Hamas militants fired 460 rockets and mortars at Israel, while the Israeli air force hit more than160 targets in Gaza—the longest and heaviest fighting since the 2014 war.[70]

Violence had been simmering since the beginning of mass protests on the Gaza-Israel border in late March by Palestinians protesting Israel's crippling blockade and demanding a right to return to lands lost to Israel in the 1948 war. Those protests intensified in violence as anger grew over the opening of the U.S. embassy in Jerusalem on May 14, with its symbolic rejection of the Palestinians' claim to a capital in East Jerusalem. Some 60 Palestinian protestors were killed and thousands injured by Israeli troops on that day alone—the deadliest day of violence in four years.[71]

Protesters lobbed grenades, flaming tires, and firebombs toward Israeli troops, who responded with tear gas and live fire. By November 13, some 170 Palestinians,

many unarmed, had been killed by Israeli fire, the Associated Press reported.[72]

In a poll published the day after the cease-fire negotiated November 13, 74 percent of Israelis said they were dissatisfied by Netanyahu's performance in the latest confrontation with Gaza. That poll also showed Netanyahu's center-right Likud party dropping in the polls for the first time after months of popularity.[73]

Netanyahu faces another threat to his political future—recommendations from Israel's police that he be indicted on corruption and bribery charges. Netanyahu is accused of accepting nearly $300,000 in gifts over 10 years, and more police recommendations are expected on bribery charges in another case.[74] If Israel's attorney general decides to press charges before an election, Netanyahu's chances could be weakened or he could be forced to step down.[75]

"He's in the fight of his life," former U.S. adviser Makovsky said after the police recommendations were released.

To survive, Netanyahu, who has vowed not to resign, needs to hold the right-wing parties in his coalition together. In a television address November 18, he warned his coalition partners considering defection that breaking up the government at a time of delicate national security would be "irresponsible."[76]

Netanyahu wants to delay the election as long as possible for "right-wing voters to forget what they feel was a failure in Gaza; and for the public storms that the indictments will create to pass," wrote political commentator Anshel Pfeffer in the Israeli daily *Haaretz*. After the police corruption charges were recommended in February, Netanyahu had maintained his popularity in the absence of an indictment; however, some political analysts anticipate an indictment could come in early 2019.[77]

Many observers say that the political necessity for Netanyahu to maintain support of the most right-wing parties in his coalition will keep him from agreeing to any long-term peace accord with the Palestinians, despite his support for a short-term cease-fire. Indeed, producing calm in Gaza through a successful cease-fire would reduce international pressure on Netanyahu to make concessions to the Palestinians, said *Haaretz* commentator Anshel Pfeffer.[78]

Is President Trump right to recognize Jerusalem as Israel's capital?

YES   **Dore Gold**
President, Jerusalem Center for Public Affairs; former Israeli Ambassador to the U.N.

Written for *CQ Researcher*, April 2018

NO   **Sam Bahour**
Managing Partner, Applied Information Management; policy adviser, Al-Shabaka, the Palestinian Policy Network

Written for *CQ Researcher*, April 2018

Since 2001, the international community has become increasingly aware of the fact that holy sites across the Middle East and South Asia have lost the immunity that they were thought to have had. The current era was ushered in by the Taliban's destruction of the 2,000-year-old statues of the Buddha in Afghanistan. It intensified with the church bombings by ISIS in Syria, Iraq, and Egypt.

This international experience is something Israelis understand well. In 1948, Jerusalem was put under siege by invading Arab armies and much of its Jewish legacy was assaulted. By the time armistice agreements were reached in 1949, some 55 synagogues and religious academies had been destroyed or desecrated. The residents of the Jewish Quarter faced exile, imprisonment, or extermination. For 19 years, Jews were not allowed to visit their holy sites in Jerusalem. These experiences hovered in the minds of Israelis in 1967 when the Israeli army was ordered to retake the Old City of Jerusalem and guarantee the security of its holy sites.

How best to resolve the question of Jerusalem has defied diplomats for decades. In 1947, the United Nations proposed that the city be internationalized. But when it was invaded in 1948, the United Nations did not lift a finger to protect its residents. Prime Minister David Ben-Gurion declared in 1949 that Jerusalem would be Israel's capital. It was hoped and expected that states would establish their embassies in Jerusalem as a result.

While President Trump did not envision the future borders of Jerusalem when he recognized the city as Israel's capital in December 2017, implicitly he gave an important boost to Israel's claim from the days of Ben-Gurion. Today, the international community has to ask itself, who will protect Jerusalem? Will it be the Fatah movement or Hamas? In 2002, a joint unit of the two Palestinian organizations invaded the Church of the Nativity in Bethlehem and took its clergy as hostages. Should they become the protectors of Jerusalem? Should we turn to internationalization again? What is the English expression? "Been there, tried that."

Only a free and democratic Israel will protect Jerusalem for all faiths. Trump is carrying out the bipartisan will of Congress, which passed the Jerusalem Embassy Act in 1995 calling on the administration to move the U.S. embassy to Jerusalem. He is also setting the stage for the protection of our common religious legacy in Jerusalem from those who threaten our common civilization.

President Trump's recognition of Jerusalem as Israel's capital ignores the city's historical and spiritual importance to Palestinian Muslims and Christians, while violating fundamental tenets of international law. Meanwhile, the decision threatens core U.S. interests in the region by contradicting America's own long-standing neutrality on this issue.

Jerusalem, al-Quds in Arabic, is the heart of Palestine for Palestinians around the world. For more than 20 years of U.S.-dominated negotiations, American negotiators have known that peace is not possible without establishing East Jerusalem as the sovereign and independent capital of Palestine. Before the Palestinians would engage in the 1991 Madrid peace conference, the United States affirmed that it did not recognize the Israeli annexation of East Jerusalem or any attempts to change its status.

Previous U.S. administrations have gone to great lengths to uphold this stringent neutrality. The arguments are always the same: Recognizing Jerusalem as Israel's capital would "critically compromise the ability of the United States to work with Israelis, Palestinians and others in the region to further the peace process." But now, in one fell swoop, Trump recognized Jerusalem in order to "take Jerusalem off the table." But in reality, he took the table altogether.

This declaration encourages maximalist Israeli claims of Jerusalem as the "eternal and undivided capital of the Jewish people." Trump has endorsed those who want to turn a political conflict into a religious war and has wholeheartedly taken the side of the right-wing Israeli government. On the other side stand the Palestinians, backed by international law.

Israel's military occupation must first end. Everyone knows how to solve Jerusalem: to have an open and shared city, with the West as Israel's capital and the East as Palestine's capital. But this U.S. administration has provided diplomatic cover to the obstinate Netanyahu government and set back a peace process already on life support.

Even as the Trump administration threatened them, nearly every country in the world weighed in following Trump's ill-fated Jerusalem Declaration, saying this move not only is illegal but puts at risk the achievement of a two-state solution.

As the Palestinian leadership says, this unprecedented and flagrantly one-sided declaration means the United States can no longer be the principal mediator. Given how recklessly Trump has acted, the global community is now contemplating how to deal with an America that is part and parcel of the problem.

While storms were buffeting the government in November, many political observers still considered Netanyahu the favorite to win an election. "People see him as a statesman even if they are sick of him," Tel Aviv consultant Scheindlin said. "He has a stature in the country that no one else seems to have."[79]

Even if Netanyahu resigns, forces opposed to a Palestinian state could continue to run the government. "Right now, nobody who stands a chance at becoming prime minister is offering a different outlook on regional foreign policy" from Netanyahu's, Daniel Levy, president of the U.S. Middle East Project, a policy institute in New York City that supports two states, said in February.[80] In a podcast discussion in mid-November, *Haaretz* analysts Landau and Pfeffer took the same view. In fact, said Landau, "The political system has become more right-wing; Netanyahu appears more moderate compared to his [coalition] partners."[81]

The number of Jewish settlers in the West Bank continues to grow. Last year, the population reached 435,159, a 3.4 percent increase over 2016, according to Bet El Institutions, a settler organization opposed to a Palestinian state. "We are changing the map," said settler leader Yaakov Katz. "The idea of a two-state solution is over. It is irreversible."[82]

However, the settlers' population growth rate has been slowing for at least the past six years, according to government statistics.[83]

That is because fewer people are moving to settlements than previously, said demographic analyst Shaul Arieli. "Israelis are voting with their feet and clearly [are] not enthusiastic about moving to the West Bank," he wrote. He said the increase has come from internal birth rates.[84]

Pro-settler parties are expected to push parliamentary bills aimed at annexing part or all of the West Bank. In January, they passed a bill in the Knesset (parliament) requiring the approval of an 80-member parliamentary "supermajority" before the government can transfer any part of Jerusalem to a "foreign entity," such as a Palestinian state. Previously, approval could be obtained with a 61-member majority and a public referendum.[85]

The pro-peace group Terrestrial Jerusalem blasted the bill, saying opponents of two states "will be able to block the will not only of any future Israeli government, but of the Israeli people as a whole."[86]

But Baruch Gordon, director of development for Bet El Institutions, says gaining full control of the West Bank is vital so that Jews can return "to our historic homeland." It's also vital for security reasons, he says, so that Israel does not repeat the mistakes it made in Gaza in 2005. In Gaza, where Israel withdrew its troops and evacuated settlers, Israel has essentially "created a Palestinian state by removing Jews. And what resulted was so catastrophic for Israel," he says, pointing to Hamas' attacks.

International Developments

In December at the United Nations, 128 countries voted to condemn the United States for its recognition of Jerusalem; only 9 countries supported the United States. In retaliation, Trump threatened to withhold billions of dollars in U.S. aid to countries that voted against the United States. However, when his administration unveiled its budget for 2019 in February, not a single country had lost funding.[87]

Meanwhile, Abbas has been refusing to meet with U.S. officials ever since Trump's Jerusalem move. Calling Trump's forthcoming peace plan—some details of which have reportedly been shared with the Palestinians—the "slap of the century," he said "we will not accept it."[88]

Tensions rose in late March as Hamas began mass protests on the Gaza Strip border at the start of Passover, with Hamas claiming that at least 15 Palestinians were killed and more than 1,400 wounded in clashes with Israeli soldiers on March 30. (Israeli officials said they could not verify those figures.) The Israeli army and security services were bracing for further protests connected with the U.S. embassy's scheduled move to Jerusalem on May 14, Israel's Independence Day, followed by the Palestinians' Nakba Day (day of catastrophe) that mourns the 1948 loss of their homelands on May 15.[89]

Tensions between the Palestinian Authority and Hamas also have been increasing following an assassination attempt on Palestinian Authority Prime Minister Rami Hamdallah during a visit to Gaza in March. A reconciliation plan, in which Hamas would turn over the administration of Gaza to the Palestinian Authority in exchange for the PA ceasing its blockade of vital services to Gaza, has still not been implemented.

Under the plan, Hamas agreed to turn over civil administration of Gaza to the Palestinian Authority. But Hamas refuses to surrender its weapons or ban armed resistance groups, something the PA is insisting upon.[90] "The Gaza Strip has been hijacked by Hamas," Abbas said in March. "They must immediately hand over everything, first and foremost security, to the Palestinian national consensus government."[91]

In the meantime, say Palestinian experts, the Palestinian Authority is depriving Gaza of vital funds and supplies to pressure Hamas. "Abbas doesn't want to bear responsibility for Gaza, as well as the rocket fire from Gaza [aimed at Israel], unless he knows he's fully in control," former Palestinian adviser Elgindy said in March. "The view in Ramallah is to keep on squeezing Hamas until it capitulates to all demands."

In early November, the Egyptian government was reportedly attempting another reconciliation between Abbas's Palestinian Authority and Hamas while pressuring Abbas to accept the cease-fire that Egypt was negotiating between Israel and Hamas. The deal would reportedly have given the Palestinian Authority eventual government control over Gaza. Palestinian officials in the West Bank had resisted the cease-fire, contending that the Palestinian Liberation Organization, which Abbas chairs, is the only legitimate group to negotiate a cease-fire with Israel.[92]

However, by the time the Israel-Gaza cease-fire was negotiated November 13, brokered by Egypt and Qatar, it was clear that Abbas had not played any role in negotiating the truce, demonstrating that he is becoming increasingly "irrelevant" to issues involving the Gaza strip, the *Jerusalem Post* reported. Abbas was reportedly "furious" with the parties that negotiated the truce, believing that direct negotiations with Hamas would only strengthen its hand in ruling the Gaza Strip, according to the *Jerusalem Post*.[93]

Abbas's irrelevancy was highlighted the week before, when Qatar sent $15 million to Gaza to pay civil servant salaries there as a way of relieving the humanitarian crisis. The Palestinian Authority had halted salary payments as part of its strict economic sanctions on Gaza.[94]

Over the weeks of Palestinian protests at the Gaza-Israel border this year, the United Nations sided with the Palestinians. On June 13, the United Nations General Assembly overwhelmingly passed a resolution castigating Israel for the deaths that had occurred among protesters at the border fence since late March. The U.N. resolution deplored the "excessive use of force" employed by the Israelis but did not explicitly criticize Hamas, whom the Israeli and U.S. governments have accused of instigating the clashes.[95]

The United States and Israel voted against the resolution, which passed 120-8 in the 193-member body. The resolution, which is not legally binding, was hailed by the Palestinian delegation as a moral victory at a moment when more than 120 Palestinians had been killed and hundreds wounded by Israeli soldiers on the other side of the fence over 10 weeks of protests, according to Palestinian Health Ministry officials.

U.S. ambassador to the United Nations, Nikki R. Haley, had proposed an amendment to the resolution criticizing Hamas, but it failed to gain the necessary two-thirds majority. She had also vetoed a similar resolution that would be legally binding in the Security Council, where the United States has veto power. Israel and the U.S. government accused Hamas of inciting the protests as a ruse to invade Israeli territory and kill civilians.[96]

U.S. Policy

The United States will no longer contribute to the U.N. agency that provides relief to Palestinian refugees, the State Department announced August 31, raising widespread criticism that it was cutting off aid in the midst of a humanitarian disaster in Gaza. The State Department called the U.N. Relief and Works Agency (UNRWA) an "irredeemably flawed operation." It has criticized the way the United Nations counts Palestinian refugees. The administration would like to reduce the number from the 5 million counted today—which includes some 700,000 Palestinians who fled or were forced to leave their homes after the 1948 war together with all their descendants—to the several hundred thousand original refugees.

UNRWA provides aid in the form of education, health care, food, and other needs to some 1.3 million Palestinians registered as refugees in the Gaza Strip, some 800,000 Palestinians in the West Bank, and other refugees in Jordan, Syria, and Lebanon. The United States contributed about one-third of a $1.1 billion budget to UNRWA in 2017. Germany and Japan pledged to donate more, but it was unlikely that would cover the U.S. cuts, the *Washington Post* reported.[97]

Saeb Erekat, secretary general of the Palestine Liberation Organization, said of UNRWA "there is an international obligation to assist and support it until all the problems of the Palestinian refugees are solved."[98]

Separately, the Trump administration announced the previous week that it was planning to cut more than $200 million in aid to Palestinians and divert it to other high-priority projects. Aid programs said they would have to cut food programs for poor Palestinians and medical aid. In a tweet the same day, Aaron Miller of the Wilson Center commented, this is the "First Administration in history to provide unqualified support to the Government of Israel while waging political/economic war on Palestinians."[99]

On March 13, the White House held a one-day conference on Gaza's struggles, attended by representatives of 20 countries, including Israel. However, the Palestinian Authority boycotted the event out of anger over U.S. policies.[100]

A White House statement issued the day after the conference said solving the humanitarian crisis is "a necessary step" to reaching a peace agreement between the Israelis and the Palestinians as well as between Gaza and the West Bank.[101]

The Palestinians remain angry over Bolton's appointment as national security adviser. With Bolton's selection, said senior Palestinian official Hanan Ashrawi, the Trump administration "has joined with extreme Zionists, fundamentalist Christians and white racists" leading to a "devastating reality for Palestine." J Street, a two-state advocacy group in Washington, said it was "horrified" by Bolton's appointment, calling him an advocate for "dangerous use of military force in the Middle East" and noting he "has opposed U.S. leadership toward a two-state solution."[102]

But Israeli Justice Minister Ayelet Shaked, of the Jewish Home party, praised Bolton's appointment. "President Trump is continuing to appoint true friends of Israel to senior positions. John Bolton stands out among them," she said.[103]

While Bolton's favored solution—returning Gaza to Egypt and the West Bank partially to Jordan—would be bitterly opposed by the Palestinians, analysts say it is unclear how Egypt, Jordan, or Israel would react.

According to a Saudi news report, Egyptian intelligence chief Abbas Kamel told a Hamas delegation in February that Egypt opposed Trump's "ultimate deal," saying "Gaza is part of Palestine and Sinai is part of Egypt." He appeared to be referring to ideas discussed in unofficial talks between American and Israeli officials, of which Egypt was informed.[104]

After a year of shuttle diplomacy, U.S. peace envoys Kushner and Greenblatt had failed to persuade leaders in Egypt, Jordan, Saudi Arabia, and other key Arab states that the United States could broker a fair peace between Israel and the Palestinians, *USA Today* reported in August. "Most of the Arab world—including Egypt and Saudi Arabia—have rejected the U.S.-proposed Deal of the Century," said Saad El Gammal, head of the Egyptian Parliament's Arab Affairs Committee.[105]

More recently, tensions between the United States and Saudi Arabia over the murder of Saudi journalist Jamal Khashoggi, which the CIA concluded was ordered by Saudi Crown Prince Mohammed bin Salman, may have dimmed prospects for Saudi Arabia as a major player, which was expected to play a key role financially in the plan, according to *Bloomberg News*.[106]

OUTLOOK
Pessimism Prevails

The mood among Israelis and Palestinians, as well as veteran negotiators, is decidedly more pessimistic about a potential peace settlement than 10 years ago.

A March poll of Palestinians found that only 9 percent expect there to be peace and a Palestinian state 10 years from now. Twenty-five percent of Palestinians anticipate a continuation of the status quo, with settlement expansion continuing.[107]

Meanwhile, most Israelis have felt little sense of urgency about changing the status quo, pollster Scheindlin said shortly after the poll was released. In the midst of intermittent rockets fired at Israel by Hamas in Gaza, "you'd think people would say, 'Stop! We can't live through it anymore.' But people say, 'Ah, well, there's terror everywhere in the world, we have our Iron Dome missile defense system, the rest of the world is not pressuring us, and we can live with the situation.'"

Even those who have spent their lives trying to negotiate peace say the ongoing conflict does not seem intolerable enough to produce an agreement. For years, "a lot of people said the status quo is not sustainable. It turns out it is sustainable," says veteran negotiator Ross.

Some veterans of the peace process suggest new tactics are needed to build trust on both sides. Former U.S.

adviser Makovsky says he now thinks Trump's predecessors made a mistake trying for "a home run," with every issue settled. What is needed, he says, is "a solid single," such as Israel stopping settlement expansion or the Palestinians agreeing to cease "martyr" payments to families of Palestinians who kill Israelis.

"If each side did one thing that was hard for them, it would at least convince their respective publics this exercise is genuine and has some promise," Makovsky says.

Dekel, who headed the negotiating team for Israeli Prime Minister Olmert in 2008, wants to go even further. He says he is tired of waiting for a comprehensive peace deal, even though he sees two states as the only way to keep Israel a "Jewish, democratic, moral state." Dekel proposes simply giving the Palestinians the land they need for a state (suggesting Gaza and 60 percent of the West Bank), to create "a two-state reality," and working out the final borders and other contentious issues later.

But that kind of unilateral action, without first bringing Palestinians to the table, will not work, says Betty Herschman, director of international relations and advocacy for Ir Amim, a Jerusalem group advocating a two-state solution. "We can't take it upon ourselves to decide."

Jerusalem resident Seidemann, who has participated in back-channel peace talks between Israelis and Palestinians for years and still hopes for a two-state solution, worries about violent religious conflict among increasingly fundamentalist Jews and Muslims.

Nevertheless, this American-born Israeli retains hope. "I'm 66 years old, and I don't think I will live to see the two-state solution. But I think it will be the ultimate outcome," he says. Noting that no one ever thought the Cold War would end or the Berlin Wall would fall, he says, "The skeptics are always right until they're wrong."

NOTES

1. Mark Landler, "Trump Recognizes Jerusalem as Israel's Capital and Orders U.S. Embassy to Move," *New York Times*, Dec. 6, 2017, https://tinyurl.com/ychf8jdj.

2. *Ibid.*; "Statement by President Trump on Jerusalem," The White House, Dec. 6, 2017, https://tinyurl.com/yb8yrkxx.

3. Rory Jones and Abu Bakr Bashir, "Palestinian Protests Pose Fresh Hurdles for Israel," *Wall Street Journal*, April 2, 2018, https://tinyurl.com/y8smk7xe.

4. Fares Akram, "Day after Cease-Fire, Gaza Border Demonstrations to Resume," Associated Press, Nov. 15, 2018, https://www.apnews.com/b23aa5dc4f7a47dfbf0cffa9c9be7634.

5. Molly Hunter, "Gaza Cease-Fire Holds, while Israel's Government May Collapse," ABC, Nov. 14, 2018, https://abcnews.go.com/International/gaza-ceasefire-holds-israels-government-collapse/story?id=59188751.

6. Lahav Harkov, "Netanyahu: Early Elections Could Bring Intifada-Level Disaster," Jerusalem Post, Nov. 18, 2018, https://www.jpost.com/Israel-News/Netanyahu-Early-election-could-bring-Intifada-level-disaster-572177. Also see Lahav Harkov, "Election Avoided? Bennett and Shaked Walk Back Resignation Threats," Jerusalem Post, Nov. 19, 2018, https://www.jpost.com/Israel-News/Election-avoided-Bennett-and-Shaked-walk-back-resignation-threats-572245.

7. Associated Press, "Hamas Abides by Cease-Fire; Restrains Protest," Nov. 16, 2018, https://abc3340.com/news/nation-world/hamas-abides-by-cease-fire-restrains-protests. Also see PBS, "Israel and Hamas Accept Cease-Fire but Deeper Issues Remain," Nov. 13, 2018, https://www.pbs.org/newshour/world/israel-and-hamas-accept-cease-fire-but-deeper-issues-remain.

8. *Haaretz* Weekly Podcast, "With Early Election Looming, Will Netanyahu Pay the Price for Gaza Truce?" *Haaretz*, Nov. 18, 2018, https://www.haaretz.com/israel-news/podcasts/haaretz-weekly-podcast-will-bibi-pay-for-gaza-truce-1.6659971.

9. Elie Podeh, "The Palestinians Also Know How to Miss Opportunities," *Jerusalem Post*, May 21, 2017, https://tinyurl.com/yamnh8kv.

10. Geoffrey R. Watson, "International Law and the 'Permanent Status' Issues," in *The Oslo Accords: A Critical Assessment* (2010), chap. 14.

11. Also see Atef Abu Saif, "Why I Stay in Gaza," *New York Times*, March 21, 2018, https://tinyurl.com/

y75l7dom. The U.N. says about $540 million is needed for humanitarian aid in the Palestinian territories in 2018. See "UN Seeks $540 million for Palestinian Aid, Mostly for Gaza," Associated Press, March 14, 2018, https://www.apnews.com/43e7035acfb44345b3aec2ab684f5206.

12. Palestinian Center for Policy and Survey Research, "Poll Summary: Palestinian-Israeli Pulse: A Joint Poll," Aug. 13, 2018, pp. 1, 5, http://www.pcpsr.org/sites/default/files/Summary_%20English_Joint%20PAL-ISR%20Poll%205_Jun2018.pdf.

13. Diana Buttu, "Issa Amro Is Merely the Latest Casualty of Palestine's War on Free Speech," *Guardian*, Sept. 20, 2017, https://tinyurl.com/yb9nprnp; "Hamas Signals Readiness to End Fatah Feuds and Hold Palestinian Elections," *Guardian*, Sept. 17, 2017, https://tinyurl.com/y9q3lj3u; and Jack Khoury, Amos Harel, and Yanif Kubovich, "Palestinian Prime Minister Survives Gaza Assassination Attempt," *Haaretz*, March 13, 2018, https://tinyurl.com/y9mjdf72.

14. David M. Halbfinger and Isabel Kershner, "Corruption Charges Suggested for Netanyahu," *New York Times*, Feb. 13, 2018, https://tinyurl.com/y9tyowaq.

15. *Haaretz* Weekly Podcast, *op. cit.*

16. "Netanyahu Says Palestinians Can Have a 'State Minus,'" *Times of Israel*, Jan. 22, 2017, https://tinyurl.com/ycovz284.

17. Rashid Khalidi, "The Middle East 'Peace Process' Was a Myth. Donald Trump Ended It," *Guardian*, Feb. 18, 2017, https://tinyurl.com/yaxrxl4p.

18. Jacob Magid, "US Envoy Tears Into Left-Wing Daily for Op-Ed Disparaging Him and Settlements," *Times of Israel*, Feb. 9, 2018, https://tinyurl.com/ycb5ktly; Peter Baker, "Trump Team Begins Drafting Middle East Peace Plan," *New York Times*, Nov. 11, 2017, https://tinyurl.com/yas5wfve; and Anne Barnard, David M. Halbfinger, and Peter Baker, "Talk of a Peace Plan That Snubs the Palestinians Roils Middle East," *New York Times*, Dec. 3, 2017, https://tinyurl.com/yd4gzgkg.

19. David Wainer and Nick Wadhams, "Trump's Middle East Plan Dealt Another Blow with Israel Turmoil," *Bloomberg News*, Nov. 15, 2018, https://www.bloomberg.com/news/articles/2018-11-15/trump-s-middle-east-plan-dealt-another-blow-with-israel-turmoil.

20. Amir Tibon, "Trump Administration's Peace Plan on Course despite Talk of Israeli Elections, Official Says," *Haaretz*, Nov. 15, 2018, https://www.haaretz.com/us-news/trump-administration-s-peace-plan-on-course-despite-talk-of-israeli-elections-1.6656568.

21. "Q&A: Why Bolton's Pick Adds to Obstacles for US Mideast Plan," Associated Press, March 29, 2018, https://tinyurl.com/yaojsalj.

22. "Full Text of Abbas' Address to the U.N. Security Council," *Times of Israel*, Feb. 21, 2018, https://tinyurl.com/ybltsrjs; Jacob Magid, "At UN Abbas Urges Multilateral Peace Effort, Lays Out Plans for Talks," *Times of Israel*, Feb. 20, 2018, https://tinyurl.com/yaveaowa.

23. "Statement by President Trump on Jerusalem," *op. cit.*

24. David Wainer and Nick Wadhams, *op. cit.*

25. "We Took Jerusalem Off the Negotiating Table, Trump Says alongside Netanyahu in Davos," *Haaretz*, Jan. 25, 2018, https://tinyurl.com/y73u6ex7.

26. Palestinian Center for Policy and Survey Research, *op. cit.*

27. *Ibid*. See also Palestinian Center for Policy and Survey Research, Public Opinion Poll No. 67, March 20, 2018.

28. Palestinian Center for Policy and Survey Research, Public Opinion Poll No. 67, March 20, 2018.

29. Khalidi, *op. cit.*

30. Ian Black, *Enemies and Neighbors: Arabs and Jews in Palestine, 1917-2017* (2017), pp. 478-80.

31. "Jerusalem Is the 'Eternal Capital' of the State of Palestine—Palestine Leader Abbas," RT, Dec. 7, 2017, https://tinyurl.com/yac495o7.

32. Khaled Elgindy, "Trump Just Sabotaged His Own Peace Process," *Foreign Policy*, Dec. 6, 2017, https://tinyurl.com/y8n9y8bb.

33. See "Unesco Adopts Controversial Resolution on Jerusalem Holy Sites," *Guardian*, Oct. 26, 2016, https://tinyurl.com/z7cseft.

34. "Full Text of Abbas' Address to the Security Council," *op. cit.*

35. Isabel Kershner, Anne Barnard, and Eric Schmitt, "Israel Strikes Iran in Syria and Loses a Jet," *New York Times*, Feb. 10, 2018, https://tinyurl.com/yal3g6m9.

36. "Trump, Netanyahu Talk Jerusalem, Iran, Mideast Peace at White House," *Haaretz*, March 5, 2018, https://tinyurl.com/y8gam4cr.

37. Jeffrey Goldberg, "Explaining the Toxic Obama-Netanyahu Marriage," *The Atlantic*, Oct. 9, 2015, https://tinyurl.com/y7vvnmb6.

38. Martin P. Bunton, *The Palestinian-Israeli Conflict: A Very Short Introduction* (2013), p. 12.

39. Peter Katel, "Israeli-Palestinian Conflict," *CQ Researcher*, June 21, 2013, p. 556.

40. Black, *op. cit.*, p. 14.

41. *Ibid.*

42. "36 Questions about the Holocaust," Simon Wiesenthal Center, https://tinyurl.com/a4veu6c.

43. Black, *op. cit.*, p. 90.

44. *Ibid.*, p. 107.

45. Bunton, *op. cit.*, pp. 53, 58.

46. *Ibid.*, pp. xiv, 60.

47. U.N. Security Council Resolution 242, Nov. 22, 1967, https://tinyurl.com/y85j3mkm.

48. "U.N. Security Council: The Meaning of Resolution 242," Jewish Virtual Library, 2018, https://tinyurl.com/ybj3nxcv.

49. "Palestine Refugees," United Nations Relief and Works Agency for Palestine Refugees, https://tinyurl.com/y8e9zvc3.

50. Mitchell Bard, "Israel-Egypt Relations," Jewish Virtual Library, https://tinyurl.com/yah7gyxg. Also see "Israel Relations: Peace Treaty between Israel & Egypt," Jewish Virtual Library, https://tinyurl.com/ybsjn2qm.

51. Katel, *op. cit.*, pp. 561, 562.

52. Bunton, *op. cit.*, p. 104.

53. "Saving Lives-Israel's Security Fence," Israel Ministry of Foreign Affairs, https://tinyurl.com/yd8zvrcm; Bunton, *ibid.*, pp. 102–3.

54. Bunton, *ibid.*, p. 103.

55. Simon Jeffery, "The Road Map to Peace," *Guardian*, June 4, 2003, https://tinyurl.com/ycqk4r28.

56. Katel, *op. cit.*, p. 562.

57. Josef Federman, "Abbas Admits He Rejected 2008 Peace Offer from Olmert," *Times of Israel*, Nov. 19, 2015, https://tinyurl.com/y8gmgaxv; Bernard Avishai, "A Plan for Peace That Still Could Be," *New York Times Magazine*, Feb. 7, 2011, https://tinyurl.com/ycrqylpj.

58. *Ibid.*, Federman.

59. Peter Baker *et al.*, "U.S. Finalizes Deal to Give Israel $38 billion in Military Aid," *New York Times*, Sept. 13, 2016, https://tinyurl.com/h3xvrzn; Raphael Ahren, "Netanyahu Initially Welcomed Kerry's Peace Initiative, Ex-US Envoy Says," *Times of Israel*, March 21, 2018, https://tinyurl.com/ycr6jodu.

60. Raphael Ahren, "In Politely Devastating Critique, Israeli Negotiator Skewers Kerry for Dooming Peace Talks," *Times of Israel*, March 2, 2017, https://tinyurl.com/ybj8zg7k.

61. "Full transcript: Kerry Blasts Israeli Government, Presents Six Points of Future Peace Deal," *Haaretz*, Dec. 28, 2016, https://tinyurl.com/yd6ngv82.

62. Black, *op. cit.*, p. 481.

63. *Ibid.*, pp. 480-81.

64. Jonathan Lis et al., "Bennett's Party Warns Netanyahu: Give Us Defense Portfolio or We'll Quit Coalition," Haaretz, Nov. 24, 2018, https://www.haaretz.com/israel-news/.premium-bennett-s-party-warns-netanyahu-give-us-defense-portfolio-or-we-ll-quit-coalition-1.6654909.

65. Associated Press, "Defense Chief's Resignation Pushes Israel toward Election," *New York Times*, Nov. 14, 2018, https://www.nytimes.com/aponline/2018/11/14/world/middleeast/ap-ml-israel-palestinians.html.

66. Anshel Pfeffer, "Why the Timing of the Israeli Election Matters So Much to Netanyahu and His

Rivals," Haaretz, Nov. 18, 2018, https://www
.haaretz.com/israel-news/.premium-why-the-
timing-of-the-israeli-election-matters-so-much-to-
netanyahu-and-his-rivals-1.6659004.

67. Lahav Harkov, "Election Avoided?" Jerusalem Post,
Nov. 19, 2018, https://www.jpost.com/Israel-
News/Election-avoided-Bennett-and-Shaked-walk-
back-resignation-threats-572245.

68. Isabel Kershner, "Renewed Clashes between Israel
and Gaza Interrupt Talk of Cease-Fire," *New York
Times*, Aug. 8, 2018, https://www.nytimes
.com/2018/08/08/world/middleeast/renewed-fire-
between-israel-and-gaza-interrupts-talk-of-cease-
fire.html

69. *Ibid.*

70. Lawahez Jabari et al., "Gaza Militants Announce
Ceasefire with Israel in a Bid to Avert War," NBC
News, Nov. 13, 2018, https://www.nbcnews.com/
news/world/hamas-threatens-step-attacks-israel-
gaza-border-ignites-n935531.

71. CBS, "Palestinians Bury Dead after Gaza-Israel
Border Clashes," May 15, 2018, https://www
.cbsnews.com/news/gaza-israel-border-protests-see-
palestinian-death-toll-mount-2018-5-15/.

72. Akram, *op. cit.*

73. "Poll: 74 Percent of Israelis Dissatisfied with
Netanyahu's Performance in Gaza Crisis,"
Haaretz, Nov. 14, 2018, https://www.haaretz.
com/israel-news/poll-74-percent-of-israelis-
dissatisfied-with-netanyahu-s-performance-in-
gaza-1.6655496.

74. Haaretz Weekly Podcast, *op. cit.*

75. Associated Press, *op. cit.* See also Halbfinger and
Kershner, *op. cit.*

76. Isabel Kershner, "Netanyahu, Citing Israel's
Security, Tries to Salvage His Government," New
York Times, Nov. 18, 2018, https://www.nytimes
.com/2018/11/18/world/middleeast/israel-netan-
yahu.html.

77. Anshel Pfeffer, *op. cit.*

78. Anshel Pfeffer, "Why Netanyahu Will Do Almost
Anything for a Gaza Cease-Fire," Haaretz, Nov. 14,
2018, https://www.haaretz.com/israel-news/

.premium-why-netanyahu-will-do-almost-
anything-for-a-gaza-cease-fire-1.6653416.

79. Isabel Kershner, "If Gaza Brings Down Netanyahu's
Government, Can He Rise Again?" *New York
Times*, Nov. 16, 2018, https://www.nytimes.com/
2018/11/16/world/middleeast/gaza-netanyahu-israel-
elections.html?action=click&module=RelatedCove
rage&pgtype=Article&region=Footer.

80. "Expert Explains What Consequences Netanyahu
Corruption Case Might Have," *Sputnik International*,
Feb. 23, 2018, https://tinyurl.com/ydyksh44.

81. Haaretz Weekly Podcast, *op. cit.*

82. Josef Federman, "Israeli Settler Leader Says
Settlements Continued to Grow in 2017," Associated
Press, Yahoo, Feb. 19, 2018, https://tinyurl.com/
y96rhwau.

83. Jacob Magid, "Settler Growth Rate Declines for
Sixth Straight Year," *Times of Israel*, Jan. 21, 2018,
https://tinyurl.com/ycwjd9gu.

84. Shaul Arieli, "The Israeli Settlement Movement Is
Failing," *Forward*, Feb. 26, 2018, https://tinyurl
.com/y9sytrar.

85. "Knesset Passes Law Requiring 80-MK Majority for
Giving Up Israeli Sovereignty over Any Part of
Jerusalem," press release, Knesset, Jan. 2, 2018,
https://tinyurl.com/y9tlvh3l.

86. "Latest Developments, New Law to Prevent Future
Compromise on Jerusalem," Terrestrial Jerusalem,
Jan. 19, 2018, https://tinyurl.com/y9fo5slt.

87. John Hudson, "Trump Threatened to Cut Off Aid
after a UN Vote," *BuzzFeed*, Feb. 13, 2018, https://
tinyurl.com/ydyzrfk5.

88. "Jerusalem Embassy: Abbas Says Trump Plan 'Slap
of the Century,'" BBC News, Jan. 14, 2018, https://
tinyurl.com/y9thk3g9.

89. Jones and Bashir, *op. cit.*; Isabel Kershner and Iyad
Abuheweila, "Israeli Military Kills 15 Palestinians in
Confrontations on Gaza Border," *New York Times*,
March 30, 2018, https://tinyurl.com/ydamfynf;
and Amos Harel, "Following Attack, Israel May
Move West Bank Separation Barrier," *Haaretz*,
March 17, 2018, https://tinyurl.com/y7cksbto.

90. "This Week in Palestine," International Middle East Media Center, Oct. 7-13, 2017, https://tinyurl.com/y7ycghex.

91. Khaled Abu Toameh, "Abbas to Hamas: You 'Hijacked' Gaza, Now Give It Back," *Times of Israel*, March 22, 2018, https://tinyurl.com/y7uozqj7.

92. TOI Staff, "Egypt Pushing for Abbas to Accept Graded Reconciliation with Hamas—Report," Times of Israel, Nov. 4, 2018, https://www.timesofisrael.com/egypt-pushing-for-abbas-to-accept-graded-reconciliation-with-hamas-report/.

93. Khaled Abu Toameh, "Israeli-Hamas Ceasefire after Gaza Violence Pushes Abbas toward Irrelevancy," Jerusalem Post, Nov. 14, 2018, https://www.jpost.com/Arab-Israeli-Conflict/Israel-Hamas-ceasefire-after-Gaza-violence-pushes-Abbas-toward-irrelevancy-571924.

94. Tovah Lazaroff, "Three Suitcases Stuffed with $15 Million Passed to Hamas in Gaza," Jerusalem Post, Nov. 8, 2018, https://www.jpost.com/Arab-Israeli-Conflict/Three-suitcases-stuffed-with-15m-passed-to-Hamas-in-Gaza-571449.

95. Rick Gladstone, "UN General Assembly Vote Castigates Israel over Gaza Deaths," *New York Times*, June 13, 2018, https://www.nytimes.com/2018/06/13/world/middleeast/israel-gaza-united-nations.html.

96. *Ibid.*

97. Karen de Young et al., "US Ends Aid to United Nations Agency Supporting Palestinian Refugees," Washington Post, Aug. 31, 2018, https://www.washingtonpost.com/world/middle_east/us-aid-cuts-wont-end-the-right-of-return-palestinians-say/2018/08/31/8e3f25b4-ad0c-11e8-8a0c-70b618c98d3c_story.html?utm_term=.c5be94db4767.

98. *Ibid.*

99. Daniel Estrin, "U.S. Cuts More Than $200 Million in Aid to Palestinians," NPR, Aug. 24, 2018, https://www.npr.org/2018/08/24/641689522/u-s-cuts-more-than-200-million-in-aid-to-palestinians.

100. Amir Tibon, "White House Kicks Off Conference on Gaza," *Haaretz*, March 13, 2018, https://tinyurl.com/y82v3c83.

101. "Readout of the Gaza Conference at the White House," The White House, March 14, 2018, https://tinyurl.com/y8b479ws.

102. "If the President Won't Reverse Course on Bolton, Congress Must Step In to Limit Bolton's Extremist Impact," press release, J Street, March 22, 2018, https://tinyurl.com/y7c68uco.

103. "Palestinians Slam Trump National Security Advisor Pick Bolton," AFP, *Times of Israel*, March 23, 2018, https://tinyurl.com/yahmjq7u.

104. Zvi Bar'el, "Why the Attempt on the Palestinian PM's Life May Accelerate Reconciliation with Hamas," *Haaretz*, March 18, 2018, https://tinyurl.com/y8lfh2zz.

105. Jacob Wirtschafter and Mina Nader, "Egypt, Saudi Arabia Less Optimistic of Trump's 'Deal of Century' to Bring Middle East Peace," USA Today, Aug. 22, 2018, https://www.usatoday.com/story/news/world/2018/08/22/enthusiasm-wanes-trumps-deal-century-middle-east-peace-deal/1047237002/.

106. David Wainer and Nick Wadhams, Bloomberg News, *op. cit.* Also see Bianca Britton, "Pence: US Is Not 'Going to Stand' for Khashoggi Killing," Nov. 18, 2018, https://www.cnn.com/2018/11/18/middleeast/jamal-khashoggi-killing-intl/index.html.

107. Palestinian Center for Policy and Survey Research, Public Opinion Poll No. 67, March 20, 2018, http://pcpsr.org/en/node/723.

BIBLIOGRAPHY
Selected Sources
Books

Black, Ian, *Enemies and Neighbors: Arabs and Jews in Palestine and Israel, 1917-2017*, Penguin, 2017.
A former Middle East editor for the *Guardian* presents a comprehensive history of the Arab-Israeli conflict, offering both points of view but ending on a pessimistic note: "No end to their conflict was in sight."

Julius, Lyn, *Uprooted: How 3,000 Years of Jewish Civilization in the Arab World Vanished Overnight*, Valentine Mitchell, 2018.

A British writer chronicles how more than 800,000 Jews were driven from their homelands in the Middle East after Israel's founding in 1948.

Ross, Dennis, *Doomed to Succeed: The U.S.-Israel Relationship from Truman to Obama*, Farrar, Straus and Giroux, 2015.

U.S. relations with Arab countries were never determined by U.S. actions on Israel and Palestine, the author argues in this history encompassing his years as an adviser and Middle East envoy during the administrations of George H.W. Bush, Bill Clinton and Barack Obama.

Schulze, Kirsten E., *The Arab-Israeli Conflict: Third Edition*, Routledge, 2017.

An associate professor of international history at the London School of Economics presents a step-by-step account of Arab-Israeli peace negotiations.

Articles

"Jared Kushner Flames Out," *New York Times*, March 1, 2018, https://tinyurl.com/y8czlrbm.

President Trump's son-in-law Jared Kushner has been discredited as a Middle East negotiator because of conflicts of interest and phone conversations in which foreign officials sought to manipulate him, according to *The New York Times*' Editorial Board.

Abrams, Elliott, "Trump Gets UNRWA Right," blog, Council on Foreign Relations, Jan. 17, 2018, https://tinyurl.com/ya3awb5x.

A former adviser to President George W. Bush says President Trump was right to cut U.N. aid to Palestinian refugees, arguing the program perpetuates the refugee crisis.

Barnard, Anne, et al., "Talk of a Peace Plan That Snubs the Palestinians Roils Middle East," *New York Times*, Dec. 3, 2017, https://tinyurl.com/yd4gzgkg.

Even before President Trump's announcement that the United States would recognize Jerusalem as the Israeli capital, rumors that his peace plan was heavily tilted toward the Israelis had roused anger among Palestinians and their supporters.

Bolton, John, "John Bolton: Trump's Jerusalem Declaration Long Overdue," *Tribune-Review*, Dec. 9, 2017, https://tinyurl.com/y8lyrakx.

The president's recently appointed national security adviser, writing while still a senior fellow at the conservative American Enterprise Institute in Washington, praised President Trump for providing an "injection of reality" into the Middle East peace process.

Elgindy, Khaled, "Trump Just Sabotaged His Own Peace Process," *Foreign Policy*, Dec. 6, 2017, https://tinyurl.com/y8n9y8bb.

A former adviser to the Palestinian leadership and now a fellow at the Brookings Institution's Center for Middle East Policy says President Trump's Jerusalem announcement was the final nail in the coffin of a moribund peace process.

Khalidi, Rashid, "The Middle East 'Peace Process' Was a Myth. Donald Trump Ended It," *Guardian*, Feb. 18, 2017, https://tinyurl.com/yaxrxl4p.

A Columbia University professor of modern Arab studies says it has long been a myth that a separate Palestinian state is an option; its fate was further sealed by President Trump's lack of endorsement of the idea and Israel's "state minus" proposal, in which Israel would retain some territory captured in 1967.

Tibon, Amir, and Noa Landau, "White House Officials Tell Haaretz Peace Plan Still on the Agenda—and Could Surprise Skeptics," *Haaretz*, March 30, 2018, https://tinyurl.com/ybdqdojd.

The Trump administration remains confident its peace plan can achieve a diplomatic breakthrough despite Palestinians' insistence that the United States can no longer act as a neutral peace broker.

Reports and Studies

"Palestinian-Israeli Pulse," Palestinian Center for Policy and Survey Research, Aug. 13, 2018, http://pcpsr.org/en/node/731.

A survey produced jointly by Palestinian and Israeli researchers finds that support for the two-state solution has slipped to a minority of both Palestinians and Jewish Israelis—and to its lowest level in a decade.

Tatarsky, Aviv, and Efran Cohen-Bar, "Deliberately Planned," Ir Amim, February 2017, https://tinyurl.com/y9lvp9ss.

A liberal Israeli advocacy group that tracks developments in Jerusalem reports that only 9 percent of the city is zoned for Palestinian residential construction, but that the city makes it so difficult for Palestinians to obtain a construction permit that many build illegally.

For More Information

Al-Shabaka, The Palestinian Policy Network, PO Box 9613, Washington, DC 20016-9997; 202-436-9103; al-shabaka.org/en. Think tank focusing on Palestinian human rights and self-determination.

American Israel Public Affairs Committee (AIPAC), 202-639-5363; www.aipac.org. Pro-Israel advocacy group with offices in all 50 states.

Americans for Peace Now, 2100 M St., N.W., Suite 619, Washington, DC 20037; 202-408-9898; peacenow.org. Sister organization of Israel peace movement organization Peace Now; advocates policies leading to a two-state solution.

Institute for Middle East Understanding, 2913 El Camino Real, #436, Tustin, CA 92782; 718-514-9662; www.imeu .org. Independent nonprofit that seeks to provide accurate information to journalists about Palestine.

Institute for National Security Studies, Haim Levanon Street, Tel Aviv 6997556 Israel; +972-3-640-0400; www .inss.org.il. Research organization focused on Israel's national security agenda that includes prominent former Israeli and U.S. government and military leaders among its staff.

Palestinian Center for Policy and Survey Research, Off Irsal Street, PO Box 76, Ramallah, Palestine; +972-2-2964933; www.pcpsr.org. Independent think tank conducting polls of Palestinians and joint polls with Israeli researchers.

Palestine Strategy Group; www.palestinestrategygroup.ps. Aims to influence and inform policy decisions related to the Palestinian national project.

Terrestrial Jerusalem, t-j.org.il. Israeli nongovernmental organization tracking developments in Jerusalem that could affect the peace process.

Washington Institute for Near East Policy, 1111 19th St., N.W., Suite 500, Washington, DC 20036; 202-452-0650; www.washingtoninstitute.org. Research institute that studies Middle East policy.

2

Saudi Arabia's Uncertain Future

Karen Foerstel

King Salman presents the golden Collar of Abdulaziz al Saud—Saudi Arabia's highest honor—to President Trump in Riyadh on May 20, 2017. Trump and Salman struck a $350 billion arms deal they said would help fight terrorism and create American jobs. But critics warn that Trump's support for the kingdom could pull the United States into one of the regional proxy conflicts between the Saudis and Iran.

From *CQ Researcher*,
March 9, 2018

As President Trump exited Air Force One in the Saudi capital of Riyadh last May, he was greeted by television cameras, a military brass band, young girls with flowers and King Salman bin Abdulaziz al Saud. Seven Saudi jets trailed red, white and blue smoke overhead.[1]

For the next two days, Trump received more than 80 gifts, including a silver dagger, swords and robes lined with tiger and cheetah fur. The king draped the golden Collar of Abdulaziz al Saud—the nation's highest honor—around the president's neck.[2]

Trump's red-carpet treatment was in stark contrast to the chilly reception a year earlier for President Barack Obama, who during his final trip to the kingdom as president was met—not by the king but by the mayor of Riyadh—in an untelevised ceremony. Obama had angered the Saudis by brokering a deal in 2015 lifting economic sanctions on the Saudis' longtime archrival Iran in return for limits on its nuclear program. The Saudis fear that eased sanctions will enable Iran to expand its power across the Middle East.[3]

"This is the beginning of a turning point in the relationship between the United States and the Arab and Islamic world," Saudi Foreign Minister Adel bin Ahmed al Jubeir said during Trump's visit. "[It] begins to change the conversation from one of enmity to one of partnership."[4]

Indeed, after years of friction, the U.S.-Saudi relationship has warmed quickly. Citing mutual opposition to Iran, Trump and the Saudi king struck a $350 billion arms deal they said would create American jobs and help fight terrorism. The thawing of relations is occurring as Saudi Arabia is aggressively ramping up its geopolitical maneuverings against Iran and its allies, leading some experts to fear that Trump's unflinching support for the kingdom could pull the United States into new Middle East conflicts.

Meanwhile, the Saudis tentatively are introducing social and economic reforms, partly to attract U.S. and other investors to help the kingdom diversify its oil-dependent economy.

Saudi Arabia's increasingly antagonistic moves toward Iran stem from a 1,400-year-old split between Shiite and Sunni Muslims.* Both countries have strict, religiously based governments: Iran is a Shiite theocracy, Saudi Arabia a theocratic monarchy where Sunnism is the state religion. Exacerbating the political power struggle, the animosity also has a racial component: The Saudis are Arabs, the Iranians Persian.[5]

The age-old rivalry has led to proxy conflicts across the region, including in Yemen, where in 2015 the Saudis intervened in a civil war on behalf of the Yemeni president against Shiite Houthi rebels. That conflict has killed more than 10,000 people, displaced 2 million and left millions on the brink of famine in what one U.N. official has called "a man-made disaster."[6]

Obama had halted the sale of cluster bombs and $400 million worth of missiles to Saudi Arabia over concerns the Saudis would use the weapons against Yemeni civilians. But the new arms deal Trump signed with the Saudis includes some of the same weapons Obama refused to sell.[7]

---

*Shiite and Sunni Muslims have been at odds since the seventh century and the death of the Prophet Muhammad. Most of the world's 1.6 billion Muslims are Sunni, who live in many more countries than Shiite Muslims, who live primarily in Iran, Pakistan, India and Iraq. After Muhammad's death, most Sunnis believed that Abu Bakr, Muhammad's father-in-law and close friend, was his rightful successor. However, a small group of Muslims, the Shiites, believed Muhammad's successor should be Ali ibn Abi Talib, his cousin and son-in-law. The Sunnis prevailed and Abu Bakr became the first Muslim caliph and successor to the prophet. Today the main difference between Shiite and Sunni Muslims remains the importance Shiites give to Ali, whom the Sunni do not recognize as the prophet's rightful successor.

"Hundreds of billions of dollars of investments into the United States and jobs, jobs, jobs," Trump tweeted about the deal. The Saudis praised the arms package as a united front against terrorism and "the face of malign Iranian influence."[8]

However, Saudi Arabia's critics question the kingdom's true commitment to fighting terrorism, since it adheres to—and spends millions of dollars spreading—Wahhabism (Salafism), an ultraconservative form of Sunnism that relies on a literal interpretation of the Quran. Violent jihadist groups such as al Qaeda, the perpetrators of the Sept. 11, 2001, attacks in the United States, have adopted an even more extremist interpretation of Wahhabism.

Besides engaging in the civil war in Yemen, the Saudis have supported Sunnis in conflicts and power struggles with Iranian-supported Shiites in:

- Syria, where the two rivals have provided money and troops to opposing sides in a civil war that has killed a half-million people and displaced 5 million. The Saudis back rebels fighting to overthrow President Bashar al Assad, who is supported by Iran.[9]

- Iraq, where Saudis have long opposed the Iran-backed Shiite-controlled government that came to power after the United States toppled Sunni dictator Saddam Hussein in 2003. The Saudis are now trying to regain a foothold there to counter Iranian influence and have pledged $1.5 billion to help Iraq rebuild.[10]

- Lebanon, where the Saudis have sought to send a strong message that they will no longer tolerate Iran's influence in the coalition government, which includes the Iranian-backed Shiite group Hezbollah. In a bizarre incident during a visit to Riyadh last November, Lebanese Prime Minister Saad Hariri, a longtime Saudi ally, was held hostage until he resigned. But Hariri rescinded his resignation after returning to Beirut, where he was welcomed as a hero.[11]

- Qatar, which the Saudis blockaded—two weeks after Trump's visit—in retaliation for alleged links to Iran and terrorism.

Trump not only expressed support for the blockade in Qatar but took credit for it, tweeting that his Saudi trip was "already paying off" because: "During my recent trip to the Middle East I stated that there can no longer be funding of Radical Ideology Leaders pointed to Qatar—look!"[12]

But Trump's overwhelming support for the blockade surprised many—including his military commanders. Qatar hosts the largest U.S. military base in the Middle East, with 11,000 personnel, and is the staging ground for airstrikes against Islamic State (ISIS) terrorists in Iraq and Syria.[13]

Some experts say Trump's belligerent stance against Iran and the nuclear deal have emboldened the Saudis to increase their aggression toward Iran.

"The Saudis are really flexing their muscles in unnerving ways," says Kristian Coates Ulrichsen, a Middle East fellow at Rice University's Baker Institute for Public Policy. "They . . . feel they have at least four years [under Trump], so there is a window of opportunity where they are determined to press their advantage to the maximum."

Meanwhile, the Saudis' oil-dependent economy faces serious challenges. Oil prices are down about 50 percent from 2014, with demand dropping as the use of renewable energy grows.[14] But in 2017 oil and oil-related industries accounted for 90 percent of the kingdom's export earnings, 87 percent of its budget revenues and 42 percent of its gross domestic product (GDP).[15]

Now 32-year-old Crown Prince Mohammed bin Salman—named heir to the throne last June 21 by King Salman, his father—is leading

Saudi Arabia Dominates in the Middle East

The largest country and fourth-largest economy in the Middle East, predominantly Sunni Saudi Arabia is part of a volatile, oil-rich region wracked by age-old conflict between Sunni and Shiite Muslims.

Religious Profile of the Region

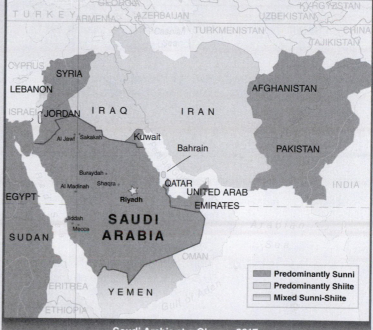

Saudi Arabia at a Glance, 2017

Area: 830,000 square miles, about one-fifth the size of the U.S.

Population: 33.5 million

Labor force: 12.3 million, about 80% of whom are immigrants, mostly from India and Pakistan

Unemployment rate: 5.8% (male), 19.5% (female)

GDP: $1.8 trillion ($55,300 per capita), with 42 percent of 2017 GDP derived from oil industry; 2017 growth projected at 0.1%

Exports: Oil and oil-related industries account for 90 percent of the kingdom's export earnings.

Religion: Muslim (85–90% Sunni), (10–15% Shiite). The government enforces a strict version of Sunni Islam.

Government: Theocratic monarchy

Sources: World Factbook; World Bank; U.S. Department of State, Worldmeters, International Labor Organization

Eight Decades of Saudi Rule

Abdulaziz ibn Saud, an Arabian tribal leader, established the Kingdom of Saudi Arabia in 1932. Since his death in 1953, six of his sons have ruled the country.

Saudi Kings (1932-Present)

King	Rule	Biographical Highlights
Abdulaziz ibn Saud	1932-1953	Established the kingdom in 1932 and began Saudi Arabia's long oil relationship with the United States in 1933.
Saud	1953-1964	Had little interest in governing and spent most of his reign abusing the kingdom's vast wealth until he was deposed by his family in 1964.
Faisal	1964-1975	Built the modern Saudi state. Assassinated in 1975 by his nephew, Prince Faisal bin Musaed bin Abdelaziz.
Khalid	1975-1982	Reigned during a time of great transition including soaring oil revenues, massive construction and religious uprisings.
Fahd	1982-2005	Ruled during the period of strongest U.S.-Saudi relations, the oil-price collapse in the 1980s, the first Gulf War and the 9/11 terrorist attacks in the United States.
Abdullah	2005-2015	Implemented many reforms: allowed women to run for office and vote in local elections; appointed 30 women to the country's highest consultative body, the Shura Council; Saudi Arabia joined the World Trade Organization during his reign.
Salman	2015-	Intervened in the civil war in Yemen; gave women the right to drive; named his son, Mohammad bin Salman, 32, as crown prince.

Sources: Pamela Engel, "Here's a who's who of the Saudi royal family," *Business Insider*, Feb. 2, 2015, https://tinyurl.com/mq7oc3o; Renee Lightner *et al.*, "Saudi Arabia's Royal Family," *The Wall Street Journal*, Dec. 3, 2017, https://tinyurl.com/y9xsdja8; "King Abdullah bin Abdulaziz al Saud Fast Facts," CNN Library, April 30, 2017, https://tinyurl.com/ybos99lh; "Ibn-Saud," and "Khalid," *Encyclopaedia Britannica*; "A Chronology: The House of Saud," Frontline, PBS, Aug. 1, 2005, https://tinyurl.com/ya9nvo2

efforts to wean his country from its dependence on oil. His economic plan, called Vision 2030, aims to grow Saudi Arabia's technology, entertainment and tourist industries.

In November, as part of an "anti-corruption" campaign designed to recoup money allegedly stolen from the government, the crown prince ordered the arrest of hundreds of fellow princes and prominent Saudi business leaders, mostly on charges of money laundering and embezzling government funds. Most have since been freed, after handing over an estimated $100 billion to the Saudi treasury.[16]

"It was a shakedown" for funds to replace dwindling oil revenues, says Thomas Lippman, a scholar at the Middle East Institute, a nonpartisan think tank that aims to increase Americans' understanding of the Middle East. "No one was doing this when oil was $100 a barrel. They were spreading the word to other people that they'd better cough it up. It was making an example while making money."

To court foreign investors and to secure support from young Saudis, who make up more than half of the population, Crown Prince Mohammed has pushed for social reforms, such as repealing a ban on women drivers and reopening public movie theaters, which were banned 35 years ago.[17]

"He has recognized, to an extent that no other Saudi leader ever has, that his country is going to have to find a different path in order to succeed in the 21st century," says Peter Mandaville, a professor of international affairs at George Mason University in Fairfax, Va. "He has realized that with the demographic equation and the pace of change that is happening in the global energy market, something rapid and dramatic is going to have to happen."

But critics of Saudi Arabia's human rights record question whether recent reforms are enough to modernize the religiously conservative country, which bans homosexuality, holds public beheadings of those convicted of capital crimes, prohibits non-Wahhabi religious expression and regularly arrests citizens who speak out against the government.[18]

"Once things settle down and people get accustomed to movies and women driving and find out this is not a big deal, . . . people will demand more, and that's when the problems arise," says Ali Alyami, executive director of the Center for Democracy and Human Rights in Saudi Arabia, a Washington-based group that promotes political reform in the kingdom. "There will be more incarceration, more people disappearing. 2017 is the beginning of the end of the Saudi royal family."

Alyami believes the kingdom is prime for an uprising and could dissolve into a patchwork of fiefdoms.

As the United States increases its support of Saudi Arabia, here are some questions geopolitical analysts, U.S. policymakers and others are asking:

Should the United States strengthen its ties with Saudi Arabia?

A week after his inauguration, President Trump approved a covert military operation in Yemen in which a U.S. Navy SEAL was killed and five others were injured. The United States is providing logistical support and intelligence to Saudi Arabia in its fight against the Houthi rebels. U.S. airstrikes and ground raids also are being launched against al Qaeda and ISIS forces, which have spread in Yemen since the Saudis injected themselves into the civil war in 2015.[19]

Yemen has become the most violent of the proxy conflicts between Saudi Arabia and Iran in the Middle East. The Saudis support Sunni groups who are fighting the Iranian-backed Houthi rebels, but other forces—including al Qaeda, ISIS and tribal separatists—are adding to the chaos and violence.

Trump has fully supported Crown Prince Mohammed's increasingly aggressive efforts to stop Iranian influence elsewhere in the region—a switch from Obama, who chose to negotiate with Iran.

"According to Saudi Arabia, Iranians are the No. 1 problem. Trump came fully on board with that," says James Gelvin, a professor of history at UCLA and author of several books on the Middle East. "Trump policy in the Middle East is fundamentally 'un-Bama': You look at what Obama did and you do the opposite."

But some veteran Middle East watchers say the new crown prince is doing what is necessary to keep Iran at bay and deserves U.S. support.

"In [the Saudis'] eyes, the last decade has seen extraordinary Iranian advances and a reluctance on the part of the United States to halt them. Thus their more assertive foreign and defense policy in Yemen, Lebanon and elsewhere," said Elliott Abrams, deputy national security adviser under President George W. Bush and now a senior fellow for Middle Eastern studies at the Council on Foreign Relations think tank in New York City. "[Crown Prince Mohammed] is taking action. He will have failures and he will make mistakes, but it is very greatly in the interest of the United States that, in the main, he succeed."[20]

Other Middle East experts worry that Trump's unflinching support of Saudi opposition to Iran could draw the United States into dangerous conflicts. "Having a mindless anti-Iranian position that targets Shiites justifies a war [in Yemen] that is not in America's interest," says Eugene Rogan, director of the Middle East Centre at St Antony's College at the University of Oxford in Great Britain.

Mandaville of George Mason University agrees, saying the Saudis' "disproportionate" sense of paranoia toward Iran threatens U.S. foreign interests. However, he says, the United States should do what it can on the domestic front to ensure that economic and social reforms do not disrupt the kingdom's status as one of the most stable nations in the Middle East.

"There are elements of the crown prince's vision that I think are valuable and where the U.S. should be supporting him," says Mandaville. "Vision 2030 is far-reaching and sweeping in its ambition. Helping the Saudis to identify which elements of that are feasible—and [which are] less realistic—that's a clear area of partnership, and crucial to ensure the Saudi political order can hold together and prosper."

Rice University's Ulrichsen cautiously agrees. "The United States should try to support Vision 2030 but insist on transparency, accountability and good governance," he says, so that it does not turn Saudi Arabia into "a one-man show" or damage the investment climate between the two countries.

The arrests last fall of powerful Saudis were carried out in the name of "anti-corruption," but Ulrichsen says the campaign could backfire. "[The crown prince] may have intended to send the message that he was cleaning house, but . . . that wasn't the message the world saw," he says. International investors "are now wondering if the assets they have in Saudi Arabia will suddenly be seized."

Others, however, say the arrests make Saudi Arabia a safer place for U.S. companies to invest. "It [was] a shakedown, but that's the only way you can get these people to pay back the money they took," says Jean-François Seznec, a senior fellow at the Global Energy Center at the Atlantic Council, a foreign affairs think tank in Washington, D.C. "There is no independent judiciary that you can use to go after people. . . . The arrests are sending mixed messages, but ultimately it will be better for anyone investing in the kingdom."

Indeed, two American tech giants—Amazon and Google's parent company, Alphabet—are considering opening data centers in Saudi Arabia. And more deals with U.S. companies could be struck this spring, when Crown Prince Mohammed is scheduled to visit the United States and meet with American business leaders.[21]

Other Saudi experts say the United States should focus on political, rather than economic, reforms in the kingdom. "It is in the U.S. interest to strengthen ties. But those ties have to serve the right strategy," says Saudi journalist Jamal Khashoggi. "In the Arab world today [that means] to embrace change, people's rights, democracy, power sharing. This relationship should serve a good cause, but I don't see it doing that right now. . . . [W]hat will serve the war on terror is bringing democracy to the Arab world."

Human rights activists complained that Trump deemphasized the kingdom's poor human rights record during his trip to Riyadh. "We are not here to lecture," he said. "We must seek partners, not perfection" in fighting terrorism.[22]

"The glaring absence of human rights from Trump's agenda will only embolden further violations in a region where governments flout the rights of their own people in the name of the fight against terror, and violate international humanitarian law in conflicts fueled in large part by U.S. arms transfers," said the human rights advocacy group Amnesty International.[23]

Is Saudi Arabia a true U.S. ally against terrorism?

In his 2011 book *Time to Get Tough: Making America #1 Again*, Donald Trump called Saudi Arabia "the world's biggest funder of terrorism." But after winning the White House, Trump agreed to sell billions of dollars' worth of weapons to the Saudis and called Iran the "leading state sponsor of terrorism."[24]

Many terrorist organizations—such as al Qaeda and ISIS—follow an even stricter interpretation of Wahhabism than the official Saudi state religion. The terrorists' version of Wahhabism opposes any interaction with the West or its cultural influences and justifies violent jihad against anyone, including Muslims, who does not subscribe to that belief.[25]

Since becoming crown prince, Mohammed bin Salman has vowed to destroy extremist ideologies and return his country to the more moderate form of Islam that existed prior to 1979. During that tumultuous year Shiite fundamentalists led a revolution in Iran, minority Shiites in Saudi Arabia revolted against Sunni authorities and Sunni fundamentalists laid siege to Saudi Arabia's Grand Mosque to protest Saudi alliances with the West. The Saudi government responded by imposing stricter adherence to Wahhabism.

But while Saudi Arabia has pledged to reform itself and work with the United States against terrorism, some experts question the strength of that alliance.

"Everyone is driven by pragmatism when it comes to combating their enemies," said Rogan of St Antony's College. "The U.S. talks about the war on terror as if it means the same thing to anyone. Al Qaeda has attacked both Saudi Arabia and the United States in the past, so the two countries are aligned in their opposition to al Qaeda. But there are other parties that Saudi Arabia supports that may not align with the United States."

Al Qaeda's founder, Osama bin Laden, was stripped of his Saudi citizenship in 1994 after calling for the overthrow the Saudi government for allowing U.S. troops to operate from bases in the kingdom. Since then, al Qaeda terrorists have conducted numerous attacks inside Saudi Arabia. But, today, Saudi troops are fighting alongside al Qaeda forces in Yemen because of their mutual opposition to the Iranian-backed Houthi rebels.[26]

Meanwhile, Saudi Arabia has spent $100 billion over the years paying clerics and building mosques and schools to spread Wahhabi beliefs around the world, says Gelvin of UCLA. "The crown prince said he'll oppose terrorism," he says. "But I'm not convinced that is the case."

Boosting terrorism probably was an unintended outgrowth of the religious spending, says Abdeslam Maghraoui, a professor of political science at Duke University in Durham, N.C. "After the Iranian revolution, Saudi Arabia felt threatened and reacted by mobilizing Sunnis and building mosques around the world," he says. "Their intent was not to create al Qaeda."

Although 15 of the 19 hijackers who attacked the United States on 9/11 were Saudis, the kingdom denies any direct link to them. It has asked a U.S. judge to dismiss lawsuits alleging that it aided the attackers.[27]

The National Commission on Terrorist Attacks Upon the United States, known as the 9/11 Commission, said in its 2004 report that it had found no evidence that Saudi officials directly supported the attacks but that the kingdom had provided "fertile fund-raising ground" for al Qaeda. Documents from a joint congressional committee investigating the attacks declassified in 2016 said some of the hijackers had received support from individuals likely "connected" to the Saudi government.[28]

"After 9/11, the Saudis . . . recognized they didn't know where [Saudi] money was coming from and going to, and they made a concerted effort to interdict these flows," says Perry Cammack, a fellow at the Carnegie Endowment for International Peace, an international affairs research organization in Washington, D.C. "I've heard senior Saudi officials privately reflect that they made some big mistakes in the '70s and '80s that came back to bite them in the 2000s."

However, Cammack adds, there are "clear benefits" for the United States in maintaining ties to Saudi Arabia: "It's the birthplace of Islam. It's important for counterterrorism."

Over the years, Saudi officials—particularly former Crown Prince Mohammed bin Nayef (known as MbN)—have cooperated closely with U.S. anti-terrorism efforts. "The information [MbN] shared with the United States over the last 15 years saved many American lives," says George Mason's Mandaville. In 2017, bin Nayef received a medal of honor from the CIA for his "excellent intelligence performance in the domain of counterterrorism."[29] Bin Nayef, who had been next in line for the throne, was pushed out last June when his cousin, Mohammed bin Salman, was named crown prince.[30]

"That has led to nervously raised eyebrows" in Washington, says Mandaville. "They're not sure they will be getting the same cooperation they had under MbN."

Others say U.S.-Saudi cooperation is essential for fighting dangerous fundamentalism based inside the kingdom. "If you're going to stop the Salafi jihadists, you need all the weapons you can get," says Greg Gause, head of the International Affairs Department at the Bush School of Government and Public Service at Texas A&M University in College Station.

One of those weapons is "confronting fundamentalism within its own Islamic tradition," he continues. "You need Saudi scholars to do that. Liberalism is not the weapon that will defeat Salafi jihadists."

Can Saudi Arabia reform its economy and society?

Last September, King Salman announced that this June, Saudi Arabia would no longer be the last nation on Earth where women are not allowed to drive.[31] Four months later Saudi activist Noha al Balawi was arrested for advocating for women's rights via social media.[32]

Women still face many restrictions in Saudi Arabia's conservative religious society. They must get permission from their husbands, fathers or other male guardians to obtain a passport, travel abroad or marry.[33] The kingdom also prohibits homosexual behavior, free speech and other social freedoms, and it beheads criminals for capital offenses, often in public.[34] The public practice of any religion other than Islam is banned, and speaking out against Islam is punishable by death.[35]

Crown Prince Mohammed's Vision 2030 promises to build "a thriving country in which all citizens can fulfill their dreams, hopes and ambitions."[36] As part of that

APF/Getty Images/Amer Hilabi (both)

In the Driver's Seat

A Saudi woman takes the wheel in a car showroom for women in Jeddah on Jan. 11, 2018 (top). Last September, King Salman announced that beginning in June women in Saudi Arabia would be allowed to drive. Women still face many restrictions in the conservative religious society. For example, they must get permission from their husbands, fathers or other male guardians to obtain a passport, travel abroad or marry. Saudi women take a selfie (bottom) at a clothing boutique in Jeddah on Nov. 28, 2017. More women than men are graduating from college in Saudi Arabia, but they comprise 80 percent of the nation's unemployed. Some experts say women's rights are not a top priority for Crown Prince Mohammed but that he knows economic success cannot occur without women's progress. Religious conservatives have pushed back against the prince's reforms, but experts say he will find support among the country's large population of young people.

These social reforms also have an economic element: More women than men are graduating from college in Saudi Arabia, but they comprise 80 percent of Saudi Arabia's unemployed.[38] If women are to get more jobs and contribute to the Saudi economy, they must be able to drive to those jobs. In addition, the theaters will create jobs, and movie-goers will spend money at the cinemas and at nearby restaurants.

Some experts say women's rights are not a top priority for the crown prince but that he knows economic success cannot occur without women's progress. "Let's not think this is some liberal progressive reformer," says Mandaville of George Mason University. "Enfranchising women [such as allowing them to drive] is an instrumental step needed for economic reform."

Some religious conservatives have pushed back against the reforms, but experts say the young prince will find support among the country's large population of young people. "The conservatives themselves include a large percentage of young people. [Yet] these young people know that things have to evolve," says the Atlantic Council's Seznec. It is not a struggle between conservatives and liberals but "more a generational battle," he says. "But at this point I don't think the pushback will be successful. I'm optimistic."

In another effort to strengthen the economy, the government announced in January it is banning foreign workers in 12 private-sector fields.[39] Currently, foreigners—mostly from India and Pakistan—comprise more than half of private-sector workers. But most send their wages back home to family members instead of pumping the money into the Saudi economy.[40]

vision, women will be allowed to drive, and Saudis will be able to attend public concerts and see movies in theaters.[37]

Another economic challenge for the country: Nearly 70 percent of Saudi citizens work for the government, which pays almost twice private-sector wage rates.[41] In addition, all Saudi citizens have long received generous government handouts, such as subsidies for utilities, free education and tax-free salaries.[42]

"Many Saudis are not interested to work in the private sector because of low salaries," said Mohammed Al Aufi, author of a study on Saudi unemployment. "The culture of shame also played a role. Most Saudis refuse to take up menial jobs as they fear it would affect their image in society."[43]

The high percentage of citizens with public-sector jobs strains government finances. To create more private-sector jobs, the crown prince hosted a conference in Riyadh last October that drew 3,500 investors and business leaders from the United States and other countries. At the conference the prince unveiled plans for Neom, a $500 billion solar-powered city run by robots.[44]

Such extravagant projects may not help Saudi Arabia transform its economy, say some experts on the kingdom. The prince "believes in a top-down approach—building futuristic cities while neglecting the status quo," says Saudi journalist Khashoggi. "Reform should be bottom up, not top down. [Saudi] cities lack infrastructure. We don't need any more white elephants. We need to fix what we have already."

Others say the prince's personal behavior raises questions about his commitment to reform. Shortly after announcing his robotic city, *The New York Times* reported that in 2015 the prince had bought the world's most expensive home (a $300 million French chateau) and a $500 million yacht. In 2017 he purchased a $450 million painting by Leonardo da Vinci—the most expensive art sale in history.[45]

"You start wondering: Why is the crown prince spending billions on his own possessions?" says Maghraoui of Duke University. "It raises doubt about the maturity of the crown prince."

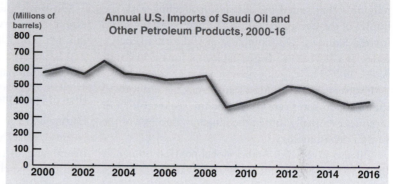

Imports of Saudi Oil Waning

U.S. imports of crude oil and other petroleum products from Saudi Arabia have declined in recent years after peaking in the early 2000s, during the wars in Afghanistan and Iraq. The United States imports about 11 percent of its oil from Saudi Arabia.

Annual U.S. Imports of Saudi Oil and Other Petroleum Products, 2000-16

(Millions of barrels)

Source: "U.S. Imports from Saudi Arabia of Crude Oil and Petroleum Products," Petroleum & Other Liquids, U.S. Energy Information Administration, Jan. 31, 2018, https://tinyurl.com/ycfkla72

But experts such as Richard Sokolsky, a former U.S. State Department official, say even minimal success would be good for the country.

"I'm skeptical that he can realize his vision," says Sokolsky, now a nonresident senior fellow with the Carnegie Endowment. "But if he realizes half or a quarter of it, Saudi Arabia will be much better off in 2030 than it is now."

BACKGROUND

Oil and Power

Saudi rulers have long understood the importance of powerful allies. The kingdom traces its beginnings to 1744, when Muhammad ibn Saud, the emir of a desert town, forged a pact with the cleric Muhammad ibn Abd al Wahhab, the father of Wahhabism.

Under the pact, Wahhab received military protection for his growing religious movement, which preached a return to conservative Islamic values with austere restrictions on women and discrimination against all other faiths (including other forms of Islam).[46] In return, Wahhab presented ibn Saud as Allah's chosen monarch.

With the support of the cleric's followers and fighters, King Saud gained control of much of the region and established a theocratic monarchy with Wahhabism as the state religion and a legal system based on Islamic law, or sharia.[47] The House of Saud has ruled the country ever since.[48]

When founding the modern kingdom of Saudi Arabia in 1932, Saudi leaders again looked for powerful allies. This time it was the United States, and oil—not religion—that sealed the alliance. Struggling with the impact of the Great Depression, the new Saudi kingdom invited Standard Oil Company of California (known today as Chevron) to begin exploring for oil in Saudi Arabia in 1933.[49]

Five years later, the Americans struck oil and formed the Arabian American Oil Company (Aramco).[50] Oil revenues eventually turned the kingdom into one of the world's richest nations.

Oil also gave Saudi Arabia global political influence. In 1945, near the end of World War II, the U.S. Department of State called Saudi oil "a stupendous source of strategic power, and one of the greatest material prizes in world history."[51] That same year, U.S. President Franklin D. Roosevelt met with Saudi King Abdulaziz ibn Saud to cement ties between the two countries. Saudi Arabia ensured U.S. access to its oil fields, which Roosevelt knew would be needed in postwar America, while the United States agreed to provide military support for the kingdom.[52]

While the two countries strengthened their military and economic ties over the next decade, relations within the Saudi royal family were less secure. In 1953, King Abdulaziz died and was succeeded as by his eldest son, Saud. The new king was an extravagant spender and more than doubled the national debt during the first five years of his rule.[53] In 1964 he was forced from the throne by his brother, Faisal, who became king.[54]

During this period, countries were gaining independence from their colonial powers and beginning to keep the revenues from the export of their natural resources. The vast majority of global oil production, however, remained under the control of seven Western oil companies—five of them American—known as the "Seven Sisters."[55] In 1960, Saudi Arabia and four other oil-producing nations—Iran, Iraq, Kuwait and Venezuela—created a cartel, the Organization of the Petroleum Exporting Countries (OPEC), which aimed to help developing countries reclaim their oil resources.[56]

OPEC demonstrated its political power in 1973, when it imposed a devastating embargo against the United States and seven other countries in retaliation for their support of Israel during the Yom Kippur war with Egypt and Syria. Gas prices in the United States nearly quadrupled.[57] OPEC lifted the embargo the following year.[58]

Oil wealth also allowed the Saudi government to export its conservative Wahhabi beliefs. From the 1960s through the 1990s, Saudi Arabia built 1,359 mosques, 210 Islamic centers, 202 colleges and 2,000 schools in non-Muslim-majority countries alone.[59]

Rise of Fundamentalism

During his reign from 1964 to 1975, King Faisal worked to modernize Saudi Arabia's economy and society, promoting infrastructure development and public education—including for girls—and introducing the country's first television broadcast.[60]

Because of his reputation as a pious Muslim, Faisal was able to cautiously push modern reforms, but the introduction of TV offended many religious conservatives. For instance, one of the king's nephews was killed by police when he led an assault on a new television station.[61]

Several years later, in 1975, the nephew's brother assassinated King Faisal in retaliation.

Faisal's successor, King Khalid, continued with many of Faisal's development programs including expanding the country's telecommunications systems and building more airports, highways, schools and hospitals. Foreign firms boosted investments in the country's petrochemical industry.[62]

John West, then-U.S. ambassador to Saudi Arabia, wrote in a 1977 memo to President Jimmy Carter that Saudi Arabia was "undergoing an almost fantasy-like experience," with the entire country changing overnight, "as though someone had rubbed Aladdin's lamp and said, 'Take this place into the Twentieth Century.'" Indeed, he added, "No country in the history of the world has ever before had such an influx of goods and services from outside in such a brief period."[63]

West warned, however, that rapid modernization was "creating tensions and frictions at all levels" that would have an unpredictable effect on the government. The United States must "understand as best we can what may happen and how it affects our interests."[64]

CHRONOLOGY

1930s-1960s *Discovery of oil in Saudi Arabia helps establish the country's global influence*

1932 Abdulaziz ibn Saud—a descendant of the Saudi emir Muhammad ibn Saud, who established a theocratic monarchy in 1744—founds the modern Kingdom of Saudi Arabia.

1938 Standard Oil Co. of California strikes oil in Saudi Arabia and forms the Arabian American Oil Co.

1945 During World War II President Franklin D. Roosevelt meets with Saudi King Abdulaziz ibn Saud and pledges military support in exchange for access to oil.

1960 Saudi Arabia and four other countries form the Organization of the Petroleum Exporting Countries (OPEC), an oil-producers' cartel.

1970s *Saudi Arabia begins modernizing, but religious fundamentalists across the region resist reforms.*

1973 OPEC imposes an oil embargo on the United States and seven other countries in retaliation for their support of Israel.

1975 Saudi King Faisal, who had pushed social and economic reforms, is assassinated by a nephew.

1979 Religious conservatives in Iran revolt and form a Shiite theocracy, inspiring Shiites in Saudi Arabia to rebel against Saudi oppression; dozens die in government crackdown. . . . Sunni fundamentalists seize Saudi Arabia's Grand Mosque and condemn the Saudi government for its Western alliances. . . . Soviets invade Afghanistan, prompting Sunnis from other countries, including Saudi Osama bin Laden, to travel to Afghanistan to help the Afghans repel the Soviets. While in Afghanistan, bin Laden forms al Qaeda terrorist group.

2000s-Present *U.S.-Saudi relations fray, but President Trump renews Saudi alliance.*

2001 Nineteen al Qaeda members—15 of them Saudis—attack the United States on Sept. 11, killing nearly 3,000 people.

2003 U.S. troops leave Saudi Arabia as Saudi citizens and al Qaeda supporters pressure the kingdom to cut ties with the West.

2011 Pro-democracy protesters topple authoritarian regimes in Tunisia, Egypt and Yemen.

2015 The Saudis strongly oppose President Barack Obama's efforts to loosen economic sanctions on Iran in exchange for restricting its nuclear program. . . . Saudis and Sunni allies launch air strikes against Shiite Houthi rebels in Yemen.

2016 Saudi Arabia executes 47 people in one day, including Nimr al-Nimr, a Shiite cleric who called for greater rights for Saudi Shiites. The execution sparks violent protests at the Saudi Embassy in Tehran, leading Saudi Arabia to cut diplomatic ties with Iran.

2017 Trump renews U.S.-Saudi friendship, traveling to the kingdom on his first international trip and signing a $350 billion arms deal with the Saudis. . . . King Salman bin Abdulaziz al Saud names his reform-minded son, Mohammed bin Salman, heir to the throne. . . . Saudis sever relations with Qatar, claiming it supports terrorists. . . . King Salman says that in June 2018 he will lift the ban on women driving. . . . Crown Prince Mohammed orders hundreds of leading Saudis arrested in anti-corruption crackdown. . . . The king announces he will lift a ban on public movie theaters. . . . Families of people killed and injured during the 9/11 terrorist attacks in the United States file lawsuits against the Saudi government claiming it supported the organizers of the attacks.

2018 First cinemas open in Saudi Arabia. . . . U.N. says Iran has violated an arms embargo and Saudi Arabia has indiscriminately killed civilians and used "the threat of starvation as an instrument of war" in Yemen. . . . Saudi, United Arab Emirates and Qatari officials plan to meet with Trump in Washington in hopes of resolving tensions. . . . For the first time, women are allowed to apply for non-combat positions in the Saudi armed forces, but they must reside with a male guardian in the same province as the job's location.

Saudis' Role in Yemen Under Fire

War "poses the specter of the richest country in the region destroying the poorest."

Yemen, one of the world's poorest countries, is on the front lines of a proxy war in the Middle East pitting Sunni-dominated Saudi Arabia against Iran's Shiite theocracy.

The roots of Yemen's troubles date to the Arab Spring of 2011, a series of demonstrations decrying poverty and political repression that began in Tunisia and spread across the Middle East. In Yemen—a small country on Saudi Arabia's southern border—protests forced President Ali Abdullah Saleh to end his 33-year rule and transfer power to Vice President Abdu Rabbu Mansour Hadi.[1]

But Hadi struggled to deal with a slew of problems, including opposition from Saleh loyalists, a separatist movement in the south, corruption, unemployment and food shortages.

Houthi rebels, who champion Yemen's Shiite minority, took advantage of the disorder to attack the government, and Hadi fled the country in 2015 leaving the Iran-backed Houthis in control. Saudi Arabia and eight other mostly Sunni Arab states began an air campaign aimed at returning Hadi to power. Since then, Yemen has become the most violent of the Saudi-Iran proxy power struggles going on across the Middle East.[2]

Since 2015, fighting in Yemen has led to the deaths of more than 10,000 people, displaced more than 2 million and triggered a cholera epidemic that has infected about 1 million. The conflict also has helped plunge the country into a famine that has put more than 7 million Yemenis, about one-quarter of the population, at risk of starvation. A Saudi blockade of Yemini ports has prevented food, medicine and other humanitarian aid from getting into the country.[3]

A United Nations report in February charged Iran with providing military support to the Houthi rebels in violation of a U.N. arms embargo, and it said the Saudi-led coalition, including the United Arab Emirates and Jordan, has conducted "indiscriminate" airstrikes that killed civilians. The coalition also has blocked ports in an effort to use "the threat of starvation as an instrument of war," the report said.[4]

But the U.N. Security Council also is considering a British resolution that praises Saudi Arabia for pledging to provide $1 billion in humanitarian aid to Yemen and $2 billion to shore up the country's war-torn economy.[5]

Human rights groups, however, say Saudi Arabia has committed war crimes by intentionally targeting civilians.[6]

Some Middle East experts say if Saudi Arabia does not end its military operations and bring stability to Yemen, there could be dire consequences for the region and beyond. "The Yemen war poses the specter of the richest country in the region destroying the poorest country in the region. It's a crime against all of our consciences," says Eugene Rogan, director of the Middle East Centre at St Antony's College at University of Oxford, England. "Saudi Arabia will have to deal with rebuilding the country. If they don't do it, it will generate shoe bombers and all the other nasties."

In 2015, Yemen was ranked 168 out of 188 countries on the Human Development Index, which measures life expectancy, education and standard of living.[7]

Several experts say the Saudis' activities pose risks for the United States. "Yemen is not only a humanitarian catastrophe, but the Saudi military campaign serves no U.S. strategic interest," says Richard Sokolsky, a former State

Indeed, Saudi Arabia and its neighbors were about to face a seismic shift in the political and social order of the Middle East. In 1979, a Shiite revolution against Iran's authoritarian regime resulted in the establishment of the Islamic Republic of Iran, a Shiite theocracy with cleric Ayatollah Ruhollah Khomeini as supreme leader.[65]

Meanwhile, in Saudi Arabia, Sunni fundamentalists seized the Grand Mosque in Mecca, one of the holiest sites in Islam, and accused the Saudi government of betraying Muslims by forging ties to Western nations. After a weeks-long standoff, the Saudi military stormed the mosque and removed the armed dissidents. More than 200 people were killed.[66] Afterwards, more than 60 dissidents were executed.

Two weeks after the siege at the mosque, Shiites, who make up about 15 percent of the Saudi population and have long faced discrimination by the government, rose up against the kingdom, in part inspired

Department official who now is a nonresident senior fellow with the Carnegie Endowment for International Peace in Washington, D.C. "The war allows greater space for al Qaeda and other jihadists, strengthens Iran's influence and increases the threat to the Saudis security."

The United States has used airstrikes and on-the-ground military personnel to attack al Qaeda and Islamic State forces that have gained a stronghold in Yemen amid the chaos. The U.S. military considers the Yemen-based Al Qaeda in the Arabian Peninsula (AQAP) the radical group's most dangerous branch.[8] The Saudis, who normally oppose al Qaeda, regularly cooperate with al Qaeda fighters in Yemen because they both oppose the Shiite Houthis.[9]

Because of Saudi links to al Qaeda, the U.S. House and Senate voted last year to curb U.S. military support to Saudi Arabia. In June, the Senate narrowly defeated—47-53—a resolution that would have blocked a $510 million sale of precision-guided munitions to the kingdom.[10] Five months later, the House overwhelming passed a non-binding resolution declaring U.S. military action in Yemen unauthorized.[11]

U.S. diplomats say the United States is pursuing "very aggressive diplomacy" to end the war. "There is no military solution to this conflict," said State Department Deputy Assistant Secretary for Arabian Gulf Affairs Tim Lenderking. "So, we're pushing everybody to move into a political process as quickly as we can."[12]

The United States, he said, has provided more than $1.3 billion in humanitarian assistance to Yemen—that country's largest humanitarian donor—and Trump's close relations with Saudi Arabia has helped to convince the Saudis to unblock a Yemeni port and allow in some humanitarian supplies.[13]

— Karen Foerstel

[1] Kathleen Schuster, "Yemen's war explained in 4 key points," *Deutsche Welle*, Nov. 8, 2017, https://tinyurl.com/y7hbgetp. For background, see Kenneth Jost, "Unrest in the Arab World," *CQ Researcher*, Feb. 1, 2013, pp. 105-132.

[2] "Yemen crisis: Who is fighting whom?" BBC, Jan. 30, 2018, https://tinyurl.com/jwtyrfj.

[3] "More than 8 million Yemenis 'a step away from famine': U.N.," Reuters, Dec. 11, 2017, https://tinyurl.com/y7zmtw3o; Shuaib Almosawa and Ben Hubbard, "Yemen's Ex-President Killed as Mayhem Rocks Capital," *The New York Times*, Dec. 4, 2017, https://tinyurl.com/y7uumelb; "Yemen: Saudi 'Aid' Plan Is War Tactic," International Rescue Committee, Feb. 22, 2018, https://tinyurl.com/yc78slbw.

[4] "February 2018 Monthly Forecast," U.N. Security Council, February 2018, https://tinyurl.com/y96ckdrx.

[5] Michelle Nichols, "U.N. Security Council mulls Saudi praise for Yemen aid pledge," Reuters, Feb. 15, 2018, https://tinyurl.com/ybwjz3aq.

[6] "Human Rights Watch Says Saudi-led Air Strikes in Yemen Are War Crimes," Reuters, Sept. 12, 2017, https://tinyurl.com/yawn339v.

[7] Kathleen Schuster, "Yemen's war explained in 4 key points," *Deutsche Welle*, Nov. 8, 2017, https://tinyurl.com/y7hbgetp.

[8] "Drone Strike Kills 7 Qaeda Suspects in Yemen," *The Nation*, Jan. 28, 2018, https://tinyurl.com/y7kxfme9.

[9] Maggie Michael and Ahmed Al-Haj, "Pro-government tribal leader among dead in US raid in Yemen," The Associated Press, Feb. 16, 2017, https://tinyurl.com/yaug8mu3.

[10] Jeremy Herb, "Senate narrowly votes to back Saudi arms sale," CNN, June 13, 2017, https://tinyurl.com/y97ehvzn.

[11] Gregory Hellman, "House declares U.S. military role in Yemen's civil war unauthorized," *Politico*, Nov. 13, 2017, https://tinyurl.com/yazrbzjx.

[12] "Special Briefing with Deputy Assistant Secretary for Arabian Gulf Affairs Tim Lenderking," U.S. Department of State, Dec. 21, 2017, https://tinyurl.com/ycxtsre9.

[13] Ibid.

by the Iranian revolution.[67] Some Shiite communities held a traditional Shiite ritual, which was illegal. Saudi security forces shot and killed several people, triggering riots in which dozens were killed and thousands arrested.[68]

The back-to-back uprisings by both Sunnis and Shiites struck fear among Saudi leaders, who rolled back many of the modernization efforts and began enforcing strict adherence to Wahhabism.[69]

In December 1979, the Soviet Union invaded Afghanistan, a predominantly Sunni country, adding to the turmoil. Saudi Arabia, supported by the United States and Pakistan, provided cash and weapons to Afghan resistance fighters, and thousands of Sunnis from across the Middle East poured into Afghanistan to fight the Soviets. One of those was Osama bin Laden, the son of a wealthy Saudi construction magnate, who spent years in Afghanistan and founded al Qaeda. When bin Laden returned to Saudi

Saudis Denounce 9/11 Suits as "Speculation, Hearsay"

Kingdom fights efforts to recover damages from terrorist attacks.

In 2016, just months before the end of his eight years in office, President Barack Obama was handed his first and only veto override.

By a vote of 97-1 in the Senate, and 348-77 in the House, Congress upheld legislation allowing families of those killed in the Sept. 11, 2001, terrorist attacks to sue Saudi Arabia for any role it might have played in the plot. Al Qaeda, the terrorist group behind the attacks, hijacked four U.S. jetliners and crashed two of them into the World Trade Center in New York City and one into the Pentagon in Northern Virginia; a fourth hijacked jetliner headed to Washington crashed in Pennsylvania. Fifteen of the 19 hijackers were from Saudi Arabia.[1]

The Justice Against Sponsors of Terrorism Act (JASTA) lifted sovereign immunity protections for foreign governments and said they could be sued for terrorism acts committed against the United States.[2] Obama vetoed the bill, fearing it could set a precedent and open the United States to lawsuits in foreign courts.[3]

Since the law's passage, dozens of suits have been filed by families of the nearly 3,000 people who died in the attacks, people who suffered injuries—such as cancer and other diseases linked to smoke from the crash sites—and businesses that suffered financial losses. Together, the suits seek billions of dollars in damages from the Saudi government.[4]

The Saudis have vehemently denied any connection to the attacks and spent $8.4 million lobbying to overturn or weaken JASTA. The money has been used to, among other things, hire U.S.-based public relations firms to raise awareness about "unintended consequences that JASTA poses to U.S. interests, including potential legal liabilities arising for U.S. military, intelligence and diplomatic personnel." Firms hired by the Saudi government have also recruited U.S. military veterans and brought them to Washington to speak out against JASTA.[5]

In January, attorneys for Saudi Arabia asked a U.S. district judge to dismiss the cases, saying they were based on "conclusions, speculation, hearsay." But lawyers for the victims gave the court sworn statements from two former FBI officials as well as former Sen. Bob Graham, D-Fla.—who co-chaired the joint congressional committee that investigated the attacks—that say Saudi officials provided support to two of the Sept. 11 hijackers.[6]

The 9/11 Commission, established a year after the attacks, "found no evidence that the Saudi government as an institution or senior Saudi officials individually funded" al Qaeda. The commission's 2004 report, however, did say that al Qaeda "found fertile fund-raising ground in the kingdom, where extreme religious views are common and charitable giving is essential to the culture and, until recently, subject to very limited oversight."[7]

Arabia after the war in 1989, he was welcomed as a hero for defending Afghan Muslims against the Soviets.[70]

But bin Laden condemned the Saudi government for allowing U.S. troops to be stationed in the kingdom during the first Gulf War (1990-1991) and was expelled in 1991. In 1994, after financing numerous terrorist bombings—including at the World Trade Center in New York City in 1993—bin Laden was stripped of his citizenship.[71]

Over the next 10 years, bin Laden created an international army of al Qaeda extremists who attacked U.S.

forces in Saudi Arabia, Somalia and Yemen and American embassies in Kenya and Tanzania. Bin Laden's holy war against the United States culminated in the 9/11 attacks, which killed nearly 3,000.[72]

Strained Alliance

After 9/11, the Saudis pledged to cooperate with the United States "in every way that may help identify and pursue the perpetrators of this criminal incident." But the George W. Bush administration reportedly grew increasingly frustrated over the lack of Saudi cooperation.

In addition, a joint inquiry by the Senate Select Committee on Intelligence and the House Permanent Select Committee on Intelligence said the U.S. intelligence community strongly suspected there were connections between Saudi government officials and some of the hijackers. Part of the committee's findings—issued in 2002 but kept classified until 2016—stated that "while in the United States, some of the September 11 hijackers were in contact with, and received support or assistance from, individuals who may be connected to the Saudi government."[8]

When Obama vetoed the JASTA bill in 2016, then-Republican presidential candidate Donald Trump slammed the move as "shameful," saying it would "go down as one of the low points of his presidency."[9] Since becoming president, however, Trump has criticized JASTA, saying it could keep the kingdom from listing shares of its national oil company, Aramco, on the U.S. stock market.

Last November, Trump told reporters he wants Saudi Arabia to do an IPO (initial public offering)—which could raise an estimated $100 billion—with the New York Stock Exchange, Nasdaq or "anybody else located in this country." But, he lamented, "right now they're not looking at it, because of litigation, risk and other risk, which is very sad, they're not looking at it."[10]

Crown Prince Mohammed bin Salman is said to prefer a listing on the New York Stock Exchange because of its large number of investors and international prestige. But Aramco legal advisers and officials—including co-chair and Saudi Energy Minister Khalid al Falih—have privately warned the crown prince that a U.S. listing could expose the kingdom to lawsuits from shareholders and 9/11 victims. Al Falih reportedly favors a listing in London, where he sees less legal risk.[11]

The IPO is the centerpiece of Saudi Arabia's plan to diversify its oil-dependent economy. The country plans to sell about 5 percent of the company to raise money for reinvestment in non-oil industries.[12]

— *Karen Foerstel*

[1] Jennifer Steinhauer, Mark Mazzetti and Julie Hirschfeld Davis, "Congress Votes to Override Obama Veto on 9/11 Victims Bill," *The New York Times*, Sept. 28, 2016, https://tinyurl.com/j793hos.

[2] "Public Law 114-222-Sept. 28, 2016," Congress.gov, https://tinyurl.com/ycbmxe2q.

[3] Steinhauer, Mazzetti and Hirschfeld Davis, *op. cit.*

[4] Jonathan Stempel, "Saudi Arabia seeks to end U.S. lawsuits over Sept. 11 attacks," Reuters, Aug. 1, 2017, https://tinyurl.com/ybsocx39.

[5] Chuck Ross, "Saudis Spent $270K At Trump Hotel In Lobbying Campaign Against 9/11 Bill," *Daily Caller*, June 4, 2017, https://tinyurl.com/y8vzjehk.

[6] Bob Van Voris, "Saudi Arabia Claims No Evidence It Aided 9/11 Plot," Bloomberg, Jan. 19, 2018, https://tinyurl.com/ya4xr77x.

[7] Tom O'Connor, "Why Doesn't Saudi Arabia Join North Korea on U.S. State Terrorism List After 9/11?" *Newsweek*, Nov. 20, 2017, https://tinyurl.com/y7mg536c.

[8] *Ibid.*

[9] Robin Wright, "The Saudi Royal Purge—with Trump's Consent," *The New Yorker*, Nov. 6, 2017, https://tinyurl.com/y9j27l3a.

[10] "Trump urges Saudi Arabia to list state oil company on N.Y. stock exchange," *Politico*, Nov. 4, 2017, https://tinyurl.com/ybbxu5a4.

[11] Maureen Farrell and Summer Said, "Aramco IPO Stalled by Indecision Over Where to List," *The Wall Street Journal*, Jan. 28, 2018, https://tinyurl.com/y6wwxm4n..

[12] Andrew Torchia, "Saudi Assures Investors that Reforms, Aramco IPO on Track," Reuters, Sept. 9, 2017, https://tinyurl.com/y7of5h6d.

For instance, the kingdom refused to let the United States use its airbases to launch strikes against al Qaeda targets in Afghanistan.[73]

Tensions between the two countries continued to grow in the post-9/11 years as the Saudi government faced increasing criticism from citizens—including those sympathetic to al Qaeda—for its ties to the United States.[74] Saudi Arabia, which had welcomed U.S. troops after Iraq invaded Kuwait in 1990, declined to join U.S. and coalition forces in the war against Iraq in 2003. The Saudis also banned U.S. airstrikes from its military bases.[75]

In April 2003, Secretary of Defense Donald H. Rumsfeld announced that all U.S. troops in Saudi Arabia—numbering 550,000 at their peak—would pull out of the country.[76] The U.S. presence had "become more of a burden than a benefit," said one U.S. diplomat.[77]

Years later, Saudi officials described their relationship with the United States during the George W. Bush administration as a "train wreck," claiming that the second U.S. war in Iraq had handed that country over to Iranian-backed Shiites.[78] Iraq's predominantly Shiite population had been governed by a Sunni minority under dictator Saddam Hussein, who was deposed in 2003 during the war.

Following Hussein's ouster, Iraq became the venue for a proxy war between Saudi Arabia and Iran, with the Saudis claiming Iraq's U.S.-backed Shiite prime minister was an agent of Iran; they supported Sunni insurgents trying to overthrow him.[79]

Barack Obama's election in 2008 did little to improve U.S.-Saudi relations. The first meeting between President Obama and King Abdullah—who had inherited the throne in 2005—grew tense when the two leaders could not agree on issues surrounding Israel and the closing of the Guantánamo Bay prison, where many Saudis were being held as terror suspects.[80]

The relationship frayed even more during the so-called Arab Spring in 2011, when massive protests across the Middle East and North Africa called for the ouster of authoritarian leaders. As tens of thousands of Egyptians gathered to demonstrate against the authoritarian President Hosni Mubarak, Abdullah wanted Obama to back the Saudis' longtime ally. Instead, Obama called for Mubarak to step down.[81]

The Saudis were furious and began to wonder if Obama would one day abandon them as well.

The Arab Spring uprisings then spread to Bahrain, where the Shiite majority threatened to topple that tiny Gulf State's Sunni monarchy. Neither Saudi Arabia nor the United States, which has a naval base in Bahrain, wanted the protesters to prevail, but the Saudis took matters into their own hands, deploying more than 1,000 troops to quell the revolt in Bahrain.[82]

To protect his own monarchy, Abdullah spent $130 billion to avert potential opposition by ordering the construction of 500,000 low-income housing units and paying government employees two months' extra salary. The kingdom also allocated $200 million to religious organizations. In return, the kingdom's highest religious official issued an order saying Islam forbade street protests.[83]

Any pretense of cordial relations between Obama and the king disappeared after Obama helped broker a deal in 2015 that lifted economic sanctions on Iran in return for limits on its nuclear program. Obama later said Saudi Arabia should "share" the Middle East with Iran.[84]

Arab Spring uprisings by Syria's Sunni majority threatened the Assad regime and opened another front in the Iran-Saudi proxy wars. The Saudis began providing funds and weapons to Sunni rebels opposing Assad, who was backed by Iran.

Tensions between Iran and Saudi Arabia continued to heat up in 2016, when the Saudis executed 47 people in a single day, including Nimr al Nimr, a Saudi Shiite cleric who opposed the royal family and called for greater rights for Shiite Muslims in Saudi Arabia.[85] The executions sparked violent protests at the Saudi Embassy in Tehran, prompting the Saudis to sever all diplomatic ties with Iran.[86]

Friends Again

After President Trump's inauguration in 2017, relations between the United States and Saudi Arabia warmed.

Days after being sworn into office, Trump phoned King Salman, and the two spoke for an hour. They agreed to join forces against terrorism and Iran's "destabilizing regional activities."[87] Two months later, Trump welcomed to the White House a high-level Saudi delegation, which proclaimed Trump "a true friend of Muslims."[88]

Trump told the delegation he would support a new U.S.-Saudi program in which the Saudis would invest more than $200 billion in U.S. energy, industry, infrastructure and technology projects over the next four years.[89] Then during Trump's visit to the kingdom in May, the Saudis struck deals with privately held U.S. companies worth tens of billions of dollars and agreed to buy $350 billion worth of U.S. arms over the next 10 years.[90]

Shortly after Trump returned from his Saudi trip, King Salman deposed Crown Prince bin Nayef and named his son Mohammed as crown prince.

The close personal relationship between Crown Prince Mohammed and Trump's son-in-law Jared Kushner has helped solidify the friendship between the two countries. Kushner traveled to the kingdom three times during the first nine months of Trump's administration.[91] The 32-year-old prince and Kushner, also in his 30s, have been given a huge amount of political authority by their fathers; U.S. officials say they are never briefed on what the two discuss.[92]

With the United States firmly behind him, the young crown prince pushed for several bold moves during Trump's first year in office. The Saudis blockaded Qatar, tried to force Lebanon's prime minister to resign and arrested Saudi princes and business leaders. The

AFP/Getty Images/Karim Jaafar

Saudi Arabia blocked its borders with Qatar two weeks after President Trump's visit—in retaliation for its alleged links to Iran and terrorism. Above is the Qatari side of the Abu Samrah border crossing with Saudi Arabia on June 23, 2017. Leaders of Qatar, United Arab Emirates and Saudi Arabia plan to meet with Trump in Washington this spring in hopes of resolving tensions.

moves sent clear messages to potential foes that Saudi Arabia—and the crown prince in particular—were forces to be reckoned with.

Along with its recent aggressive political moves, Saudi Arabia also proposed social and economic reforms in 2017, part of efforts to rebrand itself on the global market. It also held its first public concert in seven years, attended by some 8,000 men. Although women were prohibited from attending, the top religious authority warned that such concerts could potentially open the door to the mixing of sexes.[93]

CURRENT SITUATION
Social Reforms

Saudi citizens are making the most of their country's new social reforms. They kicked off 2018 by lining up to see two American animated films, "The Emoji Movie" and "Captain Underpants," during a film festival in the city of Jeddah. It was the first time in 35 years that movie theaters were open to the public, and men and women were allowed to see the movie together—an indication that Saudi society is liberalizing.

Those lucky enough to snag a ticket to one of the sold-out screenings were treated to a red carpet and popcorn in a makeshift theater at the Society for Culture and Arts in Jeddah.[94]

But Saudi movie-goers soon will be able to enjoy big screens, surround sound and reclining seats, courtesy of

London-based Vue International, the Kuwait National Cinema Co. and Front Row Entertainment of Dubai, which are planning to open more than 40 theaters in Saudi Arabia this year.[95] In addition, AMC, the world's biggest cinema chain, owned by China's Dalian Wanda Group, has agreed to "explore a range of commercial opportunities for collaboration" in Saudi Arabia.[96]

However, the country's General Commission for Audiovisual Media is expected to prohibit films with sexual or religious content.[97]

Meanwhile, women are lining up to obtain driver's licenses. Nearly 1,000 women already have signed up for training as drivers for Careem, a ride-hailing company based in neighboring United Arab Emirates, which has millions of Saudi users and wants to hire 100,000 female Saudi drivers to expand into that market.[98]

The Saudi public seems to have embraced the change: A recent survey of both male and female respondents showed that 63 percent of Saudis support allowing women to drive.[99]

Still, Saudi Arabia remains one of the most restrictive countries in the world when it comes to women's rights. The World Economic Forum's "Global Gender Gap Report" for 2017 ranks Saudi Arabia 138th among 144 countries on economic, health, education and political equality for women.[100] Male guardianship laws remain a major obstacle, although King Salman has ordered government officials to loosen the system. It requires women to have a male relative's permission for travel and many other activities of daily life.[101]

While women make up more than half of graduates from Saudi universities, they comprise less than a quarter of the Saudi workforce, a percentage the crown prince aims to raise to 30 percent.[102] And Saudi women appear eager to help achieve that goal. When it advertised 140 job openings for female passport control workers, the Saudi General Directorate of Passports received 107,000 applications—in one week.[103]

While women may be gaining some opportunities, Saudi Arabia continues to restrict free speech, religious expression and other democratic rights for both genders. Two human rights activists were sentenced to prison in January for various free-speech violations, the first human rights defenders sentenced under the leadership of Crown Prince Mohammed, who is not only heir to the throne but also heads the Ministry of Defense, the Council for

Russian President Vladimir Putin greets then-Saudi Deputy Crown Prince and Defense Minister Mohammed bin Salman at the Kremlin in Moscow on May 30, 2017. Russia hopes to finalize several multimillion-dollar deals with Saudi Arabia by this summer. Russia is among several countries, including the United States and China, with keen interest in investing in Saudi Arabia.

Economic and Development Affairs and the Supreme Council for Saudi Aramco.[104]

Saudi Arabia often uses "counterterrorism" laws to convict anyone who speaks against the government. According to Human Rights Watch, a New York-based advocacy group that tracks human rights abuses around the world, more than a dozen political activists are in jail in Saudi Arabia for peaceful activities. Since Saudi Arabia has no written penal code, defendants can be convicted on broad charges such as "trying to distort the reputation of the kingdom."

In addition, the Saudis regularly conduct public floggings of criminals, and in 2017, 138 people were executed—57 for nonviolent drug crimes—usually by beheading and often in public, according to the human rights group.[105]

"There are some real important cultural changes happening," says Cammack of the Carnegie Endowment for International Peace, "but the political stuff is going to be really, really hard."

Economic Reforms

The crown prince sees Vision 2030 as the key to long-term economic stability for Saudi Arabia. But the kingdom has tried to diversify its oil-based economy numerous times over the past 30 years, with limited success.[106]

Today, the Saudi economy is recovering from a recession, and unemployment has reached a record 12.8 percent, due largely to government measures that are reducing public sector jobs and dropping oil prices that are hurting the petroleum industry. Nearly 70 percent of Saudi citizens work for the government, including government-owned Aramco.[107] To turn things around, the kingdom must beef up its private sector while reducing public spending.

But the government has proposed its largest budget in history—$260 billion—and the public is resisting plans to increase taxes and reduce public handouts, including subsidies to keep gas prices lower.[108] In January, less than a week after the government more than doubled gasoline prices and introduced a new 5 percent sales tax on most goods, citizens complained bitterly on social media.[109] The king responded by ordering a $13 billion government stimulus package that included bonuses for all government employees, a 10 percent increase in student stipends and a tax break for first-time home buyers.[110]

"It's a prudent reaction to public opinion," says Gause at Texas A&M. "[J]arring changes to the welfare state" could trigger discontent.

The kingdom plans to offset the stimulus with some of the $100 billion in payments the crown prince's anti-corruption campaign has already collected from about 350 princes and business leaders.[111] The kingdom also is counting on future revenue from international investments.

Besides the United States, Russia and China have expressed interest in investment opportunities in Saudi Arabia. Russia wants to finalize several multimillion-dollar deals with Saudi Arabia by this summer, and a Russian-Chinese investment fund aims to participate in the Saudis' initial public offering (IPO) of Aramco. The Saudis plan to sell up to 5 percent of the giant oil firm's shares on one or more foreign exchanges. At $2 trillion, the offering is expected to be the world's largest IPO.[112]

Trump has asked the king to list the IPO on the New York Stock Exchange (NYSE), but that decision is stalled.[113] While the crown prince is said to favor the NYSE for its prestige and deep pool of investors, a U.S. listing could open Saudi books to greater regulatory scrutiny and also put it at risk of lawsuits from 9/11 victims.[114]

Could the Saudis draw the U.S. into a new military conflict?

YES

Ali Alyami
Executive Director, Center for Democracy and Human Rights in Saudi Arabia

Written for *CQ Researcher*, March 2018

It's no secret that the Saudis have long exhorted the United States to invade Iran. In 2008, then-King Abdullah called on U.S. officials to "cut off the head of the snake."

The Saudis' efforts to encourage U.S. military action against their historic foe has not lessened over the years. The regimes of Saudi Arabia and Iran have been engaged in a ferocious religious and geopolitical competition for decades. This reality continues to intensify under Saudi Crown Prince Mohammed bin Salman's leadership. The young and aggressive prince recently described the Iranian supreme cleric, Ali Khameini, as "the new Hitler of the Middle East," adding that President Trump was the "right person at the right time" to act against the Iranian threat.

Mohammed's faith in Trump to confront Iran is not surprising. Trump's administration and family empire resemble that of the Saudi royal family. In addition, the two men believe in absolute control over their countries. But the close alliance between Trump and the prince could lead the United States down a dangerous path.

Tehran has become emboldened under the nuclear deal it made with the world's superpowers. It also is gaining the upper hand in its various proxy wars with the Saudis in Yemen, Qatar and Lebanon. Given this reality, the Saudis are building Muslim and non-Muslim coalitions aimed at confronting Iran's growing influence in the Middle East. Last November, Crown Prince Mohammed hosted the 40-Sunni-nation Islamic Military Counter Terrorism Coalition in Riyadh and vowed that together they would eliminate terrorism around the world. But in reality, these countries are more concerned with dismantling Iran's military and economic infrastructures than addressing the causes of terrorism.

The United States already is entangled in the disastrous Yemen war and has fully embraced Saudi Arabia's aggression against other countries—including the United States' own military ally, Qatar. In addition, Trump's threats have led Tehran to see no opportunity for negotiations with the United States and instead to view confrontation as the only option.

As Mohammed uses the terrorism threat to woo the United States and other countries, and as Trump continues blindly to support all actions of the crown prince, a hostile environment is being created in the Gulf region that could make it impossible for Washington to avoid a military confrontation with Iran.

NO

Peter Mandaville
Professor of International Affairs, George Mason University

Written for *CQ Researcher*, March 2018

While Saudi-Iranian proxy conflicts and undisciplined diplomatic overreach by Riyadh are likely to continue for the foreseeable future, we probably will not see the United States drawn into a new regional war.

Tensions between Tehran and Riyadh have ratcheted up in recent years—with Saudi Arabia's misadventure in Yemen representing the most dramatic manifestation of this rivalry—but neither country is spoiling for a direct conflict. Although the kingdom has found the Trump administration's return to the fold somewhat reassuring, Riyadh is only too aware that Washington's basic calculus with respect to its interests in the Middle East has evolved significantly over the past decade, meaning the United States cannot be counted on to provide the absolute security guarantee it once did.

This will serve to temper Saudi ambitions. Crown Prince Mohammed bin Salman knows that major regional instability would all but guarantee that his ambitious vision for Saudi Arabia's future never comes to fruition. For its part, Iran has every incentive to moderate its drive for regional influence. With tendrils reaching across much of the Gulf Cooperation Council, Iraq, Syria and Lebanon, Tehran possesses the infrastructure needed to increase its influence in response to events.

Ultimately, however, Iran—like Saudi Arabia—is more comfortable with stability and likely more capable than its rival at calibrating its actions to avoid dangerous escalation. Both countries are aware of what is at stake. While their public diplomacy is confrontational, mature voices within their respective security establishments carefully maintain channels of communication and respect red lines.

Of course, it is impossible to rule out various wild cards that might force Washington's hand. Chief among these would be a direct threat to Israel from Iran. But Tehran waves swords at Tel Aviv when it feels vulnerable or pushed into a corner, the polar opposite of its current regional standing.

This is all the more reason to maintain the core elements of the Iran nuclear deal. It is tempting to wonder, however, whether Washington's ability to avoid being drawn into a major regional conflict might ultimately lie somewhere unexpected: in Beijing. Both Riyadh and Tehran see China as crucial to their national development plans over the coming decades, and neither is willing to risk creating a situation that frightens away lucrative capital of that magnitude.

Proxy Wars

A U.N. report in February said all sides in the war in Yemen had committed widespread human rights violations in 2017.

Along with charges that Iranian-backed Houthi rebels had used torture, arbitrary arrests and "indiscriminate" use of explosive ordinances, it said Iran had provided military support to the rebels in violation of an international arms embargo. The report condemned Saudi-led coalition forces for launching "indiscriminate" air strikes that killed civilians and for blockading ports—thus preventing food aid from entering the country in order to use "the threat of starvation as an instrument of war."[115]

But in a somewhat contradictory move, the U.N. Security Council also is considering a British resolution praising Saudi Arabia for pledging $1 billion in humanitarian aid to Yemen and $2 billion to shore up its war-torn economy.[116]

For its part, the United States is using the U.N. report to call for "consequences" against Iran for violating the arms embargo.[117]

Meanwhile, mutual opposition to Iran is leading the Saudis and Israel to forge an unusual alliance. For more than 70 years Saudi Arabia has refused to recognize Israel because of its occupation of Palestinian territories.[118] But Israeli Intelligence Affairs Minister Yisrael Katz recently called Saudi Arabia the "leader of the Arab world" and asked the Saudis to sponsor Israeli-Palestinian peace talks.[119]

Then, at a global security conference in February, Israeli Prime Minister Benjamin Netanyahu and Saudi Foreign Minister Adel Al Jubeir delivered back-to-back warnings

> **"My concern is if nothing really changes in five years, if young people still have problems finding jobs, do people lose faith in the Saudi leadership and look to an alternative?"**
>
> — *Kristian Coates Ulrichsen Middle East Fellow, Baker Institute, Rice University*

against Iran's growing and aggressive interventions across the Middle East.[120] Israel also has invited Crown Prince Mohammed to come and discuss cooperation against Iran.

"Saudi Arabia has abandoned the Palestinian issue," says Gelvin at UCLA. They may pay "lip service" to the Palestinian problem, he says, but the "Israelis are far more important to them now, because they give them more power in their fight with Iran."

The Saudis also have asked their ally Pakistan to deploy more troops to the kingdom in what many say is another effort to confront Iran. Although Pakistan's military says the deployment is simply part of ongoing security cooperation with Saudi Arabia, some Pakistani lawmakers fear it could pull their country into a direct conflict with Iran.[121]

The Saudis have been seeking Pakistani troop deployments since the outbreak of the Yemen conflict in 2015. While Sunni-dominated Pakistan has deep economic, religious and military ties to Saudi Arabia, it shares a porous border with Iran, and Shiites comprise about one-fifth of Pakistan's population. Critics warn that the deployment could upset Pakistan's Shiite community and undermine bilateral relations with Iran.[122]

In Qatar, the foreign minister asked the U.N. Human Rights Council to stop the Saudi-led blockade of Qatar's borders.[123] Leaders of the United Arab Emirates, Qatar and Saudi Arabia are planning to meet with Trump in Washington this spring in hopes of resolving tensions.[124]

And while tensions between Lebanon and Saudi Arabia have been strained since Prime Minister Hariri was detained in Saudi Arabia last November, he is scheduled to visit the kingdom in the coming weeks at the invitation of the Saudi government.[125]

OUTLOOK
"Tensions and Frictions"

The rapid political, economic and social change occurring in Saudi Arabia today is reminiscent of the "fantasy-like experience" Ambassador West described in 1977. But just as West warned 40 years ago, today's changes also risk "creating tensions and frictions at all levels."

Crown Prince Mohammed must confront several challenges inside and outside his country. While pushing social reforms needed to attract international investors, he must not alienate the kingdom's powerful religious establishment. He also faces serious threats to the economy and increased tensions with Iran.

George Mason University's Mandaville says he cannot remember a time in Saudi history that has been so intense in terms of internal and external change in the midst of regional and global upheaval. "This moment is the greatest possibility for a fundamental shift of Saudi Arabia that I have seen," he says.

Shoring up the fragile Saudi economy over the next 20 years—especially if global demand for oil declines by a projected 25 percent—will be key to ensuring long-term stability, say many observers.[126] But predictions for economic improvement, at least in the short-term, do not look good. *Bloomberg News* already ranks the Saudi economy as the 14th most "miserable" in the world and projects that it will hit the top 10 list by the end of 2018. In fact, the International Monetary Fund warned in 2015 that Saudi Arabia could face economic catastrophe in five years if sweeping financial reforms were not introduced.[127]

"My concern is if nothing really changes in five years, if young people still have problems finding jobs, do people lose faith in the Saudi leadership and look to an alternative?" asks Rice University's Ulrichsen. "We saw [in Iraq] with ISIS how ugly things can be if a state collapses. Complete collapse of Saudi Arabia is unlikely but if [the crown prince] fails to deliver, there is always a danger that fundamentalists will lash out."

Saudi journalist Khashoggi agrees jobs should be among the crown prince's top priorities. "Arab Spring was about unemployment," he says. "There will be people in the streets probably who will . . . be asking for jobs. It's the economy that will make people happy or angry."

"My sense is that the crown prince will be given the benefit of the doubt in the beginning. It might last one or two years," says Duke University's Maghraoui. "But at some point, he will have to show results. If he is just narrowing his circle of power, people will start protesting. Members of the royal family will turn against him."

But human rights advocates, such as Alyami of the Center for Democracy and Human Rights in Saudi Arabia, say they will be pushing for political reforms as well as economic changes. "The country needs to be reinvented in a different way than what Prince Mohammed has chosen to do," he says. "He is not interested in political reform. He's not interested in human rights. Women driving cars, opening movie theaters—these are basic things that should have never been denied. He has achieved nothing except giving people this mirage of reform."

If the prince fails to balance economic and political reforms, the implications could be far-reaching, says Richard Harris, a Saudi Arabia watcher who is CEO of the Hong Kong-based investment management firm Port Shelter and a columnist for the *South China Morning Post*. "We really ought to hope he succeeds whether we like him or not," says Harris, "because if he doesn't succeed what is the alternative? Civil war? Or it could be a pretender to the throne succeeding. None of that is good news for the West."

NOTES

1. Philip Rucker and Karen DeYoung, "Trump Signs 'Tremendous' Deals with Saudi Arabia on His First Day Overseas," *The Washington Post*, May 20, 2017, https://tinyurl.com/yau45v6y.

2. Ken Klippenstein, "The Insane Gifts Saudi Arabia Gave President Trump," *The Daily Beast*, Sept. 4, 2017, https://tinyurl.com/ybd6msx7.

3. Ian Black, "Obama's Chilly Reception in Saudi Arabia Hints at Mutual Distrust," *The Guardian*, April 20, 2016, https://tinyurl.com/n64do6j.

4. Rucker and DeYoung, *op. cit.*

5. Charlotte Krol and Richard Spencer, "The Sunni and Shia Muslim split explained—in 90 seconds," *The Telegraph*, Jan. 5, 2016, https://tinyurl.com/zjbfwjj.

6. "More than 8 million Yemenis 'a step away from famine': U.N.," Reuters, Dec. 11, 2017, https://tinyurl.com/y7zmtw3o. Edith M. Lederer, "Crisis that has Yemen on brink of famine is a 'man-made disaster': UN," The Associated Press, *The Globe and Mail*, Aug. 1, 2017, https://tinyurl.com/ybplrn2a.

7. Jared Malsin, "The Big Problem with President Trump's Record Arms Deal with Saudi Arabia," *Time*, May 22, 2017, https://tinyurl.com/khwevev. Michael D. Shear and Peter Baker, "Saudis Welcome Trump's Rebuff of Obama's Views," *The New York Times*, May 20, 2017, https://tinyurl.com/yatbhpm5.

8. "Trump in Saudi Arabia Signs $110B Arms Deal with Persian Gulf Ally," Fox News, May 20, 2017, https://tinyurl.com/kkjmb8r. "Remarks With Saudi Foreign Minister Adel al-Jubeir at a Press Availability," U.S. Department of State, May 20, 2017, https://tinyurl.com/y7x5osnx.

9. Alan Gomez and Kim Hjelmgaard, "Syria Explained: Why Other Countries Poked Their Noses in a Tiny Nation's Civil War," *USA Today*, Feb. 11, 2018, https://tinyurl.com/y7gb6mwp.

10. Jon Gambrell, "$30 Billion Pledged in Kuwait at Summit to Rebuild Iraq," The Associated Press, Feb. 14, 2018, https://tinyurl.com/ybrpxqn7.

11. Anne Barnard and Maria Abi-Habib, "Why Saad Hariri Had That Strange Sojourn in Saudi Arabia," *The New York Times*, Dec. 24, 2017, https://tinyurl.com/y8zgkzym.

12. Mark Landler, "Trump Takes Credit for Saudi Move Against Qatar, a U.S. Military Partner," *The New York Times*, June 6, 2017, https://tinyurl.com/y6v6jbk2.

13. Brad Lendon, "Qatar hosts largest U.S. military base in Mideast," CNN, June 6, 2017, https://tinyurl.com/y7zq9hhy.

14. Zeeshan Aleem, "Saudi Arabia's Anti-Corruption Purge Is All About Life After Oil," *Vox*, Nov. 29, 2017, https://tinyurl.com/yctqrl5f.

15. Anjli Raval and Andrew Ward, "Saudi Aramco Plans for a Life after Oil," *Financial Times*, Dec. 9, 2017, https://tinyurl.com/ycgwuyxc.

16. Aleem, *op. cit.*; Summer Said, Benoit Faucon and Georgi Kantchev, "Plea for Money Preceded Saudi Crackdown on Elites," *The Wall Street Journal*, Jan. 28, 2018, https://tinyurl.com/y78t3pjs.

17. Vivian Nereim and Sarah Algethami, "Some Saudi Millennials Won't Dance to Their Young Prince's Tune," Bloomberg, Jan. 28, 2018, https://tinyurl.com/ybdj7qsf.

18. "World Report 2018," Human Rights Watch, 2018, https://tinyurl.com/y9pmyy5o.

19. Cynthia McFadden, William M. Arkin and Tim Uehlinger, "How the Trump Team's First Military Raid in Yemen Went Wrong," NBC News, Oct. 2, 2017, https://tinyurl.com/ybyav33s.

20. "The Latest Developments in Saudi Arabia and Lebanon," Elliott Abrams testimony, Subcommittee on the Middle East and North Africa, House of Representatives, Nov. 29, 2017, https://tinyurl.com/y82s8tok.

21. Maureen Farrell, Benoit Faucon and Summer Said, "Google Weighs Unusual Bid With Giant Oil Firm Aramco to Rev Up the Saudi Tech Sector," *The Wall Street Journal*, Feb. 1, 2018, https://tinyurl.com/y7sl45uo. Tom DiChristopher, "Saudi Prince's Big Challenge on US Visit: Easing Investor Fears after Sweeping Anti-Corruption Campaign," CNBC, Feb. 6, 2018, https://tinyurl.com/yc86axxj.

22. Jon Sharman, "Donald Trump 'De-emphasised Human Rights' in Saudi Arabia Speech," *The Independent*, May 22, 2017, https://tinyurl.com/lb5fm3z.

23. "Saudi Arabia: Trump Visit Risks Giving Green Light to Violations of Human Rights," Amnesty International, May 19, 2017, https://tinyurl.com/ya6vkv4h.

24. Tom O'Connor, "Why Doesn't Saudi Arabia Join North Korea on U.S. State Terrorism List After 9/11?" *Newsweek*, Nov. 20, 2017, https://tinyurl.com/y7mg536c. "Transcript: Trump's Remarks On Iran Nuclear Deal," NPR, Oct. 13, 2017, https://tinyurl.com/y7a3xez3.

25. Galina Yemelianova, "Explainer: What Is Wahhabism in Saudi Arabia?" *The Conversation*, Jan. 30, 2015, https://tinyurl.com/ycatbw5k.

26. Tom Porter, "A Brief History of Terror in Saudi Arabia," *Newsweek*, June 24, 2017, https://tinyurl.com/ycudymjm. Gregory Hellman, "House Declares U.S. Military Role in Yemen's Civil War Unauthorized," *Politico*, Nov. 13, 2017, https://tinyurl.com/yazrbzjx.

27. Bob Van Voris, "Saudi Arabia Claims No Evidence It Aided 9/11 Plot," Bloomberg, Jan. 18, 2018, https://tinyurl.com/ya4xr77x.

28. O'Connor, *op. cit.*

29. Bethan McKernan, "CIA Awards Saudi Crown Prince with Medal for Counter-terrorism Work," *The Independent*, Feb. 13, 2017, https://tinyurl.com/zubtow7.

30. Molly Hennessy-Fiske, "In a Shake-up, Saudi King Names Son Mohammed bin Salman New Crown Prince," *Los Angeles Times*, June 21, 2017, https://tinyurl.com/y7lokv79.

31. Stephen Kalin and Yara Bayoumy, "Saudi King Decrees Women Be Allowed to Drive," Reuters, Sept. 26, 2017, https://tinyurl.com/y7qkzcaq.

32. Cristina Maza, "Saudi Arabia Feminist Activist Detained as Country Claims It Is Increasing

Women's Rights," *Newsweek*, Feb. 8, 2018, https://tinyurl.com/yapj4phj.

33. F. Brinley Bruton, "Women in Saudi Arabia Make Gains but Overall Rights Remain an Issue," NBC News, Jan. 22, 2018, https://tinyurl.com/ycnbgr7n.

34. Harriet Agerholm, "Saudi Police Arrest Men Following 'Gay Wedding' Video," *The Independent*, Jan. 11, 2018, https://tinyurl.com/y978ydxh.

35. "2011 Report on International Religious Freedom," Bureau of Democracy, Human Rights and Labor, U.S. Department of State, July 30, 2012, https://tinyurl.com/ya6ecvwe.

36. "Saudi Arabia must do something about its barbaric human rights practices," *The Washington Post*, Aug. 5, 2017, https://tinyurl.com/y7hlq925.

37. "Saudi Arabia to allow movie theaters for first time in decades," The Associated Press, Dec. 11, 2017, https://tinyurl.com/y82tye8p.

38. "Careem Signs up Nearly 1,000 Saudi Women Drivers," *Arab News*, Feb. 12, 2018, https://tinyurl.com/yat6vdo6.

39. Samuel Osborne, "Saudi Arabia Bans Foreigners from Certain Jobs to Give Citizens More Employment Opportunities," *The Independent*, Jan. 31, 2018, https://tinyurl.com/ycr9ujwm.

40. "Saudi Arabia Beyond Oil: The Investment and Productivity Transformation," McKinsey Global Institute, December 2015, https://tinyurl.com/ybt7bbku.

41. Camilla Hodgson, "The fragile balance between Saudi Arabia's ruling class and its people is 'unsustainable,'" *Business Insider*, Nov. 16, 2017, https://tinyurl.com/y8eyoo3d.

42. Sam Meredith, "Saudi Arabia Promises a Return to 'Moderate Islam,'" CNBC, Oct. 25, 2017, https://tinyurl.com/y9u4lyyd.

43. "Unemployment High in Rural Areas, Says Study," *Saudi Gazette*, Jan. 10, 2018, https://tinyurl.com/ychy9c22.

44. Ben Hubbard and Kate Kelly, "Saudi Arabia's Grand Plan to Move Beyond Oil: Big Goals, Bigger Hurdles," *The New York Times*, Oct. 25, 2017, https://tinyurl.com/ycec8y6q.

45. Nicholas Kulish and Michael Forsythe, "World's Most Expensive Home? Another Bauble for a Saudi Prince," *The New York Times*, Dec. 16, 2017, https://tinyurl.com/ya9xmxex.

46. Scott Shane, "Saudis and Extremism: 'Both the Arsonists and the Firefighters,'" *The New York Times*, Aug. 25, 2016, https://tinyurl.com/y73usout.

47. For background see Sarah Glazer, "Sharia Controversy," *CQ Global Researcher*, Jan. 3, 2012, pp. 1-28.

48. Carol E. B. Choksy and Jamsheed K. Choksy, "The Saudi Connection: Wahhabism and Global Jihad," *World Affairs*, May/June 2015, https://tinyurl.com/y95t5jso.

49. Bruce Riedel, *Kings and Presidents: Saudi Arabia and the United States since FDR* (2018), p. 23.

50. Vivienne Walt, "Inside Saudi Aramco's Kingdom of Oil," *Fortune*, Oct. 24, 2017, https://tinyurl.com/y8ssesuv.

51. "Memorandum by the Under Secretary of State (Acheson) to the Secretary of State," Foreign Relations of the United States: Diplomatic Papers, 1945, The Near East and Africa, Volume VIII, Office of the Historian, U.S. Department of State, Oct. 9, 1945, https://tinyurl.com/ycjyceaj.

52. Riedel, *op. cit.*, pp. 1-5.

53. *Ibid.*, p. 32.

54. *Ibid.*, pp. 32-35.

55. Rich Smith, "A Short History of OPEC," *The Motley Fool*, March 19, 2017, https://tinyurl.com/y8martno.

56. *Ibid.*

57. "Oil Shock of 1973-74," Federal Reserve History, https://tinyurl.com/y9t5heb2.

58. "Oil Embargo, 1973-1974," Office of the Historian, U.S. Department of State, https://tinyurl.com/zjyj3kj.

59. Shane, *op. cit.*

60. Yury Barmin, "Can Mohammed bin Salman Break the Saudi-Wahhabi Pact?" Al Jazeera, Jan. 7, 2018, https://tinyurl.com/y86nhj6o.

61. "Saudi Arabia: A Chronology of the Country's History and Key Events in the US-Saudi Relationship," Frontline, https://tinyurl.com/yb774bzt.

62. *Ibid.*

63. "Report Prepared by the Ambassador to Saudi Arabia (West)," Foreign Relations of the United States, 1977-1980, Volume XVIII, Middle East Region; Arabian Peninsula, Office of the Historian, U.S. Department of State, August 1977, https://tinyurl.com/ycgqwla2.

64. *Ibid.*

65. "Oil Dependence and U.S. Foreign Policy," Council on Foreign Relations, 2017, https://tinyurl.com/yalkgnys.

66. "Saudi Arabia: A Chronology of the Country's History and Key Events in the US-Saudi Relationship," *op. cit.*

67. Adam Coogle, "Saudi Arabia's 'War on Terror' Is Now Targeting Saudi Shiites," *Foreign Policy*, Aug. 23, 2017, https://tinyurl.com/yd8pokxl.

68. Akbar Ahmed, *The Thistle and the Drone* (2013), p. 204.

69. Barmin, *op. cit.*

70. "U.S.-Saudi Relations Backgrounder," Council on Foreign Relations, May 12, 2017, https://tinyurl.com/y7vd3dvd.

71. "Osama bin Laden," CNN, https://tinyurl.com/ypuffd.

72. "Timeline: Osama bin Laden, Over the Years," CNN, May 2, 2011, https://tinyurl.com/3ka4rm4.

73. Alfred B. Prados, "Saudi Arabia: Post-War Issues and U.S. Relations," Congressional Research Service, Dec. 14, 2001, https://tinyurl.com/yccbpfrh.

74. Sharon Otterman, "Saudi Arabia: Withdrawal of U.S. Forces," Council on Foreign Relations, Feb. 7, 2005, https://tinyurl.com/y7aotjr3.

75. Don Van Natta Jr., "The Struggle for Iraq; Last American Combat Troops Quit Saudi Arabia," *The New York Times*, Sept. 22, 2003, https://tinyurl.com/c6mtfq.

76. *Ibid.*

77. Otterman, *op. cit.*

78. Riedel, *op. cit.*, p. 152.

79. Helene Cooper, "Saudis' Role in Iraq Frustrates U.S. Officials," *The New York Times*, July 27, 2007, https://tinyurl.com/yb2apbxs.

80. Riedel, *op. cit.*, p. 153.

81. *Ibid.*, p. 158.

82. Kelly McEvers, "Bahrain: The Revolution That Wasn't," NPR, Jan. 5, 2012, https://tinyurl.com/ybet2roc.

83. Neil MacFarquhar, "In Saudi Arabia, Royal Funds Buy Peace for Now," *The New York Times*, June 8, 2011, https://tinyurl.com/624zrkh.

84. Jeffrey Goldberg, "The Obama Doctrine," *The Atlantic*, April 2016, https://tinyurl.com/hyokvh9.

85. "Saudi Arabia Executes 47, Including Prominent Cleric," NPR, Jan. 2, 2016, https://tinyurl.com/y9jvqo55.

86. Merrit Kennedy, "Who Was The Shiite Sheikh Executed By Saudi Arabia?" NPR, Jan. 4, 2016, https://tinyurl.com/ycq3bt42.

87. "Saudi king agrees in call with Trump to support Syria, Yemen safe zones: White House," Reuters, Jan. 29, 2017, https://tinyurl.com/ycrz3gkn.

88. Josh Rogin, "Trump Resets U.S.-Saudi Relations, in Saudi Arabia's Favor," *The Washington Post*, March 16, 2017.

89. Simeon Kerr and Shawn Donnan, "Trump Backs Plan to Boost Saudi Investment in the US," *Financial Times*, March 15, 2017, https://tinyurl.com/yaoac3fd.

90. Javier E. David, "US-Saudi Arabia Seal Weapons Deal Worth Nearly $110 Billion Immediately, $350 Billion Over 10 Years," CNBC, May 20, 2017, https://tinyurl.com/ycbto29o.

91. Kevin Bohn and Maegan Vazquez, "Jared Kushner traveled unannounced to Saudi Arabia," CNN, Oct. 30, 2017, https://tinyurl.com/y7pmcrqw.

92. Ben Hubbard and David D. Kirkpatrick, "The Upstart Saudi Prince Who's Throwing Caution to the Winds," *The New York Times*, Nov. 14, 2017, https://tinyurl.com/ychvfkrd.

93. Jack Moore, "Saudi Arabia's 'Paul McCartney' Plays First Jeddah Concert For Seven Years," *Newsweek*, Jan. 31, 2017, https://tinyurl.com/y98p8kzv.

94. Zahraa Alkhalisi, " 'Emoji Movie' and Popcorn: The Cinema Experience Returns to Saudi Arabia," CNN, Jan. 16, 2018, https://tinyurl.com/y7fgeglu.

95. Nick Vivarelli, "Kuwaiti Company Is Latest Entrant in Saudi Arabia Theater-Building Derby," *Variety*, Feb. 15, 2018, https://tinyurl.com/y8poh2gr.

96. Zahraa Alkhalisi, "Coming Soon to Saudi Arabia: AMC Movie Theaters," CNN, Dec. 12, 2017, https://tinyurl.com/y742pjux.

97. Vivarelli, *op. cit.*

98. Bethan McKernan, "Taxi App Signs up 1,000 New Women Drivers in Saudi Arabia," *The Independent*, Feb. 13, 2018, https://tinyurl.com/yd4y4v5t.

99. Nereim and Algethami, *op. cit.*

100. "The Global Gender Gap Report," World Economic Forum, 2017, https://tinyurl.com/ybufmzbs.

101. Adel Abdel Ghafar, "A New Kingdom of Saud?" Brookings Institution, Feb. 14, 2018, https://tinyurl.com/yabx8qez.

102. *Ibid.*

103. Ivana Kottasová, "107,000 Saudi Women Apply for 140 Passport Control Jobs," CNN, Feb. 1, 2018, https://tinyurl.com/yahqz5rg.

104. "Saudi Arabia Sentences Human Rights Activists to Prison: Amnesty," Reuters, Jan. 26, 2018, https://tinyurl.com/yda7d3ct.

105. "Saudi Arabia: Events of 2017," Human Rights Watch, https://tinyurl.com/y9pmyy5o.

106. Ghafar, *op. cit.*

107. Hodgson, *op. cit.*; "Saudi Boosts Spending to Record, Slows Austerity Drive in 2018 State Budget," Reuters, Dec. 19, 2017, https://tinyurl.com/yb39l3rd.

108. Aya Batrawy, "Saudi Arabia Heralds Biggest Spending Plans Yet Amid Deficit," The Associated Press, Dec. 19, 2017, https://tinyurl.com/y8gen88a.

109. Alaa Shahine and Vivian Nereim, "Royal Handouts Cheer Saudis But Show Struggle to Revamp Economy," Bloomberg, Jan. 5, 2018, https://tinyurl.com/yc8z8zym.

110. Zahraa Alkhalisi, "Saudi Arabia Eases Austerity After 'Very Negative' Response," CNN, Jan. 9, 2018, https://tinyurl.com/y866gjp7.

111. Said, Faucon and Kantchev, *op. cit.*

112. Rania El Gamal, "Russia Eyes Multi-million-dollar Saudi Investment Deals, Aramco IPO," Reuters, Feb. 14, 2018, https://tinyurl.com/y7eljcvf.

113. Justin Sink, Benjamin Bain and Javier Blas, "Trump Urges Saudi Aramco to List on New York Stock Exchange," Bloomberg, Nov. 4, 2017, https://tinyurl.com/ycu6ejvn.

114. Tom DiChristopher, "Massive IPO for Saudi Oil Giant Aramco Reportedly Stalled by Indecision Over Where to List Shares," CNBC, Jan. 28, 2018, https://tinyurl.com/y7kjhetd.

115. "February 2018 Monthly Forecast," U.N. Security Council, https://tinyurl.com/y96ckdrx.

116. Michelle Nichols, "U.N. Security Council Mulls Saudi Praise for Yemen Aid Pledge," Reuters, Feb. 15, 2018, https://tinyurl.com/ybwjz3aq.

117. Pamela Falk, "U.S. Ambassador Nikki Haley Pushes United Nations for 'Consequences' for Iran's 'Behavior,'" CBS News, Feb. 16, 2018, https://tinyurl.com/y9lrlvxa.

118. Rosie Perper, "Saudi Arabia May Allow Israel to Use Its Airspace—Shifting a Policy that Has Defined the Region for Decades," *Business Insider*, Feb. 9, 2018, https://tinyurl.com/y8rpxk9u.

119. Noa Landau and Hagar Shezaf, "Israeli Intel Minister to Saudi Media: Israel Can Strike Iranian Missile Plants in Lebanon, 'As Is Happening in Syria,'" *Haaretz,* Dec. 14, 2017, https://tinyurl.com/yc2nv9nj.

120. Marc Champion, Jonathan Ferziger and David Wainer, "Israel, Saudis Find Common Cause in Warning of Iran Expansionism," Bloomberg, Feb. 18, 2018, https://tinyurl.com/yan29mmv.

121. Ayaz Gul, "Pakistan Under Scrutiny for Planned Troop Deployment in Saudi Arabia," Voice of America, Feb. 16, 2018, https://tinyurl.com/y89udcye.

122. *Ibid.*

123. Barbara Bibbo, "Qatar FM Calls for an End to the Saudi-led Blockade," Al Jazeera, Feb. 26, 2018, https://tinyurl.com/ydepc9ug.

124. "Saudi, UAE, Qatari Leaders to Visit Trump in March, April," Reuters, Feb. 23, 2018, https://tinyurl.com/y9g8cueu.

125. "Saudi Envoy Invites Lebanon's PM Hariri to Kingdom," Reuters, Feb. 26, 2018, https://tinyurl.com/y85w6tx7.

126. Ernest Scheyder, "Exxon Sees Global Oil Demand Plunging by 2040 under Climate Regulations," Reuters, Feb. 2, 2018, https://tinyurl.com/ycflqytf.

127. Michelle Jamrisko and Catarina Saraiva, "These Are the World's Most Miserable Economies," Bloomberg, Feb. 14, 2018, https://tinyurl.com/ycdrlv2d; Ahmed Feteha, "Saudis Risk Draining Financial Assets in Five Years, IMF Warns," Bloomberg News, Oct. 20, 2015, https://tinyurl.com/yd9vfh2x.

BIBLIOGRAPHY
Selected Sources
Books

Aarts, Paul, and Carolien Roelants, *Saudi Arabia: A Kingdom in Peril*, C. Hurst & Co., 2015.
An academic and a journalist examine issues of employment, corruption and repression that led to the Arab Spring and ponder if Saudi Arabia will be able to avoid a similar uprising.

Al-Rasheed, Madawi, *Muted Modernists: The Struggle over Divine Politics in Saudi Arabia*, Oxford University Press, 2015.
The granddaughter of an emir overthrown by the Saud royal family offers an insider's look at the intersection of religion and politics in Saudi Arabia.

House, Karen Elliott, *On Saudi Arabia: Its People, Past, Religion, Fault Lines—and Future*, Knopf, 2012.
A Pulitzer Prize-winning reporter offers a comprehensive look at Saudi Arabia's tribal past, its complicated present and its precarious future.

Lacey, Robert, *Inside the Kingdom: Kings, Clerics, Modernists, Terrorists, and the Struggle for Saudi Arabia*, Penguin Books, 2010.
This popular book offers an insider's look at the people and culture of the conservative kingdom from the 1970s onward.

Riedel, Bruce, *Kings and Presidents: Saudi Arabia and the United States since FDR*, Brookings Institution Press, 2018.
A 30-year CIA veteran who worked for four presidents traces the changing relationship between the United States and Saudi Arabia since the founding of the kingdom in 1932.

Articles

Aleem, Zeesham, "Saudi Arabia's anti-corruption purge is all about life after oil," *Vox*, Nov. 29, 2017, https://tinyurl.com/yctqrl5f.
Crown Prince Mohammed bin Salman is pushing for social reform in hopes of shoring up his country's fragile economy.

Dreyfuss, Bob, "Does Trump Want a New Middle East War?" *Rolling Stone*, Nov. 9, 2017, https://tinyurl.com/y9v7ofqn.
A journalist argues President Trump's decision to place Saudi Arabia at the center of his Middle East policy could spark a war.

Gelvin, James L., "Why is Saudi Arabia suddenly so paranoid?" *The Conversation*, Oct. 19, 2017, https://tinyurl.com/y989l9q5.
A history professor at the University of California, Los Angeles, analyzes how the Arab Spring, the Obama administration's focus on East Asia and dropping oil prices have led to Saudi Arabia's interventions against its neighbors.

Goldberg, Jeffrey, "The Obama Doctrine," *The Atlantic*, April 2016, https://tinyurl.com/hyokvh9.
President Obama angered Saudi Arabia when he suggested the kingdom was a "free rider" that needed to "share" the Middle East with Iran.

Goldenberg, Ilan, "Here's How Both Obama and Trump Stoked the Saudi-Iranian Rivalry," *Foreign Policy*, Dec. 7, 2017, https://tinyurl.com/yber4k56.
A former State Department official looks at how Barack Obama's conciliatory strategy and Donald Trump's aggressive rhetoric have exacerbated tensions between Iran and Saudi Arabia.

Miller, Aaron David, and Richard Sokolsky, "Donald Trump Has Unleashed the Saudi Arabia We Always Wanted—and Feared," *Foreign Policy*, Nov. 10, 2017, https://tinyurl.com/ycbro4j6.
Two longtime observers explain their concerns over Saudi Arabia's newly aggressive policies.

Reports and Studies

"The Qatar Crisis," Project on Middle East Political Science, October 2017, https://tinyurl.com/ybf2wcvg.
A large collection of essays by leading scholars examines the origins and impact of Saudi Arabia's blockade of Qatar.

Ghafar, Adel Abdel, "A New Kingdom of Saud?" Brookings Institution, Feb. 14, 2018, https://tinyurl.com/yabx8qez.
A fellow at a Washington think tank looks at how economic, social and political reforms taking place in Saudi Arabia are bringing benefits to the kingdom's citizens.

House, Karen Elliott, "Saudi Arabia in Transition," Belfer Center, July 2017, https://tinyurl.com/y8q3a8ww.

A former journalist looks at the challenges and opportunities Saudi Arabia faces as it tries to transform its economy and society.

Videos

"Saudi Arabia's Game of Thrones," Wilson Center, Nov. 8, 2017, https://tinyurl.com/y9anludd.
Three experts on Saudi Arabia discuss internal politics, foreign policy and U.S.-Saudi relationships in a taped panel session.

Riedel, Bruce, "Kings and presidents: Whither the special relationship with Saudi Arabia?" Brookings Institution, Nov. 21, 2017, https://tinyurl.com/y93l7t5d.
This recording of a discussion with one of the preeminent experts on Saudi Arabia touches on a variety of issues, from the Yemen civil war to the kingdom's modernization drive.

For More Information

Atlantic Council, 1030 15th St., N.W., 12th Floor, Washington, DC 20005; 202-778-4952; www.atlantic council.org. Think tank that promotes leadership and engagement in international affairs.

Brookings Institution, 1775 Massachusetts Ave., N.W., Washington, DC 20036; 202-797-6000; www.brookings .edu. Public policy research organization that focuses on local, national and global issues.

Carnegie Endowment for International Peace, 1779 Massachusetts Ave., N.W., Washington, DC 20036; 202-483-7600; www.carnegieendowment.org. Global network of policy research centers working to advance peace in the Mideast and elsewhere.

Center for Democracy and Human Rights in Saudi Arabia, 1629 K St., N.W., Suite 300, Washington, DC 20006; 202-558–5552; www.cdhr.info. Educational organization

that promotes political enfranchisement and human rights reforms in Saudi Arabia.

Council on Foreign Relations, 58 East 68th St., New York, NY 10065; 212-434-9400; www.cfr.org. Think tank focusing on foreign policy issues.

Human Rights Watch, 350 Fifth Ave., 34th floor, New York, NY 10118; 212-290-4700; www.hrw.org. Advocacy organization that uses reporting and fact-finding to promote human rights and justice around the world.

Middle East Institute, 1319 18th St., N.W., Washington, DC 20036; 202-785-1141; www.mei.edu. Think tank focusing on the Middle East.

Wilson Center, 1300 Pennsylvania Ave., N.W., Washington, DC 20004; 202-691-4000; www.wilsoncenter.org. Congressionally chartered think tank.

3

Turmoil in Central America

Kerry Dooley Young

AP Photo/Oliver de Ros

Protesters rally in Guatemala City on Aug. 31 against a decision by Guatemalan President Jimmy Morales not to renew the mandate of a U.N.-backed commission investigating corruption in Guatemala, including potentially illegal donations to Morales' political campaign. A fledgling anti-corruption movement has emerged in recent years in several Central American countries that have long struggled with graft, poverty and weak public institutions.

From *CQ Researcher*, September 14, 2018

Rep. Kay Granger, a Republican from Texas, does not often act against President Trump's wishes. But she has openly joined colleagues to soften the White House's plan to slash foreign aid to Central America.

A key player in establishing the State and Defense department budgets, Granger has urged a deeper look at why parents in Guatemala, Honduras and El Salvador are entrusting their children to smugglers to bring them to the United States. Border agents reported more than 200,000 apprehensions of unaccompanied children from the three countries as they tried to cross the southwestern U.S. border in the past five years, according to the U.S. Customs and Border Protection.[1]

"What could be so bad that I would send my children with someone I'd never seen before, to a country I'd never been to?" asked Granger, the mother of three and grandmother of five. "I can't imagine how bad."[2]

But not all immigrants from the three countries—known collectively as Central America's Northern Triangle—have been unaccompanied children. In 2016, alone, more than 220,000 people from the three countries were caught trying to cross the U.S. border.[3] Many are fleeing violence and lawlessness, fueled by gangs and drug smugglers who act with impunity in countries plagued by deep poverty, government corruption and weak law enforcement. Teens often are bullied into serving the gangs, and ordinary citizens face extortion from which they get little official protection. Homicide rates in the three countries are among the world's highest.

A Region Rich in Natural Resources

Seven countries comprise Central America: Belize, Guatemala, Honduras, El Salvador, Nicaragua, Costa Rica and Panama. Guatemala has the largest population.

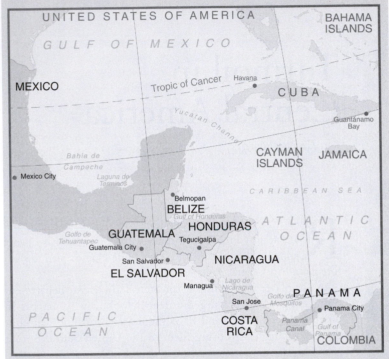

Central America At a Glance, 2017

Country	Head of State	Population	Major Exports
Belize	Queen Elizabeth II, Prime Minister Dean Oliver Barrow	360,346	Sugar, bananas, fruit juice
Costa Rica	President Carlos Alvarado	4,930,258	Tropical fruits, medical equipment
El Salvador	President Salvador Sánchez Cerén	6,172,011	Apparel, electrical capacitors, plastic lids
Guatemala	President Jimmy Ernesto Morales	15,460,732	Bananas, sugar, coffee
Honduras	President Juan Orlando Hernández	9,038,741	Apparel, coffee, insulated wire
Nicaragua	President José Daniel Ortega	6,025,951	Apparel, insulated wire, coffee
Panama	President Juan Carlos Varela	3,753,142	Passenger and cargo ships, sulfanomides

Sources: "Central America," *Encyclopedia Britannica*, 2018; CIA World Factbook, Observatory of Economic Complexity, MIT Media Lab, 2016, https://tinyurl.com/y8h2jktc

"The social network is in tatters. The fabric of society is just ripped" in the Northern Triangle countries, says Vincent T. Gawronski, a specialist in Latin American studies at Alabama's Birmingham-Southern College. "The institutions are weakened. The leaders are corrupt, and the citizens are frightened."

To help stem the flow of Central American immigrants into the United States, the Trump administration has tried several approaches. One was a short-lived policy that resulted in thousands of Central American children being separated from their parents at the border and detained. The administration also called for the cutbacks in U.S. foreign aid to the Northern Triangle countries, which Granger and colleagues have made less severe.

The administration has since backed away from its zero tolerance policy, in part due to court challenges and political pressure. Trump officials say they remain concerned about the threat of violence and poor quality of life that is causing many to flee the Northern Triangle. "If we don't resolve those issues in those three countries, we're gonna have challenges along our southern border for years and years to come," Secretary of State Mike Pompeo said at a June 2018 Senate hearing.[4]

Violence and civil conflict in those countries triggered a surge in migration to the United States in the 1980s and '90s, with many Central American immigrants ending up in poor Los Angeles neighborhoods. There, many young Salvadoran immigrants formed the Mara Salvatrucha, known as MS-13, a Central American street gang notorious for its brutal violence, members of which President Trump often refers to as "animals." Many gang members were deported during the last two decades, taking their gangs affiliations with them, which is why some analysts say the region's gang problem is a U.S. export.

Yet, in his 2018 State of the Union address, Trump called for Congress to "close the deadly loopholes" in immigration laws that allow MS-13 members "to break into our country."[5] Many experts say Trump's rhetoric about the group threatening average Americans is overblown because the 10,000 MS-13 members in the United States represent only 0.7 percent of all U.S. gang members, and their attacks in the United States largely target immigrant communities in Los Angeles, Long Island and Washington, D.C.[6]

Any serious bid to address gangs and poverty in the Northern Triangle must address the region's systemic corruption, a major underpinning of the factors driving people to try to immigrate to the United States, says Eric Olson, deputy director of the Latin American Program for the nonpartisan Wilson Center, a Washington think tank. Building effective legal and judicial institutions in the region are key to making lasting improvements, he says.

"Migrants coming to the United States don't say, 'I'm fleeing Honduras because of the failure of governance in my country,' but in fact that's what's happening," Olson says. "They may not speak of it in that way, but that's what this is about."

In recent years a fledgling anti-corruption movement has arisen in the Northern Triangle and in neighboring Nicaragua, raising hope among many Central Americans. Investigatory commissions have recommended key public officials be prosecuted for corruption—including presidents—and citizens have staged anti-government protests that sometimes have turned violent.

"There's a general mood, not just in Central America, but in the entire region, where people have had it up to here with corruption," says Adam Isacson, director for defense oversight at the Washington Office on Latin America, a human rights advocacy group. "You are seeing anti-corruption demonstrations from Brazil to Mexico."

These efforts have produced impressive results as well as, more recently, strong pushback.[7] The leader of a Honduran anti-corruption panel, Juan Jiménez Mayor,

resigned in February, citing hostility from the government as the cause.[8] Yet, in August, he congratulated the Honduran attorney general for proceeding with a case against the former president of the nation's Supreme Court.[9] Also in August, former Salvadoran president Tony Saca pleaded guilty to embezzling $301 million in public funds during his tenure as president from 2004 to 2009.[10]

In neighboring Nicaragua, hundreds of protesters died as a result of demonstrations against President Daniel Ortega, a one-time leftist rebel accused of using his office to enrich his family. In Guatemala, President Jimmy Morales announced in late August that he would not renew the mandate for a prestigious, 11-year-old anti-corruption panel backed by the United Nations that has aggressively investigated hundreds of corrupt officials and was looking into Morales' own campaign finance activities.[11]

Meanwhile, some of the Northern Triangle countries' economies have begun to show glimmers of improvement, although they still trail Costa Rica and Panama, their more prosperous and politically stable southern neighbors. The International Monetary Fund (IMF), a multilateral lender that helps countries reduce poverty, cited economic reforms this year such as pension overhaul in El Salvador, "solid, hard-earned macroeconomic stability" in Guatemala and continued relatively strong economic performance in Honduras.[12]

Panama and Costa Rica enjoy relative peace and prosperity. Costa Rica has a strong tradition of investing in education and health, and Panama's economy has benefited from its role as the home of the globally strategic shipping canal. Both countries attract much more foreign investment than the rest of Central America—with net inflows of $6 billion in Panama and $3 billion in Costa Rica in 2017, according to World Bank figures. In contrast, the three Northern Triangle countries, combined, attracted less than $3 billion in 2017.[13]

Partly as a result of the disparity in foreign investment, residents of the Northern Triangle countries are poorer than their southern neighbors. At more than $24,000, Panama has the region's highest per capita gross domestic product (GDP), which measures a country's total economic output and is a primary indicator of the economy's health, followed by Costa Rica at $17,000.

Panama, Costa Rica Lead Regional Economy

Panama's per capita gross domestic product (GDP), a measure of economic output, nearly tripled in the past 17 years to more than $24,000, fueled in part by the recent expansion of the Panama Canal, which links the Atlantic and Pacific oceans. Costa Rica had the second-highest per capita GDP in 2017, at about $17,000, while Honduras had the lowest, at slightly less than $5,000.

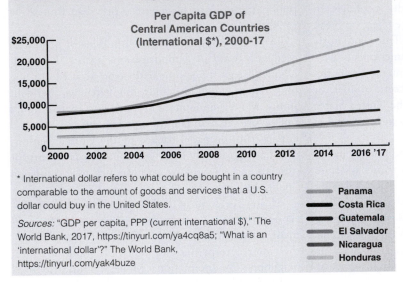

Per Capita GDP of Central American Countries (International $*), 2000-17

Legend: Panama, Costa Rica, Guatemala, El Salvador, Nicaragua, Honduras

* International dollar refers to what could be bought in a country comparable to the amount of goods and services that a U.S. dollar could buy in the United States.

Sources: "GDP per capita, PPP (current international $)," The World Bank, 2017, https://tinyurl.com/ya4cq8a5; "What is an 'international dollar'?" The World Bank, https://tinyurl.com/yak4buze

The per capita GDP in the Northern Triangle countries is far below those amounts.[14]

The region's notorious violence ticked down slightly in 2017. The homicide rate dropped to about 60 murders per 100,000 inhabitants from 81 in 2016 in El Salvador, the region's highest. Honduras and Guatemala experienced similar declines. However, the region's murder rates are much higher than Mexico's 22.5 per 100,000 in 2017—the highest in that nation's recent drug-cartel-plagued history, according to InSight Crime, a media site that partners with the Center for Latin American and Latino Studies at American University in Washington. While the rates are lower in Costa Rica and Panama—12 and 10 per 100,000, respectively—even those rates are more than double the 2016 rate in the United States of 5.3 per 100,000.[15]

As lawmakers, analysts and U.S. officials debate what to do about the instability in Central America and the illegal immigration it fosters, here are some of the questions they are discussing:

Are the Northern Triangle countries locked into a permanent cycle of poverty?

Often noted for having the world's highest homicide rate outside of a war zone, El Salvador earned a more positive accolade in the World Bank's most recent assessment of the climate for corporations doing business around the world.

In the bank's "Doing Business 2018" report, El Salvador was the only Latin American nation to make the list of top 10 countries showing the most improvement in their investment climates.[16] El Salvador now requires companies to submit their tax returns electronically, which may improve collection rates, the report said, and has strengthened the reliability of its power grid.

Such positive economic news often gets overlooked in the barrage of troubling reports about the Northern Triangle, says Ludovico Feoli, director of Tulane University's Center for Inter-American Policy and Research in New Orleans. But Guatemala, El Salvador and Honduras are far from being failed states, he says, despite facing grave challenges.

"They are in the good graces" of the IMF, Feoli says.

Indeed, the IMF's 2018 updates on each of the Northern Triangle nations cite progress toward improved economies. In addition, according to the IMF, remittances—money sent home by migrants working abroad—continue to boost the finances of the Northern Triangle countries.[17]

Still, the fund also stressed a need to tackle corruption through such measures as enhancing financial disclosures by public officials. Roger Noriega, a visiting fellow at the conservative American Enterprise Institute (AEI) in Washington who served as assistant secretary of state for Western Hemisphere affairs in the George W. Bush administration, describes endemic corruption as the "original sin" behind many of the woes of the Northern Triangle.

"There's nothing inevitable about poverty if you have political leaders committed to breaking the cycle," he says.

However, Americans' appetite for illegal drugs helps fuel the region's continued corruption and instability, says Noriega. The Mexico-based Sinaloa drug cartel relies on smaller Central American networks to move cocaine from South America to the United States, and these second-tier local criminal organizations have strong political clout. They make hefty donations to political campaigns and local charities and employ large numbers of local residents.[18]

"Business and political leaders accept a level of corruption as a normal way of doing business," Noriega says. "The result is that you have very weak, unaccountable institutions, which is how the people in power want it."

Stephanie McNulty, a Latin American specialist at Franklin and Marshall College in Lancaster, Pa., agrees that the continued demand for drugs in the United States is obstructing efforts to eradicate corruption in the Northern Triangle. In addition, many U.S. businesses rely on a continued supply of cheap, undocumented migrant labor. Such issues would need to be tackled, along with corruption, before significant improvement can occur in the economies of the Northern Triangle, she says.

"There's a web of factors that lead people to flee these countries," McNulty says. "To change that, we would need to attack all of these different pieces of the web."

Like many experts on Central America, McNulty says the work of Guatemala's United Nations-chartered anti-corruption panel is one of the region's most promising developments. Created in 2007, the International Commission Against Impunity in Guatemala, known by its Spanish acronym CICIG, has aided Guatemalan prosecutors in hundreds of corruption cases, resulting in 310 convictions, the imprisonment of two former presidents and the submission of 34 legal reforms to the Guatemalan Congress.[19]

The resignation in 2015 of President Otto Pérez Molina, charged with customs fraud, marked a major milestone for Guatemala, says Ana Rosa Quintana, senior policy analyst for Latin America and the Western Hemisphere at the conservative Heritage Foundation in Washington. "Guatemala passed that big kidney stone of having its president step down. It happened peacefully and no one died. That's huge, considering that

During a May 2018 demonstration, students from the National Autonomous University of Nicaragua demand the resignation of the country's increasingly authoritarian president, Daniel Ortega. About 300 Nicaraguans have died and 2,000 have been injured as government forces have cracked down on the protests.

people were slaughtering one another there just a few decades ago," she says, referring to the nation's civil war that lasted more than 30 years.

But Quintana doubts there will be rapid advances in fighting corruption and other major challenges for the Northern Triangle. "We're not going to see a prosperous Guatemala or Northern Triangle within one generation," she says. 'It's really going to require sustained political will in order to see the kind of changes that need to be made."

Isacson of the Washington Office on Latin America says it is unclear when, or if, the current discontent with corruption will translate into sufficient sustained public pressure to make major changes.

"Everywhere that there is a glimmer of hope, they are facing huge backlashes," Isacson says. "I don't expect any miracles in the next 10 to 15 years. They would have to make a greater effort than they are now to break out of this."

Is the United States doing enough to address the root causes of migration from Central America?

Experts on the region have seen the efforts of Guatemala's anti-corruption panel as a critical tool for combating the deeply ingrained corruption that allows high levels of crime and poverty to persist in the region. But many were disappointed by President Morales' latest bid to halt the CICIG's work.

Morales announced on Aug. 31 that he would not renew the CICIG's mandate, which expires in 2019, and he ordered that Colombian prosecutor Iván Velásquez, who has led the panel since 2013, not be allowed back into Guatemala. The panel is investigating about $1 million in allegedly illegal donations to the Morales campaign.[20] Protests erupted in Guatemala last year when Morales made another ultimately unsuccessful bid to bar Velásquez from the nation.[21]

"There are two undeniable realities in Guatemala: The people are fed up with the corruption, violence and impunity that plague that country, and those in power will do whatever they can to avoid justice," said U.S. Sen. Patrick J. Leahy, a Vermont Democrat, about Morales' latest effort to derail the commission.[22]

Morales had to back down from his 2017 bid to stop Velásquez' work due to international pressure, a court ruling and the domestic protests. The U.S. State Department issued a statement saying the CICIG should be permitted to work free from interference by the Guatemalan government, and the U.S. ambassador to the United Nations, Nikki Haley, told Morales bluntly during a visit to Guatemala that it would be in his best interest to support the commission's work.[23]

Leahy, who serves on the committee that oversees federal budgets for diplomacy and foreign aid, said Congress may reconsider how much military and domestic aid Guatemala would get if the CICIG is derailed. But Leahy opposes Trump's proposal to slash aid to the region. "The very funds we are providing to help stop migration, he threatens to cut—as if those countries can somehow solve these problems without our help," Leahy said of Trump's suggestion.[24]

Trump requested about $436 million in aid to Central America for fiscal 2019, which begins Oct. 1, down significantly from the $754 million provided in fiscal 2016, the last full year of the Obama administration.[25] That amount was up more than double from fiscal 2014, after President Barack Obama and lawmakers in both parties ramped up aid to Central America in response to waves of unaccompanied children and teenagers trying to immigrate to the United States beginning in 2014. Since then, U.S. aid to the region has been slipping, and likely will fall again, although not as much as Trump would like. A House bill proposes providing $595 million in aid to Central America for fiscal 2019, while a Senate version would give the region $515 million in aid.[26]

Trump appears to want to tie aid to control of immigration. "We're working on a plan to deduct a lot of the aid because I happen to believe that it's not so hard," he said at a meeting in May. Rep. Andy Biggs, an Arizona Republican, has five GOP co-sponsors for a bill that would cut aid to nations whose citizens are arrested at the U.S.-Mexico border by $2,000 for each person apprehended.[27]

The Trump administration also is seeking to expel a class of refugees who were granted temporary protected status (TPS) to work in the United States after natural disasters in their home countries. The program began after Hurricane Mitch devastated parts of Central America in 1998, leaving about 19,000 people dead. Under the administration's new policies, this special immigration status would disappear for about 262,000 Salvadorans on Sept. 9, 2019, and 86,000 Hondurans on Jan. 5, 2020, forcing many of these immigrants to return home.[28]

Paul J. Angelo, a former political officer at the U.S. Embassy in Honduras, contended that withdrawing TPS protection will negatively affect the returnees' home countries, which have faltering economies and inadequate public infrastructures to cope with an onslaught of returnees. To make matters worse, he wrote, 17-18 percent of each country's GDP comes from remittances from people working in the United States. "Rescinding those people's TPS eligibility won't help tackle the region's instability and grinding poverty," nor will it deter others from attempting the journey north, he wrote.[29]

At a June hearing on the State Department's fiscal 2019 budget, Secretary Pompeo told senators that it is unclear whether additional money could be well spent in Central America at this time. Even tripling the budget would not guarantee major results in addressing the root causes of migration, Pompeo said.

"I don't think the region's been lacking for American financial support," Pompeo said. "I think we've provided an awful lot of financial support to them over the past years, well intended, and I'm sure some of it effective."[30]

Studies on the effectiveness of U.S. aid to the region have shown mixed results, according to an analysis by the Wilson Center. A 2015 report cited partial wins, such as the work at Honduran outreach centers that engaged thousands of children and teenagers, but "not necessarily reaching those at highest risk or those on the margins of gang activity."[31]

But crime and poverty will persist in the Northern Triangle until corruption is stemmed, says the Wilson Center's Olson, who edited the report. "If you don't clean up government and have it function the way that it's supposed to, you end up spending a lot of money that doesn't have much impact," Olson says. "Then the people of Guatemala, Honduras and El Salvador become cynical, and the taxpayers in the United States become cynical as well."

Violence Plagues Northern Triangle

Homicide rates in Central America's Northern Triangle, composed of El Salvador, Honduras and Guatemala, were far higher in 2017 than in the United States. El Salvador, the region's most troubled country, had 60 violent deaths per 100,000 residents, compared with 5.3 in the United States.

Homicides per 100,000 Residents, 2017

El Salvador	60.0
Honduras	42.8
Guatemala	26.1
United States*	5.3

* 2016 data, the most recent available

Source: Silva Mathema, "They Are (Still) Refugees: People Continue to Flee Violence in Latin American Countries," Center for American Progress, June 1, 2018, https://tinyurl.com/y8g7fd5b

Could unrest in Nicaragua have a larger impact on the region?

Business and political leaders in the United States feared in the 1970s and '80s that the revolutionary movement headed by Nicaraguan Sandinista leader Daniel Ortega would trigger the spread of socialism in Central America. That never happened, due in part to U.S. aid provided to help neighboring autocratic governments keep domestic leftists in check.

But the potential modern-day downfall of Ortega, who first served as president from 1984-90 and was re-elected in 2006 and twice since then, could have the regional impact that his political rise did not. Now widely considered a corrupt autocrat, Ortega is being pressured by Nicaraguan civic groups and former allies in the business community to advance the date of the nation's next presidential election, which would almost certainly end his rule before his current term expires in 2022.[32]

Waves of protests have erupted since April, when environmental groups, rural residents and students denounced the government's slow and insufficient response to forest fires in the Indio Maíz Biological Reserve. Then in mid-April, Ortega's administration proposed reducing pension payments, sparking more protests, which turned violent when the government cracked down on demonstrators with tear gas and rubber bullets.[33]

About 300 people have died and 2,000 have been injured since the protests began, according to a U.N. report issued in August. At least 300 people have been prosecuted on charges such as terrorism and organized crime for having participated in or supported the protests, the report said. "Repression and retaliation against demonstrators continue in Nicaragua as the world looks away, [exposing] the fragility of the country's institutions and the rule of law," said U.N. High Commissioner for Human Rights Zeid Ra'ad Al Hussein.[34]

The U.S. Treasury Department imposed economic sanctions on three Nicaraguans this year, including two government officials it said were responsible for human rights abuses against protesters. "The violence perpetrated by the government of Nicaraguan President Daniel Ortega against the Nicaraguan people and the efforts of those close to the Ortega regime to illicitly enrich themselves is deeply disturbing and completely unacceptable," said Sigal Mandelker, the undersecretary of the Treasury for terrorism and financial intelligence. "President Ortega and his inner circle continue to violate basic freedoms of innocent civilians while ignoring the Nicaraguan people's calls for the democratic reforms."[35]

If Nicaraguans succeed in pushing out Ortega, their victory could exacerbate dissent already simmering in neighboring countries, some experts say. "Ultimately, what happens in Nicaragua may not stay in Nicaragua: If Ortega loses power, other unstable Central American countries—such as Honduras and Guatemala—could soon feel the wrath of their own dissidents," said an assessment by the geopolitical research firm Stratfor.[36]

Ortega could try to defuse domestic anger by addressing protesters' concerns, and possibly preserve his administration for another few years, the firm said. He could then try to maintain power by having his wife, Rosario Murillo, now the vice president, run for president. But Ortega's political base is weakening, and the army no longer can be counted on to provide unconditional support, according to Stratfor.

Tulane's Feoli says Honduras probably would be the most likely to be affected by the protests in Nicaragua. Tens of thousands of Hondurans protested in 2015, demanding the resignation of President Juan Orlando Hernández, alleging that public health system funds were diverted for his 2013 campaign.

"This is our Central American spring," one Honduran protester said at the time, likening the protests to the 2011 pro-democracy uprisings in the Arab world.[37] In 2017 protests erupted over the results of Orlando's re-election after international observers documented many voting irregularities.

"The president is vulnerable due to ongoing allegations of fraud in the 2017 election, which have weakened his legitimacy," Feoli says. In addition, he adds, persistent questioning by the opposition, with whom talks "have been continually delayed since they were suspended in December, has made the political crisis linger."

Other experts on Central America doubt that Nicaragua's unrest will spread because, they say, the anger in Nicaragua is unique to that country's situation. Ortega first rose to prominence as a member of the Frente Sandinista de Liberación Nacional, or FSLN, which overthrew the powerful Somoza family. When first elected in 1984, Ortega promised to implement programs to fight hunger and illiteracy and to create more private-sector jobs.

But after returning to the presidency in 2007, he began restricting the news media and aligning himself with socialist Venezuelan President Hugo Chávez.[38] Since then, his sons and daughters have been appointed to prominent government positions, and his wife was elected vice president.

Now, in 2018, protesters have been chanting: "Ortega, Somoza, son la misma cosa" ("Ortega, Somoza, they are the same thing").[39] "It's a case of a revolution gone putrid," AEI's Noriega says.

Many of those protesting Ortega's administration are Sandinistas, says the Heritage Foundation's Quintana. "These are people who supported Ortega," she says. They are protesting "the rampant corruption within the government."

Like Noriega, Quintana said she does not expect the Nicaraguan protests to spur unrest in neighboring countries, because they already have experienced their own recent uprisings. "Guatemala just went through it," she said.

It is difficult to predict what will trigger further civil protests in Central America, says Isacson of the Washington Office on Latin America. In 2015, thousands of Hondurans took to the street with signs and torches to protest allegations of presidential corruption.[40]

Anti-corruption protest "ebbs and flows," he says. "The people in Honduras who were marching . . . against corruption at that time have not come out again, and that probably owes to very unique reasons in each country."

BACKGROUND
From Empire to Republics

Central America once was home to a flourishing Mayan civilization, which stretched from modern-day Mexico into what is now Honduras and El Salvador. The Maya had highly sophisticated knowledge in astronomy and mathematics and developed an elaborate system of hieroglyphics. At its peak around A.D. 750, the Mayan city of Tikal boasted temples soaring to heights well over 100 feet and had a population of about 60,000.[41]

But by the 9th century, the Mayan civilization was in decline, possibly due to drought and deforestation.[42]

By the time the Spanish arrived in the New World, Central America was dominated by small agricultural communities. Christopher Columbus reached the region on his fourth voyage to the Americas in 1502. Mexico and Peru, with their rich silver deposits, were generally more attractive to the Spanish than Central America.[43]

The Spanish colonists brought to Central America what they called the encomienda system, in which settlers received tracts of land and control of the local population living on the land, whom the settlers were expected to convert to Catholicism. In 1542, a Catholic priest, Fray Bartolome de Las Casas, published an account of the settlers' brutal treatment of the native peoples in the Americas, including impaling them on stakes and allowing dogs to tear them apart. A new Spanish law in 1542 reflected Las Casas' call for more humane treatment of local residents of the Americas, including prohibiting forced labor, but it was not rigorously enforced.[44]

Under Spanish control, most of Central America functioned as a single governmental unit, extending from what is now the southern Mexican state of Chiapas to Costa Rica. Much of the population worked on communal lands or for landlords at subsistence level.[45]

Spain tightly controlled trade in the region. The colonies could trade only with Spain, except when trafficking in African slaves. The chief export crops included cacao, a key ingredient in chocolate, and indigo. The wealth of Panama's Nombre de Dios port attracted attacks by English raiders, including Francis Drake and Henry Morgan. Meanwhile, the British tried several times to establish a foothold on the region's Caribbean coast.[46]

Inspired by the Age of Enlightenment and the U.S. and French revolutions, Spain's colonies in Central America declared their independence in 1821, the same year Mexico won its independence after an 11-year war. Central Americans debated for several years whether to align with Mexico or dissolve into independent states. Leaders in El Salvador even inquired about joining the United States at one point. By 1842, the current configuration of nations had been established.[47]

The British established the colony of British Honduras, located north of Honduras, in 1862. It remained a British colony—the last continental possession of the United Kingdom in the Americas—until gaining full independence in 1981. It was renamed Belize in 1973. Many people of African ancestry, who descended from those enslaved in the Eastern Caribbean, took refuge in British Honduras. Today, Belize more closely resembles English-speaking Caribbean islands than its Central American neighbors.[48]

U.S. Involvement

The United States has played a significant role in the Northern Triangle countries since the 19th century, marked by repeated military interventions and U.S. corporations dominating the region's economies and politics.

During the presidency of Franklin Pierce, the United States had repeated skirmishes in Nicaragua, due in part to his efforts to try to keep the British from gaining a foothold there. These included the 1854 bombardment of the Caribbean town of San Juan del Norte, partly to protect the interests of an American steamship company.[49]

In 1856 Pierce recognized a bid by William Walker to seize control of Nicaragua. Walker was one of a series of "filibusterers" (freebooters): private American citizens who organized armed expeditions to various places in Mexico, Central America and Cuba in the 19th century. Walker sought to gain Nicaragua's entry into the Union as a slave state.[50]

But other Central American nations and the British opposed Walker. U.S. leaders eventually became wary of him, and in 1857, U.S. Marines escorted him and some followers out of Nicaragua. He repeatedly tried to return to Central America, but the British Navy caught him and turned him over to Honduran authorities, who executed him by firing squad.[51]

In 1898 the Spanish-American War sharpened America's taste for expanding its influence outside its borders, especially in its own hemisphere. In 1903, when Panama rebelled against Colombia, which had controlled Panama since its independence from Spain, President Theodore Roosevelt supported the rebels and sent U.S. naval ships to deter Colombian forces. The United States then gained the right to construct a canal across the narrow country after an earlier French-led effort failed in 1889.[52] The canal opened in 1914.

In Nicaragua, President José Santos Zelaya, who led the country from 1893 to 1909, had expansionist ambitions of his own, putting him on a collision course with the United States and neighboring countries. Zelaya tried to create a political union among Nicaragua, Honduras and El Salvador. The overthrow of Zelaya in 1909, with U.S. support, helped set the stage for two-decade U.S. Marine occupation of Nicaragua (1912-1933).[53]

Revolutionary leader Augusto César Sandino emerged as a regional folk hero after challenging the American-backed Nicaraguan government and the U.S. Marines who protected it. "From 1927 to 1933 Sandino became a popular, even charismatic, figure among peasants who, having gotten nothing out of the long U.S. occupation, fed and protected his soldiers from marine-led search parties," wrote Cornell University historian Walter LaFeber.[54]

Sandino's efforts led to the 1933 withdrawal of U.S. forces. Sandino was granted amnesty, but the National Guard assassinated him in 1934. The Nicaraguan Sandinista movement that began in the 1960s would take his name.

Sandino also inspired the Salvadoran rebel Agustín Farabundo Marti, who sought to bring communism to El Salvador. After world prices for coffee, a major export crop, plummeted in the early 1930s, a rebellion broke out in 1932. The government quickly put down the revolt and then killed tens of thousands of people in reprisals known as *la matanza*, or "the slaughter." Marti was shot for his part in the rebellion, but Salvadoran rebels in the 1980s would name their liberation group after him—El Frente Farabundo Martí para la Liberación Nacional (FMLN).[55]

In much of Honduras and Guatemala, foreign banana companies—specifically the United Fruit and Standard Fruit companies (predecessors of Chiquita and Dole, respectively)—had what some call a neocolonialist impact on the two nations' economic and political development. The companies, which built railroads and controlled huge swaths of plantation-covered lands, lobbied governments and manipulated political factions to gain favorable treatment. The United States frequently dispatched warships to the region's coastal waters to warn of the possibility of intervention if U.S. business interests were threatened.[56]

In Costa Rica, a midcentury period of unrest and a brief civil war that killed about 2,000 people produced political compromises that many experts say set the stage for the nation's future peace and prosperity. A 1949 constitution, promulgated by the administration of José Figueres Ferrer, prohibited the establishment of an army and gave women the right to vote. Figueres, who was considered left of center, might have encountered resistance from the United States if his revolution had occurred a few years later, when the U.S.-Soviet proxy standoff known as the Cold War was in full stride, says Gawronski of Birmingham-Southern College in Alabama.

In 1951, Jacobo Arbenz became president of Guatemala, backed by the army and its leftist political factions, including the Guatemalan Communist Party.

The country faced high levels of poverty and malnutrition, and 2 percent of the population controlled more than 72 percent of the nation's productive farmland. Arbenz in 1952 proposed a law that mandated the redistribution of idle lands.

The plan angered United Fruit and raised further doubts in Washington about Arbenz's relationship with communists.[57] The landed elite published anti-reform pamphlets, complaining that communists had infiltrated the government. In 1954, a coup backed by the CIA toppled Arbenz.

Cold-War Clashes

The fall of the Arbenz government was part of a long Guatemalan tradition of political dominance by the wealthy elite over the majority of the population, many of whom are Mayan. The nation faced a cycle in which social injustice led to protests and political instability, which subsequently were met by repression or military coups.[58]

In the mid-20th century, Guatemala became enmeshed in the Cold War when its leftist guerillas sought the support of Soviet-supported Communist Cuba during a 36-year civil war (1960-1996). The Guatemalan elites and military allied with the United States to thwart the insurgents. A commission chartered as part of a U.N.-led peace process later estimated that 200,000 people died during the war, most of them Mayas. "Guatemalans lived under the shadow of fear, death and disappearance as daily threats in the lives of ordinary citizens," wrote the commission.[59]

Responding to human rights violations and the continued slaughter in Guatemala, President Jimmy Carter in 1978 banned any new sales of weapons to Guatemala through the U.S. foreign military sales program and later any commercial weapons sales. But in 1983 President Ronald Reagan lifted the weapons embargo, saying the Guatemalan government had made progress toward addressing human rights abuses and was making progress toward democracy.[60] Reagan renewed the military aid to Guatemala at a time when he was seeking allies in fighting a covert war against Nicaragua's leftist Sandinista regime, which ousted U.S.-backed Nicaraguan dictator Anastasio Somoza in 1979.[61]

The Sandinistas had received extensive help from Cuba. Some who opposed communism abandoned the insurgency and joined Somoza's supporters, creating a guerrilla

CHRONOLOGY

1500s-1850s *Colonial rule gives way to U.S.-influenced independence.*

1500s Spanish colonizers arrive and settle in the region.

1820s-1850s Guatemala, Honduras, El Salvador, Nicaragua, Costa Rica and Panama declare independence from Spain and then form and break various intraregional alliances.

1930s-1940s *U.S businesses, such as the United Fruit Co., influence politics in much of Central America.*

1932 A leftist uprising in El Salvador is brutally suppressed.

1936 The dictatorial Anastasio Somoza becomes president of Nicaragua after luring rebel leader Augusto César Sandino to a meeting and having him murdered.

1949 Costa Rica adopts a constitution that abolishes the military.

1950s-1990s *An era of intense political violence takes hold in Central America.*

1954 After intense lobbying by the United Fruit Co., the CIA helps topple democratically elected Guatemalan President Jacobo Árbenz, who had sought land reform.

1060 A decades-long civil war begins in Guatemala.

1979 Sandinista revolutionaries in Nicaragua end decades of rule by the U.S.-allied Somoza family.

1980 In El Salvador, a pro-government death squad assassinates Archbishop Oscar Romero amid intensifying battles between the government and leftist guerrillas.

1987 Costa Rican President Oscar Arias Sánchez wins the Nobel Peace Prize for a plan to end civil wars in Central America. His plan—approved by Costa Rica, Guatemala, El Salvador, Honduras and Nicaragua—calls for free elections and safeguards for human rights.

1998 Hurricane Mitch devastates the Northern Triangle countries of Guatemala, Honduras and El Salvador.

2000s-Present *As violence increases in the Northern Triangle region, immigration to the United States accelerates; Central Americans begin to address systemic corruption.*

2007 Guatemala's Congress ratifies the creation of the U.N.-backed International Commission Against Impunity in Guatemala (CICIG), which proceeds to investigate hundreds of government officials for corruption.

2009 The military pushes left-leaning Honduran President Manuel Zelaya from office.

2014 The number of unaccompanied Central American children detained at the U.S.-Mexico border surges, creating a crisis for the Obama administration.

2015 Guatemala's Congress votes to end President Otto Pérez Molina's immunity from prosecution. He resigns and is arrested on charges of customs fraud.

2016 The Organization of American States and the Honduran government form the Mission to Support the Fight Against Corruption and Impunity in Honduras.

2017 Guatemalan President Jimmy Morales tries to expel Iván Velásquez, the head of the nation's anti-corruption commission, which is investigating alleged illegal financing in the president's 2015 election campaign. . . . A constitutional court blocks Morales' order, and he backs down amid protests and international criticism.

2018 Nicaragua announces a plan to cut pension benefits, spurring weeks of protests followed by violent government suppression (April). . . . Former Salvadoran President Elías Antonio Saca pleads guilty to embezzling hundreds of millions of dollars in public funds during his 2004-2009 tenure. . . . Guatemalan President Jimmy Morales announces he will not renew the CICIG's mandate and then bars the commission's head from re-entering the country (Aug.-Sept.).

Costa Rica Struggles to Meet High Expectations

Its president says the nation should be "obsessed with results."

Compared with his fellow Central American leaders, newly elected Costa Rican President Carlos Alvarado appears to have a fairly easy job. Costa Rica's long history of domestic peace and heavy investments in health and education systems routinely lift that nation well ahead of the region in international rankings of quality of life and medical care.

Costa Rica, for example, grabbed the No. 30 spot in *The Economist* magazine's "Where to Be Born" index, just beneath Spain and tied with Portugal.[1] On per capita gross domestic product (GDP), one way of measuring a nation's wealth, Costa Rica ranks 105th—ahead of such industrializing behemoths as China, Brazil and South Africa.[2]

Yet Alvarado said he worries that citizens in Costa Rica, and elsewhere in Central America, are beginning to lose faith in democracy and becoming attracted to authoritarian forms of government due to ineffective services. Alvarado, 38, who was inaugurated in May, speaks like a man racing the clock to preserve his nation's enviable circumstances.

"We need to be obsessed with results," Alvarado, a novelist and former manager for Procter & Gamble's Febreze air fresheners, said in a June speech in Washington.

The Organisation for Economic Co-operation and Development (OECD), an intergovernmental organization created to stimulate economic progress and world trade, said in 2018 that there is growing dissatisfaction among Costa Ricans regarding the quality of public services. Costa Rica faces a fiscal hurdle due to its past commitment to generous public-sector salaries and pensions, as well as laws that dedicate funding to programs such as education, says Ludovico Feoli, director of Tulane University's Center for Inter-American Policy and Research. Alvarado wants to enact spending cuts and tax reforms this year to shrink the country's fiscal deficit, which could equal 7 to 8 percent of GDP, according to the OECD.[3]

While pushing for the budget reform, Alvarado also has spoken of the need to address issues such as education and infrastructure, in part because they are "not polarizing." As Alvarado told *The Economist* magazine in April: "From Marx to Adam Smith, [all people] hate being in traffic."[4]

The last four Costa Rican administrations have tried unsuccessfully to enact similar reforms. Lacking a majority in Congress, Alvarado must negotiate with the opposition,

force known as the Contras (the "antis").[62] The Reagan administration aided the Contras, even though Congress had blocked U.S. funding for military or paramilitary operations in Nicaragua. To evade the law, Reagan aides—in a scheme that later became known as the Iran-Contra scandal—sold weapons to Iran to ransom U.S. hostages in Beirut and secretly used the proceeds to fund the Contras.[63]

Inspired by the Sandinistas' success, the FMLN emerged in the 1980s to battle U.S.-backed Salvadoran government troops, with support from Nicaragua, Cuba and the Soviet Union. Insurgents executed mayors and mined the countryside, causing many civilian deaths, but most of the killing in El Salvador was blamed on government agents, paramilitary groups and so-called death squads. For instance, in March 1980 Archbishop Oscar Romero was assassinated as he celebrated mass in

the chapel of a clinic for cancer patients. Romero had a practice of reading aloud the names of civilians who disappeared after being kidnapped by the paramilitary. He also had beseeched soldiers to ignore orders to kill their countrymen, deeming such murders immoral.[64]

In December of that year, the Salvadoran National Guard arrested, raped and murdered four American women, three of them nuns who worked with the poor and the fourth a lay missionary, according to the Commission on Truth for El Salvador, created by the United Nations in 1992 to investigate war crimes in the country.[65]

Gangs and Cartels

Instability in Central America triggered waves of immigration to the United States in the 1980s and '90s, with migrants from the region rising from 354,000 in 1980 to

and his proposal likely will be diluted, Feoli says. "But they need desperately to pass this reform to buy time, to be able to adjust gradually and avoid having more drastic measures imposed by an economic crisis," he says.

Costa Rica's central government debt almost doubled when measured as a percentage of GDP between 2008 and 2017, rising from 25 percent to 49 percent, according to the OECD. The increase was one of the largest in Latin America and amounted to about three years of government revenues.[5]

Costa Rica benefits from social reforms triggered by its 1949 constitution, which reflected the thoughts and ideals of José Figueres. Figueres helped his nation abolish its army and guarantee women the right to vote.[6]

He became Costa Rica's president in 1953 and took on the United Fruit Co., the American banana exporter that dominated Central American economic life for half a century.[7] Figueres increased the company's tax assessment from 15 percent of net profits to 35 percent and forced it to turn over all of its housing projects, schools and medical facilities to the government without compensation.[8]

Costa Rica also differed from its neighbors in terms of social development dating back to colonial times, says Stephen Johnson, regional director for Latin America and the Caribbean at the International Republican Institute in Washington, a nonpartisan organization that promotes democracy abroad.

The area where Costa Rica exists today did not have large native populations for Spanish colonists to exploit, as they did in the neighboring Northern Triangle countries of Guatemala, El Salvador and Honduras, Johnson says. Thus, the new Spanish settlers had to rely more on their own labors and build tighter connections with others, he says.

"They were attuned to helping each other," Johnson says. "So you find a communitarian spirit grew up in Costa Rica."

— *Kerry Dooley Young*

---

[1] "Birth right: Where to be born in 2013," *The Economist*, Sept. 2, 2014. https://tinyurl.com/y9xvdazq.

[2] "Country Comparison: GDP Per Capita," *The World Factbook*, CIA, https://tinyurl.com/2yckfx.

[3] Sonia Araujo and Stéphanie Guichard, "Costa Rica: Restoring Fiscal Sustainability and Setting the Basis for a More Growth-friendly and Inclusive Fiscal Policy," Organisation for Economic Co-operation and Development, July 2, 2018, https://tinyurl.com/ybawnw5q.

[4] "The unexpected victory of Carlos Alvarado," *The Economist*, April 7, 2018, https://tinyurl.com/ydgtt6a4.

[5] Araujo and Guichard, *op. cit.*

[6] José Figueres Ferrer, *Encyclopaedia Britannica*, https://tinyurl.com/y8gl7797; Katherine Stanley, "Discovering Henrietta: The Alabama woman who became Costa Rica's first lady," *Tico Times*, Feb. 29, 2016, https://tinyurl.com/yb4azk48.

[7] Peter Chapman, "Rotten Fruit," *Financial Times*, May 15, 2007, https://tinyurl.com/y9x7hgqw.

[8] Harold D. Nelson, "Costa Rica: a country study," Secretary of the Army/Library of Congress, p. 55, https://tinyurl.com/y6wm6ukn.

3.39 million in 2015, according to the Migration Policy Institute, a nonpartisan Washington think tank that studies the movement of people worldwide.[66]

Many of the young immigrants ended up in poor communities in Los Angeles where gangs such as the Mexican Mafia operated. To protect themselves, experts on gangs say, the Central Americans created their own gangs, chiefly MS-13.[67]

By the 1990s, leftist groups were reaching settlements with the governments in Central America. The Chapultepec Agreement ended the civil war in El Salvador in 1992, and in 1996 the United Nations helped the Guatemalan government reach a peace accord with leftist groups.[68]

But the end of these clashes did not mean the Northern Triangle would enjoy peace. Under a 1996 U.S. immigration law overhaul, gang members who committed crimes in the United States could be deported to their home countries. Between 2000 and 2004, an estimated 20,000 young Central American criminals were deported, bringing MS-13's crime and violence to war-torn nations struggling to rebuild.[69]

President Trump has called MS-13 a transnational criminal organization, but in the Northern Triangle countries it operates as a loose coalition of young, often formerly incarcerated men, who shake down and rob their fellow countrymen, according to Steven Dudley, a co-director of the research and media group InSight Crime.

"MS-13 is mostly about immediate gratification. It helps members eke out a living and get some perilous criminal thrills," Dudley wrote.[70] "That's why extortion is a staple. Complex supply chains? Not so much."

China Builds Influence in Central America

A diplomatic offensive seeks to curb Taiwan recognition.

El Salvador's leadership made no secret of why in August it opted to embrace diplomatic relations with China and spurn its longtime ally Taiwan. It was strictly business, not historic ties between China's Communist Party and the leftist Salvadoran governing party.

"Fundamentally, it's an interest in betting on the growth of our country with one of the world's most booming economies," Roberto Lorenzana, a Salvadoran presidential spokesman, said about the switch. "El Salvador can't turn its back on international reality."[1]

President Salvador Sánchez Cerén, a former leftist guerrilla, said talks would begin quickly with China on a wide range of issues, including trade, investment and infrastructure. "They will generate tangible benefits for the whole population," he said.[2]

Central America once stood as a bastion of support for Taiwan, an island nation locked since 1949 in a standoff with mainland China.[3] But the lure of improved relations with the growing economic giant has proven strong. The number of Taiwan's Central American allies has dwindled from seven to four over the past decade, ever since Costa Rican President Óscar Arias in 2007 switched his country's diplomatic recognition from Taiwan to China. Arias said the decision stemmed not from ideology but from a recognition of the global context in which Costa Rica operates.[4]

Panama switched sides in 2017 after a major expansion of its famous canal in 2016. Within months, a group including China Harbour Engineering Company Ltd. began building a $165 million port in Panama to accommodate cruise ships.[5]

On losing El Salvador as a diplomatic partner, Taiwan's foreign minister said his nation would not engage in "money competition," and Taiwanese officials said they decided not to give El Salvador funds for a port development project Taipei sees as unsuitable.[6]

Taiwan, formally known as the Republic of China, has been governed since 1949 by anti-communist forces who lost the Chinese civil war to Mao Zedong's communists and fled the mainland. China maintains that Taiwan is part of its territory and has threatened to annex it, by force if necessary. Taiwan intends to maintain the status quo. Amid the stalemate, the mainland government, officially known as the People's Republic of China, refuses to have diplomatic ties with any country that recognizes Taiwan.[7]

El Salvador's defection means Taiwan has diplomatic relations with only 17 nations, including four of them in Central America—Belize, Guatemala, Honduras and Nicaragua.[8] But there is strong pressure on them to change sides, said the Honduran ambassador to Taiwan, Rafael Sierra. "There's . . . a fight to get all the countries away from Taiwan," he said.[9]

The Trump administration reacted to the recognition of Beijing by Panama and El Salvador by temporarily recalling U.S. envoys to the two countries in early September and accusing China of "apparent interference" in El Salvador's domestic politics. John Feeley, the former U.S. ambassador to Panama called the recall a "serious signal" that the U.S. government fears American interests in the region "could be jeopardized" by China.[10]

Jorge Guajardo, a former Mexican ambassador to China, said it is not surprising that Central American countries might turn away from the United States, because President Trump has alienated Latin Americans with his anti-immigrant rhetoric, his policy of separating Central American border crossers from their children and his vows to cut aid to the region. Historically, the region has preferred "the U.S. as the main ally," Guajardo said. "This changed when Trump assumed the presidency. It was his call, his choice, to turn away from the region."[11]

However, in recent decades, international drug cartels have dug deeply into Central America, in part due to stepped-up international efforts to stop trafficking from Colombia and Mexico. The cartels have infiltrated the corrupt political leadership in parts of the Northern Triangle and sought to tilt local and municipal elections to ensure that drug trafficking routes are protected, experts say.[71]

Still, experts say Chinese investment abroad may prove disappointing to leaders seeking to attract new jobs and boost economic growth. In Costa Rica, for example, China built a new national soccer stadium but then brought in their own construction workers and allegedly used them to do work on another Chinese-backed project at the same time, says Jacqueline Mazza, a lecturer in the Johns Hopkins University School of Advanced International Studies in Washington and a former researcher at the Inter-American Development Bank.

While China may engage in a certain amount of "trade promotion," such as arranging for Latin American businessmen to make contacts with Chinese businesses, these relationships tend to end up benefiting China, says R. Evan Ellis, a professor of Latin American studies at the U.S. Army War College in Carlisle, Pa. "In reality, the long-term effects are almost always a significant expansion of sales of Chinese products locally," but with "very limited benefits" for the partner nation, Ellis says.

For instance, Chinese businessman Wang Jing planned to build a Nicaraguan canal intended to rival Panama's, even though Nicaragua maintained its ties to Taiwan. In 2013, Nicaraguan President Ortega signed a 50-year concession that grants Wang's HK Nicaragua Canal Development Investment Co. rights to develop a $40 billion project that includes the canal, an oil pipeline, two deepwater ports, an interoceanic railroad and two airports.[12]

Ortega ordered his supporters in Nicaragua's legislature to approve a "special law" that, according to *Miami Herald* columnist Andrés Oppenheimer, effectively turned over the country's sovereignty for 50 years—with an option to extend it for another half century—to a Chinese businessman about whom little was known.[13]

In 2015, according to Bloomberg.com, Wang lost much of his fortune, and there has been little sign of progress on the Nicaraguan projects.[14]

"The Nicaraguan canal project seems to be mysteriously disappearing," says Mazza.

Moreover, Mazza says, other Chinese business interests likely will steer clear of the Northern Triangle due to the level of violence there.

"The security situation is so severe that it is a major constraint," Mazza says. "If they don't improve the basic security conditions, nobody is going to want to invest there."

— *Kerry Dooley Young*

[1] Nelson Renteria, "El Salvador says economy prompted diplomatic switch to China from Taiwan," Reuters, Aug. 21, 2018, https://tinyurl.com/y7f2bbch.

[2] *Ibid.*

[3] Sigrid Winkler, "Biding Time: The Challenge of Taiwan's International Status," Brookings Institution, Nov. 17, 2011, https://tinyurl.com/yb9fuvrg.

[4] Kevin Casas-Zamora, "Notes on Costa Rica's Switch from Taipei to Beijing," Brookings Institution, Nov. 6, 2009, https://tinyurl.com/ybtocltd.

[5] Walt Bogdanich, "Panama Celebrates Expanded Canal's Successful First Passage," *The New York Times*, June 26, 2016, https://tinyurl.com/y8plyypq; Ben Blanchard, "After ditching Taiwan, China says Panama will get the help it needs," Reuters, Nov. 17, 2017, https://tinyurl.com/y6wbaowo.

[6] Renteria, *op. cit.*

[7] Winkler, *op. cit.*

[8] "Diplomatic Allies," Ministry of Foreign Affairs for Taiwan, undated, https://tinyurl.com/ydhgv8f7.

[9] Sarah Zheng, "Taiwan's critical battle to keep its diplomatic allies from switching sides," *South China Morning Post*, updated July 6, 2018, https://tinyurl.com/yaqx5cqs.

[10] Edward Wong, "U.S. Recalls Top Diplomats From Latin America as Worries Rise Over China's Influence," *The New York Times*, Sept. 8, 2018, https://tinyurl.com/ycrdolph.

[11] *Ibid.*

[12] Adam Williams, "Nicaragua's Canal: Chinese Tycoon Wang Jing Wants to Build It," Bloomberg, June 27, 2013, https://tinyurl.com/y9wolpn5.

[13] Andrés Oppenheimer, "Four years later, Nicaragua's $40 billion interoceanic canal remains a pipe dream," *The Miami Herald*, July 5, 2017, https://tinyurl.com/y8nwljme.

[14] *Ibid.*

In Guatemala, civic groups appealed to the United Nations for help, and in 2007 the nation's legislature cleared the way for the creation of the CICIG. Over the next 11 years, it would become one of the most trusted institutions in Guatemala as it helped local prosecutors bring dozens of corrupt officials to justice.[72]

Starting in 2014, a sudden surge in families and unaccompanied minors crossing the U.S.-Mexico border created a humanitarian crisis for the Obama administration. The number of unaccompanied young people apprehended at the border jumped from 16,067 in fiscal 2011 to 68,541 in fiscal 2014.[73]

Obama and Congress responded by more than doubling the annual aid appropriation for Central America within two years, and focusing on preventing drug crime and incorporating human rights training into all programs for police and armed forces.[74]

Meanwhile, the immigrant population from the Northern Triangle continued to climb—by 25 percent between 2007 and 2015—outpacing the 10 percent growth in the foreign-born population overall, according to the Pew Research Center, a nonpartisan Washington research organization. Federal agencies were overwhelmed by demand for shelter for apprehended children and teens. Border Patrol offices were used for daycare and military barracks for dormitories. Obama warned Central American parents in an ABC News interview: "Do not send your children to the borders. If they do make it, they'll get sent back. More importantly, they may not make it."[75]

Since his inauguration in 2017, Trump has sought to shift the focus of U.S. policies on Central America toward a greater emphasis on halting illegal immigration and cracking down on drug trafficking.[76]

CURRENT SITUATION

Zero Tolerance

In April 2018, Attorney General Jeff Sessions announced a "zero-tolerance" policy for people attempting to cross the U.S.-Mexico border, citing a 203 percent increase in illegal border crossings from March 2017 to March 2018.[77]

The Trump administration sought the prosecution of all individuals who illegally enter the United States, which had the effect of separating parents from their children when they enter the country together. The parents were referred for prosecution and the children were placed in custody. In the past, families tended to be detained together, sent back immediately or paroled into the country.

Because children cannot be held in adult detention centers, officials began separating migrant children from their parents and holding them in separate facilities, often thousands of miles apart. "If you're smuggling a child, then we're going to prosecute you, and that child will be separated from you," Sessions said.[78]

The Trump administration drew widespread criticism for its "zero tolerance" policies, which it tried to blame on Democrats, but even powerful Republicans joined in the dissent. In June, Senate Finance Chairman Orrin Hatch, a Republican from Utah, led a group of GOP senators calling for an end to the policy of separating families, emphasizing that the policy originated with the current administration.

"The current family separation crisis has multiple contributing causes, including court decisions that require release rather than detention of children—but not parents—who enter our country illegally," Hatch and colleagues said in a June 19 letter to the administration. "But the immediate cause of the crisis is your Department's recent institution of a 'zero tolerance' policy under which all adults who enter the United States illegally are referred for prosecution, regardless of whether they are accompanied by minor children."[79]

Facing intense political pressure, Trump on June 20 ordered an end to the practice of separating families at the border. "We're going to have strong—very strong—borders, but we are going to keep the families together," Trump said. "I didn't like the sight or the feeling of families being separated."[80]

The number of children and teenagers held by the U.S. government dropped from more than 2,600 to about 500 minors by the end of August 2018.[81]

In June, Sessions blocked the path to immigration for many Central Americans by removing fears of domestic abuse or gang violence as causes for granting asylum. Sessions reversed an immigration appeals court ruling that had given asylum to a Salvadoran woman who said she had been abused by her husband.[82]

"The mere fact that a country may have problems effectively policing certain crimes—such as domestic violence or gang violence—or that certain populations are more likely to be victims of crime, cannot itself establish an asylum claim," Sessions said.[83]

Ortega Prevails

As of early September, Nicaraguan President Ortega appeared to have survived a four-month-old rebellion against his rule. In August, he ordered a U.N. human rights team to leave Nicaragua after it released a report alleging human rights abuses, including rape and torture, by the Ortega government's police and prison guards. The government says the deaths of 22 police officers show the protests were not peaceful.[84]

Sparked by a briefly considered and then discarded proposal to cut pensions, the protests morphed into an expression of anger at Ortega's increasingly authoritarian rule since returning to power in 2007.

About 23,000 Nicaraguans have sought asylum in Costa Rica, triggering undercurrents of xenophobia there. The administration of Costa Rican President Carlos Alvarado is investigating whether Ortega's government, or its supporters on either side of the border, were involved in fanning the anti-immigrant flames. False rumors spread on Facebook about Nicaraguan migrants burning Costa Rican flags, for instance, along with inaccurate reports that universities were providing refugees full scholarships.[85]

Guatemala Threatens Investigation

Critics of Guatemalan President Jimmy Morales saw his Aug. 31 announcement that he would not renew the U.N.-backed CICIG's mandate as an effort to thwart the anti-corruption panel's investigation. Just days before Morales' announcement, the Guatemalan Supreme Court had ruled that a CICIG request to strip Morales of his immunity from prosecution could go to Congress for consideration.

"He is clearly worried about CICIG's corruption investigation and wants to protect himself," says U.S. Rep. Norma Torres, a California Democrat, who was born in Guatemala.

The commission's term ends on Sept. 3, 2019, but the panel's chief, Velásquez, has been banned from Guatemala. Morales has asked the U.N. secretary-general to name a replacement. A statement from the Morales administration called Velásquez "a person who attacks order and public security; affecting governance, institutionality, justice and peace in the country."[86]

The CICIG has received bipartisan support in the United States over the years, but some U.S. critics of the commission now claim it has strayed from its original mandate of investigating criminal groups, such as drug cartels, and their influence on public officials. José Cárdenas, who served on the National Security Council under George W. Bush and has close ties to the Trump administration, said under Velásquez the commission seems more interested in "high-profile, publicity-garnering

initiatives like going after Morales's brother and third cousin—I mean, come on—and then basking in the adulation . . . from the international do-gooders."[87]

The Trump administration apparently agrees. It is debating possible amendments to the CICIG's mandate, such as more narrowly redefining corruption, limiting the CICIG commissioner's term and appointing a deputy commissioner, which Guatemala would help select, sources familiar with the discussions told *The Miami Herald*. The United States has donated $44.5 million for the commission's operations since it was established in 2007, the panel's largest donor.[88]

But some CICIG supporters note that Trump's sudden interest in reining in the CICIG emerged shortly after Morales moved Guatemala's Israeli embassy to Jerusalem, following a similar move by Trump, which triggered an international uproar. "The only reason why the U.S. is all about [reforming the CICIG] is because they're so happy with Guatemala that they moved the embassy to Jerusalem," according to a source quoted by *The Herald*.[89]

After Morales' announcement ending the CICIG's mandate, Secretary of State Pompeo spoke with Morales on Sept. 6 about the need to continue fighting corruption in Guatemala and noted that the United States is preparing suggestions for reforming the commission.[90]

Daniel Wilkinson, the managing director for the Americas Division of Human Rights Watch, found Pompeo's response lacking. "Good news: @SecPompeo finally reaffirms US support for CICIG," Wilkinson tweeted. "Bad news: he's still not saying what everyone already knows—@jimmymoralesgt is destroying CICIG and, with it, any real possibility of 'cooperation in the fight against corruption and impunity.'"[91]

The United States also disappointed international CICIG supporters by failing to back a joint statement in support of Velásquez and the CICIG, issued by the G13, a group of countries and multilateral organizations representing Guatemala's largest donors.

Activists say without the CICIG, it will be harder for Guatemalans to continue their fight for land reform. "It's horrifyingly normal for rich landowners in Guatemala to force whole communities from land on which they've lived for generations, often with the help of private militias or the army," wrote Rony Morales and Michael Taylor. Morales is a community journalist with the

Should the U.S. increase aid to Central America?

YES   Michael Clemens
Co-Director, Migration, Displacement, and Humanitarian Policy and Senior Fellow, Center for Global Development

Written for *CQ Researcher*, September 2018

Since the initial coverage of the surge in unaccompanied child migrant arrivals in 2014, the public has debated the so-called root causes. Are these migrants fleeing violence, poverty or some mix of the two? What has often been missing is evidence rigorously examining this question.

Why are unaccompanied child migrants leaving the Northern Triangle (El Salvador, Guatemala and Honduras) and coming to the United States? Using unprecedented data from the Department of Homeland Security spanning 2011-16, I measured the statistical relationship between the child migration and the violence and economic indicators in their home areas. The evidence is clear: Violence is a major driver. For every 10 additional homicides in the average Northern Triangle municipality, six additional child migrants were apprehended in the United States.

Economic conditions also matter, however. In fact, they explained roughly as much migration as did homicide rates.

The bottom line is that child migrants are fleeing violence and its ripple economic and social impacts. These root causes will not be altered only by policies enacted at the U.S. border. The conditions in the origin countries must be tackled. Increased U.S. foreign aid—when appropriately targeted and based on evidence—can provide support in this, rendering more effective migration management at the U.S. border.

The United States should prioritize investments in foreign policy to reduce violence in the Northern Triangle. This will translate to a cost savings for the United States—it is more cost-effective to reduce homicides than finance the apprehension and care of unaccompanied minors.

Data-driven analysis is critical to informing targeted interventions in the Northern Triangle. More information is needed to establish forward-looking estimates around the drivers of violence and their relation to migration. These estimates can help shape the targeting of foreign aid interventions. The same is true for informing economic development support plans. Greater cooperation with Northern Triangle partners can advance U.S. interests and ensure maximum relevancy and reach of foreign aid interventions.

The evidence is clear that there is a causal relationship between less violence and less child migration. U.S. aid policy should draw on this evidence and prioritize more and better targeted spending toward violence and economic interventions in the region.

NO   Thomas Dichter
Anthropologist and Independent Development Consultant to USAID, World Bank and Others

Written for *CQ Researcher*, September 2018

After a 50-plus-year career in foreign aid, it is not easy for me to say this, but except for humanitarian aid such as disaster relief and refugee assistance, no new money should be spent.

Why? The foreign aid track record in fostering real development in the region is poor. After decades of aid, El Salvador, Guatemala, Honduras and Nicaragua (80 percent of the region by population) are in bad shape. And this despite countless short-term foreign aid projects that built schools, clinics, wells and latrines, set up vocational skills training programs, advised agricultural co-ops, funded research on cocoa and coffee production, trained teachers, provided microloans to try to increase employment, etc.

Aid agencies such as U.S. Agency for International Development boast that these inputs work, and many of them do, for a while. But I can tell you that the gains made through such projects tend to be as short-term as the projects themselves were. If donors were to go back five to 15 years after the end of their projects, they would often see little left, due to poor governance, corruption, ethnic and civil strife, lack of sustainable funding and, especially, lack of local ownership.

And on the aid side, donor fickleness is at fault. Every few years a new problem comes along that needs to be addressed (right now it is illegal migration and gang violence) along with urgent calls for more money. Foreign aid planners conveniently forget the negligible results of past magical solutions, and now have the hubris to believe they know how to solve problems such as gang violence in El Salvador.

The U.S. aid industry's concern for quick wins and quantifiable results has made short-term and simple-minded thinking the norm, pushing aside the need to understand context: the complex mix of history, political economy, social structure and culture that underlies the region's problems.

If there is an answer to the aid conundrum, it lies in the realm of country ownership. Development must now be led and owned by the countries themselves. It is their job, not ours. We can help, but with ideas, dialogue and careful thought more than with new money thrown at Band-Aid projects.

Above all, we need to remember that foreign aid is a unique business, one where the goal is to work ourselves out of a job. It is past time to begin to do that.

Union of Peasant Organizations of Verapaz in Guatemala, and Taylor is director of the secretariat of the International Land Coalition, an alliance of civil society and multilateral organizations in 77 countries, based in Rome.[92]

With the nation's elites owning the vast majority of Guatemala's land, they said, land redistribution was a major reform promised in the 1996 peace accord that ended the nation's 36-year civil war. But the issue has been largely ignored, and poverty rates have risen even as the country's gross domestic product has doubled over the past decade, they pointed out.

Land dispossession causes "relentless misery . . . and further destabilizes prospects for peace not only in Guatemala, but also in an already volatile region. It also drives families with few other options at home to attempt the perilous journey to the United States. If only for this reason, the United States should care about land reform in Guatemala."[93]

OUTLOOK
Daunting Challenges

In the next few years, the stability of Central America may rest, to a large degree, on Ortega's ability to stay in control of Nicaragua.

Ortega will do all he can to maintain power while repressing protest, says Reggie Thompson, an analyst who follows Latin America for Stratfor. That could trigger further cycles of protest and government repression, he says. "Ortega is involved in a struggle for the survival of his dynasty," Thompson says. "We're going to see him double down on some of those tactics ahead of the 2021 [presidential] vote."

For now, Ortega has hung onto his base of supporters in the military and business, Thompson says, adding, "As long as those stay at least compliant and not in open rebellion against the president, he's pretty safe relatively speaking."

Further protest likely would elicit more government repression, which could lead the United States to step up pressure on Ortega, Thompson says. There already has been significant economic disruption, with paramilitary groups interfering with transportation, he says, making it difficult for people to get to work. The unrest also will thwart investment, he says.

Meanwhile, neighboring governments are trying to manage undercurrents of dissent within their own populations, Thompson says. "The political situation isn't particularly stable" in Central America, he says. "You have populations with extreme social grievances that sometimes mobilize against the governments."

Stephen Johnson, the regional director for Latin America and the Caribbean at the International Republican Institute, a nonpartisan Washington-based group that promotes global democracy, suggested that Central Americans should look to some of their neighbors for examples of how nations can turn themselves around. For example, he said, Colombia suffered from rampant drug trafficking and armed insurgencies that killed thousands and displaced millions of citizens during the late 20th century. Yet, with help from the United States, Colombia today is much more stable and peaceful.[94]

"We tend to look at what happens through the optics of what's going on right now. It's hard to step back and take the long view and see what trends are actually at work," Johnson says.

In the Northern Triangle, there has been a gradual strengthening of governments at the local and municipal level, he says. "You've seen a deepening of some of the institutions that govern such things as public safety policy and a greater awareness of what countries have to do to ensure a competitive but fair economic environment for businesses," he says.

"It's been slow growth over time," he adds. "It's progress, but it's not going to happen overnight."

NOTES

1. "U.S. Border Patrol Southwest Border Apprehensions by Sector FY2018," Customs and Border Control, Aug. 8, 2018, https://tinyurl.com/y8e2xblr.

2. Andrea Drusch, "Trump threatens cuts to Central America aid. He'll have to go through Granger first," *Star-Telegram* (Fort Worth), June 29, 2018, https://tinyurl.com/yap46v6p.

3. Bryan Baker, "Immigration Enforcement Actions: 2016," Department of Homeland Security, December 2017, https://tinyurl.com/y7yq66t8.

4. Pompeo remarks at appropriations hearing, "Review of the FY2019 Budget Request for the Department

of State, Senate Appropriations State/Foreign Operations Subcommittee," U.S. Senate, June 27, 2018, https://tinyurl.com/yd4mlbgk.

5. José Miguel Cruz, "Five Myths: MS-13," *The Washington Post*, June 29, 2018, https://tinyurl.com/y9l7mjsy.

6. Ron Nixon, Liz Robbins and Katie Benner, "Trump Targets MS-13, a Violent Menace, If Not the One He Portrays," *The New York Times*, March 1, 2018, https://tinyurl.com/y9hsnm8c. Also see "Department of Justice Fact Sheet on MS-13," U.S. Department of Justice, April 18, 2017, https://tinyurl.com/ybk57qux; and Jane Fullerton Lemons, "Gang Violence," *CQ Researcher*, June 1, 2018, pp. 465-488.

7. "A brief golden age: The threat to Central America's prosecutors," *The Economist*, May 10, 2018, https://tinyurl.com/y7w9dlxp.

8. Malkin, Elisabeth, "Citing Hostility, Leader of Anti-Corruption Panel in Honduras Resigns," *The New York Times*, Feb. 16, 2018, https://tinyurl.com/ybk9xwuh.

9. "Encarcelan a expresidente de Corte Suprema de Justicia de Honduras por corrupción," AFP/Telemetro.com, Aug. 8, 2018, https://tinyurl.com/y75wcq4l.

10. Jakub Lewandowski, "Former Salvadoran President Tony Saca Pleads Guilty After Embezzling Hundreds of Millions of Dollars," *Newsweek*, Aug. 10, 2018, https://tinyurl.com/y8tactns.

11. John Burnett, "Guatemalan President Shuts Down Anti-Corruption Probe," "Morning Edition," NPR, Sept. 3, 2018, https://tinyurl.com/yapueb6b; "Human rights violations and abuses in the context of protests in Nicaragua," Office of the United Nations High Commissioner for Human Rights, Aug. 29, 2018, https://tinyurl.com/y8xvc56d.

12. "Guatemala: Staff Concluding Statement of the 2018 Article IV Mission," International Monetary Fund, March 19, 2018, https://tinyurl.com/yc5uekk6; "IMF staff completes 2018 Article IV mission to Honduras," International Monetary Fund, April 13, 2018, https://tinyurl.com/y8gp4uj5; "2018 Article IV Consultation—press release; Staff Report; and Statement by the Executive Director for El Salvador," International Monetary Fund, June 7, 2018, https://tinyurl.com/y8c5298v.

13. "World Bank's Foreign direct investment, net inflows," World Bank, Aug. 20, 2018, https://tinyurl.com/y9glunsc.

14. "World Bank International Comparison Database," https://tinyurl.com/y8aezqtu. Figures are adjusted for purchasing power parity.

15. Tristan Clavel, "InSight Crime's 2017 Homicide Round-Up," *InSight Crime*, Jan. 19, 2018, https://tinyurl.com/ybtercgq.

16. "Doing Business 2018 Reforming to Create Jobs," World Bank, Oct. 31, 2017, https://tinyurl.com/yaon9u4j.

17. "Guatemala: Staff Concluding Statement of the 2018 Article IV Mission," *op. cit.*; "IMF staff completes 2018 Article IV mission to Honduras," *op. cit.*; "2018 Article IV Consultation—press Release; Staff Report; and Statement by the Executive Director for El Salvador," *op. cit.*

18. Steven Dudley, "How Drug Trafficking Operates, Corrupts in Central America," *InSight Crime*, July 6, 2016, https://tinyurl.com/yd469z7z.

19. Burnett, *op. cit.*; Elisabeth Malkin, "Guatemala Arrests Ex-President and His Finance Minister in Corruption Case," *The New York Times*, Feb. 13, 2018, https://tinyurl.com/ydhyym3u; Nina Lakhani, "Guatemalan president's downfall marks success for corruption investigators," *The Guardian*, Sept. 5, 2015, https://tinyurl.com/ybw4hwlm.

20. Joshua Partlow, "Guatemala's president tries to shut down anti-corruption group investigating him," *The Washington Post*, Sept. 5, 2018, https://tinyurl.com/y8xkae6h.

21. By Elisabeth Malkin, "Protests Erupt in Guatemala Over Laws to Dilute Antigraft Campaign," *The New York Times*, Sept. 15, 2017, https://tinyurl.com/ycdr88fs.

22. Patrick J. Leahy, "Leahy REAX To The Decision Of Guatemalan President Morales To Oppose The Renewal Of The International Commission Against Impunity," U.S. Senate, Aug. 31, 2018, https://tinyurl.com/y7va93hu.

23. José Miguel Vivanco and Daniel Wilkinson, "Letter to U.S. Secretary of State Rex Tillerson," Human Rights Watch, Feb. 7, 2018, https://tinyurl.com/y8ahfbmo; "Guatemala's comedian-president fights the corruption-fighters," *The Economist*, Sept. 2, 2017, https://tinyurl.com/ybaxoag4; Statement by Heather Nauert on CICIG, U.S Department of State, Aug. 27, 2017, https://tinyurl.com/yaylz77b.

24. Sen. Patrick Leahy, "Opening Remarks At The FY19 State And Foreign Operations Appropriations Bill Markup," U.S. Senate, June 21, 2018, https://tinyurl.com/y7l3d7cc.

25. "U.S. Strategy for Engagement in Central America: An Overview," Congressional Research Service, June 25, 2018, https://tinyurl.com/y9ptdyff.

26. Peter J. Meyer, "U.S. Strategy for Engagement in Central America: Policy Issues for Congress," Congressional Research Service, June 8, 2017, p. 11, https://tinyurl.com/ybvl93dj; Haeyoun Park, "Children at the Border," *The New York Times*, Oct. 21, 2014, https://tinyurl.com/y8lnquy6.

27. Jeremy Diamond, "Trump Planning to Withhold Aid from Undocumented Immigrant Home Countries," CNN.com, May 23, 2018, https://tinyurl.com/ybmuk2yd. Text of HR 6657, Fund and Complete the Border Wall Act, https://tinyurl.com/yaf626fl.

28. Jill H. Wilson, "Temporary Protected Status: Overview and Current Issues," Congressional Research Service, Jan. 17, 2018, https://tinyurl.com/yar63ge3; Miriam Valverde, "What you need to know about the Trump administration's zero-tolerance immigration policy," *Politifact*, June 6, 2018, https://tinyurl.com/y8xtkntu.

29. Paul J. Angelo, "Donald Trump's Central America strategy is both cruel and incompetent," *The Conversation*, May 29, 2018, https://tinyurl.com/y7fmsvv5.

30. Pompeo remarks at appropriations hearing, *op. cit.*

31. Cristina Eguizábal *et al.*, "Crime and Violence in Central America's Northern Triangle: How U.S. Policy Responses Are Helping, Hurting, and Can Be Improved," Wilson Center, 2015, p. 13, https://tinyurl.com/y9wvrwqe.

32. John Otis, "Nicaraguan Leader's Former Pro-Business Allies Want Him Out," *The Wall Street Journal*, July 10, 2018, https://tinyurl.com/yby7v48l.

33. "Human Rights Violations and Abuses in the Context of Protests in Nicaragua," *op. cit.*

34. *Ibid.*

35. "Treasury Sanctions Three Nicaraguan Individuals for Serious Human Rights Abuse and Corrupt Acts," U.S. Department of the Treasury, July 5, 2018, https://tinyurl.com/y95ghrje.

36. "How Nicaragua's Protests Could Spread Elsewhere in Central America," Stratfor Worldview, May 17, 2018, https://tinyurl.com/y7b5qnel.

37. Sibylla Brodzinsky, "Our Central American Spring: Protesters Demand an End to Decades of Corruption," *The Guardian*, Aug. 14, 2015, https://tinyurl.com/y7kcwx22.

38. "Freedom in the World 2017: Nicaragua Profile," Freedom House, https://tinyurl.com/y97lo6ua.

39. Jon Lee Anderson, "Nicaragua on the Brink, Once Again," *New Yorker*, April 27, 2018, https://tinyurl.com/ydfuev5v; "Daniel Ortega is causing a blood-bath in Nicaragua," *The Economist*, July 12, 2018, https://tinyurl.com/yc5rmek7.

40. "Thousands protest against Honduran president over claims of corruption," *Deutsche Welle* (DW.com), July 18, 2015, https://tinyurl.com/yccjgb9s.

41. Ralph Lee Woodward, Jr., *Central America: A Nation Divided* (1985), p. 13; David Roberts, "Secrets of the Maya: Deciphering Tikal," *Smithsonian*, July 2005, https://tinyurl.com/ybycjbps.

42. Rachel Nuwer, "For Ancient Maya, Climate Change Giveth and Taketh Away," *The New York Times*, Nov. 8, 2012, https://tinyurl.com/yaweuhem; "The collapse of Classic Maya civilization linked to drought," press release, Durham University, Nov. 8, 2012, https://tinyurl.com/ycr78kkd; Dauna Coulter, "The Fall of the Maya: 'They Did It to Themselves,'" Science@NASA, Oct. 6, 2009, https://tinyurl.com/yc2g946m.

43. Richard A. Haggerty, *El Salvador: a country study* (1990), p. 3; Tim Merrill, *Nicaragua: a country study* (1994), p. xx, https://tinyurl.com/yajr8acl.

44. Richard F. Nyrop, ed., *Guatemala: a country study* (1983), p. 8, https://tinyurl.com/y9nyy64v; Bartolomé de Las Casas, *A Short Account of the Destruction of the Indies*, edited and translated by Nigel Griffin (1992), pp. 59, 60.

45. Hector Perez-Brignoli, *A Brief History of Central America*, as translated by Ricardo B. Sawrey A. and Susana Stettri de Sawrey (1989), p. 37.

46. Sandra W. Meditz and Dennis M. Hanratty, *Panama: a country study* (1987), p. 10, https://tinyurl.com/yadwgfky; Nyrop, *op. cit.*, pp. 11, 13.

47. *Ibid.*, Nyrop, p. 15.

48. Tim Merrill, ed., *Guyana and Belize: country studies* (1993), p. xx, https://tinyurl.com/yctpy8fh.

49. Richard F. Grimmett, "Instances of Use of United States Armed Forces Abroad, 1798-2009," Congressional Research Service, Jan. 27, 2010, https://tinyurl.com/ybaordvn; Franklin Pierce, "Second Annual Message," State of the Union, Dec. 4, 1854, The American Presidency Project, University of California, Santa Barbara, https://tinyurl.com/yac8xte2.

50. Jean H. Baker, "Franklin Pierce: Foreign Affairs," Miller Center, University of Virginia, https://tinyurl.com/y7uhs7oq; "Territorial Expansion, Filibustering, and U.S. Interest in Central America and Cuba, 1849-1861," Office of the Historian, U.S. Department of State, undated, https://tinyurl.com/ybrq5oew.

51. Merrill, *Nicaragua: a country study, op. cit.*

52. Meditz and Hanratty, *op. cit.*, p. 3.

53. Woodward, *op. cit.* Also see "U.S. Intervention in Nicaragua, 1911/1912," Archive, U.S. Department of State, https://tinyurl.com/y7oyt3sf.

54. Walter LaFeber, *Inevitable Revolutions: The United States in Central America* (1983), p. 66.

55. Donald C. Hodges, *Sandino's Communism: Spiritual Politics for the Twenty-First Century* (2014), p. 73; https://tinyurl.com/ycske65m.

56. "History," Dole Food Company, https://tinyurl.com/y8837ebo; Tim Merrill, *Honduras: a country study* (1995), p. xxvi. Also see Barbara Salazar Torreon, "Instances of Use of United States Armed Forces Abroad, 1798-2017," Congressional Research Service, October 2017, pp. 7-9, https://tinyurl.com/y9uslqfa.

57. "Foreign Relations of the United States, 1952-1954, Guatemala," Office of the Historian, Department of State, https://tinyurl.com/ybqqtobc.

58. "Guatemala, Memory of Silence: Tí'inil Nat'ab'al: Report of the Commission for Historical Clarification: Conclusions and Recommendations," Commission for Historical Clarification, United Nations, 1988, p. 18, https://tinyurl.com/k2pp3y3.

59. *Ibid.*, p. 16. Also see "Soviet Policies and Activities in Latin America and the Caribbean," CIA, 1982, p. 12, https://tinyurl.com/y8ru2mtl.

60. Bernard Gwertzman, "U.S. Lifts Embargo on Military Sales to Guatemalans," *The New York Times*, Jan. 8, 1983, https://tinyurl.com/y95dmhoh.

61. Merrill, *Nicaragua: a country study, op. cit.*, p. 29.

62. "The Contras Minus Arturo Cruz," *The New York Times*, Feb. 10, 1987, https://tinyurl.com/y8wva69b.

63. Merrill, *Nicaragua: a country study, op. cit.*, p. 47.

64. Belisario Betancur, "From Madness to Hope: The 12-Year War in El Salvador: Report of the Commission on the Truth for El Salvador," The Commission on Truth for El Salvador, p. 32, https://tinyurl.com/y8ctyocl; Scott Simon, "Oscar Romero, The Murdered Archbishop Who Inspires the Pope," NPR, Feb. 7, 2015, https://tinyurl.com/y7kqevw9; Haggerty, *op. cit.*, p. 36; Raymond Bonner, "Crisis of Conscience Moves Salvador Church," *The New York Times*, July 19, 1981, https://tinyurl.com/y9obqgmv.

65. *Ibid.*

66. Gabriel Lesser and Jeanne Batalova, "Central American Immigrants in the United States," Migration Policy Institute, April 5, 2017, https://tinyurl.com/y79r3phb.

67. Steven Dudley, "MS-13 Is a Street Gang, Not a Drug Cartel—and the Difference Matters," *InSight Crime*, March 20, 2018, https://tinyurl.com/ycggqlfy.

68. "Chapultepec Agreement Summary," Peacemaker, United Nations, https://tinyurl.com/yayn398l;

"Agreement on a Firm and Lasting Peace," Peacemaker, United Nations, https://tinyurl.com/ychc62su; Julia Preston, "Guatemala and Guerrillas Sign Accord to End 35-Year Conflict," *The New York Times*, Sept. 20, 1996, https://tinyurl.com/ybf3jk6y.

69. Ana Arana, "How the Street Gangs Took Central America," *Foreign Affairs*, May/June 2005, https://tinyurl.com/yc7kb7lt.

70. Dudley, "MS13 Is a Street Gang," *op. cit.*

71. Steven S. Dudley, "Drug Trafficking Organizations in Central America: Transportistas, Mexican Cartels, and Maras," Organized Crime in Central America: The Northern Triangle, The Wilson Center, pp. 7, 10, 18, https://tinyurl.com/ya5d6juo.

72. Elizabeth J. Zechmeister and Dinorah Azpuru, "What Does the Public Report on Corruption, the CICIG, the Public Ministry, and the Constitutional Court in Guatemala?" Latin American Public Opinion Project, Aug. 31, 2017, https://tinyurl.com/ybpty7r7.

73. William A. Kandel, "Unaccompanied Alien Children: An Overview," Congressional Research Service, Jan. 18, 2017, p. 2, https://tinyurl.com/haeb3n5.

74. "Fact Sheet: United States Support for Central American Citizen Security," White House, May 4, 2013, https://tinyurl.com/yajh5ghn.

75. D'Vera Cohn, Jeffrey S. Passel and Ana Gonzalez-Barrera, "Rise in U.S. Immigrants From El Salvador, Guatemala and Honduras Outpaces Growth From Elsewhere," Pew Research Center, Dec. 7, 2017, https://tinyurl.com/yd4txrl9; Jennifer Scholtes and Emily Ethridge, "Alone, Illegal and Underage: The Child Migrant Crisis," *Roll Call*, May 28, 2014, https://tinyurl.com/hvj8cmo; Devin Dwyer, "Obama Warns Central Americans: 'Do Not Send Your Children to The Borders,'" ABC News, June 26, 2014, https://tinyurl.com/yaee5lcv.

76. Tracy Wilkinson, "Trump administration will press Central American countries and Mexico to keep their people at home," *Los Angeles Times*, June 14, 2017, https://tinyurl.com/ydcdukul.

77. "Attorney General Announces Zero-Tolerance Policy for Criminal Illegal Entry," Justice Department, April 6, 2018, https://tinyurl.com/y96nsut6.

78. Miriam Jordan, "How and Why 'Zero Tolerance' is Splitting Up Immigrant Families," *The New York Times*, May 12, 2018, https://tinyurl.com/ybnrgwsa.

79. "Hatch, 12 Republican Senators Call on Justice Department to Halt Family Separations While Congress Works on Legislative Fix," Office of Sen. Orrin Hatch, June 19, 2018, https://tinyurl.com/y7w7l6ek.

80. "Affording Congress an Opportunity to Address Family Separation," White House, June 20, 2018, https://tinyurl.com/ya4k268y; Michael D. Shear, Abby Goodnough and Maggie Haberman, "Trump Retreats on Separating Families, but Thousands May Remain Apart," *The New York Times*, June 20, 2018, https://tinyurl.com/yd4e2dx5.

81. Nick Miroff and Maria Sacchetti, "Trump administration to circumvent court limits on detention of child migrants," *The Washington Post*, Sept. 6, 2018, https://tinyurl.com/y829ego2.

82. Katie Benner and Caitlin Dickerson, "Sessions Says Domestic and Gang Violence Are Not Grounds for Asylum," *The New York Times*, June 11, 2018, https://tinyurl.com/ydeo7hfp.

83. "Matter of A-B-, Respondent Decided by Attorney General June 11, 2018," U.S. Department of Justice, https://tinyurl.com/ycpj7osx.

84. Shannon Van Sant, "Nicaragua Expels United Nations Team After Report Critical Of The Government," NPR, Sept. 1, 2018, https://tinyurl.com/yads5afq; "Human rights violations and abuses in the context of protests in Nicaragua: 18 April-18 August 2018," Office of the United Nations High Commissioner for Human Rights, August 2018, https://tinyurl.com/y8xvc56d.

85. "Daniel Ortega tightens his grip on Nicaragua," *The Economist*, April 30, 2018, https://tinyurl.com/y92e5tuz; Joshua Partlow, "They fled violence in Nicaragua by the thousands. What awaits them in Costa Rica?" *The Washington Post*, Sept. 2, 2018, https://tinyurl.com/ycpghlsk.

86. "The Latest: Guatemalans to protest end of anti-graft body," The Associated Press, Sept. 1, 2018, https://tinyurl.com/ya7nf7a3; Perez Sonia D., "UN anti-graft investigator barred from re-entering Guatemala," The Associated Press, Sept. 4, 2018, https://tinyurl.com/yc7v5lvx.

87. Franco Ordoñez, "Trump works to thank Guatemala for moving embassy by weakening anti-corruption panel," *The Miami Herald*, July 10, 2018, https://tinyurl.com/ybb7ret8.

88. *Ibid.*

89. *Ibid.*

90. "Secretary Pompeo's Call With Guatemala President Jimmy Morales," press release, State Department, Sept. 6, 2018, https://tinyurl.com/y986yuba.

91. Daniel Wilkinson, Twitter post, Sept. 6, 2018, https://tinyurl.com/y7r7vp37.

92. Rony Morales and Michael Taylor, "Without a U.N.-backed commission, land rights activists face more deadly persecution in Guatemala," *The Washington Post*, Sept. 10, 2018, https://tinyurl.com/ybfc984g.

93. *Ibid.*

94. Stephen Johnson, "Migration Reality Check," International Republican Institute, July 17, 2018, https://tinyurl.com/ya956rqo.

BIBLIOGRAPHY

Selected Sources

Books

LaFeber, Walter, *Inevitable Revolutions: The United States in Central America*, W. W. Norton and Co., 1983.
In a classic text on the history of the region, a historian examines each country individually and presents a sweeping survey of U.S. involvement.

LeoGrande, William, *Our Own Backyard: The United States in Central America, 1977-1992*, University of North Carolina Press, 1998.
A noted academic and former congressional staffer offers a detailed look at Central America in the waning years of the Cold War.

Martínez, Óscar, *A History of Violence: Living and Dying in Central America*, Verso, 2017.
A journalist describes, through personal accounts, the effects of gangs and corruption on the daily lives of people in the region.

Reid, Michael, *Forgotten Continent: A History of the New Latin America*, Yale University Press, 2017.
A longtime Latin America correspondent for *The Economist* explores the recent social and financial history of the region.

Articles

"A brief golden age: The threat to Central America's prosecutors," *The Economist*, May 10, 2018, https://tinyurl.com/y7w9dlxp.
Politicians in El Salvador, Guatemala and Honduras likely will try to interfere with the efforts of prosecutors and special panels to address corruption.

Levitsky, Steven, and Carlos Flores, "Honduran democracy is under assault," *Los Angeles Times*, Dec. 14, 2017, https://tinyurl.com/y74r4xan.
An expert on Latin America details recent actions that he contends have undermined Honduras' already fragile democratic institutions.

Malkin, Elisabeth, "Citing Hostility, Leader of Anti-Corruption Panel in Honduras Resigns," *The New York Times*, Feb. 16, 2018, https://tinyurl.com/ybk9xwuh.
The leader of the anti-corruption panel for Honduras says his organization faced rising hostility from the nation's government.

Ordoñez, Franco, "Trump works to thank Guatemala for moving embassy by weakening anti-corruption panel," *The Miami Herald*, July 10, 2018, https://tinyurl.com/ybb7ret8.
Guatemala's president is seeking the Trump administration's support as he seeks to halt the work of an anti-corruption panel.

Reports and Studies

"Central America's Migration Crisis: What's Next for U.S. Policy?" Council on Foreign Relations, June 28, 2018, https://tinyurl.com/y9lnq94f.

A nonpartisan think tank interviews former diplomats from the Obama and George W. Bush administrations about the current situation in Central America.

Call, Charles T., "What Guatemala's political crisis means for anti-corruption efforts everywhere," Brookings Institution, Sept. 17, 2017, https://tinyurl.com/ybx2jfwx.
A researcher with appointments at the Brookings Institution and American University reports on the potential follow-on effects of a Guatemalan anti-corruption panel's work.

Eguizábal, Cristina, *et al.*, "Crime and Violence in Central America's Northern Triangle," Woodrow Wilson International Center for Scholars, 2015, https://tinyurl.com/y7v7umnj.
A team of experts from a Washington think tank says corruption, elites' resistance to paying more taxes and the absence of job opportunities remain obstacles to effective U.S. aid programs in Central America.

Labrador, Rocio Cara, and Danielle Renwick, "Central America's Violent Northern Triangle," Council on Foreign Relations, June 28, 2018, https://tinyurl.com/y9ysj6nd.

A nonpartisan think tank provides an overview of the challenges facing Central America.

Orozco, Manuel, "Recent Trends in Central American Migration," Inter-American Dialogue, May 14, 2018, https://tinyurl.com/y7a3vwpv.
An expert on migration provides key figures on immigration from Central America and explains the root causes.

Orozco, Manuel, "Report: Remittances to Latin America and the Caribbean in 2017," Inter-American Dialogue, Jan. 24, 2018, https://tinyurl.com/y7mu5zru.
An expert on migration and the flow of money from immigrants to their home countries provides an update on the status of these remittances in Central America.

Sullivan, Mark P., *et al.*, "Latin America and the Caribbean: Issues in the 115th Congress," Congressional Research Service, March 12, 2018, https://tinyurl.com/yac3u3rm.
Library of Congress' specialists on Latin America review current economic, political and security concerns in the region.

For More Information

Center for Strategic and International Studies, Americas Program, 1616 Rhode Island Ave., N.W., Washington, DC 20036; 202-887-0200; www.csis.org/programs/americas-program. Centrist think tank that offers bipartisan policy proposals on U.S. security issues in North and South America.

InSight Crime, 4400 Massachusetts Ave., N.W., Washington, DC 20016; 202-885-1000; www.insightcrime.org. News site that partners with American University's Center for Latin American and Latino Studies; provides news and analyses of crime and public safety based on its own reporting and reports from Latin American media.

Inter-American Dialogue, 1211 Connecticut Ave., N.W., Washington, DC 20036; 202-822-9002; www.thedialogue.org. Centrist think tank that studies anti-corruption efforts in the Americas.

Washington Office on Latin America, 1666 Connecticut Ave., N.W., Washington, DC 20009; 202-797-2171; www.wola.org/program/central_america. Think tank that focuses on human rights in Central and Latin America.

4

The 5G Revolution

Does the new wireless technology pose security risks?

By Kristin Jensen

A staff member manipulates a 5G remote-controlled robot at the Mobile World Congress Shanghai in June. 5G technology dramatically reduces the time needed for digital devices to communicate with each other.

In the smart city of the future, driverless cars may zip along in a synchronous, steady flow, communicating digitally with each other and with sensors embedded in the asphalt. In one vehicle, an executive might videoconference with her board of directors. In another, a man might chat with a holographic image of his wife projected from his smartphone.

But that future comes with risks. Hackers, for example, could bring autonomous cars to a standstill, or worse, send them crashing into each other.

Those contrasting scenarios represent the best hopes and biggest fears surrounding 5G, the fifth-generation telecommunications system being rolled out in the United States and around the world. 5G offers benefits—significantly faster computing speeds and responsiveness, as well as greater reach—far beyond previous advances in wireless technology. Hans Vestberg, CEO of telecom giant Verizon Communications, promised in January that 5G will "transform people, businesses and society" on the scale of a new Industrial Revolution.[1]

The new technology, for example, promises to radically increase the number of devices and services that can be linked in cyberspace, enabling a variety of innovations. But some experts are questioning whether the Trump administration and private industry are doing enough to make sure 5G networks are protected from cyberattacks that could threaten national security and consumer privacy and safety, even as the United States competes

From *CQ Researcher,*
August 2, 2019

with China and other countries to take the lead in developing those networks.

"The opportunities are going to be boundless for hackers," says James Andrew Lewis, who specializes in cybersecurity and technology issues at the Center for Strategic and International Studies, a Washington think tank.

Others worry the 5G revolution might never reach people living in low-income or rural areas, noting that a digital divide already separates those people from more affluent city dwellers. "There is this argument that 5G is only going to be deployed in areas that can afford it," says Nicol Turner Lee, a fellow at the Center for Technology Innovation at the Brookings Institution, another Washington think tank. "We have to actively address those concerns."

Still, 5G will bring far-reaching benefits, telecom companies say. Latency—the time it takes devices to respond to each other over a wireless connection—will drop to a tiny fraction of a second. The technology will allow a driverless car's artificial intelligence system to respond instantly when a pedestrian unexpectedly steps into the road, or a surgeon to perform an operation remotely, using robotic equipment.[2]

Download speeds will increase to as fast as 10 gigabits per second (Gbps), about 100 times faster than 4G technology. A two-hour movie that now takes six minutes to download will take just 15 seconds. And 5G will expand by 100 times the Internet of Things—devices ranging from refrigerators to cars, baby monitors, drones and even dog collars—that will be connected wirelessly.[3]

"This isn't just the next G—this is a technology that really is going to change the way we live, work and play," says Kevin King, director of corporate communications at Verizon.

5G also promises to change the way soldiers fight. 5G is the first generation of wireless technology that is more about connecting machines than people, says Robert Spalding, former director for strategic planning at the White House's National Security Council. That could allow soldiers to direct autonomous vehicles in combat. Earlier this year, the Pentagon asked the tech industry for help taking advantage of 5G technology.[4]

U.S. telecommunication companies such as Verizon and AT&T are building fifth-generation networks now, but 5G technology is still years away for most Americans. 5G networks will work with 4G infrastructure but will still require major capital investments. That is because 5G will use high-frequency "millimeter" radio airwaves—starting at 24 gigahertz (GHz)—in addition to lower frequencies, some of which are now used by 4G networks. Millimeter waves can carry huge amounts of data at very high speeds but cannot travel long distances and have trouble passing through buildings, trees and other obstacles.[5]

Instead of building cell towers located miles apart, 5G technology will require installing hundreds of thousands of base stations, or "small cells"—each about the size of a pizza box—on utility poles, buildings and other structures every 300 to 500 feet. In sparsely populated areas, wireless communication companies will use lower-frequency waves that can travel longer distances.[6]

Accenture, a multinational professional services company based in Dublin, said U.S. telecom companies will invest as much as $275 billion in 5G, creating 3 million jobs and boosting GDP by $500 billion. By 2026, about 800,000 small cells will be in place around the country, compared with 150,000 cell towers today, according to CTIA, a trade group in Washington that represents the international wireless telecommunications industry.[7]

Other countries, including China, are pursuing faster timetables for their 5G systems in a competition that has important global implications. Countries that lead the way in 5G will see huge economic benefits and could dictate how the technology is used around the world, experts say. China may roll out its 5G network as early as this year.[8]

The 5G competition raises national security concerns as well. U.S. officials have warned, for example, against giving Chinese telecom giant Huawei any role in developing 5G infrastructure in the United States. They say Huawei is effectively under the control of officials in Beijing who could use its equipment to hack into U.S. 5G infrastructure.

Consumer advocates also worry about 5G's security. As more devices become connected wirelessly, the security of each one becomes an issue. And since 5G technology will make people more dependent on digital services and devices, the stakes of a security breach increase.

Cyber threats will "become increasingly existential," says James Baker, former FBI general counsel and now director of national security and cybersecurity at the R Street Institute, a free market think tank in Washington. "If there's a significant cyber event in the future caused by a malicious actor, or just an accident, the implications for all of us are going to be much more profound."

In January, former Federal Communications Commission (FCC) Chairman Tom Wheeler, a Democrat appointed by President Barack Obama, blasted the Trump administration for eliminating a requirement—adopted during Wheeler's tenure—that telecommunications firms build protections against cyberattacks into the design of 5G technology.

"For the first time in history, cybersecurity was being required as a forethought in the design of a new network standard—until the Trump FCC repealed it," Wheeler wrote.[9]

Some industry advocates say such concerns are overblown. "Today's . . . networks have the most advanced security features to date, and 5G will further improve upon them," Meredith Attwell Baker, president and CEO of CTIA, said in written testimony submitted to Congress in February.[10] FCC officials say Ajit Pai, the FCC's current chairman, is working with U.S. industry and government leaders abroad to make 5G security a top priority.

Under Pai, the FCC is focused mostly on making more radio spectrum available to telecommunications companies and eliminating red tape that delays permits for 5G infrastructure. "The market, not government, is best-positioned to drive investment and innovation in the wireless space," Pai said in April.[11]

Some researchers fear, however, that market forces could worsen existing disparities in home internet access. The FCC reported in May that more than 26 percent of Americans in rural areas and 32 percent of Native Americans on tribal lands, for example, lacked high-speed internet service for home computers in 2017, compared to just 1.7 percent of those in urban areas.[12] Lee, at the Brookings Institution, says many people in rural, low-income or minority communities depend on smartphones and other mobile devices to go online.

Telecom firms get faster returns on their 5G investments in wealthier neighborhoods where people can afford to pay a premium for ultra-fast internet service. And 5G's small cells make more economic sense in densely populated areas where each cell serves a larger number of customers.[13]

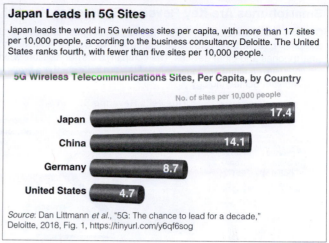

Japan Leads in 5G Sites

Japan leads the world in 5G wireless sites per capita, with more than 17 sites per 10,000 people, according to the business consultancy Deloitte. The United States ranks fourth, with fewer than five sites per 10,000 people.

5G Wireless Telecommunications Sites, Per Capita, by Country

No. of sites per 10,000 people

Country	No. of sites per 10,000 people
Japan	17.4
China	14.1
Germany	8.7
United States	4.7

Source: Dan Littmann *et al.*, "5G: The chance to lead for a decade," Deloitte, 2018, Fig. 1, https://tinyurl.com/y6qf6sog

Pai, however, has said the FCC is committed to bridging the nation's digital divide in the rollout of 5G networks, partly through programs such as the Rural Digital Opportunity Fund that will invest more than $20 billion over the next decade in high-speed internet service for rural areas. If he makes good on that pledge, minority communities should see "increased economic opportunity through improved access to social services, such as health care, education, transportation, energy and employment," Lee said.[14]

BACKGROUND

The first public call on a handheld cellular mobile phone was made in April 1973 by Martin Cooper, an executive at Motorola who led the team that developed the DynaTAC phone and used it on a New York City street to call his counterpart at rival company Bell Labs.[15]

In Japan, mobile phone company NTT DoCoMo deployed an analog cellular system in 1979, and the technology began to spread around the world. Commercial service began in the United States on a 1G analog network in 1983. The first-generation mobile phones of that era were clunky and expensive. The DynaTAC mobile phone, for example, cost almost $4,000 (about $10,000 today) and had only about 30 minutes of battery life.[16]

Cell phones became more common in the 1990s with the advent of 2G, which used digital instead of analog radio signals and gave rise to text messages.

Smartphones Are Key Revenue Source for Huawei

Chinese tech giant Huawei, the world's largest supplier of telecommunications equipment, reported a 19.5 percent jump in revenue last year, led by increased sales of smartphones and other devices. The company's carrier division, which handles telecom services, saw a slight drop in revenue from 2017. Each of the firm's three core divisions is involved with 5G technology.

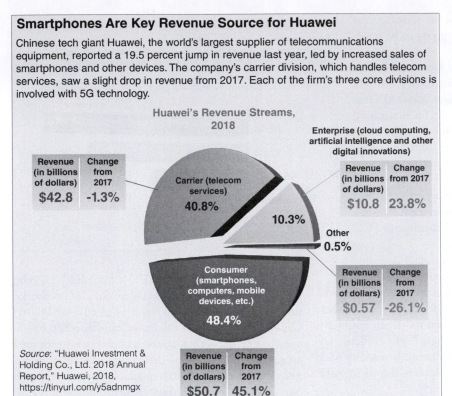

Huawei's Revenue Streams, 2018

Revenue (in billions of dollars)	Change from 2017
$42.8	-1.3%

Carrier (telecom services) 40.8%

Enterprise (cloud computing, artificial intelligence and other digital innovations)

Revenue (in billions of dollars)	Change from 2017
$10.8	23.8%

10.3%

Other 0.5%

Revenue (in billions of dollars)	Change from 2017
$0.57	-26.1%

Consumer (smartphones, computers, mobile devices, etc.) 48.4%

Revenue (in billions of dollars)	Change from 2017
$50.7	45.1%

Source: "Huawei Investment & Holding Co., Ltd. 2018 Annual Report," Huawei, 2018, https://tinyurl.com/y5adnmgx

Digital technology, encoded in numbers, is less affected by noise and deterioration than analog signals and uses radio spectrum more efficiently.[17]

In the early 2000s, in response to soaring consumer demand for faster internet browsing and data downloading, companies developed 3G technology, increasing peak data transfer speeds to 2 megabits per second (Mbps), about 1,000 times faster than 1G. The new technology helped boost sales of BlackBerry devices, which had evolved from two-way pagers first introduced in 1999 to personal digital assistants connected to email. 3G also allowed customers to connect to the internet, leading to the introduction of Apple's iPhone in 2007 and Apple's app store in 2008.[18]

Economic activity linked to mobile apps, or the "app economy," spread even more rapidly as a result of the increased speed (up to 100 Mbps) and responsiveness enabled by 4G, which was widely adopted in the 2010s and allowed apps such as the ride-sharing company Uber and social media site Instagram to flourish.[19]

The federal government and telecommunications companies have spent more than a decade researching 5G technology and installing small-cell sites. Verizon, for example, says it began building small-cell sites years ago to "densify" its 4G network in preparation for 5G.[20]

One of the first mentions of 5G technology appeared in a 2008 NASA press release that said NASA and M2Mi Corp., a technology company in Mountain View, Calif.,

CHRONOLOGY

1880s-1900s *Inventors pioneer use of telephone and wireless communication.*

1876 Inventor Alexander Graham Bell patents the telephone.

1885 Bell establishes American Telephone & Telegraph Co.

1895 Italian inventor Guglielmo Marconi harnesses wireless technology to send radio signals through the air for the first time.

1906 Canadian inventor Reginald Fessenden transmits speech wirelessly for the first time.

1910s-1930s *Regulation begins as telephones become widely adopted.*

1915 Telephone service begins between New York City and San Francisco.

1927 New York and London are linked by telephone. . . . Congress creates Federal Radio Commission to regulate the public airwaves.

1934 Communications Act of 1934 establishes the Federal Communications Commission (FCC) to oversee interstate radio communication.

1940s-1960s *New telecommunications applications are created.*

1946 Motorola and Bell System introduce the car phone.

1960s Defense Department's Advanced Research Projects Agency Network (ARPANET) paves the way for development of the internet.

1961 Soviet officials use radio waves to speak with cosmonaut Yuri Gagarin in space.

1965 NASA launches first commercial communications satellite, known as Early Bird.

1969 FCC allows MCI Telecommunications to offer long-distance service, creating AT&T's first competitor in that business.

1970s-1980s *First generation of cellular communication emerges.*

1973 Motorola executive Martin Cooper places first call on a mobile cellular phone—to a rival at Bell Labs.

1070 NTT (Nippon Telegraph and Telephone) in Japan begins operating world's first commercial cellular system.

1983 1G commercial cellular service begins in the United States using analog signals and featuring bulky, expensive phones with short battery lives.

1990s *Cell phones become widely used.*

1991 Finland's OY Radiolinja AB becomes the first company to introduce second-generation (2G) cellular service using digital signals and the Global System for Mobile Communications standard.

1992 First text message to a cell phone is sent by British engineer Neil Papworth to a Vodafone executive in England.

1996 Congress passes Telecommunications Act of 1996, loosening restrictions on industry and paving the way for more competition to emerge in telephone and broadcast services.

2000-Present *Cell phones become smart as 3G service takes hold, and broadband internet service becomes widely available.*

2002 BlackBerry personal digital assistants offer mobile telephone, email and web browsing services.

2007 Apple releases the iPhone, which lays the foundation for the modern smartphone by combining internet browsing, phone functions and portable media features.

2008 Apple opens the app store and releases the iPhone 3G.

2010s 4G becomes widely adopted and the "app economy" takes off. . . . Industry lays the groundwork for 5G.

2012 New York University establishes NYU Wireless, which focuses on 5G research.

2014 Tech companies Qualcomm and Ericsson organize North American conference for 50 professors, engineers and researchers to share work on 5G.

2016 Verizon starts testing 5G technology in collaboration with Ericsson, Intel, Nokia, Samsung and Qualcomm. . . . Qualcomm unveils the first 5G modem, called Snapdragon X50.

2017 FCC Commissioner Ajit Pai pursues a "light touch" on regulation of mobile wireless service.

2018 FCC acts to streamline local jurisdictions' permitting process for installing 5G cell sites, drawing protests from some municipalities. . . . Verizon offers 5G home service in select markets.

2019 Verizon claims it is first to launch a commercial 5G mobile network; South Korea makes the same claim. Soon after, AT&T and Sprint roll out 5G mobile phones. . . . Citing security concerns, U.S. officials make Chinese telecommunications giant Huawei ineligible to receive U.S.-made technology and encourage other countries to keep Huawei out of their 5G networks.

Chinese Telecom Giant Sparks Security Concerns Amid 5G Rollouts

"If you're a hacker, you want to go to the company that designed the network."

Many Americans do not know how to pronounce it, but those following the news over the last six months know the name: Huawei (WAH-WAY) Technologies. With 5G wireless networks poised to transform mobile communication around the world, the Chinese telecommunications giant's participation in those networks is raising security concerns in the United States and some other countries.[1]

U.S. officials and cyberespionage experts say Huawei, the world's largest telecom equipment maker, has close ties to officials in Beijing who could use the company's equipment to conduct spying operations. They say Huawei would have to turn over 5G data to China's government if government officials demanded it.[2]

"If you're a hacker, you want to be able to go to the company that designed the network" to get access, said Robert Strayer, deputy assistant secretary for cyber and international communications policy at the State Department. "That will be a huge advantage if the Chinese government decided they wanted to undertake efforts to undermine any of the critical infrastructure underlying the 5G network."[3]

In May, U.S. officials added Huawei to a blacklist—officially called the entity list—of foreign companies that are barred from receiving hardware, software and other items from U.S. firms without the government's approval. The same day, President Trump issued an executive order giving his administration expanded powers to block transactions involving information and communications technology if those transactions pose a threat to national security, a move that analysts say was primarily directed at Huawei. The firm depends heavily on U.S. parts, including microchips made by American companies Qualcomm and Intel.[4]

Trump later suggested the United States might relax restrictions on Huawei as part of an effort to restart trade negotiations with China, and Commerce Secretary Wilbur Ross said his agency will allow U.S. companies to do business with Huawei "where there is no threat to national security." But Huawei remains on the entity list.[5]

The recent U.S. actions follow the Justice Department's announcement in January of fraud and other charges against Huawei and its chief financial officer, Meng Wanzhou, for allegedly violating sanctions against Iran and lying about it to U.S. banks. Canadian authorities arrested Meng in Vancouver in December on a U.S. warrant. She has been fighting extradition ever since.[6]

In July, *The Washington Post* reported, based on leaked documents, that Huawei had partnered with a Chinese state-owned firm to secretly help North Korea build its commercial wireless network.[7]

Experts on 5G systems say U.S. officials need to make sure Huawei, a major supplier of telecommunications equipment to rural wireless companies in the United States, does

Getty Images/Jeff Vinnick

Meng Wanzhou, chief financial officer at Chinese technology giant Huawei, wears an electronic monitoring ankle bracelet as Canadian authorities escort her to a court hearing in Vancouver in May. Meng was arrested in December on a U.S. warrant that accused her of violating sanctions against Iran and lying about it to U.S. banks.

not gain access to any part of this country's 5G infrastructure.[8]

"The United States has a reasonable concern that itself and its allies do not use equipment that spies on them," says Nicholas Economides, an economics professor at New York University who has worked on 5G issues under a National Science Foundation grant.

Huawei denies that its equipment would be used for espionage or hacking. "We don't have any backdoors," Huawei founder and CEO Ren Zhengfei said in June. "We are willing to sign no-backdoor and no-spy agreements with any country."[9]

Many U.S. allies already have invested in Huawei equipment for previous generations of wireless communication networks. The company can offer many technology products at a lower price than competitors such as the Swedish telecommunications firm Ericsson and the Finnish company Nokia. That is largely because Huawei receives hundreds of millions of dollars in government subsidies each year, and because Chinese officials make a $100 billion line of credit available to the firm's customers in the developing world.[10]

The company reported total revenue of about $107 billion in 2018 and said that, as of June, it had 46 contracts around the world to install 5G networks.[11]

Australia and Japan have barred Huawei from participating in 5G development because of security concerns, but many other countries are taking a middle-of-the-road approach by excluding Huawei's involvement in only the most sensitive and central parts of their networks.[12] However, Strayer said 5G will link so many devices wirelessly that it will eliminate any distinction between a network's "core" and its "edge."

"We've basically gotten almost everybody that's thinking about running a telecom network to agree that Huawei is too risky to include in what they consider the core of their network," he said. "We're hopeful that we can convince them that there should be no untrusted technology anywhere in those networks."[13]

The U.S. actions targeting Huawei are affecting U.S. businesses. Rural telecommunication companies that rely on Huawei equipment, such as Pine Belt in Alabama and Union Wireless in Wyoming, reportedly are scrambling to get discounted pricing from Ericsson and Nokia.[14]

Huawei mobile phones are displayed at a store in Bridgend, Wales. The Trump administration has blocked Huawai from participating in the rollout of 5G networks in the United States over concerns that the company is effectively under the control of the Chinese government and poses a national security risk.

Other companies have reacted with confusion to the Trump administration's actions in May. FedEx recently sued the Commerce Department, saying delivery companies are unreasonably being held liable for delivering packages containing items that are banned because of Huawei's inclusion on the entity list.[15]

"While it's appropriate for the administration to focus our attention on the risk associated with Huawei, I worry about whether they've completely thought through the second- and third-order consequences of the steps that they've taken," says James Baker, former FBI general counsel and currently director of national security and cybersecurity at the R Street Institute, a libertarian think tank in Washington. He says the Trump administration's actions may prompt China to create domestic providers for software and hardware it normally would buy from U.S. firms, which might hurt the United States in the long run.

Huawei's Ren said the administration's actions may cost his firm about $30 billion in sales. The company had not expected such "extreme measures," but had stockpiled some parts just in case, he said. "In the next two years, we are going to switch from many old product versions to new ones," Ren said. "When this step is finished, we'll become stronger."[16]

— *Kristin Jensen*

[1] Colin Lecher and Russell Brandom, "Is Huawei a security threat? Seven experts weigh in," *The Verge*, March 17, 2019, https://tinyurl.com/yxuq5947.

[2] Arjun Kharpal, "Huawei staff share deep links with Chinese military, new study claims," *CNBC*, July 8, 2019, https://tinyurl.com/y4htz4a7; Arjun Kharpal, "Huawei says it would never hand data to China's government. Experts say it wouldn't have a choice," *CNBC*, March 4, 2019, https://tinyurl.com/y5af8rd3.

[3] "International economics and securing next-generation 5G wireless networks: A conversation with Amb. Robert Strayer," American Enterprise Institute, May 29, 2019, https://tinyurl.com/y687avsv.

[4] Graham Webster, "It's not just Huawei. Trump's new tech sector order could ripple through global supply chains," *The Washington Post*, May 18, 2019, https://tinyurl.com/yym9jjtm; Jon Fingas, "Intel, Qualcomm

and other chipmakers cut off supplies to Huawei," *engadget*, May 20, 2019, https://tinyurl.com/y4awaff3.

[5] Jim Tankersley and Ana Swanson, "Trump Administration Will Allow Some Companies to Sell to Huawei," *The New York Times*, July 9, 2019, https://tinyurl.com/y26e8b6a; Sean Keane, "Huawei remains on Commerce Department's blacklist despite Trump's deal," *CNET*, July 3, 2019, https://tinyurl.com/y3l3xfuh.

[6] Ellen Nakashima and Devlin Barrett, "Justice Dept. charges Huawei with fraud, ratcheting up U.S.-China tensions," *The Washington Post*, Jan. 29, 2019, https://tinyurl.com/yxppnfr6; "Meng Wanzhou: Huawei CFO seeks halt to extradition after Trump comments," *The Guardian*, May 8, 2019, https://tinyurl.com/y354nx77.

[7] Ellen Nakashima, Gerry Shih and John Hudson, "Leaked documents reveal Huawei's secret operations to build North Korea's wireless

Jerry Taylor, the first person in San Francisco to buy an Apple iPhone, holds up his device on June 28, 2007. The first iPhone, which combined internet browsing, phone functions and portable media features, laid the foundation for the modern smartphone.

were cooperating "to develop a fifth-generation telecommunications and networking system."[21]

In 2013, South Korean electronics giant Samsung said it had developed 5G technology that could transmit data hundreds of times faster than 4G networks and could be available by 2020. A year later, the FCC under Wheeler issued a "notice of inquiry" seeking information from the telecom industry on the radio spectrum that would be needed to accommodate 5G's use of millimeter waves.[22]

"The possibilities of 5G are very intriguing," Wheeler said in a statement accompanying the notice. "It

promises new user experiences, new deployment models, potentially even new industries. 5G will not be just better, faster and cheaper; it likely will be something fundamentally different from what is possible today."[23]

Verizon began a pilot program in 2017 to test 5G access for home and business internet service in 11 U.S. markets. Instead of using a cable, the Verizon service uses radio waves that travel from a cell site in the neighborhood to a receiver in the home, generally on or near a window.[24]

CURRENT SITUATION

Verizon made 5G home broadband service available in October 2018 in parts of Houston, Indianapolis, Los Angeles and Sacramento, Calif., and came out with a 5G-enabled smartphone in April for customers in certain parts of Chicago and Minneapolis. The company expects its network to be available in parts of more than 30 cities by the end of 2019.[25]

Other companies also are moving quickly to deploy 5G networks:

- Last December, AT&T introduced a mobile millimeter-wave 5G network for some residents of Atlanta, San Antonio and other cities. The company said it had achieved 5G speeds higher than 1.5 Gbps with a test device.[26]

network," *The Washington Post*, July 22, 2019, https://tinyurl.com/y3dvyqpm.

[8] Cecilia Kang, "Huawei Ban Threatens Wireless Service in Rural Areas," *The New York Times*, May 25, 2019, https://tinyurl.com/yxohpbnl.

[9] "A Coffee With Ren," Huawei, June 17, 2019, https://tinyurl.com/y4s2vfds.

[10] Ellen Nakashima, "U.S. pushes hard for a ban on Huawei in Europe, but the firm's 5G prices are nearly irresistible," *The Washington Post*, May 29, 2019, https://tinyurl.com/y45rkwr6; Arjun Kharpal, "Huawei tops $100 billion revenue for first time despite political headwinds," *CNBC*, March 28, 2019, https://tinyurl.com/y6yx5dvp.

[11] Kharpal, *ibid.*; "Huawei Wins 'Best 5G Core Network Technology' Award at 5G World Summit," News release, Huawei, June 13, 2019, https://tinyurl.com/y635kto2.

[12] Nakashima, *op. cit.*; "Huawei: Which countries are blocking its 5G technology?" *BBC News*, May, 18, 2019, https://tinyurl.com/y2mgkmzl.

[13] "International economics and securing next-generation 5G wireless networks: A conversation with Amb. Robert Strayer," *op. cit.*

[14] Tarmo Virki and Angela Moon, "Exclusive: In push to replace Huawei, rural U.S. carriers are talking with Nokia and Ericsson," *Reuters*, June 24, 2019, https://tinyurl.com/yxa8brcl.

[15] Rachel Siegel and Hannah Denham, "FedEx files suit against Commerce Department over Huawei restrictions," *The Washington Post*, June 25, 2019, https://tinyurl.com/yxa2gha2.

[16] "A Coffee With Ren," *op. cit.*

- AT&T says it plans to have a nationwide 5G network deployed by early 2020 using mid-band spectrum (below 6 GHz).[27]
- In May, Sprint launched a 5G network in Atlanta, Dallas, Houston and Kansas City, Mo., that uses 2.5 GHz waves on the mid-band spectrum.[28]

Those launches have helped bring the United States even with China in the 5G race, after placing third in 2018, according to a report prepared for CTIA by the British consulting firm Analysys Mason. South Korea and Japan followed closely behind. U.S. companies such as Qualcomm and Intel, which make processing chips used by Huawei and other foreign tech firms, dominate some of the technology needed for 5G.[29]

But other experts cite evidence that China still leads the world in 5G. Since 2015, China has spent about $24 billion more than the United States on 5G development, building 350,000 new cell sites compared with fewer than 30,000 in the United States, according to a 2018 report from global consulting firm Deloitte. That means China has about 14.1 sites per 10,000 people, compared with 4.7 per 10,000 in the United States.[30]

"Looking forward, China's five-year economic plan specifies $400 billion in 5G-related investment," Deloitte said. "Consequently, China and other countries may be creating a 5G tsunami, making it near impossible to catch up."[31]

Chinese companies also are leading the way in setting 5G standards and winning patents linked to the new technology. As of March, China had claimed about 34 percent of the world's 5G patents, compared with 14 percent for U.S. companies, according to the German data analytics firm IPlytics.[32]

The Defense Innovation Board, a group of educators, researchers and industry leaders that advises the U.S. secretary of defense on technology and other issues, said in an April report that four of the top 10 internet companies by revenue are Chinese, a major shift from 2009, when all 10 were American.

"5G has the potential to skew future networks even further in the direction of China if it continues to lead," the board said.[33]

It also noted that other countries developing 5G networks are following China's lead in focusing more on radio frequencies below 6 GHz than on millimeter waves. If that trend continues, semiconductors, smartphones and other equipment in much of the rest of the world will be configured for frequencies lower on the radio spectrum than the millimeter-wave frequencies that U.S. telecom companies plan to use, according to the Defense Innovation Board.[34]

"This would create security risks for [U.S. defense] operations overseas that rely on networks with Chinese components," the board said. It urged the Pentagon and FCC to "flip their prioritization" from millimeter waves to mid-band spectrum.[35]

Even apart from security risks, telecom companies cannot rely completely on millimeter waves to enable 5G throughout the United States because the waves

Are government and industry doing enough to protect 5G systems from cyberattacks?

YES

Tom Sawanobori
Senior Vice President and Chief Technology Officer, CTIA

Written for *CQ Researcher*, August 2019

The wireless industry has baked security into our networks since the beginning, and we work diligently to continually enhance our security capabilities with every generation of wireless. Today's 4G networks offer the most advanced security features to date, and 5G networks will further improve upon them.

America's wireless industry relies on network infrastructure from trusted network suppliers and invests billions of dollars in 5G innovation and advanced security—across our networks, devices, operating systems and applications—enabling a dynamic wireless experience that is more secure than ever before.

Wireless Networks: 5G's speeds, capacity and near real-time responsiveness will allow more data-intensive applications to be moved to the cloud. This network virtualization distributes network functions, reducing the risk of outages while enabling customized security features and the quick deployment of software-based security updates. In addition, limiting the amount of physical hardware needed to run the network and distributing network security to multiple locations reduce risks from potential cyberattacks.

As for the network enhancements themselves, 5G will include the use of standards-based state-of-the-art encryption algorithms, new and advanced authentication mechanisms, improved security credentials when roaming, data encoding, anti-spamming software to protect against unwanted and illegal calls and messages, strict controls for physical and IT access, and customized security updates. The wireless industry is also developing 5G Internet of Things security initiatives to protect networks, consumers and devices.

Wireless Devices: Mobile device manufacturers continue to innovate on a number of new and existing security mechanisms, including SIM card capabilities, the use of temporary identities, wireless account controls such as passwords and multifactor authentication, hardware-based cryptographic information that detects malware and authenticates system software, device anti-theft tools, and integrated authentication systems that leverage 5G's speeds and encryption capabilities.

Mobile OS and Apps: Mobile operating systems such as Android and iOS work with app developers to improve security while screening for bad applications in order to prevent the

NO

Robert Spalding
Senior Fellow, Hudson Institute

Written for *CQ Researcher*, August 2019

The answer is undeniably no, which should be obvious from the number of data breaches that the current system experiences every single day. 5G architecture is built on computing and networking technology that cannot be defended, so why should anyone expect a different outcome?

Unfortunately, the numerous engineering decisions that bring speed and connectivity to the wireless market ensure that security comes last. Not only are wireless networks themselves not impervious to attacks from hackers or an electromagnetic pulse, the data they carry is vulnerable to theft. This is one reason why America loses hundreds of billions of dollars each year in intellectual property and financial theft.

The problem becomes immensely worse with 5G. Since the 5G network is built for machines, not humans, it adds a whole new dimension for attack. While 4G features 10,000 connected devices per square mile, 5G brings 3 million. Drones, self-driving cars, medical equipment—all these devices can be used to harm humans in a potentially catastrophic manner if left unsecured.

America has entered a new age where the digital domain brings more risk than benefits as foreign governments advance their artificial intelligence, big data and social media capabilities. China and Russia have perfected these techniques and are deploying them in support of rising global totalitarianism. It is time the U.S. government fulfills its obligation to the American people to provide for the common defense by deploying a secure nationwide 5G network.

Since the telecom industry is unwilling to secure Americans' data—and large tech companies are known to exploit it—incentives and penalties are required to ensure a secure digital future. Radio technology has advanced to such an extent that it is far past time to move away from spectrum auctions. Technology today allows for dynamic sharing of spectrum. Tax breaks, rural grants and other incentives can be used to encourage the rapid deployment of a new secure 5G network.

The same can be done in the manufacturing and supply chain. Equipment manufacturers are more than willing to relocate facilities to the United States—ensuring a secure supply chain—if they are guaranteed protection from China's predatory practices.

spread of viruses and malware. OS providers and app developers will continue to advance software that protects wireless devices and consumers, including anti-malware and anti-virus software.

The wireless industry works tirelessly every single day to protect our networks. To help us secure our 5G future, we urge policymakers to continue collaborating with the wireless industry on 5G security issues. A collaborative relationship with the Department of Homeland Security based on risk assessment of cyberthreats is the best approach for government, industry and the networks of tomorrow.

The combination of American-made equipment and a new stand-alone 5G design can be the spark that unites allies and partners toward a new digital democracy.

cover such short distances, experts say. "You cannot cover 3 million square miles of the U.S. with millimeter wave—it is physically impossible," Neville Ray, chief technology officer of telecom company T-Mobile, said in April.[36]

But opening up more of the mid-band spectrum for 5G use comes with its own problems, because much of that band is already in use. The Defense Department is a major user of 3GHz and 4GHz frequencies, for example.[37]

Some 5G experts say the FCC is not acting fast enough to address the need for more spectrum, but Pai denies that.[38] He said he hopes to hold an auction in 2020 for 3.5 GHz spectrum and may repurpose a 3.7 GHz band historically used by satellite operators.[39] In June, Pai circulated a proposal to open up a 2.5 GHz band for 5G as well.[40]

The industry says such developments cannot come too fast. "We need spectrum, spectrum and spectrum," said Ken Meyers, CEO of U.S. Cellular, a telecommunications company in Chicago. "We need a lot of mid-band and we need it right away."[41]

Wireless companies also complain about the money and time they say they spend complying with thousands of federal, state and local regulations affecting installation of the small cells needed for 5G networks. The cells themselves take only an hour or two to attach to a building or utility pole, but it can take more than a year for a city or town to issue a permit, Baker, the CTIA president, said last year.[42]

It took U.S. wireless companies 30 years to deploy 150,000 cell phone towers for earlier generations of cellular technology, Baker said. "Tomorrow's 5G networks

Getty Images/MediaNews Group/*The Denver Post*/
Helen H. Richardson

Jackson Federico, a technician for Advanced Wireless Solutions, makes repairs on a cell tower near Meeker, Colo., in 2017. In urban areas, 5G technology will more often rely on "small cells" that will be installed every 300 to 500 feet, perhaps on lamp posts or utility poles.

require five times that amount in the next few years," she said. Baker said other nations get approvals for small-cell sites in weeks or even days.[43]

In September of last year, the FCC adopted rules aimed at streamlining local reviews of small-cell installation requests by setting limits on fees and review times. CTIA said in May that half of U.S. states have also passed their own laws streamlining site reviews.[44]

OUTLOOK

The first 5G benefit consumers likely will notice is that their 4G service will improve as the new generation of spectrum takes over some wireless traffic. But telecom companies are still a long way from resolving 5G's technology, infrastructure and spectrum challenges, according to Nicholas Economides, an economics professor at New York University.

"It will take years for the service to be available nationwide," Economides says.

Globally, the Swedish telecom company Ericsson projects there will be about 1.9 billion 5G mobile broadband subscriptions by the end of 2024. "5G network deployments are expected to ramp up during 2020, creating the foundation for massive adoption of 5G subscriptions," Ericsson said in a June report. However, the vast majority of mobile broadband subscriptions—about 5 billion—will still be for 4G by the end of 2024, the company said.[45]

T-Mobile and Sprint say the rollout of 5G will take place faster with their planned merger, which was approved by the Justice Department on July 26. The new company, they say, would bring 5G service to 99 percent of the country—including 90 percent of rural areas—within six years. But critics of the proposed deal say it may lead to job losses and higher wireless costs for consumers.[46]

A federal district court must still review the proposed merger, and the deal faces another hurdle: a lawsuit filed by a group of state attorneys general who say the merger would raise consumers' wireless costs by at least $4.5 billion a year.[47]

As 5G service becomes more prevalent in the United States, connecting millions more devices, the need to protect consumer data also will increase, says Gaurav Laroia, policy counsel at Free Press, a group in Washington that works to advance media and technology policies in the public interest.

Laroia says federal officials need to develop a regulatory plan for 5G networks that would penalize companies that sell or manufacture devices vulnerable to hacking. Such penalties "need to be sufficiently high that we don't accidentally walk into a situation where both consumers and the United States infrastructure at large is at risk," he says. "The danger could be exponentially greater if the number of devices is exponentially greater."

NOTES

1 "The Fourth Industrial Revolution Will Be Built on 5G, Says Verizon CEO," *Technology Breaking News*, Jan. 11, 2019, https://tinyurl.com/y6z52vfc.

2 Matthew Humphries, "China Performs First 5G Remote Surgery," *PCMag*, Jan. 15, 2019, https://tinyurl.com/y6f4rn77.

3 "The Race to 5G," CTIA, accessed July 24, 2019, https://tinyurl.com/yxg4s65u.

4 Liu Zhen, "Why 5G, a battleground for US and China, is also a fight for military supremacy," *South China Morning Post*, Jan. 31, 2019, https://tinyurl.com/y3zobemt; Robert Levinson, "Pentagon Places a Call for 5G Technology Capabilities," *Bloomberg Government*, April 19, 2019, https://tinyurl.com/y48v3byn.

5 Roger Cheng, "5G is real and lightning fast (sometimes): Here's everything you need to know," *CNET*, June 21, 2019, https://tinyurl.com/yxc5mdbq.

6 Caitlin Chin, "How Will Small Cell Regulations Impact 5G Deployment?" *National Journal*, Jan. 14, 2019, https://tinyurl.com/yxzhswz8; Shara Tibken, "Why 5G is out of reach for more people than you think," *CNET*, Oct. 25, 2018, https://tinyurl.com/y8s2c9vy.

7 "Tackling the cost of a 5G build," Accenture, Aug. 3, 2018, https://tinyurl.com/yxsw6f44; "Infrastructure," CTIA, accessed July 24, 2019, https://tinyurl.com/yx8jrt6x.

8 Milo Medin and Gilman Louie, "The 5G Ecosystem: Risks & opportunities for DoD," Defense Innovation Board, April 2019, https://tinyurl.com/y4l9kh73; Arjun Kharpal, "China gives green light for local 5G rollout amid tech tensions with US," *CNBC*, June 6, 2019, https://tinyurl.com/y2gb425y.

9 Tom Wheeler, "If 5G Is So Important, Why Isn't It Secure?," *The New York Times*, Jan. 21, 2019, https://tinyurl.com/yyydkno7.

10 "Testimony of Meredith Attwell Baker, President and CEO, CTIA, on 'Winning the Race to 5G and the Next Era of Technology Innovation in the United States,'" U.S. Senate Committee on Commerce, Science & Transportation, Feb. 6, 2019, https://tinyurl.com/yxl5u7xq.

11 "Remarks of FCC Chairman Ajit Pai at the National Spectrum Consortium 5G Collaboration Event," FCC, April 30, 2019, https://tinyurl.com/y2lgabuv.

12 "2019 Broadband Deployment Report," FCC, May 29, 2019, https://tinyurl.com/y425peh6.

13 Kim Hart, "How 5G may widen the rural-urban digital divide," *Axios*, Sept. 22, 2018, https://tinyurl.com/y59dfhn7.

14 "Pai: Closing Digital Divide is FCC Top Priority," American Hospital Association, July 25, 2018, https://tinyurl.com/yy4wdzvm; "FCC Chairman Pai Announces Major Initiatives To Promote U.S. Leadership on 5G And Connect Rural Americans To High-Speed Internet At White House Event," FCC, 2019, https://tinyurl.com/yxppyntz; Nicol Turner Lee, "Enabling opportunities: 5G, the internet of things, and communities of color," Brookings Institution, Jan. 9, 2019, https://tinyurl.com/y5gue65d.

15 Maggie Shiels, "A chat with the man behind mobiles," *BBC*, April 21, 2003, https://tinyurl.com/7fmcok2; "Motorola Demonstrates Portable Telephone To Be Available for Public Use by 1976," news release, Motorola Inc., April 3, 1973, https://tinyurl.com/yybpav83.

16 "History of Mobile Communications," NTT Docomo, December 2018, https://tinyurl.com/y3x7t5mn; "Dynatac Cellular Telephone," National Museum of American History, accessed July 24, 2019, https://tinyurl.com/yy6d4f4e; "History of Mobile Cell Phones—The First Cell Phone to Present Time," *BeBusinessed*, accessed July 24, 2019, https://tinyurl.com/ych89ywo.

17 "The Race to 5G," *op. cit.*

18 *Ibid.*; "The History and Future of 5G Networks," Community Phone, March 27, 2019, https://tinyurl.com/y62njv44; "Blackberry," National Museum of American History, accessed July 24, 2019, https://tinyurl.com/y4jh4ynl; "What is 5G?" Verizon, accessed July 24, 2019, https://tinyurl.com/yxsc2bdn; and Britta O'Boyle, "The History of Blackberry: The best BlackBerry phones that changed the world," *Pocket-lint*, Jan. 16, 2019, https://tinyurl.com/y5msvvco.

19 "The Race to 5G," *op. cit.*

20 "What is 5G?" *op. cit.*

21 "NASA Ames Partners With M2MI for Small Satellite Development," news release, NASA, April 24, 2008, https://tinyurl.com/y35zh4nj.

22 "Samsung Announces World's First 5G mmWave Mobile Technology," news release, Samsung, May 13, 2013, https://tinyurl.com/yyx3ys9f; "NOI to examine use of bands above 24 GHz for mobile broadband," FCC, Oct. 17, 2014, https://tinyurl.com/y5c5dlyw.

23 "NOI to examine use of bands above 24 GHz for mobile broadband," *ibid.*

24 Monica Alleven, "Verizon to begin 5G pilot in 1H 2017 in Atlanta, Denver, Seattle and more," *FierceWireless*, Feb. 22, 2017, https://tinyurl.com/yxfktpwx; "Verizon to deliver 5G service to pilot customers in 11 markets across U.S. by Mid 2017," news release, Verizon, Feb. 22, 2017, https://tinyurl.com/y4njqkq3; and "How 5G Home Works," Verizon, accessed July 24, 2019, https://tinyurl.com/yy6mle9g.

25 "Customers in Chicago and Minneapolis are First in the World to get 5G-Enabled Smartphones Connected to a 5G Network," news release, Verizon, April 3, 2019, https://tinyurl.com/yx8kqspe; "5G is here," news release, Verizon, Sept. 11, 2018, https://tinyurl.com/y6hpfapn; and "What is 5G?" *op. cit.*

26 "50+ Days of 5G: AT&T Provides Update," AT&T, Feb. 12, 2019, https://tinyurl.com/y2lofhwa.

27 "AT&T First to Make Mobile 5G Service Live in the U.S. on Dec. 21," news release, AT&T, Dec. 18, 2018, https://tinyurl.com/y76b8y2u; "AT&T Enhances Spectrum Position Following FCC Auction 102," news release, AT&T, June 17, 2019, https://tinyurl.com/y3c9m57v.

28 "Sprint Lights Up True Mobile 5G in Atlanta, Dallas-Fort Worth, Houston and Kansas City," news release, Sprint, May 30, 2019, https://tinyurl.com/yxrp3zd3.

29 David Abecassis, Janette Stewart and Chris Nickerson, "Global Race to 5G—Update," April 2019, https://tinyurl.com/yygz24sk.

30 Dan Littmann *et al.*, "5G: The chance to lead for a decade," Deloitte, 2018, https://tinyurl.com/y6qf6sog.

31 *Ibid.*

32 Akito Tanaka, "China in pole position for 5G era with a third of key patents," Nikkei, May 3, 2019, https://tinyurl.com/y2ebw7rs.

33 Medin and Louie, *op. cit.*

34 *Ibid.*

35 *Ibid.*

36 "CTIA 5G Summit, Videos, T-Mobile's Neville Ray," CTIA, April 4, 2019, https://tinyurl.com/y2h48q4s.

37 Medin and Louie, *op. cit.*

38 Tom Wheeler, "How the FCC lost a year in the 'race to 5G,'" Brookings Institution, June 14, 2019, https://tinyurl.com/y54pzpj9.

39 "Remarks of FCC Chairman Ajit Pai at the 7th Congreso LatinoAmericano de Telecomunicaciones Workshop on 5G," FCC, July 4, 2019, https://tinyurl.com/y2ugtrkt.

40 Ajit Pai, "A Giant Leap for 5G," FCC, June 18, 2019, https://tinyurl.com/y5cuvayw.

41 "CTIA 5G Summit, Videos, U.S. Cellular's Ken Meyers," CTIA, April 4, 2019, https://tinyurl.com/y2h48q4s.

42 "MWCA 18 Keynote: Meredith Attwell Baker," YouTube, Sept. 12, 2018, https://tinyurl.com/yyuecckw.

43 *Ibid.*

44 "The FCC's 5G FAST Plan," FCC, undated, https://tinyurl.com/yy68kcdt; Tiffany Hsu, "F.C.C. Puts 5G Rollout Rules in Federal Hands," *The New York Times*, Sept. 26, 2018, https://tinyurl.com/y5thufpx; and "A Major Milestone for U.S. 5G Leadership," Blog, CTIA, May 20, 2019, https://tinyurl.com/y525dh4b.

45 "Ericsson Mobility Report," Ericsson, June 2019, https://tinyurl.com/yy4pcvwg.

46 Christian de Looper, "The T-Mobile/Sprint merger: Everything you need to know," *Digital Trends*, July 26, 2019, https://tinyurl.com/yyen2ufk; Joe Williams, "T-Mobile, Sprint battle criticism over $26.5B merger on Capitol Hill," *Fox Business*, Feb. 13, 2019, https://tinyurl.com/y67fhvcy; and Tony Romm, "Sprint, T-Mobile receive merger approval from Justice Department," *The Washington Post*, July 26, 2019, https://tinyurl.com/y6qt78dx.

47 Yuki Noguchi, "T-Mobile And Sprint Merger Finally Wins Justice Department's Blessing," *NPR*, July 26, 2019, https://tinyurl.com/y5msotgt.

BIBLIOGRAPHY

Books

Danesi, Marcel, ed., *Encyclopedia of Media and Communication*, University of Toronto Press, 2013.
Reference text that includes contributions from more than 50 experts who explain basic concepts of media and communication, trace the field's history and discuss its major schools of thought.

Liyanage, Madhusanka, et al., eds., *A Comprehensive Guide to 5G Security*, Wiley, 2018.
Saying that security is even more important for 5G networks than for earlier generations of cellular technology, technology experts from around the world explore how to protect 5G systems from cyberattack.

Articles

Computerworld UK Staff, "A timeline of 5G development: From 1979 to Now," *TechWorld*, May 9, 2019, https://tinyurl.com/yxwlee7y.
Writers for an online information technology publication describe each succeeding generation of mobile wireless technology.

Dolcourt, Jessica, "Big four US carriers face off over 5G: We compare their peak speeds," *CNET*, June 26, 2019, https://tinyurl.com/y6qcm6b6.

A mobile technology reporter says AT&T achieved the highest peak download speeds among firms developing 5G networks, but she also notes that speed is just one aspect of a successful 5G system.

Halpern, Sue, "The Terrifying Potential of the 5G Network," *The New Yorker*, April 26, 2019, https://tinyurl.com/y5dgygzc.

A contributing writer for the magazine explains the security risks of 5G networks.

Wheeler, Tom, "If 5G Is So Important, Why Isn't It Secure?" *The New York Times*, Jan. 21, 2019, https://tinyurl.com/yyydkno7.

A former Federal Communications Commission (FCC) chairman says the Trump administration isn't doing enough to make sure 5G networks are secure and criticizes the removal of requirements that 5G technology be designed from the start to fend off cyberattacks.

Reports and Studies

"Ericsson Mobility Report," Ericsson, June 2019, https://tinyurl.com/yy4pcvwg.

The telecommunications equipment maker reports on the status of mobile networks around the world and offers predictions on 5G adoption.

"Protecting America's Next-Generation Networks," CTIA, undated, https://tinyurl.com/y357gpo9.

A trade group for wireless providers says the industry is working to make sure 5G networks are as secure as possible, partly by developing systems that will provide security updates tailored for specific mobile devices.

"The dawn of the 5G world," AT&T Business, 2018, https://tinyurl.com/yyxbv59x.

A white paper from the global telecommunications giant says 5G could enable "radically new ways to do business."

"Who is leading the 5G patent race?" IPlytics, July 2019, https://tinyurl.com/y5pakhvd.

A market intelligence company in Berlin reports on patents awarded around the world for innovations in 5G technology.

Lee, Nicol Turner, "Enabling opportunities: 5G, the internet of things, and communities of color," Brookings Institution, Jan. 9, 2019, https://tinyurl.com/y5gue65d.

A technology fellow at a Washington think tank reports on the potential for 5G technology to benefit minority and other underserved communities.

Medin, Milo, and Gilman, Louie, "The 5G Ecosystem: Risks & Opportunities for DoD," Defense Innovation Board, April 2019, https://tinyurl.com/y4l9kh73.

An organization created in part to advise the military on technological innovation looks at 5G's development and the risks posed by potential Chinese domination of the technology, while noting how the new systems can improve battlefield performance and Pentagon decision-making.

Video

"CTIA, 5G Summit," CTIA, April 4, 2019, https://tinyurl.com/y2h48q4s.

FCC Chairman Ajit Pai, White House chief economic adviser Larry Kudlow and wireless industry executives offer their perspectives on 5G at a recent industry summit.

"International economics and securing next-generation 5G wireless networks: A conversation with Amb. Robert Strayer," American Enterprise Institute, May 29, 2019, https://tinyurl.com/y687avsv.

The deputy assistant secretary of State for cyber and international communications policies talks about economic and security issues linked to 5G technology at an event sponsored by a conservative Washington think tank.

THE NEXT STEP

Access

Finley, Klint, "Schools and Phone Companies Face Off Over Wireless Spectrum," *Wired*, June 25, 2019, https://tinyurl.com/y2gfp3sx.

The federal government's plan to auction off a portion of unused wireless spectrum to satisfy demand for 5G service would unfairly favor commercial ventures over community and educational groups, critics say.

Karsten, Jack, "Building inclusion into 5G wireless networks," Brookings Institution, Feb. 5, 2019, https://tinyurl.com/yxr46fu7.

A researcher at a Washington think tank says the development of 5G technology underscores the need to make sure minority communities have the same access to high-speed internet service as other groups.

Oswald, Ed, "Will 5G fix America's rural broadband woes? We asked the experts," *Digital Trends*, July 6, 2019, https://tinyurl.com/y4bjft38.
T-Mobile and Sprint say a major selling point for their planned merger is their plan to use mid- and low-range frequencies on the radio spectrum to bring 5G to sparsely populated rural areas where high-frequency signals are impractical.

Global Competition

Herman, Arthur, "How America Can Still Win The Battle For 5G," *Forbes*, March 26, 2019, https://tinyurl.com/y5djxxtn.
A senior fellow at a conservative think tank says U.S. officials need to ramp up the pressure on other countries to deny the Chinese telecom firm Huawei a role in developing 5G networks so China will not become the dominant supplier of the new technology.

Horwitz, Jeremy, "Deutsche Telekom debuts 5G in Germany as Vodafone UK offers unlimited plans," *Venture Beat*, July 3, 2019, https://tinyurl.com/yye63wo9.
Mobile carriers Deutsche Telekom in Germany and Vodafone in Britain launched 5G service in July, allowing those countries to catch up to the United States and South Korea.

Soo, Zen, "Too early to tell who will emerge as 5G winner as tech innovation still to unfold, Cisco executive says," *South China Morning Post*, July 16, 2019, https://tinyurl.com/y65nomx9.
No one country will win the race to develop 5G networks, and smaller countries would benefit by competing to provide such service, according to the global innovation officer at a top U.S. telecom firm.

Security Concerns

Lomas, Natasha, "No technical reason to exclude Huawei as 5G supplier, says UK committee," *Tech Crunch*, July 15, 2019, https://tinyurl.com/y3a83xp8.
A parliamentary committee in Britain says that while the Chinese telecom firm Huawei should not be allowed to develop the most critical parts of Britain's 5G networks due to national security concerns, the company need not be completely excluded from the rollout of 5G.

Wieczner, Jen, "Verizon Executive Calls for Federal Privacy Rules on 5G," *Fortune*, July 16, 2019, https://tinyurl.com/yxeefq6e.
A Verizon executive says federal regulators should draft rules aimed at protecting consumers' privacy as U.S. telecom companies build out 5G networks.

Woo, Stu, and Dustin Volz, "U.S. Considers Requiring 5G Equipment for Domestic Use Be Made Outside China," *The Wall Street Journal*, updated June 23, 2019, https://tinyurl.com/yyolaawn.
Citing national security concerns, Trump administration officials are asking foreign telecom equipment manufacturers whether they can ensure that cellular equipment delivered to the United States is not made in China.

Technological Advances

Charlton, Alistair, "How 5G is crucial for autonomous cars and connected smart cities," *Salon*, March 28, 2019, https://tinyurl.com/y6jkzhsd.
5G networks will allow vast improvements in driverless cars by speeding up their response time to traffic conditions, experts say.

Daws, Ryan, "All aboard! The UK and South Korea partner on 5G public transport experience," *Telecom Tech News*, July 16, 2019, https://tinyurl.com/y3pddyp9.
5G RailNext, a consortium of public and private companies led by Cisco, has won a contract to use 5G technology to provide entertainment and travel information for public transport travelers in South Korea and Britain.

Valera, Stephanie, "World's First 5G-Powered Remote Brain Surgery Performed in China," *Geek.com*, March 18, 2019, https://tinyurl.com/y22l28gu.
A surgeon in China recently used 5G technology to perform brain surgery on a patient 1,800 miles away.

For More Information

American Enterprise Institute, 1789 Massachusetts Ave., N.W., Washington, D.C. 20036; 202-862-5800; www.aei .org. Conservative research and policy institute that promotes global free enterprise and free trade.

AT&T, 208 S. Akard St., Dallas, TX 75202; 210-821-4105; www.att.com/5g/. World's largest telecommunications company and major provider of wireless service in the United States.

Brookings Institution, 1775 Massachusetts Ave., N.W., Washington, D.C. 20036; 202-797-6000; www.brookings .edu. Centrist think tank whose research includes work on 5G and other telecommunications issues.

CTIA, 1400 16th St., N.W., #600, Washington, D.C. 20036; 202-736-3200; www.ctia.org. Trade association for U.S. wireless companies.

Federal Communications Commission, 445 12th St., S.W., Washington, D.C. 20554; 888-225-5322; www.fcc .gov. U.S. government agency that regulates interstate and international communications by radio, television, wire, satellite and cable.

Free Press, 1025 Connecticut Ave., N.W., Washington, D.C. 20036; 202-265-1490; www.freepress.net. Independent organization that works to advance media and technology policies in the public interest.

GSMA, The Walbrook Building, 25 Walbrook, London, EC4N 8AF, U.K.; 44 (0) 207-356-0600; www.gsma.com. Trade association for mobile operators worldwide; produces MWC (formerly Mobile World Congress) events and reports on 5G.

Huawei, Huawei Industrial Base, Shenzhen 518129, P.R. China; 86-755-2878-0808; www.huawei.com/us/. Chinese telecommunications equipment maker.

T-Mobile, 12920 S.E. 38th St., Bellevue, WA 98006; 425-378-4000; www.t-mobile.com/5g. Major U.S. telecommunications company owned by Deutsche Telekom.

Verizon, 1095 Avenue of the Americas, New York, NY 20013; 212-395-1000; www.verizonwireless.com/5g/. U.S. telecommunications company that says it has the nation's largest 4G LTE network.

5

Africa in Transition

Sean Lyngaas

Chocolate is poured at a cocoa processing plant in Abidjan, Ivory Coast. As the world's two largest cocoa producers, Ivory Coast and Ghana want to export finished chocolate, which has a higher value than unprocessed cocoa. But the switch to the more advanced processing has gone slowly, as it has for other African commodities elsewhere in sub-Saharan Africa, providing relatively few new jobs so far.

From *CQ Researcher,*
February 23, 2018

The gleaming skyline in Abidjan, Ivory Coast's commercial capital, is lined with towering buildings. International banks, trendy cafes and modern, well-stocked supermarkets project the image of a country on the rise. With a growth rate averaging more than 8 percent over the last five years, the West African nation is one of the continent's fastest-growing economies.[1]

After nearly a decade of civil conflict, a U.N. peacekeeping mission has left, and Ivory Coast has persuaded foreign investors to return. There was a military coup in 1999, and a 2010-2011 electoral crisis left about 3,000 people dead, but in 2015 the former French colony (also known by its French name, Côte d'Ivoire) held a peaceful presidential election.

"Our social and economic reforms benefit a growing number of Ivorians each day," President Alassane Ouattara said in 2016, shortly after beginning his second term. "Poverty is, as a result, down sharply."[2]

But like many countries—developed and developing alike—Ivory Coast is grappling with a stark gap between the rich and poor. In Abidjan's business district, well-heeled businessmen walk past impoverished women hawking fruit on the street. Forty-six percent of the population still lived in poverty in 2015, and many Ivorians are demanding to know when they will share in the country's economic growth.[3]

With its rising economic and political hopes, Ivory Coast is in some ways a microcosm of sub-Saharan Africa's recent trajectory. Steady economic growth, a growing middle class and rising democratic aspirations throughout the region have fostered an optimistic "Africa Rising" narrative.[4] The image is a drastic change from the past stereotype of a continent gripped by famine, violence and political crises. However, fissures have emerged

Economic Growth Slows

Sub-Saharan Africa's GDP growth averaged 5 percent annually from 2005 to 2014, fostering an "Africa Rising" narrative of expanding economic opportunity. But annual growth averaged just 2.2 percent for 2015 through 2017, largely because global commodity prices tumbled.

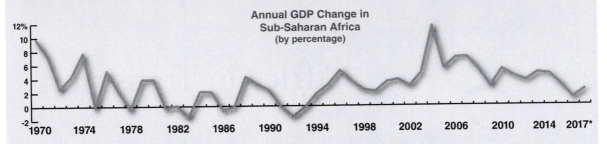

Annual GDP Change in
Sub-Saharan Africa
(by percentage)

* Projected

Sources: "GDP growth (annual %)," The World Bank Group, Jan. 25, 2018, https://tinyurl.com/yacwcspw; "Modest Growth Recovery in Sub-Saharan Africa," World Bank, Oct. 11, 2017, https://tinyurl.com/yaxmh2em

in the narrative of late, as growth has slowed, millions remain mired in poverty and some autocratic leaders have used the veneer of democracy to cling to power.

"The 'Africa Rising' story is no longer as strong as it used to be," says Jakkie Cilliers, head of African Futures and Innovation at the Institute for Security Studies in Pretoria, South Africa. "We are growing, but we're not growing rapidly enough, particularly given the demographic trends on the continent." Africa's population will double by 2050 to 2.5 billion people, according to United Nations projections, requiring the continent to create millions of new jobs.[5]

Sub-Saharan Africa's gross domestic product (GDP), a measure of the value of all goods and services produced by the region, grew at an average rate of 5 percent from 2004 to 2014, faster than those of Latin American and the Caribbean (3.2 percent) or the East Asia/Pacific region (4.8 percent). The resource-rich economies of Angola, Nigeria and South Africa have buoyed the region's growth. But because sub-Saharan Africa is so dependent on exporting raw materials, after global commodity prices tumbled in 2014, its average growth rate dropped to just 2.2 percent between 2015 and 2017.[6]

The region—located south of the Sahara Desert and composed of 46 nations—defies generalizations and differs markedly from its predominantly Arab neighbors in North

Africa. Countries range from Muslim-majority Mali in West Africa's desert region to tiny Mauritius, a volcanic island in the Indian Ocean where nearly half of the population is Hindu.[7] Sub-Saharan Africa also includes oil-rich Nigeria, with 183 million people, and South Africa, one of the continent's largest economies, ranked by the World Bank as an upper-middle-income country.[8]

The region's strong economic growth in the past decade coincided with a surge in Chinese business activity in Africa, as China sought natural resources to fuel its own rapid economic growth at home. Among other activities, Chinese state-owned companies have built roads and bridges throughout the continent, a railway connecting Kenya's two biggest cities and huge soccer stadiums in Angola and Gabon.[9]

As Africa's largest trading partner, China conducted $128 billion in bilateral trade in 2016, compared to about $48 billion in U.S.-African trade.[10] From 2001 to 2010, China's Export-Import Bank lent $62.7 billion to African countries—$12.5 billion more than the World Bank provided during that period, according to Fitch Ratings.[11]

The Chinese are "the pace-setters for African engagement" and are far ahead of the United States in that respect, says Deborah Bräutigam, director of the China Africa Research Initiative at the Johns Hopkins School of Advanced International Studies in Washington, D.C.

Critics have charged that President Trump has shown little interest in Africa and does not have clear policies toward the continent.[12] But Bräutigam says that won't make much difference. "[China is] just so far ahead of [the United States] there that we're really in their rearview mirror," she says.

China has shaken up the development narrative in Africa by using trade and investment to go beyond the typical donor-recipient relationship, according to Zambian economist Dambisa Moya.[13] China's pragmatic approach to development in Africa—one that generally comes without criticism of African governments' human rights records—contrasts with the conditions-based approach of the United States and other Western countries. And China's domestic-development model of allowing some aspects of capitalism and international trade while strictly controlling individual rights—dubbed "authoritarian capitalism"—was the second-most-popular model after American democratic capitalism in a 2014-2015 survey of 36 African countries conducted by the polling group Afrobarometer.[14]

Chinese aid to Africa is difficult to measure, but according to a database maintained by AidData, a research lab at the College of William & Mary in Williamsburg, Va., China's "official finance" commitments to Africa totaled $75 billion from 2000 to 2011.[15] This broad category of contributions includes grants for development, loans, debt relief and foreign direct investment.

As China rapidly expanded its footprint on the continent, concerns arose that Chinese aid could strengthen African autocrats and that Beijing could be trying to export its authoritarian political model. For example, a 2016 study by AidData found that Chinese aid disproportionately went to African leaders' home regions, which could bolster autocrats' power.[16]

However, Bräutigam and other experts say Chinese leaders are not interested in dictating politics in African countries. Notwithstanding close relationships between the Chinese Communist Party and political parties in South Sudan and South Africa, there is little evidence China is pushing for African countries to adopt its governing system, she says. The continent has its own autocratic governance models, including in Rwanda, where President Paul Kagame has assiduously courted investment while stamping out political dissent.

Despite some positive developments in the region, many autocrats have thrown up roadblocks to democratization. In its 2018 report, Freedom House, an independent watchdog organization based in Washington, D.C., that tracks global democracy, said that just 11 percent of sub-Saharan Africa's population lives in countries considered "free," while 52 percent lives in "partly free countries" and 37 percent in countries that are "not free."[17]

The past 18 months have been momentous for democracy in sub-Saharan Africa, with both positive and negative developments:

- In December 2016, Gambians voted longtime dictator Yahya Jammeh out of office, inspiring democracy activists across the continent.[18]

- In Kenya, the Supreme Court nullified an August 2017 presidential election on suspicions of fraud in a move analysts hailed as good for accountability and transparency.[19] However, opposition leader Raila Odinga boycotted the follow-up vote in October, claiming results would not be credible, and incumbent President Uhuru Kenyatta won easily. Tensions have remained high since then, with Odinga's supporters holding a mock inauguration of their candidate in late January, and the government shutting down TV stations planning to broadcast the event.

- In Rwanda, Kagame was re-elected in August with 99 percent of the vote in what critics called a rubber-stamp election.[20]

- South African politics have been in disarray. President Jacob Zuma, hounded by corruption allegations, resigned on Feb. 14, a day after the ruling African National Congress (ANC) party voted that he should step down. The next day, Parliament elected Cyril Ramaphosa, Zuma's successor as head of the ANC, as the country's president.[21]

This year and next promise to be pivotal for Africa's democracies, with crucial elections scheduled this year in Mali, Sierra Leone and troubled South Sudan and in 2019 in Nigeria and South Africa.

Meanwhile, several countries continue to face the persistent threat of Islamist terrorism, with Nigeria, Burkina Faso, Mali and Somalia suffering from multiple

Urban Population Rising Sharply

More than half of sub-Saharan Africa's population is expected to live in cities by 2050, up from about 40 percent today and less than 30 percent a generation ago. Experts say African governments will have to provide more mass transit and sanitation services and attract more investments in manufacturing jobs.

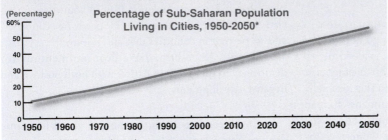

Percentage of Sub-Saharan Population Living in Cities, 1950-2050*

* Data after 2010 are projected.

Source: "World Urbanization Prospects: The 2014 Revision," Population Division, Department of Economic and Social Affairs, United Nations, June 2014, https://tinyurl.com/ycg6pdpm

As sub-Saharan African leaders, economists and activists contemplate the region's future, here are some of the questions they are debating:

Can urbanization alleviate African poverty and help foster democracy?

Africa has one of the world's highest urbanization rates. The number of African cities with half a million or more inhabitants is expected to grow by 80 percent between 2016 and 2030.[25]

Africa's cities have experienced severe growing pains, with sprawling slums emerging in places like Lagos, Nigeria, Johannesburg, South Africa, and Nairobi, Kenya, where the Kibera slum is the largest slum on the continent.[26] Poor sanitation in these shantytowns poses stiff challenges for development, and new migrants arriving from the countryside often find the going tough.

"Africa's urban environments are particularly susceptible to flooding and outbreaks of diseases such as malaria," according to UN-Habitat, the U.N. agency for human settlement.

Meanwhile, new middle- and upper-middle-class neighborhoods have sprung up in Africa's cities, revealing stark income disparities. Nevertheless, experts say urbanization can be an engine for growth.

Oxford Economics, an economic forecasting firm based in London, found that Africa's major cities accounted for nearly $700 billion, or 36 percent, of Africa's GDP in 2012, and projects that figure to reach $1.7 trillion by 2030.[27]

"We think urbanization can be a tool for sustainable development if it is properly managed," says Jean Pierre Elong Mbassi, who heads United Cities and Local Governments of Africa, an umbrella group of local governments from across the continent.

Unfortunately, he says, urban planners in many African cities have not accounted for the growth and needs of slums. His organization is trying to change that through a program that connects city planners with local governments and representatives of poorer

terror attacks. In Nigeria and Somalia, governments have shrunk the operating space of Islamist terrorist groups Boko Haram and Al Shabab, respectively, but those groups still periodically carry out successful attacks.

Some analysts have criticized how African governments have responded to terrorism. For instance, Hennie Strydom, a law professor at the University of Johannesburg in South Africa, criticizes the African Union, the continent's transnational organization, for lacking a coherent counter-terrorism strategy.[22] In addition, the G5 Sahel Joint Force, a West African coalition established a year ago, struggles with insufficient funding.

On the positive side, African countries have made substantial progress in recent years in the fight against HIV-AIDS. Eastern and southern Africa have posted the world's sharpest rate of decline in AIDS-related deaths—62 percent—from a peak of about 1.1 million deaths in 2004 to about 420,000 in 2016. The United Nations attributes the decline to wider use of anti-retroviral treatment. West and Central Africa saw a 30 percent decline in deaths over that period, according to the U.N. The United States has provided anti-AIDS drugs to millions of Africans under the President's Emergency Plan For AIDS Relief, initiated in 2003 by George W. Bush.[23]

Nonetheless, sub-Saharan Africa still accounted for about 69 percent of the world population living with HIV in 2016.[24]

neighborhoods. The program is underway in Ouagadougou and Lusaka, the capitals of Burkina Faso and Zambia respectively, and is expected to expand to other big cities across Africa.

Mbassi says cities need financial support from government institutions to tackle their urban development goals and access to credit to finance development projects. "Only if these conditions are put in place will cities become an engine for growth and development," he says. "We have to use this urbanization to boost industrialization on the continent, and a country like Ethiopia is doing it very well," he adds.

If African governments want the economic growth spurred by urbanization to be more inclusive, they need to build quality mass transit systems, according to Edward K. Brown, director of policy advisory services at the African Center for Economic Transformation, a think tank in Accra, Ghana. Urban poverty is very high, he adds, and the long commute times faced by urban residents take away from production time, he says. With funding from China's Export-Import Bank, the Ethiopian government opened sub-Saharan Africa's first light railway in 2015, designed to relieve traffic congestion in the capital, Addis Ababa.[28]

Joan Clos, the former executive director of U.N.-Habitat, has called African urbanization an "untapped tool for development and economic growth" and both "a consequence of development and also the driving force for accelerating this development." Slums, he added, "should be considered a temporary outcome of development."[29]

Urbanization also can have mixed impacts on democracy and political empowerment. For instance, according to the African research network Afrobarometer, the demand for democracy is higher (47 percent) among Africans living in urban rather than rural areas (40 percent).[30]

However, urbanization "is not simply a linear process" whereby people move to the cities and then become more democratic, explains Jeffrey Paller, an assistant professor of politics at the University of San Francisco who specializes in the politics of urbanization in Africa. Instead, his research has found, urbanization has led to competing claims for land and resources as expanding cities encroach upon existing traditional settlements. How local leaders navigate

Workers assemble Volkswagens at a recently opened factory in Nairobi, Kenya, on Dec. 21, 2016. Like the rest of the world, African countries are grappling with the long-term consequences of increased automation in manufacturing and its impact on employment.

these conflicts can affect how urban residents view democracy, he says.

Smaller cities also can be crucial in the urbanization process by connecting rural and urban areas, according to Paller. For instance, government investments in provincial universities in Ghana, Ivory Coast and Senegal have been a boon for local populations, he says.

Are sub-Saharan African economies ready to exploit manufacturing?

Historically, economies develop rapidly by industrializing. As workers move from low-yield economic sectors such as subsistence agriculture to higher-yield ones like manufacturing, economies can see major gains in productivity.

However, analysts say this structural change generally hasn't occurred in most of sub-Saharan Africa, with agriculture still providing jobs for about 60 percent of the continent's workforce.[31] "The structure of [African] economies has not changed that much," says Brown, the Ghanaian economist. "That is why you have so much poverty and inequality, because the structure of the economies has been very much primary commodity based."

Grieve Chelwa, a Zambian economist and a lecturer at the University of Cape Town's Graduate School of Business in South Africa, echoes that analysis. The growth that fueled the Africa Rising narrative was "not really based on any fundamental, structural change in terms of the way these economies function . . . [but rather] the usual growth swings that most African countries have suffered from since time immemorial," says Chelwa.

The continent's rapid growth "would have really led one to believe that you would see much more drastic reductions in poverty and inequality over the past years," says Brahima Sangafowa Coulibaly, director of the Africa Growth Initiative at the Brookings Institution think tank in Washington, D.C.

However, sub-Saharan Africa's economic growth has tended to be jobless and has not accommodated the region's surging labor force, Coulibaly adds. Sub-Saharan economies create only about 3 million jobs each year, while up to 12 million youths are entering the workforce each year, according to the African Development Bank (AfDB), which provides low-interest loans to African countries for development projects.[32]

As African policymakers plan their path to industrialization, automated technologies such as robotics are complicating the picture, leading some analysts to question whether African economies are ready to reap the benefits of this technological change.[33] For instance, as wages rise in China, manufacturing jobs could relocate to Africa, which could accelerate industrialization, according to Coulibaly. However, he adds, automation could close that "window of opportunity" if multinational companies choose to operate in countries with high-tech manufacturing rather than move their operations to low-wage countries in Africa.

And, Brown warns, while African countries adopt a "wait and see attitude" about the impact technology will have on the future of African manufacturing, that "train is already moving." If policymakers are not "much more deliberate and strategic in how they really support the local industries to create the jobs that are needed," they will not profit enough from high-tech industrialization, he says.

In recent years, some pundits thought the spread of information and communications technologies (ICT) could enable sub-Saharan economies to leapfrog early phases of development, reaping big economic benefits from ICT without the heavy up-front investments in infrastructure needed for manufacturing.[34]

However, Calestous Juma, the late Kenyan professor of international development at Harvard University's Kennedy School of Government, rebutted the notion that African economies can successfully bypass manufacturing.

"The failure of the mobile [phone] revolution to stimulate industrial development in Africa is the result, in part, of a faulty narrative that assumes that Africa can leap into the service economy without first building a manufacturing base," Juma wrote in 2017.[35]

In addition, capitalizing on ICT requires highly skilled workers, but sub-Saharan Africa's labor force is generally undereducated, Chelwa points out, which could take a generation to fix. Many firms operating in the region report that workforce skills are a constraint on expansion.[36] Only 27 percent of young people in sub-Saharan Africa have completed secondary education, according to the U.N.[37]

African policymakers want to export higher-value processed goods rather than just raw materials, so the extra value can be passed on to workers. For instance, countries such as Ghana and Ivory Coast, the world's two largest cocoa producers, want to export chocolate rather than unprocessed cocoa. But switching to agro-processing has been a slow process, providing only a fraction of employment on the continent so far.[38]

To bolster structural changes in African economies, countries must improve their export capacities and investment climates, according to John Page, a colleague of Coulibaly's at the Africa Growth Initiative. Research by Page and others has found that ICT-based services, transportation and tourism often outpace manufacturing growth in African countries. To propel their economies, African countries also need to harness the agro-industry and horticulture sectors, they argue.[39]

If African economies are to achieve long-term prosperity, those economies will need to undergo seismic shifts in how they function, according to Brown. For example, he pointed out, infrastructure projects—such as the Chinese-built railway connecting Ethiopia's capital, Addis Ababa, with the shipping port of Djibouti—are the "backbone of industrialization," but "Africa has a huge infrastructure deficit."[40]

Economist Thandika Mkandawire, of the London School of Economics, says a major challenge for African economies is that their recent growth has been fueled by consumption. "Africa's growth path has been consumption-intensive, at least when compared with the investment-driven East Asian model," Mkandawire writes. "Wal-Mart goes to Africa not to buy manufactured goods for the U.S. market, as it does in China, but to sell goods to the new middle class. The proliferation of shopping malls in Africa is the reverse side of deindustrialization—cheap imported goods have undermined local industry," he said.[41]

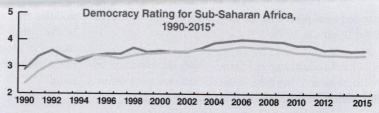

Democratic Gains at Risk

Political and civil rights have been declining in some sub-Saharan African countries since 2006, bringing down the region's overall democracy rating.

Democracy Rating for Sub-Saharan Africa, 1990-2015*

* The scoring ranges from 1 (least free and democratic) to 7 (most free and democratic).

Source: Robert Mattes and Michael Bratton, "Do Africans still want democracy?" Afrobarometer, November 2016, https://tinyurl.com/y8ryewhk

Political rights
Civil liberties

Is African democracy headed in the right direction?

With the longevity of strongmen like Vladimir Putin of Russia and Recep Tayyip Erdogan of Turkey, many observers say democracy is on the decline around the globe.[42]

"[U]nfortunately, Africa seems to be leading that global democratic recession," says Nic Cheeseman, a professor of democracy and international development at the University of Birmingham in the United Kingdom. Of the 12 countries rated by Freedom House as the worst in the world for political and civil rights, seven are in Africa: South Sudan, Eritrea, Equatorial Guinea, Somalia, Sudan, Libya and Central African Republic.[43]

But according to the Ibrahim Index of African Governance, several African governments have become more participatory in recent years.*

Ghanaians, for example, pride themselves on their reputation for holding peaceful and fair elections. They reaffirmed that reputation in December 2016 when then-President John Mahama was defeated by his long-time challenger, Nana Akufo-Addo. Mahama conceded

the day the results were announced and called for national unity.[44]

In addition, Afrobarometer found that 67 percent of those surveyed in 36 African countries preferred democracy to other forms of government. Large majorities rejected authoritarian regimes such as presidential dictatorships, one-party governments and systems of military rule.[45]

However, progress toward democratization has been uneven in sub-Saharan Africa in recent years, with some longtime autocrats being removed from office, while others have dug in their heels to stay in power. Last year sub-Saharan democracy saw positive and negative developments, including:

• In Zimbabwe, authoritarian leader Robert Mugabe, who had led the country for more than three decades, was detained in November by the military and then resigned just as parliament was to begin debating impeachment. While many Zimbabweans celebrated Mugabe's departure, the fact that it effectively occurred following a military coup underlined just how far the country has to go on the path to democracy.

• In Rwanda, democracy seemed to take another hit when autocrat Kagame, who has been president for 17 years, was re-elected. There were few opposition candidates on the ballot, and critics say Kagame has stifled dissent.

_____

* The index measures governance performance in African countries, published by a London-based foundation created by Sudanese philanthropist and businessman Mo Ibrahim.

• African democracy activists were inspired, however, by the peaceful ouster in 2017 of Gambia's longtime authoritarian leader, Yahya Jammeh, who had ruled the tiny West African nation with an iron fist for 22 years.[46] It was the first time a president had peacefully handed over power in Gambia since its independence from Britain in 1965.

That breakthrough in Gambia was accompanied by political drama. Initially, Jammeh had conceded defeat, but within days he reversed course and refused to step down. Weeks later, with troops from other West African nations heading toward the capital to oust Jammeh, he acquiesced and left the country.[47]

"The many pro-democracy activists I talk to in Cameroon and Zimbabwe and Togo and elsewhere often point to Gambia and how the opposition was able to come together and unite, which is so critical and so essential in many of these situations," says Jeffrey Smith, executive director of Vanguard Africa, a democracy advocacy group in Washington, D.C.

Zelalem Kibret, an Ethiopian lawyer who has been imprisoned for his democratic activism, echoed that sentiment. "The domino effect of what's happening in other African countries is significant. Victory for democratic activists appears to be an inspiration and a recipe for fighting against hopelessness," Kibret says, citing Jammeh's departure as inspirational for Ethiopian activists.

Kibret says civil and political liberties have been "in a downward spiral" for more than a decade in Ethiopia, the continent's second-most populous country, with about 105 million people.[48] Hundreds of anti-government protesters have been killed in clashes with security forces over the last few years.[49] But Kibret says he remains resolutely optimistic about the future, in part because Ethiopian activists haven't given up.

Along with the mixed status of democratic reforms in sub-Saharan Africa in recent years, "barely any progress" has been made in ensuring accountability during that time, with persistent corruption accounting for much of that inertia, according to the Ibrahim Index.[50]

Meanwhile, the role of foreign election observers in Africa has come under scrutiny following the controversial presidential vote in Kenya in August 2017. Observers from the African Union, European Union, the Commonwealth of Nations and a U.S. nongovernmental organization endorsed the initial round of voting, which showed that Kenyatta had been re-elected for a second term.[51]

Less than a month later, the Kenyan Supreme Court nullified the results, citing "irregularities and illegalities" in the voting.[52] Odinga, the candidate who came in second in voting, said the court's decision "put on trial the international observers who moved so fast to sanitize fraud."[53]

Smith argues that foreign election observers have clung to less-stringent, 1980s-era standards for African elections that do not reflect recent democratic advances. The observers, he says, conflate peaceful elections with those that are free and fair.

"Many of the more autocratic or abusive leaders in sub-Saharan Africa have modernized their election-rigging efforts, but international election monitoring hasn't advanced or reformed in the same way to keep up with that," Smith says. "That has led directly to the increase in voter apathy [and] the increase in disillusionment with democracy across the region."

BACKGROUND
Colonialism and Independence

A period in recent sub-Saharan African history that still reverberates today began with the Berlin Conference of 1884-85, when colonial powers such as Belgium, Britain, France, Germany and Portugal jostled for control of the area around the Congo River, a main trading artery in Africa.

Although no African delegate was invited to the conference, the resulting land grabs defined Africa for decades to come. A major outcome of the conference: Belgium's King Leopold II solidified his brutal control of the Congo, a resource-rich area many times the size of Belgium.[54]

"The Berlin Conference did not initiate European colonization of Africa, but it did legitimate and formalize the process," wrote historian Elizabeth Heath.[55]

Economic exploitation was one of the predominant dynamics of the Europe-Africa relationship.[56] After railways reached the interior of the colonies, European mining companies arrived to exploit Africa's natural resources, including gold from Ghana and diamonds from Angola.[57]

CHRONOLOGY

1800s *Europeans take control of most of the African continent*

1820 British settlers land in South Africa.

1822 American Colonization Society sends black volunteers to Africa's west coast to establish a colony for freed slaves in what eventually became Liberia.

1884 Berlin Conference sets regulations for European colonization and trade in Africa; King Leopold II of Belgium consolidates control of the Congo.

1950s-1970s *Turmoil ensues in some newly independent African countries, often complicated by proxy Cold War competition between the West and Soviet Union.*

1957 Ghana is the first sub-Saharan African country to win independence from a European power, Britain.

1960 Seventeen sub-Saharan African nations gain independence.

1961 Patrice Lumumba, the recently deposed Congolese prime minister, is assassinated with the complicity of the Belgian and U.S. governments.

1964 South African anti-apartheid activist Nelson Mandela is sentenced to life in prison for treason.

1966 Military overthrows Ghanaian President Kwame Nkrumah, a champion of the pan-Africanism movement.

1974 Portugal's five African colonies gain independence.

1975 A 27-year civil war begins in Angola.

1980s-1990s *Sub-Saharan African countries liberalize their economic policies, but their economies generally contract in the face of a debt crisis.*

1980 Liberation fighter Robert Mugabe becomes prime minister of Zimbabwe; he later becomes president.

1981 World Bank recommends strict economic reforms that many experts later say exacerbated sub-Saharan Africa's economic woes.

1987 Thomas Sankara, charismatic Marxist leader of Burkina Faso, is assassinated in a coup.

1991 Somalia's government collapses, leaving a decades-long security vacuum.

1994 Mandela becomes president of South Africa four years after being released from prison. . . . Members of Rwanda's Hutu ethnic majority murder up to 800,000 people, mostly of the Tutsi minority.

1996 Seven years of civil war begin in the Democratic Republic of Congo that eventually kills millions and involves several neighboring countries.

2000-Present *Soaring commodity prices revive African economies, but the recovery begins to falter.*

2002 African Union is established to tackle security challenges on the continent.

2003 U.S. President George W. Bush establishes AIDS relief plan in Africa.

2016 Gambian autocrat Yahya Jammeh is voted out of power after 22 years and eventually steps down in a peaceful transition that inspires African democracy activists.

2017 Kenya's Supreme Court nullifies results of August presidential election due to irregularities, the first time an African court has overturned an election. President Uhuru Kenyatta is reelected in a rerun election, which is boycotted by opposition candidate Raila Odinga. . . . In Zimbabwe, Emmerson Mnangagwa, accused of human rights abuses earlier in his career, becomes president after the military peacefully deposes Mugabe.

2018 Kenyan opposition leader Odinga declares himself the "people's president" in a mock inauguration protesting Kenyatta's re-election. . . . In South Africa, Cyril Ramaphosa, a former union leader and one of the country's richest politicians, replaces scandal-plagued Jacob Zuma as president.

Political Repression Shadows Rwanda's Economic Dreams

The Kagame regime uses authoritarianism to advance the nation's goals.

The fortunes of the small East African nation of Rwanda have changed drastically in the last two decades.

Twenty-four years after a bitter civil war that included the genocidal slaughter of an estimated 800,000 Rwandans, crime, corruption and poverty have fallen in the nation, and living standards and life expectancies have surged.[1] But President Paul Kagame's plans for an economic transformation from subsistence agriculture to high-tech, high-productivity enterprises go hand-in-hand with his authoritarianism and restrictions on civil liberties.

Kagame aims to create a large class of Rwandan entrepreneurs, make farming more productive and connect cities and towns through better infrastructure, while generating thousands of middle-class jobs.[2] But while some see Kagame's approach as a model for other African nations, his economic miracle is clouded by violence and political repression.

Under Kagame, Rwanda is effectively a one-party state in which political dissent can be dangerous.[3] Critics of the government have been murdered. Government surveillance extends to the village level via a network of informants. And some opposition candidates in the last two presidential elections have been barred from running.[4]

Critics worry that Kagame's path to economic revival could spur other African leaders to follow his autocratic lead. "[F]or many poor-country potentates, the appeal of the Rwandan model is precisely the unchecked power that [Rwanda] bestows on the president and his party," *The Economist* magazine declared.[5]

Kagame, 60, an ethnic Tutsi, took power in 2000, six years after leading the Rwandan Patriotic Front (RPF) and its Tutsi troops to victory against a Hutu government that perpetrated the 1994 genocide. He was re-elected with nearly 99 percent of the vote to a third term as president in August and can remain in power until 2034 because of a 2015 referendum that extended term limits.[6]

While Kagame's political methods have sparked criticism, his economic aspirations have garnered something akin to awe in some quarters.

According to the World Bank, Rwanda has achieved "remarkable development successes" over the last decade, including high economic growth, rapid poverty reduction and reduced inequality. For instance, GDP growth averaged about 8 percent per year between 2001 and 2015, the bank noted, one of the highest rates in sub-Saharan Africa.[7] Growth eased to 5.9 percent in 2016, but the International Monetary Fund expects it to pick up again in 2018.[8]

At the same time, Rwanda has made progress on gender equality, with women making up 64 percent of the lower house of parliament in 2016—the highest ratio in the world.[9]

The Rwandan government has used its power to tightly manage the economy. While officials have curtailed some forms of corruption, they also have cut regulations, boosting Rwanda's appeal as a place to do business.

Meanwhile, the RPF, now the ruling party, has used a private holding company, Crystal Ventures, to invest in myriad parts of the Rwandan economy, from telecommunications to real estate. Critics say the firm snatches up government contracts but that its enterprises don't always turn a profit. The firm also has spent sizable amounts on RPF's election campaigns.[10]

And despite its economic progress, Rwanda still relies on foreign aid for an estimated 30 to 40 percent of its budget. Its poverty rate—though down sharply from 57 percent in 2005—stood at 39 percent in 2014, the latest figure available.[11]

In trying to rebuild Rwanda, Kagame studied the path Singapore used to transform from a poor colonial outpost in the 1960s to the prosperous business hub it is today. Lee

Kuan Yew, Singapore's autocratic prime minister from 1959 to 1990, focused on improving public education, building quality infrastructure and attracting foreign investment while restricting civil liberties.[12] During a 2008 visit to the Southeast Asian state, Kagame called Lee "an inspiration" and later hailed him as a "visionary who has transformed Singapore and the lives of his people," adding: "This is also what we are doing in Rwanda."[13]

China, another country that combines pro-market policies with authoritarianism, also has influenced Kagame. The Chinese have built schools, government buildings, hospitals and many of Rwanda's roads, and the capital Kigali boasts a free-trade area designed to attract foreign investment, modeled after the special economic zones China created in the 1980s. A Chinese government-funded technical organization in Rwanda helps Chinese companies reach other markets in the region.[14]

Rwanda's economic successes have drawn admiration inside and outside Africa. "I hope many African nations will emulate what Rwanda is doing," then-U.N. Secretary-General Ban Ki-moon told Kagame in 2013. David Murathe, vice chairman of Kenya's ruling Jubilee Party, lauded Rwanda's stability when he said in September that Kenya could use a "benevolent dictator."[15]

And in December, a columnist for Zimbabwe's *The Standard* newspaper noted that his country's new president, Emmerson Mnangagwa, "has a reputation like that of Rwandan President Paul Kagame of being a strong man and implementer," but that his excesses "may be forgotten or forgiven" if, like Kagame, "his economic reforms work and investors are happy."[16]

But Kagame's governing strategies would not work in countries like Kenya or Zimbabwe, where opposition parties wield significant power, said Nic Cheeseman, a professor of democracy at the University of Birmingham in England and former director of the African Studies Centre at the University of Oxford.[17]

However, Uganda and Ethiopia have charted courses similar to Rwanda's "developmental authoritarianism," in which "nominally democratic governments . . . provide significant public works and services while exerting control over nearly every facet of society," according to an article in the *African Studies Review*.[18]

— *Sean Lyngaas*

[1] Marijke Verpoorten, "The Death Toll of the Rwandan Genocide: A Detailed Analysis for Gikongoro Province," *Population*, 2005/4, Vol. 60, https://tinyurl.com/yazawlm6; editorial, "Democracy Is Rwanda's Losing Candidate," *The New York Times*, Aug. 11, 2017, https://tinyurl.com/yafy6les.

[2] "Rwanda Vision 2020," Republic of Rwanda, 2012, https://tinyurl.com/y7ogb3m4.

[3] "Rwanda 2016 Human Rights Report," U.S. Department of State, 2016, p. 1, https://tinyurl.com/ydez9h6a.

[4] Anjan Sundaram, "Rwanda: Kagame's Efficient Repression," *The New York Review of Books*, Aug. 4, 2017, https://tinyurl.com/y7qac99e.

[5] "Many Africans See Kagame's Rwanda as a Model. They are Wrong," *The Economist*, July 15, 2017, https://tinyurl.com/y7an42ju.

[6] Tonny Onyulo, "Savior or dictator? Government critics challenge Rwanda's one-party state and president ahead of election," *Newsweek*, July 12, 2017, https://tinyurl.com/ycnx3jff.

[7] *Ibid.*; "Rwanda Overview," World Bank, Nov. 6, 2017, https://tinyurl.com/yb6yotoo.

[8] "Rwanda Overview," *ibid.*

[9] Gregory Warner, "It's The No. 1 Country For Women In Politics—But Not In Daily Life," NPR, July 29, 2016, https://tinyurl.com/y9s3y338.

[10] "The Rwandan Patriotic Front's Business Empire," *The Economist*, March 2, 2017, https://tinyurl.com/zsxpj3q.

[11] "Rwanda Overview," *op. cit.*; CIA World Factbook, https://tinyurl.com/2vzndc.

[12] Zarina Hussain, "How Lee Kuan Yew Engineered Singapore's Economic Miracle," BBC, March 24, 2015, https://tinyurl.com/ntdngrj.

[13] Christian Caryl, "Africa's Singapore Dream," *Foreign Policy*, April 2, 2015, https://tinyurl.com/ybzomgxs.

[14] Lily Kuo, "Rwanda is a Landlocked Country with Few Natural Resources. So Why is China Investing So Heavily in It?" *Quartz Africa*, Nov. 22, 2016, https://tinyurl.com/yawaw6cf.

[15] Killiad Msafiri, "Kenya Needs a Dictator, Says Senior Jubilee Politician," *The Standard*, Sept. 26, 2017, https://tinyurl.com/y7aekfh4 https://tinyurl.com/y7aekfh4.

[16] Paidamoyo Muzulu, "Is Mnangagwa Zimbabwe's Kagame?" *The Standard*, Dec. 4, 2017, https://tinyurl.com/yd63s83q.

[17] Nic Cheeseman, "Why Rwanda's Development Model Wouldn't Work Elsewhere in Africa," *The Conversation*, Jan. 8, 2018, https://tinyurl.com/y8fygovo.

[18] Hilary Matfess, "Rwanda and Ethiopia: Developmental Authoritarianism and the New Politics of African Strong Men," *African Studies Review*, Sept. 1, 2015, https://tinyurl.com/yabqac2g.

Africans Abroad Send Vital Support Home

Cash and technical help are lifelines for struggling communities.

When Ebola began ravaging Sierra Leone in 2014, the government warned residents of the West African nation that it planned to impose a three-day, countrywide ban on leaving their houses to keep the deadly virus from spreading. Because many Sierra Leoneans live hand-to-mouth and have no way to store food, the lockdown meant they could go hungry.

But 3,000 miles away, Memuna Janneh, a British Sierra Leonean living in London, had a plan to help. She coordinated and paid for a food distribution network, carried out with help from family and friends in Sierra Leone, that reached about 2,600 people in seven communities.

"I live in Sierra Leone for part of the year so I know people who would struggle," Janneh told *The Guardian*.[1]

Janneh's act of goodwill was part of a much larger effort by Africans who have migrated from the continent but want to help their home countries, whether through cash remittances, technical assistance or coordinated efforts like Janneh's.

For countries ravaged by poverty or conflict, the diaspora can be a lifeline. "Africans in the diaspora increasingly are transferring resources, knowledge and ideas to their home countries and integrating them in the global economy," according to the Uganda Investment Authority, which facilitates investment in the country. "These remittances and technical knowledge/experience can be an alternative source of capital to drive African economies to middle- and upper-income status."[2]

Cash remittances—money sent home by citizens living abroad—have been among the most important forms of aid, experts say. In 2014, remittances to West Africa totaled $26 billion—including $21 billion to Nigeria alone—amounting to 3.2 percent of the region's GDP, according to the African Development Bank.[3] And since 2006, remittances from West Africans abroad have exceeded the region's foreign aid.[4]

A 2017 study by the African Center for Economic Transformation, a research organization in Accra, Ghana, found that remittances to six countries—Burkina Faso, Ghana, Rwanda, Tanzania, Uganda and Zambia—more than doubled over the previous decade.[5]

Somalia, long battered by terrorism, drought and deep poverty, receives about $1.3 billion in remittances annually, more than official aid to the country.[6] To help tap diaspora resources, international organizations in 2014 set up the Somali AgriFood Fund, a seed-capital fund aimed at spurring investments in Somali agriculture, food processing and fisheries.[7] The fund put $2.3 million in capital toward projects, $993,000 of which came from investments from the diaspora, and created over 200 full-time jobs, according to the fund's website.[8]

In addition to remittances, members of the African diaspora help by acquiring new skills abroad and then returning home. Although in the past Africa has suffered from a "brain drain," in which doctors, engineers and other skilled workers leave the continent for North America or Western

The most extreme example was in the Belgian Congo, where Leopold was determined to profit from a global rubber boom in the 1890s. During Leopold's murderous reign in the Congo, as many as 10 million people died from beatings, famine, disease and overwork, in what some have described as genocide.[58]

In the early 1960s a wave of independence movements in sub-Saharan Africa crested with 38 African states gaining independence by 1965. Another seven had followed by 1975.[59]

The region's new post-independence leaders had differing ideas about the continent's role in the world. Ghana's Kwame Nkrumah, for instance, espoused a pan-Africanism that Léopold Senghor of Senegal and Félix Houphouët-Boigny of Ivory Coast shunned in favor of Union Française, in which France retained close relations with its former colonies.[60]

With independence came hopes for greater economic prosperity and political empowerment. After returning from Africa in 1960, U.N. Secretary-General Dag Hammarskjöld captured the zeitgeist by declaring Africa "a continent launched on the road to cooperative success by new and able young leaders with the help and advice of the U.N."[61]

Yet the post-colonial era was politically tumultuous, with more than 70 coups in the first three decades.[62] At

Europe, many of those workers now are returning home to live and invest in their communities.

"Most of those investments are happening in cities, or at least they're very closely linked to the urban centers of these countries," such as Abidjan, Ivory Coast; Lagos, Nigeria; and Nairobi, Kenya, according to Jeffrey Paller, a University of San Francisco assistant professor of politics who specializes in urban sustainable development in Africa.

Efforts are underway to get more diaspora money to the African countryside, where cash is needed most. The International Fund for Agricultural Development (IFAD), a United Nations agency based in Rome, established a program to help post offices in Africa provide financial services and deliver remittances.[9]

"Post offices are ideally placed to deliver remittances in rural areas, but they often lack the business model, technology and expertise to process real-time payments such as remittances in an efficient and safe manner," according to IFAD. Lowering the cost of sending remittances is crucial, the agency says. With every 1 percent drop in remittance costs, African migrants and their families can save up to $500 million, according to the agency.[10]

The explosion of mobile money accounts on the continent also can facilitate greater remittance flows, according to research from the GSM Association, a group in London that represents the interests of mobile network operators.[11]

But because some mobile money services have been susceptible to scammers, combating fraud is key if African countries are to make the most of remittances, observers say.[12] For example, the Ghanaian subsidiary of telecom giant MTN said in October that it had sanctioned 3,000 mobile money vendors for perpetrating fraud.[13]

Sean Lyngaas

[1] Katherine Purvis, "Ebola: The Story of the Sierra Leone Diaspora Response That No One is Telling," *The Guardian*, Oct. 9, 2014, https://tinyurl.com/y89pvqrp.

[2] "Africa's Diaspora: A Key to the Continent's Middle to Upper Income Status," Uganda Investment Authority, Sept. 15, 2016, https://tinyurl.com/ybts77zj.

[3] *Ibid.*

[4] "Remittances from West Africa's Diaspora: Financial and Social Transfers for Regional Development," African Development Bank, Aug. 31, 2015, https://tinyurl.com/y7xj4ehq.

[5] "Mobilizing and Managing External Development Finance for Inclusive Growth: Six Countries' Experiences and Lessons," African Center for Economic Transformation, p. 19, https://tinyurl.com/ya3ztbfy.

[6] "Diaspora Investment in Agriculture (DIA) Initiative," International Fund for Agricultural Development, February 2016, p. 3, https://tinyurl.com/y7ytxfob.

[7] *Ibid.*

[8] "Somali AgriFood Fund," 2016, https://tinyurl.com/ybqghyxg.

[9] "African Postal Financial Services Initiative," International Fund for Agricultural Development, https://tinyurl.com/ya33vscw.

[10] *Ibid.*, p. 2.

[11] "Driving a Price Revolution: Mobile Money in International Remittances," GSMA, October 2016, https://tinyurl.com/yck6wyks.

[12] Alix Murphy, "Sending Cash Home: Mobile Money is a Game-Changer," *The Guardian*, Sept. 29, 2015, https://tinyurl.com/y78uf8jw.

[13] Suleiman Mustapha, "MTN Sanctions 3,000 Agents for Mobile Money Fraud," *Graphic Online*, Oct. 27, 2017, https://tinyurl.com/y85e24bb.

any given time during the 1970s, about 40 percent of African regimes were military in nature.[63] For example, the Ghanaian military overthrew Nkrumah in 1966 after taking exception to unequal conditions among soldiers and Nkrumah's attempts to plant political spies in the army.[64]

Many of the political changes that occurred during this period were manipulated by foreign powers in Cold War proxy struggles between the West and the Soviet Union. Western democracies often found themselves supporting autocrats who opposed left-leaning or socialist revolutionaries supported by the Soviets.[65]

For example, in 1961, less than a year after the Congo gained independence, the country's first prime minister, Patrice Lumumba, was executed. He had been forced from office a few months earlier in a power struggle, and his assassination was supervised by a Belgian officer and supported by the CIA, which feared Lumumba was a Soviet sympathizer.[66] In 1987, Thomas Sankara, the captivating young Marxist president of Burkina Faso, was assassinated in a coup led by his former deputy, Blaise Compaoré, who then led the country for 27 years.[67]

Elsewhere, post-independence leaders were loath to relinquish power. In Ivory Coast, Houphouët-Boigny was president from 1960 until his death in 1993. After leading Zimbabwe to independence in 1980, Robert Mugabe held power for 37 years before being forcibly removed from office at age 93.[68]

Democratic and Economic Reforms

A wave of democratization that coursed through the continent in the late 1980s and early '90s is still being felt today. About a third of those who were in power in 1988 have been driven from office, either voluntarily or involuntarily.[69]

For instance, Mathieu Kérékou, the longtime president of the West African nation of Benin, agreed to hold elections in 1991 in the face of popular pressure, and the country adopted a new constitution. Kérékou stepped down after losing the election, a move that resonated in other African countries, particularly Francophone ones.[70]

One of the most stirring moments in modern African history occurred in 1994, when South Africans elected Nelson Mandela president. A civil rights leader during the era of harsh, legalized racial segregation known as apartheid, Mandela had been arrested for treason and spent 27 years in prison. His election was a powerful symbol of the ability of democracy to transcend racial divisions.

"For a brief moment at the beginning of the 1990s, an exhilarating sense of African renewal took hold, reminiscent of the euphoria accompanying [African] independence," wrote historian Crawford Young.[71]

There was, however, a disturbing trend associated with Africa's democratic wave. By 2004, 18 leaders who held power in 1988 were still in office, according to Young.[72] In several countries, including Cameroon, Gabon and the Democratic Republic of Congo, so-called strongmen bent the political system to their will to stay in power.

Economically, the immediate post-World War II years were relatively prosperous for the African colonies and the independent states they would become. The final decade of colonialism—the 1950s—was the only period since the beginning of European colonization that saw a significant rise in wages.[73]

Although some countries established prosperous agricultural sectors, including Ivory Coast and Mali, others neglected agriculture in favor of industrialization.[74] However, sub-Saharan Africa's predominantly agriculture-based economy and poorly educated labor force made industrialization very difficult.[75]

In 1980, African nations were almost $300 billion in debt. A widespread debt crisis ensued, leaving many African countries facing bankruptcy, thwarting development progress and causing cuts in social and economic-development spending to repay the debt.[76]

"By the mid-1980s, most Africans were as poor or poorer than they had been at the time of independence," wrote journalist and historian Martin Meredith. Per capita GDP in Ghana, for example, was barely more in 1983 than it had been at independence in 1957.[77]

To spur growth in sub-Saharan Africa, the World Bank and the International Monetary Fund (IMF) called for a fresh market-oriented strategy to economic development. The institutions offered financial support to African governments on the condition that they enact stringent economic reforms—known as structural adjustment—such as cutting budgets, privatizing state enterprises and devaluing currencies. About 40 African governments agreed to such programs during the 1980s, and foreign aid became an ever more important part of African economies.[78]

Despite the rescue packages, however, the region's per capita income fell in the 1980s by 2.2 percent annually.[79] According to economist Morten Jerven, strong economic growth generally had been the norm in Africa in the 1950s, '60s, and '70s, but after the economic crisis and structural adjustment of the 1980s, "growth became the exception."[80]

The economic legacy of colonialism in Africa is overt in some places and less obvious in others. Françafrique—the system of political patronage and close business ties between France and its former colonies in West and Central Africa—continues in various forms today.[81] In October 2017, Teodorin Obiang, the son of Equatorial Guinea's president, was found guilty of embezzlement and money-laundering after he allegedly spent more than 1,000 times his official salary on such luxuries as sports cars and a Paris townhouse.[82]

Beginning in the mid-1990s, many African countries began growing faster and in turn saw higher incomes and falling poverty rates.[83] The growth was far from uniform—some countries lagged far behind. Economist Steven Radelet has attributed the economic expansion to, among other things, better governance that bred a better business environment; better macroeconomic policies, including smaller budget deficits; and expanded trade that improved the continent's access to new technologies.[84]

And while many African economies have benefited from a boom in prices for such commodities as copper, corn and cotton, analysts say expansion in other sectors, such as telecommunications and retailing, show that the growth has not been one-dimensional.[85]

"Africa Rising"

China's rapid economic growth in the 1990s and 2000s created high demand for energy and natural resources, contributing to Beijing's growing presence in Africa. In 2000, at the prompting of then-Chinese president Jiang Zemin, the Forum on China-Africa Cooperation held its first summit. China would eventually use the forum to pledge to double its development assistance to Africa, cancel outstanding debt, set up a $5 billion African development fund and build 30 hospitals, 100 rural schools and a new headquarters in Addis Ababa for the African Union, an assembly of African countries that seeks greater unity and solidarity among its 55 members.[86]

Signs of China's growing political and cultural influence in Africa have appeared alongside its expanding economic footprint.[87] China's state-run broadcaster opened an office in Nairobi in January 2012 focusing on African news, while *China Daily*, another government-controlled outlet, distributes a newspaper supplement on the continent.[88]

Sustained growth through the first decade of the 21st century bred the Africa Rising narrative, with some foreign observers declaring that Africa had finally arrived on the world stage.[89] In a 2014 speech in Maputo, Mozambique's capital, IMF Managing Director Christine Lagarde declared, "Africa has taken its destiny into its own hands. Now is the time to build the future." She also praised sub-Saharan Africa for "showing a remarkable resilience in the face of the [2008] global financial crisis."[90]

However, after commodity prices fell in 2014 and 2015, the region's dependence on exports of raw materials eroded economic growth. From 2013 to 2016, prices of copper, corn and cotton fell more than 20 percent, while oil prices plunged 50 percent.[91] GDP growth in sub-Saharan Africa fell from 5.1 percent in 2014 to just 1.4 percent in 2016, according to the IMF.[92]

Voters took notice. In December 2016 Ghanaians voted President John Mahama out of office in an election that became a referendum on the faltering economy.

His successor, Nana Akufo-Addo, pledged to renegotiate a $918 million loan with the IMF.[93]

The dwindling growth has coincided with a migration crisis that has seen thousands of people from sub-Saharan Africa attempt perilous journeys each year to Europe and elsewhere in search of a better life.[94] Between 2014 and 2017, at least 7,000 migrants perished trying to cross the central Mediterranean Sea from North Africa, the most heavily traveled route to Europe for African migrants.[95]

The pressure is on African leaders to create more jobs at home to stem the flow of migrants.

CURRENT SITUATION
Economics and Elections

Africa's three largest economies—Angola, Nigeria and South Africa—are showing signs of rebounding from the plunge in commodity prices that began in 2014. But the recovery has been tepid in Nigeria and South Africa, where the weak economies are likely to affect key elections in 2019.

Oxford Economics projects that GDP growth in Nigeria and South Africa in 2018 will be just 2.6 percent and 1.6 percent, respectively.[96]

Nigeria's slow growth is due to low global energy prices and inconsistent oil production due to periodic interruptions, according to Oxford Economics.

Experts say Nigeria's sluggish economy is likely to affect the presidential election in 2019. Critics of President Muhammadu Buhari, 75, who spent months in London receiving medical treatment in 2017, say he should not seek re-election, arguing the country needs younger leadership.[97] Opposition candidates see an opportunity to capitalize on the country's recent economic woes, and new political movements are springing up to tap into discontent with both the ruling and main opposition parties.

A lack of economic reform, the potential for violence in the oil-producing south and political jockeying prior to the election overshadow Nigeria's economic recovery, according to BMI Research, a London-based economic consultancy.[98] And despite being weakened by a military campaign in recent years, the Boko Haram terrorist group still carries out occasional mass-casualty bombings in its stronghold area in northeastern Nigeria.[99]

Two suicide bombings killed at least nine people in Maiduguri, Nigeria, on Oct. 29, 2016. Nigeria, along with Burkina Faso, Mali and Somalia, face the persistent threat of Islamist terrorism. While Nigeria has shrunk the operating space of Boko Haram and Somalia has done the same with Al Shabab, both domestic terrorist groups still periodically carry out successful attacks in those countries.

Meanwhile the South African economy suffers from weak consumer demand and lackluster business investment, according to the Organisation for Economic Co-operation and Development (OECD), an economic research institution in Paris composed of 35 member countries.[100]

The government also is dealing with fallout from a corruption probe into the Gupta brothers, powerful businessmen and associates of former President Zuma. South African police have raided the Gupta family home in connection with an investigation of the brothers' business holdings. A 2016 report from an anti-corruption watchdog accused the Guptas of trying to influence the appointment of cabinet ministers and of illegally being awarded government contracts.[101]

South Africa ranks 64th of 176 countries on Transparency International's Corruption Perception Index, in which higher numbers indicate greater corruption levels. Nigeria ranks 136th and Angola 164th.

Looking to cast a new course before 2019 elections and ditch an unpopular president dogged by scandal, a faction of the ANC ratcheted up pressure on Zuma to resign in February. After days of resisting, Zuma finally resigned on Feb. 14 in a televised address to the nation in which he said he had not been "the epitome of perfection," but added, "if truth be told, none of us are."[102]

His successor, Ramaphosa, a former union leader and one of the country's richest politicians, has called for an overhaul of the sluggish economy and a crackdown on corruption. "At the state level we must confront the reality that critical institutions of our state have been targeted by individuals and families," said Ramaphosa, in what some observers take to be a thinly veiled reference to Zuma and the Guptas.[103]

"From a political perspective, South Africa needs to urgently address economic roadblocks if the country is to avoid medium-term growth stagnation," says Gary van Staden, a senior political analyst at NKC African Economics, a political and economic risk firm based in South Africa. Delays in clearing up overtly political issues have been "regrettable and damaging, but we remain optimistic that once the political impasse is resolved we should be in a position to make some progress."

In Angola, the diamond- and oil-rich former Portuguese colony on Africa's southwestern coast, a battle is taking shape between newly elected President João Lourenço and the powerful dos Santos family. After succeeding repressive José Eduardo dos Santos, who ruled the country for 38 years, last September, Lourenço is moving to purge dos Santos allies and family members from positions of power. Lourenço has sacked the former intelligence and police chiefs and removed the former president's daughter, Isabel dos Santos, from her post as chair of the state-owned oil company. Analysts say he is fulfilling campaign promises to fight corruption and government-run monopolies.[104]

Despite the optimism surrounding Lourenço's crackdown on corruption, he faces a formidable task in rejuvenating Angola's oil-based economy. The economy grew at 1.1 percent in 2017, after zero growth the previous year, making that two-year economic performance the worst since Angola's 27-year civil war ended in 2002.[105]

Elsewhere on the continent, the fallout from last year's presidential election in Kenya has created a political crisis for a key Western ally with a multiparty democracy. The endgame of opposition leader Odinga, who rejected the election results that awarded President Kenyatta another term, remains unclear, analysts say.

AT ISSUE

Does foreign aid reliably spur sustained economic growth in sub-Saharan Africa?

YES Steven Radelet
*Donald F. McHenry Chair in
Global Human Development;
Director, Global Human Development
Program, Georgetown University*

Written for *CQ Researcher*, February 2018

NO Ryan C. Briggs
*Assistant Professor, Department of Political
Science, Virginia Tech*

Written for *CQ Researcher*, February 2018

There is growing evidence from independent researchers demonstrating that aid programs have helped spur growth and development in sub-Saharan Africa. Of course, aid programs do not always work, and no one claims they should be the major driver of growth. But there is now lots of empirical evidence showing the positive effects of aid on development and growth.

Aid programs have saved millions of lives in Africa, particularly programs on HIV/AIDS, malaria and child vaccination. Critics of aid tend to overlook the fact that most aid programs are aimed at health, education, food security and emergency relief, which have been very successful. Only a minority of programs focus on economic growth.

Still, the relationship between aid and growth is an important question that has been the focus of much debate over the years. The key drivers of growth are effective leadership in recipient countries and efforts by people in those countries to build strong economic and political institutions, invest in education and health and create more economic opportunities for people.

Aid programs cannot be the centerpiece of growth, but they can help support growth by investing in infrastructure, increasing agricultural productivity (partly through new technologies) and helping build financial systems. Aid has been particularly helpful in spurring growth during post-conflict reconstruction in countries such as Liberia, Sierra Leone, Mozambique and Rwanda.

The empirical evidence on aid and growth was hotly contested a decade ago, but in recent years the preponderance of research has shown a positive relationship between the two. *The World Bank Economic Review* in October 2016 provided an extensive review of that growing evidence, showing that sustained aid equivalent to 10 percent of GDP raises a country's growth rate by 1 percentage point, on average. For a country growing annually at 3 to 4 percent per capita, that extra growth is an important addition. Even *The Economist* magazine, long skeptical of aid, has changed its tune in recent years, concluding that most evidence shows aid boosts growth.

Aid programs do not always work. Neither do all business investments, diplomatic efforts or military efforts. And much can be done to improve aid programs. They are not a magic bullet to end poverty, but overall they have had a positive impact in spurring growth and development in Africa.

Foreign aid programs are not a reliable tool for spurring sustained economic growth. However, aid can reliably reduce poverty and is a valuable component of a broader development strategy.

The first problem with trying to use aid to increase growth is theoretical: There is no consensus on why economies grow or how to increase growth. Thus, trying to use aid to increase growth is like trying to navigate an expensive car through a city without a map. You might reach your destination, but that will be due largely to luck and clever improvisation. Aid is similar. We lack the theoretical knowledge required to use aid reliably to increase sustainable growth.

Second, we might think we have stumbled into reliable ways to use aid to boost growth if we see historical evidence that aid causes an increase in growth. This evidence exists, but it exists alongside research showing that aid does nothing or even hurts growth. This cacophony of clashing results is typical in research areas where scientists cannot randomize things, and it is difficult to find "natural experiments."

The countries or time periods with more aid are not like the countries or time periods with less. Thus, while we can see correlations in the data, it is incredibly hard to understand if aid is causing changes in growth. This means that we lack the information needed to learn how to better use aid to boost growth. And we cannot rely on theory for guidance, because we do not understand economic growth well enough.

But while aid is an unreliable tool for spurring sustained growth, it can be relied upon to lessen many dimensions of poverty. Anti-malarial bed nets, vaccines and anti-retroviral medication have saved tens of millions of lives. And cash transfers directly to the poor look very promising. But there is not much evidence that such effective, reliable anti-poverty work is moving the needle on long-run macroeconomic growth.

While aid can help reduce poverty, my research has shown that aid often does not reach the poorest people in Africa. Rather, it seems to flow to the relatively rich parts of those countries. We should devote more attention to ensuring that aid actually reaches the people who can benefit most from it.

Aid is a useful part of a broader development strategy aimed at combating poverty, even though it is unlikely to boost economic growth.

During Odinga's mock inauguration in Nairobi in late January, the government shut down local broadcasting stations and defied a court order to allow broadcasts to resume. The government also cracked down on the political opposition, declaring one opposition group an "organized criminal group."

"What we have seen is an emboldened opposition that is willing to take risks, and an administration that is often caught without a plan and therefore lashes out, often with deadly consequences," says Ken Opalo, an assistant professor at the Edmund A. Walsh School of Foreign Service at Georgetown University. Dozens of people died in post-election violence after the disputed 2017 election, and 1,200 died in violence that broke out following the disputed 2007 presidential election.[106]

After first criticizing the mock inauguration, the U.S. State Department urged government restraint. "We remain deeply concerned by [the Kenyan government's] intimidation and restriction of the media, and decision to disregard court orders to allow full resumption of broadcasting," tweeted State Department spokesperson Heather Nauert. "These actions undermine democracy and the rule of law. We have raised our concerns at the highest level."[107]

Other sub-Saharan countries, however, are taking note of the Kenyan court's decision to overturn the election results, according to Cheeseman, the University of Birmingham professor. "Other leaders in other African states, having seen what happened in Kenya, will be more carefully watching their judiciaries and more carefully thinking about how their judiciaries can get in the way of . . . elections," Cheeseman says.

Zambian President Edgar Lungu, for example, has warned Zambia's judges not to try to prevent him from running in the 2021 election.[108]

Tensions and Crises

Politics in the Democratic Republic of Congo (DRC) and Zimbabwe are unsettled.

The vast, mineral-rich DRC in Central Africa is often described as a "powder keg" because of the political uncertainty wrought by President Joseph Kabila's refusal to leave office after his second term, mandated by the constitution, and reflected in simmering armed conflicts in the country's east.[109]

"We don't see any leadership in Africa that is prepared to engage with a crisis that is happening [in the DRC]," says Cilliers of the Institute for Security Studies. "We know the DRC is going to explode. We know that, but nobody is engaged on it."

Ongoing fighting between government and rebel forces has triggered a humanitarian crisis.[110] Every day, 330 Congolese refugees enter Uganda fleeing the violence in eastern Congo, according to the U.N. Some 5 million Congolese have been displaced by the violence, most of whom are living in domestic camps for displaced persons. About 7.7 million people inside the country—nearly 10 percent of the population—face extreme hunger.[111]

The U.N. Security Council is worried about the "continued deterioration of the security situation and the worrisome humanitarian situation" in the DRC, said Council President Kairat Umarov of Kazakhstan.[112]

Meanwhile, observers across southern Africa are watching how things unfold in Zimbabwe now that Mugabe is gone. His successor, Emmerson Mnangagwa, has promised to attract foreign investors to the economy. "My government is committed to open Zimbabwe out to investment by building a free and transparent economy which benefits Zimbabweans and is welcoming to outsiders," said Mnangagwa.[113]

Mnangagwa also is promising that Zimbabwe will hold "free and fair" presidential elections in 2019, as scheduled.[114] A former vice president known as "The Crocodile" for his guerrilla tactics against the British during Zimbabwe's war for independence, Mnangagwa was in charge of internal security in Zimbabwe in the mid-1980s, when troops killed an estimated 20,000 civilians.[115]

The big question confronting Zimbabwe, according to the University of Birmingham's Cheeseman, is whether Mnangagwa, who is blamed for a crackdown on opposition parties in 2008, can change Zimbabwe's flawed political system.[116]

Meanwhile, sub-Saharan Africans who face unemployment or conflict at home continue to risk their lives to make the dangerous journey across the Mediterranean Sea to Europe. The years-long migrant crisis has resulted in thousands of drownings—more than 3,100 in 2017 alone—as well as detentions and deportations of thousands more by European immigration authorities.[117] But many Africans remain undeterred and vow to try the journey again if their prospects do not improve soon.[118]

Often they get stuck in Libya, the jumping-off spot for catching a smuggler's boat to Europe, where some end up being auctioned off as slaves, according to a CNN exposé last November. The report sent shockwaves across the region, with multiple African countries recalling their ambassadors to Libya in outrage.[119]

European leaders want African countries to help stem the migrant tide by creating jobs and bolstering security. The European and African unions have developed an emergency plan to break up smuggling networks and repatriate migrants, and Guinean President Alpha Conde has called for "humane solutions to this migration crisis that taints relations between the North and the South."[120]

OUTLOOK
Guarded Optimism

As commodity prices stabilize and domestic demand picks up, the World Bank projects GDP growth in sub-Saharan Africa will rise from an estimated 2.4 percent in 2017 to 3.5 percent in 2019.[121]

However, the outlook for the region's three biggest economies—Angola, Nigeria and South Africa—remains bleak, growing an average of no more than 2 percent annually through 2022, according to Coulibaly, the Brookings Institution scholar. That's not enough to keep up with population growth, he says. This slow growth could have particularly troubling implications for Nigeria as the country grapples with Boko Haram, he adds.

On the political side, experts are generally guardedly optimistic about the trajectory of democracy in sub-Saharan Africa. "I think it is inevitable," Cilliers, of the Institute for Security Studies, says of further democratization in the region. "As education levels rise, as income levels rise, people want to control their destinies and the destinies of their children."

Cheeseman, of the University of Birmingham, forecasts diverging trends for both democracy and governance on the continent. "We will see divergence for the next 5 to 10 years—with some states becoming increasingly democratic, others becoming increasingly authoritarian," he says. There also will be better economic management, he predicts, but declining respect for civil liberties as some governments seek to use development as a way to excuse repressive political systems.

Meanwhile, Bräutigam, the scholar of Chinese engagement in Africa, predicts that the rate of Chinese economic engagement in Africa will wane somewhat. Although bilateral trade has tapered off, she says, Beijing's economic footprint in Africa will continue to be strong. "The Chinese economy will continue to need elements that are available in Africa, and African countries are going to continue to be interested in the construction opportunities available from Chinese companies," she says.

Chinese companies have tended to favor their own nationals for mid-level and management jobs at their construction projects in sub-Saharan Africa. Journalist Howard W. French, who covered both China and Africa for *The New York Times* and has written a book on China in Africa, says that will have to change if African countries are to reap more from their relationship with Beijing.

"For whatever progress there's been, much more needs to be done in order to make many of these [Chinese-backed] projects truly sound value propositions for African nations," French says. "They should bargain much harder for mid- and upper-level training in the more sophisticated construction trade, in engineering and in project management."

Climate change also will be a major challenge to Africa's development in the coming years, according to multiple studies. A sample of 30 African countries found that two-thirds of them are warming faster than the world as a whole. Losses in crop yield and total output could be 20 to 30 percent by 2050.[122]

The ability of African countries to connect their young, often entrepreneurial populations with the global economy will be a key to the region's success, according to analysts.

"If Africans are successful at accelerating our participation in the global technology revolution, we will not only begin to solve Africa's most pressing challenges, we will in fact begin to solve the world's," wrote Seni Sulyman, Nigeria director for the tech company Andela.[123]

NOTES

1. "GDP Growth (Annual %)—Côte d'Ivoire," World Bank, 2018, https://tinyurl.com/y9dehsu8.

2. "Message à la Nation de SEM Alassane Ouattara, Président de la République," Abidjan.net, Jan. 2, 2016, https://tinyurl.com/yd86fmcb.

3. "Côte d'Ivoire: 2016 Article IV Consultation-Press Release; Staff Report; and Statement by the Executive Director for Côte d'Ivoire," International Monetary Fund, June 10, 2016, https://tinyurl.com/y9q29l2z. And see Sean Lyngaas, "'Social Discontent' Grips Ivory Coast as Economic Gains Pass Many By," *The New York Times*, March 28, 2017, https://tinyurl.com/ycrhz6hm.

4. Jeffrey Gettleman, "'Africa Rising?' 'Africa Reeling' May Be More Fitting Now," *The New York Times*, Oct. 17, 2016, https://tinyurl.com/ydaoq5ub.

5. "World Population Prospects, The 2017 Revision," Department of Economic and Social Affairs, United Nations, 2017, p. 1, https://tinyurl.com/ydhrcnn4.

6. "GDP growth (annual %)—Sub-Saharan Africa," World Bank, 2017, https://tinyurl.com/yc4xuzda; "GDP growth (annual %)—Latin America and Caribbean," World Bank, 2017, https://tinyurl.com/y8e9bufw; "GDP growth (annual %)—East Asia and Pacific," World Bank, 2017, https://tinyurl.com/y8mzzwab.

7. "Mauritius," *CIA World Factbook*, Jan. 23, 2018, https://tinyurl.com/24y37s.

8. "Africa Population 2018," *World Population Review*, https://tinyurl.com/ybjt8wqq.

9. Kimiko de Freytas-Tamura, "Kenyans Fear Chinese-Backed Railway Is Another 'Lunatic Express,'" *The New York Times*, June 8, 2017, https://tinyurl.com/y9g8y8z3. Also see Rachel Will, "China's Stadium Diplomacy," *World Policy Journal*, Summer 2012, https://tinyurl.com/6wp6rnn; and Howard W. French, *China's Second Continent: How a Million Migrants are Building a New Empire in Africa* (2014), p. 53.

10. "Data: China-Africa Trade," China Africa Research Initiative, School of Advanced International Studies, Johns Hopkins University, December 2017, https://tinyurl.com/yby6dohf.

11. "China Lends Africa More Than World Bank," ESI Africa, Jan. 3, 2012, https://tinyurl.com/y9bdg78n.

12. John Campbell, "Trump's Dangerous Retreat from Africa," *Foreign Policy*, Nov. 3, 2017, https://tinyurl.com/ycxatb9w.

13. David Pilling, "Chinese Investment in Africa: Beijing's Testing Ground," *Financial Times*, June 13, 2017, https://tinyurl.com/y9ak68dl.

14. Mogopodi Lekorwe *et al.*, "China's Growing Presence in Africa Wins Largely Positive Popular Reviews," *Afrobarometer*, Dispatch No. 122, Oct. 24, 2016, https://tinyurl.com/yb2ynpvq.

15. Austin Strange *et al.*, "China's Development Finance to Africa: A Media-Based Approach to Data Collection," Center for Global Development, Working Paper 323, April 2013, p. 1, https://tinyurl.com/yb2tv8br.

16. Axel Dreher *et al.*, "Aid on Demand: African Leaders and the Geography of China's Foreign Assistance," October 2016, AidData Working Paper 3 Revised, AidData, 2016, https://tinyurl.com/y8mrtx5s.

17. "Freedom in the World 2018," Freedom House, Jan. 16, 2018, p. 19, https://tinyurl.com/ydalfp3w.

18. Chiekh Sadibou Mane and Thierry Gouegnon, "Gambians Celebrate After Voting Out 'Billion Year' Leader," Reuters, Dec. 2, 2016, https://tinyurl.com/y88d8jt2.

19. Rael Ombuor and Paul Schemm, "Kenya's Supreme Court Annuls Presidential Election Result for Irregularities, Orders New Vote," *The Washington Post*, Sept. 1, 2017, https://tinyurl.com/y9o359cp.

20. Jason Burke, "Paul Kagame Re-elected President with 99% of Vote in Rwanda Election," *The Guardian*, Aug. 5, 2017, https://tinyurl.com/yd8j4l5p.

21. Wendell Roelf, "Ramaphosa Elected President of South Africa, Vows Anti-Corruption Fight," Reuters, Feb. 15, 2018, https://tinyurl.com/ybnza7g2.

22. Hennie Strydom, "The African Union Lacks a Coherent Plan to Fight Terrorism," *The Conversation*, May 13, 2015, https://tinyurl.com/y9huysw2. "Finding the Right Role for the G5 Sahel Joint Force," International Crisis Group, Report No. 258, Dec. 12, 2017, https://tinyurl.com/ybs8ck53.

23. "UNAIDS Data," Joint United Nations Program on HIV/AIDS, 2017, p. 5, https://tinyurl.com/ya8l5r6z.

24. "Global HIV and AIDS Statistics," Avert, 2017, https://tinyurl.com/kusdl78; Abdesslam Boutayeb, "The Impact of HIV/AIDS on human development in African countries," *BMC Public Health*, Vol. 9, Supplement 1, Nov. 18, 2009, https://tinyurl.com/y7vq5e6u.

25. "The World's Cities in 2016," United Nations, 2016, p. 5, https://tinyurl.com/zz3t9y9.

26. Tim McDonnell, "Slum Dwellers in Africa's Biggest Megacity Are Now Living in Canoes," NPR, May 15, 2017, https://tinyurl.com/ycy93up7.

27. "Bright Continent: The future of Africa's opportunity cities," Oxford Economics, 2012, p. 2, https://tinyurl.com/ycykc3at.

28. "Light Rail Transit in Addis Ababa," Centre for Public Impact, April 7, 2016, https://tinyurl.com/y7tojyof.

29. "Africa's Cities of the Future," *Africa Renewal*, April 2016, pp. 4, 11, U.N. Department of Public Information, https://tinyurl.com/ya2gjm4e.

30. Michael Bratton and Robert Mattes, "Do Africans Still Want Democracy?" *Afrobarometer Policy Paper No. 36*, November 2016, p. 11, https://tinyurl.com/y8ryewhk.

31. "Why Africa's Development Model Puzzles Economists," *The Economist*, Aug. 17, 2017, https://tinyurl.com/ybgu36xd. "African Economic Outlook 2017," African Development Bank, Organisation for Economic Co-operation and Development, U.N. Development Programme, 2017, p. 77, https://tinyurl.com/yadkjfaw.

32. "Jobs for Youth in Africa," African Development Bank Group, May 2016, https://tinyurl.com/y8zx7a57.

33. Lynsey Chutel, "Robots are Set to Take Africa's Manufacturing Jobs Even Before It Has Enough," *Quartz Africa*, July 26, 2017, https://tinyurl.com/yb4aaytm.

34. Calestous Juma, "Leapfrogging Progress: The Misplaced Promise of Africa's Mobile Revolution," *Breakthrough Journal*, Summer 2017, https://tinyurl.com/yanqnqxb.

35. *Ibid.*

36. "Africa's Pulse," The World Bank Group, October 2017, vol. 16, p. 50, https://tinyurl.com/y94n9tnm.

37. "Secondary Education," UNICEF, January 2018, https://tinyurl.com/ycvwgtal.

38. Akinyi Ochieng, "The World's Two Largest Cocoa Producers Want You to Buy Their Chocolate, Not Just Their Beans," *Quartz Africa*, May 12, 2017, https://tinyurl.com/ya24kpn3. "Agriculture Powering Africa's Economic Transformation," African Center for Economic Transformation, 2017, p. 25, https://tinyurl.com/yd95yklz.

39. "Foresight Africa: Top Priorities for the Continent in 2018," Africa Growth Initiative, Brookings Institution, January 2018, https://tinyurl.com/ycth86pm.

40. "Ethiopia-Djibouti Electric Railway Line Opens," BBC, Oct. 5, 2016, https://tinyurl.com/jog3xfe.

41. Thandika Mkandawire, "Can Africa Turn from Recovery to Development?," *Current History*, May 2014, https://tinyurl.com/yb5kubvb.

42. For background, see Suzanne Sataline, "Democracy Under Stress," *CQ Researcher*, Oct. 20, 2017, pp. 869-892.

43. "Freedom in the World 2018," Freedom House, p. 6, Jan. 16, 2018, https://tinyurl.com/ydalfp3w.

44. Sean Lyngaas, "With Election Defeat, Ghana's President Becomes Casualty of Faltering Economy," *The New York Times*, Dec. 9, 2016, https://tinyurl.com/yabye478.

45. Bratton and Mattes, *op. cit.*

46. "State of Fear: Arbitrary Arrests, Torture, and Killings," Human Rights Watch, Sept. 16, 2015, https://tinyurl.com/yd75e9ep.

47. Dionne Searcey and Jaime Yaya Barry, "Yahya Jammeh, Gambian President, Now Refuses to Accept Election Defeat," *The New York Times*, Dec. 9, 2016, https://tinyurl.com/y9uegtvm. "Ex-President Yahya Jammeh leaves The Gambia after losing election," BBC News, Jan. 22, 2017, https://tinyurl.com/ycou2n2q.

48. "Ethiopia," *CIA World Factbook*, Jan. 30, 2018, https://tinyurl.com/3d6bhw.

49. "Report: 669 Killed in Ethiopia Violence Since August," *Al Jazeera*, April 18, 2017, https://tinyurl.com/ldjqrcp.

50. "2017 Ibrahim Index of African Governance," Mo Ibrahim Foundation, p. 35, 2017, https://tinyurl.com/ybdnmnut.

51. Lily Kuo and Abdi Latif Dahir, "Foreign Election Observers Endorsed a Deeply Flawed Election in Kenya. Now They Face Questions," *Quartz Africa*, Sept. 6, 2017, https://tinyurl.com/y869zajh.

52. Maggie Fick and Katharine Houreld, "Kenya Supreme Court: presidential election contained irregularities," Reuters, Sept. 1, 2017, https://tinyurl.com/y87a89b2.

53. Laura Smith-Spark and Farai Sevenzo, "Kenya Supreme Court Nullifies Presidential Election, Orders New Vote," CNN, Sept. 2, 2017, https://tinyurl.com/yay64cj3.

54. Martin Meredith, *The Fortunes of Africa* (2014), p. 393. Adam Hochschild, *King Leopold's Ghost* (1998), p. 86.

55. Henry Louis Gates and Kwame Anthony Appiah, eds., *Encyclopedia of Africa* (2010), https://tinyurl.com/kmkca2p.

56. "Colonial Powers in Sub-Saharan Africa," *Geopolitical Futures*, June 2016, https://tinyurl.com/yccm6t6w.

57. Meredith, *op. cit.*, p. 493.

58. Hochschild, *op. cit.*, pp. 159, 161. Andrew Osborn, "Belgium Confronts Its Colonial Demons," *The Guardian*, July 18, 2002, https://tinyurl.com/yd36ovvb.

59. John Reader, *Africa: A Biography of the Continent* (1997), p. 663.

60. Meredith, *op. cit.*, p. 61.

61. Crawford Young, *The Post-Colonial State in Africa* (2012), p. 351.

62. Reader, *op. cit.*, p. 663.

63. Young, *op. cit.*, p. 496.

64. Meredith, *op. cit.*, p. 191.

65. For background, see Jason McLure, "Sub-Saharan Democracy," *CQ Researcher*, Feb. 15, 2011, pp. 79-106.

66. Meredith, *op. cit.*, p. 110.

67. Mohamed Keita, "Why Burkina Faso's Late Revolutionary Leader Thomas Sankara Still Inspires Young Africans," *Quartz Africa*, May 31, 2015, https://tinyurl.com/y6vumlmj.

68. Joseph Winter, "Robert Mugabe: Is Zimbabwe's Ex-President a Hero or Villain?" BBC, Nov. 21, 2017, https://tinyurl.com/y8orq5ef.

69. Young, *op. cit.*, p. 674.

70. *Ibid.*, p. 674.

71. *Ibid.*, p. 702.

72. *Ibid.*, p. 703.

73. *Ibid.*, p. 380.

74. Meredith, *op. cit.*, pp. 618-619.

75. Gareth Austin, "African Economic Development and Colonial Legacies," *International Development Policy Review*, 2010, pp. 11-32.

76. Henry F. Jackson, "The African Crisis: Drought and Debt," *Foreign Affairs*, Summer 1985, https://tinyurl.com/y9mykbwo.

77. Meredith, *op. cit.*, p. 621; Austin, *op. cit.*

78. Meredith, *op. cit.*, p. 623.

79. *Ibid.*

80. Morten Jerven, *Africa: Why Economists Get It Wrong* (2015), p. 88.

81. Pierre Haski, "The Return of Françafrique," *The New York Times*, July 21, 2013, https://tinyurl.com/y7kw5uyo.

82. "Paris Court Gives Equatorial Guinea President's Son Suspended Sentence in Graft Trial," France 24, Oct. 27, 2017, https://tinyurl.com/ybcn3tgh.

83. Steven Radelet, "Africa's Rise—Interrupted?" International Monetary Fund, June 2016, vol. 53, no. 2, https://tinyurl.com/y7nhskss.

84. Radelet, *op. cit.*

85. Acha Leke *et al.*, "What's Driving Africa's Growth," McKinsey & Company, June 2010, https://tinyurl.com/ybxk5mef.

86. French, *op. cit.*, p. 12.

87. For background, see Karen Foerstel, "China in Africa," *CQ Global Researcher*, Jan. 1, 2008, pp. 1-26.

88. "About CCTV Africa," Jan. 11, 2012, CCTV.com English, https://tinyurl.com/ybcbplfo.

89. Brahima Sangafowa Coulibaly, "In Defense of the 'Africa Rising' Narrative," Brookings Institution June 27, 2017, https://tinyurl.com/y8fvuutg.

90. Christine Lagarde, "Africa Rising—Building to the Future, Keynote Address by Christine Lagarde, Managing Director, IMF," International Monetary Fund, May 29, 2014, https://tinyurl.com/ycrupplb.

91. Radelet, *op. cit.*

92. "Regional Economic Outlook: Restarting the Growth Engine," International Monetary Fund, May 2017, https://tinyurl.com/y9yt3sb6.

93. Lyngaas, "With Election Defeat, Ghana's President Becomes Casualty of Faltering Economy," *op. cit.*; Kwasi Kpodo, "UPDATE 2-Ghana's new government says it will review $918 million IMF deal," Reuters, Jan. 20, 2017, https://tinyurl.com/y7aj2yc4.

94. Dirke Köpp and Babou Diallo, "Senegal: Migrants Leaving in Thousands," *DW*, April 30, 2015, https://tinyurl.com/qzbfflf.

95. See Frank Laczko, Ann Singleton and Julia Black, eds., "Fatal Journeys: Improving Data on Missing Migrants, Vol. 3, Part 1," International Organization For Migration, 2017, Table 2, p. 8, https://tinyurl.com/yd7m95r4.

96. "Research Briefing: Africa," Oxford Economics, January 2018, p. 2.

97. "Muhammadu Buhari Gears Up for a Second Presidential Term," *The Economist*, Jan. 31, 2018, https://tinyurl.com/ya3rzv3r.

98. "Political Risk Analysis—Key Political Risks Could Derail Recovery," BMI Research, November 2017, https://tinyurl.com/ycdllwz2.

99. Ruth Maclean, "Nigeria Mosque Attack: Suicide Bomber Kills Dozens," *The Guardian*, Nov. 21, 2017, https://tinyurl.com/yasotvjq.

100. "OECD Economic Surveys: South Africa," Organisation for Economic Co-operation and Development, July 2017, p. 10, https://tinyurl.com/y7hd2ykr.

101. Alexander Winning, "Factbox: South Africa's Divisive President—Zuma's Many Scandals,"

Reuters, Feb. 14, 2018, https://tinyurl.com/yasyc25t; Joseph Cotterill, "Net Closes on South Africa's Guptas as Zuma's Power Wanes," *Financial Times*, Jan. 27, 2018, https://tinyurl.com/ydexx523.

102. Norimitsu Onishi, "Jacob Zuma Resigns as South Africa's President," *The New York Times*, Feb. 14, 2018, https://tinyurl.com/yblwbgcg.

103. Alexander Winning and James Macharia, "South Africa's new ANC leader Ramaphosa aims to fight corruption," Reuters, Dec. 20, 2017, https://tinyurl.com/ybpggr3l.

104. Henrique Almeida and Pauline Bax, "Lourenço Proves He's No One's Puppet in Angola," Bloomberg, Jan. 17, 2018, https://tinyurl.com/y7nekljf; Stephen Eisenhammer, "Angola's Lourenço Replaces Police and Intelligence Chiefs," Reuters, Nov. 20, 2017, https://tinyurl.com/y8rp3fct; Candido Mendes and Henrique Almeida, "Angola's President Fires Dos Santos' Daughter as Sonangol Boss," Bloomberg, Nov. 15, 2017, https://tinyurl.com/y8mcr8xa.

105. Almeida and Bax, *op. cit.*

106. John Aglionby, "Kenya death toll rises in post-election violence," *Financial Times*, Aug. 13, 2017, https://tinyurl.com/y9fymk6m.

107. Heather Nauert, Feb. 8, 2018, https://tinyurl.com/yd7dg3ob.

108. Merrit Kennedy, "Congo a 'Powder Keg' as Security Forces Crack Down on Whistling Demonstrators," NPR, Dec. 21, 2016, https://tinyurl.com/y9jpjnea.

109. "Zambia president warns judges not to follow Kenya's lead," *Daily Nation*, Nov. 3, 2017, https://tinyurl.com/y99crske.

110. For background, see Josh Kron, "Conflict in Congo," *CQ Global Researcher*, April 5, 2011, pp. 157-182.

111. "DRC Congo Violence Sees Surge in Refugees Fleeing Eastwards," United Nations High Commissioner for Refugees, Jan. 30, 2018, https://tinyurl.com/y7z3em9e.

112. "Security Council Press Statement on Democratic Republic of the Congo," United Nations, Jan. 16, 2018, https://tinyurl.com/ycfozrf8.

113. "Emmerson Mnangagwa Vows to Open Zimbabwe to Investors," Al Jazeera, Dec. 21, 2017, https://tinyurl.com/yacz3tcj.

114. Anita Powell, "Mugabe's Presumptive Successor, Emmerson Mnangagwa, is Called 'the Crocodile,'" Voice of America, Nov. 21, 2017, https://tinyurl.com/y7q4ovcf. Jason Burke, "Emmerson Mnangagwa Promises 'Free and Fair' Elections in Zimbabwe," *The Guardian*, Nov. 24, 2017, https://tinyurl.com/y9gmmv9q.

115. Sebastian Mhofu, "Zimbabwe Activists Seek Truth About 1980s Massacres," Voice of America, Jan. 10, 2018, https://tinyurl.com/yagsbdnz.

116. Jason Burke, "Zimbabwe Activists Fear Post-Mugabe Human Rights Crackdown," *The Guardian*, Nov. 26, 2017, https://tinyurl.com/ya9ys4ns.

117. For background, see Sarah Glazer, "European Migration Crisis," *CQ Researcher*, July 31, 2015, pp. 649-672. "Mediterranean Migrant Arrivals Reached 171,635 in 2017; Deaths Reach 3,116," International Organization for Migration, Jan. 5, 2018, https://tinyurl.com/y72gcfpa.

118. Nellie Payton, "Rescued from Libya, Jobless Senegalese Migrants Likely to Return," Thomson Reuters Foundation, Dec. 5, 2017, https://tinyurl.com/yasjwa6e.

119. Nima Elbagir *et al.*, "People for Sale," CNN, Nov. 14, 2017, https://tinyurl.com/ya3bzvn7; Thiam Ndiaga, "Burkina Faso Recalls Ambassador to Libya Over 'Slave Markets' Report," Reuters, Nov. 20, 2017, https://tinyurl.com/yb88hn4g.

120. James McAuley and Isaac Stanley-Becker, "Can Africa Thwart the Next Migration Crisis? European Leaders Think So," *The Washington Post*, Aug. 28, 2017, https://tinyurl.com/y7o9nojd; Marine Pennetier and Andreas Rinke, "EU, U.N., African Leaders Draw up Emergency Plan for Migrants in Libya," Reuters, Nov. 30, 2017, https://tinyurl.com/y7qxooas; Joe Bavier, "EU's Tusk: Africa, EU Must Cooperate to End 'Horrifying' Migrant Abuses," Reuters, Nov. 29, 2017, https://tinyurl.com/y7afjfxl.

121. "The World Bank in Africa," World Bank, Oct. 11, 2017, https://tinyurl.com/y72lfygp.

122. "Foresight Africa," *op. cit.*

123. Seni Sulyman, 'Why Africa is the Key to Advancing Human Potential," CNN, Oct. 17, 2017, https://tinyurl.com/y9qwxr4l.

BIBLIOGRAPHY
Selected Sources
Books

French, Howard W., *China's Second Continent: How a Million Migrants are Building a New Empire in Africa*, Vintage, 2015.
A journalist tells the story of China's growing engagement in Africa through the eyes of enterprising Chinese migrants who have started new lives on the continent.

Jerven, Morten, *Africa: Why Economists Get It Wrong*, Zed Books, 2015.
A Norwegian economist challenges conventional wisdom on historical economic growth patterns in Africa.

Meredith, Martin, *The Fate of Africa: A History of The Continent Since Independence*, PublicAffairs, 2011.
A journalist who spent decades in Africa chronicles its tumultuous post-independence years.

Meredith, Martin, *The Fortunes of Africa: A 5,000-Year History of Wealth, Greed, and Endeavor*, PublicAffairs, 2014.
A journalist, historian and biographer traces the saga of Africa's wealth and its plundering over five millennia.

Young, Crawford, *The Postcolonial State in Africa: Fifty Years of Independence, 1960-2010*, The University of Wisconsin Press, 2012.
A professor emeritus of political science at the University of Wisconsin-Madison breaks down five decades of ebbs and flows in African history into digestible chunks.

Articles

Cheeseman, Nic, "Why Rwanda's development model wouldn't work elsewhere in Africa," *The Conversation*, Jan. 8, 2018, https://tinyurl.com/y8fygovo.
A professor of democracy and international development at the University of Birmingham in the United Kingdom rebuts claims that Rwanda's authoritarian development model would work in other African countries.

Coulibaly, Brahima Sangafowa, "In defense of the 'Africa Rising' narrative," Brookings Institution, June 27, 2017, https://tinyurl.com/y8fvuutg.
The director of the Africa Growth Initiative at a Washington think tank argues that the recent slowdown in economic growth in sub-Saharan Africa is not as worrisome as some claim.

Elbagir, Nima, *et al.*, "People for Sale: Where lives are auctioned for $400," CNN, Nov. 14, 2017, https://tinyurl.com/y9jzsryy.
A CNN investigation reveals that smuggling rings in Libya are auctioning off would-be migrants as slaves.

Gettleman, Jeffrey, "'Africa Rising'? 'Africa Reeling' May Be More Fitting Now," *The New York Times*, Oct. 17, 2016, https://tinyurl.com/ydaoq5ub.
A journalist tries to reconcile relatively strong economic performance in many African countries with political unrest on the continent.

Kuo, Lily, "Africa is changing China as much as China is changing Africa," *Quartz Africa*, Jan. 8, 2018, https://tinyurl.com/ybl7omr7.
Chinese engagement in Africa is more complex and multi-faceted than many realize, according to a reporter based in Kenya.

Pilling, David, and Joseph Cotterill, "Jacob Zuma, the Guptas and the Selling of South Africa," *The Financial Times*, Nov. 30, 2017, https://tinyurl.com/ya7nazzy.
Two journalists explain how rampant corruption has led to political disillusionment in South Africa.

Reports and Studies

"African Transformation Report 2017: Agriculture Powering Africa's Economic Transformation," African Center for Economic Transformation, 2017, https://tinyurl.com/yd95yktz.
A think tank in Ghana reports on agriculture's potential to transform the economies of many African countries.

Austin, Gareth, "African Economic Development and Colonial Legacies," International Development Policy, 2010, https://tinyurl.com/ycet9nfh.
A professor of African economic history at the London School of Economics and Political Science traces the myriad ways colonialism has affected African economies.

Coulibaly, Brahima S., ed., "Foresight Africa: Top Priorities for the Continent in 2018," Africa Growth Initiative, Brookings Institution, January 2018, https://tinyurl.com/ycth86pm.
A think tank in Washington provides a collection of essays by experts on Africa, including some sitting African presidents, answering complicated questions about how the continent can grow rapidly and equitably.

Mattes, Robert, and Michael Bratton, "Do Africans still want democracy?" *Afrobarometer Policy Paper No. 36*, November 2016, https://tinyurl.com/y8ryewhk.
The director of the Democracy in Africa Research Unit at the University of Cape Town (Mattes) and a professor of political science and African studies at Michigan State University (Bratton) offer a rich dataset on attitudes toward democracy in Africa.

For More Information

Africa Research Institute, 55 Tufton St., London, United Kingdom, SW1P 3QL; +44 (0)207 222 4006; https://www.africaresearchinstitute.org. Delivers timely analysis of trends in African politics.

African Center for Economic Transformation, Castle Road, Ridge PMB CT4, Cantonments Accra, Ghana; +233 (0) 302 210 240; and 1776 K St., N.W., Suite 200, Washington, DC 20006; 202-833-1919; http://acetforafrica.org. Think tank with a deep roster of experts on the economic challenges facing Africa.

African Union, P.O. Box 3243, Roosevelt St. (Old Airport Area), W21K19, Addis Ababa, Ethiopia; +251 11 551 77 00; https://au.int. Multilateral African organization with 55 member countries that promotes democracy in Africa.

Institute for Security Studies, Block C, Brooklyn Court, 361 Veale Street, New Muckleneuk, Pretoria, South Africa 0181; +27 12 346 9500/2; https://issafrica.org. Think tank that specializes in African security issues.

REPOA, 157 Mgombani St., Regent Estate, P.O. Box 33223, Dar es Salaam, Tanzania; +255 (22) 270 0083; www.repoa.or.tz. Independent research institution, formerly called Research on Poverty Alleviation, focusing on poverty reduction and inequality.

United Nations Development Program in Africa, Main Bole Road, Olympia Roundabout, DRC St., P.O. Box 60130, Addis Ababa, Ethiopia; www.africa.undp.org. The main African bureau of the U.N. agency dedicated to development.

UN-Habitat Regional Office for Africa, P.O. Box 30030, GPO, Nairobi, 00100, Kenya; 254-20 7621234; https://unhabitat.org/roaf/. The African office of the U.N. agency dealing with urban development challenges.

6

India Today

Jonathan Broder

A child sits in the remains of his house, one of 250 structures demolished in June during a slum clearance in Bangalore. The city is India's technology hub and a primary economic driver, but it also exemplifies the nation's income disparity problem. India is producing a growing number of billionaires, but one-fifth of the population lives in extreme poverty.

From *CQ Researcher*,
October 5, 2018

Last July, Kaalu Ram, 26, was searching for a job in Bangalore—a city of 10 million people in southern India—just as false rumors about child abductions were spreading virally throughout the country on social media.

Suddenly, the poor, uneducated residents of one Bangalore neighborhood convinced themselves that the stranger in their midst was a kidnapper. As Ram walked under an overpass, locals overpowered him, bound his hands and feet and dragged him through the street where a frenzied mob kicked and beat him, some with cricket bats. He died on the way to the hospital.

Ram was one of nearly two dozen victims of such mob violence since May, triggered by false kidnapping rumors spread on the internet.[1]

Such deaths underscore some of the major challenges confronting India's Prime Minister Narendra Modi as he seeks another five-year term next year: There is the tendency toward mob violence in the sprawling nation of 1.3 billion people deeply riven by differences in income, education, religion, language and caste. And while India's growing middle class may live in modern, brightly lit cities, 22 percent of the population still lives in extreme poverty.[2]

Bangalore, known as India's Silicon Valley, is a classic example of the economic split plaguing modern India. It is home to one of the world's most educated workforces and the country's high-tech industry, which is a major economic driver of the nation's $2.6 trillion economy—the world's sixth largest.[3] But every month an estimated 1 million young Indians like Ram enter the country's official job market, which can absorb only a fraction of them, according to Shailesh Kumar, Asia director

India Is World's Largest Democracy

India is the world's largest democracy, the second most populous country after China, and it has the world's fastest growing major emerging economy. Its population of 1.3 billion is nearly 80 percent Hindu but includes more than 180 million Muslims.

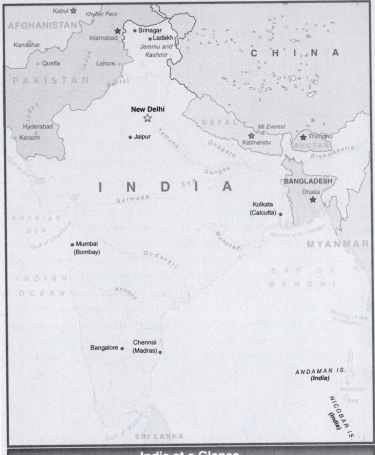

India at a Glance

Area	1.2 million square miles, just over one-third the size of the United States
Population	1.28 billion (July 2017 est.)
Unemployment rate	8.8 percent (2017 est.)
Average per capita GDP	$1,939 (2017)
Annual GDP growth rate	7.3 percent (2018-19 est.)
Religion	Hindu—79.8 percent; Muslim—14.2 percent; Christian—2.3 percent; Sikh—1.7 percent; other and unspecified—2 percent (2011 est.)

Sources: "The World Factbook," Central Intelligence Agency, https://tinyurl.com/ypn8hx; "GDP per capita (current US$)," World Bank Group, https://tinyurl.com/y967okgt

for the Eurasia Group, a global business consultancy. Millions more remain either unemployed or underemployed in the "informal" or off-the-books economy. And although the middle class has expanded significantly over the past 25 years, slums such as those surrounding Bangalore are a reminder that 260 million Indians still live on less than $1.90 a day.[4]

Modi led his right-wing, Hindu nationalist Bharatiya Janata Party (BJP) to a sweeping victory in 2014 by promising to reduce poverty and create jobs, in part by overhauling the over-regulated economy and by combating chronic corruption. But to achieve those goals he faces additional hurdles besides the growing income disparity exemplified by Bangalore. Rising crime is a major social concern, polls show, and farmers have been staging angry protests about the alarming rates at which they have been losing their land due to high bank interest rates and low crop prices. Internationally, meanwhile, fears that India is being eclipsed in the region by China, its economically and militarily stronger northern neighbor, have led Modi to strengthen India's armed forces and strategic ties to the United States.[5]

Most analysts agree Modi has largely delivered on economic growth. India's gross domestic product (GDP), the value of goods and services produced by the country, has grown at an impressive annual rate of 7.3 percent, on average, under Modi's watch.[6] His most notable economic achievements, analysts say, include a long-promised nationwide tax on goods and services that replaced a hodgepodge of state business taxes and the first comprehensive bankruptcy law, which is enabling banks to address a mountain of bad loans that have hampered lending and investment.

And, in a radical assault on counterfeiting, bribery and tax evasion, Modi introduced a demonetization policy in 2016 that overnight banned the country's largest currency bills and required people to exchange them at banks for new bills or old ones of smaller denominations. To make the exchange, people had to open a registered bank account and, most importantly, explain how they got their cash. Those who could not credibly account for their money face investigation.[7]

"He's done very well, given the rocky economic situation he inherited when he took office," says Arvind Panagariya, a senior official in Modi's government until last year and a former chief economist at the Asian Development Bank, a Manila, Philippines-based multilateral institution that provides subsidized loans to developing Asian countries. For instance, under Modi's watch India's annual inflation rate has fallen from 10 percent to about 4 percent, he says.

However, critics say Modi has failed to overhaul India's restrictive land, labor and trade laws and failed to privatize failing state-run industries. Labor-rights advocates also say he has done little to prevent the exploitation of Indians working at clothing factories for major U.S. and multinational brands, such as Gap, Hugo Boss and H&M.[8]

Modi is promising voters his policies will produce sustained double-digit economic growth, but economists such as Kumar say that will not happen without major reforms. "The most they can hope for is low- to mid-sevens or possibly 8 percent growth," says Kumar.

Modi's critics also say he has used his fierce Hindu nationalism in the predominantly Hindu country to suppress India's Muslim minority. For weeks, they charge, Modi ignored a recent wave of virulent intolerance by Hindus, including violent mob attacks against Muslims accused of eating beef or slaughtering cows, considered sacred by Hindus. He also failed to intervene when the state of Uttar Pradesh published a government tourism booklet last year deliberately dropping any mention of the Taj Mahal, the state's storied mausoleum built by the 17th-century Muslim emperor Shah Jahan.[9] And Modi's party recently appointed a Hindu priest who has

referred to Muslims as "two-legged animals" as the state's chief minister. Uttar Pradesh is India's most populous state and a springboard to national office.[10]

"They took one of the most extreme figures in the party and gave him one of the most important jobs in Indian politics," says Sadanand Dhume, an India expert at the American Enterprise Institute, a conservative think tank in Washington. "It clearly sent a signal that extremism pays in the BJP."

The religious strife also plays out in perennial tensions between India and its predominantly Muslim archrival, Pakistan, creating the ever-present potential for armed conflict. The neighboring nuclear powers have fought three wars and countless skirmishes over the disputed region of Kashmir, and India accuses Pakistan of supporting decades of terrorist attacks in India by Kashmiri separatists.

Meanwhile, Modi has carefully maintained a cordial, if strained, relationship with neighboring China, India's major trading partner and principal geostrategic rival. The two countries have several unresolved border disputes, over which they fought a brief war in 1962. Also complicating New Delhi's relations with Beijing: China maintains close ties with Pakistan and is adopting an increasingly assertive economic posture across South Asia, which India has dominated for decades.

China recently has established major footholds in Sri Lanka, Bangladesh, Nepal and the Maldive islands as part of an ambitious $900 billion infrastructure project of roads, railways, ports and shipping routes designed to connect China to markets and raw materials across Asia, Europe, Africa and Latin America. Fearing that China's so-called Belt and Road Initiative (BRI) will undermine India's stature in the region, Modi so far has rejected Beijing's invitation to participate in the project and instead has noted that a BRI spur is being built on disputed land in Pakistan.[11]

Such concerns have prompted India to build up its military capabilities and draw closer to the United States, which also wants to restrain China's regional aspirations. U.S. and Indian concerns also overlap regarding Pakistan, a longtime U.S. ally that American intelligence officials say is covertly supporting militant groups in Afghanistan, including the Taliban, a domestic insurgency that Washington and New Delhi have spent nearly two decades trying to help Afghanistan quash.[12]

Other aspects of India-U.S. relations have been fraught. The Trump administration has not ruled out imposing economic sanctions on India if it proceeds with plans to buy an advanced S-400 Russian anti-aircraft missile system. And after President Trump imposed tariffs in May on imported steel and aluminum, some of which comes from India, New Delhi retaliated with levies on U.S.-made motorcycles and several other U.S. imports.

A much larger issue, however, is Washington's renewed sanctions on Iran, aimed at choking off Iranian oil exports in an effort to force Tehran to permanently abandon what U.S. officials say are its nuclear weapons ambitions. Iran denies it has such ambitions. India, the second-largest consumer of Iranian oil, has told the United States it cannot afford to stop importing oil from Iran.

Meanwhile, India, which used to abstain in international forums on many global issues, has increasingly been willing to use its soft power to try to shape world events. For example, in 2015 India stopped opposing carbon emission caps and announced at the Paris climate change conference that it would implement an ambitious solar energy program to radically reduce the country's dependence on fossil fuels. A new multilateral organization called the International Solar Alliance, which raises money for the program, is now headquartered in India.[13]

Yet, despite its economic and military clout and its status as the world's second most populous country after China, India still does not have a permanent seat on the United Nations Security Council, something New Delhi—and many experts—strongly feel it deserves. Experts say politics and geopolitical rivalries have prevented India's accession to a permanent seat.

Amid these challenges, here are some key questions being asked about India's economic and geopolitical future:

Can India's economic growth be sustained?

India will remain the world's fastest growing major emerging economy for the next few years, according to the World Bank's latest three-year projection. As the country adjusts to Modi's demonetization policy and his goods and services tax, the nation's GDP is expected to grow by 7.3 percent in 2018 and 7.5 percent in 2019 and 2020, the bank says.[14]

"India's economy . . . is robust, resilient and has potential to deliver sustained growth," said Ayhan Kose, director of the World Bank's Development Prospects Group, which produces the global lender's macroeconomic forecasts.[15]

The favorable forecasts are consistent with an economic trajectory that has been rising, along with an expanding middle class, since 1991, when India abandoned its socialist model and embraced free-market principles.

The extent of middle-class growth, however, varies wildly, depending on how that economic label is defined. A study by two Mumbai University economists found that between 2004 and 2012 the middle class—defined as people spending between $2 and $10 a day—doubled in size to 600 million, or nearly half of the nation's population.[16] An analysis by Euromonitor International, a global business research firm based in London, said the number of Indian households with high disposable incomes—more than $10,000 a year—rose twentyfold over the 25 years from 1990 to 2015—from 2.5 million to 50 million.[17]

Gross Domestic Product Doubled in Past Decade

India's gross domestic product (GDP), a measure of all goods and services produced within a country, rose from $1.2 trillion in 2007 to $2.6 trillion last year.

India's GDP, 1996-2017
(in current $US, seasonally adjusted)

(in $ Trillions)

Source: "GDP (current US$)," The World Bank, updated Sept. 21, 2018, https://tinyurl.com/ycxp3rqe

The country's healthy economic growth rate, however, fails to reflect the poverty that continues to afflict one in five Indians and their growing anger about what they regard as Modi's failure to provide them with jobs and better lives.

Vikram Nehru, an economics professor at the Johns Hopkins School of Advanced International Studies in Washington, says the economic growth statistics reflect only workers in the country's official economy—those with government or industry jobs. "The majority of Indians belong to the unofficial economy," he says, toiling as subsistence farmers, street peddlers, unregistered factory workers or in other jobs that barely earn them a living.

Nonetheless, economists generally agree that rising consumption by the growing middle class, government spending and increased foreign direct investment likely will keep India's economy humming along at a growth rate of 7 percent to 8 percent for at least another five years and probably longer. But this will only happen, they caution, if oil prices do not rise significantly and if the government that emerges after next year's elections does not create new economic hurdles.

"India can continue to perform quite well, but there are some caveats," says Rajiv Biswas, the Singapore-based chief economist for Asia at IHS Markit, a global business intelligence firm. "Inflation could grow if oil prices go significantly higher." India is particularly vulnerable because it imports 70 percent of its oil, he says.

Much also depends on how the government spends its $350 billion fiscal 2019 budget, says the Eurasia Group's Kumar. Before Modi, most government spending went to subsidies and welfare, he says. "Now a third of the budget goes to infrastructure—roads, railways and ports—which makes getting goods to market faster and doing business easier," he says.

Large amounts of foreign direct investment, which totaled a record $60 billion last year, according to Kumar, also helps drive growth. Similar investments will continue for the next three or four years, he says.

Many economists say Modi's policies, such as the goods and services tax, the new bankruptcy law and demonetization, have improved some of the fundamental architecture of India's hidebound economy. For example, the bankruptcy law will enable the speedy dissolution of failing enterprises, which used to take between 10 and 25 years, says Panagariya, the former

A technician sets up a display of surveillance equipment during a space technology expo in Bangalore on Sept. 6, 2018. India is considered a world leader in technology.

AFP/Getty Images/Manjunath Kiran

Modi official who is currently an economics professor at Columbia University in New York. During that period, the failed companies would be in government receivership and were forced to continue paying employees.

That discouraged new startups, says Panagariya, "unless you could be sure you were going to succeed, [because] if you failed, you wouldn't be able to exit." The new law also has enabled India's largely government-run banks to start cleaning up $114 billion in debts from bad loans, he adds. "This was a very big reform with very substantial long-term implications," Panagariya says.

But he and other economists caution that the bankruptcy law will take years to contribute to India's economic growth because it undoubtedly will be challenged in the nation's notoriously backlogged courts. "It takes years to bring cases to court," largely due to a shortage of judges, Panagariya says. "And lawyers are paid by the day, so they have an incentive to drag out cases."

It will also take time for the complicated new tax law to bolster economic growth, economists add. Instead of a single, flat tax, the law imposed four different tax rates for various classes of goods and services, allowed numerous exceptions and required businesses to file returns 37 times a year. Thus, the tax will raise costs and cause confusion initially, experts say, but once businesses get used to the new regime it could add a couple of percentage points to economic growth. Meanwhile, the demonetization policy already is adding to government coffers, they say.

While Modi has promised he will help India attain 10 percent growth into the next decade, economists say restrictive trade policies and rigid land and labor laws must be overhauled before that can happen. In addition, India has some of the world's most restrictive trade policies, says Nehru. "After the initial flurry of economic liberalization in 1992," Nehru says, "things have been going backwards" in recent years, and "tariffs have increased under the Modi regime as the elections draw near."

Moreover, Nehru says, under India's labor laws companies with 100 or more workers must obtain government permission to fire someone, which is rarely given. A new law allows companies to hire temporary contract workers but retains protections for existing workers. "Firms which aren't doing well can't shrink," Nehru says, "and their inability to reallocate their resources reduces growth."

The lack of an eminent domain law, which would allow local governments to secure land rights for major infrastructure projects, also hampers development. A 2013 law required the government to study the long-term impact of such projects on local residents before a project can begin, Nehru says. The Modi government tried to soften those requirements in 2015 but abandoned the effort amid heavy opposition.

Nevertheless, many economists agree, barring some unforeseen development, India will enjoy a long period of sustained growth at rates that more developed economies would welcome.

"If future governments keep current policies in place and don't create more obstacles," says Panagariya, "we'll have 7 to 8 percent growth for the next two to three decades."

Are India and China destined to be locked in conflict?

On Aug. 15, 2017, a violent brawl erupted between Indian and Chinese troops high in the Himalaya Mountains after a Chinese patrol briefly crossed into Indian-held territory in Ladakh, a disputed area where the two countries had fought a border war more than 50 years ago.[18] This time, there was no shooting; the soldiers merely punched, kicked and threw rocks at each other before retreating behind their respective forward lines.

Still, the clash heightened tensions between the two nuclear-armed countries at a time when they already were locked in another territorial standoff 2,400 miles away on India's northeastern border with China and Bhutan, a tiny kingdom that relies on India for protection.[19]

New Delhi and Beijing soon announced they had agreed to pull back their forces from both disputed areas. Indian Prime Minister Modi and Chinese President Xi Jinping then held follow-up talks in China and vowed to avoid further border standoffs and maintain peace between their two countries.[20]

The situation illustrates that Indian and Chinese leaders aim to prevent their differences from escalating into armed conflict, despite the unresolved border disputes and other major irritants such as China's close ties with Pakistan. Another is India's support for the exiled Tibetan religious leader, the Dalai Lama, whom the Chinese accuse of agitating for Tibetan independence.

"They both recognize that they have a clash of interests that must be managed," says Arzan Tarapore, an expert on Indian national security of the National Bureau of Asian Research, a Seattle think tank that focuses on Asian economic, political and security issues.

Border disputes aside, experts say the two Asian giants—each with more than a billion people—are locked in a strategic and ideological competition reflecting the ambitions of Modi and Xi. Both seek to proclaim their nation's centrality on the world stage and offer their country as a model for others, says Daniel S. Markey, a former senior State Department official who coordinated South Asia policy during the George W. Bush administration.

Yet Modi has carefully struck a balance between competition and cooperation with China. In June, he emphasized India's strategic partnerships with the United States, Japan and other regional powers but dismissed the view that those relationships aim to contain China.[21] "India does not see the Indo-Pacific region as a strategy or as a club of limited members," Modi said.[22]

Still, much of New Delhi's relationship with Washington has been defense-oriented. Over the past 10 years, India has bought nearly $20 billion worth of American-made weapons and regularly joined U.S.-led naval exercises in the Pacific. The two countries also agreed recently to deepen their strategic and operational cooperation, enabling multibillion-dollar Indian purchases of U.S. weapons.

Nevertheless, experts say, India remains wary of appearing too close to the United States. "Nobody in India wants to pick a fight with China," says the American Enterprise Institute's Dhume. "And certainly nobody in India wants to become a pawn for an American confrontation with China."

Even so, India remains particularly concerned about the inroads China has made in the region via its BRI projects. According to Gateway House, a Mumbai think tank focusing on Indian foreign relations, China has invested or committed more than $150 billion in infrastructure projects and financial systems in Bangladesh, the Maldives, Myanmar, Pakistan, Nepal and Sri Lanka—countries India once considered within its orbit.[23]

For example, according to Gateway House, China is spending $62 billion in Pakistan to build the China-Pakistan Economic Corridor, a network of roads, rail lines, fiber-optic cables and power stations that will link southwest China to Pakistan's Arabian Sea port of Gwadar, which is being expanded to handle Chinese commercial and military ships. India worries the project could bring Chinese troops into Pakistan, analysts say, and that the broader BRI plan could block India's access to important energy resources in Kazakhstan, Turkmenistan and the Persian Gulf.

In response, India has partnered with Japan to provide development aid to countries in Southeast Asia and Africa, increased military exercises with Singapore and agreed to modernize the Indonesian port of Sabang, strategically located to control passage to the Indian Ocean via the Malacca Strait.[24]

In Oman, a sultanate on the tip of the Arabian Peninsula, Indo-Chinese competition for strategic advantage is playing out in unusually close proximity. Less than a

Poverty Rate Fell Sharply

India's rate of extreme poverty—the percentage of the population living on less than $1.90 per day—fell by more than 15 percentage points between 2004 and 2011, based on the most recent census.* But one in five Indians lives below the poverty threshold, and unrest is growing in the countryside, where most of the poor live.

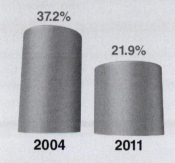

Percentage of India's Population Living in Extreme Poverty, 2004-11

37.2% 2004
21.9% 2011

* Based on 2011 purchasing power parity.

Source: "Poverty headcount ratio at national poverty lines (% of population)," World Bank, updated Sept. 21, 2018, https://tinyurl.com/ycexux6d

mile apart in the dusty Arabian Sea town of Duqm, Chinese and Indian workers are building separate port facilities to accommodate their respective commercial and military ships. Both China and India buy much of their oil from Gulf countries.

"So now you have a competition of influence taking place, a competition for friends, a competition of economic partnership, and it's only going to get worse," says the Eurasia Group's Kumar. "I don't believe India and China will go to war over their border disputes. But everywhere else in the region, it's going to be a constant battle for position."

Should India have a permanent seat on the U.N. Security Council?

Prime Minister Modi used his first speech to the U.N. General Assembly in 2014 to renew his country's call for a major overhaul of the Security Council, the United Nations' premier body for maintaining global peace and security.[25]

He called for a more "participative" Security Council that reflects today's geopolitical realities. By warning that the United Nations risked irrelevance if it did not modernize, Modi was seen by many as calling for India to be granted permanent membership on the council.[26] Since then, India repeatedly has argued for a permanent seat in meetings with leaders of the council's five permanent member countries: the United States, Russia, China, France and the United Kingdom. Each has veto power over council decisions, including whether to add new members.

India argues that as the world's second most populous country, the largest democracy and the sixth largest economy, it should have a permanent council seat. Militarily, India is a nuclear power with the world's fourth largest conventional armed forces.[27] Moreover, as

AFP/Getty Images/Narinder Nanu

An Indian soldier guards a remote post on the India-Pakistan border in October 2016. The two countries have fought over the territory of Kashmir since independence from Britain in 1947. A disputed border with China adds to the tensions along India's northern boundary.

a charter member of the U.N., India has been a leading contributor of forces to U.N. peacekeeping missions for 60 years, Indian officials point out.

Under the current rules, the Security Council has 15 members—the five veto-wielding permanent members, and 10 nonpermanent members who join the council on a rotating basis for two years each but who do not exercise veto power. When the United Nations was formed in 1945, the Security Council had six nonpermanent members. That was expanded to 10 in 1965 to provide greater geographic representation, the only time the council has been revamped.[28]

Nevertheless, the council "does not reflect even the most basic realities of a world in which the population has grown from 2.3 billion . . . to over 7 billion" and the number of member countries nearly quadrupled, from 51 to 193, wrote former Indian ambassador to Denmark, Neelam Deo, and researcher Karan Pradhan in a commentary for Gateway House.[29]

So far, the United States, Russia, France and Britain have given India verbal support for its Security Council bid but have taken no action. Markey, the former South Asia policy coordinator at the State Department, describes such support as a "friendly gesture" meant to convey backing for India's rise as a world power. But the lack of any follow-through on the issue reflects the recognition that China's refusal

to support India's bid means it is highly unlikely it will be approved, he says.

China, a close ally of India's longtime foe Pakistan, "has no interest in having India become a permanent member of the Security Council," Markey says. "So you've got one veto-wielding member of the Security Council that opposes India." China also opposed India's membership in the Nuclear Supplier Group, a multilateral organization that seeks to control the export of material and technology used to produce nuclear weapons, he points out. "And the Security Council is much more significant than that organization."

Besides international rivalries, internal U.N. politics also are blocking changes that would allow India and other major powers, such as Japan, Germany and Brazil, to become permanent council members, Dhume says. "Nobody on the Security Council wants to leave it, and a whole bunch of countries don't want any Security Council expansion," he says. "So the Italians don't want the Germans to get in, the Pakistanis don't want India to get in, and the Argentines don't want the Brazilians to get in. And the Chinese don't want the Indians or the Japanese to get in."

Panagariya, the former Modi government official, says if the Security Council were to expand the permanent membership, the new members' rivalries would likely negate their votes, ultimately diluting the council's authority. "Rising powers like India understand that by the time they get their seat at the table, that table may not be relevant anymore," he says. "So they've begun asking 'What's the point of the Security Council anyway?'"

India's failure to make headway with Security Council membership has prompted it to join alternative multilateral organizations, such as the Asian Infrastructure Investment Bank, which China launched to fund its BRI plan. Indian officials say membership in such organizations affords New Delhi a larger voice in shaping regional and global events.

BACKGROUND
From Colonialism to Nonalignment

In 1820, India was the world's second-largest economy after China, accounting for 16 percent of global GDP, according to British historian Angus Maddison. India's popular cloth exports dominated the global trade in textiles and apparel.[30]

But in 1858, after a series of small wars that eventually brought the entire subcontinent under British control, India became a British colony, known as the Raj. The British imposed heavy tariffs on the cloth exports, while allowing raw Indian cotton into Britain duty-free. As a result, Britain eventually overtook India as the world largest textile manufacturer.

During the colonial period, the British built a railway system in India, but the industrial revolution largely bypassed the subcontinent. India's agrarian economy fell behind as Western countries grabbed larger shares of global output. "At the beginning of the 20th Century, 'the brightest jewel in the British Crown,' was the poorest country in the world in terms of per capita income," wrote former Indian Prime Minister Manmohan Singh.[31]

After a nonviolent movement led by activist Mahatma Gandhi, India gained independence from Britain in 1947. Jawaharlal Nehru, the country's first prime minister, decided to base India's economy largely on the Soviet model, with government-directed industrialization, power generation and infrastructure construction. In 1951, India nationalized private companies in an effort to curb corporate excesses, such as the exploitation of workers, and to harness business to the needs of the state. But the move, coupled with a blizzard of regulations and red tape, smothered private enterprise. By 1952, Singh said, India's share of the world economy had dwindled to just 3.2 percent, down from 3.8 percent at independence.[32]

In foreign policy, Nehru resisted taking sides in the Cold War rivalry between the United States and the Soviet Union, preferring a pacifistic, "nonaligned" course. But the policy backfired when the United States aligned with Pakistan and began providing it with weapons in a move to block the spread of communism in the subcontinent.[33]

In 1962, Chinese troops seized a slice of the disputed Himalayan territory of Kashmir, sparking a brief border war that ended in a humiliating defeat for India. The area China claimed, one of two territorial disputes with India, was mostly a glacier, but it held symbolic significance to Beijing, which saw it as part of Chinese-controlled Tibet.

India's bitterest foe, however, was neighboring Pakistan, a predominantly Muslim country that separated from Hindu-majority India as part of India's independence agreement with Britain. The violent nature of the partition, in which more than 15 million people were displaced according to their religion and up to 2 million killed in brutal sectarian violence, created much of the ongoing hostility that still plagues India-Pakistan relations.[34] The two countries fought major wars in 1947 and 1965 over the disputed territory of Kashmir, a predominantly Muslim territory that became part of India after partition, despite Pakistan's protests.

Under Nehru, India's economic growth eventually averaged 4.1 percent annually until his death in 1964.[35] After his daughter, Indira Gandhi, became prime minister in 1966, annual growth fell to 2.9 percent for more than a decade as she nationalized banks and tightened government controls. An Arab oil embargo that sent world energy prices skyrocketing in 1973 only deepened India's economic problems.[36]

In the 1950s, droughts and food shortages made India synonymous in the West with starving children. But after U.S. agronomists developed new high-yield grain varieties in the early 1960s, India dramatically increased the quantity and quality of its agricultural output. By 1979, India was self-sufficient in grain.

Although officially nonaligned, Gandhi drew closer to the Soviet Union in an attempt to balance the pressures she felt from China and the U.S.-Pakistan alliance. In 1971, she signed a Treaty of Peace, Friendship and Cooperation with Moscow, which supplied India with all of its weapons and invited Indian academics to participate in scientific exchanges.[37]

But India's socialist economy remained relatively stagnant, growing by only 3.5 percent a year for three decades.[38]

Economic Liberalization

In 1974, Gandhi ordered the Indian police to crush a nationwide railway strike. In 1975, as labor unrest persisted and her Congress Party lost popular support, Gandhi declared martial law, jailing tens of thousands of political opponents and muzzling the media.

Voters retaliated in 1977 parliamentary elections, ousting Gandhi's Congress Party from power for the first time. But the new government soon faltered, and the Congress Party returned to power in 1980 with Gandhi again at the helm.[39]

She implemented some modest economic reforms, but in June 1984 she ordered troops to storm the Sikh Golden Temple complex in the northern city of Amritsar, where armed Sikh militants had holed up. Sikhs saw the raid as an attack on their religion and strongly criticized the action. Five months later, Gandhi's own Sikh bodyguards assassinated her.

Gandhi's son, Rajiv, succeeded her as prime minister and implemented additional economic reforms that boosted growth before he left office in 1989. Then in 1991, the former prime minister was campaigning again when he was assassinated by militants seeking a separate Tamil state in Sri Lanka, which India opposed.

Burdened with mounting public debt, India suffered a full-blown financial crisis in 1991 when oil prices soared after the Persian Gulf War. Then-Finance Minister Manmohan Singh informed Prime Minister Narasimha Rao that India's foreign currency coffers were nearly bare, with only enough to buy two more weeks of fuel supplies.[40]

The crisis allowed Rao and Singh to scrap the country's socialist framework, relax regulations and embrace free-market principles and the globalized economy. India's average annual economic growth rate rose to 6.3 percent between 1992 and 1999, lifting millions out of poverty and planting the seeds of a new Indian middle class.[41]

Part of India's economic growth stemmed from the burgeoning information technology sector. Headquartered in Bangalore, Indian IT companies utilized the country's large pool of skilled, low-cost, English-speaking workers, the internet and satellite communications to attract Western corporations seeking to outsource their business operations and administrative tasks. According to the World Bank, per capita GDP in India rose from $340 in 1992 to $430 in 1999, a 26 percent increase.[42]

Nuclear Player

India, which had detonated its first nuclear bomb in 1974, conducted five underground nuclear weapons tests in May 1998 and declared itself a nuclear power. Two weeks later, Pakistan joined the nuclear club with five of its own successful tests.

In response, the U.N. Security Council urged the two countries to abandon their nuclear weapons programs. President Bill Clinton imposed economic and military sanctions on both countries and cancelled a planned visit to India.[43]

But by 2000, conditions had changed. The Cold War was long since over, globalization and the internet were linking people and economies, and India's GDP was growing at a healthy 5.5 percent annual clip. Most importantly, the United States recognized that India was playing a bigger political and economic role in Asia. Clinton visited India that March and lifted many of the sanctions.

After President George W. Bush took office in 2001, India gained additional strategic importance to the United States as a potential counterweight to China's growing regional dominance. To woo India, Bush officially recognized it as a nuclear power in 2005.

Meanwhile, the Congress Party in 2004 had won a plurality, led by another member of the Gandhi dynasty: Rajiv's Italian-born widow Sonia Gandhi. But the left-wing coalition government that the party formed spooked financial markets, reflecting fears India would return to its well-worn socialist path. To restore confidence, the Congress Party gave the premiership to Singh, the former finance minister and mastermind of India's shift to a free-market economy.

During Singh's subsequent two five-year terms, India's GDP growth accelerated, exceeding 9 percent from 2005 to 2008. It dropped to 6.7 percent in 2009, due largely to the global financial crisis, then rose to more than 8 percent in 2010-11. But growth slumped again after the government rejected further free-market reforms due to opposition from its leftist coalition partners.[44]

Singh's tenure also was marred by an upswing in deadly terrorist attacks, many by Pakistani-backed militants. In 2006, seven bomb blasts tore through local trains in Mumbai, killing 187 people and wounding more than 800. In 2008, Islamist terrorists based in Pakistan attacked civilian targets, killing 175 people and wounding nearly 300. These were among scores of terrorist attacks in India since 1980 that have killed more than 3,300 people.[45]

Singh and the Congress Party went into the 2014 elections with his government burdened by multiple corruption scandals, which many analysts say were major factors in the BJP victory that brought Modi to power.[46]

CHRONOLOGY

1947-1964 *A newly independent India embraces socialist economic policies and a pacifist, nonaligned foreign policy.*

1947 India gains independence from Britain after a nonviolent movement led by Mahatma Gandhi. . . . Muslims form separate state of Pakistan amid bloody sectarian violence.

1948 A Hindu extremist assassinates Gandhi.

1962 China defeats India in brief border war along their disputed frontiers with Tibet and Kashmir.

1964 Nehru dies in office.

1966-1989 *Indira Gandhi tightens Soviet-style state control of the economy and represses political opponents.*

1966 Nehru's daughter, Indira Gandhi (no relation to Mahatma Gandhi), becomes prime minister. . . . India launches a "Green Revolution" using higher-yield seeds and irrigation and eventually becomes self-sufficient in grain production.

1971 India and the Soviet Union sign a Treaty of Peace, Friendship and Cooperation, cementing the Kremlin's role as India's main arms supplier. . . . India and Pakistan go to war, leading to East Pakistan's independence as the new nation of Bangladesh.

1974 India becomes the first nation outside of the five permanent members of the U.N. Security Council to conduct a nuclear weapons test.

1977 Voters reject Gandhi and her Indian National Congress party.

1980 Government unravels; Gandhi is returned to office.

1984 Gandhi is assassinated by two of her Sikh bodyguards five months after she orders the army to storm the Golden Temple in Amritsar, the Sikh religion's holiest site. . . . Her son, Rajiv, becomes prime minister.

1989 Rajiv Gandhi voted out of office.

1991-Present *India embraces free-market principles, paving the way for economic growth and a larger international role.*

1991 Amid a financial crisis, India begins to liberalize its economy. Former Prime Minister Rajiv Gandhi is assassinated in a suicide bombing.

1998 India conducts a second nuclear test, prompting Pakistan to announce its own successful nuclear tests. Western nations impose economic sanctions on both countries. . . . Hindu nationalist Bharatiya Janata Party (BJP) comes to power at the head of a coalition government.

1999 India and Pakistan fight over Kashmir for the third time.

2001 Terrorist attack on the Indian Parliament by Pakistan-backed Kashmiri separatists raises fears of nuclear war with Pakistan.

2004 Congress Party unseats the BJP-led coalition in national election. Economist and former Finance Minister Manmohan Singh becomes prime minister.

2007 Economy grows by 9.2 percent, the fourth year of high growth. . . . Percentage of Indians living in extreme poverty falls to one quarter, from one third in 2004.

2008 Islamist terrorists from Pakistan kill 175 people in 12 coordinated shooting and bombing attacks over four days in Mumbai.

2014-2016 BJP returns to power. Narendra Modi becomes prime minister and begins to overhaul tax, bankruptcy and anti-corruption laws.

2017 In response to China's aggressive moves in South Asia, India signs military cooperation agreements with the United States.

2018 Modi, who is running for re-election, launches new nationwide health care initiative.

2019 Parliamentary elections are scheduled for May.

Indian Women Face Rampant Violence, Discrimination

One study found bias costs India's economy $900 billion a year.

India is one of the few countries where women have served as prime minister and chief ministers—the equivalent of state governors in the United States—and fill half the seats on local government councils. When *Forbes* magazine issued its 2018 list of the world's billionaires, six were Indian women.[1]

Yet Indian women routinely are victims of blatant, brutal and sometimes legal gender discrimination and violence in homes, schools and workplaces, according to experts, and that bias severely retards the country's economic growth.

Gender bias begins before birth. At all levels of Indian society, the culture traditionally prizes sons over daughters. In poor families, the bias stems from the inability to afford the high cost of the dowries that are typically demanded from a bride's family by the groom's family. As a result, if a pregnant woman learns that her unborn child will be female, an abortion often takes place. India has 37 million more men than women, according to its 2011 census, its most recent, and the proportion of female newborns continues to plummet.[2]

Child marriage, though illegal, is still widespread. According to the United Nations, more than a quarter of Indian girls are married by the time they reach 18, the legal age to wed; 7 percent are married by age 15. In addition, more than 7,000 brides are burned to death or forced to commit suicide each year by their grooms' families for not delivering adequate dowries, according to India's National Crime Records Bureau, but fewer than 35 percent of the perpetrators are convicted.[3]

According to the Indian government, an Indian woman is raped every 21 minutes, and crimes against women have increased 34 percent in the past four years. But experts say most rapes are never reported, and spousal rape is not a crime in India.[4]

In addition, lower-caste and Muslim women are often the victims of so-called honor killings if they become romantically involved or engaged to upper-caste or Hindu men. Faced with the "dishonor" of a mixed marriage, the man's relatives simply kill the woman, according to New Delhi-based feminist columnist Kavita Krishnan.[5]

A Thompson Reuters Foundation poll this year named India as the world's most dangerous country for women, up from fourth place seven years ago, mostly due to the risk Indian women face from sexual violence and harassment; cultural, tribal and traditional practices; and being forced into sex slavery or domestic servitude.[6] A spokesperson for the poll says the risks apply to both urban and rural women.

Violence is not the only obstacle Indian women face due to their devalued status in Indian culture. Economists say the Indian government does a poor job of integrating women into the job market, which hinders economic growth. A 2015 study by the McKinsey Global Institute, a private-sector think tank in New York, said Indian women represent only 24 percent of India's formal labor force, compared with an average of 40 percent worldwide. As a result, women account for only 17 percent of India's gross domestic product (GDP), far below the global average of 37 percent, the study said.[7]

In fact, if women had full parity in the Indian workforce, it would boost the economy by roughly $900 billion a year, according to Dhruva Jaishankar, an expert on India at the Brookings Institution think tank in Washington and its New Delhi branch. India's average annual economic growth of 7.7 percent during 2003-13 could have been 11.6 percent if women had fully participated in the workforce, he said.[8]

Economic Reforms

Modi came into office promising to crack down on corruption and revive the economy. But some foreign governments were troubled by his reputation as a Hindu nationalist. As the top official of the western state of Gujarat in 2002, Modi had been blamed for stirring up Hindu mob violence against Muslims, which left 1,000 people dead. The accusations, which Modi denied, rendered him persona non grata in the United States, Britain and several other EU countries until he won the premiership.[47]

Education is a major challenge to women achieving parity in the workplace, experts say. Girls and boys attend primary and secondary schools in equal numbers, but males account for a greater share of higher education students because female students often marry at an early age. Only 42 percent of Indian university students are female.[9]

Some multinational corporations operating in India have taken steps to increase women's participation in the workforce. The Indian branch of Unilever, the global household products giant, has encouraged women who left their jobs to raise children to return as part-time consultants, with the option to resume full-time employment.[10] But a June 2018 study by several European labor rights groups found that many Indian factories that produce apparel for major U.S. and European brands, such as Gap and Hugo Boss, foster working conditions tantamount to modern forms of slavery, especially for female workers.[11]

India does not have anti-gender discrimination employment laws. Thus, many women who try to find jobs find that employers prefer to hire males. A World Bank study of more than 800,000 Indian help-wanted ads posted online between 2007 and 2017 found that many employers specified they were seeking a man. Employers were willing to hire women as receptionists, beauticians, nursemaids or cooks, jobs that tend to be lower in status and pay, the study found. Notable exceptions were customer service call center jobs and administrative work, some of which offered women salaries that were 19 percent higher than those offered to male applicants.[12]

Sadanand Dhume, an India expert at the American Enterprise Institute, a conservative think tank in Washington, says Prime Minister Narendra Modi's government has experimented with several technological approaches to reducing gender inequality and violence, with mixed results. To combat rape, for instance, the government two years ago required all mobile phones sold in India to include a panic button that can be pressed if help is needed, to alert police or a person chosen by the phone user.

The government's faith in technology reflects "a peculiar Indian tendency to seek silver-bullet solutions for complex problems" that instead require education about outdated notions about violence against women, Dhume says.

— Jonathan Broder

[1] Luisa Kroll and Kerry Dolan, "The Billionaires 2018," *Forbes*, March 6, 2018, https://tinyurl.com/yat97ht6.

[2] Dhruva Jaishankar, "The Huge Cost of India's Discrimination Against Women," *The Atlantic*, March 18, 2013, https://tinyurl.com/ybjzu6tq; Simon Denyer and Annie Gowen, "Too Many Men," *The Washington Post*, April 18, 2018, https://tinyurl.com/ybvfgag8.

[3] "Child Marriage Around the World: India," Girls Not Brides, undated, https://tinyurl.com/y8zxzhc2; Chayyanika Nigam, "21 lives lost to dowry every day across India; conviction rate less than 35 per cent," *India Today*, April 22, 2017, https://tinyurl.com/ydcnaedm.

[4] Sorcha Pollak and Rahul Bedi, "Indian government tries to curb violence against women," *Irish Times*, March 15, 2017, https://tinyurl.com/ybax8jrw; Sunita Toor, "How to stop violence against women in India—it starts with training police officers," *The Conversation*, Jan. 23, 2018, https://tinyurl.com/ydd8xxx9.

[5] Kavita Krishnan, " 'Honour' crimes in India: An assault on women's autonomy," Aljazeera, March 14, 2018, https://tinyurl.com/y9gza2s4.

[6] Belinda Goldsmith and Meka Beresford, "Exclusive: India most dangerous country for women with sexual violence rife: global poll," Reuters, June 25, 2018, https://tinyurl.com/y8wokojk.

[7] Jonathan Woetzel *et al.*, "The Power of Parity: Advancing Women's equality in India," McKinsey Global Institute, November 2015, https://tinyurl.com/ydzehzm5.

[8] Jaishankar, *op. cit.*

[9] *Ibid.*

[10] Anne-Birgitte Albrectsen, "Here's how companies are fighting gender bias in the workplace," World Economic Forum, Jan. 9, 2018, https://tinyurl.com/ybplsc64; "Unilever: Global Reach With Local Roots: Creating a Gender-Balanced Workforce in Different Cultural Contexts," *Catalyst*, Jan. 24, 2013, https://tinyurl.com/ycjuvonw.

[11] Vishy Anulag, ed., "Case closed, problems persist," Homeworkers Worldwide, India Committee of the Netherlands, Centre for Research on Multinational Corporations, June 2018, https://tinyurl.com/y9ze2t5u.

[12] Afra R. Chowdhury *et al.*, "Reflections of Employers' Gender Preference in Job Ads in India," World Bank Group, March 2018, https://tinyurl.com/y8bb5sjp.

Modi quickly began implementing his campaign promises, pushing through several changes credited with improving the structure of India's economy.

Modi's government relaxed India's foreign investment regulations, particularly those affecting pharmaceuticals, e-commerce and defense, attracting a record annual average of $60 billion in foreign direct investment during his first three years in office, compared to $36 billion the year before he took power.[48] Modi began to modernize India's creaking infrastructure and set new standards for

India Struggles to Achieve Renewable Energy Goals

Reliance on fossil fuels, other challenges stand in the way.

All across India, solar panels are cropping up on the roofs of factories, airport operations centers and on irrigation pumps. Large tracts of land have been transformed into some of the world's biggest solar parks, and the southern state of Tamil Nadu now hosts one of the world's largest onshore wind farms. Even a few of India's famously antiquated railroad locomotives are now solar-powered, as is the official residence of Prime Minister Narendra Modi.[1]

These projects are part of Modi's ambitious plan to install 227 gigawatts of clean, renewable energy by 2022.[2] That would replace all of the 222 gigawatts of power currently produced by coal plus two-thirds of India's installed power capacity of 345 gigawatts.[3] With additional pledges to sell only electrical vehicles in India by 2030 and cut by one third the 2005 level of the country's greenhouse gas emissions by the same year, Modi hopes to become a global leader in the use of green energy technology to fight climate change.[4]

So far, however, the government has installed equipment to generate just 70 gigawatts of renewable energy, and projects that could generate another 40 gigawatts of green power are either under construction or still up for bidding. The slow pace has put Modi's plan behind schedule, prompting many sustainable energy experts to question whether India can meet his ambitious deadlines.

Standing in his way, experts say, are several major obstacles, including infrastructure challenges, competing demands for government funds and the country's continued reliance on fossil fuels for its energy needs.

"There are many, many operational constraints to the plan in terms of land availability, transmission connections, who's going to buy and pay for those [transmission] towers, and so forth," said Vinay Rustagi, managing director of Bridge to India, a renewable energy consulting firm.[5]

Ever since India signed on to the Paris climate accords in 2015, Modi has sought to make India a global leader in renewable energy. At the Paris meeting, he announced the formation of the International Solar Alliance, a coalition of 121 countries that India now leads, to promote worldwide collaboration on developing solar power technology. Since then, he has repeatedly emphasized the need for nations to act against climate change.

A shortage of money is not one of the obstacles Modi faces, according to energy experts. The World Bank has pledged more than $1 billion to support India's development of more efficient solar panels, solar-energy parks, transmission lines to distribute power from sun-rich areas and other initiatives to expand solar power.[6] In March, the European Union kicked in another 800 million euros ($940 million) for clean energy projects in India.[7] And these amounts were supplemented with $10 billion in public and private invest-

worker mobility, particularly in global services trade. The new goods and services tax transformed India into a single market, and the new comprehensive bankruptcy law began to pay dividends.

"Before Modi came along, they never had a concept of Chapter 11, and now they do," the Eurasia Group's Kumar says. "If you're a bank, you can now foreclose on properties and corporate borrowers if the loans are failing."

Modi also introduced biometric ID cards to counter the epidemic of fraud in government-run food programs.

Many families had been using multiple ration cards or forged cards to receive more than their share of food aid. "The biometric IDs have put a stop to that abuse, saving the government as much as $6 billion annually," says Panagariya, the former Modi government official.

His boldest and most controversial move was aimed at corruption. His 2016 demonetization, introduced overnight without warning, banned the largest denominations of bank notes. Black marketeers had to pay delinquent taxes to exchange their large bank notes for

ment in India's solar industry in 2017, according to a March report by the Mercom Capital Group, a Bangalore-based clean energy consulting firm.

The slowdown is due in part to the government's diversion of funds to cover revenue losses caused by its shaky implementation of a new goods and services tax, according to Mongabay-India, a conservation and environmental news site. In addition, government tariffs on imported Chinese solar panels have created a shortage of solar equipment.

"A number of changes are required" in India's solar policies, said S.P. Gon Chaudhuri, an Indian energy consultant. "Those changes have not taken place . . . yet, [so] there is a slowdown."[8] Yet without such changes, he said, India cannot hit its renewable energy targets.

Rahul Tongia, a sustainable energy expert at the Brookings Institution's New Delhi branch, said India also must overcome a major structural hurdle before it can scale up its renewable energy capacity. India's electricity grid will need to be able to store renewable energy and ramp it up or down as needed, he said. This variability and non-controllability, he said, is "the core of one of the challenges" of renewable energy.[9]

The power grid also presents problems for Modi's electric vehicle strategy, said Denes Csala, an energy storage expert at Britain's Lancaster University. India's solar and wind power alone will not be enough to power those vehicles, he said, so the country will still need its fossil-fuel power plants. "Effectively, India will replace petrol with coal and may even need to expand coal power, thus actually increasing emissions," he said.[10]

More than 80 percent of India's energy comes from coal and imported oil. "India couldn't replace that overnight," said Csala. "Even if it wanted to, there are not enough wind turbines and solar panels in the world" to do that. As a result, he said, "the transition to renewable energy could take decades."[11]

Besides, in a sign that India is not planning to abandon fossil fuels anytime soon, he pointed out, Russia's state-owned Rosneft oil company invested $13 billion in India's Essar Oil in 2016 and another $25 billion to lay a gas pipeline from Siberia to India.[12]

— *Jonathan Broder*

[1] Dénes Csala, "India wants to become a solar superpower—but its plans don't add up," *The Conversation*, Nov. 11, 2016, https://tinyurl.com/yab9gd5b.

[2] Michael Safi, "India's huge solar ambitions could push coal further into shade," *The Guardian*, June 29, 2018, https://tinyurl.com/y8aeh7z9.

[3] "Power Sector in India," India Brand Equity Foundation, September 2018, https://tinyurl.com/ya5ulp79.

[4] Jackie Wattles, "India to sell only electric cars by 2030," CNN Money, June 1, 2017, https://tinyurl.com/y7m69zmn; Anjali Jaiswal, "India Leads on Climate Action as Trump Exits Paris Agreement," National Resources Defense Council, https://tinyurl.com/y7h6re22.

[5] Safi, *op. cit.*

[6] "World Bank to Back India's Solar Power Initiative," The Associated Press, Voice of America, June 30, 2016, https://tinyurl.com/yabxlkcy.

[7] Frédéric Simon, "India takes lion's share of EU bank funding for solar power," Euractiv.com, March 13, 2018, https://tinyurl.com/y8vfhnsh.

[8] Sapna Gopal, "Will India be able to meet its renewable energy targets by 2022?" *Mongabay-India*, March 5, 2018, https://tinyurl.com/ydxskefh.

[9] "Rahul Tongia on the Indian Power Grid," Brookings India, Jan. 15, 2015, https://tinyurl.com/y8t3oyes.

[10] Csala, *op. cit.*

[11] *Ibid.*

[12] *Ibid.*

new bills or be left holding piles of worthless currency. "The number of taxpayers has increased . . . much faster than it ever did in the past," Panagariya says.

But the government failed to privatize inefficient state-owned companies, and Modi could not muster support to overhaul India's restrictive land and labor laws. His campaign promise to create 10 million new jobs remained unfulfilled.

"So there's some things they did right, and credit is due," says the American Enterprise Institute's Dhume.

"But . . . they basically shied away from any kind of serious reforms dealing with land and labor, and their privatization record was dismal. On trade, they went backward by raising tariffs on numerous imports."

Modi's foreign policy record also has been mixed. He updated a 10-year defense cooperation agreement with the United States in 2014, and Washington declared India a "major defense partner" in 2015. New Delhi and Washington also signed a major agreement to share logistics during joint naval exercises and reimbursements. But

Rescue workers and onlookers survey a collapsed bridge in Kolkata in September. As India, a country of 1.3 billion people, modernizes, the government is pouring money into building or replacing roads, ports and railways.

the increased security cooperation with the United States prompted domestic criticism that it would erode the nation's "strategic autonomy"—the updated term for India's traditional nonaligned posture.

Meanwhile, Modi has strengthened ties with India's South Asian neighbors, resolved a decades-long border dispute with Bangladesh and deepened ties with Afghanistan. India also began building a port in the Iranian coastal town of Chabahar, in an effort to create a sea-land route from Iran to Afghanistan that bypasses Pakistan. U.S. officials consider the route an important alternative if tensions with Pakistan prompt Islamabad to close the sea-land supply route from Karachi to Afghanistan used by the U.S. military.

But Modi's initial hopes of improving relations with Pakistan and China have not panned out.

In a goodwill gesture after winning election, Modi invited then-Pakistani Prime Minister Nawaz Sharif to his May 2014 inauguration. However, in August, as bilateral talks between the two countries were to begin, Pakistan's ambassador to India invited Muslim separatists from disputed Kashmir to a reception at the Pakistani embassy in New Delhi. Modi promptly canceled the talks. Relations deteriorated further after Pakistan-based militants launched several attacks inside India that killed dozens of Indian soldiers. Modi, who had vowed during his campaign to adopt a hard line toward Islamabad's provocations, retaliated with a series of military strikes inside Pakistan.

India's relations with China remained strained over Chinese military incursions into disputed territories.

Yet under Modi, China became India's largest trading partner, further complicating relations. But as China sought to broaden its economic, military and political reach in the region, Modi added a security element to India's trade relations with other Southeast Asian countries. The Indian navy begin making port calls in Indonesia and Malaysia, near the strategic Strait of Malacca. New Delhi also began selling weapons to Vietnam and holding joint naval exercises with Singapore and Japan.

CURRENT SITUATION

Income Disparity

As Modi gears up for parliamentary elections in May, he appears on course for another five-year term, with nearly an 80 percent job-approval rating, according to a Gallup poll released in July.[49]

Under India's parliamentary system, the voters elect political parties, not individuals. The leader of the winning party becomes prime minister. If the winning party doesn't capture a majority of seats in India's lower house, it must form a coalition government with smaller parties.

The Gallup poll also showed 54 percent of Indians see economic conditions improving and 86 percent feel satisfied with the amount of freedom in their lives—higher than at any point in the past decade.[50] Foreign investment is strong, the Indian stock market is soaring and economic growth is galloping along.

Yet it does not feel that way to huge numbers of Indians. Hundreds of millions of farmers and lower-caste Indians, who make up the country's enormous underclass, see their lives getting worse while a handful of millionaires, billionaires and upper-class professionals are getting richer. Indeed, according to the Gallup poll, only 3 percent of Indians rank their lives today and in the future as "thriving."[51]

Justin Lall, a polling analyst and strategic partnerships manager at Gallup, said, "Indians rate their lives worse now than they have at any point in the history of Gallup's global tracking."[52]

Analysts attribute the discrepancy between Indians' optimism about their economy and government and their pessimism about their own lives in large part to the growing income gap between the rich and the poor.

A January report by Oxfam, a global development and anti-poverty organization, said India's richest 1 percent now hold 73 percent of the country's wealth—up from 58 percent the previous year—while wealth has risen by just 1 percent among the 670 million Indians who make up the country's poorest half.[53]

India has 119 billionaires collectively worth $440.1 billion, according to *Forbes* magazine. But average per capita annual income in 2017 was $1,939, according to the World Bank.[54] "It is alarming [that] the benefits of economic growth in India continue to concentrate in fewer hands," said Nisha Agrawal, Oxfam India's CEO.[55]

Another Gallup survey, released in August, found that 37 percent of Indian adults have at times not had enough money to buy food during the past year, double the 18 percent with similar complaints in 2012, before Modi came to power. In India's eastern states, the nation's poorest, nearly half of the population struggles to afford food, the survey found.[56]

In 2014, Modi's promises of improved living standards won him strong support in India's rural areas, where 70 percent of Indians live.[57] The nation's 263 million farmers deserted the Congress Party in droves in response to Modi's promises of higher crop prices.[58] With agriculture employing the majority of the country's 520 million-strong workforce, farmers were a key factor in the BJP's electoral success.[59]

But Modi may not be able to count on the farm vote again. Since he came into office, commodity prices have plummeted, fuel costs have risen and tightened credit in India's mostly government-run banks have made it difficult for farmers to borrow money to buy seed, fertilizer and pesticides.

"There was a wave for Modi in 2014, but farmers are disenchanted with him now," said Uday Vir Singh, 53, a sugar cane grower in Kairana, in Uttar Pradesh state. "Modi promised to double farmers' income but our earning has halved because of his apathy and anti-farmer policies," such as cuts in crop subsidies by Modi's pro-business BJP and the party's reluctance to address the credit crunch.[60]

Over the past several months, roughly a half million subsistence farmers, many with less than five acres of land, have staged protests demanding loan forgiveness and higher prices for their crops. The government sets commodity prices in India.

According to Palagummi Sainath, a journalist and author who focuses on India's rural economy, public-sector banks have been rejecting small farmers' loan requests since the 1990s, forcing them to borrow from unscrupulous street-corner lenders who charge annual interests of up to 60 percent. As a result, nearly 15 million farmers lost their farms between 1991 and 2011, according to Sainath.

Between 2011 and 2015, farmers' ranks shrank by another 26 million, according to a June 2017 study by the McKinsey Global Institute, a private sector think tank based in New York. Many of the dispossessed farmers, Sainath said, have ended up in India's impoverished underclass, working as agricultural laborers.[61]

"We need freedom from debt," said Abhimanyu Kohar, national coordinator of the National Farmers Big Union, which organized the protests. "We are not asking for dole; we are not criminals. The farmer is in debt today not because he has messed up but because of the flawed policies of the government."[62]

Another large rural constituency unhappy with Modi and his party—the 250 million Dalits, members of India's lowest caste once known as "untouchables"—could be another potent force in next year's elections. Despite a system of affirmative action that aimed to lift India's lower castes, Dalits continue to suffer job discrimination and physical attacks when they violate age-old caste taboos. In late March, a mob in Gujarat murdered a Dalit youth for riding a horse, something Dalits once were prohibited from doing.[63]

Although India's 2,000-year-old caste system was outlawed at independence, the rigid, Hindu system of social stratification endures. It divided people into five categories according to their work and social status. At the top were the Brahmins, which traditionally included priests and teachers, followed by rulers and warriors, merchants and farmers, and laborers. The fifth category was the Dalits, who worked as street sweepers and latrine cleaners.[64]

For centuries, the apartheid-like system determined every aspect of Hindu life: Upper and lower castes lived in segregated communities and intermarriage was strictly forbidden. Last names indicated one's caste, which was

Is a close strategic partnership with the U.S. good for India?

YES
Arzan Tarapore
Nonresident Fellow, National Bureau of Asian Research

Written for *CQ Researcher*, October 2018

A close strategic relationship with the United States is the most effective way to secure India's strategic interests. As the past decade of deepening relations has illustrated, U.S. material and political support augments and multiplies India's rising power in at least three ways.

First, it gives India access to state-of-the-art military equipment and technology transfers. India's most capable acquisitions in recent years have been from the United States, including M-777 artillery, P-8I maritime patrol aircraft and C-130J and C-17 transport aircraft, which extend the range of Indian forces. In the future, this may include co-development of aircraft carriers and satellites. The partnership is a vital resource for military modernization and military-industrial development—clearly exceeding what India could achieve independently or with other partners.

Second, the partnership allows India to more effectively tackle its security interests. U.S. intelligence sharing, for example, has given India insight into terrorist threats and Chinese military activity. Combined military exercises, such as Malabar, a trilateral naval exercise conducted off the coast of Guam this year, help India prepare for coordinated military operations in the Indian Ocean.

Third, the partnership gives India political support as its power rises. The United States is actively encouraging India's growing influence in the region. A more tense relationship between the two countries—as existed in previous decades—might have prompted the United States to thwart India's rise. Washington has supported India's membership in regional and global governance institutions and has encouraged U.S. allies, such as Japan and Australia, to deepen their own strategic partnerships with India.

These benefits do not—as many Indian critics claim—compromise India's sovereignty. Agreements, such as the recently signed pact enabling the transfer of encrypted communications between Indian and U.S. forces, help facilitate Indian military activity but do not bind India politically. The partnership will never be a formal alliance so it imposes no strategic obligations.

Meanwhile, India is free to pursue an independent foreign policy, as demonstrated by its continued close relations with Russia and Iran. The United States may be statutorily obligated to sanction India for buying arms and energy from Russia and Iran, but the United States may yet waive those sanctions for the sake of preserving positive bilateral relations. Thus, a closer strategic partnership offers India and the United States a better chance of managing such periodic policy differences.

NO
Brahma Chellaney
Professor and Head of Strategic Studies, Center for Policy Research, New Delhi, India

Excerpted from the *Hindustan Times*, September 2018

The United States has emerged as India's most important partner in the Indo-Pacific region. However, in India's neighborhood, Washington and New Delhi are still not on the same page. . . .

The United States and India have become key partners in seeking to create a free, open and democracy-led Indo-Pacific. The critical missing link in this strategy, however, is the South China Sea, which connects the Indian and Pacific oceans. U.S. reluctance to impose tangible costs on China's continued expansionism in the South China Sea has emboldened Chinese inroads in the Indian Ocean. . . .

India [also] has emerged as a prime victim of two new sets of U.S. economic sanctions—on Iran and on Russia. The new sanctions directly impinge on India, a longstanding significant buyer of Russian weapons and the second-largest importer of Iranian oil after China.

The twin U.S. pressures on the energy and defense fronts have made India acutely aware of the risks of aligning itself closer with Washington. After ensnaring India in its Iran and Russia sanctions, Washington has sought to save the promising Indo-U.S. strategic partnership by throwing in concessions. In reality, the concessions are intended as tools of leverage.

For example, the Pentagon's top Asia official, characterizing Indian media reports as "misleading," has made it clear that India can expect no waiver from Russia-related sanctions if it signs major new defense deals with Moscow. The congressional waiver crimps India's leeway with its stringent conditions, including a six-monthly presidential certification specifying the other side's active steps to cut its inventory of Russian military hardware.

On the Iran-related sanctions, no waiver for India is [yet] in sight. With global shipping operators already pulling back from business with Iran and oil prices rising, India's energy-import bill is increasing. U.S. sanctions threaten to affect even India's Pakistan-bypassing [transit] corridor to Afghanistan via Iran. . . .

The Trump administration is clearly seeking to influence India's arms-procurement and energy-import policies [and is] pressuring New Delhi to buy more American weapons, although the United States has already emerged as [India's] largest arms seller.

The United States and India will remain close friends. Washington, however, must fully address Indian concerns over the extraterritorial effects of its new sanctions on Iran and Russia. Make no mistake: Washington has introduced a major irritant in the bilateral relationship.

unalterable and handed down for generations. Affirmative action programs instituted by successive governments have failed to eradicate job and housing discrimination against the lower castes, particularly in the countryside.

A week after the horse-riding Dalit youth was murdered, hundreds of thousands of Dalits rioted in New Delhi—burning buses, blocking railroad tracks and hurling bricks at police. They were protesting a court ruling that many said swept away some of the hard-fought protections they had won against discrimination.[65]

To help dampen the anger of the Dalits and the farmers, Modi announced in September that he was providing free health care to half a billion poor Indians.[66] He also aims to provide a toilet for every household by next March, the 150th birthday of Mahatma Gandhi.

In September, however, police arrested five activists for India's disadvantaged, charging links to an outlawed group of Maoists who've been waging a 50-year insurgency in the impoverished central state of Chhattisgarh. Modi's opponents say the arrests are an effort to quash dissent ahead of next year's elections and a test of civil liberties in India.[67]

U.S. Ties

In foreign policy, Modi is drawing closer to an unofficial alliance with the United States, defying critics who have expressed concerns about losing India's traditional autonomy in international affairs.

In September, the United States and India signed a major agreement to share encrypted communications, enabling U.S. weapons sales to India and greater operational coordination during military exercises. Just before the high-level talks began, New Delhi announced it will purchase 24 Lockheed Martin maritime helicopters at an estimated $1.8 billion. The announcement follows sizeable purchases of U.S.-made military hardware over the past decade, as well as India's regular participation in joint naval exercises with U.S. forces.[68]

Meanwhile, U.S. aerospace companies are vying for a $15 billion deal to supply 110 jet fighters to India's air force, but Modi insists the planes be manufactured in India, according to Indian defense officials.[69]

The deepening security ties dovetail with Washington's focus on the importance of India and the

A member of India's lowest caste, the Dalits—formerly known as "untouchables"—attacks a bus in April during protests in Bhopal against an Indian Supreme Court ruling the Dalits say reduced their legal protections. India's Hindu caste system is officially outlawed, but the country's 260 million Dalits continue to face prejudice and violence.

Indian Ocean in U.S. strategic thinking, given China's expanding influence in the region. To underscore the region's significance, the Pentagon's U.S. Pacific Command has been renamed the Indo-Pacific Command.[70] The ties also fit with India's efforts to modernize its conventional ground and air forces, build a modern navy capable of projecting power on the high seas and reassert its military primacy throughout the Indian Ocean.

Still, New Delhi has been careful not to align itself too closely with Washington. Unlike Japan and South Korea, India has no defense treaty with the United States and has not sought one. "India has a neuralgic opposition to alliances," says Tarapore, the Indian national security expert. "It will not go into an alliance with the U.S. or any other country." But to maintain its strategic autonomy, India has maintained "good, productive relations with a bunch of countries so that India isn't beholden to any one power."

For example, India has diversified its weapons suppliers to include Russia and Israel, among others, and has reached agreements with the Seychelles and Oman to build naval bases in those countries as counterweights to the port China is building on Pakistan's coast.[71]

Even so, India and the United States remain at odds over the Trump administration's threats to sanction India for buying Iranian oil and for its plans to purchase an advanced Russian air defense system. It is unclear whether the U.S. administration, which continues to threaten punitive sanctions against any country that does business with Tehran and Moscow, will exempt India from those sanctions.

OUTLOOK
Rapid Urbanization

India-watchers foresee one of two scenarios in the country's future, depending on whether it continues to overhaul its economy and education systems, exercises adroit political leadership—and benefits from sheer luck.

The first scenario depicts a bright future in which India's leaders preserve and advance Modi's liberalizing economic policies, encourage tolerance and government spending to harness urbanization and the massive influx of young people into the workforce. Over the next 30 years, experts say, about half a billion people will move from the countryside to the cities. Historically, urbanization has fostered increased literacy and economic growth, expanding the middle class.[72]

About a million young people will be entering the workforce every month for the next decade. With the right policies, economists say, they will find jobs and produce what economists call a "demographic dividend" as they increase productivity and savings.

India could become one of the world's most powerful countries if it "gets its act together" and increases economic efficiency, creates jobs, improves the education system and builds a national ideology that includes diversity and civic bonds that are "not just based on identity," says the American Enterprise Institute's Dhume. "Then you're talking about a young, dynamic, growing middle-income country, which will play a larger role on the global stage."

Many experts say India's economic future will also affect the balance of power in Asia, with a strong India providing a prosperous and democratic example for the region's developing countries instead of China's authoritarian model.

Still, even within optimists' rosy scenario, security experts do not expect India's border disputes with China to be resolved. "The challenge over the next decade will be to manage that issue so it doesn't turn into a big war, and I predict there won't be a big war," says Tarapore. "But that irritant will remain."

The alternative scenario is nothing short of a dystopian nightmare, analysts say: Urbanization produces scattered islands of wealth, but the vast majority of Indians lack jobs and must deal with inadequate government services and neglected infrastructure. Many of the nation's youth, feeling betrayed by government promises to reduce income inequality, retreat to their religious, regional and caste identities, aggravating sectarianism.[73]

Such a future could have incendiary implications. The sharp decline in life satisfaction amid the steady GDP growth already mirrors conditions in Egypt just before the 2011 uprising there, says Lall, the Gallup analyst. "You could have a weak economy that eventually plateaus; a fairly low level of income; and the demographic dividend . . . turns into a demographic disaster as unemployed youth resort to violence and India's politicians adopt more nativist and chauvinist policies," says Dhume.

"These are the two poles," he says. "In reality, things tend to fall somewhere in the middle." The big question is whether India will fall more toward the positive or the negative side, he says. "Frankly, the jury is still out."

NOTES

1. "India 'WhatsApp child abduction rumours': Five more lynched," BBC (See video, "The India WhatsApp video driving people to murder"), July 2, 2018, https://tinyurl.com/ycju5tsg; Mattha Busby, "2,000-strong mob kill engineer over child kidnapping rumors in India's latest lynching," *The Independent*, July 16, 2018, https://tinyurl.com/y9535xsp.

2. "The World Factbook: India," Central Intelligence Agency, https://tinyurl.com/ypn8hx; "Poverty headcount ratio at national poverty lines (% of population)," World Bank, https://tinyurl.com/ycexux6d.

3. "2018 India Staff Report," Asia and Pacific Department, International Monetary Fund, Aug. 6, 2018, p. 5, https://tinyurl.com/yas8dfo9.

4. Poverty Calculation Net (povcalnet), World Bank, undated, https://tinyurl.com/ybvo7zfy. The $1.90 figure is based on 2011 purchasing power parity.

5. "Crime is top domestic issue in India," Global Attitudes and Trends, Pew Research Center, Nov. 13, 2017, https://tinyurl.com/ydyvlerx.

6. "Global Economic Prospects, Regional Outlook, South Asia," The World Bank, 2018, https://tinyurl.com/yde9cdfv.

7. Geeta Anand and Hari Kumar, "Narendra Modi Bans India's Largest Currency Bills in bid to Cut Corruption," *The New York Times*, Nov. 8, 2016, https://tinyurl.com/yd8gcufd.

8. Vicky Anning, ed., "Case closed, problems persist," Homeworkers Worldwide, India Committee of the Netherlands and Centre for Research on Multinational Corporations, June 2018, https://tinyurl.com/y9ze2t5u.

9. Ravneet Ahluwalia, "Taj Mahal Dropped From Tourism Booklet By State Government," *The Independent*, Oct. 3, 2017, https://tinyurl.com/ybsbr3k7.

10. Ellen Barry and Suhasini Raj, "Firebrand Hindu Priest Ascends India's Political Ladder," *The New York Times*, July 12, 2017, https://tinyurl.com/y9vwygqc.

11. Press Trust of India, "India refuses to endorse China's Belt and Road Initiative," *The Hindu*, June 10, 2018, https://tinyurl.com/ydcfojow.

12. Vanda Felbab-Brown, "Why Pakistan supports terrorist groups, and why the US finds it so hard to induce change," Brookings Institution, Jan. 5, 2018, https://tinyurl.com/y9yxabnl.

13. Arthur Neslen, "India unveils global solar alliance of 120 countries at Paris climate summit," *The Guardian*, Nov. 30, 2015, https://tinyurl.com/y7qyje5i.

14. Press Trust of India, "World Bank sees India as fastest growing economy for next 3 years," *The Mint*, June 8, 2018, https://tinyurl.com/ybwom3rs.

15. *Ibid.*

16. Madhura Karnik, "600 million people are now part of India's middle class—including your local carpenter," *Quartz*, July 29, 2016, https://tinyurl.com/y8dvytqv.

17. Keith Breene, "6 Surprising Facts about India's exploding middle class," World Economic Forum, Nov. 7, 2016, https://tinyurl.com/y99lttse.

18. "Video Shows Clashes Of Indian, Chinese Soldiers At Ladakh," YouTube, Aug. 19, 2017, https://tinyurl.com/y9uwno3z.

19. "India and China troops clash along Himalayan border," BBC News, Aug. 16, 2017, https://tinyurl.com/ya4kwu92.

20. Dipanjan Roy Chaudhury, "There won't be a war at Doklam as India and China agree to disengage," *The Economic Times*, Aug. 29, 2017, https://tinyurl.com/y9byg9r2.

21. "Indo-Pacific Region Not a Club of Limited Members: Modi," *The Wire*, June 2, 2018, https://tinyurl.com/yd33m3la.

22. *Ibid.*

23. Amit Bhandari and Chandni Jindal, "Chinese Investments in India's Neighbourhood," Gateway House, March 12, 2018, https://tinyurl.com/ydgd7fwb.

24. "India and Indonesia Agree Naval Cooperation at Sabang," *The Maritime Executive*, May 30, 2018, https://tinyurl.com/y7f8vax4.

25. "India's Modi calls for reform in speech to UN," BBC News, Sept. 27, 2014, https://tinyurl.com/ydy6x9a4.

26. *Ibid.*

27. Logan Nye, "The Top 10 Militaries of the World in 2017," Military.com, Aug. 4, 2017, https://tinyurl.com/y8mphgvk.

28. "Election of five non-permanent members of the Security Council," United Nations, undated, https://tinyurl.com/ycp5rh9c.

29. Neelam Deo and Karan Pradhan, "Should India Give Up on the UN Security Council?" *The Diplomat*, Nov. 9, 2014, https://tinyurl.com/yad8n9hr.

30. Jeffrey Sachs, *The End of Poverty* (2005), p. 173.

31. Ken Moritsugu, "India Rising," *CQ Researcher*, May 2007, pp. 101-124; Manmohan Singh, "Of Oxford, Economics, Empire and Freedom," *The Hindu*, July 10, 2005, https://tinyurl.com/yarsc38j.

32. Tariq Ali, *The Nehrus and the Gandhis: An Indian Dynasty* (2005), p. 87; Singh, *op. cit.*

33. Ali, *ibid.*, pp. 93-101.

34. William Dalrymple, "The Great Divide: The violent legacy of Indian Partition," *The New Yorker*, June 29, 2015, https://tinyurl.com/ydfp6bk9.

35. Arvind Virmani, *Propelling India from Socialist Stagnation to Global Power: Vol. I* (2006), p. 43.

36. Moritsugu, *op. cit.*

37. Stephen P. Cohen, *India: Emerging Power* (2001), p. 41.

38. Moritsugu, *op. cit.*

39. Ali, *op. cit.*, pp. 181-187.

40. Kamal Nath, address to the 79th general meeting of the Federation of Indian Chambers of Commerce and Industry, Jan. 9, 2007.

41. Arvind Panagariya, "India in the 1980s and 1990s: A Triumph of Reforms," p. 11, International Monetary Fund, March 2004, https://tinyurl.com/y8xvx6eg.

42. "GNI per capita, Atlas method (current US$), 2018, The World Bank, 2018, https://tinyurl.com/y7g4ttac.

43. Strobe Talbott, *Engaging India* (2004), p. 52.

44. "GDP Growth Rate of India (Constant Prices) during 2001-02 to 2013-14," Open Government Data Platform India, CommunityData.gov.in, Feb. 4, 2015, https://tinyurl.com/yah6f64h.

45. "List of terrorist incidents in India," Wikipedia, https://tinyurl.com/nhnm5t2.

46. Reetika Syal, "The UPA-II Report Card," *The Hindu*, Oct. 18, 2016, https://tinyurl.com/y9v3uapv.

47. Priyamvada Gopal, "Narendra Modi's Transformation From International Outcast to India's Prime Minister," *The Nation*, May 21, 2014, https://tinyurl.com/yadem7w9.

48. "3 Years of Modi rule: FDI inflows jump to $60 billion in 2016-17 from $36 billion in 2013-14," *Financial Express*, May 19, 2017, https://tinyurl.com/yckwwfaz.

49. Justin Lall, "Indians' Life Satisfaction Goes Bust as Economy Booms," Gallup, July 1, 2018, https://tinyurl.com/ybpfr5ny.

50. *Ibid.*; "Mega Times Group poll: 71.9% of Indians say they will vote for Narendra Modi for PM again in 2019," *Times of India*, May 26, 2018, https://tinyurl.com/ydxn5x9h.

51. Lall, *op. cit.*

52. *Ibid.*

53. "Richest 1 percent bagged 73 percent of wealth created last year—poorest half of India got 1 percent, says Oxfam India," press release, Oxfam, Jan. 22, 2018, https://tinyurl.com/y72pmwb8.

54. Luisa Kroll and Kerry Dolan, "The Billionaires 2018," Forbes, March 6, 2018, https://tinyurl.com/yat97ht6; "GNI per capita," *op. cit.*

55. "Richest 1 percent bagged 73 percent of wealth created last year—poorest half of India got 1 percent, says Oxfam India," *op. cit.*

56. Steve Crabtree, "Indians' Life Ratings Depend on Which India They Live in," Gallup, Aug. 30, 2018, https://tinyurl.com/y84k4jvl.

57. Mayank Bhardwaj, "As election looms, Modi's popularity wanes in rural India," Reuters, June 3, 2018, https://tinyurl.com/ybe7ku9g.

58. *Ibid.*

59. "Labor force, total," The World Bank, 2018, https://tinyurl.com/ybfh2fgv.

60. Bhardwaj, *op. cit.*

61. P. Sainath, "In India, Farmers Face a Terrifying Crisis," *The New York Times*, April 13, 2018, https://tinyurl.com/ydarybt8.

62. Zeenat Saberin, "Why are Indian farmers protesting?" Aljazeera, June 5, 2018, https://tinyurl.com/y9lm395e.

63. Jeffrey Gettleman and Suhasini Raj, "Lower-Caste Fury Shakes India, and Hints at Fiery Election Ahead," *The New York Times*, April 6, 2018, https://tinyurl.com/yb54tmxs.

64. Kallie Szczepanski, "History of India's Caste System," ThoughtCo, Sept. 29, 2018, https://tinyurl.com/y9hmgfk8; BBC, "What is India's caste system?" July 20, 2017, https://tinyurl.com/yantvagk.

65. Gettleman and Raj, *op. cit.*

66. Vindu Goel and Hari Kumar, "India Wants to Give Half a Billion People Free Health Care," *The New York Times*, Feb. 1, 2018, https://tinyurl.com/ycfqoypg.

67. Joanna Slater, "India's government is arresting lawyers and activists amid accusations of plotting to overthrow Modi," *The Washington Post*, Sept. 28, 2018, https://tinyurl.com/ybsk5akd.

68. Rajesh Roy and Bill Spindle, "U.S., India Look to Patch Up Rocky Relationship With Diplomacy, Defense Deals," *The Wall Street Journal*, Sept. 4, 2018, https://tinyurl.com/y7vmvtzy.

69. *Ibid.*

70. Idrees Ali, "In symbolic nod to India, U.S. Pacific command changes name," Reuters, May 30, 2018, https://tinyurl.com/yar9bpbe.

71. Indrani Bagchi, "Access to Omani port to help India check China at Gwadar," *Times of India*, Feb. 14, 2018, https://tinyurl.com/ybvsohw8.

72. Milan Vaishnav, "An Indian Nightmare: Is New Delhi Ready for the Twenty-First Century?" *Foreign Affairs*, March 1, 2018, https://tinyurl.com/y7529nzb.

73. *Ibid.*

BIBLIOGRAPHY

Selected Sources

Books

Ayres, Alyssa, *Our Times Has Come: How India Is Making Its Place in the World*, Oxford University Press, 2017.
A former U.S. diplomat traces India's economic liberalization and its rise as a global power.

Crabtree, James, *The Billionaire Raj: A Journey Through India's New Gilded Age*, Tim Duggan Books, 2018.
A former Mumbai bureau chief for Britain's *Financial Times* explores India's new billionaire class and the economic policies that created it.

Goswami, Namrata, *India's Approach to Asia: Strategy, Geopolitics and Responsibility*, Pentagon Press, 2015.
An Indian defense expert at New Delhi's Institute for Defence Studies and Analyses examines India's security issues, including its border disputes with China, military modernization and its strategic relations and rivalries with major powers.

Poonam, Snigdha, *Dreamers: How Young Indians Are Changing Their World*, Viking, 2018.
An Indian journalist profiles her country's Millennials and their uncertain future in a country with a booming economy but few opportunities.

Articles

"India refuses to endorse China's Belt and Road Initiative," *The Hindu*, June 10, 2018, https://tinyurl.com/ydcfojow.
India turned down China's invitation to participate in its pan-Asian infrastructure initiative, alleging the Pakistan spur is being built on disputed territory.

"World Bank sees India as fastest growing economy for next 3 years," *The Mint*, June 8, 2018, https://tinyurl.com/ybwom3rs.
The World Bank projects "robust" growth for India as factors holding back growth fade.

Bagchi, Indrani, "Access to Omani port to help India check China at Gwadar," *Times of India*, Feb. 14, 2018, https://tinyurl.com/ybvsohw8.
India seeks port privileges in the Omani port of Duqm as a way to balance China's maritime presence in Pakistan.

Barry, Ellen, and Suhasini Raj, "Firebrand Hindu Priest Ascends India's Political Ladder," *The New York Times*, July 12, 2017, https://tinyurl.com/y9vwygqc.
Two reporters explain the growing appeal of Hindu nationalism in Indian politics.

Chaudhury, Dipanjan Roy, "There won't be a war at Doklam as India and China agree to disengage," *Economic Times*, Aug. 29, 2017, https://tinyurl.com/y9byg9r2.
India's border disputes with China are unlikely to provoke a war but will remain a source of tension.

Doshi, Vidhi, "India launches ambitious health-care program for poor," *The Washington Post*, Sept. 24, 2018, https://tinyurl.com/yclh9a9t.
The Indian government introduces a massive health care program for a half billion poor people, noting it is unclear how much it will cost.

George, Steve, "Gender discrimination kills 239,000 girls in India each year, study finds," CNN, May 15, 2018, https://tinyurl.com/yaqsful9.
A study published in the British medical journal, *The Lancet*, finds that nearly a quarter million girls up to age five die every year in India due to neglect and gender bias.

Lall, Justin, "Indians' Life Satisfaction Goes Bust as Economy Booms," Gallup, July 1, 2018, https://tinyurl.com/ybpfr5ny.
A Gallup Poll analyst cites India's enormous income inequality as the reason most Indians are unhappy despite the country's economic progress.

Safi, Michael, "India's huge solar ambitions could push coal further into shade," *The Guardian*, June 29, 2018, https://tinyurl.com/y8aeh7z9.
India announces plans to develop 100 gigawatts of solar power to underscore its commitment to reducing greenhouse gases, even though the country lacks the infrastructure and the demand for so much solar power, a British journalist writes.

Reports and Studies

Anning, Vicky, ed., "Case closed, problems persist," Homeworkers Worldwide, India Committee of the Netherlands and Centre for Research on Multinational Corporations, June 2018, https://tinyurl.com/y9ze2t5u.
A study by three labor rights organizations finds that despite efforts by Western clothing companies to ensure fair treatment of all workers in their supply chains, female workers in India are still the victims of discrimination.

Chowdhury, Afra R., *et al.*, "Reflections of Employers' Gender Preference in Job Ads in India," World Bank Group, March 2018, https://tinyurl.com/y8bb5sjp.
A team of social scientists examines how job ads in India expose blatant gender bias.

Kang, Kenneth H., and Seán Nolan, "India: 2018," International Monetary Fund, Aug. 6, 2018, https://tinyurl.com/yanfktbv.
The International Monetary Fund's Asia and Pacific Department predicts robust growth for at least the next three years.

For More Information

Centre for Policy Research, Dharma Marg, Chanakyapuri, New Delhi 110021, India; 91-11-2611-5273; www.cprindia.org. Organization that researches Indian public policy issues.

Institute for Defence Studies and Analyses, 1 Development Enclave, Delhi Cantt, New Delhi 110010, India; 91-11-2614-6653; www.idsa.in. Think tank that studies Indian national security issues.

Institute of Peace and Conflict Studies, B-7/3 Lower Ground Floor, Safdarjung Enclave, New Delhi 110029, India; 91-11-4100-1900; www.ipcs.org. Organization that researches South Asian security issues.

National Bureau of Asian Research, 1819 L St., N.W., Ninth Floor, Washington, DC 20036; 202-347-9767; www.nbrDC@nbr.org. Research institution that studies strategic, political, economic and other issues affecting U.S. relations with Asia.

World Bank, 1818 H St., N.W., Washington, DC 20433; 202-473-1000; www.worldbank.org. International finance group that provides economic analysis and subsidized loans to developing countries.

7

The Future of Cash

Will digital payment systems replace paper currency?

By Hannah H. Kim

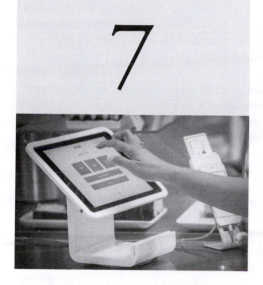

Jamie Birdwell-Branson does not remember a time when she regularly used cash to buy things. "I've always just used my debit card," says the 30-year-old freelance writer and editor who lives in Toledo, Ohio. "I've always thought it was more convenient because I have an actual record online of every single thing I'm purchasing."

It doesn't always work. On a holiday road trip last year, she and her husband stopped at a toll plaza outside Oklahoma City. Her husband, who was driving, handed his card to the man in the toll booth, who "just looked completely befuddled," she says. "It was like he had never been confronted with this modern mystery of a debit card before."

But such cash only facilities may be a dying breed. In a typical week, Birdwell-Branson routinely uses her debit card to pay for almost every transaction, from her morning coffee to her gym membership to weekly grocery purchases. "I get really salty" about having to take out cash, she says. "I'm 99.99 percent cashless."

The rise of digital payment systems and electronic banking has led to debates among economists, business experts and the public about the future of cash. Advocates of a cashless economy argue that the physical wallet and its contents will soon become historical artifacts. A cashless society, in which all financial transactions will be conducted through transfers of digital information, could be a more efficient, practical and traceable money system, they argue.

From *CQ Researcher,*
July 19, 2019

Critics of a cashless economy, however, say the nation is ill-equipped for such a transition. Barriers to banking and technology may deny portions of the population access to basic goods and services, they say. Some people will want to continue to use cash for a variety of reasons, such as for budgeting or privacy, the critics also point out. Others may not have the access, finances or skills to acquire formal banking services or a smartphone, or simply do not like banks.

"We have fierce individualism in this country, and cash is a part of that in many parts of the country," says Sarah Jane Hughes, a professor of commercial law at Indiana University's Maurer School of Law in Bloomington.

Cash is still the most frequently used payment instrument in the United States, but mainly for transactions of less than $10, according to a 2018 study by the Federal Reserve Bank of Boston. The study found that while debit cards, cash and credit cards were the most popular payment instruments, the adoption of mobile apps and online accounts for making payments was steadily increasing. About half of U.S. consumers used mobile or online methods in 2017.[1]

"It's inevitable that [payments] are going to become more digitized and that cash is going to eventually wither," says Michael Best, an assistant professor of economics at Columbia University. "It will end up being that cash gets used only for very small, or very illegal, transactions."

Cashless payments include a wide range of fund transfer methods: credit and debit cards, prepaid cards, bank account transfers, bank and traveler's checks, money orders, direct deduction from income and cryptocurrency such as bitcoin. They also include mobile apps linked to credit and debit cards, as well as transactions connected to a user's credit card or bank account that are made through online payment intermediaries such as PayPal and Venmo.[2]

The trend toward cashless payments may be accelerated by Facebook's announcement in June that it would create its own Libra cryptocurrency in partnership with digital and credit card companies.[3]

The dollar is the U.S. national currency. Its value is backed by collateral held by the Federal Reserve, the central bank of the United States, most of it in the form of government securities.[4] The Federal Reserve's Board of Governors determines how much new currency will be produced each year, and the Treasury Department's Bureau of Engraving and Printing prints U.S. currency.[5] About $1.70 trillion is in circulation, according to the Federal Reserve.[6]

The Treasury's U.S. Mint produces coinage. But due to the rising prices of metals, the cost of producing pennies and nickels has exceeded their worth since 2006, resulting in financial losses to the Mint, according to the U.S. Government Accountability Office.[7] In 2015, a penny cost about 1.7 cents to make, while a nickel cost 8 cents to produce.[8]

The Federal Reserve Bank of Chicago estimates that demand for

Fewer Americans Using Cash

The share of U.S. adults who say they do not use cash in their typical weekly transactions increased 5 percentage points from 2015 to 2018, while the proportion who made almost all purchases with cash fell 6 points.

How U.S. Adults Made Weekly Purchases, 2015 and 2018

2015: 24% (All/almost all with cash), 51% (Some with cash), 24% (None with cash)

2018: 18% (All/almost all with cash), 52% (Some with cash), 29% (None with cash)

● All/almost all with cash ● Some with cash ● None with cash

Note: Nonresponses not shown. The margin of error is plus or minus 1.5 percentage points.

Source: Andrew Perrin, "More Americans are making no weekly purchases with cash," Pew Research Center, Dec. 12, 2018, https://tinyurl.com/yyq9awl6

U.S. currency will increase by at least 1.7 percent, and as much as 10.2 percent, by 2028. If the lower estimate proves correct, the main reason will be increased consumer adoption of new payment technologies, the bank said. If the higher projection is borne out, it will be because of increased foreign use of U.S. dollars.[9]

The dollar is also the global economy's reserve currency, the currency that other nations hold, in part to pay for purchases of oil and other commodities that are priced in dollars. As the world's most popular currency, the dollar is accepted for routine transactions in many countries, even North Korea.[10] U.S. dollars are seen as a secure form of currency in many other countries, especially those with unstable political or financial systems, according to a 2018 report by the Federal Reserve Bank of Chicago.[11] Some nations, such as Ecuador, have even adopted the dollar as their official currency.[12]

"There are places around the world that don't enjoy the sound banking systems that we have in the U.S., so they're more likely to use cash than to rely on deposit accounts to make payments," says William J. Luther, a director at the American Institute for Economic Research, a Massachusetts-based think tank.

According to research by Federal Reserve economist Ruth Judson, while overall demand for U.S. currency continues to grow, demand for smaller denominations, including the $20 bill, has been slowing, which may be the first indication of a declining domestic need for cash.[13]

Cash serves another purpose: it is the medium of choice for illicit activities. This helps explain two seemingly contradictory trends: a steady increase in the demand for U.S. dollars, most notably the $100 bill, even as the average value of consumer purchases made in cash declines. In 2017, the $100 bill became the most widely circulated note in circulation, even exceeding the $1 bill.[14]

"Eighty percent of the value of all U.S. cash in circulation is in $100 bills," says Campbell Harvey, a professor of finance at Duke University. "But most people don't carry $100s. They're hard to use, because retailers don't want to accept them because of counterfeit risk. Where are these $100 bills?" Cash critics say the rising demand for $100 bills is directly tied to paper currency's utility for activities such as money laundering, tax evasion and purchases of illegal goods.

The proliferation of cashless payment methods, as well as payment service providers (PSPs) such as PayPal that facilitate online money transfers, has given consumers and business owners more ways to conduct cashless transactions than in the past. The global payments market grew 11 percent in 2017, topping $1.9 trillion, according to the consulting firm McKinsey, which identified the Asia-Pacific region as dominating the revenue pool. The report predicted increased growth in the payments market as more emerging economies continue to invest in electronic money systems.[15]

Cashless payment methods are not as widely used in the United States as in some other parts of the world, where both cards and mobile wallets are so popular that cash use is declining rapidly. Sweden is the world's most cashless society; most payments are made with debit cards or a mobile payment app called Swish—which allow the user to make a purchase by withdrawing an amount directly from a checking account.[16] The country could become completely cashless by 2023, according to researchers at the Copenhagen School of Economics.[17]

In China, mobile payment apps have drastically changed day-to-day transactions in cities over the last five years. Some stores, markets and food stalls in urban centers no longer accept paper currency.[18] More than three-fourths of Chinese smartphone users made a mobile purchase in 2017, according to the market research firm eMarketer. Earlier this year, China's central bank and other regulatory bodies released a joint report announcing an initiative to make mobile payments accessible in rural areas by the end of 2020.[19]

"There are societies much more cashless than the U.S. We're behind," says Daniel Levine, the director of the Avant-Guide Institute, a business consultancy on trends influencing the global marketplace. "We have technological challenges and societal challenges."

Nevertheless, payment card transactions have grown rapidly in the United States since 2000, according to the most recent annual payments study by the Federal Reserve. The yearly growth of total card payments accelerated in 2017 from the study's previously reported increases. Remote payments are also increasing faster than in-person payments, which suggests a changing pattern in how U.S. consumers buy and spend.[20]

The payment habits of younger U.S. consumers are leading the cashless trend. A 2018 study by the Pew

Research Center, a Washington-based research organization, found that more than one-third of adults under age 50 made no cash purchases during an average week.[21] A survey by the credit card and banking company Capital One found that Millennials, defined as those born between 1981 and 1996, were the demographic most likely to report that they "rarely or never" carried cash and that paying with cash was "inconvenient."[22]

Polls that have attempted to measure public perception regarding the outlook of cash show conflicting results. A 2016 Gallup poll found that 62 percent of respondents expected the United States to become a cashless society within their lifetime.[23] But a 2018 study by YouGov, an international public opinion and market research firm, found that only one in five U.S. adults believed that their payments will become completely cashless within their lifetime. Among those who expressed that belief, almost half said the United States would transform into a cashless society within five years.[24]

"It really doesn't make any sense that in the future we're going to be using paper," says Harvey, the Duke professor. "Physical cash will be a legacy."

Stella Adams, the CEO of S J Adams Consulting, a fair housing and lending consulting firm in Durham, N.C., disagrees. "We need cash," she says. "Cash is protected by the Federal Reserve. It has gotten the full faith and credit of the United States behind it."

As economists, businesses, payments specialists and the public debate the future of cash, these are some of the questions they are asking:

Are cashless payment policies discriminatory?

In recent years, some brick-and-mortar businesses have experimented with becoming cash free. In 2017, clothing shops Everlane and Bonobos, the hair salon Drybar and fast-casual restaurants Sweetgreen, Dos Toros and Shake Shack stopped accepting cash, according to a report by the market research company eMarketer. Many of these businesses were in metropolitan areas where digital-only branding appealed to younger consumers. However, public criticism that cashless businesses are discriminatory and a legislative backlash have halted the trend.[25]

The growing acceptance of online and mobile banking, as well as e-commerce businesses such as Amazon, have normalized the idea of conducting financial transactions digitally. Within the last two decades, a number of payment service providers have emerged to allow more businesses to accept cashless transactions. Notable PSPs include PayPal, which facilitates worldwide money transfers, and Square, which offers point-of-sale and mobile payment services.

Before PSPs, businesses that accepted credit or debit cards and other electronic funds had to open a traditional merchant account with a bank. This required processing service fees, equipment, software and security features that were prohibitively expensive for many small businesses.[26] The advent of PayPal, Square and other payment service technologies made it more convenient and affordable for a variety of businesses to accept card and electronic transactions, and even allowed solo service providers, such as street musicians, to accept cashless payments.

"Cash transactions are becoming less and less popular

Debit Cards Dominate Noncash Payments

Non-prepaid debit cards have become the most common method of cashless transaction in the United States, increasing from 25 billion payments in 2006 to almost 70 billion in 2017, the latest year for which data is available, according to Federal Reserve estimates.

U.S. Noncash Payment Methods, 2006-17, in billions*

* Estimates for electronic funds transfers and check payments were not available for 2016 and 2017.
Source: "Payment Research," Board of Governors of the Federal Reserve System, last updated Jan. 18, 2019, Fig. 1, https://tinyurl.com/y227vzgd

Legend:
- Non-prepaid debit cards
- Credit cards
- Electronic funds transfers*
- Checks*
- Prepaid debit cards

every day, and businesses who refuse to adapt are doomed to fail," says Nate Masterson, CEO of the e-commerce business Maple Holistics, which sells hair care products.

But in some instances there has been a backlash against brick and mortar businesses that do not accept cash. Critics assert that cashless payment policies exclude people who rely on paper currency and who may not have bank accounts. In the face of this reaction, many no-cash pioneers, such as Apple, the brick-and-mortar convenience store chain Amazon Go and the salad chain Sweetgreen, have reversed their policies.

Many of the first cashless brick-and-mortar businesses were urban fast-casual restaurants. Sweetgreen announced its decision to go cashless in late 2016 with a blog post titled, "Welcome to the Future—It's Cashless."[27] Sweetgreen said it was going the no-cash route because the level of cash transactions at its restaurants was declining anyway and that eliminating cash handling could discourage theft and improve employee efficiency.

Just over two years later, Sweetgreen reversed its payments policy in response to growing criticism. In a statement, the company said its cashless policy "had the unintended consequence of excluding those who prefer to pay or can only pay with cash."[28]

Federal law is silent on the question of whether businesses must accept cash.[29] But in May 2019, lawmakers introduced two pieces of legislation in Congress to stop businesses from going cashless. Rep. David Cicilline, D-R.I., introduced the Cash Always Should Be Honored (Cash) Act, which would authorize the Federal Trade Commission to enforce a ban on cashless establishments. The bill has attracted nine co-sponsors, all Democrats. Rep. Donald Payne, D-N.J., introduced a similar bill called the Payment Choice Act that would allow consumers to sue stores for not accepting cash.[30]

The bills follow recent action by some state and municipal governments to stop businesses from going cashless. In March, New Jersey became the second state to ban cashless stores (Massachusetts was the first), and in the same month Philadelphia became the first major U.S. city to do so.[31] Other cities, including New York, Chicago, San Francisco and Washington, are considering similar measures.[32]

New Jersey Assemblyman Paul Moriarty, who supported his state's law, said he did so because "a ban on

A Sweetgreen restaurant in Washington, D.C., gets ready for business. The fastcasual chain stopped accepting cash in late 2016 but reversed course in April amid criticism that the move discriminated against customers who lack access to digital payment methods or simply prefer cash.

cash is discriminatory. It marginalizes the poor, marginalizes young people who haven't established credit yet. People prefer to pay in cash, and people . . . don't want every aspect of life noted by a credit card company, right down to a stick of gum."[33]

Supporters of cash payments argue that card and digital payment systems have adoption barriers that may exclude some people. For example, they say, those under the age of 18 may be forced to rely on cash because they cannot open a bank account without a parent or guardian.[34]

The so-called unbanked—adults who do not have a bank or credit union account—also rely on cash. About 5 percent of adults in the United States are unbanked, according to a 2018 Federal Reserve report. And about 18 percent of those who do participate in traditional banking services are considered underbanked, which the Fed defined as having used an alternative financial service, such as a check-cashing service.[35]

Advocates of policies to promote greater economic equality argue that many bank accounts have maintenance and overdraft fees that are prohibitive for people of modest means.[36] "We are not prepared," says Adams, the fair lending consultant. "We currently do not have the financial infrastructure in place that has addressed the needs of low- or moderate-income communities and workers as it relates to movement into a cashless society."

A 2018 Pew study found a sharp divide along income lines regarding the use of cash. Those with a yearly

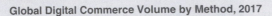

Mobile Payments Popular Worldwide

Mobile app payments accounted for more than 30 percent of the value of worldwide commercial digital transactions in 2017, with the Asia-Pacific region leading other parts of the world.

Global Digital Commerce Volume by Method, 2017

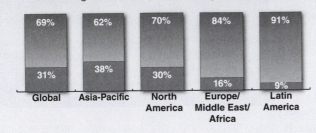

	Global	Asia-Pacific	North America	Europe/Middle East/Africa	Latin America
Web Browser	69%	62%	70%	84%	91%
Mobile App	31%	38%	30%	16%	9%

Source: Sukriti Bansal et al., "Global payments: Expansive growth, targeted opportunities," McKinsey & Co., October 2018, Exhibit 4, https://tinyurl.com/y28cjrg5

household income of at least $75,000 were more than twice as likely to say they made no purchases with cash during a typical week than those making less than $30,000 annually, Pew found.[37]

Some owners of cashless establishments argue that their policies are not discriminatory. "We are inclusive of all because anyone can go get a prepaid card and load cash on it and then eat with us, if they want," said Jeremiah Dupin, who runs a restaurant in Kansas City, Mo., that specializes in poke, a Hawaiian raw-fish salad.[38]

Can cashless transactions be private and secure?

While digital payment methods create transaction records for each user, cash can be anonymous, providing a measure of privacy to the purchaser. Internal Revenue Service (IRS) rules require a cash transaction to be reported only when it exceeds $10,000.[39] Cash is also essentially untraceable.

In addition, noncash transactions and the systems that process them are vulnerable to cyberattacks. Such attacks on financial service firms are more frequent than in other industries, and increased by more than 70 percent worldwide in 2017 over the previous year, according to a report by HTF Market Intelligence, a consulting firm based in India.[40] A 2018 survey by the International Monetary Fund found that businesses ranked cyber risks as the greatest threat to the broader economy, outranking geopolitical threats or the impact of new regulations.[41]

Many of the biggest cyberattacks on record have targeted databases that store sensitive personal and financial information. When stolen, such information can be used for identity theft and fraud. One of the largest data breaches was the 2017 hack involving Equifax, the consumer reporting agency, in which more than 150 million customer records were stolen, including Social Security numbers, birthdates and credit card data.[42]

Cybersecurity consultant Tom Arnold says it is difficult to measure how well databases that store personal information are protected. "Sadly, there are so many of them," says Arnold, who is co-founder of Payment Software Co., a California-based security firm. "Whether it's a government database, or a bank's database, or an individual company that has a database—are they tested? Have they really been examined? And what's coming in the future that might cause them a problem is hard to tell. Consumers still have to be vigilant."

Government regulations in the United States protect consumers against being held responsible for the losses due to credit card fraud and theft, according to the Federal Deposit Insurance Corporation, the government agency that insures bank deposits.[43] "If consumers weren't indemnified, and were actually carrying the brunt of the loss, they wouldn't use [payment cards] because it would be too dangerous," Arnold says. As a result, he says, credit card issuers and other payment companies support such regulations, "and that's frankly why they charge fees. They're trying to cover that loss that the industry is carrying as a burden." (Credit card companies charge some cardholders annual service fees and charge businesses per-transaction fees.)

Those fees also give banks and credit card companies a strong financial interest in promoting the idea of a cashless future, critics of the cashless trend argue. Brett Scott, author of *The Heretic's Guide to Global Finance: Hacking the Future of Money*, wrote that financial institutions are trying to steer consumers toward digital banking.

"Payments companies such as Visa and Mastercard want to increase the volume of digital payments services they sell, while banks want to cut costs," wrote Scott. "Branches require staff. Replacing them with standardized self-service apps allows the senior managers of financial institutions to directly control and monitor interactions with customers."[44]

Some payment processors, such as Visa and Mastercard, as well as intermediaries such as PayPal, offer user protections.[45] The payment processors' contract usually requires the issuing bank to absorb the cost of a fraudulent transaction, according to NerdWallet, a personal finance website directed toward Millennials. The bank could shift the burden of reimbursement to the business that allowed the fraudulent transactions to take place. While a large bank or business may be able to cover serious fraud reimbursement costs, the liabilities could jeopardize the solvency of smaller regional banks as well as smaller businesses.[46]

Other critics say a society that relies too heavily on cashless payments creates privacy concerns. While federal financial privacy laws limit the amount of personal and payment information a financial institution can share with unaffiliated third parties, banks that issue credit or debit cards monitor consumer spending for fraud detection, risk management and marketing. Privacy advocates have raised concerns about how financial institutions could excessively monitor this data. For example, credit card issuers have used detailed credit card information—such as the types of stores where consumers have shopped—to determine how much customers can borrow and at what interest rates.[47]

"Cash is the ultimate privacy protector," says Paul Stephens, a director of policy and advocacy for the Privacy Rights Clearinghouse, a San Diego-based consumer advocacy group. "Once you start bringing in other forms of payment, there are opportunities for you to be tracked, both by the company that you are paying and by the issuer of the credit card or debit card. And then when you bring a digital payment into the picture, you're adding yet another entity."

Most peer-to-peer payment services—digital services that allow payments to be sent directly from one user to another, such as Venmo, Zelle and Facebook Payments—reserve broad rights to sell

Supporters of Venezuelan presidential candidate Henri Falcón hold replica $100 bills at a rally in Caracas in 2018. Falcón, who lost the election, called for swapping Venezuela's devalued currency for the U.S. dollar. American banknotes are favored during times of political upheaval as a way to safeguard assets.

Getty Images/Bloomberg/Wil Riera

users' data to third parties for purposes that include targeted advertising.[48]

"You need to look at what is being done with your personal information by that new entity," Stephens says. "Are they just acting as an intermediary and passing the information through without utilizing it in any manner, or are they monetizing that data?" Stephens says that many privacy policy statements sent to consumers are written in highly legalistic language and often do not help inform consumers on how their information is being used.

Will Cash Become Obsolete?

Demand for cash increases during periods of economic and political uncertainty. During the 1990s and early 2000s, greater demand for U.S. currency coincided with political and economic upheaval in Germany, the former Soviet Union and several Latin American countries as well as in the aftermath of the Sept. 11 terrorist attacks in the United States, according to research by Federal Reserve economist Judson.[49]

She noted that demand for dollars declined around 2002, coinciding with the introduction of the European Union's euro and the stabilization of economies in countries around the eurozone and the former Soviet Union. Then, as the global financial crisis struck in 2008, demand for U.S. dollars increased once again, both internationally and domestically.

Demand for cash continues to grow today.[50] Luther of the American Institute for Economic Research says foreigners may use U.S. dollars in their home countries for both day-to-day transactions and to safeguard their money. "If you're in a kleptocracy and you hold your wealth in a bank account, that's pretty easy to confiscate," he says. "If you're holding your wealth in the denominated assets of the domestic currency, and that currency experiences really high inflation rates unexpectedly, then you see your wealth eroded."

For some economists, such as Kenneth Rogoff of Harvard University, the anonymity that cash affords is why it is used for illegal economic activity. "The biggest use of cash—really, by far—in the world is in large-scale real estate transactions, where people are trying to launder money," he said.[51]

In his 2016 book *The Curse of Cash: How Large-Denomination Bills Aid Crime and Tax Evasion and Constrain Monetary Policy*, Rogoff argued for a society that relies less on cash, although not one that is completely cashless. Phasing out large-denomination bills, such as the $100 bill, will help to crack down on the underground economy, he said in an interview with *Quartz* last year.

"If someone wants to buy something for a couple thousand dollars and not have anyone know about it, that's one thing. If they want to buy a $40 million

Activists in Mumbai, India, protest on the second anniversary of the removal of 500- and 1,000-rupee notes from circulation. Prime Minister Narendra Modi invalidated the notes to crack down on tax evasion and financial crimes, but critics say the move was poorly planned.

apartment in Trump Tower or pay off a bribe of $150,000 in cash, you want to make that hard," Rogoff said.[52]

Columbia University's Best says there is an international dimension to cash real estate purchases. High-wealth U.S. citizens who may try to hide some of their earnings from the IRS "don't have big piles of cash sitting around to buy real estate with," Best says. "On the other hand, if you think about oligarchs from countries with a weaker rule of law who might actually have large piles of cash and want to park it in real estate in Manhattan, those transactions are likely to be taken first in cash."

Best thinks transitioning to a cashless economy in order to reduce tax evasion would mainly affect small-business owners and self-employed individuals. "It's important to note that tax evasion by very, very high-wealth individuals or very large corporations has nothing to do with the ability to use cash," Best says.

In an effort to crack down on tax evasion and other financial crimes, Indian Prime Minister Narendra Modi in 2016 removed his country's two highest-value notes from circulation. The 500 and 1,000 rupee notes (worth about $7 and $14 respectively), which made up about 85 percent of India's currency in circulation, were "demonetized," or invalidated by the government. The move led to street protests, long lines at banks and ATM machines and cash shortages.[53]

Critics of India's demonetization efforts argue that the move failed to expose unreported wealth. While cashless payments and direct tax collection did increase in the year following demonetization, some analysts said cash use in India has not decreased, and that there had been increases in direct tax collection in the past.[54] "In large part it didn't go well because it wasn't very well planned," Best says. "There's a very large informal economy in India that operates on cash, and so when you withdraw a bunch of the banknotes, it actually seriously disrupts a lot of economic activity."

The eurozone's 19 member countries stopped issuing the 500 euro note (worth about $570) this year. The decision to stop printing the note was made by the European Central Bank (ECB) in 2016, due to the denomination's use in illegal activities. However, in Germany and Austria, the least cashless countries in Europe, the ECB's move was controversial, and both nations delayed the phaseout of the note by three months.[55]

Some critics of going cashless argue that an electronic money system can give too much power to the state, citing past examples when U.S. government agencies used electronic payment systems to police activities. In 2010, the government pressured Visa, Mastercard, PayPal and other financial enterprises to stop processing donations to the whistleblower site WikiLeaks after the organization released thousands of State Department cables.[56]

"How much do you trust government and corporate authorities to run a public banking system in a liberal and open manner, and to not use that power to punish either political ideologies or social behaviors they don't like?" wrote Jeff Spross, a business and economics journalist.[57]

Public distrust of corporate banks also remains a long-standing issue. Even nearly a decade after the 2008 financial crisis, Millennials continued to feel skeptical of big banks and credit issuers, according to a 2017 survey conducted by the World Economic Forum, the international economic think tank. Less than a third of the 30,000-plus respondents said they agreed with the statement that banks are fair and honest.[58]

For many people, the financial crisis demonstrated "that banks can't be trusted, and your money is only as safe as the government allows you to believe," said Tom Lee, co-founder and managing partner of Fundstrat, a New York-based market research firm. "That's why Millennials today have so little trust in banks, because of what their parents went through."

Analysts say that enduring distrust in banks is partly why new payment technologies have flourished among younger consumers.[59]

BACKGROUND
Establishing the Dollar

In the country's early history, money took many forms of chaotic value. In colonial America, there was no standard unit of currency. And because the colonists had an unfavorable balance of trade with the mother country, Great Britain, most British money circulating in the colonies was quickly returned to England to pay for imports.

For everyday purchases, colonists used the Spanish dollar, which circulated throughout the New World, especially from trade in the West Indies and Mexico.[60]

They also used commodities—such as tobacco leaves, beaver skins, sugar, rice and shells—as money. However, these items' supply and demand varied widely, which made them unreliable stores of value.[61]

In the 18th century, local colonial governments issued two types of paper currency: commodity-backed money and fiat money. Commodity-backed money included paper notes issued by land offices, which allowed colonists to use their land as collateral for debts and to pay interest in gold and silver coins.[62] Colonial governments also issued fiat money, or money without intrinsic value but with value established by users' faith in the issuing party.

One example of fiat money was the Continental, currency issued by the Continental Congress in 1775 to help finance the Revolutionary War and backed by anticipated tax revenues.[63] Continentals quickly lost their value, however, because the Continental Congress did not properly manage the amount in circulation and the British mounted a massive counterfeiting effort.[64] By 1781, Continentals had become worthless and ceased to circulate.[65]

After the federal government was established in 1789, Treasury Secretary Alexander Hamilton helped create a modern financial system for the new country and defined the U.S. dollar as backed by reserves of gold and silver. Hamilton also founded a national bank, the Bank of the United States, prompting state legislatures to charter more local banks. By the mid-1790s, a banking system had taken root in the United States that facilitated the growth of the national economy.[66]

However, the Bank of the United States was politically controversial. State governments reaped revenue from local banks through chartering fees, taxes and dividends earned from investments in the banks. Some state bankers resented how a national bank could compete directly with local banks.[67]

Congress rejected renewal of the national bank's charter in 1811. The Second Bank of the United States was established five years later, but President Andrew Jackson vetoed its rechartering in 1832, and the United States ceased to have a central bank until passage of the Federal Reserve Act of 1913.[68]

Throughout the first half of the 19th century, the country also lacked uniformity in banknotes. The national government provided currency only in coins, while individual banks issued several denominations

CHRONOLOGY

1600s-1860s *U.S. experiments with early forms of banking and currency.*

1600s American colonists use the Spanish dollar coin, commodity money (such as animal pelts or other objects of widely accepted value) and paper money issued by colonial governments as mediums of exchange.

1775 Continental Congress issues Continental currency to help finance the American Revolution, but it quickly depreciates and is worthless by 1781.

1791 Treasury Secretary Alexander Hamilton founds the First Bank of the United States, partly to create a common currency.

1811 Congress narrowly rejects renewal of the First Bank of the United States' charter, partly because state banks fear competition from a national bank.

1816 Second Bank of the United States is established . . . President Andrew Jackson vetoes its recharter in 1832 and redistributes its money among various state banks in 1836, ending the bank's operations.

1861 President Abraham Lincoln's government issues demand notes, a type of paper money, to finance Union participation in the Civil War . . . The Confederacy, initially formed by seven states that seceded from the United States, issues its own paper currency, the Confederate States dollar.

1862 United States notes, also known as legal tender notes, replace demand notes as paper currency.

1863 The National Banking Act of 1863 establishes a national banking system and currency, and an 1865 revision levies a tax that effectively abolishes state-backed currencies.

1900s-1960s *The credit card industry take shape.*

1913 The Federal Reserve Act establishes the Federal Reserve system, which introduces Federal Reserve notes, the paper currency now used throughout the United States.

1928 First credit cards, made of metal and called Charga-Plates, are issued by certain stores to select customers.

1944 Bretton Woods Conference, organized by Allied nations to create an international monetary policy after World War II, establishes the U.S dollar as the global reserve currency and ties the dollar's value to U.S gold reserves.

1950 Diners Club introduces the first credit card that can be used at a wide variety of establishments.

1955 Stanford Research Institute develops an automated bookkeeping system to speed up check processing.

1958 Bank of America issues its first BankAmericard credit cards in Fresno, Calif., an effort that goes national in 1966 and is renamed Visa in 1976.

1966 A group of California banks launch Mastercard.

1969 Chemical Bank installs the nation's first ATM on Long Island, N.Y. . . . Advances in electronic banking technology make Federal Reserve notes of $500 and above obsolete.

1970s-1990s *Banking and credit card payments move online.*

1971 President Richard Nixon severs the link between the U.S dollar and gold, ending the Bretton Woods system.

1978 First National Bank of Seattle issues nation's first debit card, which functions like a check.

1984 Landmark Banking Corp. establishes a nationwide ATM and debit card system.

1994 Stanford Federal Credit Union in California becomes the first financial institution to offer online banking. . . . In the first e-commerce sales transaction, a Philadelphia resident uses a credit card to buy a CD through a New Hampshire website called NetMarket.

1995 E-commerce websites Amazon and eBay launch.

1999 PayPal is established as part of a Palo Alto, Calif., company called Confinity to facilitate worldwide money transfers.

2000s-Present *Mobile payment apps debut.*

2008 Blockchain is introduced as the digital ledger for bitcoin cryptocurrency.

2010 Online payments processing company Square launches in San Francisco, expanding the number of brick-and-mortar stores and independent businesses that accept credit card and electronic payments. . . . Technology company Stripe launches in San Francisco to allow people and companies to make and receive credit card payments over the internet.

2011 Google Wallet (now known as Google Pay) debuts, allowing customers to make purchases using a mobile device.

2013 The iPhone 5S offers a fingerprint scanner that Apple later adapts to authenticate Apple Pay online purchases.

2017 The $100 bill becomes most popular U.S. currency in circulation around the world.

2019 States and cities increasingly enact laws requiring most brick-and-mortar businesses to accept cash to prevent discrimination against people who do not use banks.

---

of their own paper money. By 1860, there were several thousand different banknotes circulating in the country, each printed with the name of an individual bank and its promise to redeem the note in coins. The value of these banknotes fell the further they traveled from the issuing bank, and counterfeit currency thrived.[69]

In 1861 and 1862, Abraham Lincoln's Union government issued the country's first general circulation of paper money, called demand notes, as a way to pay for the costs incurred during the Civil War. The demand notes were printed with green ink, leading to the name "greenbacks." In 1862 they were replaced by United States notes, also known as legal tender notes.[70] The Confederacy issued its own currency.

The National Banking Act of 1863 and its revisions in 1864 and 1865 established a national banking system and currency. Yet even with the issuance of United States notes, about 200 different currencies were still in circulation in the Union states alone. But with the creation of a new banking system, chartered by the federal government rather than by individual states, a common national currency could be issued and accepted across state lines. Banknotes became a liability of the federal government, rather than that of state-backed banks.[71] However, the country still lacked a central bank to oversee monetary policy, which contributed to a series of financial panics following the Civil War.[72]

The Federal Reserve Act of 1913 established the Federal Reserve system, a central bank with 12 regional banks to oversee monetary policy—management of the nation's money supply and interest rates—and promote economic stability.[73] The Fed, as it came to be known, operated a national check-clearing system and introduced Federal Reserve notes denominated in U.S. dollars, the type of banknote still used today.[74] The Fed was authorized to print new currency, set interest rates and buy and sell U.S. Treasury debt.[75]

International recognition of the U.S. dollar as the world's reserve currency emerged at the end of World War II. In 1944, delegates from the Allied nations gathered in Bretton Woods, N.H., to establish an international monetary system and stabilize exchange rates.[76] At the time, the United States controlled two-thirds of the world's gold, which gave U.S. negotiators leverage to successfully argue that the Bretton Woods system should rest on both gold and the U.S. dollar. An international payments system was developed in which all other currencies were defined by their relationship to the dollar, which was convertible to gold.[77] This forced other countries to keep sufficient reserves of U.S. dollars, as well as other securities, to maintain fixed exchange rates.[78]

In the early 1970s, when some countries and currency traders increasingly began demanding gold for the dollars they held, the United States did not have enough gold to cover the global volume of dollars at the set price of $35 per ounce. In 1971, President Richard M. Nixon severed the link between the dollar and gold. This ended the Bretton Woods system and transitioned the U.S. dollar from a representative currency—money that could be exchanged for items of value such as

Sweden Moves Toward National E-Currency

E-krona may be offered to public for everyday use

Sweden is well on its way to becoming the world's first cashless society.

Use of cash continues to decline in the country of 10 million. Only 13 percent of Swedes paid for their most recent purchase in cash, according to a 2018 survey by the Riksbank, the country's central bank.[1] Researchers at the Copenhagen School of Economics have predicted that cash could be obsolete in Sweden by 2023.[2]

To prepare for that possibility, the Riksbank will operate a pilot project from 2019 to 2021 to test the need for a state-backed electronic currency called "e-krona"—named after the country's basic monetary unit—that would be offered to households and companies as a complement to cash.[3]

A shopper uses a Swedish 50 kronor note at a grocery store in Stockholm. Cash may be obsolete in Sweden by 2023, one study has predicted. The government is researching ways to prepare for a cashless society.

Sweden's move away from cash is rooted in the country's culture of trusting institutions and new technologies, said Claire Ingram Bogusz, a researcher at the Stockholm School of Economics. "The convenience of having your bank account, your money at your fingertips and increasingly on your smart watch vastly outweighs any concerns that [Swedes] have about security or about being tracked," Bogusz said.[4]

The e-krona project aims to address concerns that the Riksbank has linked to the rapid decline in use of cash. An electronic currency could, for example, provide a parallel system to help the country weather severe economic downturns, some experts say.[5] Swedish officials "want to ensure that the market of payments will continue to function no matter the circumstances, [such as] financial crises, or even in the case of a war," says Konstantinos Georgantas, a researcher at the Warwick Business School in the United Kingdom who has studied Sweden's e-krona initiative.

In 2018, Swedish financial authorities asked banks to continue offering cash to citizens, as government officials figure out ways to deal with the potential consequences of a cashless society.[6] A cashless money system can marginalize groups of people who rely on paper currency, such as the elderly, people with disabilities and those without bank accounts. It could also be vulnerable to cyberattacks or power outages, critics of the cashless trend say.[7] The e-krona would reduce this vulnerability by creating an independent, alternative payment system, Riksbank Governor Stefan Ingves said last year.

precious metals—to a fiat currency, or money with a value based upon the perceived stability of the government issuing it.[79]

Payment Technologies Evolve

With the circulation of money came the problem of how to use it to efficiently transact business. In the late

The Swedish government has warned citizens that giving up on cash completely may not be wise, and it distributed leaflets advising households to set aside some cash in case of a national crisis.[8]

For daily transactions, however, the Riksbank project proposes letting Swedes access e-krona that is stored on a card or a mobile app or held in an account at the Riksbank. Both options will be supported by an electronic platform that will contain an underlying central register for recording transactions. The register will make e-krona transactions traceable, the bank's second report on the e-krona project said.[9]

The Riksbank has said that e-krona will differ from bitcoin and other cryptocurrencies because, while cryptocurrencies have no official issuer, e-krona would be issued by the central bank and have the same value as banknotes and coins.[10]

The bank is considering a variety of technical systems to support e-krona, with particular emphasis on security and reliability, the second project report on e-krona said.[11]

The Riksbank will also explore changes to banking laws that would allow the bank to issue e-krona to the public. While the central bank currently offers money in the form of electronic transfers to commercial banks, "we're not supposed to offer accounts to citizens, so Parliament will need to make a decision on whether to allow this," said Monika Johansson, a lawyer and adviser at the Riksbank's payments department.[12]

The Swedish Parliament would also have to act to include e-krona in the country's definition of legal tender, according to Trijo, a Swedish cryptocurrency news site.[13] If e-krona becomes legal tender, the Riksbank would become a source of competition with private banks and payment service providers, experts say. "The Riksbank now is basically the bank of banks," Georgantas says. "Its customers are the banks themselves. But [Riksbank] would open up to the public and let people move their money into the central bank. The pushback from the commercial banks is expected to be strong."

A majority of Swedes were skeptical of the e-krona initiative, a 2018 survey conducted by the Swedish social research firm Sifo found. Despite the declining use of cash, seven out of 10 respondents said they wanted paper currency around as a payment option, the survey found.[14]

Bogusz, the Stockholm School of Economics researcher, said digital security and surveillance issues have created

some skepticism about a completely cashless society. "There is a very, very large number of people who . . . don't think that the state should be trusted as blindly as many do," she said.[15]

While Sweden is a forerunner in cashless commerce, some 40 other countries are also experimenting with or planning to research state-issued electronic currencies, according to the World Economic Forum.[16]

—*Hannah H. Kim*

[1] "The Riksbank's e-krona project, Report 2," Sveriges Riksbank, October 2018, https://tinyurl.com/y6ldc36s.

[2] Kyree Leary and Chelsea Gohd, "Sweden could stop using cash by 2023," World Economic Forum, Oct. 11, 2017, https://tinyurl.com/yxfeurt6.

[3] "The Riksbank's e-krona project, Report 2," op. cit.

[4] Maddy Savage, "Sweden's Cashless Experiment: Is It Too Much Too Fast?" *NPR*, Feb. 11, 2019, https://tinyurl.com/y4brvled.

[5] "Ingves: The e-krona and the payments of the future," Sveriges Riksbank, June 11, 2018, https://tinyurl.com/yxnpy2jj.

[6] "All banks should be obliged to handle cash," Riksbank, Oct. 22, 2018, https://tinyurl.com/y4h44ooc.

[7] Liz Alderman, "Sweden's Push to Get Rid of Cash has Some Saying, 'Not So Fast,'" *The New York Times*, Nov. 21, 2018, https://tinyurl.com/yxof7dsz.

[8] *Ibid.*; "Ingves: The e-krona and the payments of the future," op. cit.

[9] "The Riksbank's e-krona project, Report 2," op. cit.

[10] "Differences between e-krona and crypto-assets," Sveriges Riksbank, Oct. 18, 2018, https://tinyurl.com/y4gvpfn7.

[11] "The Riksbank's e-krona project, Report 2," op. cit.

[12] Amanda Billner, "There Are Plans for 'e-Krona' in Cash-Shy Sweden," *Bloomberg*, Oct. 26, 2018, https://tinyurl.com/yxb4j58a.

[13] Christian Ploog, "Swedish central bank wants new definition of 'legal tender'—but cryptocurrencies are out of the question," *Trijo News*, April 30, 2019, https://tinyurl.com/y4nau5po.

[14] "Most Swedes don't want country to go cash free: poll," *The Local Sweden*, March 19, 2018, https://tinyurl.com/y4ft3l7a.

[15] Savage, op. cit.

[16] "Central Banks and Distributed Ledger Technology: How are Central Banks Exploring Blockchain Today?" World Economic Forum, March 2019, https://tinyurl.com/y4jm7bn3.

18th century, banknotes with face values of $500 or higher were used in the United States primarily for interbank transfers and real estate purchases.[80] In 1780, North Carolina issued the first $500 note; in

1781, Virginia printed $2,000 notes.[81] With the absence of federal paper money, the U.S. government issued high-denomination Treasury notes to fund short-term national debts in periods of financial stress,

Mobile Payment Systems Attract Younger Consumers

"GenZers want their mobile wallets to think for them."

Younger Americans have embraced the digital wallet—but they want more than just convenience from it, experts in payment trends say.

Millennials (defined as those born between 1981 and 1996) and Generation Z consumers (born after 1996) make up more than 70 percent of U.S. mobile payment users, a survey by the Pew Research Center, a Washington research organization, found.[1] About a third of Millennials believed the future will be cashless, according to a 2015 survey by LinkedIn, the online social network, and Ipsos, a global market research firm.[2]

Experts say that the high adoption rates of payment service technologies among younger consumers will continue to reshape the finance industry. A cashless society is "a matter of time," although it will not arrive immediately, said Michael Vaughan, the chief operating officer at payment service provider Venmo. "It's going to take our lifetime and our kids' lifetime before you start to see this work itself out."[3]

Millennial and Gen Z consumers have payment preferences that contrast sharply with those of their parents' and grandparents' generations, according to a 2017 study by the global consulting firm Accenture. Younger adults and teenagers grew up in the digital age and are the leading adopters of new payment technologies, the study found.[4]

Gen Z is "likely to be the first generation to forgo the leather wallet for the digital wallet," the Accenture report said. "GenZers want their mobile wallets to think for them. One example would be a wallet that automatically chooses the card that offers the best reward or savings."[5]

But some researchers warn that mobile payments may encourage risky attitudes regarding spending and debt. Millennials who use mobile payment apps were more likely to be poor money managers than those who do not use such apps, according to a 2017 study by researchers at the George Washington University School of Business. App users, for example, were more likely to overdraw their checking accounts and accrue fees on their credit cards, the study found.[6]

The George Washington study does not argue that there was a causal relationship between using mobile payments and increased spending or debt, says Annamaria Lusardi, the lead researcher on the study and academic director of the university's Global Financial Literacy Excellence Center. But consumers using cashless payment systems may be less aware of the consequences of spending than those who use cash, she says. "What

such as the War of 1812 and the Mexican War of 1846-48.[82]

In 1865, the government printed the first gold certificates, a form of U.S. paper currency backed by gold held by the Treasury.[83] In 1934, the Treasury printed the $100,000 gold certificate for official transactions between Federal Reserve banks.[84] The last high-denomination bills of $500, $1,000, $5,000 and $10,000 were printed in 1945 but discontinued in 1969 due to lack of use.[85] While the main purpose of these bills was for bank transfer payments, the Federal Reserve banks in 1918 had begun using an electronic funds transfer network using a

Morse code system, which later evolved into the Federal Reserve Wire Network.[86]

The post-World War II economic and population boom increased consumer demand for products, as well as the volume of bank checks that had to be processed.[87] The number of checking accounts opened by American consumers roughly doubled between 1939 and 1952.[88]

In 1950, check clearing—the process in which funds move from a repository account to a recipient account—was so slow and labor intensive that it threatened to overwhelm banks' operational capacities. By 1955, the

could happen is that people who are prone to using mobile payments are also those who pay less attention to their finances," Lusardi says.

While Millennials are the first cohort to widely embrace digital payments, they are less inclined to use credit cards and are actually more debt-averse than older generations, experts say.[7] Analysts attribute the aversion to credit cards largely to the 2007-09 financial crisis and to the cost of paying off student loans.[8]

Members of Gen Z, the oldest of whom were children during the crisis, also have developed a more conservative approach to finances and debt, researchers say. More than 75 percent of them, including teenagers, are working, and more than 30 percent have their own bank account, according to a study by Raddon Research, an Illinois-based research firm.[9]

Even as the economy has stabilized in recent years, Lusardi says that there continues to be consequences from the high amount of debt that adults carry. "It's a constraint on people and what they can do," Lusardi says. "Young people start their economic life in debt, [which can result in] loss of opportunities, whether that's being an entrepreneur or undertaking some careers."

In the first quarter of 2019, U.S. consumer debt rose for the 19th consecutive quarter to reach $13.67 trillion, according to the Federal Reserve Bank of New York. However, average credit card balances fell by 2.5 percent.[10]

The younger generations' attitudes toward payment technologies and debt may indicate that there is a demand for services in budgeting, savings and planning that financial technologies and financial literacy programs can address. "It is obvious that we are moving toward an economy where information and knowledge is truly essential," Lusardi says. "Technology gives us a lot more opportunities, and we need to be able to use these opportunities well."

— *Hannah H. Kim*

[1] "Who Uses Mobile Payments?" The Pew Charitable Trusts, May 2016, https://tinyurl.com/y6hadpms; Michael Dimock, "Defining generations: Where Millennials end and Generation Z begins," Pew Research Center, Jan. 17, 2019, https://tinyurl.com/y93zo8fk.

[2] Jeff Desjardins, "How Affluent Millennials are Changing the Finance Industry," *Visual Capitalist*, Dec. 1, 2015, https://tinyurl.com/y68laebj.

[3] Kate Rooney, "Venmo executive says we're still 'decades away' from a cashless society," *CNBC*, June 15, 2018, https://tinyurl.com/y2wsoeg5.

[4] "Generation Z is beginning to change the payment ecosystem," BBVA, June 12, 2018, https://tinyurl.com/y5okfuyq.

[5] *Ibid.*

[6] Annamaria Lusardi, Carlo de Bassa Scheresberg and Melissa Avery, "Millennial Mobile Payment Users: A Look Into Their Personal Finances and Financial Behaviors," The George Washington University Global Financial Literary Excellence Center, April 2018, https://tinyurl.com/y4vjynwb.

[7] "Digitalization Among Factors Pushing Millennial Credit Preferences Toward Auto and Personal Loans," TransUnion, Aug. 30, 2017, https://tinyurl.com/y3llj9mq.

[8] "Why Millennials Are Ditching Credit Cards," *Bloomberg*, Feb. 27, 2018, https://tinyurl.com/y6t2zwt5.

[9] Penny Crosman, "8 things banks need to know about Gen Z," *American Banker*, July 6, 2018, https://tinyurl.com/y32ntu5t.

[10] "Household debt and credit report," Federal Reserve Bank of New York, accessed May 15, 2019, https://tinyurl.com/pe4juck.

Stanford Research Institute, a scientific research organization, developed an automated check bookkeeping and proofing system, which laid the groundwork for future payment systems.[89]

The credit card was another major development in payment technologies. The first credit cards originated in 1928 as metal cards issued by individual stores to select customers, who paid the full balance each month.[90] In the 1940s, department stores introduced credit cards with revolving credit, which allowed cardholders more time to pay balances while continuing to charge new purchases to their accounts.[91]

In 1950, Diners Club introduced the first universal credit card, which could be used at a variety of establishments. American Express, the financial services company, launched a paper credit card in 1958.[92] Banks began issuing credit cards in the late 1950s. Bank of America issued the BankAmericard in California in 1958, which evolved into a national plan in 1966 and was renamed Visa in 1976.[93] Also in 1966, a group of California banks launched the credit card company Mastercard.[94]

The automated teller machine (ATM), first introduced by Barclays Bank in London in 1967, allowed consumers more convenient ways to access their bank accounts without a bank teller's assistance. Two years later, Chemical Bank installed an ATM in Long Island, N.Y.[95]

The debit card was first issued in 1978 by the First National Bank of Seattle. Credit card use paved the way for debit card adoption, and in 1984 Landmark Bank created a nationwide ATM and debit card system.[96]

In the 1990s, as computer use increased and more Americans gained access to the internet, the first online banking and shopping platforms emerged. In 1994, Stanford Federal Credit Union began offering customers online banking.[97] That same year, the Internet Shopping Network and NetMarket made the first retail transactions over the internet, requiring customers to download software to securely transmit their credit card information online.[98] In 1995, the e-commerce websites Amazon and eBay opened and gradually normalized the practice of paying for things online.[99] PayPal was launched as part of a Palo Alto, Calif., company called Confinity in 1999 to support worldwide money transfers.[100]

Throughout the 2000s, online banking and shopping grew rapidly, and consumer habits shifted toward making more financial transactions over the internet.[101] The number of U.S. consumers who bought or researched a product online roughly doubled between 2000 and 2007, according to a Pew report. And the share of Americans who used online banking grew from 9 percent to 39 percent over the same period, the report said.[102]

Also in 2008, an unidentified person, or group of people, released a white paper titled "Bitcoin: A Peer to Peer Electronic Cash System" under the pseudonym Satoshi Nakamoto. Bitcoin, the first cryptocurrency, utilized a digital ledger called blockchain to record and protect the security of transactions. Blockchain offered a secure, decentralized network through which the public could use a currency system separate from government regulation or monetary policy.[103]

In 2010, financial service providers, such as the mobile payment company Square Inc. and the online payments processing company Stripe, emerged to allow online and brick-and-mortar businesses more ways to process card and digital payment transactions.[104] In 2011, the debut of the Google wallet allowed consumers to pay for goods with their mobile device rather than a physical card.[105]

In 2013, Apple introduced a biometric security feature in the form of a fingerprint scan to unlock its iPhone 5S. Soon after, Apple's iPhone payment service, Apple Pay, used a fingerprint scan to authenticate transactions.[106] The mass adoption of mobile devices has played a key role in the wide acceptance of biometric security features in mobile devices and digital financial services.[107]

CURRENT SITUATION
Banking Barriers

In April, an Amazon executive announced to employees that Amazon Go will begin accepting cash.[108] The first Amazon Go store had opened in 2016 on the e-commerce giant's campus in Seattle with no cashiers or checkout lines. The stores automatically detected products removed from the shelves, and customers were charged via a mobile app upon exiting.

Amazon Go's reversal of its no-cash policy came as a growing number of cities and states banned most cashless retail stores and restaurants.[109]

Some retail business owners assert that the process of cash handling and reconciliation has become more difficult because banks themselves are moving away from cash. "The number one obstacle we're seeing right now in the industry is that banks have been resistant to handling customers' cash," said Dean Fox, a director of finance at Paradigm Investment, which owns the chain restaurants Hardee's and Jersey Mike's.

Fox said many banks have stopped counting cash at the time of deposit, postponing the tallying until later. This causes delays for retail businesses in verifying the amount of cash they have at the close of business, he said.[110]

Owners of cashless businesses have argued that eliminating cash improves workers' safety and operational efficiency. Going cashless also frees up workers' time to serve customers rather than having to make change, go on bank runs or manage accounting books. Eliminating cash also reduces losses from robberies or employees' difficulties in counting change, they said.

At a New York City Council hearing in February, industry representatives from three cashless businesses spoke against a ban on cashless establishments. "By not keeping any cash in our stores our employees feel safer, especially in our preopening and closing hours when our stores are relatively empty," said Annamária Ferencz, a regional director for ByChloe, a vegan restaurant chain.

In response, council member Ritchie Torres said: "Some of these businesses have endured for more than 100 years, accept cash and are able to operate smoothly and efficiently and safely in the Bronx, which is probably much tougher than some of the neighborhoods in which you operate." Council members have not yet scheduled a vote on the cashless ban.[111]

Despite the backlash against cashless establishments, some experts argue that laws banning cashless brick-and-mortar businesses are not long-term solutions.[112] They point to underlying issues regarding financial inclusion for people without bank accounts or credit cards, such as the accessibility and affordability of banking services. "The future does not lie in" banning cashless businesses, Rogoff, the Harvard professor, said. "The future lies in giving people free debit cards and financial inclusion."[113]

Adams, the fair lending consultant, points to barriers that inhibit financial inclusion, such as lack of access to bank branches and digital services. "Many of the unbanked and underbanked live in banking deserts, so they don't have ready access to banking services," Adams says. "A lot of the unbanked are also in digital deserts, and so access to some of the alternatives is also very difficult for them."

Mehrsa Baradaran, a law professor at the University of Georgia who specializes in banking law, argues in her book *How the Other Half Banks: Exclusion, Exploitation and the Threat to Democracy* that the democratization of credit should not be left to the discretion of commercial banks, but should become a responsibility of the government. She supports a 2014 proposal by the U.S. Postal Service Inspector General's Office that post offices could serve as a public banking option, especially in low-income communities underserved by commercial banks.

"There have never been barriers to entry at post offices, and their services have been available to all, regardless of income," Baradaran wrote. "And so, it is not unreasonable to suggest that as America's oldest instrument of democracy in action, the post office can once again level the playing field."[114]

Some political analysts have suggested that postal banking will become a part of the economic agenda for the Democratic Party in the 2020 presidential campaign.[115] In April 2018, Sen. Kirsten Gillibrand, D-N.Y., announced legislation to create a postal bank.[116] In May, Sen. Bernie Sanders, I-Vt., and Rep. Alexandria Ocasio-Cortez, D-N.Y., outlined a plan to create postal banking services as part of the Loan Shark Prevention Act, which aims to combat predatory lending.[117] Gillibrand and Sanders are presidential candidates.

Adams says she thinks the United States will become a cashless society at some point in the future, but that fundamental changes must first be made regarding the accessibility of banking and credit.

"Moving to a cashless society also means that we have to move to a different model in terms of fees and services on using apps or debit cards," she says. "You want to make sure that when we go to a cashless society, that we're not cheating workers out of their fair wage by using fees to access the money [they] earn."

Financial education experts argue that cashless transactions can make people, including children and young adults, less aware of the value of money, hindering their ability to make sound financial decisions. "The fact that we don't see cash, that we don't even feel the payment, makes [us] less focused on it," says Annamaria Lusardi, the academic director of the Global Financial Literacy Excellence Center at George Washington University.

Studies have shown that shoppers spend more and make poorer buying decisions when making noncash payments. Consumers are willing to pay up to double for an item when using a credit card, a 2000 study by the Massachusetts Institute of Technology's Sloan School of Management found.[118] A 2010 study by Cornell University's Johnson Graduate School of Management found that consumers felt parting with physical currency was more "painful" than paying for items with a credit or debit card, where payment could be delayed. The study also found that credit card payments weakened impulse control and resulted in shoppers buying more unhealthy foods than when they paid in cash.[119]

Blockchain Investigations

Some cashless advocates believe cryptocurrencies such as bitcoin can serve as a cash alternative for consumers seeking anonymity in digital payments. Bitcoin investment data published in 2018 by Chainalysis, a blockchain analyst company, however, reported that most cryptocurrency was held as an investment rather than as a medium for exchange.[120]

Will paper currency become obsolete in the United States?

YES
Nash Foster
CEO and co-founder, Pyrofex Corp.

Written for *CQ Researcher*, July 2019

Civilizations have used metal coinage for more than 5,000 years and paper money for nearly 1,500 years, but the explosive growth in mobile technology and the internet promises to make these ancient methods of payment obsolete within just a few years.

Money has always been used to conduct transactions, but both savings and debt also have social meaning, affecting social rank and people's perceptions. Moreover, while Americans are accustomed to doing business with global corporations, transactions still occur often between friends and acquaintances and are a natural part of our everyday social network.

No wonder, then, that the inherently social nature of internet communications affects how we think about and use money. Some applications are explicitly social, such as Venmo's default public wallet that lets friends see how one is spending money. Other applications, such as WePay, simply leverage the existing social network technologies to facilitate easier and faster payments. And the coming cryptocurrency revolution will allow people to interact with self-executing smart contracts that use the internet's social features for everything from small-scale credit formation to high-speed securities trading. All of these features allow money to perform its social function more thoroughly and flexibly than ever before. In some deep sense, this makes digital money "more real" than physical currency could ever be.

To observe the obsolescence of physical cash, we need only look at existing statistics. Across a variety of retail environments— from department and discount stores to gas stations and restaurants—debit and credit cards already have begun to dwarf the use of cash. According to data from payment processor TYTS, there are no retail environments remaining that use cash for most transactions. Optimistic predictions about how quickly Americans would move to a cashless society notwithstanding, the use of cash continues to plummet precipitously. The Federal Reserve reported that between 2011 and 2016, the share of Americans using cash for all transactions dropped from 19 percent to 10 percent.

It is hard to imagine a world where paper money and coinage ceased to exist. Technologies as venerable as these rarely die completely. But they are often relegated to performing extremely limited functions that exploit their few advantages over improved technologies. In an increasingly social world, where payments are increasingly integrated into our mobile-first, internet-driven lives, it seems inevitable that cash will become obsolete, and statistics suggest this future is already closer than many think.

NO
Brett Scott
Journalist and author of The Heretic's Guide to Global Finance: Hacking the Future of Money

Written for *CQ Researcher*, July 2019

There are no citizens campaigning for the end of cash, but there are large companies doing so. For decades, banks and payments companies such as Visa have waged a "war on cash" for commercial reasons. Recently, for example, Amazon lobbied against legislation in Philadelphia requiring businesses to accept cash. Critics of the city's policy say it damages "innovation." What they really mean is that it hampers *automation*—cash doesn't play well with Amazon's desire for fully automated systems.

The digital payments industry tries to present cash as the horse-drawn carriage of payment methods, but for many people, cash is more like a bicycle: They may not use it for every transaction, but they enjoy keeping it as an option. In advance of hurricane landfalls, demand for cash spikes by up to 500 percent because people don't want their money trapped in cyberspace when the electricity goes down. As the saying goes, cash doesn't crash.

"Going cashless" actually refers to the process of becoming more dependent on the banking system. Digital payment firms like the term "cashless society" precisely because it is so misleading—like referring to whisky as beer-less alcohol. We should instead call it the *bankful society*, since cashless payments is just a convoluted way of saying bank transfers.

In many countries, though, the payments industry helps determine how the issue is framed. Every time the media interviews me on the dangers of the bankful society, the interviewer inevitably says, "but surely we all just want convenience," as if the only thing people value is laziness. This channels the biased terms of debate established by the industry and ignores the deep politics of being dependent on banks' digital money.

It is actually not obvious that digital payment is much more convenient than cash, especially when the electricity goes out. Regardless, it's the wrong focus. Maintaining good body posture and eating healthily also appear "inconvenient" in the short term. Likewise, maintaining the resilience, privacy and openness of our payments system can superficially appear inconvenient. But if convenience means becoming dependent on financial institutions that have repeatedly proven they do not have our best interests at heart, it is not something to strive for.

The people least concerned about having banks insert themselves into every transaction (enabling fine-grained financial surveillance) are high-status urban professionals who consider it obvious that everyone should desire institutionally mediated, frictionless commerce—and that the spread of digital payments is thus a *gentrification* process. If you don't believe me, just look at which shops lead the anti-cash charge.

Blockchain technology, the ledger in which crypto-currency transactions are recorded, may provide the future infrastructure for central banks and other financial institutions to address issues regarding privacy, security and cyber resilience. Blockchain is a type of distributed ledger technology (DLT), a system in which transactions are recorded via multiple computers rather than in a centralized database.[121]

Ashley Lannquist, the project lead of blockchain and DLT at the World Economic Forum, says consumers are deterred from using cryptocurrency in everyday transactions because of logistical difficulties and low merchant acceptance, as well as the hope that cryptocurrency value may increase over time. "I think many countries like the U.S. will see greater use of mobile phone apps and cashless transactions, mostly from non-DLT-based services," Lannquist says. "We'll also likely see an increase in DLT-based payments, but I think adoption will remain challenged."

Dozens of central banks currently are researching blockchain and other types of DLT to investigate long-standing interests, including retail central bank digital currency—a form of state-backed electronic currency—and to improve payments system efficiency and security, according to a 2019 white paper published by the World Economic Forum.[122]

The Bank of France has already successfully deployed a DLT-based application to automate and digitize a system for smart contracts, according to the white paper.[123] (A smart contract is a self-executing agreement in which the terms are written into computer code and automatically take effect when the conditions are fulfilled.)[124] Some central banks, such as South Korea's, are conducting blockchain research with peer institutions in an effort to transition into a "coin-free society," reported TokenPost, a South Korean news site.[125]

Lannquist says central bank researchers are still investigating whether DLT could help lower—or increase—risks of cyberattacks. However, the case for DLT improving operational resilience is the clearest, she says. "Because data and transactions are stored and operate in a decentralized manner across several 'nodes' or computers, the system has greater data redundancy and robustness against hardware faults in one or two servers," Lannquist says.

Duke's Harvey says blockchain is facilitating the issuance of new currencies that can compete with the state-issued money system. "Traditionally, the idea was to collateralize [currency] with gold, silver, public stocks, land," Harvey says. While the U.S. dollar is a fiat currency, blockchain-based cryptocurrencies can be collateralized by a variety of assets.

JPMorgan Chase, the largest bank in the United States, announced in February a successful pilot of its own digital coin, called JPM Coin, based on blockchain technology. While each JPM Coin is backed by U.S. dollars held in designated accounts at JPMorgan Chase, its primary use will be for instantaneous payments.[126] Paper money "is called a banknote because banks used to issue the currency," Harvey says. "Now, we're going back to that system, where every bank will have their own currency."

In June, Facebook announced it would develop a cryptocurrency called Libra with the goal of making it a stable global currency. Scheduled to launch in early 2020, Libra will be backed by a reserve of real assets, such as gold, and the interest on the assets will ensure low fees for users, Facebook said. Libra will be governed by an association that includes founding members that invested at least $10 million each into the project, among them Visa, Uber, eBay and PayPal.[127]

OUTLOOK
More Ways to Pay

While cash use will vary throughout the world in the coming decades, many experts think the future of consumer payments in the United States will include a greater variety of digital payment systems and currencies.

"We're obviously headed in a direction where there is going to be more digital payments," says Stephens of the Privacy Rights Clearinghouse. "It sets up a number of challenges for both legislators and regulators to come up with a framework that can protect consumers who are going to be using digital payments."

Hughes, the Indiana University law professor, thinks the future of payments in the United States may not be in cash, cards or even with mobile devices. "The idea that the phone is going to be the principal repository of potential tools for payment purposes may be short-sighted," she says.

Levine, the global trends consultant, foresees a future in which "we won't have cards. It'll be biometric," such as Apple's fingerprint scan. "It's starting now. There are biometric payments already. One thing in the forefront is that the culture has to get used to it to accept it."

Arnold, the cybersecurity expert, says a variety of institutions, including financial services, airport security and border protection, are increasingly using biometric authentication. He cited the Face ID security feature debuted by Apple's iPhone X in 2017 that uses facial recognition to unlock the device, which then authorizes payments in the mobile wallet Apple Pay.

"It's always been a very interesting marketplace to watch and to track when you see relatively new behaviors," Arnold says. "It's a long time to evolve a payment system."

Payment analysts say U.S. consumers have been more reluctant to adopt mobile payments than those in other countries.[128] "We still have so many people who like the payment services that they have," says Hughes. "Unlike some parts of the world, we have so many choices that it keeps us from being ready adopters of new options. In a sense, even cards are legacy systems."

Some banking experts think the U.S. electronic payments system is fragmented and inefficient compared to other advanced economies, and that cash will remain more popular in the United States for longer than elsewhere. The global ubiquity of the U.S. paper dollar also places the United States in a unique position, experts say.

Researchers say governments that oversee large cash-based informal economies will likely become more interested in transitioning to electronic money systems. "The sheer scope of the problem is there is so much tax evasion in countries with big informal sectors," says Best, the Columbia economist. "The fact that more and more transactions are electronic does seem extremely promising to crack down on tax evasion."

Globally, the future role of cash will evolve as competition from cashless payments continues to increase. "As superior transaction technologies come along, the use of cash is declining," Rogoff said. "And I think we'll reach a tipping point where, regardless, central banks are going to find themselves having to buy back a lot of the cash supply. But that could take three or four decades. I would just say, we're doing a lot of damage [by transitioning to cashless payments] now."[129]

NOTES

1. Claire Greene and Joanna Stavins, "The 2016 and 2017 Surveys of Consumer Payment Choice: Summary Results," Federal Reserve Bank of Boston, 2018, https://tinyurl.com/y3r2ksre.

2. *Ibid.*

3. Mike Isaac and Nathaniel Popper, "Facebook Plans Global Financial System Based on Cryptocurrency," *The New York Times*, June 18, 2019, https://tinyurl.com/yxt8tv7y.

4. "Is U.S. currency still backed by gold?" Board of Governors of the Federal Reserve System, Aug. 2, 2013, https://tinyurl.com/ln238o3.

5. "How much does it cost to produce currency and coin?" Board of Governors of the Federal Reserve System, Dec. 27, 2018, https://tinyurl.com/ckn6ovr.

6. "How much U.S. currency is in circulation?" Board of Governors of the Federal Reserve System, April 2, 2019, https://tinyurl.com/6udsz4u.

7. "U.S. Coins—Implications of Changing Metal Compositions," United States Government Accountability Office, December 2015, https://tinyurl.com/yxsfagb9.

8. Jeanne Sahadi, "Pennies and nickels cost more to make than they're worth," *CNN Business*, Jan. 11, 2016, https://tinyurl.com/y54k73ku.

9. Thomas Haasl, Sam Schulhofer-Wohl and Anna Paulson, "Understanding the Demand for Currency at Home and Abroad," Federal Reserve Bank of Chicago, 2018, https://tinyurl.com/yyru28lw.

10. Jieun Kim, "US Dollars Become Currency of Choice Among Well-Heeled North Koreans," *Radio Free Asia*, Feb. 21, 2018, https://tinyurl.com/y9ebz3by.

11. Haasl, Schulhofer-Wohl and Paulson, *op. cit.*

12. Kabir Chibber, "Here are all the countries that don't have a currency of their own," *Quartz*, Sept. 15, 2014, https://tinyurl.com/yyajt5cd.

13. Ruth Judson, "The Death of Cash? Not So Fast: Demand for U.S. Currency at Home and Abroad,

1990-2016," Board of Governors of Federal Reserve System Division of International Finance, March 2017, https://tinyurl.com/yyoyaxz3.

14. Taylor Telford and Jeanne Whalen, "There are more $100 bills than $1 bills, and it makes no cents," *The Washington Post*, March 4, 2019, https://tinyurl.com/y537meas.

15. Sukriti Bansal *et al.*, "Global payments 2018: A dynamic industry continues to break new ground," McKinsey & Co., October 2018, https://tinyurl.com/y36d8kdq.

16. "Sweden—The First Cashless Society?" Swedish Institute, April 1, 2019, https://tinyurl.com/y3ooyg4h.

17. Kyree Leary and Chelsea Gohd, "Sweden could stop using cash by 2023," World Economic Forum, Oct. 11, 2017, https://tinyurl.com/yxfeurt6.

18. Yuan Yang, "Why millennials are driving cashless revolution in China," *Financial Times*, July 17, 2018, https://tinyurl.com/y3gl3do9.

19. Rita Liao, "China wants its rural villages to go cashless by 2020," *TechCrunch*, Feb. 22, 2019, https://tinyurl.com/y2qqpk7f; "eMarketer Projects Surge in Mobile Payments in China," eMarketer, Nov. 2, 2017, https://tinyurl.com/y23qzcsx.

20. "The Federal Reserve Payments Study: 2018 Annual Supplement," The Federal Reserve, December 2018, https://tinyurl.com/y46vbe2l.

21. Andrew Perrin, "More Americans are making no weekly purchases with cash," Pew Research Center, Dec. 12, 2018, https://tinyurl.com/y2h9tbun.

22. Rick Maughan, "Americans barely carry around cash anymore," *New York Post*, March 22, 2018, https://tinyurl.com/y4ynumho.

23. Art Swift and Steve Ander, "Most Americans Foresee Death of Cash in Their Lifetime," Gallup, July 15, 2016, https://tinyurl.com/y23hdpp4.

24. "Cashless Research Report Press Release," Global Acceptance Transaction Engine, April 26, 2018, https://tinyurl.com/y2vx4wtn.

25. Krista Garcia, "Are Consumers Ready for a Cashless Society?" eMarketer, Dec. 7, 2018, https://tinyurl.com/y4nrr8o8.

26. Frank Kehl, "How To Accept Credit Card Payments For Your Small Business," Merchant Maverick, May 7, 2018, https://tinyurl.com/y4zhowz8.

27. "Welcome to the Future—It's Cashless," Sweetgreen, Dec. 27, 2016, https://tinyurl.com/y4bhwfvb.

28. "Back to the Future—It's Cash," Sweetgreen, April 25, 2019, https://tinyurl.com/yxfdqf6e.

29. "Is it legal for a business in the United States to refuse cash as a form of payment?" Board of Governors of the Federal Reserve System, June 17, 2011, https://tinyurl.com/kj8229m.

30. Marianne Wilson, "Federal legislation introduced to ban cashless stores," *Chain Store Age*, May 17, 2019, https://tinyurl.com/y459om8h.

31. "New Jersey Enacts Law Barring Cashless Stores," NBC New York, March 18, 2019, https://tinyurl.com/y5auojq7; "Section 10A," The 191st General Court of the Commonwealth of Massachusetts, accessed May 7, 2019, https://tinyurl.com/y2b2waze.

32. Rebecca Bellan, "As More Cities Ban Cashless Businesses, New York Wants to Follow," *CityLab*, March 6, 2019, https://tinyurl.com/yyf8jjwr.

33. "Cashless Ban: New Jersey Requires Businesses to Accept Cash," *CBS New York*, March 18, 2019, https://tinyurl.com/y2r78j4m.

34. Justin Pritchard, "Bank Accounts for People Under 18," *The Balance*, Jan. 18, 2019, https://tinyurl.com/yxco5bgl.

35. "Report on the Economic Well-Being of U.S. Households in 2017," Board of Governors of the Federal Reserve System, May 2018, https://tinyurl.com/y2uj7ehw.

36. Annie Harper, "This Nasty Bank Fee Makes It Much Harder to Climb Out of Poverty," *Money*, Oct. 18, 2017, https://tinyurl.com/y54oys4n.

37. Perrin, *op. cit.*

38. Jelisa Castrodale, "Owner of Cashless Poke Restaurant Argues Anyone Without a Bank Account Is a Tax Evader," *Vice*, March 22, 2019, https://tinyurl.com/y5ldts6j.

39. "Report of Cash Payments Over $10,000 Received in a Trade or Business—Motor Vehicle Dealership Q&As," IRS, July 23, 2018, https://tinyurl.com/y3bebzbl.

40. "Cybersecurity in Financial Services Market Is Booming Worldwide—IBM, Accenture, Airbus," *MarketWatch*, Sep. 8, 2018, https://tinyurl.com/y2qnxjwj.

41. Antoine Bouveret, "Cyber Risk for the Financial Sector: A Framework for Quantitative Assessment," International Monetary Fund, June 22, 2018, https://tinyurl.com/y4b2kgu6.

42. "Timeline of Cyber Incidents Involving Financial Institutions," Carnegie Endowment for International Peace, accessed May 7, 2019, https://tinyurl.com/y3tr7nu2.

43. "Consumer Protection Topics—Billing Errors and Resolution," Federal Deposit Insurance Corporation, Feb. 29, 2016, https://tinyurl.com/yxpfybx5.

44. Brett Scott, "The cashless society is a con—and big finance is behind it," *The Guardian*, July 19, 2018, https://tinyurl.com/y5udefwc.

45. Justin Pritchard, "Protection From Electronic Banking Fraud and Errors," *The Balance*, Dec. 20, 2018, https://tinyurl.com/y3k6qp36.

46. Lindsay Konsko, "Who Pays When Merchants Are Victims of Credit Card Fraud?" *NerdWallet*, June 3, 2014, https://tinyurl.com/yyh4ce72.

47. "Regulations," Board of Governors of the Federal Reserve System, Dec. 28, 2016, https://tinyurl.com/y38mk4r5; Connie Prater, "What you buy, where you shop may affect your credit," creditcards.com, June 12, 2009, https://tinyurl.com/yjcbqnb.

48. "Peer-to-Peer Payments Are Generally Safe, But Consumers Must Be Aware of Risks," *Consumer Reports*, Aug. 6, 2018, https://tinyurl.com/y5aznyze.

49. Judson, *op. cit.*

50. *Ibid.*

51. John Detrixhe, "Kenneth Rogoff wrote the book on getting rid of paper money," *Quartz*, Nov. 19, 2018, https://tinyurl.com/yxu6399x.

52. *Ibid.*

53. Patrick W. Watson, "India's Demonetization Could Be The First Cash Domino To Fall," *Forbes*, Dec. 1, 2016, https://tinyurl.com/y383jqux.

54. Shadab Nazmi, "India election 2019: Did the ban on high-value banknotes work?" *BBC*, March 12, 2019, https://tinyurl.com/y6x39tcu.

55. Alexander Pearson, "Eurozone banks stop issuing € 500 notes, but cash-loving Germany delays," *Deutsche Welle*, Jan. 27, 2019, https://tinyurl.com/y5dapd5z.

56. Kim Zetter, "Wikileaks Wins Icelandic Court Battle Against Visa for Blocking Donations," *Wired*, July 12, 2012, https://tinyurl.com/y677g9cw.

57. Jeff Spross, "Should America go cash-free?" *The Week*, April 16, 2018, https://tinyurl.com/yypdqpp6.

58. "Global Shapers Survey," World Economic Forum, 2017, https://tinyurl.com/y2vyqn9t.

59. Kate Rooney, "After the crisis, a new generation puts its trust in tech over traditional banks," *CNBC*, Sep. 14, 2018, https://tinyurl.com/y57k752b.

60. Sharon Ann Murphy, "Early American Colonists Had a Cash Problem. Here's How They Solved It," *Time*, Feb. 27, 2017, https://tinyurl.com/yyh9tq7x.

61. Ron Michener, "Money in the American Colonies," Economic History Association, Feb. 1, 2010, https://tinyurl.com/y26x33pz.

62. Murphy, *op. cit.*

63. Eric P. Newman, *The Early Paper Money of America—Fifth Edition* (2008), p. 62.

64. Andrew Glass, "Congress issues Continental currency, June 22, 1775," *Politico*, June 22, 2018, https://tinyurl.com/y2r5599w.

65. Newman, *op. cit.*, p. 74.

66. Richard Sylla, "The US Banking System: Origin, Development, and Regulation," The Gilder Lehrman Institute of American History, accessed April 16, 2019, https://tinyurl.com/y24wyott.

67. *Ibid.*

68. Andrew T. Hill, "The Second Bank of the United States," Federal Reserve History, Dec. 5, 2015, https://tinyurl.com/y5nnvt82.

69. Sylla, *op. cit.*

70. "Currency Notes," U.S. Bureau of Engraving and Printing, accessed April 16, 2019, https://tinyurl.com/y5d97b48.

71. David A. Dieterle and Kathleen C. Simmons, eds., *Government and the Economy: An Encyclopedia* (2014), p. 249.

72. *Ibid.*, p. 250.

73. "1913 Federal Reserve Act," Investopedia, March 14, 2019, https://tinyurl.com/yxfftpy4.

74. Sylla, *op. cit.*

75. "1913 Federal Reserve Act," *op. cit.*

76. "The Bretton Woods Conference, 1944," U.S. Department of State Archive, accessed April 16, 2019, https://tinyurl.com/y3njt339.

77. Michael D. Bordo, "The Operation and Demise of the Bretton Woods System; 1958 to 1971," Hoover Institution, February 2017, https://tinyurl.com/y4ngltcg.

78. "Reserve Currency," Investopedia, Feb. 7, 2018, https://tinyurl.com/y5jeoqxy.

79. "Nixon and the End of the Bretton Woods System, 1971-1973," U.S. Department of State Office of the Historian, accessed April 16, 2019, https://tinyurl.com/y2ul58rs; "Fiat Money," Investopedia, June 25, 2019, https://tinyurl.com/y58r6xob.

80. Janet Nguyen, "Here's why we stopped using $1,000 bills," *Business Insider*, Aug. 13, 2017, https://tinyurl.com/yyc95nep.

81. Newman, *op. cit.*, p. 326.

82. Arthur L. Friedberg and Ira S. Friedberg, *Paper Money of the United States. A Complete Illustrated Guide with Valuations* (2017), p. 6.

83. "U.S. Currency: History of the BEP and U.S. Currency," U.S. Bureau of Engraving and Printing, accessed April 18, 2019, https://tinyurl.com/3h2qorx.

84. "U.S. Currency: $100,000 Gold Certificate," U.S. Bureau of Engraving and Printing, accessed April 18, 2019, https://tinyurl.com/4y5hy9y.

85. "U.S. Currency: Denominations Above The $100 Note," U.S. Bureau of Engraving and Printing, accessed April 18, 2019, https://tinyurl.com/y3kcrnbp.

86. "The Fedwire Funds Service," The Federal Reserve, July 2014, https://tinyurl.com/yyfjqw5n.

87. Amy Weaver Fisher and James L. McKenney, "The Development of the ERMA System: Lessons from History," *IEEE Annals of the History of Computing*, 1993, https://tinyurl.com/y3gj9def.

88. Matt Phillips and Quartz, "The Spectacular Decline of Checks," *The Atlantic*, June 5, 2014, https://tinyurl.com/y2ssqmey.

89. Fisher and McKenney, *op. cit.*

90. Asma Salman and Nauman Munir, "Relationship between the Incentives Offered on Credit Card and its Usage," *Journal of Finance, Accounting and Management*, January 2015, https://tinyurl.com/y5echlxk.

91. "Credit Cards," Encyclopedia.com, accessed April 18, 2019, https://tinyurl.com/y2rpwvqa.

92. "The Story Behind the Card," Diners Club International, accessed July 15, 2019, http://tinyurl.com/y4z9yzgn; "American Express—Our Story," American Express, Sept. 13, 2012, https://tinyurl.com/y4zfuw8e.

93. "Credit Cards," *op. cit.*

94. Jay MacDonald and Taylor Tompkins, "The history of credit cards," creditcards.com, July 11, 2017, https://tinyurl.com/y3ezhfxm.

95. Kevin Wack and Alan Kline, "The evolution of the ATM," *American Banker*, May 23, 2017, https://tinyurl.com/yxmzrchp.

96. Eric Tilden, "A Detailed History of Debit Cards," *PocketSense*, Nov. 8, 2018, https://tinyurl.com/y2xcfmsa.

97. Skip Allums, *Designing Mobile Payment Experiences: Principles and Best Practices for Mobile Commerce* (2014), p. 13.

98. Alorie Gilbert, "E-commerce turns 10," *CNET Magazine*, Aug. 11, 2004, https://tinyurl.com/y6xfh2qn.

99. Harry McCracken, "1995: The Year Everything Changed," *Fast Company*, Dec. 30, 2015, https://tinyurl.com/y4xbbbmu.

100. Mark Odell, "Timeline: The Rise of PayPal," *Financial Times*, Sept. 30, 2014, https://tinyurl.com/y6czt46e.

101. Jeffry Pilcher, "Infographic: The History Of Internet Banking (1983-2012)," *The Financial Brand*, Oct. 2, 2012, https://tinyurl.com/y56zztsh.

102. John B. Horrigan, "Part 1. Trends in Online Shopping," Pew Research Center, Feb. 13, 2008, https://tinyurl.com/y33owbpn.

103. Bernard Marr, "A Very Brief History Of Blockchain Technology Everyone Should Read," *Forbes*, Feb. 16, 2018, https://tinyurl.com/y2w9p6a5.

104. Eric Rosenberg, "Square vs. Stripe (SBUX, TWTR)," June 25, 2019, Investopedia, https://tinyurl.com/y5qxym3x.

105. Angela Scott-Briggs, "What is a Mobile Wallet, Origin and History in Financial technology?" *TechBullion*, Nov. 29, 2016, https://tinyurl.com/y57u7d9z.

106. Fionna Agomuoh, "Password-free smartphones are no longer the stuff of science fiction—they're everywhere," *Business Insider*, Dec. 27, 2017, https://tinyurl.com/y3kshkfz.

107. "Biometric Authentication in Payments," Promontory Financial Group and Visa, November 2017, https://tinyurl.com/y5fnjmlx.

108. Eugene Kim, "Amazon exec tells employees that Go stores will start accepting cash to address 'discrimination' concerns," *CNBC*, April 10, 2019, https://tinyurl.com/y6cjcu55.

109. *Ibid.*

110. Liz Carey, "How Restaurants Can Improve Their Cash Operations," *QSR Magazine*, June 21, 2018, https://tinyurl.com/y6evhhlf.

111. Erika Adams, "Restaurant Chains Push Back Against New York's Proposed Cashless Ban," *Skift Table*, Feb. 15, 2019, https://tinyurl.com/yymv6ezt.

112. Bellan, *op. cit.*

113. *Ibid.*

114. Mehrsa Baradaran, *How the Other Half Banks: Exclusion, Exploitation, and the Threat to Democracy* (2015).

115. Kevin Wack, "Postal banking is back on the table. Here's why that matters," *American Banker*, April 26, 2018, https://tinyurl.com/y47yv4dt.

116. "Gillibrand Announces Major New Legislation To Create A Postal Bank To Wipe Out Predatory Payday Lending Industry Practices, Ensure All Americans Have Access to Basic Banking Services," news release, Office of Sen. Kirsten Gillibrand, April 25, 2018, https://tinyurl.com/y2hlem67.

117. "Senator Sanders and Representative Ocasio-Cortez Unveil the Loan Shark Prevention Act to Protect Consumers," news release, Office of Sen. Bernie Sanders, May 9, 2019, https://tinyurl.com/y49rxgyx.

118. Drazen Prelec and Duncan Simester, "Always Leave Home Without It: A Further Investigation of the Credit-Card Effect on Willingness to Pay," MIT Sloan School of Management, June 8, 2000, https://tinyurl.com/yxgokpzz.

119. Manoj Thomas, Kalpesh Kaushik Desai and Satheeshkumar Seenivasan, "How Credit Card Payments Increase Unhealthy Food Purchases: Visceral Regulation of Vices," Cornell University Johnson Graduate School of Management, September 2010, https://tinyurl.com/yyla8zuy.

120. "Bitcoin Investors and Speculators Hold Their Positions Over the Summer," *Chainalysis Blog*, Sept. 24, 2018, https://tinyurl.com/yyxwjulz.

121.. Oliver Belin, "The Difference Between Blockchain & Distributed Ledger Technology," Tradeix, accessed May 12, 2019, https://tinyurl.com/y25wcj2h.

122. "Central Banks and Distributed Ledger Technology: How are Central Banks Exploring Blockchain Today?" World Economic Forum, March 2019, https://tinyurl.com/y4wmmysc.

122. *Ibid.*

124. "Smart Contracts," Investopedia, updated April 26, 2019, https://tinyurl.com/y5w4dr62.

125. Shin Yoonjin, "The Bank of Korea— 'Cryptographic money will advance the society

without coin,' " *Tokenpost*, May 1, 2018, https://tinyurl.com/y3gqxtd2.

126. "J.P. Morgan Creates Digital Coin for Payments," J.P. Morgan, Feb. 14, 2019, https://tinyurl.com/y2wmu74o.

127. "Libra White Paper," Libra Association, accessed June 28, 2019, https://tinyurl.com/y5qz87x9.

128. John Detrixhe, "A complete guide to a world without cash," *Quartz*, Nov. 13, 2018, https://tinyurl.com/y6zcukw3.

129. Detrixhe, "Kenneth Rogoff wrote the book on getting rid of paper money," *op. cit.*

BIBLIOGRAPHY

Books

Batiz-Lazo, Bernardo, and Leonidas Efthymiou, eds., *The Book of Payments: Historical and Contemporary Views on the Cashless Society,* Palgrave Macmillan, 2016.
Two business professors edit a collection of essays about the conceptual origins of cashless societies and the future of payment systems around the world.

Friedberg, Arthur L., and Ira S. Friedberg, *Paper Money of the United States: A Complete Illustrated Guide with Valuations,* Clifton: Coin & Currency Institute, 2017.
The authors, brothers and highly regarded numismatists, offer a comprehensive guide to the use of paper money throughout U.S. history.

Murphy, Sharon Ann, *Other People's Money: How Banking Worked in the Early American Republic,* Johns Hopkins University Press, 2017.
A history professor at Providence College in Rhode Island explains the development of banking in America and the evolution of the modern financial system.

Rogoff, Kenneth S., *The Curse of Cash*, Princeton University Press, 2016.
A Harvard University economist argues that large-denomination paper currency is mainly used to finance illicit economic activity.

Articles

Alderman, Liz, "Sweden's Push to Get Rid of Cash Has Some Saying, 'Not So Fast,'" *The New York Times*, Nov. 21, 2018, https://tinyurl.com/yxof7dsz.
Financial authorities in Sweden are asking banks to continue making cash available until the government determines exactly how going cash-free will affect retirees, immigrants and others.

Bellan, Rebecca, "As More Cities Ban Cashless Businesses, New York Wants to Follow," *CityLab*, March 6, 2019, https://tinyurl.com/y6molnuj.
A culture writer says a growing number of cities are barring businesses from going cashless because many minorities and low-income people do not use banks.

Jeong, Sarah, "How a Cashless Society Could Embolden Big Brother," *The Atlantic*, April 8, 2016, https://tinyurl.com/ybzx33ss.
A technology reporter investigates how U.S. government officials have used electronic money systems and data on consumer transactions to conduct surveillance and censorship operations.

Kim, Eugene, "Amazon exec tells employees that Go stores will start accepting cash to address 'discrimination' concerns," *CNBC*, April 10, 2019, https://tinyurl.com/yy23u3se.
Amazon Go stores, which were initially designed to automate payments and make cashiers unnecessary, will begin accepting cash in response to criticisms that the stores discriminate against customers who do not use banks, a technology journalist reports.

Zhou, Youyou, and John Detrixhe, "Here's what's happening with electronic money around the world," *Quartz*, Nov. 15, 2018, https://tinyurl.com/y4bdc2la.
Two technology journalists find that cash usage varies widely in 37 countries.

Reports and Studies

"Biometric Authentication in Payments: Considerations for Policymakers," Promontory Financial Group, November 2017, https://tinyurl.com/y5fnjmlx.
A white paper produced for Visa outlines the ongoing development of biometric authentication in financial services.

Judson, Ruth, "The Death of Cash? Not So Fast: Demand for U.S. Currency at Home and Abroad, 1990-2016," Division of International Finance, Board of Governors of Federal Reserve System, March 2017, https://tinyurl.com/y4dyktcq.
A senior economic project manager at the Federal Reserve says growth in international demand for U.S. currency continues to be strong while domestic demand appears to be slowing.

Kahn, Charles, "Payment Systems and Privacy," Economic Research, Federal Reserve Bank of St. Louis, Oct. 15, 2018, https://tinyurl.com/y57xhqnr.
A research fellow at the Federal Reserve Bank of St. Louis says that, as use of electronic payments increases, central banks may shift from providing privacy for transactions to regulating how different electronic payment apps offer such privacy.

Lusardi, Annamaria, Carlo de Bassa Scheresberg and Melissa Avery, "Millennial Mobile Payment Users: A Look into their Personal Finances and Financial Behaviors," Global Financial Literacy Excellence Center, The George Washington University School of Business, April 30, 2018, https://tinyurl.com/y692evud.
University researchers say Millennials who use mobile payment apps tend to be poorer financial managers than those who do not use the apps.

Perrin, Andrew, "More Americans are making no weekly purchases with cash," Pew Research Center, Dec. 12, 2018, https://tinyurl.com/yyq9awl6.
A survey finds that 29 percent of U.S. adults made no cash purchases in a typical week last year, up from 24 percent in 2015.

THE NEXT STEP

Generational Differences

Jones, Rupert, "Cashless Britain: over-55s and low earners at risk of being left behind," *The Guardian*, March 23, 2019, https://tinyurl.com/yxkg5jvm.
Nearly three-quarters of British adults over age 55 never use mobile banking apps, according to a recent survey by a multinational professional and management consulting company.

Lunden, Ingrid, "Step raises $22.5M led by Stripe to build no-fee banking services for teens," *TechCrunch*, June 6, 2019, https://tinyurl.com/yxz8lmtn.
A new mobile app aims to help educate teenagers on banking, financial planning and the value of currency in an increasingly cashless society.

Weisbaum, Herb, "Sallie Mae launches new credit cards aimed at millennials and Gen Z. Are they right for you?" *NBC News*, June 25, 2019, https://tinyurl.com/y4gpl7a6.
Student lender Sallie Mae recently unveiled three credit cards designed to appeal to younger consumers with features such as spending alerts and rewards to help college students earn good credit scores.

Illegal Activity

"How Prepaid Cards Played A Role In El Chapo's Global Drug Operation," PYMNTS.com, Feb. 13, 2019, https://tinyurl.com/y5vkyry4.
The infamous drug kingpin used prepaid debit cards, each often holding as much as $9,900, to more easily and cleanly transport the massive amounts of cash generated by his drug empire.

Bown, Jessica, "What's the new weapon against money laundering gangsters?" *BBC*, April 2, 2019, https://tinyurl.com/y4vvcg2h.
Criminals are using specialist software and cryptocurrency to launder money, pushing law enforcement agencies to use artificial intelligence software to pinpoint and fight this activity.

Noguchi, Yuki, "Bags of Cash, Armed Guards and Wary Banks: The Edgy Life of a Cannabis Company CFO," *NPR*, April 10, 2019, http://tinyurl.com/yxe6crxm.
Federal law lags behind states' legalization of cannabis, creating complex financial barriers for cannabis companies struggling to operate without much bank support, says one company's chief financial officer.

Security and Privacy

DeNisco Rayome, Alison, "Half of online banks allow hackers to steal your money," *TechRepublic*, April 5, 2019, https://tinyurl.com/yyygfefr.

Almost all online banks are vulnerable to unauthorized-access attacks on client and company information, and more than three-quarters have flawed two-factor authentication, according to a recent report by a global security solutions provider.

Newman, Lily Hay, "A New Breed of ATM Hackers Gets In Through a Bank's Network," *Wired*, April 9, 2019, https://tinyurl.com/y6s7vhcc.
Hackers have developed new methods to gain access to the international payment network SWIFT through manipulating ATMs and initiating fraudulent transfers and cashouts.

Nguyen, Vicki, et al., "Instant fraud: Consumers see funds disappear in Zelle account scam," *NBC News*, June 11, 2019, https://tinyurl.com/y3e8negr.
Scammers have stolen thousands of dollars from consumers by exploiting the ease and simplicity of a digital banking service used by banks such as Chase and Bank of America.

Technology and Innovation

"Two of Japan's biggest convenience store chains launch their own mobile payment services," *The Japan Times*, July 1, 2019, https://tinyurl.com/yxa6n774.
Seven-Eleven Japan and FamilyMart now have mobile payment apps that allow customers to scan their phones at the register to pay for items, and are using the data from the transactions for product development.

Ehrbeck, Tilman, "Momentum Is Building For A 21st-Century Digital Banking Infrastructure," *Forbes*, June 3, 2019, https://tinyurl.com/y5q22hjz.
Tech giants such as Amazon and Facebook are making forays into the financial industry, seeking to disrupt the current banking infrastructure, says the chair of a United Nations advisory council on inclusive financial development.

Sharma, Alkesh, "Standard Chartered aims to build new digital capabilities with 5G inclusion," *The National*, July 2, 2019, https://tinyurl.com/y63fbvl2.
A British multinational bank has announced plans to integrate 5G technology with its mobile and digital banking platforms to enhance customer services.

For More Information

American Institute for Economic Research, 250 Division St., Great Barrington, MA 01230; 888-528-1216; www.aier.org. Independent political and economic think tank that has researched the declining use of cash.

Board of Governors of the Federal Reserve System, 20th Street and Constitution Avenue, N.W., Washington, DC 20551; 202-452-3000; www.federalreserve.gov. U.S. central bank that sets monetary policy and determines the amount of new currency produced each year.

George Washington University Global Financial Literacy Excellence Center, Duqués Hall, Suite 450, 2201 G St., N.W., Washington, DC 20052; 202-994-7148; www.gflec.org. University research center dedicated to advancing financial knowledge.

Sveriges Riksbank, SE-103 37 Stockholm, Sweden; +46-8-787-00-00; www.riksbank.se/en-gb. Sweden's central bank, which is researching the development of an electronic currency to largely replace cash.

United States Mint, 801 9th St., N.W., Washington, DC 20220; 800-872-6468; www.usmint.gov. Treasury Department agency that produces U.S. coinage.

U.S. Bureau of Engraving and Printing, 14th and C Streets, S.W., Washington, DC 20228; 202-874-3188; www.moneyfactory.gov. Treasury Department agency that produces U.S. paper currency.

World Economic Forum Centre for the Fourth Industrial Revolution, 1201 Ralston Ave., San Francisco, CA 94129; 415-704-8848; www.weforum.org/centre-for-the-fourth-industrial-revolution. Global organization developing policy frameworks to address challenges related to emerging technologies.

8

European Union at a Crossroads

Will political divisions tear the EU apart?

By Jonathan Broder

Signs outside the British Parliament denounce the 2016 decision by U.K. voters to leave the European Union. Some analysts say the Brexit debacle has increased public support for the EU throughout Europe.

From *CQ Researcher*, April 5, 2019

The European Union (EU) was founded in 1993 in a burst of hope and unity, the culmination of a decades-long quest for greater European integration. But today, a resurgence of nationalist and populist fervor is threatening the core values, and future, of the 28-nation federation.

In France, violent fuel tax protests by an amorphous group called the *gilets jaunes*, or yellow vests, have metastasized into a potent populist movement that demands greater social justice for low-skilled workers left behind by Europe's economic integration. Those populists now imperil the pro-EU presidency of Emmanuel Macron.[1]

In Germany, a far-right party hostile to the EU scored major gains in regional elections in October at the expense of the ruling coalition. In response, German Chancellor Angela Merkel, who has long been regarded as Europe's de facto leader, announced she would step down as head of her party, the Christian Democratic Union (CDU), and retire from politics when her term as chancellor ends in 2021.[2]

In the United Kingdom, chaos is engulfing the government as Prime Minister Theresa May struggles with a mutinous Cabinet and a fractured Parliament over how to implement the island nation's 2016 Brexit vote to leave the EU—a decision favored by

181

nationalists who say they want Britons, not EU officials in Brussels, to chart their trade, immigration and fiscal paths.[3]

Until now, Germany, the U.K. and France, with their strong economies and pro-European governments, were regarded as the EU's primary engines. But many political analysts say their difficulties are stark reminders that even Europe's most stable governments may not be strong enough to withstand the populist wave that spread across the Continent in the wake of two crises: the 2009 European debt crisis and the 2014-16 refugee crisis that saw more than a million African and Mideast migrants flee to European shores.

"For the first time in my professional career, I'm afraid—existentially—for Europe," says Charles Kupchan, the top National Security Council adviser on European affairs under former President Barack Obama and now a senior fellow at the Council on Foreign Relations.

A major test looms in May, when elections are scheduled for the European Parliament, the EU's legislative branch. Polls show that populist parties seeking to return more sovereignty to member states pose a major challenge to the European integrationists who have dominated the rule-making body.[4]

"Never, since World War II, has Europe been as essential," Macron wrote in a newspaper column urging voters to support the EU. "Yet never has Europe been in so much danger."[5]

In addition to populism and the political troubles of Merkel, May and Macron, the EU is facing numerous other challenges:

• Splits between its wealthier, creditor northern members and poorer, debtor members in the south, as well as between traditionally democratic Western European nations and more authoritarian Eastern European members, such as Hungary and Poland.

• Slowing economic growth throughout the Union. Italy already is in recession, and the EU as a whole is likely to fall into recession later this year or in 2020, according to economists. The European Central Bank in mid-March cut its forecast for economic growth in the eurozone, the 19 countries that use the euro currency, from 1.7 percent to 1.1 percent.[6]

• German-French tensions over the EU's direction. Macron is pushing for a common EU fiscal policy, but Merkel has resisted because she wants Germany to keep control over its own financial affairs.

• Worsening relations with the Union's erstwhile closest ally, the United States.

Unlike his predecessors, President Trump has called the EU a "foe" on trade, portraying it as "a vehicle for Germany" to "beat the United States when it comes to making money."[7]

Hoping to weaken the EU's collective bargaining power, Trump praised Brexit, imposed tariffs on European steel and aluminum and threatened additional levies on European cars—a move that would spur retaliation and a trade war, says David O'Sullivan, the outgoing EU ambassador to the United States.[8]

Meanwhile, U.S. Secretary of State Mike Pompeo urged European nations in December to reassert their sovereignty over the EU to protect their national interests.[9]

Ivo Daalder, a former U.S. ambassador to NATO, says the Trump White House is the first administration that does not support the EU and the principle of shared economic and political sovereignty that underpins the federation.

"In the European Union, sovereignty is explicitly shared," says Daalder, citing the EU's single market as the most powerful manifestation of continental integration. Pompeo's "calling for the end of shared sovereignty is calling for the end of the European Union," he says.

For all its challenges, however, the EU still has much going for it, many analysts say. The common market has removed border controls between member nations, allowing the free flow of people, goods and services, capital and labor. The EU's economic integration has created the world's second-largest market after the United States.[10] And in recent years, the EU has begun speaking as a single voice on political issues ranging from human rights to support of the Iran nuclear deal.

"People have anticipated the demise of the EU every year since its founding, but at the end of each year, the EU is somehow still around," says Bart Oosterveld, an expert on Europe at the Atlantic Council, a Washington think tank that focuses on trans-Atlantic issues. The federation's economic and political integration, he says, has benefited millions of Europeans.

Europeans' support for the EU is generally strong, according to a September 2018 Eurobarometer poll by the European Parliament: More than two-thirds of respondents said their country has benefited from EU membership.[11]

Populist parties in France, Germany and Italy, inspired by Britain's Brexit vote, were calling for their own referendums on leaving the EU. But after watching how chaotic and costly the U.K.'s exit has become, they have tempered their political objectives. Rather than leave the EU, they now say they want to overhaul it from the inside by running for seats in the European Parliament.

"Brexiteers have done Europe no end of good," said Denis MacShane, a writer and former minister for Europe in the government of former British Prime Minister Tony Blair. "Frexit and Grexit and Italexit and all the rest of it are gone."[12]

Populism, however, remains a potentially serious threat to the EU mission. When Merkel opened Germany's borders to refugees in 2015 and provided billions of euros for their resettlement, her humanitarian gesture and an EU-imposed quota system designed to resettle migrants across member states backfired because of the hostility these policies generated. In the 2017 national elections, the far-right Alternative for Germany party (AfD) became the third-largest party in the Bundestag, Germany's parliament, effectively forming the main opposition.[13]

In Britain, the refugee issue helped fuel populist demands for the Brexit referendum. In France, the far-right Nationalist Front of Marine Le Pen called for a similar vote. Meanwhile, southern European countries, some still struggling under the EU's austerity dictates that followed the 2009 debt crisis, saw the EU's refugee resettlement mandate as an added burden.[14] And in central Europe, defiant member states simply refused to take any refugees, says Rachel Ellehuus, the deputy director of the Europe program

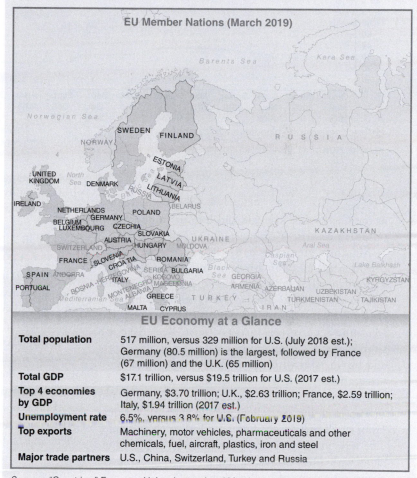

EU Economy Under Pressure

The European Union (EU) remains a global economic powerhouse, with a gross domestic product (GDP) second only to that of the United States. But the EU economy is slowing, and the United Kingdom—with the EU's second-largest economy behind Germany's—could leave the 28-nation federation as early as this spring. Founded in 1993, the EU encompasses a single market with free movement of goods, services and people.

EU Member Nations (March 2019)

EU Economy at a Glance

Total population	517 million, versus 329 million for U.S. (July 2018 est.); Germany (80.5 million) is the largest, followed by France (67 million) and the U.K. (65 million)
Total GDP	$17.1 trillion, versus $19.5 trillion for U.S. (2017 est.)
Top 4 economies by GDP	Germany, $3.70 trillion; U.K., $2.63 trillion; France, $2.59 trillion; Italy, $1.94 trillion (2017 est.)
Unemployment rate	6.5%, versus 3.8% for U.S. (February 2019)
Top exports	Machinery, motor vehicles, pharmaceuticals and other chemicals, fuel, aircraft, plastics, iron and steel
Major trade partners	U.S., China, Switzerland, Turkey and Russia

Sources: "Countries," European Union, last updated March 28, 2019, https://tinyurl.com/h887qhw; "Europe: European Union," CIA World Factbook, Central Intelligence Agency, last updated March 15, 2019, https://tinyurl.com/y2efwtxl and https://tinyurl.com/27j377; and "European Union Unemployment Rate," Trading Economics, undated, https://tinyurl.com/y9rtfx8f

Europeans See Value in EU Membership

A record 68 percent of European Union (EU) citizens say membership in the 28-nation federation has benefited their country. Analysts cite Brexit—the U.K.'s plan to leave the Union—as a factor in the EU's growing popularity because fallout from the exit plan has strengthened other nations' commitment to the federation.

Percentage Who Say Their Nation Has Benefited from EU Membership, 2007–18

Benefited
Not benefited
Don't know

Source: "Parlemeter 2018: Taking Up the Challenge," European Parliament, October 2018, p. 21, https://tinyurl.com/yxnkb4l2

With Merkel, May and Macron all preoccupied with their domestic political challenges, Europe's three major leaders no longer are focused on an EU agenda in any meaningful, consistent way, says Ellehuus, a former principal director for European policy at the Pentagon.

"The people who are normally the engines of Europe are not there to drive it," she says. As a result, she says, "the EU is in a state of flux."

Amid such challenges, here are some of the key questions that policymakers, political analysts and others are asking about the European Union:

at the Center for Strategic and International Studies (CSIS), a centrist Washington think tank.

Macron's victory over Le Pen in France's 2017 presidential election brought temporary relief to European allies who had feared another populist upheaval following Brexit, says Quentin Lopinot, a senior French Foreign Ministry official. He notes that Macron, a European integrationist, won Merkel's support for his proposal to create a European army and began talks with her on additional steps toward integration.

But today, Macron is fighting for his political life, and Le Pen is urging the yellow vests to support National Front candidates for the European Parliament elections. The new movement's calls for Macron's resignation, along with direct democracy and greater national sovereignty, echo many of Le Pen's demands.[15]

Meanwhile, political experts say Russia is trying to weaken the EU by supporting the Continent's nationalist-populists. Over the past decade, they note, Russia has provided populist parties with financial, political and propaganda support as part of its long-standing effort to exploit Europe's divisions and undercut its liberal institutions. "They're very good at figuring out the vulnerabilities in these countries," says Lopinot.

Is the EU in danger of unraveling?

As the U.K. prepares to leave the EU and member countries gear up for European parliamentary elections, bitter differences over immigration, budgets and democratic values have raised the specter of a vote that could produce a paralyzed Parliament, possibly leading to the EU's eventual collapse.

Unless Britain's Parliament can agree on a plan for a smooth exit, the country is in danger of crashing out of the EU under a "hard Brexit" that some analysts have called the geopolitical equivalent of a major amputation without anesthesia. But hard or soft, they say, the result will be an EU that is weaker economically because of the trade barriers that will go up between Britain and the Continent, disrupting labor flows, supply chains and financial services.

In a December 2017 study, a group of Dutch and British economists determined that Brexit's economic impact would fall heaviest on nations geographically closest to Britain—Ireland, the Netherlands and Belgium—as well as those with the highest volumes of trade with Britain, such as France, Germany and Sweden. The study said these countries faced losses ranging from 5 percent to 10 percent of their GDP from Britain's exit from the EU. The remaining EU member states faced 1 percent to 4 percent losses to their GDPs.[16]

"There will be a shock," says William Reinsch, a CSIS expert on the European economy. "It will cost a lot of money," for businesses on both sides of the English Channel to adapt to the new rules governing trade, customs and border inspections, "and the new equilibrium will be far less efficient than the old equilibrium."

The parliamentary elections also pose a major challenge. The EU Parliament, once a mere consultative body, has matured into a formidable check on the European Commission, the executive arm of the EU, and the national governments of member states on issues ranging from trade and environmental standards to the democratic rule of law. Until now, older lawmakers from centrist parties who favor European economic and political integration have dominated it.

This year's new class of legislators, however, is likely to be younger and contain many members from populist parties that are hostile to the EU and want their nations to claw back sovereignty from Brussels, particularly on immigration, fiscal policy and judicial affairs, analysts say.

Many will come from populist movements that have sprung up in nearly every EU member state, mostly since the 2009 debt crisis. Their political targets: Middle Eastern and African migrants; the liberal, cosmopolitan elite; and EU bureaucrats, whom the populists deeply resent over the immigration mandates and other requirements they have imposed, such as legalizing gay marriage, implementing smoking bans and passing strict limits on budget deficits.

"The other parties—the Social Democrats, the Christian Democrats, the Left and the Greens—they don't talk about these issues," said Hugh Bronson, an Alternative for Germany politician. "There has never been a discussion about security. There was never a big discussion in Parliament [over such questions as,] Shall we open the borders? Can we do this? . . . Now a party like the AfD comes along and says, 'OK, now we are going to address this.'"[17]

Populist parties are strongest in Hungary, Italy and Sweden, where they serve in the national governments.

A girl runs near a refugee camp on Lesbos, a Greek island in the Mediterranean Sea, in August 2018. An influx of refugees and migrants from the Middle East and Africa beginning in 2014 has fueled a rise in anti-immigrant sentiment and boosted populist movements across Europe.

AFP/Getty Images/Aris Messinis

Populist parties also are a growing presence in Austria, Denmark, Finland, Spain and Slovakia. In France and Germany, these parties form the principal opposition.

According to a January study by the *Politico Europe* news organization, euroskeptics—those who are critical of the EU—from nearly a half dozen far-right and far-left parties are expected to win more than a third of the European Parliament's 705 seats.[18] That is enough to block policy initiatives on financial matters, social welfare and migration, effectively halting European integration, says Daalder, now president of the Chicago Council on Global Affairs, a think tank that focuses on international issues.

"If the Parliament can't get anything done, that will have a major impact on the ability of the European Union to function," Daalder says. "Ultimately, as countries increasingly focus on their own narrow national interests and they become much more resistant to share sovereignty and make compromises, there would be [a political] collapse."

O'Sullivan, the outgoing EU ambassador to the United States, cautions against dire scenarios. "Support for the European Union across all our member states is at an all-time high in terms of public opinion," he says. "So there are conflicting trends across the body politic."

Sixty-one percent of European Union citizens said EU membership is "a good thing," according to the May 2018

Eurobarometer poll, an increase of 4 percentage points from 2017. But the 2018 poll also showed that half of EU citizens believe things "are going in the wrong direction," an 8 percentage-point increase over poll results six months earlier.[19]

Despite such stresses, Daalder reckons Europe's center will hold. A major reason, he says, is Trump's antipathy toward the EU, which is making many Europeans appreciate the Union's value.

"There's a real understanding that maintaining the European Union is vitally important because the member states can't necessarily count on the United States for their security," Daalder says. "And if the EU wants to compete economically in a world with China and the United States as competitors, they've got to remain united; otherwise, they'll be eaten up. So the strategic rationale for the Union is only becoming stronger."

Other political experts warn that populism's allure should not be underestimated. Pointing to Italy, the Council on Foreign Relations' Kupchan calls its election of a populist government last year "as concerning as any development" on the Continent.

"Italy is a founding member of the EU. It's a large economy, and yet the center has not held there," he says. "If it can happen in Italy, it can probably happen anywhere."

Can the crucial Franco–German alliance survive?

On Jan. 22, French President Macron and German Chancellor Merkel met in the cavernous 14th-century town hall in the German city of Aachen to sign the Franco–German Treaty of Cooperation and Integration.[20]

The ceremony was laden with historical significance. Aachen was the home of Charlemagne, the Frankish king who united much of Western Europe during the early Middle Ages. The signing also echoed a foundational event 56 years earlier, when French President Charles de Gaulle and West German Chancellor Konrad Adenauer signed the first Franco–German friendship pact in Paris after centuries of enmity.[21]

The earlier pact, known as the Élysée Treaty, institutionalized the post-World War II Franco–German partnership, placing it at the center of efforts to integrate Europe economically and politically ever since. But now, a half century later, with

the U.K. preparing to leave the EU and populism and nationalism threatening to weaken it, Merkel and Macron felt the need to reassure other integrationists that France and Germany would continue to guide the European project.

"We reaffirm that we want to tackle the great challenges of our time hand-in-hand," Merkel said after signing the document, which pledges Franco–German cooperation on European political and economic issues, defense projects and common foreign and security policies.[22]

Political experts say the treaty builds on a foundation of close Franco–German cooperation during some of the EU's most challenging moments. They point out that during the debt crisis, senior aides to Merkel and then-French President Nicolas Sarkozy conferred daily as they successfully created the European Stability Mechanism, a bailout fund for struggling economies in the eurozone.

And when British officials tried to divide European countries as they negotiated the United Kingdom's exit from the EU, France and Germany led the resistance to those attempts, says the Atlantic Council's Oosterveld. "The fact that Europe maintained a unified front in those negotiations couldn't have happened without close coordination between the French and the Germans," he says.

Oosterveld says the Franco–German partnership remains strong. "I don't currently see anyone in political circles in either France or Germany who would actively work to loosen that alliance," he says.

French President Emmanuel Macron (left) and German Chancellor Angela Merkel sign a treaty of friendship in Aachen, Germany, on Jan. 22. With the EU facing numerous challenges, the leaders of the federation's two most powerful member nations reaffirmed their support for the Union.

But other political experts say the Aachen treaty papers over deep differences between the two countries that threaten to weaken their alliance.

Since entering office in 2017, Macron has pushed for greater European economic integration by proposing a common budget for the eurozone. He also proposed a banking union and a large pool of funds for bailouts in the event of another debt crisis. But Merkel has refused to go along.

"Merkel and Macron fundamentally disagree about what the next big steps are in terms of European economic integration," says Daalder of the Chicago Council on Global Affairs. "Macron argues that if you have a single monetary policy—the euro—you need to have a single fiscal policy, which makes perfect sense. But Merkel, as the leader of Europe's strongest economy, wants to maintain German control over [her nation's] fiscal policy and not surrender it to European control. Germany's economic hegemony is simply not something she's willing to give up in order to advance European integration."

Merkel also has resisted Macron's pleas to boost German spending, which economists say would stimulate more demand across the EU. Now Italy has fallen into recession, Germany is close to it, and the rest of Europe is facing a cyclical downturn with growth in China slowing, says Reinsch, CSIS's European economy expert.

Most recently, Macron and Merkel have been locked in a dispute over European arms exports to Saudi Arabia. Germany's arms embargo on Saudi Arabia over last October's killing of Saudi journalist Jamal Khashoggi may jeopardize a joint Franco–German program to develop a fighter jet, as well as a large Eurofighter warplane order from Riyadh that includes parts made in Germany. France has imposed no such embargo, and Macron has slammed the German sanctions as "pure demagoguery."[23]

"As long as we don't have unified European rules for arms exports, we will always have this problem," said Tim Stuchtey, executive director of the Brandenburg Institute

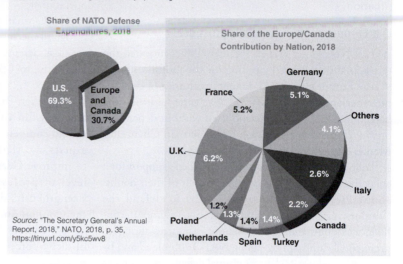

U.S. Pays Bulk of NATO Bill

The United States supplied 69 percent of NATO's defense budget in 2018, more than double the share that Canada and the military alliance's 27 European members collectively provided. Most nations have been slowly increasing their military spending since 2014.

Share of NATO Defense Expenditures, 2018

U.S. 69.3%

Europe and Canada 30.7%

Share of the Europe/Canada Contribution by Nation, 2018

Germany 5.1%
France 5.2%
Others 4.1%
U.K. 6.2%
2.6%
Italy
1.2%
2.2%
Poland
1.3% 1.4% 1.4% Canada
Netherlands Spain Turkey

Source: "The Secretary General's Annual Report, 2018," NATO, 2018, p. 35, https://tinyurl.com/y5kc5wv8

for Society and Security, a think tank in Potsdam, Germany, that focuses on European security issues. "It will be difficult to square French and British attitudes about arms exports with German moral imperatives."[24]

Perhaps the most debilitating threat to the Franco–German partnership, experts say, is Merkel and Macron's political difficulties at home, which have limited their ability to support each other's initiatives or compromise on their differences. In the face of anti-immigrant sentiment in France, Macron has done nothing to advance Merkel's efforts to formulate an EU-wide immigration policy. And in an attempt to appease the yellow vest protesters, Macron lifted his fuel tax, which would have added the equivalent of 29 cents to the $10.13 per gallon the French pay for gasoline or diesel—half of which already goes to taxes. Macron's capitulation to the protesters damaged his credibility with the fiscally conservative Merkel.[25]

But the Atlantic Council's Oosterveld says that the yellow vests have been losing support in France lately, improving Macron's chances for survival, while Merkel's likely successor, CDU leader Annegret Kramp-Karrenbauer, is a strong advocate of Franco–German cooperation. Still, he cautions against any assumptions that the Aachen treaty signals a reinvigoration of the alliance.

"You can argue that in France and Germany, the center is holding for now," Oosterveld says. "But these days, you have to watch and worry. It's not a very reassuring situation."

Is a European army a realistic prospect?

Last November, French President Macron jolted the trans-Atlantic alliance by calling for the mobilization of a "true European army." Speaking in advance of ceremonies marking the end of World War I, he said the time had come for Europe to defend itself without depending on the United States. A week later, German Chancellor Merkel echoed Macron's call.[26]

Political analysts say Macron and Merkel's support for a collective European force is a direct result of their doubts about President Trump's willingness to defend the Continent against Russia. Trump first shook European confidence in long-standing U.S. security guarantees during his presidential campaign by calling NATO "obsolete" and by refusing to endorse its charter's mutual defense commitment when he attended his first NATO summit as president in May 2017. A month later, he reversed himself on the defense commitment, but his announcement in February that the United States would withdraw from a Cold War-era nuclear arms treaty with Russia has added fresh urgency for the call to create a European force.[27]

Under that treaty, Russia and the United States eliminated their medium- and short-range ballistic missiles, which had primarily targeted each side's European allies. Without the treaty, Europe will once again find itself within range of these missiles.

"When I see President Trump announcing that he's quitting a major disarmament treaty, who is the main victim? Europe and its security," Macron said. Because of Trump's policies, he said, Europe needs to defend itself.

But defense experts say, at best, a European force is a long-term prospect. Most European nations, they say, are spending a paltry amount on defense. European members of NATO pledged to devote 2 percent of GDP to military spending by 2024, but only six nations—Estonia, Greece, Latvia, Lithuania, Poland and the United Kingdom—have met that target, according to a NATO report published in March.[28]

One of the smallest defense spenders is Germany, whose military has become a shell since the end of the Cold War in 1991. The German Defense Ministry acknowledged late last year that the majority of the military's newly acquired weapons systems—tanks, fighter jets, helicopters, transport planes and warships—are not operational.[29]

The German government is likely to break Merkel's pledge to increase military spending. Under a new budget plan, defense spending, now at 1.2 percent of GDP, would rise to 1.37 percent in 2020, but then gradually decrease to 1.25 percent by 2023.[30]

Moreover, Paris and Berlin disagree over the shape and mission of a European army and whether it should compete with or complement NATO, security experts say. Merkel views a continental army as a way to improve Germany's defense capabilities, raise the level of professionalism in its armed forces and strengthen its defense industries. Significantly, says the Council on Foreign Relations' Kupchan, Merkel has scaled back her views regarding the independence of such a force and now regards it as a complement to NATO.

By contrast, says the Chicago Council on Global Affairs' Daalder, Macron views the army as a new reserve of soldiers that France can call upon to help protect its interests in places such as North Africa.

"Macron wants a coalition of capable and willing nations to provide troops and equipment to help out in Mali," Daalder says, referring to the former French colony in North Africa where French and European troops are backing the government's fight against Islamist militants. "So it's two very different views."

Eastern and central European capitals, meanwhile, worry that a European force would alienate the United States, whose military is still seen as the only credible guarantor of their survival against a Russian attack.[31]

"We believe that the United States is indispensable in European security," said Bartosz Cichocki, Poland's deputy foreign minister for security affairs.[32]

With Russia on their borders, NATO countries in Eastern and central Europe worry Trump could use a European army as a pretext to end U.S. participation in the rotation of NATO forces across the region. Poland has even told the Pentagon it is ready to spend $2 billion to build a U.S. military base on its soil and call it Fort Trump if the president agrees to permanently station a brigade-size—1,500 to 3,200 troops—contingent of American soldiers there.[33]

Because of all these political and economic obstacles, some defense experts doubt a European army will happen.

But German Defense Minister Ursula von der Leyen maintains that "Europe's army is already taking shape" with the launch of several defense cooperation initiatives. One is the $15 billion European Defense Fund, which aims to boost Europe's defense industries so they can better compete with U.S. arms makers. Another is the Permanent Structured Cooperation initiative, or PESCO, a collection of some three dozen defense projects that is working to standardize the weapons and equipment used by different European armies. A third is the European Intervention Initiative, which envisions an EU rapid deployment force.[34]

Supporters of a European army reject the argument that it would undermine the Trump administration's support for NATO. "This is just a red herring," says Kupchan, who points out the Pentagon quietly backs the idea. "The more capable Europe is," he says, "the more the United States will value the partnership because they will bring more to the table."

Most importantly, say other advocates, such a force would go a long way toward bolstering the EU's self-confidence in its defense capabilities.

"We Europeans have talked ourselves into believing that we cannot achieve a degree of strategic autonomy," says Bastian Giegerich, director of defense analysis at London's International Institute of Strategic Studies. "That's wrong. Yes, it would take a lot of money; yes, it would take a lot of time. But collectively, there's enough potential, and there's enough political will, to actually try and achieve this."

With initiatives such as the European Defense Fund, "we've done more in the past three years to strengthen our security and defense capabilities than we've probably done in the previous 30 years," says O'Sullivan, the outgoing EU ambassador to the United States.

BACKGROUND
A United States of Europe

After World War II, fears that a rebuilt Germany or renewed European rivalries might lead to new wars prompted Europeans to find ways to keep the peace.

Some historians credit former British Prime Minister Winston Churchill with providing the solution in a speech he delivered in 1946.

"We must build a kind of United States of Europe," Churchill said, arguing that a democratic federal union of European nations would bind Germany and other countries to its institutions.[35]

Belgium, France, Germany, Holland, Italy and Luxembourg took the first step toward union when they created the European Coal and Steel Community, a free trade zone for those key industrial resources. The idea behind its formation was to rebuild Europe's heavy industry and to control Germany, which was eager to restore its manufacturing base.[36]

Britain was invited to join, but the Labour government decided against membership out of a desire to maintain economic independence.[37]

To manage the new industrial community, the founding treaty created a governing body that included an executive authority with a common assembly to formulate policy, a legislative council of ministers and a court of justice to interpret the treaty and resolve disputes. These would grow into the EU's key governing bodies.[38]

The six states making up the industrial community hit their first bump in the mid-1950s, when they proposed expanding their union to include a European

Allied bombing during World War II left Dresden, Germany, in ruins. Efforts to ensure a peaceful—and unified—Western Europe eventually led to the creation of the European Union in 1993.

defense community. The proposal envisioned a joint European army overseen by new supranational defense minister. But in 1954, France rejected the initiative, and it was scrapped.[39]

In 1957 the same six nations signed two treaties in Rome that bound them closer together. One accord established the European Atomic Energy Community, which facilitated cooperation on research and development of nuclear energy. The second created the European Economic Community (EEC), which established a common market that required the six nations to overhaul their respective trade laws.[40]

The changes included the abolition of all internal tariffs to allow the free movement of goods, services, capital and labor. In addition, the treaty required the six governments to eliminate protectionist regulations that favored domestic industries and to fall in line behind a common international trade policy.[41]

Meanwhile, the rivalry between France and the United States complicated membership. The U.K., which saw its economic growth lag the EEC's, reconsidered its earlier decision to remain outside the EEC and asked to join in 1963. But French President de Gaulle torpedoed its bid, concerned Britain would act as a proxy for the United States.[42]

Membership in the EEC expanded in the 1970s and 1980s. Replacing de Gaulle in 1969, George Pompidou reversed the veto on Britain, which was admitted in 1973, as were Denmark and Ireland. Greece joined in 1981, followed by Spain and Portugal in 1986.[43]

EU's Debut

On Feb. 7, 1992, the leaders of EEC member countries gathered in the Dutch city of Maastricht to sign the treaty that officially created the European Union. The treaty then went to each member state for ratification. It met with resistance in Britain, Denmark and France, where voters feared their countries would lose control over their affairs. An amended version won approval from all member states and went into effect in November 1993.[44]

Under the Maastricht Treaty, the EU consisted of three main elements. The first gave the European Community broad powers as the central component of the new European Union. The treaty also established common EU citizenship, which gave a citizen of one EU country the right to vote in the elections in another EU nation.

The treaty paved the way for replacing national currencies with a euro currency and created new monetary institutions, including the European Central Bank. The accord laid out the conditions member countries had to meet to join the monetary union. These included annual budget deficits below 3 percent of GDP, low inflation and stable exchange rates.[45]

The second element required EU members to implement a common foreign policy and, where possible, a common defense policy. Any joint military action required unanimity. The third element mandated enhanced cooperation in domestic and judicial affairs, including immigration, asylum and residency policies.[46]

In 1995, the EU expanded to include Austria, Finland and Sweden, leaving Iceland, Norway and Switzerland as the only major Western European nations outside the bloc.

In 1999, 11 countries—Austria, Belgium, Finland, France, Germany, Ireland, Italy, Luxembourg, the Netherlands, Portugal and Spain—adopted the euro, handing over control of their exchange rates to the European Union. Greece, which initially failed to qualify, was admitted in 2001. During that period, internal borders between EU member states came down.[47]

Limited Membership

With the Cold War's end, many countries in central and Eastern Europe, along with Turkey and Cyprus, asked to join the EU. But because of their underdeveloped economies, these countries did not qualify for full membership. So the EU came up with a limited membership category, which allowed these countries to join some of the EU's integrated areas, such as the free trade zone, but restricted their membership in others, such as the eurozone.[48]

Some Western European members feared that opening the door even partially to these countries would further dilute consensus on issues ranging from foreign policy and security to rule of law and cultural issues. This was particularly the case with Turkey, which had strained relations with EU member Greece and a poor human rights record.

In addition to the controversy over a multitiered membership system, the EU faced other unresolved issues. These

CHRONOLOGY

1940s *The vision of a united Europe is born.*

1945 World War II ends, leaving Europe in ruins.

1946 Former British Prime Minister Winston Churchill calls for a "United States of Europe" to avoid another continental war.

1948 Belgium, Luxembourg and the Netherlands form the Benelux customs union, a precursor to pan-European organizations . . . . U.S. undertakes the Marshall Plan to reconstruct Western Europe.

1949 NATO is formed, creating a U.S.-led defense alliance in Western Europe.

1950s-1960s *Europe takes halting steps toward union.*

1951 Benelux countries, plus Germany, France and Italy, form the European Coal and Steel Community, a free trade zone for those key resources.

1954 France rejects a proposal to form a European Defense Community.

1957-58 Treaties of Rome create the European Economic Community (EEC), a common market that requires member nations to overhaul their trade laws, and the European Atomic Energy Community to facilitate the development of nuclear energy.

1961 France rejects Britain's bid to join the EEC, because of the U.K.'s close ties to the United States; France rejects a second British bid in 1967.

1968 The EEC establishes a full customs union.

1970s-1980s *More countries join the European Economic Community.*

1973 France relents and allows Britain, along with Denmark and Ireland, to join the EEC.

1979 First direct elections to European Parliament are held. . . . European Monetary System is created, linking EEC members' currencies.

1981 Greece joins the EEC; Portugal and Spain follow five years later.

1990s-2007 *The European Union (EU) replaces the EEC.*

1992 Maastricht Treaty creates the EU and takes effect a year later after the 13 member nations approve an amended treaty.

1995 Austria, Finland and Sweden join the EU.

1999–2002 A common euro currency is introduced in 11 countries, creating a eurozone. . . . Convention on the Future of Europe convenes to draft an EU constitution.

2004 Draft constitution is signed. . . . Cyprus, Malta and eight Eastern European nations, including Hungary and Poland, join the EU.

2005 France and the Netherlands reject draft constitution.

2007 Treaty of Lisbon is signed, modifying the constitution. It takes effect in 2009 after ratification by all EU members. . . . Bulgaria and Romania join the EU.

2009-Present *Debt crisis and populism threaten EU.*

2009-12 A debt crisis begins in Greece and spreads to Italy and other European nations, threatening the euro's survival. The crisis leads to EU bailouts and severe austerity measures for Greece, Spain, Portugal, Cyprus and Ireland; populist movements opposing the EU grow in response.

2013 Croatia joins the EU, bringing membership to 28 countries.

2014-16 Large numbers of Middle Eastern and African refugees arrive on the Continent, intensifying the populist backlash against the EU.

2016 British voters, citing a need to control their borders and economy, vote to leave the EU.

2017 Pro-EU politician Emmanuel Macron is elected French president. . . . Far-right Alternative for Germany party becomes the third-largest party in Germany's parliament.

2018 German Chancellor Angela Merkel, considered the de facto EU leader, announces she will retire when her current term ends in 2021. . . . Number of migrants illegally entering Europe falls to 150,000, down from 1.5 million in 2015.

2019 EU agrees to a Brexit delay (March). . . . European Parliament is scheduled to hold elections, in which populists are predicted to make substantial gains (May).

EU Seeks to Restrict Flow of African Migrants

Critics say the policies are fueling a humanitarian crisis in Libya.

For the past two years, the Libyan coast guard has been operating a fleet of swift patrol boats, courtesy of the European Union (EU) and Italy, to intercept African migrants and refugees headed for the Italian coast. Since the operation began in 2017, the Italian-trained Libyans have apprehended thousands at sea and sent them to detention centers in Libya.[1]

The EU also is providing hundreds of millions of euros to Niger and Sudan to intercept migrants and asylum-seekers as smugglers guide them across the Sahara to the Libyan coast. Once in custody, the Africans are then taken to one of a half-dozen EU-funded transit centers in Niger, where those seeking European asylum remain until their applications are processed. The others are returned to their home countries, says Kathleen Newland, a migration expert at the Migration Policy Institute, a Washington think tank.

The Libyan patrol boats, the Niger transit centers and the partnerships with African countries are some of the measures that make up the European Agenda on Migration, the EU's official policy to control the flow of migrants into the Continent.

A principal aim of the EU is "to push the [migration] crisis as far away from its borders as possible," said the Center for Strategic and International Studies (CSIS), a centrist Washington think tank, in a report on the crisis.[2]

EU officials consider the strategy largely a success. The number of illegal arrivals in Europe dropped to 150,000 in 2018, according to a March EU report—the fewest since 2015, when 1.5 million people fleeing war-ravaged Syria and other Middle Eastern countries came ashore in the world's worst refugee crisis since World War II.[3]

But human rights groups say the EU is complicit in the tragedy unfolding at Libya's government detention centers. Migrants intercepted at sea are held against their will under horrific conditions, according to a January report by Human Rights Watch. The advocacy group said that as many as 10,000 detainees suffer from "severe overcrowding, unsanitary conditions, malnutrition and lack of adequate health care." In addition, the report said, the detainees, including children, are regularly subjected to beatings, rape, extortion and forced labor.[4]

The report also said the EU has done little to pressure Libya to improve detainees' treatment.

"Fig-leaf efforts to improve conditions do not absolve the EU of responsibility for enabling the barbaric detention system in the first place," said Judith Sunderland, associate director of Human Rights Watch's Europe and Central Asia division.[5]

The EU's March report acknowledged "appalling conditions" in the detention centers, but said the EU has joined a task force with United Nations and African Union officials to help the detainees. So far, the EU said,

Migrants wait inside the Ganzour shelter in Libya on Sept. 5, 2018. With support from the EU, the Libyan coast guard has intercepted refugees and migrants crossing the Mediterranean and placed them in Libyan detention centers. Human rights groups have called conditions in the centers horrific.

AFP/Getty Images/Mahmud Turkia

the task force has facilitated the return of 37,000 migrants to their home countries and evacuated another 2,500 of the most vulnerable to the EU-funded transit centers in Niger.[6]

The transit centers provide migrants with food, water and shelter, as well as medical, psychological and social assistance, according to Newland. "Stay [at the transit centers] is voluntary," she says, adding that migrants who choose to go home receive travel documents, transportation and money.

Since 2016, when the EU struck a deal with Turkey that sharply reduced migrant flows from the Middle East, the bulk of Europe-bound migrants and asylum-seekers have come from Africa, primarily Sudan, Nigeria and Eritrea. Until 2017, Libya's loosely controlled Mediterranean coast, teeming with human traffickers, was the principal departure point for Europe.

In response, Italy and the EU teamed up that year with Libya's government to block the migrant trail. Together, Rome and Brussels spent more than 90 million euros (about $101 million) to provide the Libyan coast guard with patrol boats and training. It also provided 230 million euros to Niger, 100 million to Sudan and an unspecified amount to tribes along Libya's southern border, for their help in interdicting migration traffic.[7]

A total of 23,000 migrants and refugees arrived in Italy from Libya in 2018, down from nearly 119,000 in 2017, according to the International Organization for Migration.[8]

The EU's report said the bloc has made far more progress in preventing migrants from reaching Europe through its partnerships with African countries than it has in integrating those who already have landed in Europe.[9]

Rachel Ellehuus, deputy director of the Europe program at CSIS, says the EU's 28 member states have been unable to agree on a one-size-fits-all immigration policy.

"The policies, in terms of who you accept, how they're processed, that's all still happening at a national level," Ellehuus says.

Germany, France and the Scandinavian countries are Europe's leaders in granting asylum to refugees whose claims of fleeing political persecution have been vetted, according to Ellehuus. They also provide skilled migrants with work permits but deport those who do not meet their requirements. Those who do not qualify as political refugees are

deported as well. By contrast, many people who successfully crossed the Mediterranean still languish in overcrowded camps in Italy and Greece, their bids for asylum or work permits unaddressed. Hungary refuses to take in any migrants.

"There is a fundamental need for an EU-wide approach," the EU report said. "It must be based on strong guarantees that each Member State will deal with the asylum applications it is responsible for."[10]

But in a bid to mollify Italy, which has refused to take in any more refugees rescued at sea, Brussels announced in late March that it will suspend EU maritime patrols that have been conducting such rescue operations and provide only aerial surveillance and continued support for the Libyan coast guard.[11]

— *Jonathan Broder*

[1] Giovanni Legorano and Jared Malsin, "Migration from Libya to Italy, Once Europe's Gateway, Dwindles After Clampdown," *The Wall Street Journal*, March 10, 2019, https://tinyurl.com/y3dzgcg3; Judith Sunderland and Hanan Salah, "No Escape from Hell: EU Policies Contribute to Abuse of Migrants in Libya," Human Rights Watch, Jan. 21, 2019, https://tinyurl.com/yyh4b7pg.

[2] Heather A. Conley and Donatienne Ruy, "Crossing Borders: How the Migration Crisis Transformed Europe's External Policy," Center for Strategic and International Studies, August 2018, p. 11, https://tinyurl.com/y64eywxo.

[3] "Progress Report on the Implementation of the European Agenda on Migration," European Commission, March 6, 2019, https://tinyurl.com/y2pk2yzd.

[4] Sunderland and Salah, *op. cit.*

[5] "Libya: Nightmarish Detention for Migrants, Asylum-Seekers," Human Rights Watch, Jan. 21, 2019, https://tinyurl.com/y5hafoqg.

[6] "Progress Report on the Implementation of the European Agenda on Migration," *op. cit.*

[7] Legorano and Malsin, *op. cit.*

[8] "Mediterranean Migrant Arrivals Reach 113,145 in 2018; Deaths Reach 2,242," International Organization for Migration, Dec. 21, 2018, https://tinyurl.com/y4y43kls.

[9] "Progress Report on the Implementation of the European Agenda on Migration," *op. cit.*

[10] *Ibid.*

[11] "EU recalls ships helping in Mediterranean refugee rescues," Al Jazeera, March 27, 2019, http://tinyurl.com/y423x5ap.

Europe Defies U.S. on Iran Nuclear Deal

Administration threatens "severe consequences" if Continent circumvents sanctions.

Of all the disputes roiling the U.S.-European relationship, no issue has divided the two sides as starkly—or as politically dangerously—as their quarrel over the Iran nuclear deal, experts say.

With the United Kingdom, Germany and France's recent creation of a special financial mechanism to allow continued trade with Iran in defiance of renewed U.S. sanctions, the increasingly acrimonious disagreement risks sparking a diplomatic war between European Union (EU) members and the United States, these experts warn. Such a battle, they say, could result in a serious European challenge to the United States' long-standing dominance over the global banking system and weaken the U.S. position in global affairs.

"The dirty little secret of U.S. financial hegemony is that it rests on far more shallow foundations than its most enthusiastic proponents realize," said Henry Farrell, an associate professor of political science and international relations at George Washington University.[1]

The dispute centers on the 2015 deal in which Iran agreed to scale back its nuclear program in exchange for relief from crippling international economic sanctions. Signatories to the pact were the Obama administration, the other four permanent members of the United Nations Security Council—the United Kingdom, France, Russia and China—Germany and the EU.

As a candidate, President Trump denounced the deal as shortsighted, saying it failed to address Iran's missile program, its support for terrorism and its military activity in the Middle East. Last May, Trump pulled the United States out of the accord and reinstated U.S. sanctions on Tehran.[2]

The administration imposed what are known as secondary sanctions, which stipulate that any company or country that trades with Iran will be barred from doing business with all public or private U.S. entities. Because the U.S. dollar is the preferred international reserve currency and the United States controls the New York-based SWIFT bank wire system used to move dollars around the world, the Treasury Department can easily discover who is doing business with Iran.

Faced with the choice of trading with Iran or losing access to the huge U.S. market, dozens of foreign companies such as France's Total SA oil company already have severed their business ties with Tehran. As a result, Iran's oil exports have been reduced by half, its rial currency has lost more than half its value and its inflation rate has soared to 47.5 percent.[3]

Although the Trump administration has tried to rally international support for its "maximum pressure" campaign against Iran, the International Atomic Energy Agency, U.N. Secretary-General António Guterres and, most recently, U.S. Director of National Intelligence Dan Coats have all said that Iran has upheld its end of the nuclear deal. Therefore, other signatories say they are bound to do so as well.

Like Trump, the Europeans condemn Iran's missile program, assassination plots and what they call its Middle East meddling. But they say it will be much harder to contain Iran if President Hassan Rouhani withdraws from the nuclear accord.

To help keep the accord alive, Britain, Germany and France in January introduced a "special purpose vehicle" to enable Tehran to continue doing business with the rest of

included determining the authorities of large and small member nations and balancing the EU's drive to achieve deeper European integration against the need to maintain the national character of member states. To resolve these issues, EU leaders decided they needed a constitution.[49]

Inspired by the 1787 convention in Philadelphia that wrote the U.S. Constitution, the Convention on the Future of Europe, consisting of 105 members representing national governments and EU bodies, met in Brussels in 2002 to draft the document.

"After 50 years devoted to economic integration culminating in the crowning achievement of the single currency, we are now at the start of a second phase which might also last for 50 years," said former French President Valery Giscard d'Estaing, the convention chairman.[50]

the world. The new company allows foreign companies and Iran to conduct trade through barter, thereby avoiding use of the dollar and the American banking system. The company is called INSTEX, for Instrument in Support of Trade Exchanges, and has the EU's support.[4]

Vice President Mike Pence has demanded the Europeans abandon the Iran accord. "The time has come for our European partners to withdraw from the disastrous Iran nuclear deal and join with us as we bring the economic and diplomatic pressure," he told the annual Munich conference on international security in February.[5]

The question now, experts say, is what the administration will do to enforce its demand. The threat of a harsh American response to INSTEX came from Treasury Undersecretary Sigal Mandelker. "Those that engage in activities that run afoul of U.S. sanctions risk severe consequences, including losing access to the U.S. financial system and the ability to do business with the United States," she warned in an op-ed.[6]

So far, however, the Europeans have refused to back down. "Iran is one of those issues where there is a strong divergence of views between the European side and the U.S.," says David O'Sullivan, the outgoing EU ambassador to the United States. "We are firmly committed to the [pact], and we will remain committed."

INSTEX's utility in resisting U.S. sanctions policy does not stop with Iran, former officials said. Europe and the United States also have clashed over American sanctions against Russia, whose natural gas supplies have made European leaders less willing to punish Moscow for its bad international behavior.

The Trump administration and Congress have threatened additional sanctions against European nations if they move ahead with the Nord Stream 2 natural gas pipeline, a project that will increase the flow of Russian gas to Europe. Trump worries Europe, especially Germany, is becoming overly reliant on energy supplied by an ideological enemy. He also wants Europe to buy U.S. gas.[7]

If the dispute over U.S.-Russia sanctions comes to a head, European governments and companies will be able to utilize INSTEX, said Jarrett Blanc, a former U.S. State Department official who is now a senior fellow with the Carnegie Endowment for International Peace, a Washington think tank.

"This is the nightmare scenario of the U.S. pushing its financial power so far that our allies and partners feel compelled to build financial alternatives to New York and the dollar, with profound political and economic effects," Blanc said. "In the worst case, the U.S. could lose the capacity to sanction transactions that threaten our interests and the profit centers that accrue from providing global services for simple banking."[8]

— *Jonathan Broder*

[1] Henry Farrell, "Trump may be about to call Europe's bluff on Iran. Europe isn't bluffing," *The Washington Post*, Feb. 25, 2019, https://tinyurl.com/y3jvcc9r.

[2] Mark Landler, "Trump Abandons Nuclear Deal He Long Scorned," *The New York Times*, May 8, 2018, https://tinyurl.com/y7u4oy5s.

[3] Alex Lawler, "Despite sanctions, Iran's oil exports rise in early 2019: sources," Reuters, Feb. 19, 2019, https://tinyurl.com/y2kuz5as; Thomas Erdbrink, "Iran's Economic Crisis Drags Down the Middle Class Almost Overnight," *The New York Times*, Dec. 26, 2018, https://tinyurl.com/ybbjghj4; and "Iran Inflation Rate," Trading Economics, https://tinyurl.com/y9rrrg27.

[4] Ellie Geranmayeh and Esfandyar Batmanghelidj, "Trading with Iran via the special purpose vehicle: How it can work," European Council on Foreign Relations, Feb. 7, 2019, https://tinyurl.com/yyf2fqou.

[5] Linda Givetash, "Pence renews criticism of U.S. allies, urging action on Iran and Venezuela in Munich speech," NBC News, Feb. 16, 2019, https://tinyurl.com/y23kckau.

[6] Sigal Mandelker, "Europe's trust in Iranian promises is severely misplaced," *The Hill*, Feb. 22, 2019, https://tinyurl.com/y636l7mx.

[7] "US threatens sanctions over Russia-Germany gas pipeline," Agence France Presse, *The Straits Times*, Jan. 13, 2019, https://tinyurl.com/y39gajg8.

[8] Jarrett Blanc, "Trump Risking Financial Disaster for America," *Politico*, Jan. 13, 2019, https://tinyurl.com/y7b3tw87.

In 2003, the convention produced a draft constitution that greatly expanded the EU's powers. One provision gave the EU sole authority to negotiate most treaties on members' behalf. The draft was then sent to member states, all of whom had to agree on ratification for the constitution to take effect.[51]

Meanwhile, the EU the following year admitted eight former communist countries: the Czech Republic, Estonia, Hungary, Latvia, Lithuania, Poland, Slovakia and Slovenia, along with Cyprus and Malta.

In 2005, France and the Netherlands rejected the draft constitution, scuttling its chances. The EU then declared a two-year "period of reflection" before it considered any further constitutional efforts.[52]

In 2007, Bulgaria and Romania came on board, bringing the EU's membership to 27. By this time, the

EU had achieved an unprecedented level of economic and political integration, with its executive, legislative and judicial institutions operating as a democratic, federal system at a supranational level. But the business of the constitution remained unfinished, and in June of that year, EU officials decided to draft a treaty that would replace the failed constitution. By October, they had finished. The treaty was signed in December and later ratified by all member states.[53]

For the first time, the treaty clarified the EU's powers. Under its exclusive authority, the EU alone could legislate; under shared authority, member states could write and adopt legally binding measures if the EU had not done so; and with its supporting authority, the EU could adopt measure that support or complement the policies of member states.[54]

The accord retained some provisions from the draft constitution, including the power to sign international treaties. And for the first time, it created a formal procedure for member states to withdraw from the EU.[55]

2009 Debt Crisis

Amid a global economic downturn, several EU members were unable to repay or refinance their government debts in 2009. Starting in Greece, the debt crisis spread to Portugal, Ireland, Italy and Spain, threatening the survival of the euro and, according to some analysts, the EU itself.

At first, the EU and the International Monetary Fund implemented stopgap measures to prevent the crisis from spreading, but it became clear that a much larger response was needed. In 2010, German Chancellor Merkel and French President Sarkozy, representing the eurozone's two largest economies, put together a bailout package for Greece. Similar rescues for Ireland, Spain, Portugal and Cyprus followed. The terms, however, were harsh, requiring these countries to drastically cut government spending and public services and raise taxes.[56]

The debt crisis also exposed weaknesses in enforcement provisions of the Maastricht Treaty governing the eurozone. In 2012, EU leaders drew up tougher regulations in which member states that failed to limit government deficits to 3 percent of GDP would face automatic penalties.[57]

The measures calmed markets, and the financial threats facing the eurozone receded. But the austerity measures turned many Europeans against the EU and stoked a wave of populism that took a high political toll. By 2012, more than half of the governments in the eurozone's 17 member states either collapsed or changed hands.

In 2013, Croatia joined the EU, becoming its 28th member.

In 2014, the populists who had changed the political complexion of so many eurozone governments turned their sights on the EU itself. In the elections for the European Parliament that year, euroskeptics won up to 25 percent of the chamber's seats. EU leaders were suddenly confronted by a bloc of euroskeptics who were calling for less economic and political integration and a return of sovereignty to member states.[58]

Populist sentiment intensified in 2015 as a result of the migrant crisis, during which hundreds of thousands of refugees and migrants from the Middle East and Africa came ashore on the Greek islands and Italy, all seeking asylum in the EU. Populist leaders such as the Netherlands' Geert Wilders and France's Le Pen stoked anti-immigrant fears, blaming them for terrorist attacks in Brussels and Paris.[59]

Under pressure from the anti-immigrant U.K. Independence Party and euroskeptics in his own Conservative Party, former British Prime Minister David Cameron agreed to hold a referendum on the country's continued membership in the EU. On June 23, 2016, a narrow majority of British voters chose to leave the EU. The following day, Cameron announced he would resign as prime minister, and in July, he was succeeded by his former home secretary, Theresa May.[60]

Even though May had voted to remain in the EU, she said she felt obligated to implement the Brexit vote. She invoked Article 50, the provision in the EU charter under which a member can withdraw from the Union. The declaration began a two-year countdown in which Britain was to depart the EU by March 29, 2019.[61]

During that period, May met with EU leaders in an effort to negotiate what many called a "soft Brexit"—arrangements that would cause the least amount of dislocation for the U.K. The biggest sticking point was how to deal with the border between Northern Ireland, which also would withdraw as part of the U.K., and the Republic of Ireland, which would remain in the EU.

Neither side wanted a return of checkpoints and customs posts at the border for fear they could disrupt the unimpeded flow of people and trade and reignite the sectarian conflict between Protestant and Catholic Irish.

Unable to find a solution, May and the EU agreed to a "backstop"—an agreement that whatever the outcome of trade talks between Britain and the EU, no hard Irish border would result. The agreement also stipulated that the U.K. would remain in the EU customs union and the backstop would continue indefinitely, ending only when Britain and the EU reached a final deal.[62]

British euroskeptics denounced the plan, fearing it could leave Britain tied to the EU indefinitely with no say over its rules and no freedom to negotiate trade deals with other countries. May said it was the best deal she could get.[63]

May had planned to ask Parliament to ratify the deal in December 2018, but facing certain defeat, she canceled the vote and appealed for more support. On Jan. 15, 2019, May did put the plan to a vote and suffered a 202-432 loss, the biggest defeat for a prime minister in modern British history. A revote in March 2019 produced a similar result.[64]

CURRENT SITUATION

Brexit Chaos

The Brexit drama continues to dominate the EU agenda.

On March 21, EU leaders agreed to extend the deadline for the U.K.'s departure to May 22 if British Prime Minister May could persuade Parliament to accept her plan for leaving the bloc. But if May could not do so, the EU said it would make the deadline April 12.[65]

With little prospect for the passage of May's plan, Parliament voted on March 25 to take control of the Brexit process from the prime minister and explore alternative policy proposals, including one to hold a second Brexit referendum. But after a series of nonbinding "indicative votes," no proposal garnered a majority.[66]

Then, in an extraordinary last-gasp bid to win over opponents of her plan, May offered to resign if Parliament approved it—a move that would have handed the plan's implementation to her successor. But when the plan came up for a vote on March 29, Parliament decisively rejected it for a third time.

As things now stand, Britain will leave the EU on April 12 without any agreement. But members of Parliament believe it is more likely that the government will ask the EU for another deadline extension. May also has hinted she may call for a general election over the issue.[67]

May is now trying a different approach. On April 2, after a seven-hour Cabinet meeting, the embattled prime minister announced she would seek a May 22 deadline extension to allow her time to work out a Brexit compromise with the opposition Labour Party. May's hope is that a combination of votes from Labour and less doctrinaire members of her Conservative Party will produce a new Brexit deal that can win parliamentary approval. "It requires national unity to deliver the national interest," May said.[68]

Analysts say her approach is politically risky because Labour supports keeping the U.K. inside the European Union's customs union. That means a deal with Labour likely would leave Britain more closely tied to the EU, angering hard-line conservatives and weakening support for her government within her own party. As of April 3, no agreement had been reached between May and Labour.

The other ongoing drama is the European Parliament election scheduled for May. As campaigning begins in the EU member states, a major battle is shaping up between the supporters of continued European integration and the euroskeptics.

In France, President Macron is urging voters to reject nationalism and Brexit-style proposals. "The trap is not being part of Europe," he warned.[69]

The French leader proposed a far-reaching agenda for the EU, including a defense treaty that would increase the bloc's military spending. He also said he wants Europe to take the lead in fighting climate change, proposing a target of zero emission of carbon dioxide by 2050.

Macron called for the establishment of an EU agency with responsibility to protect each member state's voting machinery from cyberattack. In a direct swipe at Russia, he urged the EU to ban foreign powers from financing European political parties. And in a nod to rising anti-immigrant sentiment across the Continent, Macron called for stricter border controls.[70]

But Macron's ambitious plans for the EU stand in sharp contrast to his political troubles at home.

As the yellow vest demonstrations continue, Macron scrapped the fuel tax and announced a package of measures worth about 10 billion euros (about $11.4 billion) to boost workers' and retirees' benefits. He also undertook a two-month "grand debate," in which he held town hall meetings across the country to listen to the public's views on France's economic and democratic issues and to explain the rationale for his economic policies.[71]

Polls show Macron's popularity is rising, up to 31 percent from a low of 23 percent in December. But the yellow vests have announced they will field a dozen candidates for the European Parliament elections, opening another populist front against the French leader's pro-European agenda.[72]

Le Pen, leader of France's populist National Rally party, is campaigning for Europe's populist parties in the European Parliament. Confident of a strong showing, she has portrayed these far-right parties as the future of the European Union—one that will include eliminating policies that she says sacrifice national sovereignty, borders and identity for a globalized world that leaves many Europeans behind.

"Today Europe has taken a turn," Le Pen told a political rally in Nanterre, a suburb of Paris, in February. "We can legitimately envision today changing Europe from the inside, modifying the very nature of the European Union, because we consider ourselves powerful enough."[73]

Merkel Speaks Out

In Germany, the customarily reserved Merkel no longer feels compelled to hold back when speaking publicly about another major European concern: President Trump's treatment of the EU as an adversary.

In a speech at the Munich Security Conference in February, Merkel delivered a scathing critique of Trump's policies, accusing him of strengthening Russia and Iran with his plan to withdraw U.S. troops from Syria. She rejected U.S. demands that European allies pull out of the Iran nuclear deal and castigated Trump for withdrawing from the Intermediate-Range Nuclear Forces (INF) Treaty—a move that she said would put European states in the crosshairs of rival U.S. and Russian missile forces.[74]

Merkel also alleged that under Trump, the U.S.-led global order "has collapsed into many tiny parts."[75]

"The relationship between Europe and the United States is as bad as it has ever been," says Daalder, who attended the security conference.

Republican and Democratic lawmakers have supported Trump's decision to withdraw from the nuclear treaty, citing U.S. intelligence reports that Russia's deployment of a medium-range cruise missile has violated the accord. "The Russian Federation brazenly violated the INF treaty and has been unwilling to take the steps necessary to come back into compliance," said Sen. Robert Menendez of New Jersey, ranking Democrat on the Senate Foreign Relations Committee.[76]

The specter of automobile tariffs is the most urgent issue between the EU and the United States, trans-Atlantic analysts say. Many analysts believe Trump will impose tariffs, primarily to punish Germany, the largest European exporter of cars to the United States and one of the principal targets of Trump's anger over the ballooning U.S. trade deficit.

European carmakers exported 1.2 million automobiles worth 37.3 billion euros to the United States in 2018, according to the European Automobile Manufacturers Association. But the trade group added that the European and U.S. auto industries have been integrated for decades. In 2018, the U.S. plants of European carmakers produced 3 million cars, accounting for 27 percent of total U.S. car production. More than half of those cars were exported to third countries, the trade group said, helping to improve the U.S. trade balance, the association said.[77]

"Automobiles are the largest manufactured item that Europe exports," says Reinsch, the European economist at CSIS. The European auto industry "employs thousands of workers. A 25 percent tariff would have an enormous impact on the EU economy."

The Council on Foreign Relations' Kupchan says Germany and France have experienced slower growth in the past few quarters and could join Italy in a recession. With the slowdown in China, analysts say, the EU is likely to fall into a recession by 2020. But a U.S. auto tariff, which would affect France, Sweden, Italy and the U.K. as well as Germany, would push it there that much faster, with unwelcome political repercussions.

"It's a problem, because if you were to point to the two main causes of the populism and discontent, number one would be immigration, and the second would be economic insecurity," Kupchan says. "It's particularly troubling for France, where Macron really needs to deliver and get the economy jump-started."

Is the European Union in danger of unraveling?

YES
Charles A. Kupchan
Senior Fellow, Council on Foreign Relations;
Professor of International Affairs,
Georgetown University

Written for *CQ Researcher*, April 2019

The project of European integration is passing through a perilous moment. Is the European Union (EU) likely to unravel? No. Is the EU at risk of unraveling? Most certainly yes.

A combination of economic insecurity and immigration is fueling a populist revolt against Brussels and political establishments across the EU. Britain is already in the process of quitting the EU—and making a hash of it. Poland, Hungary and Italy all have populist, euroskeptic governments determined to roll back power from Brussels. Although Italy has not (yet) gone down the illiberal path followed by Poland and Hungary, it is in some ways the bigger story. Italy is a founding member of the EU, with one of the Union's largest economies. That the political center has not held in Italy suggests that centrist, pro-EU parties are vulnerable everywhere.

So far, the center has held in most other EU member states. Although they are weakening as populist parties on the left and right gain market share, center-left and center-right parties still call the shots in most countries. The same goes for elections to the European Parliament scheduled for May. Populist parties are poised to make significant gains, but centrist, pro-EU parties are likely to do well enough to form a stable governing coalition.

The key question is what lies ahead. Will disaffection deepen, drawing more voters to the populist extremes, or will the center hold, if not rebound? The most likely scenario is that centrist parties will maintain power in France, Germany and most other member states. But uncertainties abound. Will French President Emmanuel Macron prove adept at jump-starting the country's economy and facing down unemployment? German Chancellor Angela Merkel, who has anchored European politics for more than a decade, is preparing to step aside. What comes next?

Europe's fate rides on its ability to tackle many of the same challenges facing the United States. As automation advances, the Atlantic democracies need to ensure that workers earn a living wage. Immigration continues to roil politics, requiring new policies that enjoy popular support. Addressing inequality and communal fragmentation are key to sustaining pluralism, multiethnic tolerance and social cohesion.

Europeans should not be complacent about the fate of their Union. The EU needs to demonstrate that it can deliver prosperity and security to its citizens. In so doing, it can re-legitimate the project of integration among European publics.

NO
Ivo Daalder
President, Chicago Council on Global Affairs

Written for *CQ Researcher*, April 2019

Following the end of the world's most devastating war, which had left the Continent destroyed and destitute, Europe after 1945 set out to build a new order in which differences between nations would be settled by peaceful means rather than by force of arms.

The result was the European project—ever-growing cooperation among European nations that culminated in the creation of the European Union, uniting 28 diverse countries into a single economic market, governed by executive and legislative bodies that derive their legitimacy from the voters and individual member states. It has proven to be an extraordinary experiment of international cooperation, one that effectively eliminated war from a continent whose history was forged by centuries of armed conflict.

That Union is now under severe stress, mainly as a result of the domestic politics and divisions among its member states, including in each of the six largest members. Growing populist and nationalist movements have ascended to power in Italy and Poland and shown increased strength in France, Germany and Spain. In Britain, such sentiment expressed itself in a nationwide vote in favor of leaving the Union altogether.

To many observers, these political developments bode ill for Europe's future—that after a steady march of ever closer European integration, the Union will now disintegrate into its constituent parts. There are at least three reasons why these fears are misplaced.

First, the international environment is making the case for European cooperation and unity stronger with each passing day. Recognition is growing among Europeans that unity is the best, if not the only, way to thwart the ambitions of a rising China (now seen by the EU not just as a large market but also as a "strategic rival"). And growing fissures across the Atlantic enhance the imperative of European cooperation as continued reliance on the United States becomes increasingly questionable.

Second, the fallout from Brexit, including its inordinate costs for Britain's politics and economy, has markedly increased support for the EU in all European countries (including, paradoxically, in Britain itself). Indeed, two out of three European adults now have a favorable view of the Union.

Finally, for the vast majority of Europeans, the project has worked. European cooperation has brought more prosperity, greater freedom and lasting peace for more than 500 million people. These successes are not something anyone is prepared to give up.

Italy recently defied both the Trump administration and Brussels by signing on to China's Belt and Road Initiative, a trillion-dollar infrastructure program designed to link markets in Europe, Asia and Africa to China. Concerned over Beijing's growing influence, Washington and Brussels have urged EU countries not to join the initiative. But Rome, still deeply in debt from the 2009 debt crisis, found China's offers of investment in Italy's ports, energy and telecommunications sectors too attractive to resist, analysts said.[78]

Meanwhile, Reinsch says, Trump's tariff threats have insulted Germany. "The biggest car exporter from the U.S. right now is BMW, the second is Daimler-Benz. They ship to Europe tens of thousands of cars from their factories in Alabama and South Carolina," he says. "They have more employees in the U.S. than lots of American companies. They're totally exercised about this."

O'Sullivan, the outgoing EU ambassador to the United States, says if Trump moves ahead with automobile tariffs, the EU will retaliate by imposing $24 billion in tariffs on U.S. exports. He calls the administration's national security rationale for U.S. tariffs "patently absurd."

Administration officials defend the use of tariffs, saying they are driven by Trump's belief that EU members routinely take advantage of the United States. "We have wonderful relationships with a lot of people. But nobody treats us much worse than the European Union," Trump said last year, noting on another occasion that the United States had a $15 billion trade deficit with the EU. "The European Union was formed in order to take advantage of us on trade, and that's what they've done."[79]

Security Threats

On the security front, defense experts say the EU faces an ongoing terrorism threat from North Africa and the Middle East, as well as Russian interference in the form of loans and other political assistance to populist and nationalist parties across the Continent. They say Russia routinely wages sophisticated online disinformation campaigns aimed at weakening Western institutions.

Last September, the European Parliament approved a report that said democracy, the rule of law and fundamental rights are under "systematic threat" in Hungary and recommended sanctions against the government of Prime Minister Viktor Orbán. The report cited Orbán's efforts to curtail judicial independence, press freedom and the rights of Roma (also known as Gypsies), Jews, migrants and refugees. The report also accused Orbán of corruption.[80]

Hungary could temporarily lose its EU voting rights, and Orbán's government could be required to repay 43 million euros in what investigators say were misappropriated EU development funds.[81]

Orbán has denounced the threatened EU sanctions, challenging Brussels' authority over EU member states. "European policy is distorted," he said. "The essence of Europe is not in Brussels but in the member states, and if the institutions don't respect the member states, that is depressing."[82]

The report has gone to the EU Council, the body's highest executive authority, for a final ruling.

OUTLOOK
Populism's Impact

Many analysts say populism could decide the EU's future.

Determined to return greater sovereignty to their nations, populists could in May establish a bloc of parties in the European Parliament strong enough to thwart initiatives meant to advance the Continent's integration.

"Just how large will the populist representation be—under 20 percent, more than 30 percent?" asks Daalder, of the Chicago Council on Global Affairs. "The future health of the European project will be judged in some large measure by that."

At the moment, the populist movement appears ascendant, with polls showing EU voters are poised to send more populists from both the left and right than ever before. Europe traditionally has had coalition governments made up of parties from both sides of the political spectrum.

But some experts doubt the populists will be able to influence key policies and appointments, saying right-wing and left-wing populists may be too divided to form a cohesive political force.

Still, "it would be a mistake to assume that means their impact will be minimal," Mujtaba Rahman, director of European analysis for the Eurasia Group, a political and economic consultancy, wrote in a recent commentary for *Politico*'s European edition. "If populists perform well in the May election, it will be much harder than it was in 2014 [after the last European Parliament elections] for the pro-European establishment to simply dust itself off and carry on."[83]

Since 2014, Hungary, Italy and Poland have elected populist governments, enabling them to make appointments to the European Commission. Coalition governments in several other member states include populist parties, giving them a say in their country's commission choices.

Against that backdrop, Daalder predicts three possible scenarios over the next five years. The first envisions a weak populist showing in the elections and broad agreement among European centrists that the EU must make a major leap forward in economic integration if it is to compete successfully with China and the United States.

"That means getting Germany to agree with Macron's proposals for integrating the eurozone's monetary and fiscal policies, as well as his vision for a European army," Daalder says. "And that's not very likely."

The second scenario is one in which European integration moves forward at different speeds. The wealthier northern countries—Belgium, France, Germany, Luxembourg, the Netherlands and the Scandinavian members—accelerate their economic and security cooperation while the other member states integrate more slowly. Depending on the election outcome, Daalder says, such a compromise is possible.

In the third scenario, he says, the EU stumbles into a dystopian future.

"The EU becomes more contentious, and there are more differences that make policymaking more difficult," he says. "There's a sense of stalemate in the Union, with not much happening and everyone increasingly focusing on their own narrow national interests."

The Council on Foreign Relations' Kupchan warns that if the member states go down that road, the EU's eventual collapse is not out of the question. "Then all bets are off," he says. "Europe returns to its old ways."

NOTES

1. David A. Andelman, "Can Macron survive France's 'yellow vest' revolution?" bdnews24.com, Dec. 8, 2018, https://tinyurl.com/yy4quccs.

2. Griff Witte, "Germany's Angela Merkel says she won't run again for party leader or chancellor," *The Washington Post*, Oct. 29, 2018, https://tinyurl.com/y3awhrf9.

3. Tom McTague, "British politics goes over a cliff," *Politico Europe*, March 28, 2019, https://tinyurl.com/ycn5vmbp.

4. Ryan Heath *et al.*, "Europe in pieces: Where voters disagree," *Politico Europe*, Jan. 23, 2019, https://tinyurl.com/ycwvlf5d.

5. Sylvie Corbet, "France's Macron makes pro-European plea before EU elections," The Associated Press, *Star Tribune*, March 4, 2019, https://tinyurl.com/y2xydj59.

6. David McHugh, "European Central Bank joins global push to help economy," The Associated Press, March 7, 2019, http://tinyurl.com/y6hw5csd.

7. Maegan Vazquez, "Trump calls the EU a 'foe' of the United States," CNN, July 16, 2018, https://tinyurl.com/y6wbp7wq; Ben Jacobs, "Donald Trump: EU was formed 'to best the US at making money,' " *The Guardian*, July 23, 2016, https://tinyurl.com/jm4qbu3; and "Donald Trump takes swipe at EU as 'vehicle for Germany,' " *Financial Times*, Jan. 15, 2017, https://tinyurl.com/y3laar64.

8. Emily Tamkin, "Outgoing E.U. ambassador on Trump tactics: 'This is not maybe the best way to build an alliance,' " *The Washington Post*, Feb. 22, 2019, https://tinyurl.com/y2dqt5as; "Donald Trump and the New World Order," *Der Spiegel*, Jan. 20, 2017, https://tinyurl.com/hqnnuww.

9. Michael R. Pompeo, "Restoring the Role of the Nation-State in the Liberal International Order," U.S. Department of State, Dec. 4, 2018, https://tinyurl.com/y4hbbh5g.

10. "Gross domestic product at market prices," Eurostat, European Commission, 2019, https://tinyurl.com/yyul2tq4.

11. "Parlemeter 2018: Taking Up the Challenge," European Parliament, October 2018, p. 21, https://tinyurl.com/yxnkb4l2.

12. Steven Erlanger, "The Messier Brexit Gets, the Better Europe Looks," *The New York Times*, Jan. 30, 2019, https://tinyurl.com/yc2zgghg.

13. Matthew Goodwin, David Cutts and Thomas Raines, "What Do Europeans Think of Muslim Immigration?" Chatham House, Feb. 7, 2017, https://tinyurl.com/h7jbpjl; Amanda Taub, "What the Far Right's Rise May Mean for Germany's Future," *The New York Times*, Sept. 26, 2017, https://tinyurl.com/y98vcdfn.

14. Ian Dunt, "It's a Brexit World: Tide of anti-immigrant sentiment sweeps globe," politics.co.uk, Aug. 11, 2016, https://tinyurl.com/y27o6d6n.

15. Geert de Clercq, "France's Le Pen launches EU campaign with appeal to 'yellow vests,'" Reuters, Jan. 13, 2019, https://tinyurl.com/y48kl9ns.

16. Wen Chen *et al.*, "The continental divide? Economic exposure to Brexit in regions and countries on both sides of The Channel," *Regional Science*, March 2018, https://tinyurl.com/y9977uev.

17. "German elections: How right-wing is nationalist AfD?" BBC, Oct. 13, 2017, https://tinyurl.com/yxujlhsu.

18. Heath *et al.*, *op. cit.*

19. "Democracy on the Move: European Elections— One Year To Go," European Parliament, May 2018, https://tinyurl.com/y3gj9nay; "Parlemeter 2017: A Stronger Voice—Citizens' Views on Parliament and the EU," European Parliament, Nov. 10, 2017, https://tinyurl.com/yxenat6v.

20. Guy Chazan, "Macron and Merkel sign Aachen treaty to deepen Franco–German ties," *Financial Times*, Jan. 22, 2019, https://tinyurl.com/yxuf7lfp.

21. *Ibid.*

22. "Merkel and Macron seal friendship pact," *Der Spiegel*, Jan. 22, 2019, https://tinyurl.com/yaax8s9w.

23. "Germany's moral qualms about arms sales infuriate its allies," *The Economist*, March 2, 2019, https://tinyurl.com/y2duezdn.

24. Andrea Shalal and Sabine Siebold, "German halt to Saudi arms sales could put squeeze on Eurofighter," Reuters, Oct. 23, 2018, https://tinyurl.com/y4vdzoj4.

25. Stephen Pope, "Long Live Gilets Jaunes As Macron's Makes A Fuel Tax U-Turn," *Forbes*, Dec. 6, 2018, https://tinyurl.com/y6n2b5nb.

26. Katrin Bennhold and Steven Erlanger, "Merkel Joins Macron in Calling for a European Army 'One Day,'" *The New York Times*, Nov. 13, 2018, https://tinyurl.com/ydhry8eh.

27. Rosie Gray, "Trump Declines to Affirm NATO's Article 5," *The Atlantic*, May 25, 2017, https://tinyurl.com/mmlqrho.

28. "The Secretary General's Annual Report: 2018," NATO, 2018, https://tinyurl.com/y5kc5wv8; Michael-Ross Fiorentino, "NATO Pledge: Which European countries spend over 2% of GDP on defence?" euronews, March 14, 2019, https://tinyurl.com/y6c8gypd.

29. "German Army to be fully equipped for combat . . . in 13 years—Defense Chief," RT, Jan. 5, 2019, https://tinyurl.com/y55fz6ck.

30. Bojan Pancevski and Laurence Norman, "Germany Plans to Renege on Pledge to Raise Military Spending, Defying Trump," *The Wall Street Journal*, March 18, 2019, https://tinyurl.com/yykr5pbo.

31. Yaroslav Trofimov, "Is Europe Ready to Defend Itself?" *The Wall Street Journal*, Jan. 4, 2019, https://tinyurl.com/y7ke5z7q.

32. *Ibid.*

33. Trofimov, *op. cit.*; Rod Powers, "How The U.S. Army Is Organized," The Balance Careers, Dec. 18, 2018, https://tinyurl.com/y6xtm7op.

34. "The Paper Euro-army," *The Economist*, Jan. 31, 2019, https://tinyurl.com/y5r8dyj8.

35. "Winston Churchill, speech delivered at the University of Zurich," Sept. 19, 1946, https://tinyurl.com/y3y355zu.

36. Ina Sokolska, "The First Treaties," Fact Sheets on the European Union, European Parliament, 2019, https://tinyurl.com/y4b2mqjt.

37. Matthew J. Gabel, "European Union," Encyclopeadia Britannica, Jan. 24, 2019, https://tinyurl.com/y5yxzakr.

38. Sokolska, *op. cit.*

39. "The failure of the European Defense Community (EDC)," CVCE.eu, 2019, https://tinyurl.com/y42rbulz.

40. Sokolska, *op. cit.*

41. *Ibid.*

42. Gabel, *op. cit.*; "Common Market Founded," History.com, Feb. 9, 2010, https://tinyurl.com/y2amm9mq.

43. "Common Market Founded," *ibid.*

44. Morgane Griveaud, "Why is the Maastricht Treaty considered to be so significant?" E-International Relations Students, May 29, 2011, https://tinyurl.com/yxbksmp7.

45. *Ibid.*

46. *Ibid.*

47. Cynthia Kroet, "A timeline of the eurozone's growth," *Politico Europe*, Dec. 26, 2014, https://tinyurl.com/y5xrc2fk.

48. Gabel, *op. cit.*

49. *Ibid.*

50. "Interview with Valéry Giscard d'Estaing from Le Figaro," CVCE.eu, Jan. 22, 2003, https://tinyurl.com/yyr8m2e7.

51. "EU draft constitution agreed," BBC, June 13, 2003, https://tinyurl.com/y5ff4bq5.

52. "Dutch say 'devastating no' to EU constitution," *The Guardian*, June 2, 2005, https://tinyurl.com/yyvuh2gg.

53. Gabel, *op. cit.*

54. Roberta Panizza, "The Treaty of Lisbon," Fact Sheets on the European Union, European Parliament, October 2018, https://tinyurl.com/yyxoamh7.

55. *Ibid.*

56. Michael Ray, "Euro-zone debt crisis," Encyclopaedia Britannica, Sept. 3, 2017, https://tinyurl.com/yyuzsj2f.

57. *Ibid.*

58. Kristin Archick, "The 2014 European Parliament Elections: Outcomes and Implications," CRS Insights, July 24, 2014, https://tinyurl.com/y2lydlnx; Andrew Grice and Nigel Morris, "European election results 2014: Farage and UKIP top poll as Europe swings to the right," *The Independent*, May 26, 2014, https://tinyurl.com/y4v9qob8.

59. Charlotte McDonald-Gibson, "Europe's Anti-Immigrant Parties Make Hay From Paris Terrorist Attack," *Time*, Jan. 8, 2015, https://tinyurl.com/yyyc3c6e.

60. Paul Dallison, "Theresa May takes over as British prime minister," *Politico Europe*, July 13, 2016, https://tinyurl.com/yxznoaeo.

61. Curt Mills, "Brexit Officially Begins," *U.S. News & World Report*, March 29, 2017, https://tinyurl.com/yyeoa95z.

62. Kevin Doyle and Shona Murray, "Brexit deal reached: No hard border for Ireland as 'sufficient progress' made on talks," *The Independent*, Dec. 8, 2017, https://tinyurl.com/y63tufwu.

63. Ylenia Gostoli, "Brexit: the backstop and why some oppose it," Al Jazeera, Feb. 5, 2019, https://tinyurl.com/yawprelx.

64. Jonathan Broder, "Can Theresa May and Angela Merkel Resist the Forces They Helped Create?" *Newsweek*, Jan. 24, 2019, https://tinyurl.com/ycm9tm2y; "The Brexit Plan Failed Again: What Happened, and What's Next?" *The New York Times*, March 12, 2019, https://tinyurl.com/y25eelaf.

65. Stephen Castle and Steven Erlanger, "E.U. Approves Brexit Extension, but Chaotic Departure Still Looms," *The New York Times*, March 21, 2019, https://tinyurl.com/y2xo869w.

66. Danica Kirka and Jill Lawless, "UK lawmakers prepare to vote on alternatives to Brexit deal," The Associated Press, *The Washington Post*, March 27, 2019, https://tinyurl.com/y6kmovph.

67. Max Colchester and Jason Douglas, "May's Brexit Deal Is Rejected for a Third Time by Lawmakers," *The Wall Street Journal*, March 29, 2019, https://tinyurl.com/y6yua4ak.

68. "Brexit: Theresa May meets Jeremy Corbyn to tackle deadlock," BBC, April 3, 2019, http://tinyurl.com/y2qegkel.

69. Corbet, *op. cit.*

70. *Ibid.*

71. Sophie Law, "Yellow Vest activists set bins ablaze while police pelt mobs with tear gas," *Daily Mail*,

March 2, 2019, https://tinyurl.com/yxbrrfej; James McAuley, "Macron hoped a 'grand debate' would curb the yellow vests. It may or may not have worked," *The Washington Post*, March 17, 2019, http://tinyurl.com/y6exdbcp.

72. "L'Observatoire politique," Les Echos/Radio Classique, March 7, 2019, https://tinyurl.com/yygx6jjk; Nicholas Vinocur, "Why the Yellow Jacket movement is a gift to Macron," *Politico Europe*, Jan. 28, 2019, https://tinyurl.com/y92uo55m; and McAuley, *ibid*.

73. Elaine Ganley, "France's Le Pen Boasts Far-Right Power for EU Elections," *U.S. News & World Report*, Feb. 15, 2019, https://tinyurl.com/y284znpy.

74. Steven Erlanger and Katrin Bennhold, "Rift Between Trump and Europe Is Now Open and Angry," *The New York Times*, Feb. 17, 2019, https://tinyurl.com/yxwno378.

75. Griff Witte and Michael Birnbaum, "Trump foreign policy under attack from all sides at European security conference," *The Washington Post*, Feb. 16, 2019, https://tinyurl.com/y446bc57.

76. "Menendez Statement on Trump Administration's Withdrawal from Nuclear Treaty," Office of Sen. Bob Menendez, Feb. 1, 2019, https://tinyurl.com/yyfbhoyc.

77. "EU-US Automobile Trade: Facts and Figures," European Automobile Manufacturers Association, March 2019, https://tinyurl.com/y43fu4ru.

78. Jason Horowitz, "Defying Allies, Italy Signs On to New Silk Road With China," *The New York Times*, March 23, 2019, https://tinyurl.com/y4pha7jv.

79. Lesley Stahl, "President Trump on Christine Blasey Ford, His Relationships With Vladimir Putin and Kim Jong Un and More," "60 Minutes," Oct. 15, 2018, https://tinyurl.com/y7dddnmw; Gabriela Galindo, "Trump: EU was 'set up' to take advantage of U.S.," *Politico*, June 28, 2018, https://tinyurl.com/y9grdxjv.

80. Keno Verseck, "Hungary's Viktor Orban challenges EU over Article 7 sanctions," Deutsche Welle, Sept. 25, 2018, https://tinyurl.com/y4dk4gcc.

81. Bernd Riegert, "EU wants to hit Viktor Orban where it hurts: the wallet," Deutsche Welle, April 7, 2018, https://tinyurl.com/y2dt7efy.

82. "Hungary PM Orban criticizes EU sanctions threat," *Daily Sabah*, May 19, 2017, https://tinyurl.com/y5la74ld.

83. Mujtaba Rahman, "Populism's rising tide," *Politico Europe*, Jan. 28, 2019, https://tinyurl.com/yaevc8sq.

BIBLIOGRAPHY
Books

Clarke, Harold D., Matthew Goodwin and Paul Whiteley, *Brexit: Why Britain Voted to Leave the European Union*, Cambridge University Press, 2017.
Three political scientists explore the social and political forces that led to the United Kingdom's vote in 2016 to quit the European Union (EU).

Drozdiak, William, *Fractured Continent: Europe's Crises and the Fate of the West*, W.W. Norton & Co., 2017.
A former chief European correspondent for The Washington Post examines the political, economic and ethnic fractures that the author says could pull Europe apart.

McCormick, John, *Understanding the European Union: A Concise Introduction*, Red Globe Press, 2017.
An Indiana University political science professor reviews the history and structure of the EU and its current challenges.

Verhofstadt, Guy, *Europe's Last Chance: Why the European States Must Form a More Perfect Union*, Basic Books, 2017.
A former Belgian prime minister argues for an overhaul of the EU to ensure it more closely resembles the federal system in the United States.

Articles
Crawford, Alan, "Trump's Foreign Policy Discord Drives Wedge Between Vital Allies," Bloomberg, Feb. 14, 2019, https://tinyurl.com/y3wtlt8n.

A journalist writes that President Trump's policies on Iran, trade and global security have alienated Washington's European allies.

Erlanger, Steven, "The Messier Brexit Gets, the Better Europe Looks," *The New York Times*, Jan. 30, 2019, https://tinyurl.com/yc2zgghg.
The Times' chief European correspondent reports on how political chaos in Britain over Brexit has dampened enthusiasm among EU skeptics for similar votes in other European countries.

Trofimov, Yaroslav, "Is Europe Ready to Defend Itself?" *The Wall Street Journal*, Jan. 4, 2019, https://tinyurl.com/y7ke5z7q.
A journalist describes the EU's efforts to form a European army and the political divisions that stand in the way.

Reports and Studies

Conley, Heather A., and Donatienne Ruy, "Crossing Borders: How the Migration Crisis Transformed Europe's External Policy," Center for Strategic and International Studies, Oct. 18, 2018, https://tinyurl.com/y4dldp32.
The EU decided in the wake of the 2014-16 refugee crisis to focus on blocking migration routes in Africa and the Middle East to Europe, according to experts at a centrist Washington think tank.

Dennison, Susi, and Pawel Zerka, "The 2019 European Election: How Anti-Europeans Plan to Wreck Europe and What Can Be Done to Stop It," European Council on Foreign Relations, February 2019, https://tinyurl.com/y6hrgsr8.
Researchers at a European think tank present various strategies to blunt the nationalist influence of euroskeptic critics of the EU who are expected to control more than one-third of the seats in the European Parliament after May elections.

Goodwin, Matthew, David Cutts and Thomas Raines, "What Do Europeans Think of Muslim Immigration?" Chatham House, Feb. 7, 2017, https://tinyurl.com/h7jbpjl.
Three political scientists present research that points to widespread public anxiety over migration to Europe from mainly Muslim countries.

Grevi, Giovanni, "Shaping Power: A Strategic Imperative for Europe," European Policy Center, Feb. 22, 2019, https://tinyurl.com/yxdb9v3e.

A senior fellow at a pro-EU think tank in Brussels analyzes how updating the EU's industrial, social and fiscal policies can strengthen Europe's ability to compete with the United States and China.

Heath, Ryan, *et al.*, "Europe in pieces: Where voters disagree," *Politico Europe*, Jan. 23, 2019, https://tinyurl.com/ycwvlf5d.
Journalists examine the issues dividing Europeans today and assess their impact on this spring's European Parliament elections.

Megerisi, Tarek, "Order From Chaos: Stabilising Libya the Local Way," European Council on Foreign Relations, July 19, 2018, https://tinyurl.com/y3r55l3h.
A visiting fellow at a think tank focusing on European security explores how a partnership between European governments and nongovernmental organizations and local authorities in Libya can restore order to that country and help stem the flow of refugees to Europe.

THE NEXT STEP
Brexit

Chrisafis, Angelique, and Jennifer Rankin, "EU must learn from Brexit and reform, says Emmanuel Macron," *The Guardian*, March 4, 2019, https://tinyurl.com/yydcz6eh.
French President Emmanuel Macron has called for a major overhaul of the European Union (EU) in response to Brexit, proposing protections against internet threats, a higher minimum wage and a new defense treaty, among other things.

McCann, Allison, *et al.*, "Where Europe Would Be Hurt Most by a No-Deal Brexit," *The New York Times*, Feb. 7, 2019, https://tinyurl.com/yd5hshhw.
If the United Kingdom departs from the European Union under a worst case scenario—with no official withdrawal agreement with the EU—Northern Europe's economy would suffer the most because of tariffs, labor shortages and banking complications, according to a *New York Times* analysis.

Meredith, Sam, "'Last chance': EU leaders issue ultimatum to Britain over no-deal Brexit," CNBC, March 22, 2019, https://tinyurl.com/y3th2gc2.

The European Union will grant a two-month Brexit delay if the British Parliament passes the current withdrawal agreement. If lawmakers don't act, the EU will force Britain to leave on April 12 with no deal in place and greater harm to the U.K.

Migration

"Operation Sophia: EU to scale back Mediterranean rescue mission," euronews, March 27, 2019, http:// tinyurl.com/y69zy3vd.
The EU plans to end its naval patrols that intercept African migrants who are crossing the Mediterranean Sea to Europe, but it said it will extend its air patrols.

Roth, Clare, "EU Commission strikes back at Hungarian migration campaign 'fiction,'" Reuters, Feb. 28, 2019, https://tinyurl.com/y655rxv7.
The EU accused Hungarian Prime Minister Viktor Orbán of spreading misinformation by claiming that the European Commission and American billionaire George Soros conspired to encourage mass immigration to Europe.

Smith-Spark, Laura, "Illegal migration to EU falls to lowest level in 5 years—but spikes in Spain," CNN, Jan. 5, 2019, https://tinyurl.com/y9xj3p45.
The number of migrants crossing the western Mediterranean Sea from Morocco to Spain jumped in the past two years after Italy cut off access to the central Mediterranean crossing.

Populist Threat

Mason, Josephine, "As worries about populism in Europe rise, investors bet on stock market volatility," Reuters, March 21, 2019, https://tinyurl.com/ y4452lhs.
International investors say populists' expected strong showing in the upcoming European Parliament elections could lead to big swings in European stock markets.

Tomek, Radoslav, and Peter Luca, "Populists Slapped as Slovaks Poised to Elect Pro-EU President," Bloomberg, updated March 18, 2019, https://tinyurl .com/y68z6zn2.
Slovakia's presidential runoff election features two candidates who favor European integration, a stark contrast to its populist neighbors.

Wilkes, William, "Europe's Populist Right Threatens to Erode Climate Consensus," Bloomberg, Feb. 25, 2019, https://tinyurl.com/yyxdvw9r.
Several right-wing populist parties that cast doubt on climate change or deny that humans contribute to it could jeopardize the EU's environmental policies, says a Bloomberg reporter.

Tariffs

Byrd, Haley, "Trump eyes auto tariffs in EU standoff," CNN, March 20, 2019, https://tinyurl.com/ y4eoprwj.
President Trump has threatened to enact auto tariffs if trade negotiations with the EU do not succeed in opening the European market to U.S. agriculture products.

Pandey, Ashutosh, "Malaysia threatens to raise stakes in EU palm oil spat," Deutsche Welle, March 27, 2019, https://tinyurl.com/yyf57kxy.
A proposed EU free trade pact in Asia is in jeopardy after Malaysia challenged the Union's plan to phase out palm oil, the country's main agricultural export, due to environmental concerns.

Wishart, Ian, and Emma Ross-Thomas, "How a 'Customs Union' Could Define Post-Brexit Trade," *The Washington Post*, March 27, 2019, https:// tinyurl.com/y5m9sew3.
The United Kingdom might form a customs union—an agreement allowing the free flow of goods—with other nations to avoid EU tariffs.

For More Information

Atlantic Council, 1030 15th St., N.W., 12th Floor, Washington, DC 20005; 202-778-4952, www.atlanticcouncil.org. Think tank that promotes the trans-Atlantic alliance through policy papers and briefing seminars.

Center for Strategic and International Studies, 1616 Rhode Island Ave., N.W., Washington, DC 20036; 202-887-0200; www.csis.org. Think tank that focuses on defense and security, regional studies and transnational challenges, including those involving the European Union (EU).

Confrontations Europe, 227 Boulevard Saint-Germain, 75007 Paris, France; +33 (0) 1 43 17 32 83; http://confrontations.org. Think tank that seeks to foster economic growth and influence European policy through papers, seminars and conferences.

European Council on Foreign Relations, 159-165 Great Portland St., London W1W 5PA; +44 (0) 20 7227 6860; https://www.ecfr.eu. Think tank that researches European foreign and security policy.

European Parliament Think Tank, 60 Rue Wiertz / Wiertzstraat 60, B-1047, Brussels, Belgium; +32 (0) 2 28 42111; www.europarl.europa.eu. Research department of the European Parliament that assists members in their parliamentary work.

European Policy Centre, 14-16 Rue du Trône/Troonstraat, B-1000, Brussels, Belgium; +32 (0) 2 231 03 40; www.epc.eu. Think tank that promotes European integration through issue papers, policy briefs and commentaries, as well as the journal *Challenge Europe*.

Migration Policy Institute Europe, 155 Rue de la Loi, 1040 Brussels, Belgium; +32 (0) 2235 2113; www.migrationpolicy.org. Think tank that provides research and policy proposals to European governments and nongovernmental organizations on immigration.

Notre Europe-Institut Delors, 18, Rue de Londres 75009 Paris, France; +33 1 44 58 97 97; http://institutdelors.eu. Think tank that contributes to the debate on the EU through political, economic and social analyses and proposals.

9

U.S. Foreign Policy in Transition

Is the United States relinquishing its global supremacy?

By Bill Wanlund

AP Photo/Jim Mone

Michael Petefish stands inside a soybean bin at his farm near Claremont, Minn., in July 2018. When President Trump imposed $250 billion in tariffs on Chinese exports, China responded with its own tariffs. The trade war, which has cooled, has hurt some U.S. farmers. China is the largest buyer of American soybeans.

From *CQ Researcher*, March 29, 2019

At an annual security conference of the United States' European allies in February, a gathering that normally celebrates trans-Atlantic unity, German Chancellor Angela Merkel delivered a harsh assessment of U.S. foreign policy.

Merkel criticized the Trump administration's unilateral approach to international affairs, specifically questioning U.S. plans to pull troops out of Syria and Afghanistan and a decision to abandon the 31-year-old intermediate-range nuclear weapons treaty with Russia. Both actions, she said, would endanger Europe while strengthening Moscow's position.

The liberal world order—the U.S.-led system of institutions and alliances created after World War II and credited with establishing postwar global peace and prosperity—"has collapsed into many tiny parts," Merkel said.[1]

Attendees gave the German leader a standing ovation, in contrast to the cool reception that met Vice President Mike Pence hours later when he extended greetings from Trump. In that speech, Pence defended the administration's foreign policy, saying that under President Trump, "America is leading the free world once again." Pence also urged Europeans to "do more" in their own defense and "stop undermining" U.S. sanctions against Iran by joining the U.S.

Global Approval of U.S. Leadership Plunges

After falling to a new low of 30 percent in the first year of Donald Trump's presidency, median global approval of U.S. leadership remained largely unchanged in 2018, according to surveys of adults across more than 130 countries and areas of the world. The 2018 rating was down 17 percentage points from 2016, the final year of Barack Obama's administration, and 3 points less than the previous low of 34 percent in the final year of the George W. Bush presidency.

Median Global Assessment of U.S. Leadership, 2007-18

Source: Julie Ray, "Image of U.S. Leadership Now Poorer Than China's," Gallup, Feb. 28, 2019, http://tinyurl.com/y67ozzpf

agrees that U.S. foreign policy has needed adjusting. "Trump clearly was elected to pull back our responsibilities around the world," he says. "The country has been in that mood for the last 10 years at least."

A recent survey by the Eurasia Group Foundation, a New York City research organization, supports Nau's view, identifying a "public desire for a more restrained U.S. foreign policy." Only 18 percent of respondents agreed that "promoting and defending democracy around the world" is the best way to help sustain global peace, while 34 percent said the path to peace means focusing on "domestic needs and the health of American democracy."[4]

Trump's worldview appears to coincide with the 34 percent, according to Thomas Shannon, who retired last year as undersecretary of State for political affairs, the State Department's highest position for a career diplomat. "Trump believes we live in a dangerous, complicated world in which America has carried a huge security burden, and a large economic burden in managing the world trading system," says Shannon, now senior international policy adviser for the Washington law firm Arnold & Porter. "He thinks that over time this has disadvantaged the U.S., and that even allies and partners have taken advantage of this relationship for their own benefit."

To correct that perceived imbalance, Trump has, among other things:

- Pulled out of three international agreements signed by President Barack Obama: the Paris climate agreement aimed at limiting planet-warming carbon emissions; the 2015 treaty to limit Iran's nuclear weapons; and the Trans-Pacific Partnership (TPP), a free-trade agreement, which had covered 12 Pacific region nations.
- Questioned how fairly the United States has been treated by international organizations such as the 70-year-old North Atlantic Treaty Organization (NATO) military alliance.

withdrawal from a 2015 agreement to halt Iran's development of nuclear weapons.[2]

Trump is changing the U.S. role on the global stage. Unlike his postwar predecessors, who tended to promote U.S.-style democracy and other values overseas through multinational alliances and agreements, Trump prefers fewer international commitments and a foreign policy focused on protecting U.S. jobs and interests.

The president's supporters say America's largesse has reached its limit and that the United States should use its economic and political might to its advantage. Trump's critics say the United States is withdrawing from global leadership, which they argue means a decline of democracy, a return to cutthroat international economic competition and a heightened threat of conflict. The debate has led to a re-evaluation of U.S. priorities and the nation's place in the world.

Trump has vowed to extract the United States from what he views as economically harmful international agreements and limits on U.S. sovereignty. "From this moment on, it's going to be America First," he said in his inaugural address. "We will seek friendship and goodwill with the nations of the world—but it is the right of all nations to put their own interests first."[3]

Henry Nau, a professor of political science and international affairs at George Washington University,

- Initiated a series of trade disputes with China.
- Renegotiated a trade agreement among the United States, Canada and Mexico.
- Aggressively tried to limit U.S. immigration, both legal and illegal.
- Withdrawn from the agreement to ban land-based intermediate-range missiles, originally signed in 1987 by President Ronald Reagan and Soviet leader Mikhail Gorbachev.

Critics of the administration worry about the long-term impact of Trump's embrace of anti-immigrant populist leaders in Eastern Europe and Italy who question the value of the European Union and his praise for autocrats with questionable human rights records—such as Russian President Vladimir Putin and the leaders of Egypt, Brazil, the Philippines and Saudi Arabia.

For instance, shortly after his inauguration President Trump traveled to Saudi Arabia—his first overseas trip as president—and a year later welcomed Saudi Crown Prince Mohammed bin Salman to the

U.S. Abandons Key International Agreements

President Trump has begun or concluded withdrawal from five major treaties and agreements, involving climate change, trade and nuclear arms. In addition, Trump, who during his presidential campaign threatened to withdraw from the North American Free Trade Agreement (NAFTA), negotiated a revised version of the pact, now called the U.S.-Mexico-Canada Agreement (USMCA), which awaits congressional approval.

Top International Agreements the U.S. Has Abandoned or Altered, as of 2019

Agreement /Treaty	Description	Status
Intermediate-Range Nuclear Forces (INF) Treaty	Established 1987; required the U.S. and Soviet Union to destroy all land-based missiles with ranges between 300 and 3,400 miles. U.S. obligations suspended in February, with formal withdrawal in six months. The U.S. and Russia have accused each other of violating the treaty.	Withdrawing
North American Free Trade Agreement (NAFTA)	Established 1994 among the U.S., Canada and Mexico; eliminated tariffs and other restrictions among the three countries. The Trump administration has negotiated a new version, the USMCA, which the White House says provides more advantages for the U.S. workforce and economy.	Renegotiated; awaiting congressional approval
Joint Comprehensive Plan of Action (Iran nuclear deal)	Agreement reached July 2015 among Iran, the U.S., the U.K., France, China, Russia and Germany; limited Iran's nuclear program development and allowed international inspections in exchange for the lifting of economic sanctions. In May 2018 Trump announced that the U.S. was withdrawing from the deal and reinstated U.S. sanctions against Iran.	Withdrawn
Paris Agreement on Climate Change	Adopted December 2015 by 195 countries; set universal goals on limiting climate-warming emissions. Trump said the agreement put the U.S. at a disadvantage. The agreement prevents official withdrawal until 2020.	Withdrawing
Trans-Pacific Partnership (TPP)	Established 2016 by 12 countries bordering the Pacific Ocean; designed to reduce tariffs and foster free trade and economic growth among members. Trump said the agreement is unfair to U.S. workers. The remaining 11 countries have moved forward with the deal, renaming it the Comprehensive and Progressive Agreement for Trans-Pacific Partnership.	Withdrawn

Sources: Zachary B. Wolf and JoElla Carman, "Here are all the treaties and agreements Trump has abandoned," CNN, Feb. 1, 2019, https://tinyurl.com/yau3v64d; "The Intermediate-Range Nuclear Forces (INF) Treaty at a Glance," Arms Control Association, https://tinyurl.com/6oxqkas; "Paris Agreement," European Commission, https://tinyurl.com/zxwwpa2; Colin Dwyer, "The TPP Is Dead. Long Live the Trans-Pacific Trade Deal," NPR, March 8, 2018, https://tinyurl.com/yy23bs6u; "North American Free Trade Agreement (NAFTA)," Office of the U.S. Trade Representative, https://tinyurl.com/yy2grr44; F. Brinley Bruton, "What is the Iran nuclear deal?" NBC News, May 10, 2018, https://tinyurl.com/ya3cshut

White House. In both instances, Trump hailed the kingdom's help in fighting terrorism and the thousands of American jobs that would be created by Saudi Arabia's

AFP/Getty Images/Jonathan Nackstrand

A U.S. Marine gets ready for a NATO-led training exercise in Norway in November 2018. More than 30 NATO partner countries participated in the joint exercise. President Trump caused a stir last year when he told a NATO summit that the United States was prepared to "go our own way" if other members did not pay more toward the alliance.

large purchases of U.S. military equipment, but did not mention the kingdom's poor human rights record.

"Saudi Arabia is a very wealthy nation, and they're going to give the United States some of that wealth, hopefully, in the form of jobs, in the form of the purchase of the finest military equipment anywhere in the world," he told reporters during Salman's White House visit.[5]

Trump's actions and policies could spell the end of the economic and social progress enjoyed by most of the world since 1945, says Robert Kagan, a senior fellow at the centrist Brookings Institution think tank, who has served as a foreign policy adviser in Republican administrations. "I fear we will find ourselves where we were between the world wars, where no one is keeping the order and everything fell apart," says Kagan, author of *The Jungle Grows Back: America and Our Imperiled World.*

Others disagree. "The [U.S.] economy is booming, the military is rapidly recovering from 15 years of overextension, and the Trump administration is concluding trade deals in record time," wrote Salvatore Babones, an American associate professor of sociology and social policy at the University of Sydney in Australia.[6]

Meanwhile, foreign public approval of the United States has "plummeted" since Trump's election, according to the Pew Research Center's 2018 Global Attitudes Survey. It found "widespread opposition to [Trump's] policies and a widely shared lack of confidence in his

leadership." Seventy percent of respondents in 25 countries said they had "no confidence" in Trump's leadership, compared to 27 percent who said they did.[7]

"People generally aren't interested in seeing the U.S. disengage, or wall itself off from the rest of the world," says Richard Wike, Pew's director of global attitudes research.

James Poulos, executive editor of The American Mind, an online publication of the conservative Claremont Institute think tank in Upland, Calif., says a poor global image "is obviously not what you want to achieve in your foreign policy, but you do have to put the prosperity and security of America at the top of your priorities list."

The ranks of professional diplomats have thinned under Trump, who says he prefers to rely on his own instincts and one-on-one rapport rather than experts when dealing with foreign leaders. "I talk to a lot of people . . . but my primary [foreign policy] consultant is myself, and I have a good instinct for this stuff," Trump said during the 2016 campaign.[8]

The State Department lost 60 percent of its career ambassadors during the first 11 months of the Trump administration, and 59 of the nation's 188 ambassadorships remained unfilled as of March, according to the American Foreign Service Association, a professional organization representing diplomats. In comparison, in February 2011, two years into the Obama administration, 14 of 173 ambassadorships were vacant.[9]

"No national security institution can withstand the unprecedented loss of highly skilled senior officers . . . without weakening America's capacity to lead globally," says the association's president, Barbara Stephenson. She blamed Trump's first secretary of State, former ExxonMobil CEO Rex Tillerson, who slashed the department's budget, eliminated many positions and halved promotion rates.[10]

Besides diminishing U.S. influence, the administration has "hollowed out American diplomacy and only deepened the divisions among Americans about our global role" at a time when the international landscape is shifting, wrote former Deputy Secretary of State William J. Burns in his new book, *The Back Channel: A Memoir of American Diplomacy and the Case for its Renewal.*

"The United States is no longer the only big kid on the geopolitical block," Burns, now president of the Carnegie Endowment for International Peace, said on CBS News' "Face the Nation." "It's a moment when diplomacy, when our alliances, our capacity for building coalitions—what sets us apart from lonelier powers like China or Russia—is more important than ever. And my concern is that we are squandering those assets right now."[11]

But Randall Schweller, director of the Program for the Study of Realist Foreign Policy at Ohio State University, said, "Trump is merely shedding shibboleths and seeing international politics for what it is: . . . a highly competitive realm populated by self-interested states concerned with their own security and economic welfare."[12]

Trump's foreign policy, he said, "seeks to promote the interests of the United States above all [and] has given the lie to the notion that many of the institutions of the postwar order actually bind the United States, and he has walked away from them accordingly."[13]

As Trump pursues his "America First" approach to foreign policy and U.S. citizens sort out their views on the direction of that policy, here are some of the questions being asked:

Is the United States relinquishing its global supremacy?

Since the dissolution of the Soviet Union and the end of the Cold War in 1991, the United States has enjoyed pre-eminence as the world's superpower—"the indispensable nation," as former Secretary of State Madeleine Albright described it.[14]

But some historians and foreign policy experts say the Trump administration has undercut U.S. global supremacy by withdrawing from the nation's leadership role in multilateral organizations and agreements, opening a power vacuum that authoritarian countries such as China and Russia will fill.

The president has been "demolishing," one by one, "the essential pillars of U.S. global power that have sustained Washington's hegemony for the past 70 years," said Alfred McCoy, a history professor at the University of

Wisconsin-Madison and author of *In the Shadows of the American Century: The Rise and Decline of U.S. Global Power.* Trump has done that, McCoy said, by weakening post-World War II alliances such as NATO and "withdrawing the United States, almost willfully, from its international leadership, most spectacularly with the Paris climate accord but also very importantly with the Trans-Pacific Partnership."[15]

In 2018, McCoy said that by relying on his "strikingly inept version of one-man diplomacy" and favoring "narrow national interest over international leadership," Trump had undercut the U.S. strategic position at a time when China was pushing relentlessly to dominate the vast Eurasian continent.[16]

But Babones, at the University of Sydney, praised Trump's foreign policy moves. "Trump has [delivered] an as-yet-uninterrupted string of foreign-policy successes," he wrote. North Korea "hasn't launched a rocket in 10 months; America's NATO allies are finally starting to . . . increase defense spending; . . . and the U.S. embassy in Israel moved to Jerusalem in May without sparking the Third Intifada predicted by Trump's opponents."[17]

Other scholars say the days of U.S. dominance were waning long before Trump was elected. Canadian political scientist Robert Muggah, for instance,

China Seen as Growing U.S. Rival

More than two-thirds of respondents say China plays a more important role in the world than it did a decade ago, according to a 2018 survey conducted across 25 countries. But a plurality still calls the United States the world's leading economic power, and a substantial majority prefers U.S. leadership.

Median Global Opinion on Balance of Power Between the U.S. and China, 2018

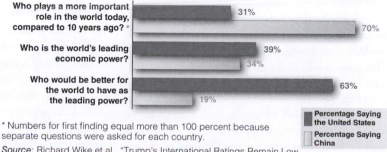

Who plays a more important role in the world today, compared to 10 years ago? * — 31% / 70%

Who is the world's leading economic power? — 39% / 34%

Who would be better for the world to have as the leading power? — 63% / 19%

Percentage Saying the United States

Percentage Saying China

* Numbers for first finding equal more than 100 percent because separate questions were asked for each country.

Source: Richard Wike et al., "Trump's International Ratings Remain Low, Especially Among Key Allies," Pew Research Center, Oct. 1, 2018, https://tinyurl.com/y95dqags

predicted in 2016 that by 2030 there would be "no single hegemonic force" overseeing international peace, but rather a handful of countries—such as the United States, Russia, China, Germany, India and Japan—exhibiting "semi-imperial tendencies." This broadening of global power has been caused in part by "a vicious backlash against globalization" triggered by the 2008 worldwide financial crisis, said Muggah, co-founder of the Igarape Institute, a nonpartisan research organization in Rio de Janeiro.[18]

This redistribution of power is "profoundly disrupting the global order," Muggah said. The United States and the European Union are ceding influence to China and India, whose economies are growing more rapidly, and postwar alliances are yielding to new regional coalitions, he wrote. Muggah added, "While these reconfigurations reflect regional political, economic and demographic shifts, they also increase the risk of volatility, including war."[19]

Brookings' Kagan says that if the United States withdraws from its role as an indispensable nation, conflicts will result thousands of miles away. "We will find ourselves, as we did in the world wars, economically affected by these conflicts and then sucked into them."

Gordon Adams, a professor emeritus at the American University School of International Service, said the United States is not relinquishing its global supremacy; rather, the world is undergoing an inevitable post-World War II and post-Cold War rebalancing of power.

"The power of other countries has grown, giving them both the ability and the desire to [affect] global affairs independently of U.S. desires," Adams wrote last June. "This global trend spells the end of the 'exceptional nation' Americans imagined they were since the nation was founded and the end of the American era of global domination that began 70 years ago."[20]

But in an interview Adams says the fears of a U.S. decline are exaggerated. "Everybody focuses on China and says the U.S. is declining, but it isn't about declining," he says. "It's about a shift in the power balance."

Tufts University assistant professor of political science Michael Beckley believes the United States is not about to be pushed off its perch. In his 2018 book, *Unrivaled: Why America Will Remain the World's Sole Superpower,* Beckley wrote that the United States "will remain the world's only superpower for many decades,

and probably throughout this century," because of its economic and military advantages.[21]

China, America's most powerful economic competitor for global pre-eminence, he said, has an inefficient economy that "is barely keeping pace" as its wealth is eroded by "the burden of propping up loss-making companies and feeding, policing, protecting and cleaning up" after its 1.4 billion people. By contrast, the United States "is big and efficient, producing high output at relatively low costs" with much lower welfare and security costs but five to 10 times the military capabilities of China, Beckley wrote.[22]

Russia, meanwhile, wants to expand its influence beyond Eastern Europe but is likely to remain only a regional power, Beckley says in an interview, because its military and economic strength is much weaker than that of the United States. "The U.S. holds all the high cards, [with] the best fundamentals for being able to amass wealth and military power in the decades ahead," he says.

Is President Trump playing into Vladimir Putin's hands?

Since the collapse of the Soviet Union in 1991, every U.S. president has vowed to ease tensions between Russia and the United States.[23]

"The post-Cold War era has been punctuated by high-profile attempts to reset the relationship," says Alexander Cooley, director of the Harriman Institute for the Study of Russia, Eurasia and Eastern Europe at Columbia University. But those efforts have tended to fail, he says, "because they don't get at the structural sources of U.S.-Russian discord"—Russia's desire to control the former Soviet states and satellites of Central and Eastern Europe where the United States has been promoting democratic reforms.

President Trump has said that he and Russian President Vladimir Putin would "end up having an extraordinary relationship. Getting along with Russia is a good thing, not a bad thing."[24]

But Trump's critics say he has a puzzling history of soft-pedaling criticism of Putin, despite a string of apparent provocations, including Russia's interference in the 2016 U.S. presidential elections, its 2014 incursion into Ukraine and its support for Syrian President Bashar al-Assad, whom the United States opposes in that country's civil war.

The CIA, FBI and National Security Agency unanimously concluded with "high confidence" that the Russians interfered in the 2016 presidential election to aid Trump's candidacy. But after a private, two-hour meeting with Putin in Helsinki in 2018, Trump stunned U.S. intelligence officials by saying he didn't see "any reason" that Russia would have meddled in the elections and was inclined to believe Putin's "extremely strong and powerful . . . denial" of such activity.[25]

Many Republican and Democratic leaders were astounded. "No prior president has ever abased himself more abjectly before a tyrant," said the late Republican Sen. John McCain of Arizona.[26] (Trump later said he "misspoke" and that he had meant to say he saw no reason Russia "wouldn't" have interfered in the elections.[27])

Trump also has likened America's conduct to Russia's with regard to political assassinations. In February 2017, for instance, he appeared to excuse allegations that Putin has had political opponents and journalists assassinated, saying, "There are a lot of killers. You think our country's so innocent?"[28]

Vladimir Frolov, a Russian foreign affairs analyst, has called Trump "God's gift that keeps on giving." He added: "Trump implements Russia's negative agenda by default, undermining the U.S.-led world order, U.S. alliances, U.S. credibility as a partner and an ally. . . . Russia can just relax and watch and root for Trump, which Putin does at every TV appearance."[29]

But George Washington University's Nau says that despite Trump's friendly words about Putin, the administration's actions toward Russia have been tough, such as endorsing the placement of NATO forces, including U.S. troops, in Poland and the Baltic states, on Russia's borders. "How's that coddling Russia?" Nau asks. "And he's given lethal weapons to the Kiev government in Ukraine, a big step Obama never would have taken."

Trump supporters also point out that the administration continues to enforce sanctions against Russia for its 2014 invasion of Ukraine and its cybercrime-related activities, human rights violations, weapons proliferation, support for Syria, trade with North Korea and terrorism-related activities.[30]

"Trump is dealing with Russia in the right way," says James Carafano, director of the Douglas and Sarah Allison Center for Foreign Policy Studies at the Heritage Foundation,

a conservative think tank. "Trump is consistently saying to Putin, 'I'm here to safeguard American interests.'"

But critics point out that Trump did not stand up to Russia until March 2018, after Congress pressured him to use the Countering America's Adversaries Through Sanctions Act, which Congress had passed in August 2017. Trump had signed the legislation reluctantly, complaining that it "improperly encroaches on executive power."[31]

Some of Trump's critics have asked whether the president's business interests in Russia—including a proposal to build a Trump Tower in Moscow—have affected his approach to Putin, something the president has repeatedly denied. [32] But Trump's former attorney, Michael Cohen, told the House Oversight Committee Feb. 27 that Trump "knew of and directed the Trump Moscow negotiations throughout the campaign, and lied about it . . . because he stood to make hundreds of millions of dollars" on the project.[33]

Stephen Sestanovich, a professor of international diplomacy at Columbia University and a former State Department official, said, "We can't rule out the more sinister and sordid explanations of [the Trump-Putin] 'bromance.'" But some explanations for the mutual attraction are not mysterious, he said. "Putin's got this record as a bad-boy statesman that puts him outside the bounds of polite society in Europe and America. Trump admires that."[34]

Are post-World War II alliances and structures suited for today's foreign policy challenges?

Some foreign policy experts say that, with notable exceptions, the world has enjoyed 70 years of relative peace and prosperity, due largely to international political, economic and military structures and alliances established after World War II by U.S. and other Western leaders. The goal of the liberal international order was to prevent the Soviet Union from expanding communism into other countries and to promote democracy, human rights and free-market economies.

The international order was defended by NATO—a military alliance established in 1949 that now has 29 member countries—and was implemented through economic rules and standards of behavior established by the United Nations (U.N.), World Bank, International Monetary Fund and General Agreement on Tariffs and

Trade (GATT)—the predecessor of the World Trade Organization (WTO).

Many historians say the U.S. architects of those institutions felt it was in the nation's long-term interest to surrender some sovereignty to advance global harmony. Without such institutions, they say, the world would revert to the chaotic political rivalries and unregulated trade practices that twice led to global war.

The institutions enable national leaders "to better manage the kind of conflicts that would otherwise have spun up into wars," says E. Anthony Wayne, former assistant secretary of State for economic and business affairs. Abandoning them, he says, means "the world becomes more like a jungle."

But since the fall of the Soviet Union, some foreign policy experts have questioned whether these institutions should be scrapped, or at least retooled, to deal with modern problems such as terrorism, climate change, religious and ethnic conflicts and migration.

"The world has changed in profound ways over the last several decades, and . . . our alliance structures were built for another time," says former diplomat Shannon. "Although they're still useful, we are rethinking the world and America's purpose in it, a discussion which the president, in his own way, is driving by his behavior."

Indeed, Trump's skepticism about NATO has led some Europeans to wonder whether Europe should start looking after its own security needs. French President Emmanuel Macron and German Chancellor Merkel have called for consideration of a military force run by the 28-member European Union. "The days where we can unconditionally rely on others are gone," Merkel said.[35]

Trump caused a stir last July when he told a NATO summit meeting that the United States was prepared to "go our own way" if other member states did not pay more to fund the organization. Trump said he told the gathered leaders, "The United States is paying close to 90 percent of the costs of protecting Europe. . . . You got to pay your bill." (The United States paid nearly $7 billion of NATO's costs in 2017.)[36]

His threats got results. NATO renewed a 2014 pledge that every member would spend at least 2 percent of its gross domestic product on national defense, as is required under the NATO charter, by 2024. Since 2014, annual defense spending by non-U.S. members has increased by $14.6 billion, an average of 1.47 percent of members' GDP. The U.S. spends 3.5 percent of its GDP on defense.[37]

In January, NATO Secretary-General Jens Stoltenberg said members had agreed to increase their defense spending by $100 billion. "There is no doubt that [Trump's] very clear message is having an impact," Stoltenberg said. "And the message was that . . . President Trump [is] committed to NATO, but we need fair burden sharing."[38]

Trump also has criticized the WTO, which sets rules and adjudicates international trade disputes. In October 2017 he complained that the organization "was set up for the benefit of everybody but us. . . . [W]e lose . . . almost all of the lawsuits." [39] He threatened to withdraw the United States from the 164-member body "if they don't shape up."[40]

But Dan Ikenson, director of the libertarian Cato Institute's Herbert A. Stiefel Center for Trade Policy Studies, has studied WTO trade disputes in which the United States was either the complainant or the defendant. "There is no anti-American bias" in the WTO's Dispute Settlement Body, he said. The United States won 91 percent of the 114 complaints it filed with the WTO from 1995 to March 2017, a higher success rate than of any other country, he found, and lost in 89 percent of the 129 cases filed against it.[41]

Dennis Shea, U.S. ambassador to the WTO, has said certain outdated WTO procedures should be reformed, including rules that allow China to protect its domestic industries while "creating disadvantages for foreign companies."

In addition, two-thirds of WTO members—including China, Saudi Arabia, Brunei and Qatar—are allowed to claim special privileges because they classify themselves as developing countries. On Feb. 15, Shea proposed that the WTO withhold special treatment from countries classified as "high income" by the World Bank or other institutions, including any state accounting for 0.5 percent or more of world trade.[42]

The WTO is unlikely to undertake serious reform because all member states must approve any rule changes, "a formidable roadblock," according to the Center for Strategic and International Studies, a Washington think tank. Yet, a failure to enact major reform proposals "could lead to the disintegration of key pillars of the organization," the center concluded.[43]

BACKGROUND

Isolationism

As George Washington left the presidency in 1796, he counseled fellow citizens about the risks of foreign entanglements. "Steer clear of permanent alliances with any portion of the foreign world," he advised. Take a neutral path, he said, by avoiding both "permanent, inveterate antipathies against particular nations, and passionate attachments for others."[44]

In its early years, the United States generally clung to an isolationist policy, except with regard to the 1823 Monroe Doctrine, which declared that the Western Hemisphere was America's sphere of influence. In 1898, the United States used that doctrine to justify going to war against Spain, siding with Cuban revolutionaries seeking independence from the colonial power. The Spanish-American War ended with Cuba nominally independent and Spain ceding Puerto Rico, the Philippines and Guam to the United States as territories.[45]

In the early 20th century, the United States reverted to isolationism but was thrust into global pre-eminence by its involvement in two world wars, despite early efforts to remain neutral. In 1914, when World War I broke out in Europe, President Woodrow Wilson declared that the United States would remain neutral. But after German submarine attacks on U.S. vessels, Wilson abruptly reversed direction in 1917.[46]

Even before the war ended, Wilson—in his 1918 "Fourteen Points" speech—called for diplomatic transparency, freer trade, arms reduction and "a general association of nations [to provide] mutual guarantees of political independence and territorial integrity," the founding principles of the League of Nations, championed by Wilson. Isolationist sentiment returned after the war ended, however, and the Senate refused to ratify the treaty. In fact, Congress passed four Neutrality Acts in the 1930s, aiming to keep the United States neutral by avoiding financial dealings with belligerents.[47]

Isolationism still reigned in the late 1930s and early '40s, when President Franklin D. Roosevelt was forced to heed public sentiment against entering World War II until Dec. 7, 1941, when Japan bombed the U.S. naval base at Pearl Harbor. Public opinion changed overnight, and Congress declared war on Japan the next day. Germany declared war against the United States four days later.

In 1944, before World War II ended, Roosevelt led a move to establish an array of major international institutions designed to prevent future wars and promote economic stability. Among those were two largely U.S.-financed international lending institutions: the World Bank, which provides aid to less developed nations, and the International Monetary Fund, which lends funds to help countries out of short-term currency crises. Roosevelt also pushed for establishment of the U.N., an international organization to promote global peace, which was created on Oct. 24, 1945, with the United States as a permanent and powerful member of its enforcement arm, the Security Council.[48]

Containment

After the war, Roosevelt's successor, President Harry S. Truman, began to identify U.S. interests as global and espoused the Truman Doctrine—vowing "to support free peoples who are resisting attempted subjugation by armed minorities or outside pressures."[49] As the Cold War emerged between the United States and the Soviet Union, the doctrine morphed into one of containment—using whatever diplomatic, economic and military means were necessary to contain the spread of Soviet communism. Often, the United States ended up siding with anti-communist dictators, such as when it helped the authoritarian Greek government put down an insurgency during a civil war in the late 1940s.

The Truman Doctrine also led to the Marshall Plan in 1948, and the Korean War in the early 1950s.

The Marshall Plan, named for its architect, Secretary of State George C. Marshall, provided $13 billion between 1948 and 1951 to help rebuild war-torn Europe. Besides jump-starting Western Europe's economic recovery, the aid program required recipient countries to exclude communists from their governments and to purchase supplies from U.S. manufacturers whenever possible. The total gross national product among recipient nations increased by 32 percent during the four years the plan was in effect.[50]

Also under Truman, the United States in 1949 joined Canada and 10 European countries to form NATO. In response, in 1955 the Soviet Union created the Warsaw Pact, an alliance with its Eastern European satellite states, several of which would join NATO after the Soviet Union's collapse in 1991.

C H R O N O L O G Y

1700s-1800s *Early America adopts an isolationist foreign policy.*

1796 George Washington warns against "permanent alliances."

1823 Monroe Doctrine establishes principle that Western Hemisphere is U.S. sphere of influence.

1898 Spanish-American War ends with Cuba nominally independent and the U.S. with three territories: Puerto Rico, Guam and the Philippines.

1900-1945 *U.S. participates in two world wars, beginning its ascent as a superpower.*

1917-18 U.S. enters World War I; President Woodrow Wilson pushes for a League of Nations to foster international cooperation and prevent future wars.

1919 Isolationist Congress refuses to join new League of Nations.

1935-1939 Congress passes four Neutrality Acts aimed at keeping the U.S. out of foreign conflicts.

1941 Japanese bomb Pearl Harbor; U.S. declares war on Japan, and Germany in turn declares war on U.S.

1944 Bretton Woods conference lays plans for postwar world economic system, including the World Bank and International Monetary Fund.

1945 World War II ends; United Nations is established to promote world peace.

1946-1980s *In Cold War, U.S. foreign policy focuses on multilateralism and containment of communism.*

1947-50 President Harry S. Truman adopts a containment policy to limit Soviet expansion by aiding Greece and Turkey, introducing Marshall Plan to rebuild Europe and guaranteeing the security of Western Europe by joining the North Atlantic Treaty Organization (NATO).

1950-53 North Korea, aided by the Soviet Union, attacks South Korea. U.S.-led coalition intervenes on behalf of the South; truce leaves Korea divided.

1962 Cuban missile crisis leads the U.S. and the Soviet Union to brink of nuclear war.

1965 U.S. support for South Vietnam against communist North Vietnam leads to a major escalation of American forces. Protracted war results in domestic calls for retrenchment.

1972 President Richard M. Nixon promotes opening to China and détente with the Soviet Union while maintaining containment strategy.

1978 President Jimmy Carter makes support for human rights a major foreign policy objective.

1982 President Ronald Reagan adopts hawkish foreign policies by increasing military spending, calling the Soviet Union an "evil empire" and vowing to support democracy in communist countries.

1983 U.S. invades Grenada, claiming it is enabling "Soviet-Cuban militarization" in the Caribbean.

1986-87 Investigations reveal the Reagan administration illegally sold weapons to Iran and supported anti-communist insurgents in Nicaragua.

1987 U.S. and Soviet Union sign Intermediate-Range Nuclear Forces (INF) Treaty, agreeing to destroy all land-based missiles with ranges between 300 to 3,400 miles.

1990s-2000s *Cold War ends, leaving U.S. as sole superpower; rise of jihadist terrorism forces U.S. foreign policy to focus on the Middle East.*

1991 Iraq invades Kuwait; U.S.-led, U.N.-sanctioned coalition ousts Iraqis. Soviet Union collapses.

1994 U.S., Mexico and Canada sign landmark North America Free Trade Agreement (NAFTA).

2001 Sept. 11 terrorist attacks prompt President George W. Bush to launch NATO-backed attack on Afghanistan, which is protecting Osama bin Laden, the architect of the attacks and leader of al Qaeda, a jihadist group.

2002 Bush widens the conflict by declaring the right to "prevent or forestall" attacks by terrorists or others.

2003 Bush invades Iraq in search for weapons of mass destruction (none are found) and ousts President Saddam Hussein. Years of U.S. occupation, chaos and ethnic violence ensue.

2006 Iran enriches uranium, triggering U.N. sanctions amid fears it will develop nuclear weapons; North Korea announces it has carried out its first nuclear test.

2009 Barack Obama begins presidency; calls for "new beginning" in U.S. relations with Muslim world.

2010-Present *Pro-democracy movement sweeps Middle East.*

2011-12 U.S. troops withdraw from Iraq; Arab Spring protests depose dictators in Tunisia, Libya and Egypt but spark prolonged civil war in Syria.

2015 Obama signs international agreement to curb Iran's nuclear weapons development and the Paris climate accord to limit carbon emissions.

2016 Obama signs Trans-Pacific Partnership (TPP) to lower trade barriers in 12 Pacific countries. Donald Trump is elected president, vowing to follow an "America First" foreign policy.

2017 Trump withdraws U.S. from TPP; announces intention to leave climate accord and demands that NATO allies pay their share for maintaining the alliance.

2018 Trump withdraws U.S. from Iran nuclear deal, renegotiates NAFTA, meets North Korean leader Kim Jong Un to discuss removing nuclear weapons from Korean peninsula and embarks on trade war with China.

2019 Second Trump-Kim meeting ends without denuclearization agreement; U.S. and Russia announce they are pulling out of INF agreement.

In 1950, the West's fears of aggressive communist expansion seemed to be realized when North Korea, backed by the Soviet Union (and later communist China), attacked South Korea. The United States, backed by U.N. troops, joined South Korea in the conflict. An inconclusive truce ended the fighting in 1953.

During most of the Cold War, the United States avoided direct military confrontations with the Soviet Union or China but often backed anti-communist governments or insurgents in proxy wars. But in October 1962, during President John F. Kennedy's administration, Soviet bombers and launch sites for medium-range missiles capable of reaching the United States were discovered in Cuba. A tense two-week standoff raised the specter of nuclear war between the two superpowers. Eventually, Soviet Premier Nikita Khrushchev agreed to remove the Soviet launchers and bombers in exchange for a U.S. pledge that it would not invade Cuba; the United States also removed its Turkey-based nuclear missiles targeting the Soviet Union.

Realpolitik

In the 1960s, Presidents Kennedy and Lyndon B. Johnson viewed the conflict in Vietnam between the communist North and pro-Western South as a critical test of U.S. containment policy. The so-called domino theory, first articulated by President Dwight D. Eisenhower in 1954, held that if Vietnam fell to the communists, nearby countries would follow.[51]

A small U.S. military presence in South Vietnam in the 1950s grew to 16,000 by 1963 and continued to increase. During U.S. involvement in the war, which officially ended in 1973, more than 2.7 million U.S. troops had served in Vietnam. Richard M. Nixon, elected president in 1968, initially expanded the war but eventually worked to end U.S. involvement. By the time the United States pulled out, the war had cost more than 58,000 American lives and an estimated $168 billion in military operations and economic aid.

There were other costs as well. The U.S. role in the war prompted sometimes-violent street protests at home and abroad and diminished world confidence in U.S. superiority. America turned inward, and the term "Vietnam syndrome" described the ensuing U.S. reluctance to intervene abroad.

The Nixon administration, under the direction of National Security Adviser and later Secretary of State Henry Kissinger, adopted Realpolitik—the theory that practical considerations rather than ideology should govern foreign relations. This approach enabled the

Populist Governments Are Up Fivefold

"The economic approach in Brussels and in Washington is failing."

Populist politicians—who practice a brand of nationalistic politics that claims to represent "the people" instead of society's "elites"—are on a global roll.

Twenty governments, including the United States, now have populists either in charge of, or as part of, a governing coalition—a fivefold increase since 1990, according to the Tony Blair Institute for Global Change, an international affairs research center in London. "Whereas populism was once found primarily in emerging democracies, populists are increasingly gaining power in systemically important countries," the institute's researchers said.[1]

Some experts say that while President Trump, a populist, did not cause the global rise in populism, his friendliness toward and praise for populist leaders are fueling it. "There's a lot of speculation about Trump's effect on populist movements and leaders," says Leslie Vinjamuri, head of the U.S. and the Americas Program at Chatham House, a London-based international affairs think tank.

One of Trump's first foreign visitors to the White House was Nigel Farage, the right-wing British populist who helped engineer Brexit, the successful referendum calling for the United Kingdom to withdraw from the European Union (EU).[2] Anti-EU sentiment is a major tenet of today's European populists, and Trump has said EU trade policies have made the European Union a "foe" of the United States.[3]

Brazil's far-right populist president, Jair Bolsonaro, sometimes called "the Trump of the Tropics," endeared himself to the American president with a Trump-like attack on "fake news" and a campaign vow to "make Brazil great." Trump said he intended to designate Brazil a "major non-NATO ally," which would give it preferential treatment in buying U.S. military equipment and receiving other security assistance.[4]

Trump also has established warm relations with Viktor Orbán, the prime minister of Hungary, and Polish President Andrzej Duda, populists who have been critical of the EU. Orbán, who has cracked down on the press, the judiciary and nonprofit groups to create what he calls an "illiberal" state, was the first world leader to endorse Trump's election.[5] Duda, who has overseen efforts to put Poland's judicial system under the control of the ruling party, reportedly has offered the United States $2 billion toward construction of a U.S. military base in Poland that he proposed calling Fort Trump.[6]

Vinjamuri says populist leaders like Orbán and Duda "serve to drive a wedge through Europe's internal coherence in the post-Cold War period." Max Bergmann, a policy analyst at the Center for American Progress, a liberal think tank in Washington, says that could "allow countries like Russia and China to build ties within Europe," serving as beachheads for them to weaken U.S. alliances there.

Getty Images/Pool/Chris Kleponis

Newly elected Brazilian President Jair Bolsonaro presents President Trump with a national soccer team jersey during a meeting at the White House on March 19, 2019. Critics say Trump's embrace of Bolsonaro and other populist leaders is helping to fuel a rise in nationalistic politics.

Some say Trump's rhetoric encourages populists abroad. So too, they say, does his association with right-wing political strategist Steve Bannon and senior policy adviser Stephen Miller, known for his hardline views on immigration.[7]

Bannon, a controversial former adviser to Trump with ties to extreme right-wing U.S. groups, has established a populist think tank in Brussels called The Movement to promote anti-EU populist politicians. In March 2018, Bannon told supporters of France's extreme right-wing National Front Party, led by populist politician Marine Le Pen, "Let them call you racist, let them call you xenophobes, let them call you nativist. Wear it as a badge of honor."[8]

Bergmann has attributed the current wave of populism to the 2008 financial crisis, which he called "the biggest economic calamity since the Great Depression." Even 10 years later, he says, there is "general angst in parts of the U.S. as well as Europe [and] a steeper divide between economic winners and losers. That angst is the sense that the economic approach in Brussels [the EU headquarters] and in Washington is failing," particularly on behalf of industrial workers.

Bergmann says right-wing populists do not usually have an economic plan but that they do have scapegoats—typically immigrants. Politicians on both sides of the Atlantic, he says, can say, " 'Hey—you know why things are bad? It's because the elites favor these open borders and cultural dilution.' " Populists in the United States and Europe are appealing to a day when their countries were more ethnically and culturally homogeneous, he says.

But others see expanding populism as a sign of citizen participation in a healthy democracy. James Miller, professor of liberal studies and politics at The New School, a university in New York City, said, "Popular insurrections and revolts in the name of democracy have become a recurrent feature of global politics [and] form the heart and soul of modern democracy as a living reality."

At various times and "in virtually every country," he continued, "crowds of ordinary people unite to demand a fairer share of the common wealth [and more truly] democratic institutions." Such revolts "against remote elites are essential to the vitality, and viability, of modern democracy."[9]

Yves Leterme, former prime minister of Belgium and secretary-general of the International Institute for Democracy and Electoral Assistance, a democracy-promotion think tank in Stockholm, and Sam van der Staak, head of the institute's Europe program, also find some positive features in populism. Populist parties have "made reforming the political system a key part of their agenda," they wrote, and have championed policies that give citizens "who feel alienated by their government a sense of control."

Mainstream parties that "embrace populism's better ideas will be the ones who survive to shape the political future," they said.[10]

— *Bill Wanlund*

[1] Jordan Kyle and Limor Gultchin, "Populists in Power Around the World," Tony Blair Institute for Global Change, Nov. 7, 2018, https://tinyurl.com/yyu3gl55.

[2] Simon Shuster, "The Populists," *Time*, Dec. 24-31, 2018, https://tinyurl.com/ydyrtad2.

[3] Erin Corbett, "Donald Trump Calls the European Union a 'Foe' of the U.S.," *Fortune*, July 15, 2018, https://tinyurl.com/y23qnwqy.

[4] Rebecca Ballhaus and Samantha Pearson, "Trump, Meeting With Bolsonaro, Backs Stronger Ties With Brazil," *The Wall Street Journal*, March 25, 2019, https://tinyurl.com/yyrgxr64.

[5] Ishaan Tharoor, "Hungary's right-wing leader hopes Trump will bring him in from the cold," *The Washington Post*, Nov. 30, 2016, https://tinyurl.com/y64cmjzw. John Shattuck, "How Viktor Orban degraded Hungary's weak democracy," The Conversation, Jan. 11, 2019, https://tinyurl.com/y97g8obm.

[6] Jeremy Diamond, " 'Fort Trump'? Polish President urges US to consider opening base," CNN, Sept. 19, 2018, https://tinyurl.com/ycbt76ll. Marc Santora and Joanna Berendt, "Poland Overhauls Courts, and Critics See Retreat from Democracy," *The New York Times*, Dec. 20, 2017, https://tinyurl.com/yctccpfu.

[7] Dan Merica, "Stephen Miller is crucially important to the immigration debate—or maybe not," CNN, Jan. 22, 2018, https://tinyurl.com/y5d7qp7u.

[8] Daniel Politi, "Bannon: "Let Them Call You Racist . . . Wear It as a Badge of Honor," *Slate*, March 10, 2018, https://tinyurl.com/y3gx494d. Joshua Green and Richard Bravo, "Europe's Crisis of Confidence Opens Door to Bannon-Style Chaos," Bloomberg, Jan. 13, 2019, https://tinyurl.com/ydy83br2.

[9] James Miller, "Could populism actually be good for democracy?" *The Guardian*, Oct. 11, 2018, https://tinyurl.com/ydc7qlgs.

[10] Yves Leterme and Sam van der Staak, "What populists get right," *Politico*, June 26, 2018, https://tinyurl.com/y4wpvakn.

Economic Sanctions Can Be Double-Edged

"There's a danger in overusing" them.

Countries commonly use economic sanctions—restrictions on commerce imposed on countries, companies or individuals—as a nonmilitary method of inducing them to change their behavior.

The United States is by far the world's leader in applying sanctions. As of Feb. 1, it was enforcing sanctions on 20 countries and some 6,300 individuals, according to the U.S. Treasury Department.[1]

Sanctions typically target certain commercial activities with an entire country or certain industries or companies in a country, or they block the financial assets of individuals such as terrorists, drug traffickers or corrupt government officials. An embargo—or a complete ban on all commercial activity with one or more countries—is another type of sanction. Sanctions usually are designed to enhance the sanctioning country's security or to punish another country's behavior, such as human rights violations or aggression against another nation.

"Sanctions often are used if diplomacy and words alone are insufficient but use of military force is too costly or extreme to effect the changes they want against a government that is behaving badly," says Bryan Early, an associate professor of political science at the University at Albany, State University of New York, who researches sanctions.

Nigel Gould-Davies, a lecturer in international relations at Bangkok's Mahidol University, cites the international sanctions imposed on Russia in 2014 for its incursions into Ukraine as having proved "more effective, more quickly, than their advocates expected."[2]

Russia has not returned Crimea or withdrawn from Ukraine, he said, but the sanctions, imposed by the United States, the European Union and others, had three goals: to deter further Russian military aggression; to reaffirm international norms and condemn their violation; and to encourage Russia to reach a political settlement with Ukraine. "Judged against those goals, sanctions have largely worked," Gould-Davies said.[3]

But sanctions achieve their goals only about one-quarter to one-third of the time, studies show.[4]

Sanctions fail, Early says, when the sanctioned countries "find other states willing to support them for geopolitical reasons." For instance, he says, communist Cuba has survived a U.S. embargo since 1960 with support from the Soviet Union during the Cold War and later from China and Venezuela.

Former State Department economics official E. Anthony Wayne agrees that sanctions can fail. "There's a danger in overusing sanctions," he says. "Eventually, the people you're sanctioning will just find other ways to get around the U.S. economy."

And unilateral sanctions—those imposed by only one country—in particular often do not work, he says. "It takes pressure from all different angles to make a country change," he says. "Unilateral sanctions can harm individuals, so the sanctions that target specific companies and individuals do have an impact, but it's rare that they can bring a whole country to change its ways."

Wayne argues that the Trump administration may be over-relying on unilateral sanctions and neglecting diplomatic efforts needed to get other countries to join in. The United States has imposed unilateral sanctions on several countries, including those already under multilateral sanctions, such as Russia and North Korea. When President Trump pulled the United States out of the 2015 Iran nuclear deal last year, he announced that he was reinstating the tough U.S. sanctions suspended by the agreement. Under the renewed sanctions, U.S. companies could no longer trade with Iran, and neither could any foreign company wanting to continue doing business with the United States.[5]

staunchly conservative Nixon in 1972 to be the first U.S. president to visit the People's Republic of China, a communist nation since 1949. The normalization of U.S.-China relations helped widen a rift between China and Russia that strengthened the U.S. position in the Cold War. Also in 1972, Nixon went to the Soviet Union, initiating a series of arms control measures and a period of détente between the two rivals.[52]

During his administration, President Jimmy Carter sought to make protecting human rights a major foreign policy objective, and Congress ordered the State Department to produce an annual report evaluating

Trump's unilateral move did not sit well with the European signatories to the nuclear agreement. To avoid the renewed U.S. sanctions, Britain, Germany and France in late January created a complicated workaround mechanism called the Instrument in Support of Trade Exchanges (INSTEX). It would allow Iran to continue doing business with other countries by paying for goods through a barter system, avoiding use of the dollar and the U.S. banking system.[6] It is unclear how successful INSTEX will be.

In the meantime, the renewed sanctions have hurt Iran's economy: Oil exports, Iran's main source of income, have dropped 60 percent since Trump reinstated sanctions, and Iran's economy is expected to shrink by 3.6 percent this year.[7]

Despite the U.S. withdrawal from the nuclear deal, Iran so far has continued to abide by the terms of the agreement, according to CIA Director Gina Haspel and the International Atomic Energy Agency, which monitors nuclear weapons activity worldwide.[8]

Early says sanctions can have unintended consequences: Authoritarian regimes often are willing to allow their populations to suffer the negative economic consequences created by sanctions in order to advance their objectives. "Broad-based sanctions are . . . good at inflicting broad-scale harms against their targets, but they're not very good at actually forcing the regimes to change their behavior," he says.

Sanctions also have been associated with a range of social and political harms, says Early, such as making governments more repressive when leaders "use the restrictions imposed on them as an excuse for consolidating their authoritative regimes. So, even if the sanctions don't force the government to change their policies, they can, inadvertently but effectively, do harm to the country."

— *Bill Wanlund*

An Iranian man burns a dollar bill in November 2018 outside the former U.S. embassy in Tehran during a demonstration marking the anniversary of the 1979 Iran hostage crisis. President Trump pulled the United States out of the 2015 Iran nuclear deal, and the administration has imposed unilateral economic sanctions on Iran.

AFP/Getty Images/Atta Kenare

[1] "Sanctions Programs and Country Information," Research Center, U.S. Department of the Treasury, https://tinyurl.com/ybsocltu.

[2] Nigel Gould-Davies, "Sanctions on Russia Are Working," *Foreign Affairs*, Aug. 22, 2018, https://tinyurl.com/y77eyswz.

[3] *Ibid.*

[4] Bryan Early, *Busted Sanctions: Explaining Why Economic Sanctions Fail* (2015), p. 5.

[5] "Remarks by President Trump on the Joint Comprehensive Plan of Action," The White House, May 8, 2018, https://tinyurl.com/y3t2xsg3.

[6] Ellie Geranmayeh and Esfandyar Batmanghelidj, "Trading with Iran via the special purpose vehicle: How it can work," European Council on Foreign Relations, Feb. 7, 2019, https://tinyurl.com/yyf2fqou.

[7] Doyle McManus, "Trump's sanctions are hurting Iran's economy, but that doesn't mean they're working," *Los Angeles Times*, Feb. 13, 2019, https://tinyurl.com/y6aegdhl.

[8] "IAEA says Iran adhering to terms of nuclear deal," Agence France-Press, Feb. 22, 2019, https://tinyurl.com/y343kmp4.

countries' human rights practices. Carter enjoyed some success in the troublesome Middle East by brokering the Camp David Accords, a peace agreement that ended hostilities between Israel and Egypt. However, his presidency never recovered from the humiliation of the seizure of 52 U.S. diplomats and citizens in Tehran, Iran, by Islamic fundamentalists in 1979. The hostages were held for 444 days and then released on Jan. 20, 1981—the day Carter's successor, Ronald Reagan, was inaugurated.[53]

In his two terms, Reagan maintained a hawkish foreign policy, increasing military spending, branding the Soviet Union an "evil empire" and vowing to support democracy

A man with a pickax swings at the Berlin Wall separating communist East Berlin from democratic West Berlin on Nov. 9, 1989. The wall's demise helped usher in the end of the Cold War and a rebalancing of global power.

in communist countries. In 1983, he sent troops to Grenada to oust a Marxist military junta. His administration also illegally sold weapons to Iran and used the proceeds to support anti-communist insurgents in Nicaragua.[54]

Meanwhile, reform-minded Soviet Premier Gorbachev had begun to restructure the hidebound Soviet system. In 1987, he and Reagan signed the Intermediate-Range Nuclear Forces (INF) Treaty, representing the first time the superpowers had agreed to eliminate an entire category of nuclear weapons.[55]

Also in 1987, speaking near the Berlin Wall separating democratic West Berlin from Soviet-controlled East Berlin, Reagan challenged Gorbachev to "tear down this wall."[56]

Two years later, East German citizens themselves began to dismantle the wall, and the authorities did not intervene. That year, the nominally independent Eastern European countries that were part of the Warsaw Pact, such as Poland and Hungary, began to distance themselves from the Soviet Union. Two years later, Soviet republics such as the Baltic states and Ukraine would be moving toward independence.

In January 1991, the United States, under President George H. W. Bush, led a U.N.-authorized coalition to expel the Iraqis from Kuwait, which they had invaded the previous August to seize its oil fields. After a six-week campaign, the coalition had routed the Iraqis, but Bush decided not to remove Iraqi dictator Saddam Hussein from power,

believing it would be too costly and could have fractured the coalition, created solely to oust Iraq from Kuwait.

On Christmas Day that year, the Union of Soviet Socialist Republics was officially dissolved, ending the Cold War.

War on Terror

Bill Clinton's presidency opened in 1993 amid a changed world. The Soviet Union's collapse left the United States without its archenemy. International problems arose, but they lacked the clear-and-present-danger character that would rally public support for intervention.

For instance, in Bosnia in 1993 Orthodox Christian Serb fighters conducted a brutal ethnic cleansing program against Muslims. Faced with conflicting advice and sketchy intelligence, Clinton waited until 1995 to initiate a U.S.-led NATO bombing campaign against Bosnian Serb targets, finally bringing the Serbs to the negotiating table. The resulting Dayton Accords brought peace, backed by a 60,000-member NATO force. An estimated 100,000 people had died in the civil war, about 80 percent of them Muslims.[57]

During the Clinton administration, al Qaeda jihadist leader Osama bin Laden demanded that U.S. military forces leave Saudi Arabia and issued a "Fatwa" against the United States in 1998, declaring that killing "Americans and their allies—civilians and military—is an individual duty for every Muslim who can do it in any country."[58] About six months later, Qaeda suicide truck-bombers struck U.S. embassies in Kenya and Tanzania, killing 224. Clinton responded by bombing suspected Qaeda targets in Afghanistan and Sudan. Two years later, Qaeda operatives rammed an explosives-filled boat into the USS *Cole*, a Navy destroyer refueling in Yemen, killing 17 sailors.[59]

Qaeda bombers again struck the United States, in devastating fashion, early in the administration of Clinton's successor, George W. Bush. To root out those responsible for the Sept. 11, 2001, terrorist attacks, the United States, with NATO support, invaded Afghanistan, where bin Laden and al Qaeda were based.[60] Bush also declared a worldwide war on terror and instituted several fundamental changes in U.S. foreign policy, notably opting for unilateral action instead of multilateral initiatives and espousing a doctrine of preventive or pre-emptive war.

In March 2003, the United States led a 30-nation coalition of mostly European countries, recruited by Bush and Secretary of State Colin Powell, to invade Iraq over what later proved to be unfounded claims that Iraq was stockpiling weapons of mass destruction. Hussein was deposed (and later executed by Iraqis), but no such weapons were found. The invasion damaged America's global standing.

By the time the United States left Iraq in 2010, more than 4,400 Americans and tens of thousands of Iraqi civilians had died. Years of conflict followed, fed by political and ethnic rivalries and jihadist terrorist attacks, creating fertile ground for the Islamic State to establish a caliphate there in 2014.[61]

Shortly after his inauguration in 2009, President Obama tried to repair damaged relations with the Middle East, proposing in a speech in Cairo "a new beginning between the United States and Muslims around the world, one based on mutual interest and mutual respect."[62] His foreign policy aimed to use diplomacy rather than force, and he maintained a cool relationship with Putin and other authoritarian leaders.

Despite his noninterventionist stance, Obama ordered an 18-month "surge" of 30,000 troops to Afghanistan to train the Afghan military in their fight against al Qaeda and the Taliban, domestic religious militants who had controlled most of the country before the U.S.-led invasion in 2001. He also authorized a special operations raid in Abbottabad, Pakistan, on May 2, 2011, that found and killed bin Laden.

Although al Qaeda's influence has diminished, the Islamic State and other terrorist groups have filled the void—many based in Afghanistan, where the United States has been fighting for more than 17 years.[63]

Obama also had to respond to pro-democracy demonstrations that churned the Middle East, especially Egypt, during the Arab Spring of 2011-12. Eventually, dictators in Tunisia, Libya and Egypt were deposed, but protests in Syria sparked a prolonged civil war.

After weeks of massive public demonstrations in Egypt, Obama called for Egyptian President Hosni Mubarak to step down, which he eventually did. But Obama offered only a tepid response to government crackdowns on protesters in Bahrain, home to two U.S. Navy facilities. He helped the opposition in Libya depose dictator Moammar Gadhafi, but later said he regretted not foreseeing the chaos that followed Gadhafi's overthrow.[64]

Obama also promoted the downfall of President Bashar al-Assad in Syria, and warned him in August 2012 that the United States would respond if he crossed "a red line" by using chemical weapons against Syrian civilians. A year later, Assad did use such weapons, killing hundreds of people in two sarin gas attacks in the Damascus suburbs. Obama sought congressional authorization for a retaliatory missile strike, but Congress refused to vote on the request, and Obama in the end did not act. That decision was "a serious mistake" that "impacted American credibility," Obama's Secretary of Defense Robert Gates later said.

Instead, the United States and Russia negotiated a deal in which Assad agreed to give up his chemical weapons, which he did, but he later used similar weapons.[65]

Obama's signature foreign policy achievements both occurred in 2015: signing the international agreement under which Iran agreed to limit its nuclear weapons development in return for the lifting of economic sanctions and the completion of the Paris climate accord, in which 195 countries agreed to limit carbon emissions that are warming the planet.[66]

During Obama's last year in office, the United States signed the Trans-Pacific Partnership (TPP), an agreement to lower trade barriers among 12 countries in the Pacific region.[67]

"America First"

President Trump came into office with vastly different ideas about multilateral agreements, vowing to scrap or amend those that he felt did not protect American interests and workers. He also differs in how he treats and negotiates with dictators such as Putin and North Korea's Kim Jong Un, both of whom he has praised as being strong.

Right away Trump made it a point to distinguish his administration from that of his predecessor. He immediately pulled out of the TPP and later the Iran nuclear deal and the Paris climate accord. Trump also renegotiated the 24-year-old North American Free Trade Agreement (NAFTA) among the United States, Mexico and Canada, which he called "a bad joke." Congress has yet to ratify the new United States-Mexico-Canada Agreement.[68]

And, in a Cairo speech laying out the administration's Middle East policy, Secretary of State Mike Pompeo criticized Obama for "willful blindness" to "the danger of the [Iran] regime" when he signed the 2015 nuclear agreement, and for criticizing Israel.[69]

A longtime critic of what he sees as China's discriminatory trade barriers, theft of intellectual property and economic espionage, Trump imposed $250 billion worth of tariffs on Chinese imports, demanding that China mend its ways. China retaliated with $110 billion in import tariffs on U.S. products.[70]

On Dec. 1, 2018, Trump and Chinese President Xi Jinping agreed to a 90-day "truce," since extended, while the two countries negotiated a range of economic irritants. Without an agreement, Trump threatened to raise tariffs on another $200 billion of Chinese products, and China said it would respond with punitive measures.[71]

Trump has also made removing North Korea's nuclear threat a top foreign policy goal. His relationship with Kim had a rocky start: Trump threatened "fire and fury" if Kim continued provocative missile tests and belittled Kim as "Rocket Man;" Kim called Trump a "mentally deranged U.S. dotard."[72]

Then the two met in Singapore in June 2018 to discuss removing nuclear weapons from the Korean Peninsula, the first-ever meeting between leaders of the two countries. Although no concrete steps toward denuclearization took place, both sides made concessions: North Korea paused its nuclear weapons-testing program and dismantled some weapons-making facilities, and the United States cancelled scheduled joint military exercises with South Korea.

As the Trump-Kim relationship grew warmer, Trump told a campaign audience in West Virginia that Kim had sent him "beautiful letters" and "we fell in love."[73]

CURRENT SITUATION

North Korea and China

Expectations for an agreement with North Korea were high in February, when Trump and Kim met again in Hanoi, Vietnam. Trump had scheduled a signing ceremony before the talks had even started. But the summit ended early after Kim reportedly insisted that the United States lift nearly all U.S. economic sanctions on his country before he would start incrementally dismantling his nuclear weapons program.[74]

However, North Korean Foreign Minister Ri Yong Ho disputed this account, saying his country had only demanded partial relief from the sanctions in exchange for closing its main nuclear complex, and that the talks ended when the United States demanded further disarmament steps. An unidentified State Department official said Ri was only "parsing words" and that the North Koreans had asked for the lifting of all sanctions except those on weapons.[75]

After walking out of the summit, Trump told a press conference that lifting sanctions before Pyongyang has dismantled its nuclear program would allow Kim to continue producing weapons of mass destruction, and "we couldn't do that."[76]

White House National Security Adviser John Bolton said Trump had simply rejected "a bad deal."[77] Even some of Trump's critics agreed. "The president did the right thing by walking away," said Obama's vice president, Joe Biden.[78]

Days after the summit collapsed, South Korean and U.S. intelligence officials said satellite imagery showed that North Korea appeared to have rebuilt a satellite rocket launching facility it had dismantled as a confidence-building measure after the first summit, and that the work had begun even before the Feb. 27-28 Hanoi meeting.[79]

Two weeks later North Korean Vice Foreign Minister Choe Son Hui told reporters in Pyongyang that the United States, with its "gangster-like stand," had thrown away "a golden opportunity." In addition, she said, "we understood very clearly that the United States has a very different calculation to ours."[80]

John Delury, an expert on East Asia at Seoul's Yonsei University, said Choe's comments did not necessarily mean further negotiations would be abandoned, noting that there was no name-calling or insults and that Choe praised Kim's relationship with Trump. "A lot of this is rhetoric or posturing, but both sides have been careful not to fling mud," he said. "This is each side reminding each other what's at stake."[81]

On March 22, Trump tweeted that he was rolling back new sanctions his administration planned to impose on North Korea.[82] The decision apparently surprised the president's foreign policy advisers, and White House spokesperson Sarah Sanders said only, "President Trump likes Chairman Kim, and he doesn't think these sanctions will be necessary."

On March 25, Sanders told reporters: "The sanctions that were in place before are certainly still on. They are

Should the United States continue promoting democracy abroad?

YES

Thomas Carothers
Senior Vice President for Studies, Carnegie Endowment for International Peace

Written for *CQ Researcher*, March 2019

NO

Henry R. Nau
Professor of Political Science and International Affairs, Elliott School of International Affairs, George Washington University; Author, Conservative Internationalism: Armed Diplomacy Under Jefferson, Polk, Truman and Reagan

Written for *CQ Researcher*, March 2019

Analyses of the role of democracy promotion in U.S. foreign policy often emphasize the tension between American ideals and interests abroad. Ideals may be nice, the argument typically goes, but hard interests, above all security, need to take priority.

This is not a useful framing. Supporting democracy abroad is not just about living up to U.S. ideals. Just as importantly, it is about advancing hard U.S. interests. Most of America's closest security relationships are with democracies. Most of our geopolitical rivals are non-democracies. Of course, there are exceptions. Certain nondemocracies are useful security partners. But when our security partners are repressive and corrupt, we have to be significantly concerned about the destabilizing anger and radicalism they generate internally.

A more democratic world is one in which the United States has more allies and fewer adversaries. Regions dominated by democracies, such as Europe, South Asia and Latin America, are places where the United States has stable, productive partnerships. Regions dominated by autocracies, such as the Middle East, the former Soviet Union and parts of Asia, are sources of geopolitical conflict and competition.

Thus, for example, supporting democratic reform in Ukraine is not just a good thing to do for the Ukrainian people; it increases the chances that the Ukrainian government will productively balance the country's ties with Russia and friendly relations with the West. Stabilizing the democratic experiment in Tunisia is not just some idealistic venture; it is crucial to helping head off potentially dangerous radicalization or civil conflict. A more democratic Venezuela is less likely to ally itself with Russia and China, shelter drug trafficking or precipitate a regional humanitarian crisis, as Venezuela's authoritarian regime has done in recent years.

Making support for democracy an integral part of U.S. foreign policy does not mean full-bore democracy promotion everywhere all the time, pushing our political model on others and going it alone. Nor does it mean intervening militarily at great cost as in Afghanistan and Iraq—those interventions were primarily motivated by security concerns and were not representative cases of democracy promotion. Instead, it means—or it should mean—modulating U.S. pro-democracy diplomacy and assistance to take account of local political conditions and the overall balance of U.S. interests. It also means supporting homegrown efforts to advance democracy and working closely with other governments engaged in democracy support, as well as with relevant international organizations and nongovernmental organizations, on a broad positive-sum approach.

Under current circumstances the United States should defend, not promote, democracy. And that defense should be targeted on Eastern Europe and the Korean Peninsula, not everywhere across the globe.

The United States pursued a more aggressive policy after World War II when it confronted an existential threat from an anti-democratic power, the Soviet Union. Germany and Japan became enduringly democratic for the first time in their history. And the United States did so again when it emerged from the Cold War as the world's sole superpower. More than 60 countries became democratic, some durably (South Korea), others still struggling (Poland).

The United States paid a disproportionate price for these gains. U.S. soldiers manned the ramparts of freedom around the world and died or were wounded too frequently in long wars in Vietnam, Iraq and Afghanistan. U.S. workers moved relentlessly from one job to another to accommodate exports and create jobs for other countries. And U.S. society heaved under the disruption of immigrant flows that totaled more than 59 million from 1965 to 2015. In the end, the United States benefitted from this liberal world order. It defeated communism, grew wealthier and became a less racist and more diverse society.

But enough is enough. Circumstances have changed. Today the United States neither faces an existential threat nor enjoys unchallenged pre-eminence. Terrorism is not the equivalent of a new Cold War, democratic allies are now equal in wealth and technology, and authoritarian powers—China and Russia—challenge the United States regionally rather than globally.

In these circumstances, defending, not expanding, democracy is the strategic imperative. While Europe is whole and free for the first time ever, Russia strikes to weaken it. Moscow seizes territory in Ukraine and menaces struggling democracies in Poland, Hungary and the Baltic states. China extinguishes freedom at home and bulldozes peaceful aspirations in the South China Sea and on the Korean Peninsula. If Ukraine succumbs to Russian thuggery and Korea stabilizes or unites under the authoritarian talons of China, all the postwar gains of democracy may be lost.

Thus, holding out the prospects of freedom in Ukraine and Korea far outweigh the loss or gain of freedom anywhere else in the world. In the Middle East and elsewhere, the United States should counter threats but not deploy large numbers of U.S. forces and resources to build democratic nations. Circumstances allow the United States to take a break. The American people have earned it.

very tough sanctions. The president just doesn't feel it's necessary to add additional sanctions at this time. . . . The president likes him [Kim]. They want to continue to negotiate and see what happens."[83]

Harry Kazianis, director of Korean studies at the conservative think tank Center for the National Interest, said Trump might be trying to reduce tensions between Washington and Pyongyang and keep North Korea from pulling out of the negotiations.[84]

But an unnamed administration official quoted in *The New York Times* denied Trump made the decision in order to speed progress toward an agreement, telling reporters, "It would be a mistake to interpret the policy as being one . . . where we release some sanctions in return for piecemeal steps toward denuclearization. That is not a winning formula and it is not the president's strategy."[85]

The Trump administration has tried to get China, which accounts for 90 percent of North Korea's trade, to pressure Kim to dismantle its nuclear arsenal.[86] However, U.S. relations with China have been complicated by the ongoing trade dispute.

Negotiations during the trade-war truce reportedly have shown signs of progress, and Trump extended the original March 1 deadline. Trump and Xi are expected to meet in late spring or early summer at Trump's Mar-a-Lago resort in Florida.

Both sides have suffered during the trade war. American farmers and manufacturers have lost sales due to increased tariffs on their exports to China. But some economists say that China, with its slowing economy and greater reliance on exports, has been hurt more than the United States.[87]

Trans-Atlantic Relations

Trump has said he is not worried about his low popularity in Europe. "I shouldn't be popular in Europe," he said in January. "I'm not elected by Europeans; I'm elected by Americans."[88]

Doug Bandow, a senior fellow specializing in foreign policy at the libertarian Cato Institute in Washington, agrees that it doesn't matter if Trump is unpopular abroad. "If another country is irritated because the U.S. says 'You should be capable of defending yourself,' that doesn't strike me as a major problem," he says.

But Leslie Vinjamuri, head of the U.S. and the Americas Program at Chatham House, a nonpartisan think tank in London, says Trump's skepticism toward NATO could alter trans-Atlantic diplomacy "for a long time," because "reliability and predictability are at issue."

In March, former Vice President Richard B. Cheney, who served under Republican President George W. Bush, sharply criticized Trump's foreign policy at a private retreat sponsored by the American Enterprise Institute, a conservative think tank. Cheney told Vice President Pence that Trump's policies feed "this notion on the part of our allies overseas, especially in NATO, that we're not long for that continued relationship," according to *The Washington Post*.[89]

Cheney also complained about reports that Trump plans to demand that Germany, Japan, South Korea and other countries that host U.S. troops pay the full cost for such deployments—plus 50 percent. Noting that NATO countries are fighting alongside U.S. soldiers in Afghanistan, Cheney said that foreign relations are "a lot more complicated than just: 'Here's the bottom line. Write the check.'"[90]

Pence defended the administration's policies. "I think there is a tendency by critics of the president and our administration to conflate the demand that our allies live up to their . . . commitments and an erosion in our commitment to the post-World War II order," Pence said. "This president is skeptical of foreign deployments and only wants American forces where they need to be."[91]

Two days later, signaling bipartisan support for the alliance, congressional leaders said they were inviting NATO chief Stoltenberg to address a joint session of Congress in April to celebrate the 70th anniversary of the organization.[92]

Not all European countries are dissatisfied with Trump. He gets favorable ratings in Poland and Hungary, where anti-immigrant, nationalist leaders have emerged. Hungarian-American writer Boris Kálnoky explained Eastern Europeans' affinity for Trump: "We like plainspoken men who have the [guts] to say what they're thinking. If they're vulgar, so much the better." The president also "represents the idea that the United States is, and should remain, the most powerful country in the world," which is a "powerful guarantee of our security," he said.[93]

Western European allies were disappointed on Feb. 1, when Trump announced the United States was withdrawing from the INF Treaty on midrange nuclear weapons with Russia. German Chancellor Merkel said it was "unavoidable" after "years of violations of the terms of the treaty by Russia." However, she lamented, the pact "directly affects our security . . . and we are left sitting there."[94]

Trump and Putin say each other's country has repeatedly violated the treaty. Trump also has noted that China, which is not a signatory, is developing intermediate-range missiles. "If Russia's [building its arsenal] and if China's doing it, and we're adhering to the agreement, that's unacceptable," he said.[95]

Terrorism and Iran

Secretary of State Pompeo's Jan. 10 Middle East policy speech in Cairo stressed concern for Israel and a desire to strengthen relations with Saudi Arabia, Egypt and other countries friendly to the United States. He promised to reduce the threat to Israel from Lebanon-based Hezbollah militants and to stifle Iran's "deadly ambitions."[96]

A month later, Pompeo told a Middle East summit in Warsaw, Poland: "You can't achieve stability in the Middle East without confronting Iran." Israeli Prime Minister Benjamin Netanyahu echoed those sentiments, but he also called the summit a group of nations "sitting down together with Israel in order to advance the common interest of war with Iran."[97]

Democratic Sens. Tom Udall of New Mexico and Richard Durbin of Illinois worry about just such a scenario. Trump is "barreling toward war with Iran," they said, using "false narratives that Iran is not meeting its obligations under the nuclear deal." The senators said Trump is being egged on by Pompeo and Bolton, whom they called "committed advocates of virtually unchecked interventionism."[98]

In a March 5 *Washington Post* op-ed, Udall and Durbin said Trump's breach of the Iran nuclear deal had left the United States isolated and that Congress must "end the growing threat of a national security calamity, return our country to diplomacy and rebuild international trust in U.S. foreign policy." The two are preparing to introduce bipartisan legislation to restrict U.S. funds from being used to attack Iran.[99]

Carnegie president Burns said pulling out of the Iran deal "added to the fissures between us and our closest European allies, [and] in a way it's done Vladimir Putin's work for him" by sowing discord among the allies.[100]

Meanwhile, on Dec. 19, 2018, Trump unexpectedly announced the "full and rapid" withdrawal of the 2,200 U.S. troops from Syria, declaring that ISIS had been defeated—and prompting the resignation of Defense Secretary Jim Mattis, who disagreed with the decision. On Jan. 6, Trump backtracked, saying "we won't be finally pulled out until ISIS is gone."[101]

Such actions exemplify Trump's shoot-from-the-hip approach to diplomacy and its negative consequences, critics say.[102]

"Careless talk about the fight against ISIS being over is counterproductive [and] undermines our counterterrorism efforts and undermines our partners" in the region, says Daniel Benjamin, former State Department coordinator for counterterrorism and now director of Dartmouth College's John Sloan Dickey Center for International Understanding.

On March 23, U.S.-backed forces announced they had driven ISIS fighters out of the last territory they had been occupying in Syria. However, U.S. intelligence officials say ISIS is far from finished as a fighting force. According to Russ Travers, deputy director of the National Counterterrorism Center, about 14,000 armed and active ISIS fighters remain in Syria and Iraq.[103]

"A lot of ISIS has gone to ground and obviously there needs to be more engagement there" before it is no longer a threat, Benjamin says.

Venezuela

Trump told the U.N. General Assembly last year, "The United States will not tell you how to live or work or worship."[104] But events in Venezuela have put that pledge to the test.

On Jan. 23, Trump pronounced the regime of Venezuelan President Nicolas Maduro, re-elected last May in a vote widely regarded as rigged, "illegitimate." Trump said he considered Juan Guaidó, president of the legislative National Assembly, the lawful interim president. Some 50 other Latin American and European countries also support Guaidó.[105]

On Jan. 29, the administration announced sanctions effectively blocking imports of oil from Venezuela's state-owned oil company, the country's biggest revenue source. Venezuela, with the world's largest proven oil reserves, shipped 500,000 barrels of crude a day to the United States in 2018, representing about 75 percent of the cash it received for its crude exports.[106]

"Trump said the United States wouldn't interfere in other countries' business," says Thomas Carothers, a senior vice president at the Carnegie Endowment, "but when it comes to countries we can't get along with, he points to their internal values and says that's a problem. There's an inconsistency."

OUTLOOK

End of 'Unipower'

Foreign policy experts tend to agree that Trump's presidency has coincided with a disruption in the international order that prevailed during much of the postwar period. They are far less united, however, on what will replace that order or on Trump's ultimate impact on the world.

American University's Adams, who calls himself a foreign policy "realist," says the United States' days as a "unipower" are over, but through no fault of its own. "Power is rebalancing. We couldn't have prevented the rebalancing of global power after the Cold War," he says. "It's not something brought on by Donald Trump," but his role has been "that of accelerant."

Ohio State's Schweller, who also calls himself a foreign policy realist, says, "For the U.S., there really are very few threats right now," although China is a looming competitor. Terrorism, meanwhile, is "a side show, a minor discomfort [but] not something we should spend too much time focusing on in our foreign policy. We're currently in a threat trough, so the U.S. should act accordingly and retrench."

It is unclear whether Trump's nationalism has left an indelible stamp on how the United States conducts diplomacy. For Thomas Wright, director of the Center on the United States and Europe at Brookings, the next presidential election is key.

If Trump is defeated in 2020, he predicts, "a lot of U.S. foreign policy would revert to some version of internationalism." But if Trump is re-elected, "over time he will be able to get his agenda through, and a lot of people will say America has fundamentally changed, and we will have to adjust accordingly."

But Carnegie's Burns is optimistic that American diplomacy will return to a place of legitimacy "over the medium term," regardless of how much it is "belittled and disdained today."[107]

Salman Ahmed, a senior fellow at the Carnegie Endowment, has some advice for U.S. leaders: "The strategic and economic rationale for the U.S. acting abroad is less clear than in the past. Those with responsibility for clarifying it would be wise to step back and try to understand what Americans think about it."

Ahmed is overseeing a series of state-level case studies to record how middle-class Americans view foreign policy and its impact on their economic well-being. He says those views are more nuanced than the country's political polarization would suggest.

"People get it," he says. "They know the 1960s aren't coming back. They have legitimate questions, though. What's going to happen to their town if it was dependent on a labor-intensive, heavy manufacturing practice which has gone away? Whatever caused it—trade and economic policies or something else—something has radically changed for them."

Former diplomat Shannon says, "In many ways, we're experiencing the end of a certain structure of the world order . . . driven by social and economic changes.

"We're kind of at a moment of re-founding, where the American people want a larger conversation with our collective leadership about what we're doing in the world," Shannon says. "And whether you like him or not, the president is the catalyst of that discussion."

NOTES

1. Griff Witte and Michael Birnbaum, "Trump foreign policy under attack from all sides at European security conference," *The Washington Post*, Feb. 16, 2019, https://tinyurl.com/y36tgvxs.

2. "Remarks by Vice President Pence at the 2019 Munich Security Conference, Munich, Germany," The White House, Feb. 16, 2019, https://tinyurl.com/y2qz66up; Katrin Bennhold and Steven Erlanger, "Merkel Rejects U.S. Demands That Europe Pull Out of Iran Nuclear Deal," *The New York Times*, Feb 16, 2019, https://tinyurl.com/yx8skap6.

3. Donald J. Trump, "Inaugural Address," The White House, Jan. 20, 2017, https://tinyurl.com/yxo997ez.

4. Mark Hannah, "Worlds Apart: U.S. Foreign Policy and American Public Opinion," Eurasia Group Foundation survey, February 2019, https://tinyurl.com/y58w7mbs.

5. Steve Holland and Yara Bayoumy, "Trump praises U.S. military sales to Saudi as he welcomes crown prince," Reuters, March 20, 2018, http://tinyurl.com/y5x7jxwz.

6. Salvatore Babones, "Trump's Foreign Policy Successes Show Principled Realism in Action," The National Interest, Sept. 26, 2018, https://tinyurl.com/y6ebcr38.

7. Richard Wike et al., "Trump's International Ratings Remain Low, Especially Among Key Allies," Pew Research Center, Oct. 1, 2018, https://tinyurl.com/y95dqags.

8. Eliza Collins, "Trump: I consult myself on foreign policy," Politico, March 16, 2016, https://tinyurl.com/yax7xahb.

9. "Tracker: Current U.S. Ambassadors," American Foreign Service Association, March 13, 2019, https://tinyurl.com/gppkm54; Twenty-nine of the 59 unfilled positions have nominees awaiting Senate confirmation; another six are in countries with which the U.S. currently does not exchange ambassadors: Belarus, Bolivia, Eritrea, Sudan, Syria and Venezuela; "Lists of Chiefs of Mission as of February 2011," U.S. State Department, https://tinyurl.com/yx9axkmk.

10. Barbara Stephenson, "Time to Ask Why," The Foreign Service Journal, December 2017, https://tinyurl.com/y53ctxvy.

11. "Face the Nation," CBS News, March 10, 2019, https://tinyurl.com/y2kevn5z.

12. Randall Schweller, "Three Cheers for Trump's Foreign Policy," Foreign Affairs, Sept./Oct. 2018, https://tinyurl.com/y44ncnfx.

13. Ibid.

14. "Interview with Secretary of State Madeleine Albright," "Today Show," NBC News, Feb. 19, 1998, https://tinyurl.com/y2248a2l.

15. Jeremy Scahill, "Donald Trump and the Coming Fall of American Empire," The Intercept, July 22 2017, https://tinyurl.com/ydyp3qut.

16. Alfred W. McCoy, "The World According to Trump Or How to Build a Wall and Lose an Empire," Tikkun, Jan. 16, 2018, https://tinyurl.com/y4v6bf95.

17. Babones, op. cit.

18. Robert Muggah, "America's dominance is over. By 2030, we'll have a handful of global powers," World Economic Forum, Nov. 11, 2016, https://tinyurl.com/y4amv59w.

19. Ibid.

20. Gordon Adams, "A new world is dawning, and the US will no longer lead it," The Conversation, June 26, 2018, https://tinyurl.com/yynaao49.

21. Michael Beckley, Unrivaled: Why America Will Remain the World's Sole Superpower (2018), p. 1.

22. Ibid., p. 5.

23. Robert E. Hamilton, "The Reset that Wasn't: The Permanent Crisis of U.S.-Russia Relations," Foreign Policy Research Institute, Dec. 14, 2018, https://tinyurl.com/y5nxwkp8.

24. Jordan Fabian, "Trump: 'Getting along with Russia is a good thing,'" The Hill, July 16, 2018, https://tinyurl.com/yczb87re.

25. Jeremy Diamond, "Trump sides with Putin over US intelligence," CNN, July 16, 2018, https://tinyurl.com/y84yl3nn.

26. Jessica Taylor, "'Disgraceful,' 'Pushover,' 'Deeply Troubled': Reaction To The Trump-Putin Summit," NPR, July 16, 2018, https://tinyurl.com/y7z96jk4.

27. Brian Naylor, "Trump Walks Back Controversial Comments on Russian Election Interference," NPR, July 17, 2018, https://tinyurl.com/yay5mwsh.

28. Sophie Tatum, "Trump defends Putin: 'You think our country's so innocent?'" CNN, Feb. 6, 2017, https://tinyurl.com/yxara4ff.

29. Neil MacFarquhar, "Glee in Russia Over Trump's Foreign Policy Largess," The New York Times, Dec. 21, 2018, https://tinyurl.com/y7rcafwq.

30. "U.S. Sanctions on Russia, Updated January 11, 2019," Congressional Research Service, https://tinyurl.com/y33m9u3b.

31. Kevin Liptak, "Trump administration finally announces Russia sanctions over election meddling," CNN, March 15, 2018, https://tinyurl.com/yaf93q4k; "Statement by President Donald J. Trump on Signing the 'Countering America's Adversaries Through Sanctions Act,'" The White House, Aug. 2, 2017, https://tinyurl.com/y2uv2prs.

32. John Haltiwanger and Sonam Sheth, "Here's a glimpse at Trump's decades-long history of business ties to Russia," Business Insider, Dec. 15, 2018, https://tinyurl.com/y6s6d9zy; Donald J. Trump, Twitter post, Jan. 11, 2017, https://tinyurl.com/y37ewy4k.

33. "Testimony of Michael D. Cohen, Committee on Oversight and Reform, U.S. House of Representatives, Feb. 27, 2019," CNN, https://tinyurl.com/y2mjpflp.

34. "5 Questions with Foreign Policy Expert Steve Sestanovich on the Trump-Putin Summit," Columbia News, July 13, 2017, http://tinyurl.com/y4klsrdw.

35. Katrin Bennhold and Steven Erlanger, "Merkel Joins Macron in Calling for a European Army 'One Day,'" The New York Times, Nov. 13, 2018, https://tinyurl.com/ydhry8eh.

36. David M. Herszenhorn and Lili Bayer, "Trump's whiplash NATO summit," Politico, July 12, 2018, https://tinyurl.com/yayp9evp; Donald Trump (transcript), "Trump Confirms He Threatened to Withdraw from NATO," CSPAN, Aug. 22, 2018, https://tinyurl.com/ybbswx69; Lucie Béraud-Sudreau, "The US and its NATO allies: costs and value," Military Balance Blog, International Institute of Security Studies, July 9, 2018, https://tinyurl.com/y4detsz7.

37. "Defence Expenditure of NATO Countries (2011-2018)," NATO, July 10, 2018, https://tinyurl.com/y65x4j5a.

38. Julie Allen, "Nato members increase defence spending by $100 billion after Donald Trump called them 'delinquents,'" Telegraph, Jan. 27, 2019, https://tinyurl.com/y89vgrfn; Brent D. Griffiths, "NATO head: Trump 'committed' to the alliance," Politico, Jan. 27, 2019, https://tinyurl.com/yaf42wzg.

39. Ian Schwartz, "Full Lou Dobbs Interview: Trump Asks What Could Be More Fake Than CBS, NBC, ABC and CNN?" Real Clear Politics, Oct. 25, 2017, https://tinyurl.com/yyjvhscl.

40. John Micklethwait, Margaret Talev and Jennifer Jacobs, "Trump Threatens to Pull U.S. Out of WTO If It Doesn't 'Shape Up,' " Bloomberg, Aug. 31, 2018, https://tinyurl.com/y6tqxctb.

41. Dan Ikenson, "US Trade Laws And The Sovereignty Canard," Forbes, March 9, 2017, https://tinyurl.com/y3kebsbq.

42. "Statement of the United States by Ambassador Dennis Shea at the 14th WTO Trade Policy Review of the United States of America," Office of the U.S. Trade Representative, Dec. 17, 2018, https://tinyurl.com/y9k4tmkp; Tom Miles, "U.S. drafts WTO reform to halt handouts for big and rich states," Reuters, Feb. 15, 2019, https://tinyurl.com/y4vsb8uy.

43. Jack Caporal and Dylan Gerstel, "WTO Reform: The Beginning of the End or the End of the Beginning?" Center for Strategic and International Studies, Oct. 23, 2018, https://tinyurl.com/yxpkjppv.

44. "Transcript of President George Washington's Farewell Address (1796)," Ourdocuments.gov, https://tinyurl.com/y8ufm2e6.

45. "1898: The Birth of a Superpower," Office of the Historian, U.S. Department of State, https://tinyurl.com/y669brmx.

46. "Wilson's War Message to Congress, April 2, 1917," Brigham Young University document archive, https://tinyurl.com/ybmbkn9n.

47. "President Wilson's Fourteen Points, Address to Congress," Jan. 8, 1918, Yale Law School—Lillian Goldman Law Library, https://tinyurl.com/y6s8gkw3. "The Neutrality Acts, 1930s," Office of the Historian, U.S. Department of State, https://tinyurl.com/ych68pxj.

48. Sandra Kollen Ghizoni, "Creation of the Bretton Woods System," Federal Reserve History, https://tinyurl.com/yxocydeh; "The United Nations," The Eleanor Roosevelt Papers Project, The George

Washington University, https://tinyurl.com/y7t983va.

49. "President Harry S. Truman's address before a joint session of Congress, March 12, 1947," Yale Law School—Lillian Goldman Law Library, https://tinyurl.com/6781rja.

50. "Marshall Plan: Reconstructing Europe," BBC News, Jan. 6, 2005, https://tinyurl.com/yxo6ob5b.

51. "Domino Theory," The Vietnam War, May 4, 2016, https://tinyurl.com/yxvcn2uf.

52. Laura Deal, "Nixon Goes to China," The Wilson Center, Feb. 21, 2017, https://tinyurl.com/y3mkl5ph; "Nixon's Foreign Policy," Office of the Historian, U.S. Department of State, https://tinyurl.com/y2alhk65.

53. "1977-1981: The Presidency of Jimmy Carter," Office of the Historian, U.S. Department of State, https://tinyurl.com/yxutb9ld.

54. "The Iran-Contra Affair," PBS, https://tinyurl.com/y4jznprt.

55. Daryl Kimball, "The Intermediate-Range Nuclear Forces (INF) Treaty at a Glance," Arms Control Association, Feb. 2, 2019, https://tinyurl.com/6oxqkas.

56. Peter Robinson, "Tear Down This Wall," Prologue, U.S. National Archives, Vol. 39, No. 2, Summer 2007, https://tinyurl.com/y783bcrr.

57. Ivo Daalder, "Decision to Intervene: How the War in Bosnia Ended," The Brookings Institution, Dec. 1, 1998, https://tinyurl.com/jxqcn7w.

58. Marc Sageman, *Understanding Terror Networks* (2004), p. 19.

59. Steve Coll, *Ghost Wars: The Secret History of the CIA, Afghanistan, and Bin Laden, From the Soviet Invasion to September 10, 2001* (2004), pp. 405-409, 466-468, 534-537.

60. Jens Stoltenberg, "NATO's Vital Role in the War on Terror" *The Wall Street Journal*, May 24, 2017, https://tinyurl.com/y5os7cv6.

61. "Iraq War Timeline," Council on Foreign Relations, https://tinyurl.com/y295tqqg.

62. "Remarks by the President at Cairo University, 6-04-09," The White House, June 4, 2009, https://tinyurl.com/yxbkk64k.

63. Brian Michael Jenkins, "Five Years After the Death of Osama bin Laden, Is the World Safer?" Rand, May 1, 2016, https://tinyurl.com/yyp9szjd; "Remarks by the President in Address to the Nation on the Way Forward in Afghanistan and Pakistan," The White House, Dec. 1, 2009, https://tinyurl.com/y3gvkwnk.

64. Helene Cooper and Robert F. Worth, "In Arab Spring, Obama Finds a Sharp Test," *The New York Times*, Sept. 24, 2012, https://tinyurl.com/yxjr5nat.

65. Pamela Engel, "Former US defense secretary: Obama hurt US credibility when he backed down from his red line on Syria," *Business Insider*, Jan. 26, 2016, https://tinyurl.com/y68h7j8g.

66. Kelsey Davenport, "The Joint Comprehensive Plan of Action (JCPOA) at a Glance," Arms Control Association, May 2018, https://tinyurl.com/y9mvd9qd; "Statement by the President on the Paris Climate Agreement," The White House, Dec. 12, 2012, https://tinyurl.com/y8c36tqb.

67. Barack Obama, "President Obama: The TPP would let America, not China, lead the way on global trade," *The Washington Post*, May 2, 2016, https://tinyurl.com/y5a98rh5.

68. Mark Landler, "Trump Abandons Iran Nuclear Deal He Long Scorned," *The New York Times*, May 8, 2018, https://tinyurl.com/y7u4oy5s; "United States-Mexico-Canada Agreement," Office of the U.S. Trade Representative, https://tinyurl.com/y3vfe8qx.

69. "A Force for Good: America Reinvigorated in the Middle East," Secretary of State Michael Pompeo in Cairo, Egypt, Jan. 10, 2019, U.S. Department of State, https://tinyurl.com/y9w5qafw.

70. Dorcas Wong and Alexander Chipman Koty, "The US-China Trade War: A Timeline," China Briefing, Feb. 7, 2019, https://tinyurl.com/y2suzjkc.

71. Zhou Xin and Orange Wang, "Donald Trump can outgun China on trade tariffs but Beijing has other ways to fight back," *South China Morning Post*, June 19, 2018, https://tinyurl.com/y6gqel2s.

72. Matt Stevens, "Trump and Kim Jong-un, and the Names They've Called Each Other," *The New York Times*, March 9, 2018, https://tinyurl.com/ybt8koxr.

73. Chris Mills Rodrigo, "Trump: Kim Jong Un and I 'fell in love,'" *The Hill*, Sept. 29, 2018, https://tinyurl.com/ybkf52yl.

74. Carmin Chappell, "Trump schedules joint agreement signing ceremony with North Korean dictator Kim Jong Un at end of Vietnam summit," CNBC, Feb. 27, 2019, https://tinyurl.com/yxw5hoe5; Kim Tong-Hyung, "North Korea says it will never give up nukes unless US removes threat," The Associated Press, *Military Times*, Dec. 20, 2018, https://tinyurl.com/y4qft3v5.

75. Deirdre Shesgreen and John Fritze, "North Korea contradicts Trump's account of negotiations. State Dept. official says NK is 'parsing words,'" *USA Today*, Feb. 28, 2019, https://tinyurl.com/yybnsec8.

76. Alex Ward, "Transcript of Trump's North Korea summit press conference in Vietnam," *Vox*, Feb. 28, 2019, https://tinyurl.com/yyh9m5vs.

77. Felicia Sonmez, "John Bolton: North Korea summit was not a failure," *The Washington Post*, March 3, 2019, https://tinyurl.com/yyqjq2cr.

78. Laura Litvan, Daniel Flatley, Anna Edgerton and Bloomberg, "Trump Gets Bipartisan Praise for Walking Out of Summit With Kim," *Fortune*, Feb. 28, 2019, https://tinyurl.com/y4ox34zs; Sara Gray, "Biden praises Trump for 'walking away' from the North Korea summit with no nuclear deal," *Business Insider*, March 1, 2019, https://tinyurl.com/y2t7ppub.

79. Simon Denyer and Carol Morello, "North Korea Threatens to Suspend Denuclearization Talks with the United States," *The Washington Post*, March 15, 2019, http://tinyurl.com/y5qh5wn5.

80. *Ibid.*

81. *Ibid.*

82. Donald J. Trump, Twitter post, March 22, 2019, https://tinyurl.com/y5l7y843.

83. "Sarah Sanders on the Mueller Report," C-Span, March 25, 2019, http://tinyurl.com/y2sdkp6j.

84. Roberta Rampton, "Trump decides against more North Korea sanctions at this time: source," Reuters, March 22, 2019, https://tinyurl.com/y36axjbw.

85. Alan Rappeport, "Trump Overrules Own Experts on Sanctions, in Favor to North Korea," *The New York Times*, March 22, 2019, https://tinyurl.com/y63v947l.

86. Randy Kluver, Robert Hinck and Skye Cooley, "China more friend than foe to U.S. in North Korea denuclearization," UPI, Nov. 14, 2018, https://tinyurl.com/yarmpwy6; Atsuhito Isozaki, "Why Kim Jong Un Has Turned to 'Tributary Diplomacy,'" *The Diplomat*, Jan. 23, 2019, https://tinyurl.com/y9u87wte.

87. Will Martin, "Lost jobs, shrinking growth, and rotting crops—here are the ways Trump's trade war is hurting America," *Business Insider*, Nov. 28, 2018, https://tinyurl.com/yxgt4s3y; Milton Ezrati, "Trade War from the Chinese Side," *Forbes*, Oct. 3, 2018, https://tinyurl.com/y5ch36w6.

88. "Remarks by President Trump in Cabinet Meeting," The White House, Jan. 2, 2019, https://tinyurl.com/yyl8rkaq.

89. Robert Costa and Ashley Parker, "Former vice president Cheney challenges Pence at private retreat, compares Trump's foreign policy to Obama's approach," *The Washington Post*, March 12, 2019, https://tinyurl.com/y5yoljbx; Nick Wadhams and Jennifer Jacobs, "Trump Seeks Huge Premium From Allies Hosting U.S. Troops," Bloomberg, March 8, 2019, https://tinyurl.com/y4puqg39.

90. Costa and Parker, *ibid.*

91. *Ibid.*

92. Jake Sherman, "Pelosi, McConnell to invite NATO's secretary-general to address Congress," *Politico*, March 11, 2019, https://tinyurl.com/y3d4j5lg.

93. Boris Kálnoky, "My Europe: Why Eastern Europeans like Donald Trump," Deutsche Welle, Nov. 12, 2018, https://tinyurl.com/y6qhkk4k.

94. Shervin Taheran, "Select Reactions to the INF Treaty Crisis," Arms Control Now, Feb. 1, 2019, https://tinyurl.com/y4lj9qmc.

95. "US has violated INF Treaty since 1999, Lavrov tells Putin," TASS, Feb. 2, 2019, https://tinyurl.com/

y43to72c; Amy F. Woolf, "Russian Compliance with the Intermediate Range Nuclear Forces (INF) Treaty: Background and Issues for Congress, Updated Feb. 8, 2019," Congressional Research Service, https://tinyurl.com/hwkzn8y; Zeke Miller and Michael Balsamo, "Moscow says U.S. nuke treaty pullout would be 'very dangerous step,'" The Associated Press, Oct. 21, 2018, https://tinyurl.com/y5pgnau4.

96. "A Force for Good: America Reinvigorated in the Middle East," *op. cit.*

97. Tom Udall and Richard J. Durbin, "Trump is barreling toward war with Iran. Congress must act to stop him," *The Washington Post*, March 5, 2019, https://tinyurl.com/y2u6lvf8.

98. *Ibid.*

99. *Ibid.*

100. "Face the Nation," *op. cit.*

101. Kathy Gilsinan, "Trump Is Rushing the Syria Withdrawal—And That Could Backfire," *The Atlantic*, Jan. 11, 2019, https://tinyurl.com/ycfoy2zp; Francesca Paris, "Trump Adviser Bolton Says U.S. Withdrawal From Syria Is Conditional on Defeat of ISIS," NPR, Jan. 6, 2019, https://tinyurl.com/ybwf52fh.

102. Stephen Collinson, "Shocking Syria withdrawal plan is pure Trump," CNN, Dec. 21, 2018, https://tinyurl.com/yadpavy7.

103. Mark Katkov and Larry Kaplow, "Analysis: The End Of The 'Caliphate' Doesn't Mean The End Of ISIS," NPR, March 22, 2019, https://tinyurl.com/y299grlt.

104. "Remarks by President Trump to the 73rd Session of the United Nations General Assembly, New York, NY," The White House, Sept. 25, 2018, https://tinyurl.com/yc3xfnrr.

105. William Neuman and Nicholas Casey, "Venezuela Election Won by Maduro Amid Widespread Disillusionment," *The New York Times*, May 20, 1918, https://tinyurl.com/yban46hs; "Statement from President Donald J. Trump Recognizing Venezuelan National Assembly President Juan Guaido as the Interim President of Venezuela,"

The White House, Jan. 23, 2019, https://tinyurl.com/ycrz8ejv; Amy Mackinnon, "Maduro vs. Guaidó: A Global Scorecard," *Foreign Policy*, Feb. 6, 2019, https://tinyurl.com/yxzay7yc.

106. Jeremy Diamond and Allie Malloy, "Trump approves sanctions on Venezuelan oil company," CNN, Jan. 29, 2019, https://tinyurl.com/yafcnrse; Devika Krishna Kumar and Collin Eaton, "Venezuelan oil exports to U.S. still a primary source of cash" Reuters, Jan. 25, 2019, https://tinyurl.com/ydzyzxpm.

107. From interview on "The 11th Hour with Brian Williams," MSNBC, March 12, 2019, https://tinyurl.com/y67bwkne.

BIBLIOGRAPHY

Books

Beckley, Michael, *Unrivaled: Why America Will Remain the World's Sole Superpower*, Cornell University Press, 2018.
A Tufts University political scientist says the United States' overwhelming wealth and military might, if used wisely, will assure its continued international dominance.

Daalder, Ivo H., and James M. Lindsay, *The Empty Throne: America's Abdication of Global Leadership*, Public Affairs, 2018.
The president of the Chicago Council on Global Affairs (Daalder) and senior vice president at the Council on Foreign Relations (Lindsay) argue that the United States has abandoned its commitment to alliances, free trade, democracy and human rights.

Kagan, Robert, *The Jungle Grows Back: America and Our Imperiled World*, Knopf, 2018.
A senior fellow at the Brookings Institution warns that rising nationalism threatens the relative peace, prosperity and progressive character of the post-World War II years.

Simms, Brendan, and Charlie Laderman, *Donald Trump: The Making of a World View*, I. B. Tauris, 2017.
Two British historians explain that President Trump's foreign policy views, far from being impulsive and improvised, were formed in the 1980s and are deeply rooted in American history.

Articles

Allison, Graham, "The Myth of the Liberal Order," *Foreign Affairs*, July/August 2018, https://tinyurl.com/ybk6nu8p.
A professor at the John F. Kennedy School of Government at Harvard University says as the U.S. share of global power shrinks, it must coexist with China, Russia and other emerging powers with their own ideas of how the world should be run.

Cox, Michael, "Understanding the Global Rise of Populism," LSE Ideas, Feb. 12. 2018, https://tinyurl.com/y4jjw4r8.
A professor of international relations at the London School of Economics dissects various theories on why populism is on the rise and on its possible consequences.

Nau, Henry R., "Trump's Conservative Internationalism," *National Review*, Aug. 28, 2017, https://tinyurl.com/yytv6zsw.
A professor of international affairs at George Washington University writes that the president's unilateral foreign policy, based on national sovereignty rather than international institutions, is what the United States needs now.

Nye, Joseph S., "A Time for Positive-Sum Power," *The Wilson Quarterly*, Fall, 2018, https://tinyurl.com/y4rgqnb6.
The former dean of Harvard's Kennedy School of Government and a former Defense Department official urges a return to multilateralism in U.S. dealings with China and in other foreign policy challenges.

Plattner, Marc F., "Illiberal Democracy and the Struggle on the Right," *Journal of Democracy*, Vol. 30, No. 1, January 2019, https://tinyurl.com/y6qt7er4.
The founding co-editor of the *Journal of Democracy* and co-chair of the Research Council of the International Forum for Democratic Studies writes that the rise of right-wing populist parties in Europe and Latin America threatens liberal democracy.

Reports and Studies

"National Security Strategy of the United States of America," The White House, December 2017, https://tinyurl.com/y6rtr789.

The Trump administration outlines its plans to defend the homeland from economic, military and diplomatic threats, both foreign and domestic.

"Summary of the 2018 National Defense Strategy of The United States of America," U.S. Department of Defense, Jan. 19, 2018, https://tinyurl.com/y8a3laof.
The Pentagon analyzes defense challenges facing the United States and the military's response.

Cimino-Isaacs, Cathleen D., Rachel F. Fefer and Ian F. Fergusson, "World Trade Organization: Overview and Future Direction," Congressional Research Service, updated Feb. 15, 2019, https://tinyurl.com/y64vvn7b.
Analysts from the research arm of Congress examine the history of the World Trade Organization and the challenges it faces in today's economic and political environment, emphasizing the role of the United States.

Kyle, Jordan, and Limor Gultchin, "Populists in Power Around the World," Tony Blair Institute for Global Change, Nov. 7, 2018, https://tinyurl.com/yyu3gl55.
Two researchers at the nonpartisan institute define populism, evaluate its impact and track its growth in a global database.

Mazarr, Michael J., et al., "Understanding the Emerging Era of International Competition: Theoretical and Historical Perspectives," RAND Corp., 2018, https://tinyurl.com/y2vkb476.
Researchers examine the Trump administration's national security strategy in the context of the new military, economic and political competition facing the United States.

THE NEXT STEP

North Korea

Denyer, Simon, "North Korea denounces scaled-back U.S.-South Korea military exercises," *The Washington Post*, March 7, 2019, https://tinyurl.com/y4faokx8.
In the latest indication of increased tension between the United States and North Korea, Pyongyang condemned a U.S.-South Korean military exercise, even though it was reduced in scope.

Perez, Evan, and David Shortell, "North Korean-backed bank hacking on the rise, US officials say," CNN, March 1, 2019, https://tinyurl.com/y43nq9ze.
The bite of U.S. economic sanctions has driven North Korea to resort to digital bank heists, according to U.S. officials.

Shin, Hyonhee, " 'All-or-nothing' U.S. approach toward North Korea won't work: Moon adviser," Reuters, March 12, 2019, https://tinyurl.com/yxvcw9tx.
While both sides bear responsibility for the failed North Korea-U.S. summit, the United States "made excessive demands" by abruptly toughening its stance to demand complete North Korean denuclearization, says a South Korean national security adviser.

Russia

Pancevski, Bojan, "How a Russian Gas Pipeline Is Driving a Wedge Between the U.S. and Its Allies," *The Wall Street Journal*, March 10, 2019, https://tinyurl.com/y4ufknps.
The Trump administration plans to impose sanctions on companies and investors involved in a natural gas pipeline project that would increase German consumption of Russian gas.

Sonne, Paul, "U.S. military to test missiles banned under faltering nuclear pact with Russia," *The Washington Post*, March 13, 2019, https://tinyurl.com/yylu8mvx.
The United States is preparing to test a ground-launched cruise missile previously banned by the Intermediate-Range Nuclear Forces Treaty shortly after the U.S. withdrawal from the accord takes effect this summer.

Zengerle, Patricia, "U.S. senators to try again to pass Russia sanctions bill," Reuters, Feb. 13, 2019, https://tinyurl.com/y2afa74h.
A bipartisan group of senators has proposed legislation that would impose new sanctions on Russia's banks, cyber sector and energy industry.

Sanctions

Domm, Patti, and Tom DiChristopher, "US sees room to be more aggressive on sanctions and take Iran oil exports to zero," CNBC, March 13, 2019, https://tinyurl.com/y2clyoc9.

Market projections that show global oil supply exceeding demand may enable the United States to increase its pressure on Iranian energy exports, a State Department official said.

Weissenstein, Michael, and Matthew Lee, "Trump symbolically tightens embargo on Cuba," The Associated Press, March 4, 2019, https://tinyurl.com/y2b4lkh6.
The Trump administration is allowing lawsuits against some Cuban businesses and government agencies, but the effect is likely to be largely symbolic because most of the targeted entities are not connected to the U.S. legal or financial systems.

Wyss, Jim, "As U.S. sanctions against Venezuela mount, what's the human toll?" *Miami Herald*, updated March 12, 2019, https://tinyurl.com/y3ekuonv.
The United States is increasing its economic pressure on the regime of Venezuelan leader Nicolas Maduro, but there is debate about whether the strategy is appropriate given the increased suffering it is causing.

Trade War

Wei, Lingling, and Bob Davis, "U.S., China Close In on Trade Deal," *The Wall Street Journal*, March 3, 2019, https://tinyurl.com/y66l647v.
China is prepared to ease tariffs and other restrictions on U.S. goods if the United States lifts most of the trade sanctions it imposed last year, say a Beijing-based finance reporter and a *Wall Street Journal* senior editor.

Weinraub, Mark, "Why U.S. growers are betting the farm on soybeans amid China trade war," Reuters, March 14, 2019, https://tinyurl.com/y649y6wn.
U.S. farmers are still planting soybeans, despite losing their biggest market because of the U.S.-China trade dispute, because of a lack of good alternatives.

Wu, Wendy, "Casualties of trade war: Chinese in US denied licences to work with sensitive technologies," *South China Morning Post*, March 12, 2019, https://tinyurl.com/yxdoxdxv.
Heightened U.S. concerns over technology security may be preventing Chinese-born workers from getting technology access work permits, says a Beijing-based reporter.

For More Information

Brookings Institution, 1775 Massachusetts Ave., N.W., Washington, DC 20036; 202-797-6000; www.brookings .edu. Bipartisan think tank concerned with issues of national and international policy.

Carnegie Endowment for International Peace, 1779 Massachusetts Ave., N.W., Washington, DC 20036-2103; 202-483-7600; https://carnegieendowment.org. U.S. think tank analyzing global policy issues.

Center for American Progress, 1333 H St., N.W., 10th Floor, Washington, DC, 20005; 202-682-1611; www .americanprogress.org. Think tank providing liberal perspective on global and domestic policy issues.

Center for Security and International Studies, 1616 Rhode Island Ave., N.W., Washington, DC 20036; 202-887-0200; www.csis.org. Bipartisan think tank that researches and highlights U.S. and international strategic topics.

Council on Foreign Relations, 58 East 68th St., New York, NY 10065; 212-434-9400; www.cfr.org. Nonpartisan foreign affairs membership organization, publisher and think tank.

Heritage Foundation, 214 Massachusetts Ave., N.E., Washington DC 20002-4999; 202-546-4400; www.heritage .org. Conservative public-policy think tank that promotes public policies, including foreign policies, based on the principles of free enterprise, limited government, traditional American values and a strong national defense.

National Security Archive Gelman Library, Suite 701, The George Washington University, 2130 H St., N.W., Washington, DC, 20037; 202-994-7000; https://nsarchive .gwu.edu. An independent nongovernmental research institute and library that collects and publishes declassified government documents, including those on U.S. foreign policy, acquired through the Freedom of Information Act.

Peterson Institute for International Economics, 1750 Massachusetts Ave., N.W., Washington, DC 20036; 202-328-9000; https://piie.com. Independent nonprofit think tank researching and analyzing global trade and economic issues.

Royal Institute of International Affairs, Chatham House, 10 St James' Square, London SW1Y 4LE; +44 (0)20 7957 5700; www.chathamhouse.org. Nongovernmental, nonpartisan British institute that analyzes major international issues from a European perspective.

U.S. Institute of Peace, 2301 Constitution Ave., N.W., Washington, DC 20037; 202-457-1700; www.usip.org. Congressionally funded, nonpartisan think tank researching and promoting nonviolent solutions to global challenges.

Woodrow Wilson International Center for Scholars, Ronald Reagan Building and International Trade Center, One Woodrow Wilson Plaza, 1300 Pennsylvania Ave., N.W., Washington, DC 20004-3027; 202-691-4000; www .wilsoncenter.org. Nonpartisan think tank that researches and presents programs on international issues.

10

Future of Puerto Rico

Barbara Mantel

Statehood supporters in San Juan celebrate on June 11, 2017, after 97 percent of participants in a nonbinding referendum backed statehood over two other options: remaining a commonwealth or pursuing independence. But opponents of statehood dismissed the results, noting that more than three-quarters of registered voters did not participate. Ultimately, it is up to Congress to decide Puerto Rico's political fate.

From *CQ Researcher,*
January 28, 2018

Surveying the flattened trees, flooded streets and ruined homes in their native Puerto Rico, Jarold Correa and Yumari Rivera decided they had had enough.

The couple, in their 30s, moved to Miami in mid-October 2017 with their two young sons to live with Rivera's brother. They are part of a massive exodus of more than 100,000 Puerto Ricans to date, according to demographers, that began after Hurricane Maria walloped the island on Sept. 20, 2017, only two weeks after Hurricane Irma's wind and rain knocked out more than half the island's power.[1]

Maria was Puerto Rico's most powerful storm in nearly 90 years. It destroyed much of the island's antiquated power grid, damaged or destroyed nearly 500,000 homes and devastated the island's struggling economy.[2] The Puerto Rican government said 64 people died as a result of the hurricane, but independent analyses put the toll at more than 1,000.[3]

After Maria's maximum 155 mph winds blew out windows and doors in their home in Gurabo, Correa and Rivera found shelter elsewhere on the island. "We were shifting among relatives' houses," recalls Rivera. "It was so difficult."

Lack of power forced them to permanently close their hair salon in nearby San Juan. But their barbershop, which had a generator and is now reconnected to the electric grid, remains open. They supervise employees remotely from Miami, and Correa makes monthly visits. The couple, who plan to expand their business to Miami, say they are unsure whether they will return to Puerto Rico to live.

Puerto Rico's Economy Is Shrinking

Puerto Rico's annual gross national product (GNP)—the value of all goods and services—has fallen every year since 2007 except 2012, when growth was a modest 0.5 percent. The outlook remains bleak in the wake of Hurricanes Irma and Maria, which destroyed the power grid in September and forced thousands of businesses to close for months.

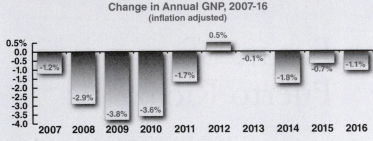

Change in Annual GNP, 2007-16
(inflation adjusted)

Source: "Economic Activity Index ('GDB-EAI')," Government Development Bank for Puerto Rico, p. 4, July 2017, https://tinyurl.com/y9sd4zbk

Four months after Maria hit, Puerto Rico is still struggling to recover. Hospitals are functioning again and most schools are open, at least part time. But hundreds of thousands of homes remain damaged or uninhabitable, and only about 60 percent of islanders have their electricity back on. The U.S. Army Corps of Engineers, the federal agency helping Puerto Rico repair its electric grid, estimates that it will take until the end of May to completely restore power.[4]

The slow and wrenching recovery has thrown into harsh relief the island's 11-year recession and the resulting migration, stoked by the storm, of Puerto Ricans to the mainland. It also has drawn renewed attention to the Puerto Rican government's $73 billion debt and its neglect of the island's infrastructure. And it has revived a long-standing debate over whether residents would be better off if Puerto Rico were to become the 51st state or an independent nation instead of remaining a U.S. commonwealth.

As a commonwealth, Puerto Rico elects its governor and legislators, who control most internal affairs, while Washington determines the island's foreign relations, maritime laws and immigration policies. Puerto Ricans are U.S. citizens, but they cannot cast ballots for president and do not receive the same level of federal benefits

as state residents. They enjoy full rights if they move to the states. The island has no voting representatives in Congress.

Ultimately, it is up to Congress to decide Puerto Rico's political fate, but it has never acted on any of five nonbinding referendums held on the island since 1967, many of which have been plagued by controversy over their wording and have yielded varying results. Last week, Puerto Rico Gov. Ricardo Rosselló, whose New Progressive Party (PNP) favors statehood, sent a delegation to lobby Congress to allow Puerto Ricans to hold a binding vote, which would force Congress to act.[5]

Meanwhile, Puerto Rico's economy has been shrinking for 10 of the past 11 years. November's unemployment rate was 10.8 percent, compared with 4.1 percent in the rest of the United States. And inflation-adjusted median household income was $20,078 in 2016, about half that of Mississippi, the poorest state.[6]

In June 2016, President Barack Obama signed a controversial bill creating the federal Financial Oversight and Management Board to oversee Puerto Rico's finances. Last May, Puerto Rico filed for bankruptcy after it announced it could no longer make payments on its public debt, which almost doubled in size over the past decade as the recession reduced revenue and the government borrowed to pay for essential services.[7]

Debate rages about the root causes of Puerto Rico's spiraling problems. Prime contenders include the island's "neocolonial" status, uncompetitive labor laws and, some critics say, an inept or even corrupt government.

The island needs "to demand that sovereignty over Puerto Rico be in our hands. Not in Washington, not in Wall Street, and not in the hands of the political lackeys and our local oligarchy," said Déborah Berman-Santana, a retired professor of geography and ethnic studies at Mills College in Oakland, Calif., and a permanent resident of Puerto Rico who supports independence.[8]

But Cesar Conda, former chief of staff to U.S. Sen. Marco Rubio, R-Fla., and a principal of Navigators

Global, a lobbying and public relations firm in Washington, says statehood, not independence, would lessen the island's economic woes because Puerto Rico would receive the same federal benefits as other states.

"Why is there a different treatment of American citizens who live in Puerto Rico? It's just ridiculous," says Conda.

Some conservative analysts say political status is not the issue. Instead, they say Puerto Rico needs to make sweeping changes to its economy, such as lowering its minimum wage below $7.25 an hour, the federally mandated minimum wage, and loosening labor protections to make the island competitive with its Caribbean neighbors.

"I hope this would be like the alcoholic who hits rock bottom and who says, 'OK, we're bankrupt now, we really got to change the way we're doing things,'" said Andrew Biggs, a resident scholar at the American Enterprise Institute, a conservative think tank in Washington. Biggs is a member of the federal oversight board.[9]

The island has strengths: high literacy, robust tourism and a manufacturing base that exports pharmaceuticals, medical devices, rum and other goods.

But Puerto Rico was hit with a triple whammy beginning in 2006 when Congress finished phasing out a tax break that had lured U.S. factories to the island; the economy of the United States, Puerto Rico's biggest trading partner, sank into a deep recession; and a local real estate boom went bust, devastating banks and construction jobs.[10]

Then came Hurricane Maria, which tore through the agricultural sector and countless businesses. Puerto Rico could suffer up to $95 billion in damages and lost economic output, or roughly 130 percent of its annual gross national product, because of the hurricane, according to global research firms.[11] And it could take a quarter-century for inflation-adjusted per capita income to return to pre-hurricane levels, said Solomon Hsiang and Trevor Houser, directors of the Climate Impact Lab, a collaboration of climate scientists, economists and other experts.

"But this doesn't have to become Puerto Rico's destiny," said Hsiang and Houser. "Sufficient, timely, sustained and well-designed disaster relief from Washington can help mitigate Maria's impact."[12]

However, Washington and Puerto Rico are wrangling over how many billions of aid dollars the island should receive, while both are being blamed for the ongoing humanitarian crisis. Puerto Ricans and international aid groups say the Trump administration and the Federal Emergency Management Agency (FEMA), which leads disaster relief efforts, are mishandling relief efforts.

"Maria survivors are encountering enormous challenges navigating [FEMA's] bureaucratic and opaque assistance process and lack sufficient information on whether, when, and how they will be assisted," said Washington-based Refugees International in a scathing December report.[13]

At the same time, critics accuse the Puerto Rico Power Authority (PREPA), the government-run electric utility, of being corrupt and inept. In November, Ricardo Ramos, its executive director, resigned amid a furor over recovery efforts and PREPA's awarding of a $300 million no-bid contract to a tiny Montana firm, Whitefish Energy Holdings, to lead the power-restoration effort. Ramos canceled the contract shortly before resigning.

In the meantime, the flow of islanders to the mainland United States continues unabated, contributing, along with a declining birth rate, to the island's depopulation from a high of 3.8 million people in 2004 to 3.3 million by July 2017.[14] The Center for Puerto Rican Studies at Hunter College in New York City estimates that after Maria, between 114,000 and 213,000 Puerto Ricans will leave the island annually to live on the mainland in the next few years, with no significant migration in the other direction. The result could be a 14 percent population loss by the end of 2019.[15]

The chances of these new emigrants eventually returning to Puerto Rico are slim, says center director Edwin Meléndez. "There is such a deterioration in the quality of life in Puerto Rico right now—security, safety, schools, government services, entertainment—that the factors to induce people to go back are just not there."

Meléndez calls the population loss a "disaster" for Puerto Rico. "If you reduce the population, you reduce demand for goods and services. It then gets harder for economic recovery," he says.

As Puerto Rico struggles with its myriad problems, here are some of the questions experts, islanders and others are debating:

Islanders Flee to U.S. Mainland

Puerto Rican migration to the U.S. mainland has soared since Hurricane Maria devastated the island in late September. Nearly 40 percent of the migrants are estimated to have headed to Florida, where Gov. Rick Scott declared a state of emergency last fall, saying the newcomers needed housing and job assistance, crisis counseling and legal advice.

Migration from Puerto Rico to U.S. Mainland, 2013-19

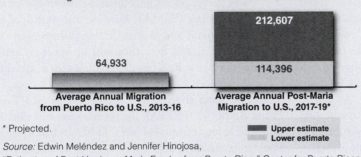

Average Annual Migration from Puerto Rico to U.S., 2013-16: 64,933

Average Annual Post-Maria Migration to U.S., 2017-19*: Upper estimate 212,607; Lower estimate 114,396

* Projected.

■ Upper estimate
■ Lower estimate

Source: Edwin Meléndez and Jennifer Hinojosa, "Estimates of Post-Hurricane Maria Exodus from Puerto Rico," Center for Puerto Rican Studies, Hunter College, City University of New York, October 2017, https://tinyurl.com/yaqoxtgu

Have the hurricane recovery and relief efforts been sufficient?

Ten days after Maria devastated the island, San Juan Mayor Carmen Yulín Cruz made a televised plea to President Trump for help.

"We are dying, and you are killing us with the inefficiency and the bureaucracy," said Cruz.[16]

Trump pushed back, praising his administration's efforts and criticizing the island government. "Such poor leadership by the Mayor of San Juan and others in Puerto Rico who are not able to get their workers to help," he tweeted.[17]

So the finger-pointing began for the months it is taking to repair the electrical grid, process disaster relief funds and provide clean water, food, health care and temporary housing to those in need. Critics have assailed FEMA and the Trump administration for a lack of urgency.

"If this were happening in the continental United States, if we were in Connecticut 100 days after a hurricane and half the state didn't have power, there would be riots in the street," said U.S. Sen. Christopher Murphy, D-Conn., after a January trip to the island.[18]

But FEMA's defenders say its hands are somewhat tied by the 1988 Stafford Act, which requires local authorities to take the lead in the wake of a disaster. The problem, FEMA's defenders say, is that the law assumes that a state or territorial government has functioning computers, telephones and an available workforce. Puerto Rico had few of those, Gov. Rosselló said in November.

"Maria wiped out [the capital of] San Juan, leaving our . . . government unable to communicate and effectively in the dark," said Rosselló. No one was able to take charge early on, resulting in relief supplies stuck on ships docked at the island's ports, he told a congressional hearing.[19]

In addition, FEMA is stretched thin as it responds to the aftermath of hurricanes in Texas and Florida and wildfires in California. "My staff is tapped out" and working around the clock, said FEMA Administrator Brock Long in November. "We are doing the best that we can do and trying to move as quick as we can."[20]

Still, experts on the ground and observers on the mainland say FEMA and the agencies it directs during disasters, such as the Army Corps of Engineers, could have done better in Puerto Rico. FEMA eventually stepped into the leadership breach and began coordinating the disaster response, but not always well, say critics.

Shannon Scribner, acting director for humanitarian programs and policy at Oxfam America—a Boston-based relief organization that has a small team in Puerto Rico providing water filters to individuals and communities—praises the Corps of Engineers for its rapid clearing of roads. But on flights to Puerto Rico in the fall, she says she noticed something missing. "You didn't see a lot of blue tarps on the roofs to keep the rain and mold out, even though such a large percentage of homes were destroyed," she says. In early October, FEMA awarded a $30 million contract to a tiny Florida company for tarps and plastic sheeting, but the material was never delivered.

"It's completely unacceptable, and it cries out for a professional and independent review of the inspector general of the Department of Homeland Security," FEMA's parent agency, said Rep. Sean Maloney, D-N.Y., in early December. The situation has improved since then, and the federal government says 51 percent of the needed tarps have been installed as of Jan. 7.[21]

Scribner and others say the federal government has moved more slowly in Puerto Rico than on the mainland. "I'm not attributing the inadequate response to racial considerations," says Pedro Cabán, chair of the Latin American, Caribbean and U.S. Latino Studies Department at the University at Albany, State University of New York. "Instead, I see the larger issues involved, the growing inconsequence of Puerto Rico to the United States' economic and strategic policies."

In its defense, the Corps of Engineers has said it signed contracts with repair companies in record time but that supplies have been slow in arriving.

"Puerto Rico is competing for supplies with Texas and Florida, whose electrical grids were similarly ravaged by hurricanes," said Army Corps spokesman Luciano Riviera shortly before Christmas. Hurricane Harvey struck Texas in August and Hurricane Irma hit Florida in September. By Jan. 8, for example, only 12,000 of the nearly 31,000 transmission poles and about 412 of 6,000 transformers ordered had arrived in Puerto Rico.[22]

Meanwhile, Corps officials, accompanied by armed federal agents, seized materials the Corps discovered unaccounted for at a PREPA warehouse on Jan. 6. PREPA later said the Corps had access to that warehouse all along, and Gov. Rosselló has asked the U.S. Justice Department to investigate to determine the facts. This week, Puerto Rico's electric utility workers' union accused the Corps of hoarding materials at one of its warehouses, which the Corps denied, according to *The Intercept*.[23]

Some observers say PREPA is mostly to blame for the power problems.

PREPA was not only broke before Maria made landfall but also dysfunctional, said Ramon-Luis Nieves, an attorney and former chairman of the Committee on Energy in the Puerto Rican Senate, who testified before Congress in November. Each new political administration would award "loyalists with

San Juan Mayor Carmen Yulín Cruz appealed to President Trump for disaster relief 10 days after Hurricane Maria hit. "We are dying, and you are killing us with the inefficiency and the bureaucracy," she said. In reply, Trump praised his administration's efforts and criticized local officials, including Cruz. Amid the post-storm fingerpointing, clean water, food, health care and roof tarps have been slow to arrive.

numerous management and technical posts at PREPA," which was known for its generous employee benefits, said Nieves.[24]

The Whitefish scandal was a prime example of the utility's troubled governance, say its critics. Rather than pursue mutual aid from other U.S. public power utilities as is typical after a disaster, PREPA signed the no-bid contract in early October with Whitefish and agreed to pay it 17 times the going hourly wage for its subcontracted electrical linemen. A company spokesman said Whitefish's overhead costs justified the extra money. After PREPA canceled the contract at the end of the month, it reached mutual aid agreements with New York and Florida to send thousands of utility workers.[25]

Several congressional committees are investigating the Whitefish episode, and, reportedly, so is the FBI.[26]

Should Puerto Rico's new fiscal plan include tough austerity measures?

On Jan. 24—about a month behind schedule—the Puerto Rican government is supposed to present a five-year fiscal plan, which is meant to be a template for the government's budget and the basis for restructuring $55 billion of the commonwealth's debt in a kind of bankruptcy process. (The balance of the government's

$73 billion debt is owed by its power utility, sewer authority and other government agencies, which will be submitting their own fiscal plans.)

Analysts say the plan, if approved by the federal Financial Oversight and Management Board, is sure to draw the ire of mutual funds, hedge funds and individual investors who bought Puerto Rico's bonds: Under the plan, they are expected to receive zero or near-zero payments over the next five years.

"Bondholders will then protest in court, and the judge will have to rule," says Matt Fabian, a partner at Municipal Market Analytics, a bond research firm in Concord, Mass. "I have no idea how it will end up."

The judge presiding over Puerto Rico's bankruptcy is Laura Taylor Swain of the U.S. District Court for the Southern District of New York. In 2016 Congress passed the Puerto Rico Oversight, Management, and Economic Stability Act (PROMESA), which created the oversight board and provided the legal basis for Puerto Rico to seek bankruptcy protection.

This will be Puerto Rico's second fiscal plan under PROMESA. The first, from last March, became obsolete because of Hurricane Maria, and the oversight board called for a new one.

Virtually no one liked the original fiscal plan—not bondholders, students or government employees. It called for a combination of spending cuts and modest tax hikes resulting in a projected cash-flow surplus of $7.9 billion over 10 years to allow payment of about 25 percent of the $3.35 billion owed, on average, annually to bondholders over that time period. The spending cuts of $25.7 billion over the decade involved, among other measures, reducing support for municipalities and schools, scaling back health benefits and possibly furloughing government workers.[27]

Economist Brad Setser, a senior fellow at the Council on Foreign Relations, a New York City-based think tank, says the plan was too optimistic in its assumptions, even before Maria wrecked the island. It overestimated the ability of a weak economy to handle austerity measures and the willingness of Puerto Ricans to remain on the island during tough economic times, he says. Specifically, the plan projected that economy activity, adjusted for inflation, would stabilize after contracting by 12 percent over six years. And it expected outmigration to significantly slow.[28]

But a group of institutional bondholders and bond insurers complained the fiscal plan was too pessimistic and underestimated both what the government could raise and what it could afford to pay creditors. "The Fiscal Plan fails to account for potentially significant additional revenues generated from improved tax collection and compliance reforms," it wrote in a March letter to the oversight board.[29]

Bondholders are bracing for the worst when the plan is released, fearing Puerto Rico will cut payments to bondholders to zero, as expected. But others say that would be just fine.

"There is a strong justifiable case for zero debt service, at least in the foreseeable future," because of the hurricane damage and the island's protracted recession, says Jason Miller, who led efforts by the Obama White House to address Puerto Rico's fiscal crisis and is the CEO of the Greater Washington Partnership, a group of business, academic and civic leaders.

The plan's details are anybody's guess because of all the assumptions Puerto Rico's government must make. Among other things, it will have to estimate migration numbers, and it does not yet know the amount of the latest emergency disaster relief that Congress might approve. The government also does not know the full impact of Maria on the island's income tax and sales tax revenues. Finally, it does not know how U.S. corporations in Puerto Rico will react to the tax overhaul bill that President Trump signed in December.

The overhaul places a 10.5 percent minimum corporate tax on income earned overseas, and it imposes a 12.5 percent tax on income derived from intangible assets, such as patents, that U.S. companies earn offshore. Both taxes would apply to Puerto Rico because Congress treated the island in the bill as an overseas entity.

Puerto Rico legislator Rafael Hernandez, a member of the opposition Popular Democratic Party (PPD), said the intangible assets tax, in particular, "leaves Puerto Rico without any kind of protection or any advantages" against global competitors such as Singapore and Ireland.[30] Gov. Rosselló has called the new taxes "potentially devastating," but Sen. Rubio of Florida, who voted for the bill, says the governor is mistaken. "We're talking to multiple employers there," Rubio said in December. "They've told us that the cost of moving [from Puerto Rico] would be higher than what they would save by moving."[31]

Setser and Miller say the new plan should not include further cuts to government spending. "Asking an island where the economy has already absorbed a really big blow to incur additional austerity will only add to the downturn," says Setser.

And both men say it is imperative that the United States provide adequate disaster relief, invest in modernizing Puerto Rico's infrastructure and treat the island the same as states when it comes to social welfare programs and the earned income tax credit. The tax credit applies to low- to moderate-income working individuals and couples but is not available to Puerto Rican residents.

But Fabian says Congress is unlikely to make all of these structural changes. Additional austerity measures are inevitable, he says. "The economic contraction is painful."

Should Puerto Rico become a state?

On a Sunday last June, Puerto Rico held its fifth referendum since the 1960s on its political status. Ninety-seven percent of Puerto Ricans who voted said Puerto Rico should become the 51st state—the second time voters backed statehood after choosing commonwealth status in the first three referendums.

But more than three-quarters of registered voters did not participate, after proponents of independence or remaining a commonwealth called for a boycott, saying the wording on the ballot for current territorial status was slanted.*[32]

Poverty Bedevils U.S. Territory

Puerto Rico is mired in a decade-long recession as it struggles with slumping housing values, a debt crisis and the aftermath of Hurricanes Irma and Maria, which harmed the island's manufacturing and tourism. Poverty and unemployment rates are more than double those on the U.S. mainland.

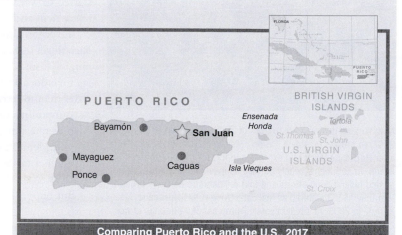

Comparing Puerto Rico and the U.S., 2017

	Puerto Rico	United States
Population	3.3 million; 29.5% under age 25, 19.5% over 65	326.6 million; 32% under age 25, 15.6% over 65
Urbanization rate	93%	82%
Government	U.S. commonwealth	Constitutional federal republic
GDP*	$105 billion	$18.6 trillion
Median annual household income	$20,078*	$57,617
Unemployment rate	10.8%	4.1%
Poverty rate*	43.5%	12.7%
Trade*	$71.9 billion exports (medical equipment, electronics, rum, etc.), $43.3 billion imports (machinery, clothing, food, etc.)	$1.4 trillion exports (computers, telecommunications equipment, industrial supplies, etc.); $2.2 trillion imports (consumer and industrial goods, etc.)

* 2016 figures.

Source: The World Factbook, CIA, 2017, https://tinyurl.com/2yn3sp

---

* The territorial option read: "With my vote, I express my wish that Puerto Rico remains, as it is today, subject to the powers of the Congress and subject to the Territory Clause of the United States Constitution that in the Article IV, Section 3 states: 'The Congress shall have Power to dispose of and make all needful Rules and Regulations respecting the Territory or other Property belonging to the United States and nothing in this Constitution shall be so construed as to Prejudice any Claims of the United States, or of any particular State.'"

New Yorkers demonstrate in front of Trump Tower on Oct. 3, 2017, to protest President Trump's visit to Puerto Rico two weeks after Hurricane Maria and express support for the beleaguered island. In comments widely derided as insensitive, the president lauded federal relief efforts and told residents to be "very proud" that they hadn't endured a "real catastrophe" like Hurricane Katrina in 2005. At a relief center, Trump handed out bags of rice and "shot" rolls of paper towels into the crowd like basketballs, *USA Today* reported.

The historically low turnout has not stopped Gov. Rosselló from promising to press the results with Washington.

"It is certainly the responsibility of all U.S. citizens to ask themselves if we believe in democracy, if we believe in rights and equality which are the pillars of our society, how can we still have a colonial territory with more than 3 million citizens that don't have access to the same rights and the same political power?" said Rosselló in October.[33]

But a week before the vote, Puerto Rican Sen. José Nadal Power, whose Popular Democratic Party favors remaining a commonwealth, called the referendum a waste of "millions of dollars" and "not a good use of the time and energy we must devote to solving the fiscal and economic crisis of Puerto Rico."[34]

Statehood's proponents, however, argue that the change in status would bring the island tremendous economic benefits.

"It would provide certainty for business to invest in Puerto Rico, certainty that they otherwise don't have today," says Conda, the former chief of staff to Sen. Rubio.

"Just look at Alaska and Hawaii," says José Fuentes, a former attorney general in Puerto Rico and chairman of the Puerto Rico Statehood Council, an advocacy group based in Washington. "Once it was determined that they were on the road to statehood, big U.S. companies started to want to get in, and once they became states, investment and real estate went through the roof."

Advocates also say that statehood would allow Puerto Rico to get its fair share of federal spending on programs ranging from Medicare to Social Security because formulas for allocating federal funds are more generous to states than to territories. In 2014, the U.S. Government Accountability Office (GAO) estimated that if Puerto Rico were a state, its funding for Medicare, Medicaid, the Supplemental Nutrition Assistance Program and Supplemental Security Income would increase by as much as $5.4 billion, or 76 percent.[35]

But opponents say statehood would carry significant costs.

"Puerto Rico under PROMESA has a bankruptcy procedure, and that is not something that a state would enjoy," says Desmond Lachman, a resident scholar at the American Enterprise Institute. "That bankruptcy protection is very important when the territory is more than $70 billion in debt." While U.S. law allows municipalities to declare bankruptcy, states cannot.

In addition, Puerto Ricans currently pay federal income tax only on income earned outside the island. The GAO calculated that in 2010, Puerto Ricans paid $20 million in income taxes. That figure would have ballooned to as much as $2.3 billion if Puerto Rico were a state.[36]

Ultimately, the net addition of a few billion dollars is a paltry sum compared to the tens of billions that are needed for reconstruction and recovery after the hurricane, says Lachman. "I don't see an overwhelming argument that if Puerto Rico became a state they would suddenly solve their economic problems."

In any case, Congress could decide to change the formulas for federal funding for territories without conferring statehood, say statehood critics.

"Theoretically, that's true. But we've been trying for 40 years and haven't been able to make that happen," says Fuentes. "If Puerto Ricans could vote for president and had two U.S. senators and five voting members of the House of Representatives, that political power alone would increase tremendously the amount of federal resources that flowed to the island."

That prospect bothers some, who worry that Puerto Ricans, 44 percent of whom live in poverty, are already too dependent on federal support.[37]

"Does statehood for Puerto Rico imply increased reliance and dependency on federal transfers and funds?" asks Cabán of the University at Albany. "Or would it lead to a fundamental economic transformation of Puerto Rico that is necessary to address the very serious problem of poverty and unemployment? The jury is still out on that."

Ultimately, Puerto Rico has to break away from its almost exclusive reliance on investment from abroad and an economy that exports virtually all that it produces and imports virtually all that it consumes, he says. While only a tiny minority of Puerto Ricans support independence, Cabán says it may be the best route for transforming the economy.

Pulling off dramatic economic change may sound utopian while achieving independence faces huge barriers, Cabán admits. These include determining whether the U.S. dollar would remain the currency and whether Puerto Rico would fall outside the U.S. tariff system.

"There are a lot of questions, but I think they can all be resolved," says Cabán.

BACKGROUND

Spanish Colonial Rule

The Taínos were the dominant indigenous inhabitants of Puerto Rico when Europeans first made contact in the late 15th century. This subgroup of Arawak Indians called the island Boriken, which translates to Borinquén, or land of the valiant lord, in Spanish. Skilled at hunting and fishing, they farmed cassava (a plant whose roots can be eaten or used to make flour and breads), garlic and potatoes, among other crops, worshiped a hierarchy of deities, and had a complex social system consisting of chiefs, noblemen and workers.[38]

In 1493, the Italian explorer Christopher Columbus claimed Borinquén for the Spanish crown during his second voyage to the New World. In 1507, Spanish nobleman Juan Ponce de León established the first European settlements on the island.[39]

The conquerors soon found gold on the island that they began to call Puerto Rico, Spanish for rich port. They forced the Taínos to work the mines and farm cassava plantations, and the Taínos eventually rebelled and attacked several Spanish settlements. The Spaniards responded by burning indigenous villages and branding the foreheads of Taínos prisoners, reducing them to slaves, according to historian Fernando Picó.[40]

Suicide, migration, harsh working conditions and exposure to European diseases took an enormous toll on the Taínos. Before Columbus' arrival, inhabitants of Puerto Rico numbered about 100,000, but by 1531 only 1,545 Taínos remained.[41]

Many of the survivors intermingled with Spanish settlers and a growing number of African slaves, who were first brought to the island in the early 16th century, wrote anthropologist Jorge Duany. African slaves worked in the gold mines, on plantations and as domestic servants. They built the island's forts and churches and eventually "became the backbone of the sugar industry in Puerto Rico and the rest of the Caribbean," Duany said.

By 1550, the island's gold mines were exhausted and sugar was not yet a great revenue source. Thus, Puerto Rico's primary role within the Spanish empire was not economic but strategic. The capital city of San Juan became a military bastion.[42]

In the mid-18th century, the Spanish crown instituted economic reforms in Puerto Rico, and the cultivation of sugar, coffee, tobacco and cotton expanded. By 1870, Puerto Rico was producing 7 percent of the world's sugar. Growing European demand and rising prices turned coffee into the island's leading crop by the 1890s. Still, most Puerto Ricans remained rural and poor, despite the fact slavery had been abolished in 1873. The illiteracy rate was high, schools were few and housing was inadequate.[43]

During most of the Spanish colonial era, the royally appointed governor ruled the island and assigned lieutenants to each main town. "Except for a short period of democratization in the early 1800s, the entire colonial system was highly centralized, hierarchical, and monarchical," wrote Duany.[44]

In 1869, political parties were allowed in Puerto Rico. The Liberal Reformist Party was the first to form in 1870, followed by the Conservative Party a year later.

The former called for rights equal to Spain's provinces while the latter supported the status quo. In 1876, dissatisfied members of the Liberal Reformist Party who wanted some form of self-government formed the Autonomist Party. Spanish authorities persecuted and occasionally jailed its members.[45]

By the late 19th century, Spain was under pressure from independence fighters in Cuba and feared the United States would invade that Spanish colony to support the rebels, protect U.S. sugar interests and project U.S. naval power in the Caribbean. In an attempt to neutralize the independence movement, Spain issued the Autonomous Charter of 1897. It granted Spanish citizenship to Puerto Ricans and Cubans and allowed them each to elect a parliament, which could pass laws on local matters as well as sign international treaties and impose tariffs.[46]

However, the Puerto Rican governor, as the king's representative, continued to wield great power, according to former Puerto Rican judge José Trías Monge. The governor commanded the armed forces and could "suspend freedom of speech, the press, and assembly, arrest people, order searches and seizures, and temporarily shelve other major civil liberties," he wrote.[47]

U.S. Rule

Puerto Rico's experiment with autonomy was short-lived. Spain and the United States went to war in April 1898, primarily in Cuba but also in other parts of Spain's Caribbean and Pacific empire. Resistance was minimal when U.S. troops landed in Puerto Rico in July. In August, an armistice was proclaimed, and in December Spain ceded Puerto Rico, as well as the Philippines and Guam, to the United States.[48]

The U.S. Department of War dismantled Puerto Rico's autonomous government, and in 1900 Congress passed the Foraker Act to establish the legal framework for the island's governance. The law, named for Republican Sen. Joseph Benson Foraker of Ohio, assumed that Puerto Ricans were incapable of self-governance and concentrated most legislative, executive and judicial power in the hands of officials appointed by the U.S. president. Puerto Ricans had the right to elect members to a lower chamber of a bicameral legislature.[49]

Previously, under a 1787 land ordinance and the U.S. Constitution, U.S. territories eventually became states on equal footing with existing states.[50] But the Foraker Act made no promise of statehood to Puerto Rico. The policy departure was the result of Foraker's skillful manipulation of "legislators' racial enmity for the inhabitants of new possessions acquired in 1898," wrote the University at Albany's Cabán.[51]

In 1901, the U.S. Supreme Court ruled that Puerto Rico and other territories annexed after 1898 were "unincorporated" territories—they would receive fundamental constitutional protections, including free speech and due process of law, but not the full range of constitutional protections enjoyed by U.S. citizens. The court also affirmed that the U.S. Constitution endowed Congress with the sole responsibility to determine the territories' political status.[52]

In 1917, Congress passed the Jones-Shafroth Act, which granted U.S. citizenship to Puerto Ricans without altering the island's status as an unincorporated territory. The act established a bill of rights for Puerto Rico and an elected bicameral legislature. But Congress could veto any law the Puerto Rican legislature passed, and the U.S. president continued to appoint the governor and several other high-ranking government officials. Puerto Ricans still could not vote in presidential elections and had only a nonvoting representative in Congress, called the resident commissioner of Puerto Rico, whom Puerto Ricans elected to a four-year term in the House of Representatives.

Under U.S. rule, Puerto Rican politics continued to center on the status issue. The pro-statehood Republican Party, founded in 1899 by physician José Celso Barbosa, initially dominated the Puerto Rican legislature, but in 1904 control switched to the Union Party, co-founded that year by journalist Luis Muñoz Rivera. It agitated for greater autonomy.[53] In 1922, independence supporters broke from the Union Party to form the Nationalist Party. Ten years later, the Republican Party, in a coalition with socialists, regained control of the legislature. That same year, Luis Muñoz Marín, son of Luis Muñoz Rivera, helped to form the Liberal Party, which demanded immediate independence.[54]

Meanwhile, U.S. corporations quickly gained control of the island's sugar industry and expanded it, concentrating land ownership in fewer hands. During this period, world coffee prices fell as Brazil and other countries expanded production, and wages on Puerto Rico's coffee plantations sank to near-starvation levels. By the

CHRONOLOGY

Before 1900 *Four hundred years of Spanish colonial rule ends.*

1493 Christopher Columbus claims for Spain the island of Borinquén, later renamed Puerto Rico.

1507 Spanish nobleman Juan Ponce de León establishes the first European settlements on the island.

1897 Spain grants Spanish citizenship to Puerto Ricans and allows them to elect a parliament.

1898 U.S. declares war on Spain (April); in December, Spain cedes Puerto Rico to the United States in the Treaty of Paris.

1900-1952 *Puerto Ricans get limited U.S. citizenship rights.*

1900 Foraker Act establishes colonial rule in Puerto Rico under which the president appoints the governor and other officials while Puerto Ricans elect the lower legislative chamber.

1917 Jones-Shafroth Act establishes an elected bicameral legislature and grants U.S. citizenship to Puerto Ricans, but they cannot vote for president and have only a nonvoting representative in Congress.

1938 Luis Muñoz Marín founds the Popular Democratic Party (PPD), which later supports commonwealth status.

1942 Puerto Rican legislature begins Operation Bootstrap by passing the Industrial Incentives Act, which exempts factories producing goods never before made in Puerto Rico from local taxes.

1946 Independence Party is founded.

1947 Congress gives Puerto Ricans the right to elect the island's governor.

1950 Two Puerto Rican nationalists who favor independence for the island attempt to assassinate President Harry S. Truman in Washington.

1952 Puerto Rico is declared a commonwealth, with its own constitution, although Washington still controls foreign policy and maritime laws.

1954 Four nationalists open fire from a spectators' gallery in the U.S. House, wounding five members.

1960s-Present *Puerto Ricans vote on the island's status.*

1967 In a nonbinding referendum, islanders vote to remain a commonwealth.

1968 New Progressive Party, which favors statehood, is founded (PNP).

1976 Congress approves Section 936 of the Internal Revenue Code, which allows U.S. corporations operating in Puerto Rico to avoid federal income taxes.

1996 Because of a drop in tax revenue, Congress repeals Section 936, which is phased out by 2006.

2004 Puerto Rico's population peaks at 3.8 million.

2006 The repeal of Section 936, a busted local real estate boom and the coming U.S. recession propel Puerto Rico into a prolonged downturn.

2012 A majority of voters choose statehood in a contested referendum.

2015 Puerto Rican emigration to the United States, propelled by a local recession, accelerates amid a worsening governmental debt crisis.

2016 Congress creates a federal oversight board for Puerto Rico's finances and allows Puerto Rico to declare a form of bankruptcy. . . . Emigration and a low birth rate reduce the population to 3.4 million.

2017 Puerto Rico seeks bankruptcy protection (May). . . . Puerto Ricans overwhelmingly choose statehood in a referendum boycotted by supporters of independence and commonwealth status (June). . . . Hurricanes Irma and Maria devastate the island (September), creating an estimated $100 billion in damage and leading more than 100,000 Puerto Ricans to leave for the United States by year's end.

2018 Puerto Rico submits a revised fiscal plan. . . . Thousands of Puerto Ricans still lack electricity.

Puerto Rico Seeks
Exemption From Shipping Law

Jones Act is "strangling" island's economy, critic says.

An arcane shipping law passed in 1920 could become a victim of Hurricane Maria, if Puerto Rico supporters get their way.

The devastating storm, they say, has dramatized the importance of exempting the island from the Merchant Marine Act. Known as the Jones Act after its sponsor, the law allows only U.S.-flagged ships, constructed in the United States and owned and crewed by U.S. citizens, to carry goods between U.S. ports, including Puerto Rico.[1]

As Puerto Ricans struggled to purchase food, fuel and other critical supplies immediately after the hurricane, some members of Congress urged the Department of Homeland Security to grant Puerto Rico a temporary waiver from the law, as it did for Texas and Florida after hurricanes in August and September, in a bid to boost the recovery effort. A week after Maria hit, the Trump administration granted a 10-day waiver, which it declined to renew.

"We believe that extending the waiver is unnecessary to support the humanitarian relief efforts on the island," said David Lapan, a Homeland Security Department spokesman. "There is an ample supply of Jones Act-qualified vessels to ensure that cargo is able to reach Puerto Rico."[2]

But the law's critics say Puerto Rico should be permanently exempted from the Jones Act because it impedes the flow of goods to the island and hurts its economy. By restricting competition with lower-cost foreign carriers, they say, the act unfairly raises the cost of shipped goods in Puerto Rico, Hawaii and Alaska, which are heavily dependent on oceangoing vessels for imports. The law's defenders say it protects the domestic shipping industry and is essential for national defense.

The Jones Act is "strangling" Puerto Rico's economy, said Nelson A. Denis, a former New York state Assembly member and the author of *War Against All Puerto Ricans: Revolution and Terror in America's Colony.* "Thanks to the law, the price of goods from the United States mainland is at least double that in neighboring islands."[3]

Not true, said the American Maritime Partnership, a Washington-based organization representing vessel owners, shipbuilders and others in the shipping industry. "The supposed 'cost' of Jones Act shipping in Puerto Rico has been wildly exaggerated."[4]

The U.S. Government Accountability Office (GAO), which provides auditing and investigative services for Congress, has conducted the most recent study of the Jones Act's impact on Puerto Rico. However, the 2013 report failed to draw firm conclusions, and both sides have quoted from it to support their position.

"The Act may result in higher freight rates—particularly for certain goods—than would be the case if service by foreign carriers were allowed," the GAO said. At the same time, "the law has helped to ensure reliable, regular service between the United States and Puerto Rico—service that is important to the Puerto Rican economy." That "on-time" and predictable service allows many of the island's importers to deliver goods directly to store shelves and to minimize high warehouse and inventory costs, the GAO said.[5]

Ultimately, the law's net effect on the prices Puerto Ricans pay for goods shipped from the mainland may be

---

time of the 1930s worldwide depression, Puerto Rico was a land "foundering in despair," said historian Arturo Morales Carrión.[55]

Economic Development

The 1930s saw strikes by farmworkers, factory workers and bus drivers. Per capita income was unchanged from the turn of the century, and industrialization was almost non-existent. Literacy, school attendance and life expectancy had improved but remained shockingly low compared to the mainland.[56] The decade's social unrest laid the groundwork for the island's political and economic transformation.

As a result of struggles within the Liberal Party, Muñoz Marín and his followers in 1938 founded the Popular Democratic Party (PPD), which drew support

impossible to determine. "So many factors influence freight rates and product prices that the independent effect and associated economic costs of the Jones Act cannot be determined," the GAO concluded.[6]

Even if the Jones Act distorts the flow of free trade, other concerns make it worth keeping, said Loren Thompson, chief operating officer of the Lexington Institute, a conservative think tank in Arlington, Va., which is funded primarily by defense contractors. "The law is more important to national security than the critics seem to realize," said Thompson.[7]

Protecting the U.S. shipping industry provides the Navy with a reserve fleet and crew in time of war, he said. In addition, without the Jones Act, foreign ships and mariners would take over critical transport of iron ore in the Great Lakes needed for steel or of oil along the nation's coastlines, "raising major security concerns," Thompson said.[8]

But the Heritage Foundation, a conservative think tank in Washington, said these arguments have not "held up to actual maritime practices." For example, during the Persian Gulf conflict of 1990-91, foreign-flagged vessels carried one-fifth of military supplies, and the U.S. military routinely leases foreign-built vessels to execute missions, it said. The Heritage Foundation has called for the law's repeal.[9]

In its report, the GAO said Congress will have to make complex policy trade-offs when deciding the Jones Act's fate and that it will be doing so without precise information. The Federal Reserve Bank of New York, in a 2012 examination of Puerto Rico's troubled economy, suggested exempting the island from the law for five years to assess the costs and benefits of a permanent exemption.[10]

But several members of Congress reject a trial period. In late September, Republican Sens. John McCain of Arizona and Mike Lee of Utah introduced legislation, which was reported out of committee and placed on the Senate calendar in October, to permanently exempt Puerto Rico from the law.[11] McCain had introduced a bill in 2010, 2015 and July 2017 calling for the repeal of the law entirely.

"For years, I have fought to fully repeal the Jones Act, which has long outlived its purpose to the benefit of special interests," said McCain. "It's time for Congress to take action, end this injustice, and help our fellow citizens in this time of need."[12]

— Barbara Mantel

[1] Jones Act, Transportation Institute, https://tinyurl.com/y8yz3aq5.

[2] "DHS Says Extension of Puerto Rico Jones Act Waiver Not Needed," Reuters, Oct. 5, 2017, https://tinyurl.com/ybvmt3w7.

[3] "The Jones Act: The Law Strangling Puerto Rico," *The New York Times*, Sept. 25, 2017, https://tinyurl.com/ybdro2s6.

[4] "Fact Sheet: Domestic Maritime Industry Is Dedicated to Puerto Rico," American Maritime Partnership, https://tinyurl.com/yabzwcvl.

[5] "Puerto Rico: Characteristics of the Island's Maritime Trade and Potential Effects of Modifying the Jones Act," U.S. Government Accountability Office, March 2013, pp. 10, 28-29, https://tinyurl.com/ycz7tjnr.

[6] *Ibid.*, p. 29.

[7] Loren Thompson, "Why Repealing The Jones Act Could Be A Disaster For The U.S." *Forbes*, Oct. 17, 2017, https://tinyurl.com/yb93vgr6.

[8] *Ibid.*

[9] Brian Slattery, Bryan Riley and Nicolas D. Loris, "Sink the Jones Act: Restoring America's Competitive Advantage in Maritime-Related Industries," Heritage Foundation, May 22, 2014, p. 2, https://tinyurl.com/y7crmngs.

[10] "Puerto Rico: Characteristics of the Island's Maritime Trade and Potential Effects of Modifying the Jones Act," *op. cit.*; "Report on the Competitiveness of Puerto Rico's Economy," Federal Reserve Bank of New York, June 29, 2012, p. iv, https://tinyurl.com/yddtw8x8.

[11] "S.1894," Congress.Gov, 2017, https://tinyurl.com/ybp87pde.

[12] "McCain & Lee Introduce Legislation to Permanently Exempt Puerto Rico From the Jones Act," press release, Office of Sen. John McCain, Sept. 28, 2017, https://tinyurl.com/yahjuftf.

from laborers, the lower- and middle-classes and intellectuals. The party put aside the status debate to concentrate on social and economic reform. It gained control of the legislature in 1940 and swept elections for the next 28 years.[57]

In 1941, Muñoz Marín was elected Senate president, and the PPD-controlled legislature "soon produced a series of far-reaching measures," over the opposition of the sugar industry and business groups, wrote Puerto Rico scholars César J. Ayala and Rafael Bernabe. With the support of Rexford Tugwell, Puerto Rico's governor from 1941 to 1946, the legislature instituted land reform and created a planning board, a government bank and an industrial development company.[58]

The following year, with passage of the Industrial Incentives Act, it began Operation Bootstrap, a program

To Fix Grid, Experts Call for Changes to U.S. Law

Massive overhaul of island's "antiquated" electric system proposed.

An army of 4,000-plus workers from Puerto Rico and the mainland is laboring to repair the island's devastated electric grid, which suffered back-to-back blows in September when two hurricanes struck within two weeks of each other.[1]

The federal government is bearing much of the recovery costs, under parameters set by the Stafford Disaster Relief and Emergency Assistance Act of 1988. But Puerto Rico's governor, several members of Congress and the Federal Emergency Management Agency (FEMA), which leads federal disaster relief efforts, say the law needs to be changed if Puerto Rico is to avoid another hurricane-driven catastrophe.

"The Stafford Act allows me to rebuild communities to a pre-disaster standard," said FEMA Administrator Brock Long at a congressional hearing in late November. But that does not make much sense for Puerto Rico because the island's electric grid before the storms hit was "antiquated," with "massive amounts of deferred maintenance," said Long.[2] The median age of the island's state-owned power plants is more than 40 years old, only 15 percent of its transmission lines were built to withstand Category 4 hurricanes, and the grid is overly reliant on expensive imported fuel oil and diesel, leading to electric bills for residents and businesses that are more than double the U.S. average.[3]

Long told Congress that FEMA needs the additional authority to make Puerto Rico's infrastructure modern and resilient.[4]

Congress should revise the Stafford Act to give Long the authority he wants, says U.S. Rep. Elizabeth Esty, D-Conn., who sits on the Transportation and Infrastructure Committee, and not just because of Puerto Rico. "With the aging infrastructure that we have in so many parts of America, it is essential we build and rebuild [after disasters] in ways that are more durable, that are cybersecure, that are using better technologies, better materials and the like," she says.

In the meantime, a group of energy experts has come up with an ambitious plan to overhaul Puerto Rico's electric grid. The Puerto Rico Energy Resiliency Working Group, a collaboration among several New York-based electric utilities, two national laboratories, the U.S. Department of Energy and the Puerto Rico Electric Power Authority, among others, issued its report in December.

"The magnitude of devastation to the Puerto Rico electric power system presents an unprecedented opportunity to rebuild and *transform* the system to one that is hardened, smarter, more efficient, cleaner, and less dependent on fossil fuel imports," the group wrote.[5]

Its recommendations aim to improve the ability of the electric grid to withstand storms and to increase the grid's

of export-led industrialization. The law exempted from local taxes factories producing goods never made before in Puerto Rico, while the government supplied financial support for factory construction and worker training.

U.S. manufacturers, including textile, clothing and footwear producers, flocked to the island, lured by the tax incentives, low wages, a dollar-based currency and tariff-free access to the U.S. market. Investment tripled between 1950 and 1960 and then quadrupled over the next decade. Economic growth, meanwhile, averaged more

than 4 percent annually between 1955 and 1975, and wages increased.

But Operation Bootstrap helped to accelerate the decline of Puerto Rico's agricultural sector and the migration of laborers to urban areas and the United States. Between 1950 and 1970, net migration to the United States totaled 605,550 people, about one-quarter of the island's 1950 population.[59]

Tugwell also recommended that Puerto Ricans be allowed to elect their governor. Congress complied in 1947. Muñoz Marín was elected the following year.

resiliency so it can continue operating even after a storm causes widespread damage. The recommendations include:[6]

- Upgrading as many as 350 of 2,478 miles of overhead transmission lines to withstand stronger winds;

- Placing some transmission lines underground;

- Designing the transmission system so it can take energy from large solar operations and other renewable power sources and from smaller microgrids—grids that can operate autonomously;

- Concentrating solar arrays and microgrids at critical sites, including hospitals, police departments, fire stations and wastewater and water treatment plants;

- Relocating substations to higher ground and installing protective barriers;

- Instituting modern grid controls and automated distribution systems.

The proposal's estimated price tag is $17.6 billion, and the rebuilding process could take up to 10 years, the group said.[7] Before the two September hurricanes struck, the Puerto Rico Electric Power Authority estimated it needed more than $4 billion to upgrade its power plants and reduce reliance on imported oil.[8] Even if Congress modifies the Stafford Act to allow these improvements, it is unclear whether it will approve such a high level of funding.

But spending additional money now can save money later, says Esty. "If you look at Hurricane Irma [last September], you can see how Florida sustained much less damage than it might have, in part because of the lessons of the 1980s and '90s and powerful storms then," she says.

"Florida responded by revising its building codes and beefing up the requirements for infrastructure, construction, the electric grid and flood control."

Democrats in both the House, on Nov. 3, and the Senate, on Nov. 28, introduced bills to amend the Stafford Act to allow federal funds to be used for modernizing infrastructure after a natural disaster. In the meantime, Congress could issue a short-term waiver for Puerto Rico, says Esty.

"But I think we will certainly need a longer-term fix," she says.

— Barbara Mantel

[1] Frances Robles and Patricia Mazzei, "Parts of Puerto Rico Won't Have Power for 8 Months. What's the Holdup?" *The New York Times*, Dec. 23, 2017, https://tinyurl.com/ybfbwxq8.

[2] "FEMA Funding: Brock Long," C-Span, Nov. 30, 2017, https://tinyurl.com/ybjqojr9.

[3] Steven Mufson, "Hurricane Maria has dealt a heavy blow to Puerto Rico's bankrupt utility and fragile electric grid," *The Washington Post*, Sept. 20, 2017, https://tinyurl.com/ybzocfl2; "FEMA Funding: Brock Long," *ibid.*

[4] "FEMA Funding: Brock Long," *op. cit.*

[5] "Build Back Better: Reimagining and Strengthening the Power Grid of Puerto Rico," Puerto Rico Energy Resiliency Working Group, Dec. 11, 2017, p. 5, https://tinyurl.com/yalfm76m.

[6] Emma Foehringer Merchant, "Group of Energy Heavyweights Unveils Plan for Puerto Rico's Future Grid," Greentech Media, Dec. 12, 2017, https://tinyurl.com/y9lra42u.

[7] "Build Back Better: Reimagining and Strengthening the Power Grid of Puerto Rico," *op. cit.*, pp. 7, 41.

[8] Mufson, *op. cit.*

By this time, he had abandoned his insistence on independence and, in 1950, proposed that Puerto Ricans draft a constitution to establish greater self-governance.[60] The U.S. Congress passed a law to set the process in motion.

Some favoring statehood objected, but the pro-independence Nationalist Party presented the most vigorous opposition. Some nationalists turned to violence that claimed 28 lives in Puerto Rico; two nationalists attempted to assassinate President Harry S. Truman in Washington in 1950; and four nationalists opened fire

from a spectators' gallery in the U.S. House, wounding five members, in 1954.[61]

Nevertheless, Puerto Ricans elected members to a constitutional convention, which spent five months writing a constitution. After it was approved by Puerto Ricans, Congress and Truman in 1952, Puerto Rico officially became a U.S. commonwealth.

"The Commonwealth formula did not substantially alter the Island's legal, political, and economic dependence on the United States," wrote Duany. But commonwealth supporters argued that Puerto Ricans had exercised their right to self-determination and now had their own constitution and that future negotiations with the United States could lead to greater autonomy.[62]

Status Debate

The status debate has remained one of the defining issues of island politics, with Puerto Ricans jostling over statehood versus independence and the status quo. But since the 1960s, support for independence has waned for two reasons, analysts say: Family ties to the Puerto Rican population on the mainland and islanders' dependence on federal transfer payments, such as government health insurance and food stamps (currently known as the Supplemental Nutrition Assistance Program), have both grown.

The statehood party, now called the New Progressive Party (PNP), and the PPD have been the two main political parties in Puerto Rico for decades. Since 1968, the PNP has won seven of the 13 gubernatorial elections. It gained in popularity as the transition to an urban, industrialized economy undercut the PPD's agrarian base and the PPD's leadership failed to strengthen the commonwealth's autonomy.[63]

Puerto Rico held five referendums on its status between 1967 and 2017. Given a choice between a commonwealth, statehood or some form of independence, the majority of Puerto Ricans who voted in the first three referendums chose commonwealth. In 2012, the referendum consisted of two questions. In the first, 54 percent of voters said they wanted a status change, and in the second 61 percent chose statehood, but nearly half a million voters left the second question blank.

Last June, 97 percent favored statehood, but the opposition parties had called for a boycott of the referendum, and less than a quarter of registered voters turned out. In any case, the referendums are nonbinding and Congress has not acted.[64]

Meanwhile, Operation Bootstrap has run out of steam, according to Duany.[65]

In its first decade, Operation Bootstrap attracted labor-intensive, light manufacturing to the island, followed in the 1960s and early 1970s by capital-intensive industries, such as oil refining and petrochemicals, which collapsed after the 1973 international oil crisis.

The third and current phase was initiated in 1976 when Congress approved Section 936 of the Internal Revenue Code, allowing U.S. corporations operating in Puerto Rico to avoid federal income taxes. Pharmaceutical and electronics companies opened manufacturing plants on the island, quadrupling their profit margins. However, in 1996, Congress repealed Section 936 because of a drop in federal tax revenues and the disappointing number of Puerto Rican jobs it created in these technology-intensive sectors. Congress phased out the tax break by 2006.[66]

Some factories shut down, but dozens of U.S. companies remained, in part because they continued to enjoy federal tax benefits as long as they kept their profits in Puerto Rico. Manufacturing currently makes up nearly half of the island's economy. Nevertheless, the impact of the 2006 tax break phase-out, coupled with the 2007-09 U.S. recession and the bursting of a local residential real estate bubble, helped to precipitate the worst economic crisis in Puerto Rico since the Great Depression. The island's economy has yet to recover.

Tourism has been the one bright spot for Puerto Rico, the only industry to escape the recession, accounting for 7.1 percent of the economy, according to the government's tourism agency.[67] At least, that was the case before Hurricane Maria struck. While cruise ships have begun to return to the island and many hotels have reopened, most rooms in the December high season were occupied by relief workers.

CURRENT SITUATION
House Passes Bill

In Puerto Rico, all eyes are on Congress as it debates how to help the struggling island.

The U.S. House of Representatives in late December passed an $81 billion emergency disaster aid bill to help communities in Texas, Florida, Puerto Rico and the U.S. Virgin Islands recover from a brutal hurricane season and in California to rebuild after wildfires. That amount is nearly double the $44 billion in emergency disaster relief that the White House proposed in November, which lawmakers from both sides of the aisle called grossly inadequate.

It is unclear how much of the $81 billion would end up in Puerto Rico because the bill does not designate where the money would go. Instead, the legislation would distribute funds through grants to local communities that successfully apply.

The legislation would certainly not give Puerto Rico the amount it has said it needs. In November, Gov. Rosselló asked Congress to pass a $94.4 billion disaster relief package for Puerto Rico alone. He requested $46 billion to rebuild nearly 500,000 homes, $30 billion to repair infrastructure and $17.9 billion for long-term recovery programs to make Puerto Rico's electric grid more resilient.[68]

Nevertheless, Jenniffer González, Puerto Rico's resident commissioner in the House, supports the bill and expects Congress will provide additional financial help.

"This is not the last allocation of funds that will benefit the island, as Congress will work on a fourth measure of supplemental aid for Puerto Rico in 2018," said González.[69]

If the House bill becomes law, Congress would have approved a record $130 billion in emergency disaster funding since September to replenish the accounts of FEMA and other government agencies, far more than was spent on recovery efforts after Hurricanes Katrina in 2005 and Sandy in 2012.[70]

Dozens of House Democrats supported the bill, including many from affected states, allowing it to pass 251-169. But others, such as Rep. Nita Lowey of New York, the ranking Democrat on the powerful House Appropriations Committee, called it a waste of time. Lowey accused Republican leaders of creating a "poor product that will not be enacted into law."[71]

Democrats' main complaint is that the bill does nothing to address a shortfall in dollars for Medicaid—the health insurance program for low-income individuals—in Puerto Rico. The island, whose fragile health care system took a big hit from the September hurricanes, is subject to an annual cap in federal Medicaid funding. All five U.S. territories—Puerto Rico, the U.S. Virgin Islands, Guam, American Samoa and the Commonwealth of the Northern Mariana Islands—have been subject to such a cap since they were first included in the nation's social insurance programs in 1950.[72]

"Congress must lift the Medicaid cap . . . and ensure all evacuees receive the care they need," said Rep. Frank Pallone Jr. of New Jersey, the top Democrat on the Energy and Commerce Committee.[73]

But Rep. Tom Cole, R-Okla., a top House appropriator, said the disaster funding is meant for emergency aid only and that addressing the Medicaid cap could come later.[74]

Refrigerated trailers in San Juan serve as backup morgues, installed by the Federal Emergency Management Agency (FEMA). The Puerto Rican government said 64 people died as a result of Hurricane Maria, but independent analyses put the toll at more than 1,000.

The House bill faces an uncertain future in the Senate. Minority Leader Chuck Schumer, D-N.Y., has voiced reservations similar to those of House Democrats about Medicaid.

Senate Democrats Act

Meanwhile, a group of liberal senators in November introduced a more comprehensive measure to address the needs of Puerto Rico and the U.S. Virgin Islands.

U.S. Sen. Bernie Sanders, I-Vt., and six Democrats cosponsored the Puerto Rico and Virgin Islands Equitable Rebuild Act. The $146 billion bill would address a wide range of concerns raised by the Puerto Rican government and its supporters in Congress. Among other things, the bill would:

• Ensure the electric grids are rebuilt so they can withstand hurricanes and other storms and use more renewable sources of energy;

• Make Puerto Rico and the Virgin Islands eligible for the same Medicare and Medicaid benefits as states;

• Appropriate funds to rebuild and improve schools as well as improve veterans' services;

• Make significant investments in infrastructure to spur economic growth;

• Provide grants to clean up environmental contamination from the hurricanes, prior pollution and past military bombing exercises on the Puerto Rican island of Vieques.

Should Puerto Rico become a state?

YES
Andrés L. Córdova
Professor of Law, Inter American University of Puerto Rico

Written for *CQ Researcher*, January 2018

Whether Puerto Rico should become a state raises questions that intertwine matters of history with the rights of American citizens to organize as a political entity with voting representation in Congress, on equal footing with American citizens in the 50 other states. It is, fundamentally, an issue of democracy and political equality.

Puerto Rico became an American territory by virtue of the Treaty of Paris of 1898 between the United States and Spain after the Spanish-American War. Between 1901 and 1922, the Supreme Court decided the well-known "insular cases," which declared that Puerto Rico was an unincorporated territory under Article IV, Section 3 of the U.S. Constitution, and to which not all constitutional rights apply.

Although Congress granted American citizenship to Puerto Ricans in 1917, the Supreme Court reiterated in 1922 that the island remained an unincorporated territory, meaning Puerto Rico was not entitled to the full protection of the guarantees contained in the 14th Amendment.

This decision finds no textual support under the Constitution. In fact, from the Northwest Ordinance of 1787 to 1901, all U.S. territories were eventually incorporated as states. A plain reading of the Constitution brings into question the historical context of such a racially and ethnically charged distinction made at the turn of the 20th century.

In the summer of 2016, the Supreme Court handed down two opinions that reaffirmed Puerto Rico's territorial status: *Commonwealth of Puerto Rico v. Sanchez Valle* and *Commonwealth of Puerto Rico v. Franklin California Tax-Free Trust.*

The principal opposition party to statehood, the territorial Popular Democratic Party (PPD), has traditionally claimed that in 1952 Puerto Rico achieved some sort of sovereignty independent from Congress when the latter authorized the Constitution of the Commonwealth of Puerto Rico and local self-government. The recent Supreme Court decisions, 2016 congressional legislation creating a Financial Oversight Board to attend to Puerto Rico's fiscal and economic crisis, and the island government's filing for bankruptcy-like protection have proven this claim to be a dangerous illusion. The devastation caused by Hurricane Maria in September highlights our lack of effective political representation in Congress.

Puerto Rico's political alternatives are clear: statehood, continued territorial status or independence, of which statehood commands a clear majority of the electorate. Congress needs to act on the democratic will of its citizens.

NO
Sen. José Nadal Power
Popular Democratic Party (PPD), Senate of Puerto Rico

Written for *CQ Researcher*, January 2018

The admission of Puerto Rico as the 51st state would collapse the island's finances.

As a commonwealth, Puerto Rico governs its internal revenues, an authority that U.S. states do not have. This allows the commonwealth's government to implement its own fiscal policy and economic development strategies. As a result, island-based individuals and corporations do not pay federal income taxes on Puerto Rico-sourced income. Taxes that under statehood would be paid to the federal government are currently paid by individuals and corporations to the commonwealth.

In March 2014, the Government Accountability Office (GAO) released a report stating that under statehood, "Puerto Rico residents would be subject to federal tax on all their income." The report confirms that the two largest sources of revenue for the Puerto Rico government—individual and corporate income taxes—would be substantially affected by statehood.

The GAO further says that if Puerto Rico had been a state in 2010, individuals would have paid from $2.2 billion to $2.3 billion in federal income taxes. In addition, "if Puerto Rico had been a state in 2009, estimated corporate income tax revenue from businesses that filed a Puerto Rico tax return for that year (or their parent corporation in the United States) would have ranged from $5.0 to $9.3 billion."

This reality creates an unsolvable dilemma. The payment of individual and corporate taxes to the federal government on top of the commonwealth's tax rates would be unbearable to taxpayers. To solve that problem, the commonwealth's taxes would have to be drastically reduced, depriving the Puerto Rico government of its main sources of income for its $9 billion annual budget.

Moreover, the report anticipates many corporations leaving Puerto Rico for lower-tax jurisdictions. It is inconceivable that Puerto Rico, with its current fiscal and economic challenges, could afford the costs that come with statehood. When admitting Hawaii to the union, Congress took into consideration the fact that "the proposed new State ha[d] sufficient population and resources to support State government and at the same time carry its share of the cost of the Federal Government."

The same cannot be said about Puerto Rico. The statehood debate is a distraction from urgent discussion of new economic development measures.

Puerto Rico needs to focus on economic growth.

"It is unconscionable that in the wealthiest nation in the world we have allowed our fellow citizens to suffer for so long," Sanders said. "The full resources of the United States must be brought to bear on this crisis, for as long as is necessary."[75]

But close followers of Puerto Rico's finances said the legislation's chance of passage is slim.

"This goes beyond normal Federal Emergency Management Agency funding and begs the question if other areas suffering from natural disasters should also receive enhanced funding," said Howard Cure, managing director of municipal bond research at Evercore Wealth Management, an investment advisory firm in New York. "Since there are no Republican sponsors on the bill, I don't think there is strong chance of passage."[76]

Immigrants in Florida

Just weeks after Hurricane Maria struck Puerto Rico, Republican Gov. Rick Scott declared a state of emergency in Florida's 67 counties. Scott was anticipating a wave of Puerto Rican evacuees, who would need housing assistance, crisis counseling, unemployment assistance and legal advice.[77] Florida is the destination of choice for many Puerto Ricans fleeing the island.

But the exact number who are making Florida their home is difficult to determine. Scott and other Florida politicians have taken to quoting numbers compiled by the Florida Division of Emergency Management from airline statistics. More than 302,000 people flew from Puerto Rico to Orlando, Miami and Tampa between Oct. 3 and Jan. 4.[78]

But researchers say the airlines' figures are not a good proxy for migration from Puerto Rico to Florida because it's unclear how long arrivals will remain and the statistics include other travelers, such as aid workers, journalists and contractors.

Rich Doty, a demographer at University of Florida's Bureau of Economic and Business Research, and university colleagues estimate that, as of early January, about 50,000 Puerto Ricans had moved to Florida since Hurricane Maria, based on school enrollment and requests for state aid.[79]

Whatever the final migration number, the state is scrambling to find affordable housing and to make room in elementary and secondary schools for student arrivals, as well as help evacuees find jobs. It is offering in-state college tuition for Puerto Rican transfer students.

In late December, U.S. Rep. Darren Soto, D-Fla., formed a regional task force to tackle the challenges faced by Puerto Ricans new to Central Florida, where most have congregated. Housing is the most critical issue, Florida officials said. Orlando, for instance, has the fourth-worst shortage of affordable rental housing out of the country's 50 largest metropolitan areas, according to a 2017 study.[80]

Some motel owners are interested in converting their units into affordable apartments, but officials said long-term solutions will take time.

"Our ability to provide affordable housing is something that is going to happen over the next two to five years, not over the next two to five months," said state Rep. Rene Plasencia, a Republican. "So we need to look at options to help people now, and those options may not be in this particular area." Plasencia suggested that central Florida counties direct evacuees to other parts of the state where jobs and housing are more plentiful.[81]

Many of the arrivals have children who are registering for school. More than 10,000 children from Puerto Rico have enrolled in Florida schools since Hurricane Maria, more than double the largest number in any of the previous 15 years, according to the Center for Puerto Rican Studies.[82]

"A lot of schools are not used to having English-language learners. Their principals are asking, 'What do we do?'" said Ingrid Carias, director of English for Speakers of Other Languages (ESOL) and World Languages in Duval County, Fla. As a result, the county is hiring Spanish-speaking paraprofessionals to help these students with language arts and to assist classroom teachers with instruction in math, science and other core subjects.

"Paraprofessionals are able to come to a class to help these students feel validated," Carias said.[83]

But the state was already facing a shortage of such paraprofessionals as well as teachers in math and science before the disaster in Puerto Rico. The arrival of teachers from Puerto Rico is helping to alleviate that shortage.

Meanwhile, at the request of Puerto Rico Gov. Rosselló, FEMA has extended its Transitional Shelter

Assistance Program, which pays for displaced families to live in hotels temporarily in Puerto Rico and on the mainland, beyond its Jan. 13 expiration date through March 20.[84]

OUTLOOK

Future Statehood?

Fuentes of the Puerto Rico Statehood Council says he is hopeful that Congress will pass legislation within the next several years to put Puerto Rico on the path to statehood. The bill could establish conditions the island would have to meet to become the 51st state, such as a certain level of English proficiency among islanders and economic stability, he says.

The American Enterprise Institute's Lachman is doubtful statehood is coming. "So long as you've got a Republican-controlled Congress, they're not going to want Puerto Rico to have statehood because they don't see it as part of their constituency."

But Conda of Navigators Global says, "The notion that [the island] would automatically be a blue state isn't backed up by the facts. It would be a purple state," with both political parties enjoying strong support.

Neither party wants Puerto Rico as a state, says the University at Albany's Cabán. "In the past 120 years, the United States has never made a move towards statehood, so why would it do so now, when the economic conditions in Puerto Rico are so poor?" he asks.

Puerto Rico's economy could temporarily rebound next year as reconstruction efforts provide a stimulus that outweighs the ongoing disruption from Hurricane Maria, says Setser of the Council on Foreign Relations. But Congress must start treating Puerto Rico the same as states in terms of Medicaid and other federal programs to slow the migration of Puerto Ricans to the mainland, he says.

"If the population continues to decline and the declining population leads to lower [government] revenues and that leads to a need for future austerity, you're going to return to a quite negative [economy]," says Setser.

Miller of the Greater Washington Partnership says Puerto Rico's economic prospects are highly dependent on Congress' willingness to allocate money to rebuild and modernize the island's electric grid and transportation and health care systems.

But time is of the essence, he says. "If the steps are taken in the next 12 months, despite all of the challenges that Puerto Rico has faced both before and since the hurricane, there is real potential for a growing economy."

Scribner of Oxfam America agrees that infrastructure investment is key to Puerto Rico's economic future. "If we don't do that, then people will continue to leave Puerto Rico," she says.

Still, the future of manufacturing, currently the biggest slice of the island's economy, is uncertain, says Fabian of Municipal Market Analytics. Manufacturers are going to be thinking long and hard about where—and even whether—to locate on the island "because this is probably not going to be the last storm hitting Puerto Rico," he says.

NOTES

1. Edwin Meléndez, Jennifer Hinojosa and Nashia Roman, "Post-Hurricane Maria Exodus from Puerto Rico and School Enrollment in Florida," Center for Puerto Rican Studies, December 2017, p. 1, https://tinyurl.com/y9n3upfu; Edwin Meléndez and Jennifer Hinojosa, "Estimates of Post-Hurricane Maria Exodus from Puerto Rico," Center for Puerto Rican Studies, October 2017, p. 2, https://tinyurl.com/yaqoxtgu.

2. Ricardo Rosselló, "Build Back Better: Puerto Rico," November 2017, p. 2, https://tinyurl.com/y95ok7oe.

3. Alexis R. Santos-Lozada, "Why Puerto Rico's death toll from Hurricane Maria is so much higher than officials thought," *The Conversation*, Jan. 3, 2018, https://tinyurl.com/yb3oq66r.

4. "El 97% de las escuelas han reabierto tras el paso de María," Puerto Rico Department of Education, https://tinyurl.com/ydgc9ecr; StatusPR, https://tinyurl.com/yc7tzkju; and Christopher Flavelle, "Puerto Rico Grid Fix Won't Meet Governor's Plan, Corps Says," Bloomberg News, Dec. 13, 2017, https://tinyurl.com/y6wg3g4q.

5. Rafael Bernal, "Puerto Rico announces shadow congressional delegation," *The Hill*, Jan. 10, 2018, https://tinyurl.com/y98qzaww.

6. "Economic Activity Index ('GDB-EAI')," Government Development Bank for Puerto Rico,

p. 4, July 2017, https://tinyurl.com/y9sd4zbk; "Economy at a Glance: Puerto Rico," Bureau of Labor Statistics, https://tinyurl.com/yb32w7b5; and "Median Household Income in the Past 12 Months (In 2016 Inflation-adjusted Dollars)," U.S. Census Bureau, https://tinyurl.com/yd2thqtj.

7. Heather Long, "Puerto Rico's crisis: How did it get so bad?" CNN Money, May 12, 2016, https://tinyurl.com/yd6ubj4s.

8. Michael Nevradakis, "Puerto Rico's Recovery Efforts Stymied by Colonial Status," MintPress News, Nov. 11, 2017, https://tinyurl.com/y9v9rdgu.

9. Lee Fang, "After Hurricane Maria, Key Republican Compares Puerto Rico to 'The Alcoholic Who Hits Rock Bottom,'" *The Intercept*, Nov. 14, 2017, https://tinyurl.com/y7r44rmc.

10. Brad W. Setser, "Puerto Rico Before Maria," Council on Foreign Relations, Oct. 2, 2017, https://tinyurl.com/yagrmn8t.

11. Jill Disis, "Puerto Rico could be a $95 billion storm for Puerto Rico," CNN, Sept. 28, 2017, https://tinyurl.com/yb5r9nhj.

12. Solomon Hsiang and Trevor Houser, "Don't Let Puerto Rico Fall Into an Economic Abyss," *The New York Times*, Sept. 29, 2017, https://tinyurl.com/y7sphhgy.

13. Alice Thomas, "Keeping Faith with Our Fellow Americans: Meeting the Urgent Needs of Hurricane Maria Survivors in Puerto Rico," Refugees International, December 2017, p. 1, https://tinyurl.com/y7av3578.

14. "La población de Puerto Rico redondea a 3.3 millones en el 2017," Estadísticas.PR, Dec. 20, 1017, https://tinyurl.com/ycpf4u89.

15. Meléndez and Hinojosa, "Estimates of Post-Hurricane Maria Exodus from Puerto Rico," *op. cit.*

16. Phil Helsel and Saphora Smith, "Puerto Rico Crisis: San Juan Mayor Pleads for Federal Aid, Trump Hits Back," NBC News, Sept. 30, 2017, https://tinyurl.com/y7jxmqw5.

17. Gabriel Stargardter and Dave Graham, "Trump lays blame on Puerto Ricans for slow hurricane response," Reuters, Sept. 30, 2017, https://tinyurl.com/y74dce8d.

18. Mike Savino, "Murphy returns from Puerto Rico saying 'island still in crisis,'" *The Record Journal*, Jan. 4, 2018, https://tinyurl.com/ybgnjam2.

19. Ricardo Rosselló, "Hurricane Recovery Efforts in Puerto Rico and the U.S. Virgin Islands," written statement, Senate Committee on Energy and Natural Resources, Nov. 14, 2017, pp. 3-4, https://tinyurl.com/y82wl92t.

20. "Hearings: Supplemental Oversight—FEMA," U.S. House Committee on Appropriations, Nov. 30, 2017, https://tinyurl.com/yd7v7j9h.

21. "Lawmaker wants audit of award for Hurricane Maria tarps," The Associated Press, Dec. 1, 2017, https://tinyurl.com/y88jkm5l; U.S. Army Corps of Engineers, Twitter post, Jan. 8, 2017, https://tinyurl.com/y6wc4sot.

22. Pablo Venes, "93 Days Later, Puerto Rico Can't Get Supplies to Turn on the Power," *Daily Beast*, Dec. 22, 2017, https://tinyurl.com/yatguluv; Danica Coto, "More equipment, crews head to Puerto Rico for power boost," The Associated Press, Jan. 8, 2018, https://tinyurl.com/ya5798ez.

23. Kate Aronoff, "Puerto Rico Utility Workers Charge That Federal Government Is Hoarding Reconstruction Supplies," *The Intercept*, Jan. 16, 2017, https://tinyurl.com/yd8g5j37.

24. "Testimony of Ramon-Luis Nieves, Esq., former Senator and Chairman of the Committee on Energy, Senate of Puerto Rico," U.S. House Subcommittee on Energy, Committee on Energy and Commerce, Nov. 2, 2017, pp. 3-4, https://tinyurl.com/y6w5vmng.

25. Frances Robles, "The Lineman Got $63 an Hour. The Utility Was Billed $319 an Hour," *The New York Times*, Nov. 12, 2017, https://tinyurl.com/y7fyd3ck.

26. Andrew Scurria, "FBI Is Probing Puerto Rico Power Contract," *The Wall Street Journal*, Oct. 30, 2017, https://tinyurl.com/ybhefqwk.

27. "Fiscal Plan for Puerto Rico," Puerto Rico Fiscal Agency and Financial Advisory Authority,

March 13, 2017, p. 8, https://tinyurl.com/yahre-upc; Gregory Makoff and Brad W. Setser, "Puerto Rico Update: PROMESA, Population Trends, Risks to the Fiscal and Economic Plan—and Now Maria," Centre for International Governance Innovation, September 2017, pp. 3-4, https://tinyurl.com/ydhh5oz9.

28. Makoff and Setser, *ibid.*, p. 4.

29. "Letter to Oversight Board," March 27, 2017, https://tinyurl.com/kw8krgk.

30. "Puerto Rico fears economic downturn from new tax overhaul," The Associated Press, Dec. 21, 2017, https://tinyurl.com/ybw68ble.

31. Marc Caputo, Colin Wilhelm and Lorraine Woellert, "Rubio, Puerto Rico governor spar over tax reform," *Politico*, Dec. 19, 2017, https://tinyurl.com/yac4zzre.

32. Ed Pilkington, "Puerto Ricans vote in favour of being 51st US state, but doubts remain," *The Guardian*, June 11, 2017, https://tinyurl.com/y87od7aq.

33. Molly Hennessy-Fiske, "Can Puerto Rico's governor convince Trump his island should be a state?" *Los Angeles Times*, Oct. 3, 2017, https://tinyurl.com/y6v8skhp.

34. Darran Simon and Susannah Cullinane, "(Some) Puerto Ricans vote for US statehood," CNN, June 12, 2017, https://tinyurl.com/yaebudfa.

35. "Puerto Rico: Information on How Statehood Would Potentially Affect Selected Federal Programs and Revenue Sources," U.S. Government Accountability Office, March 2014, https://tinyurl.com/ybwfvbv4.

36. *Ibid.*

37. "Quick Facts: Puerto Rico," U.S. Census Bureau, https://tinyurl.com/ycqx9os4.

38. Jorge Duany, *Puerto Rico: What Everyone Needs to Know* (2017), pp. 9-11; "Taino Indian Culture," Welcome To Puerto Rico, https://tinyurl.com/yd53v9fr.

39. Fernando Picó, *History of Puerto Rico: A Panorama of Its People* (2006), pp. 34-36.

40. *Ibid.*, pp. 36-38.

41. Duany, *op. cit.*, p. 11.

42. *Ibid.*, pp. 11-12, 14, 17-18.

43. *Ibid.*, pp. 15, 17-18, 24-25, 27. Also see Kenneth Jost, "Puerto Rico's Status," *CQ Researcher*, Oct. 23, 1998, pp. 929-952.

44. Duany, *op. cit.*, p. 17.

45. José Trías Monge, *Puerto Rico: The Trials of the Oldest Colony in the World* (1997), pp. 10-12.

46. Duany, *op. cit.*, p. 40.

47. Monge, *op. cit.*, p. 14.

48. Jost, *op. cit.*

49. Duany, *op. cit.*, pp. 45-46.

50. See Barbara Mantel, "Managing Western Lands," *CQ Researcher*, April 22, 2016, p. 370.

51. Pedro Cabán, "Puerto Ricans as Contingent Citizens: Shifting Mandated Identities and Imperial Disjunctures," *Centro Journal*, Spring 2017, p. 250.

52. *Ibid.*, pp. 250-251; "Puerto Rico," History, Art & Archives: U.S. House of Representatives, https://tinyurl.com/ybr8hkd7.

53. Jost, *op. cit.*

54. Monge, *op. cit.*, pp. 77-78, 83.

55. Arturo Morales Carrión, *Puerto Rico: A Political and Cultural History* (1983), pp. 152-153; Duany, *op. cit.*, pp. 45, 165.

56. César J. Ayala and Rafael Bernabe, *Puerto Rico in The American Century: A History Since 1898* (2007), p. 138; Monge, *op. cit.*, p. 99.

57. *Ibid.*, Monge, pp. 100-101.

58. Ayala and Bernabe, *op. cit.*, pp. 144-145.

59. Jost, *op. cit.*; Duany, *op. cit.*, p. 69.

60. Ayala and Bernabe, *op. cit.*, p. 148.

61. Doug Stanglin, "Six decades ago, shots rained down on Congress," *USA Today*, Oct. 22, 2014, https://tinyurl.com/ybzq4adl; Jost, *op. cit.*

62. Duany, *op. cit.*, pp. 73, 74.

63. *Ibid.*, p. 79.

64. Vann R. Newkirk II, "Puerto Rico's Plebiscite to Nowhere," *The Atlantic*, June 13, 2017, https://tinyurl.com/yb3s5shb.

65. Duany, *op. cit.*, p. 98.

66. *Ibid.*, pp. 93, 97-98.

67. Dennis Costa, "Tourism Contribution to Puerto Rico GDP Grows to 7.1%," *Caribbean Business*, March 1, 2016, https://tinyurl.com/y7ul2pxc.

68. Rosselló, *op. cit.*, p. 3.

69. "U.S. Senate postpones disaster aid bill until January," *Caribbean Business*, Dec. 26, 2017, https://tinyurl.com/yb28c2u6.

70. Mike DeBonis, "House eyes $81 billion disaster funding package as shutdown deadline looms," *The Washington Post*, Dec. 19, 2017, https://tinyurl.com/yc9p8gyx.

71. Sarah Ferris, "Mammoth disaster aid package could languish for weeks," *Politico*, Dec. 21, 2017, https://tinyurl.com/yc6pre4f.

72. Vann R. Newkirk II, "The Historical Exclusion Behind the Puerto Rico Bankruptcy Crisis," *The Atlantic*, May 2, 2017, https://tinyurl.com/ycz5te8h.

73. Nathaniel Weixel, "Dem rips disaster package for failing to address Medicaid in Puerto Rico, Virgin Islands," *The Hill*, Dec. 19, 2017, https://tinyurl.com/yafqeo86.

74. *Ibid.*

75. "Sanders, Colleagues Unveil Legislation to Rebuild Puerto Rico and Virgin Islands," press release, Office of Sen. Bernie Sanders, Nov. 28, 2017, https://tinyurl.com/y9vqgpk8.

76. Robert Slavin, "Sanders' Puerto Rico bill dwarfs requests from Gov. Rosselló, Trump," *The Bond Buyer*, Nov. 29, 2017, https://tinyurl.com/ycfavadc.

77. "Gov. Scott Declares State of Emergency for Hurricane Maria to Support Puerto Rico," news release, Office of Gov. Rick Scott, Oct. 2, 2017, https://tinyurl.com/y843wb85.

78. Florida Division of Emergency Management, Twitter post, Jan. 4, 2018, https://tinyurl.com/y7egurgp.

79. Paul Brinkmann, "How many Puerto Ricans have moved to Florida? State's numbers questioned," *Orlando Sentinel*, Jan. 6, 2018, https://tinyurl.com/y7tzdcf9.

80. Jeff Weiner, "U.S. Rep. Darren Soto launches task force on Puerto Rican arrivals to Central Florida," *Orlando Sentinel*, Dec. 28, 2017, https://tinyurl.com/ycd3b5z9; Andrew Aurand *et al.*, "The Gap: A Shortage of Affordable Homes," National Low Income Housing Coalition, March 2017, p. 8, https://tinyurl.com/y9vrabvg.

81. Scott Powers, "Puerto Rico evacuees to Florida need immediate, long-term housing, task force concludes," *Florida Politics*, Dec. 28, 2017, https://tinyurl.com/y9ug3evw.

82. Meléndez, Hinojosa and Roman, *op. cit.*, p. 3.

83. Denise Smith Amos, "Duval gains 200 new students with language needs from Puerto Rico, other hurricane-hit areas," *Florida Times-Union*, Dec. 15, 2017, https://tinyurl.com/y78cxeka.

84. "Transitional Sheltering Assistance Request #1 For FEMA DR-4336-PR; FEMA DR-4339-PR," Federal Emergency Management Agency, Dec. 29, 2017, https://tinyurl.com/ycujnhx2.

BIBLIOGRAPHY
Selected Sources
Books

Ayala, César J., and Rafael Bernabe, *Puerto Rico in the American Century: A History Since 1898*, University of North Carolina Press, 2007.
Two scholars explore the island's economic, political, cultural and social past.

Duany, Jorge, *Puerto Rico: What Everyone Needs to Know*, Oxford University Press, 2017.
An anthropologist describes the milestones and important people in Puerto Rico's history.

Picó, Fernando, *History of Puerto Rico: A Panorama of Its People*, Markus Wiener Publishers, 2006.
A historian traces Puerto Rico's history from its geological formation to the 21st century.

Articles

Brinkmann, Paul, "How many Puerto Ricans have moved to Florida? State's numbers questioned,"

Orlando Sentinel, Jan. 6, 2018, https://tinyurl.com/y7tzdcf9.

State officials have quoted airline figures of more than 300,000 people flying from Puerto Rico from Florida since Maria, but demographers estimate that the number of migrants is much smaller.

Fang, Lee, "After Hurricane Maria, Key Republican Compares Puerto Rico to 'The Alcoholic Who Hits Rock Bottom,'" *The Intercept*, Nov. 14, 2017, https://tinyurl.com/y7r44rmc.

A member of the federal Financial Oversight and Management Board says Puerto Rico has to change its ways.

Ferris, Sarah, "Mammoth disaster aid package could languish for weeks," *Politico*, Dec. 21, 2017, https://tinyurl.com/yc6pre4f.

The House passed an $81 billion emergency disaster relief bill for several states and Puerto Rico, but Senate Democrats say the aid does not go far enough.

Foehringer Merchant, Emma, "Group of Energy Heavyweights Unveils Plan for Puerto Rico's Future Grid," Greentech Media, Dec. 12, 2017, https://tinyurl.com/y9lra42u.

A group of energy experts has introduced a plan to bring Puerto Rico's energy grid into the modern age.

Helsel, Phil, and Saphora Smith, "Puerto Rico Crisis: San Juan Mayor Pleads for Federal Aid, Trump Hits Back," NBC News, Sept. 30, 2017, https://tinyurl.com/y7jxmqw5.

San Juan's mayor accused the Trump administration of neglect after Hurricane Maria slammed the island in September.

Newkirk II, Vann R., "Puerto Rico's Plebiscite to Nowhere," *The Atlantic*, June 13, 2017, https://tinyurl.com/yb3s5shb.

Experts doubt that Puerto Ricans who backed statehood in a 2017 referendum will get their wish because of questions about the referendum's legality and other roadblocks.

Slavin, Robert, "Sanders' Puerto Rico bill dwarfs requests from Gov. Rosselló, Trump," *The Bond Buyer*, Nov. 29, 2017, https://tinyurl.com/ycfavadc.

A group of Senate Democrats seeks a $146 billion aid package for Puerto Rico and the U.S. Virgin Islands.

Stargardter, Gabriel, and Dave Graham, "Trump lays blame on Puerto Ricans for slow hurricane response," Reuters, Sept. 30, 2017, https://tinyurl.com/y74dce8d.

President Trump has accused Puerto Rican officials of poor leadership in the wake of Hurricane Maria.

Reports and Studies

"Build Back Better: Reimagining and Strengthening the Power Grid of Puerto Rico," Puerto Rico Energy Resiliency Working Group, Dec. 11, 2017, https://tinyurl.com/yalfm76m.

Energy experts outline a $17 billion plan for rebuilding and modernizing Puerto Rico's electric grid in the wake of September's hurricanes.

"Puerto Rico: Information on How Statehood Would Potentially Affect Selected Federal Programs and Revenue Sources," U.S. Government Accountability Office, March 2014, https://tinyurl.com/yaq5l494.

If Puerto Rico were a state, it would receive about 76 percent more in federal payments for welfare and other programs, but its residents would pay significantly more in federal income tax, according to a government agency.

Cabán, Pedro, "Puerto Ricans as Contingent Citizens: Shifting Mandated Identities and Imperial Disjunctures," *Centro Journal*, Spring 2017, https://tinyurl.com/yc6bokn7.

Racism, strategic considerations and territorial policies figured prominently in the U.S. decision to impose limited citizenship on Puerto Ricans, says a specialist on Puerto Rico.

Nieves, Ramon-Luis, "Testimony of Ramon-Luis Nieves, Esq., former Senator and Chairman of the Committee on Energy, Senate of Puerto Rico," Subcommittee on Energy, Committee on Energy and Commerce, U.S. House of Representatives, Nov. 2, 2017, https://tinyurl.com/y6w5vmng.

A former member of Puerto Rico's Senate says the island's electric utility is corrupt and dysfunctional.

For More Information

Brookings Institution, 1775 Massachusetts Ave., N.W., Washington, DC 20036; 202-797-6000; brookings.edu. Centrist think tank that deals with public policy, including issues on Puerto Rico.

Center for Puerto Rican Studies, Hunter College, 695 Park Ave., Room E1429, New York, NY 10065; 212-772-5688; centropr.hunter.cuny.edu. Studies the Puerto Rican experience in the United States and the island's history and culture.

Council on Foreign Relations, 58 E. 68th St., New York, NY 10065; 212-434-9400; cfr.org. Think tank on foreign affairs, including Puerto Rico.

Municipal Market Analytics, 75 Main St., Concord, MA 01742; 512-575-4562; mma-research.com. Independent research firm providing analysis and commentary on municipal conditions and bonds in Puerto Rico and elsewhere.

New Progressive Party (PNP), https://twitter.com/pnp_pr. Political party in Puerto Rico that seeks statehood.

Oxfam America, 226 Causeway St., 5th Floor, Boston, MA 02114; 800-776-9326; oxfamamerica.org. Global organization that works to end poverty and responds to disasters, including in Puerto Rico.

Popular Democratic Party (PPD), PO Box 9020436, San Juan, PR 00902; 787-721-2000; https://www.ppdpr.net. One of two main political parties in Puerto Rico; it wants the island to remain a commonwealth.

Puerto Rico Institute of Statistics, 57 Calle Quisqueya, 2nd Floor, San Juan, PR 00917; 787-993-3336; www.estadisticas.pr. Government agency that collects and analyzes economic and demographic statistics.

Puerto Rican Statehood Council, 750 9th St., N.W., Washington, DC 20001; 202-494-1427; www.pr51st.com. Advocacy group that lobbies for statehood.

11

Global Tourism Controversies

Barbara Mantel

Getty Images/LightRocket/Leisa Tyler

Tourists gather for selfies in front of Rome's famed Trevi Fountain in 2016. Popular destinations are struggling with crowds, litter, environmental damage and traffic jams. Some places are fining inappropriate behavior or using social media to steer visitors to less crowded sites.

From *CQ Researcher,*
November 9, 2018

The historic Trevi Fountain is one of Rome's most iconic tourist destinations, made famous by actress Anita Ekberg's saunter through the water in Federico Fellini's 1960 film, *La Dolce Vita.* These days, tourists swarm the low walls of the baroque fountain and the surrounding piazza at all hours, dangling their feet in the water, buying souvenirs from armies of street vendors and jostling one another as they pose for photos.

In August, the severe overcrowding resulted in a brawl as two women, a 19-year-old tourist from the Netherlands and a 44-year-old American, threw punches after competing for the same spot to take selfies. Family members joined in until police broke up the fight.[1]

The incident is one sign of a troubling global phenomenon: Tourism has grown so much in recent decades—international tourist arrivals have nearly doubled since 2000, reaching 1.3 billion in 2017—that the throngs of visitors can overwhelm local communities.[2] Crowds, long lines, litter, environmental degradation and traffic jams are becoming more common in places as varied as European cities, Caribbean and Asian islands and U.S. national parks.

Disgruntled residents of Amsterdam, Venice, Barcelona and other European cities have taken to the streets in protest to demand that government officials take action. Slogans such as "tourists go home" and "tourists are terrorists" have been spray painted on buildings. In 2016, Skift, an online service providing news and research to the travel industry, coined the term "overtourism" to describe the crush of tourists and its negative effects on local life.[3]

Europe Is Top International Destination

France was the most visited country in the world last year, with 87 million international tourist arrivals, up 5 percent from 2016. Spain was second, with 82 million visitors. The United States had 76 million arrivals in 2016, the latest year for which data were available.

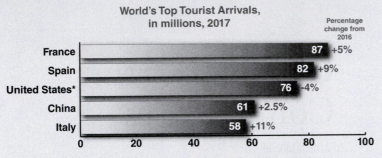

World's Top Tourist Arrivals, in millions, 2017

Country	Arrivals (millions)	Percentage change from 2016
France	87	+5%
Spain	82	+9%
United States*	76	-4%
China	61	+2.5%
Italy	58	+11%

* Tourist arrival figure is from 2016 and the percentage change is for the first nine months of 2017.

Source: "UNWTO Tourism Highlights 2018," World Tourism Organization (UNWTO), August 2018, https://tinyurl.com/ybv9olde

continue to promote tourism growth despite the ecological and social limits of living on a finite planet."[6]

In Utah, for instance, the state's international advertising campaign promoting its national parks helped attract record numbers of visitors in recent years, but it also contributed to overcrowding, according to experts. Two national parks in Utah, Zion and Arches, are now considering requiring reservations to enter in hopes of controlling the crowds.

Even when places want to preserve their character and slow tourism growth, doing so is not always easy because they typically do not control the ports and airports.

"Kauai's niche is that we're the rural getaway kind of place, and we need to keep it that way," said Jim Braman, chair of the Hawaii Lodging and Tourism Association's chapter on the island of Kauai. "We're looking at who can we talk to about the number of flights, and that's controlled by the state and the feds."[7]

Overtourism can happen anywhere, says Justin Francis, CEO of Responsible Travel, an online travel agency in Brighton, England. "It is a mistake to think that overtourism applies only to U.S. national parks with enormous number of visitors or large European cities," he says. "An extra 100 tourists in the tiny town where I live could start causing problems." Responsible Travel arranges trips it says minimizes the harms of tourism and maximizes the benefits, including providing volunteer opportunities (known as volunteer tourism) and responsible travel to natural areas (known as ecotourism).

Travel's growth shows no sign of slowing because population, affluence and ease of travel are all increasing. Arrivals by international tourists jumped 6 percent in the first half of 2018, compared with the same period last year, according to the World Tourism Organization (UNWTO), a United Nations agency in Madrid that promotes sustainable tourism—tourism that attempts to minimize its impact on the environment and local culture while helping to generate income, employment and ecosystem conservation. That figure is expected to reach

But government officials, the tourism industry and residents do not agree on how to respond. The travel industry, officials note, is vital to local economies. In some places, such as Hawaii, tourism can be the largest single contributor to a region's gross domestic product (GDP).[4]

Rather than stifle tourism, some experts say, governments and communities should cooperate to better manage it. "In Amsterdam, the inhabitants are very resentful, but the visitors didn't organize their red light district and permit cannabis shops to open. The residents did," said Tom Jenkins, CEO of the European Tour Operators Association, a trade group based in London. "It's a planning problem, not a tourism problem."

Last year, Amsterdam began restricting new shops in its city center, such as bike rental outlets, that cater to tourists, a move Skift called "a solid first step."[5]

Others say better management, while necessary, is insufficient. Officials should limit tourist numbers, they argue, by reducing cruise ship visits, capping tourist beds or turning away visitors once a marketplace, square or national park becomes saturated.

Tourism "is addicted to growth," said Freya Higgins-Desbiolles, senior lecturer in tourism management at the University of South Australia, and "tourism authorities

1.8 billion arrivals in 2030. Last year, the top destinations, in order of popularity, were France, Spain, the United States, China and Italy.[8]

Tourism is rising in all those destinations except for the United States, which saw a drop last year "that coincided with mixed messages emerging from U.S. government policies and presidential rhetoric about tourism and foreign visitors," said journalist Elizabeth Becker, author of *Overbooked: The Exploding Business of Travel and Tourism*.[9]

Meanwhile, China tops a different list. Its citizens take the most international trips of any country in the world and Chinese tourists are the biggest international spenders.[10] Countries are working hard to encourage Chinese tourists to visit. "France has eased Chinese visa requirements," and Switzerland has as well, says Richard Butler, professor emeritus of tourism at the University of Strathclyde in Scotland.

Butler says many factors are behind the growth in international travel, including global prosperity. A 2017 report from the Brookings Institution, a research organization in Washington, documents what it calls an unprecedented expansion of the global middle class.

"The rate of increase of the middle class, in absolute numbers, is approaching its all-time peak," wrote Homi Kharas, a Brookings senior fellow and the report's author. "In two or three years, there might be a tipping point where a majority of the world's population, for the first time ever, will live in middle-class or rich households."[11]

Another factor is "the advent of low-cost air carriers and the sheer amount of cruise ships out there that has made it cheap and easy to travel and that has liberated the movement of tourists across the globe," says Rachel Dodds, a professor of hospitality and tourism management at Ryerson University in Toronto. In the United States, domestic airfares fell 44 percent, after adjusting for inflation, between 1980 and 2016.[12]

Technology is perhaps one of the more fraught contributors to tourism's growth. "Rating and review sites, social media, destination rankings and other channels are

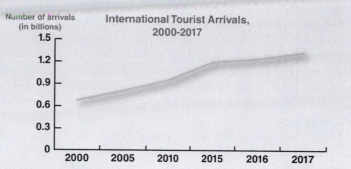

International Tourism Boom

The number of international tourist arrivals worldwide—visitors staying overnight in a foreign country—has nearly doubled since 2000, according to a United Nations agency that compiles travel statistics.

International Tourist Arrivals, 2000-2017

Number of arrivals (in billions)

Source: "World Tourism Barometer," World Tourism Organization (UNWTO), October 2018, https://tinyurl.com/yaetlvd5

creating and reinforcing interest in travel, particularly to top destinations and the most popular sites," McKinsey & Co., a management consultant company in New York, said in a recent report. But there is a flip side. "For endangered destinations such as the Great Barrier Reef [in Australia], awareness of the threat can lead more people to visit 'while they still can,' which can exacerbate the problem."[13]

Technology also is making it easier for travelers to book accommodations online, either at hotels or at short-term vacation rentals through websites such as Airbnb. Those sites, and Airbnb in particular, often are accused of exacerbating overcrowding in heavily visited cities by making thousands of relatively low-cost rooms and apartments available to travelers.

Airbnb says its home-sharing model actually can lessen overcrowding because it disperses visitors over a wider area. The travel industry, meanwhile, stresses tourism's economic benefits. "As one of the world's largest economic sectors, travel and tourism creates jobs, drives exports and generates prosperity across the world," said Gloria Guevara Manzo, president and CEO of the World Travel & Tourism Council in its latest annual economic impact report.

The council is a membership organization in London representing more than 150 travel and tourism companies worldwide. It estimates that travel and tourism generated 3.2 percent of the world's economic activity in 2017 and supported more than 118 million jobs, or 3.8 percent of total employment. Travelers also boost revenues for localities through hotel taxes and other fees.[14]

And tourism has cultural benefits, says Butler. "You get museums that are built or expanded partly as tourist attractions, and locals can benefit from them," he says. "Tourism may be a threat to the environment in some places, but tourism may be the reason they were designated a national park or a World Heritage Site in the first place."

Some of the cities suffering the most from overtourism are World Heritage Sites, including Venice and Dubrovnik, a historic city on Croatia's coast. World Heritage Sites are United Nations-designated places of cultural, scientific or historical significance and are protected by international treaties. Research also shows that many World Heritage Sites face catastrophic flooding linked to climate change and that tourism's contribution to climate change is greater than thought.[15]

Against this backdrop, here are some questions that politicians, residents, tourism officials and environmentalists are asking about global tourism:

Should overcrowded destinations limit the number of tourists?

Two years ago, Thailand temporarily closed some of its most popular islands to the public to reverse tourism-linked damage to coral reefs. Last year, Dubrovnik began turning away daily tourists from its overcrowded old town once 8,000 pedestrians had entered the area. Starting next year, Barcelona will limit the number of tourist beds in its busiest districts, and the Greek island of Santorini will cap the number of daily cruise ship visitors.

"The electricity grid and water supply are at their limit. Garbage has doubled in five years," said Santorini Mayor Nikos Zorzos. "If we don't control the crowds, it will backfire and ruin us."[16]

Not surprisingly, turning away tourists is controversial. In Barcelona, where tourism accounts for 12 percent of the city's gross domestic product, Manel Casals, director general of the Barcelona Hotel Association, said discouraging overnight guests will not reduce overcrowding. That's because the majority of Barcelona's tourists are day-trippers arriving by cruise ship, car or public transportation, Casals said.[17]

Most communities facing complaints that hordes of tourists are making these places unlivable are stopping short of limiting tourist numbers. For example, Amsterdam is imposing fines on drunken behavior while Venice is promoting the city's less visited sites in its "detourism" campaign.[18]

The problem often is not tourism but bad local management, says Rochelle Turner, director of research at the World Travel & Tourism Council. Turner cites the Greek island of Corfu as an example, where uncollected garbage piled up along roadsides this summer and tour operators received an unprecedented number of complaints about the trash.

"The island didn't have the required waste facilities or the people to manage that waste," says Turner. A landfill closed in February and licensing problems reportedly kept a new one from operating.[19]

On its website, Turner's organization suggests several strategies that tourist destinations can take to reduce overcrowding and its ill effects. They include building better infrastructure; raising tourist taxes to pay for that construction; providing tourists with better information, such as real-time crowd data so visitors can avoid visiting popular sites when they are most crowded; and dispersing tourists to less visited sites, as London's "Do London Like a Londoner" website tries to do with its suggestions of alternative restaurants, museums and nightspots.[20]

"You're taking people to destinations that might not be in the guidebooks," says Turner. "And you have to make sure they are well signposted, well lit and there is the right transportation to get people there."

Managing the flow of tourists is another tactic. Cruise ships are blamed for much of the overcrowding in port cities, such as Venice and Dubrovnik, because they can unload thousands of tourists all at once. The largest cruise ship in the world, the *Symphony of the Seas*, can carry more than 6,000 passengers, for example.[21] Rather than ban cruise ships or limit their numbers, cities can work with cruise lines to stagger arrivals, says Sarah Kennedy, spokeswoman for the Cruise Lines International Association, the industry trade association in Washington.

"We are working closely with the mayor of Dubrovnik to help manage the schedule of cruise ships," says

Kennedy. "The cruise lines have adapted their itineraries to change the days and the times that they are coming into the city." Kennedy says this is a new project for the association, and it is identifying other markets and regions with which to work on schedule changes.

But Francis of Responsible Travel says better management is not the full answer to overtourism. "All the ideas put forth by [the tourism council] for managing tourism should be happening anyway, but that will not solve the problems," says Francis. "Each destination has a [tourism] capacity, and no matter how good the management is, it will eventually be exceeded."

As a result, some places should reduce the number of cruise ships, while others should cut back the number of home rentals to tourists or restrict large tour groups from certain sites, says Francis. Barcelona, for instance, now bans tour groups of more than 15 from entering its iconic La Boqueria food market at peak times. Butchers and fishmongers had complained that packs of selfie-taking tourists who bought very little were clogging the venue and preventing residents from reaching their stalls.[22]

"Travel is a privilege, not a right," says Francis.

But Megan Epler Wood, director of the International Sustainable Tourism Initiative at Harvard University, says closing doors creates the potential for government corruption. "There is always someone who's going to change that limit for money, be it legal or illegal," she says, pointing to Ecuador's Galápagos Islands in the Pacific Ocean as an example. Critics, including tour operators who worry that the islands' fragile ecosystem is at risk, charge Ecuador with lax enforcement of laws and regulations, including tourism limits.[23]

Whatever tactics destinations eventually adopt, they first must do a better job of measuring tourism's impact on residents, the environment, the cultural heritage and tourists themselves, and then devise a long-term plan for managing it, many experts and tourism officials agree.

"Do we have those systems in place? The answer is no," says Epler Wood, who teaches tourism master planning at Harvard. "Do we think we can get them in place? The answer is yes."

It is going to require that the tourism industry, residents and local, regional and national governments work together, says Francis. "And that concerted effort has been in short supply until now," he says.

Royal Caribbean's *Symphony of the Seas*—the world's largest cruise ship—docks in Malaga, Spain, in March 2018. The influx of passengers from massive cruise ships can inundate port cities. Cruise lines are working to stagger arrivals to help relieve the congestion, but critics say such steps do not go far enough.

Should U.S. national parks require reservations for entry?

More than 60,000 people descended on Zion National Park in southwest Utah during Memorial Day weekend. Visitors waited two hours for the park's free shuttle buses, hikers thronged trails and trash cans overflowed. "This park has become a nightmare," wrote a commenter on Zion's Facebook page.[24]

Famed for its narrow canyons and soaring sandstone cliffs, Zion is one of the country's most popular national parks. A record 4.5 million people visited in 2017, a 70 percent increase over a decade. But park officials say visitors are trampling vegetation and eroding soil. Traffic jams are common, shuttles are routinely overcrowded and trails and campgrounds need serious repair.[25]

"It's overwhelming," said park spokesman John Marciano. "It's just going to be loved to death."[26]

In response, Zion is considering a drastic step: limiting the number of people allowed into the park each day by instituting an online, year-round reservation system. In many parks, reservations are required for campground spaces and permits for wilderness hiking, but capping visitor numbers would be a first for a major national park.

Overcrowding is a problem across the park system, from Glacier in Montana to the Great Smoky Mountains in Tennessee and North Carolina: In 2010, some 281 million people visited the national park system. In 2017,

National Park Attendance Climbs

The number of visits to the U.S. national park system rose to nearly 331 million last year, up 18 percent from 2010. Overcrowding has led to calls for limits on visitors at some parks.

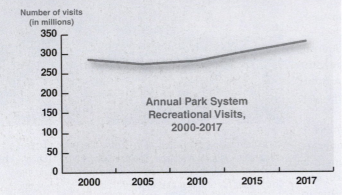

Annual Park System Recreational Visits, 2000-2017

Source: "National Park Service," National Park Service, 2017, https://tinyurl.com/yab8olrm

the total was nearly 331 million, an 18 percent increase. But so far, only three national parks—Acadia in Maine and Zion and Arches in Utah—are considering requiring advance reservations for parking or entry. The proposals are controversial. By law, the National Park Service must strike a difficult balance, conserving the environment while allowing for a park's enjoyment by visitors.[27]

"These are irreplaceable resources. We have to protect them by putting some strategic limits on numbers, or there won't be anything left," said Joan Anzelmo, a retired Park Service superintendent in Wyoming.[28]

But Michael Liss, a real estate developer in Moab, Utah, the gateway town for Arches National Park—so named because of its more than 2,000 natural sandstone arches—says advance reservation systems would destroy people's freedom to travel. "Can you imagine showing up at the Grand Canyon and the sign says, 'Sorry, you need a reservation to get in'? It's just not right."

Others say park reservations could hurt local businesses that depend on high tourist numbers during peak season.

Liss, the former managing director of a luxury travel outfitter, chairs the Moab Transit Authority Study Committee, created by Grand County in response to

Arches' proposal. With proper design, the park could handle three times the current number of visitors, he says.

His committee has come up with an alternative plan to reduce car congestion inside the park and human traffic on its trails: refurbish two underused entrances; build parking lots on government land outside Arches' three entrances; create a voluntary shuttle system to ferry people from the parking lots to points within the park; mobilize a fleet of smaller vehicles to disperse hikers to less crowded areas; build new trails to accommodate them; and add bike paths.

Parking fees would subsidize shuttle operations, and the state could cover construction and vehicle costs. "I think we could get funding from the Utah Department of Transportation because this is literally what powers our local economy," says Liss.

Federal funding would almost certainly not be available, says Holly Fretwell, director of outreach at the Property and Environment Research Center, a research institute in Bozeman, Mont., that favors free-market solutions to environmental problems. "We already have a deferred maintenance backlog of almost $12 billion in our national parks," she says.

Arches presented its plan late last year, received public comments and is preparing to submit a final version to regional Park Service administrators. A shuttle service will not be included, says Jeffrey G. Olson, a National Park Service spokesman in Washington. Park officials determined that a voluntary shuttle system could initially reduce vehicles inside the park by up to 25 percent, "but the growth in visitation annually would undo that effect within two or three years," Olson says.

Fretwell says the National Park Service should use pricing to address overcrowding. In June it increased entrance fees at the 117 fee-charging national parks by $5 a vehicle to help pay for maintenance. Fretwell says the Park Service can do more.

"I enter Yellowstone National Park and pay $35 to go in and out of the park for seven days. And I can take as many people as I can cram in my car on any of those days," says Fretwell. "That's ridiculous."

Instead, national parks should charge a daily rate per person that is high enough in peak season to encourage people to visit at other times of year and to contribute more to covering costs, she says.

"The problem with that is the parks are an American heritage for all people," says Jeffrey Marion, a recreation ecologist with the U.S. Geological Survey and an adjunct professor at Virginia Tech University in Blacksburg, Va. Using pricing as a mechanism to reduce use would favor the wealthy and undermine recent strides in diversifying park visitation, says Marion. Visitors to national parks have historically been overwhelmingly white, according to government surveys.[29]

Fretwell says the government could devise a system to give lower-income people a discount, although she did not offer details.

Before parks raise fees, require reservations, add shuttles or build more trails, they should determine their capacity to sustainably host visitors, says Jeff Ruch, executive director at Public Employees for Environmental Responsibility (PEER) in Silver Spring, Md., a nonprofit group that works to ensure that environmental laws are enforced and defends government whistleblowers. Then each park needs to establish goals, such as the desired number of visitors on trails, says Ruch.

The National Parks and Recreation Act of 1978 mandates such long-range planning, but a 2016 PEER study found that of the 10 most visited national parks, only Yosemite had established so-called carrying capacities, and then only for its wilderness zones.[30]

"The fact that [parks are] not affirmatively planning . . . is a form of malpractice," says Ruch.

Do Airbnb and the home-rental market contribute to "overtourism"?

Eleven-year-old Airbnb, based in San Francisco, matches property owners seeking short-term renters with vacationers looking for a place to stay and has more than 5 million vacation rental listings in 191 countries. It has revolutionized how travelers book accommodations and where they choose to stay, from a single room in someone's home to an entire apartment or house.[31]

By its estimates, 22 percent of all overnight guests in Kyoto, Japan, booked through Airbnb in 2017. Airbnb captured 18 percent of the market in Barcelona, and 12 percent in Amsterdam. Its relatively low-cost

Barcelona residents protest higher housing costs and "overtourism," which they blame partly on the home-sharing industry. Critics say Airbnb and similar websites are worsening housing shortages by encouraging local owners to rent to tourists instead of residents. The industry denies its practices drive up housing costs and says its rentals actually disperse tourists over a wide area.

accommodations are the biggest draw, according to a study in the *Journal of Travel Research* that surveyed users of the platform.[32]

The company's jaw-dropping growth has attracted scrutiny from government officials and growing complaints from residents who blame it for contributing to gridlocked streets, packed sidewalks and boorish tourist behavior.

"Airbnb has definitely added an extra 15 percent in visitor numbers this year, which means in August we were close to being full," said Malcolm Bell, a tourism official in Cornwall, one of Britain's top summer holiday spots. The number of Airbnb listings in the county has grown from 17 in 2016 to 9,000 in August, according to the tourist board, and the result has been traffic jams and overflowing parking lots, Bell said.[33]

"The last thing we want is for local people to become increasingly annoyed and frustrated with tourists," he said. "We want visitors to have the best experience possible, and if they don't, then they won't come back."

But blaming tourist crowds on Airbnb and its competitors in the home-sharing industry—HomeAway, VRBO, 9flats and Wimdu, among others—is too easy, says Daniel Guttentag, director of the Office of Tourism Analysis at the College of Charleston in South Carolina.

"It probably is a factor, but I think it's a small factor," he says. About 95 percent of Airbnb renters that Guttentag surveyed for a research project said they would have been traveling anyway.

Airbnb contends that the company actually helps to mitigate overcrowding by making lodging available in rural areas in need of sightseers' money and dispersing tourists within cities. "In many places, two-thirds and in other cities upward of 75 percent of our listings are outside of traditional tourist areas," says Clark Stevens, director of Airbnb's Office of Government Affairs and Strategic Partnerships. Shops and restaurants in those less visited neighborhoods benefit because tourists often spend money near where they sleep, he says.

But neighbors in residential areas often do not appreciate the influx of tourists made possible by peer-to-peer rentals, says Guttentag. They may have been able to avoid the tourist throngs in the city center, "but now it's a very different feeling, having tourists next door or in an apartment on the floor above or seeing them come through the lobby," he says. In fact, complaints by neighbors about noisy, drunken or disrespectful rental guests became so intense that Airbnb two years ago opened a dedicated webpage to register grievances. It also promised to suspend or remove those listings with continual complaints.[34]

Many hosts recognize the need to keep neighbors happy. One advice site for Airbnb hosts suggests they leave their cellphone number for neighbors to call, set clear guest rules and install a noise alarm that pings the host's cellphone. "I used it this week to let a guest know they were being too loud," wrote one host. "I definitely think it is a helpful tool."[35]

Overcrowding and noise are not the only charges against Airbnb and the growth in short-term tourist rentals. Several cities have accused the online marketplace of contributing to rising housing costs as professional operators turn apartments into permanent vacation rentals, shrinking the supply of apartments available to residents. Studies in New York City, Montreal and elsewhere document the trend, but Airbnb has attacked their methodology.

"The majority of our hosts are sharing the home in which they live, not removing permanent housing from the market," Airbnb said earlier this year in response to a New York City study that attributed 9 percent of the rise in rents over a seven-year period to Airbnb.[36]

But researchers point out that even a small minority of professional hosts operating large enough numbers of multiple Airbnb listings can affect residential housing costs.[37]

Cities are increasingly regulating Airbnb and cracking down on short-term rentals. Palma, the capital of Mallorca, a Spanish island in the Mediterranean, has banned Airbnb completely. Amsterdam limits whole-home rentals to 60 days a year and London to 90 days a year. Tokyo legalized home-sharing only in 2017 and capped it at 180 days per year per rental.

In Berlin, hosts need a permit to rent 50 percent of their main residence short-term. Barcelona requires short-term rentals to be licensed but is issuing no new licenses. And hosts in San Francisco must register with the city.[38]

But local officials are struggling to enforce these regulations, says Guttentag. Even though Airbnb's listings are public, addresses are not, so it can be difficult to track down violators. In negotiating regulations with cities, Airbnb has often agreed to become involved in enforcement. For example, it purged more than 4,500 unregistered listings in San Francisco, about 40 percent of the total, the day after the registration requirement went into effect in January.[39]

Jonathan Tourtellot, founder and CEO of the Destination Stewardship Center, a nonprofit in Lovettsville, Va., says he has told Airbnb that it should make it easier for the public to differentiate between hosts who are sharing their homes and professionals who are renting multiple listings as a business. Tourtellot, whose group grades more than 400 destinations around the world on the stewardship of their natural and cultural resources, wrote the foreword to a recent Airbnb report assessing its economic contribution in eight destinations.

Consumers can then decide for themselves how they want to contribute to the economy of the places they visit, says Tourtellot.

BACKGROUND

Earliest Tourism

Imperial Rome was the first culture that had regular tourism, according to Maxine Feifer, who wrote a history of world travel. An unprecedented period of peace and prosperity across the Roman Empire in the second century allowed some Romans to pursue travel for pleasure and culture. Bureaucrats and officials, who possessed the means and ability to take time off from work, traveled in the spring and fall when the government recessed for weeks at a time.

Inns along the way served their needs, and an extensive network of well-paved roads meant that "a carriage ride was frequently smoother in the second century than in the eighteenth," wrote Feifer. Popular destinations included Greece, Asia Minor—modern-day Turkey—and Egypt, all within the empire's borders.[40]

By the late fifth century, this tourist infrastructure was in shambles. The Roman Empire had collapsed into small warring kingdoms and fiefdoms under the weight of a complex web of pressures, including incompetent emperors, marauding invaders and plague. Trade and commerce were negligible, paved roads were reduced to muddy tracks, inns were closed and banditry was common. "It was hazardous to travel and difficult to find what a tourist might have wanted to see," Feifer said.[41]

Seven hundred years passed before tourism began to revive. In 1096, the Crusades, a series of religious wars spanning nearly 200 years, were launched at the urging of the Roman Catholic Church to pry the Holy Lands from Muslim control. The often ruthless campaigns failed in their territorial aims, but they brought treasure and wealth to the church. Newly built monasteries and churches, particularly in France and Rome, attracted specialized tourists—pilgrims seeking pardon for their sins and relief for their ailments.[42]

"By the thirteenth and fourteenth centuries, pilgrimage was a mass phenomenon, practicable and systemized, served by a growing industry of networks of charitable hospices," wrote Feifer.

During the 15th century, travel books began to appear, containing descriptions of culture and natural wonders in addition to chronicles of pilgrimages. Services akin to travel agencies and tour operators also eased the pilgrims' way. Nevertheless, the journey for many tourists could be grueling, particularly for Germans and the English as they crossed the Alps to reach their destinations.

Beginning in the 16th century, the Protestant Reformation shifted travelers' attention increasingly away from Catholic shrines and churches toward the secular. During this period, the European tourist was

Tourists celebrate the opening of Disneyland in Anaheim, Calif., on July 17, 1955. The post-World War II era saw a sharp rise in tourism. With incomes growing and the interstate highway system taking shape, middle-class families increasingly explored the country by car.

typically a well-off male student who visited churches, monuments, theaters and museums in as many European cities as possible. Italy, the home of the Renaissance, was often the final destination. The goal was to learn, and proof of a student's status was necessary to receive the discounted entrance fees accorded to students at many tourist sites.[43]

Arrival of Modern Tourism

Modern tourism—"the pursuit of pleasure and an escape from everyday realities"—grew out of an elite, largely English travel experience called the Grand Tour, which reached its peak between 1748 and 1789, said historian Eric G.E. Zuelow of the University of New England.

"Vast numbers of young Englishmen, and a few Englishwomen, ventured to Paris, Rome, Venice, Florence and Naples," and some continued to Berlin, Vienna, Geneva and Prague, said Zuelow. Most travelers sought to gain knowledge and were accompanied by tutors, but the Grand Tour "gradually reflected something altogether new, a hedonistic approach to consuming that was less evident during the previous century," wrote Zuelow. Drinking and gambling were common, prostitutes were ubiquitous and venereal disease was a constant threat.[44]

In the 19th century, tourism began to spread beyond the elite because of the Industrial Revolution and cultural changes. As the middle class grew, workers had the income and leisure time to take vacations, a relatively new concept in Western culture. Accompanying this rising wealth were technological advances that made traveling more accessible.

Railway construction for steam-powered trains took off in the United Kingdom during the first half of the 19th century. By 1843, roughly 2,000 miles of track had been lain. Sixteen years later, the mileage had climbed to nearly 10,000. The British also built tracks to crisscross India, part of its global empire. Other countries followed suit, and railways spread across Africa, China, Russia, Latin America and the United States, where a transcontinental railroad was completed in 1869. Fifty years later, the U.S. railway network contained 127,000 miles of track.[45]

Speed and comfort improved rapidly. By the 1870s, American George Mortimer Pullman's company was manufacturing train cars with more wheels and springs. It leased five classes of cars to railroads, including sleeping and dining room cars.[46]

The steam engine also transformed travel by water. Steam-powered ships took travelers along lakes, rivers and coastlines and eventually across the oceans. By the mid-19th century, Canadian Samuel Cunard and his Scottish business partner Robert Napier owned a fleet of trans-Atlantic ships carrying mail and passengers.

As technology advanced, ships became larger, faster and more luxurious. "The greatest ships of the steam age . . . were floating grand hotels," wrote Zuelow.

Still, third-class passengers, sleeping in open berths in steerage and typically immigrants rather than tourists, far outnumbered first-class passengers and generated most of the profits. To attract middle-class tourists, shipping lines in the 1920s created tourist and cabin classes, "opening long-distance ocean voyages to younger and less affluent tourists," said Zuelow.[47]

As the railroads and steamships expanded, British cabinetmaker Thomas Cook started a tour company, taking middle-class customers on domestic and European excursions. His innovations included packaging the trips with lodging and food and making the routes a circular journey.[48]

In the United States, the spread of railroads and steamships led to the development of mass tourism destinations, one of the first being Niagara Falls. But within decades, tourists began to complain about overcrowding and blight as hotels, souvenir stands and entertainment pavilions dominated the area. In response, the New York Legislature in 1885 appropriated funds to establish the Niagara Reservation, and landscape architect Frederick Law Olmsted was hired as its designer. His plan restored the landscape by removing previous development and creating paths and overlooks that framed the views.[49]

In 1864, Yosemite became the first protected parkland, and it too became a popular destination as tourists took advantage of the newly completed transcontinental railroad to reach California. In 1872, Yellowstone was designated the first national park. Yosemite became a national park in 1890 and Mount Rainier followed in 1899.

President Theodore Roosevelt (1901-09) was the driving force behind the creation of five additional national parks, 150 national forests, 51 federal bird reserves, four national game preserves and 18 national monuments (including the Grand Canyon National Monument).[50]

The government recognized that the creation of national parks and the associated tourism would generate money, encourage people to visit the West and help heal the nation after the Civil War, Zuelow said.[51]

Planes, Trains, and Automobiles

Like the steam engine, the development of the internal combustion engine in the late 19th century revolutionized tourism because it further eased travel. During the first few decades of the 20th century, car enthusiasts formed automobile clubs in the United States and in Europe, Australia, South America and Africa. Nine clubs met in Chicago in 1902 and founded the American Automobile Association (AAA), a membership organization known for its maps, traveler guides, insurance and safety campaigns.[52]

Motor clubs lobbied for better roads and for access to U.S. national parks. In 1908, Mount Rainier became the first national park to allow cars, but supervisors at other parks worried that allowing cars would turn visitors into mere day-trippers, cheapen the park experience and damage the environment. The car lobby, however,

CHRONOLOGY

1814-1890 *Steam-powered trains and ships spur tourism.*

1814 English mechanic George Stephenson builds the first practical steam locomotive, which hauls eight coal-laden wagons at 4 mph.

1825 The first public passenger steam train makes its inaugural run in England.

1840 A Cunard Line steamship begins regular passenger service between Liverpool, England, and Boston, helping to make the trans-Atlantic crossing popular with wealthy tourists.

1859 Nearly 10,000 miles of railroad track crisscrosses the United Kingdom.

1867 Pullman Palace Car Co. of Chicago starts producing train cars, eventually manufacturing luxury sleeping and dining cars and attracting more tourists to rail travel.

1869 The U.S. completes its first transcontinental railroad, making it easier for travelers to reach Western territories.

1872 Congress establishes Yellowstone as the first national park.

1890 Yosemite becomes a national park, followed by Mount Rainier nine years later.

1900-1935 *Automobiles and air travel transform tourism.*

1900 French tire company Michelin starts publishing its touring guide to restaurants and hotels.

1908 Mount Rainier becomes the first national park to allow cars.

1926 Air Commerce Act allows the U.S. Commerce Department to regulate the nascent airline industry; within 10 years several airlines are launched, including United Airlines.

1935 Imperial Airways in the U.K. offers globe-circling flights, with stops in parts of the British Empire. . . . The number of gas stations in the U.S. reaches 200,000, boosting the travel industry.

1955-Present *Mass tourism develops, and with it overcrowding.*

1955 Disneyland, a major tourist attraction, opens in Anaheim, Calif.

1963 The United Nations holds a conference to examine the role of tourism in economic development.

1970 U.S. economic output is double what it was in the 1950s, when the economy started to boom; the rising living standards spurred a tourism increase.

1973 Organization of Arab Petroleum Exporting Countries (OPEC) proclaims an oil embargo, causing fuel prices to rise, hurting the travel industry.

1978 Airline Deregulation Act in the U.S. leads to lower airline fares and greater travel.

1985 Ryanair, Europe's first budget airline, is established; others follow in Europe and the U.S.

2000 Travel website TripAdvisor is founded in Needham, Mass.

2007 Home-sharing company Airbnb is founded in San Francisco. . . . A global recession begins; over the next year, international tourism arrivals decline by 4 percent, from 936 million.

2009 Many countries begin to recover from the recession; international tourism arrivals rise nearly 7 percent.

2016 Protesters hold anti-tourism marches in several European cities . . . . More cities begin to regulate short-term vacation rentals, which some blame for contributing to "overtourism."

2017 International tourist arrivals top 1.3 billion. . . . U.N. declares the International Year of Sustainable Tourism for Development. . . . Three U.S. national parks propose limiting visitors because of record overcrowding.

2018 Protests against overtourism in European cities continue. . . . Research finds that dozens of World Heritage Sites on the Mediterranean coast are threatened by rising seas as a result of climate change. . . . Congress is poised to vote on legislation to allocate $6.5 billion for repairs to National Park Service lands.

Ecotourism Seeks to Conserve and to Give Back

But critics say the practice falls short of its lofty goals.

Twenty-four years after civil war and genocide devastated Rwanda, "ecotourists" are flocking to this central African nation, where they can stay in luxury lodges and view spectacular sights, including volcanoes, golden monkeys and the main attraction—mountain gorillas.

The experience is not cheap, and that is partly by design.

To see the gorillas, an endangered species, a visitor must acquire a government-issued permit costing $1,500. A portion of that money—currently 10 percent—goes to communities near the national parks where the gorillas live to help build schools, clinics and housing.

For ecotourists, that fee is money well spent, said Paul Charles, CEO of The PC Agency, a travel marketing firm in London. "Those who go want to be tourist-philanthropists," he said. "They want to give back to local communities."[1]

The International Ecotourism Society (TIES), an advocacy group in Washington that promotes ecotourism, defines it as "responsible travel to natural areas that conserves the environment, sustains the well-being of the local people, and involves interpretation and education."[2]

But ecotourism, which grew out of environmental movement of the 1970s and surged to popularity in the 1980s, has long had critics, who say many hotels, lodges and tour companies use the term indiscriminately to lend a sheen to their businesses, a practice known as "greenwashing."

To define ecotourism and set standards for the travel industry, TIES developed principles for ecotourism businesses to adopt, including:

- "Minimize physical, social, behavioral and psychological impacts.

- "Build environmental and cultural awareness and respect.

- "Provide direct financial benefits for conservation.

- "Generate financial benefits for both local people and private industry.

- "Deliver memorable interpretive experiences to visitors that help raise sensitivity to host countries' political, environmental and social climates.

- "Design, construct and operate low impact facilities.

- "Recognize the rights and spiritual beliefs of the Indigenous People . . . and work in partnership with them."[3]

Megan Epler Wood, director of the International Sustainable Tourism Initiative at Harvard University and a consultant who helped develop these principles, says ecotourism has scored numerous successes globally. In addition to gorilla-watching tours in Rwanda, she cites environmentally conscious whale-watching expeditions in Mexico's Baja California Peninsula.

"It's just absolutely classic," says Epler Wood, who returned recently from the region. "My guide was Mexican and had gotten an advanced degree on whale behavior at a university in Baja, and the local, so-called *lancheros*

was strong, said Zuelow, and soon roads penetrated every national park.

The expanding networks of roads around the world prompted motor clubs and others to begin publishing touring guides. In 1900, the Michelin rubber company in France, which produced automobile tires, introduced its eponymous red guidebook that eventually used a star system to rate the best hotels and restaurants. More-affordable automobiles, such as the Model T in 1919, opened up tourism to more people.[53]

Soon, air travel would revolutionize the travel industry yet again. In the United States, the Air Commerce Act of 1926 allowed the U.S. Department of Commerce to "certify aircraft, license pilots, and issue and enforce air traffic regulations," according to a brief history of the airline industry. "Within 10 years, many modern-day airlines, such as United and American, had emerged as major players."[54]

Overseas, the Dutch airline KLM pioneered long-distance flights with service from Amsterdam to Djakarta, Indonesia, in 1929. By 1935, the British

[boatmen] were running the small boats." The Mexican government helped by building better docking facilities for the *lancheros*, she says. "There is often a public-private aspect to ecotourism."

Epler Wood says the last accurate reckoning of ecotourism's size was conducted in 2002, which the United Nations proclaimed the International Year of Ecotourism. The U.N. then estimated it to be about 5 percent of global tourism. Even if that remains unchanged, she says, the absolute number of ecotourists must be significantly higher today, as overall international tourism has soared.

Critics are skeptical about ecotourism's goals and effectiveness. "Claims that we can protect nature, benefit local communities and also bring national revenues to [these places] are faced with a different reality on the ground," according to the Third World Network, a research and advocacy group for developing nations. "From Thailand to Belize, ecotourism has opened the doors to more forest destruction."[4]

Anita Pleumarom, coordinator of the Tourism Investigation & Monitoring Team in Bangkok, Thailand, a private group that campaigns for social and ecological justice in tourism, said "ecotourism is fraught with romantic and delusional beliefs," and the concept remains vague. No one, she said, has conducted empirical studies of how widely travel companies using the term have adopted ecotourism principles.[5]

Epler Wood agrees that such research does not exist. "I can only go by the work I've done in over 35 countries," she says. "I've dealt with thousands of business, and I don't see [greenwashing] very often."

Ecotourism's biggest weakness, says Epler Wood, is not greenwashing but the frequent lack of government planning for tourism development that occurs just outside protected wildlife areas. It can result in sprawl, she says.

Pleumarom's assessment is harsher: "Many people and communities whose territories have been turned into playgrounds for ecotourists have seen their remaining patches of natural forest disappear," watersheds polluted and wildlife harmed "because of a plethora of tourism-related development projects and rapidly expanding numbers of tourists."[6]

Travelers interested in ecotourism can check to see whether their hotel, lodge or tour operator is certified as "sustainable." But they will want to be sure the certification body is legitimate, says Epler Wood. The Global Sustainable Tourism Council is a nonprofit in Washington that accredits certification bodies that meet its standards.

The problem is that certification is fairly rare, says Epler Wood. She urges prospective travelers to question tour companies, hotels and ecolodges about their greenhouse gas emissions and wildlife policies and whether their guides and suppliers are local.

"If the company has nothing in response, then move on," she says.

— *Barbara Mantel*

[1] Laura Powell, "Rwanda Is Making a Push for the Right Number of High-Spending Visitors," *Skift*, June 12, 2018, https://tinyurl.com/ybpeffet.

[2] "What is Ecotourism?" International Ecotourism Society, https://tinyurl.com/y7gdb6mo.

[3] "Principles of Ecotourism," International Ecotourism Society, https://tinyurl.com/y7gdb6mo.

[4] "2002: International Year of Reviewing Ecotourism," Third World Network, https://tinyurl.com/yar6gnnz.

[5] Anita Pleumarom, "Ecotourism—an unsustainable delusion," Briefing Paper 88, Third World Network, December 2016, pp. 1-3, https://tinyurl.com/y9vndxsj.

[6] *Ibid.*

Imperial Airways offered flights that circled the globe, linking the British Empire from India to Asia.[55]

The Great Depression of the 1930s and World War II in the early 1940s badly hurt the tourism industry, but the slowdown was only temporary. When the war ended in 1945, the world economy grew and consumer spending rebounded.

Mass Tourism

On July 17, 1955, animator and film producer Walt Disney opened Disneyland on 160 acres of former orange groves in Anaheim, Calif. Disney designed his theme park to appeal to families.[56] After World War II, Americans were having more children in what became known as the Baby Boom. With incomes rising and roads improving as the nation built an interstate highway system, middle-class families explored the country by car and visited tourist destinations such as Disneyland. In Britain, Scandinavia and France, the same pattern held. European families increasingly took vacations by car, and entrepreneurs built campgrounds, seaside cottages and American-style motels.[57]

Social Media Helps Drive Tourism

"People say the information is more up-to-date, more relevant to them."

Over the past two years, Chinese tourists have been drawn to the white chalk cliffs that border the English Channel in East Sussex, England, inspired by the windswept landscape's appearance in social media and films. This summer, South Korean day-trippers discovered the cliffs, a two-hour drive south of London, after an actress from their homeland posted photos and a video of herself standing near their edge.

"When we search for London on social media, it's the first thing we see," said Hyeon Hui Shin, a 28-year-old South Korean tourist visiting the cliffs.[1]

Social media is transforming tourism, says Richard Butler, professor emeritus of tourism at the University of Strathclyde in Glasgow, Scotland. Facebook, Twitter, Instagram, YouTube, Snapchat and TripAdvisor are some of the platforms that allow travelers to browse photos, ratings and feedback when deciding where to visit. Critics, however, say social media has its downsides: It can exacerbate "overtourism," in which popular sites are overrun with visitors, and lead to safety issues, such as when selfie-taking daredevils get too close to a cliff's edge.

But for its users, social media is a net positive. "People say the information on social media is more up-to-date, more relevant to them and more fun" than the information from tour operators, on destination websites and in guidebooks,

says Ulrike Gretzel, a senior fellow at the University of Southern California Center for Public Relations who studies social media and tourism. And people view it as more trustworthy than information from the tourism industry because it comes from other travelers, she adds.

Among Millennials, born between the early 1980s and 1990s, 86 percent are "inspired to book a trip based on content they viewed online," and 87 percent "use Facebook for travel inspiration; more than 50 percent use Twitter or Pinterest," according to a report by marketing consultancy FutureCast.[2]

Travel companies and tourism boards are catching on and creating social media campaigns to reach potential customers directly. For example, the regional tourism board in East Sussex, England, has hired a Chinese student to post about its chalk cliffs on the Chinese social media platform WeChat.[3]

A recent university report advised tourism operators in Southwest Australia seeking Asian visitors to start telling interesting stories on social media. "It is important that attractions in Australia's Southwest become more iconic by combining the unique features of the region with building popular social media moments," said the study's lead author, Michael Volgger, a senior fellow in tourism marketing at Curtin University in Perth.[4]

Travel was harder for African-American tourists during this era because of segregation. Many relied on *The Green Book*, which was published annually beginning in 1936 by postal worker Victor Hugo Green. The guide listed those motels, restaurants and other businesses that would safely serve black travelers.[58]

The popularity of air travel, meanwhile, was climbing. After World War II, passenger aircraft became bigger, faster and more fuel-efficient, and to fill the planes, the first trans-Atlantic "tourist class fare" was introduced. By 1957, more passengers were crossing the Atlantic by air than by sea. A sustained level of prosperity in the United States and Western Europe helped to fuel continued growth in tourism. From 1960, global tourism

grew by more than 10 percent a year and by 1974 tourist spending accounted for 6 percent of international trade.[59]

But two oil crises in the 1970s made traveling more expensive and interrupted the growth in worldwide tourism. In the United States, for example, the average price of gasoline rose from 39 cents a gallon in 1973, not adjusted for inflation, to $1.19 cents a gallon in 1980.[60]

In the late 1970s, airfares began to drop sharply, after Europe eased regulations on the airline industry and Laker Airlines in Britain began offering cheap, one-way trans-Atlantic flights for 59 pounds (about $75 today). "The company demonstrated that there was a vast market for cheap tickets and competitors quickly offered lower prices," wrote Zuelow.[61]

Social media also is important to tourists, especially Millennials, once they reach their destinations. "It's a little bit of a security blanket for some people to let their friends and family know where they are, and for others, it can be a feedback and status kind of thing," says Gretzel. In the Millennial travel report, 43 percent of Millennials reported that "the comments and 'likes' they receive from social media are as important or more important than a trip itself."[5]

But the desire of many tourists to take clever selfies to post on Instagram, Facebook or other social media has led to dangerous behavior and even deaths. In the past six years, 259 people have died while taking selfies, according to a study by the All India Institute of Medical Sciences, a group of public medical colleges in New Delhi. (The study did not say how many were tourists.)[6]

"In many places, people are climbing things they're not supposed to, they're jumping into fountains, and they're ignoring warning signs," says Gretzel.

While social media can lead tourists to less crowded destinations that may welcome the influx, social media-using visitors also can overwhelm spots that are unprepared for the sudden attention. For example, Philip Evans, the head of tourism at the local council in East Sussex, said the visiting throngs threaten the chalk cliffs, which are crumbling in places.[7]

Social media also can concentrate tourists at already-crowded sites. "If you go to Pinterest, there are hundreds of posts about the 10 most photo-worthy spots in Los Angeles," says Gretzel. Those posts drive tourists to those areas, exacerbating an already irritating problem for residents, she says.

But social media also can be part of the solution, according to Gretzel. "In many ways, social media is a blessing for destinations," she says, "because this data allows officials to see where people are going and to potentially manage, and also anticipate, where problems might occur if suddenly there is hype around a certain place."

In addition, government and tourism officials can work with so-called influencers, such as celebrities, to change travel patterns. "They can expose the influencers to different, less crowed places and therefore redirect their followers as well," says Gretzel, citing Melbourne, Australia, and Switzerland as two places that are pursuing this strategy.

— Barbara Mantel

[1] Amie Tsang, "How Asian Social Media Transformed a Quiet U.K. Walking Spot," *The New York Times*, Oct. 12, 2018, https://tinyurl.com/y7qumbz9.

[2] Skyler Huff and Leah Swartz, "The Millennial Brief on Travel & Lodging," *FutureCast*, October 2016, p. 13, https://tinyurl.com/y89b3c88.

[3] Tsang, *op. cit.*

[4] "Social media key: tourism report," *The West Australian*, Oct. 22, 2018, https://tinyurl.com/y9qawrpq.

[5] Huff and Swartz, *op. cit.*

[6] Agam Bansal *et al.*, "Selfies: A boon or bane?" *Journal of Family Medicine and Primary Care*, July-August 2018, https://tinyurl.com/ydcq3b6k.

[7] Tsang, *op. cit.*

In the United States, Congress passed the Airline Deregulation Act of 1978, and for the first time, U.S.-based airlines were allowed to fully compete on price. Deregulation gave rise to a new kind of airline—low-cost, no-frills carriers such as Southwest and the now defunct People Express—and the average roundtrip domestic airfare fell about 16 percent over the next decade, after adjusting for inflation.[62]

The rise of the internet in the 1990s provided a further boost to tourism. "The internet's ability to automate transactions—cutting out the middleman function of ticketing agents—in turn allowed airlines to run a tighter and more streamlined ship," according to the European online travel site eurocheapo. "In no time at all, cheap fares became the expectation."[63]

Travelers turned to online search engines such as Expedia.com, which was founded as a division of Microsoft in 1996, to compare and book airfares, hotel rooms and rental cars.

Soon the internet was allowing travelers to talk to one another. TripAdvisor started in an office above a pizzeria in Needham, Mass., a little more than 18 years ago and has grown into the world's most visited travel website. Its user-generated reviews can make or break hotels, restaurants and attractions.

Similarly, Airbnb, another "disruptor" in the travel industry, began small. In 2007, its founders, Joe Gebbia and Brian Chesky, were having trouble making rent on the San Francisco loft they shared and decided to lay down three air mattresses and advertise them for rent for $80 each a night to out-of-towners. The company is now a multibillion-dollar business operating worldwide.

A series of deep recessions began in 2007 and ended for most countries within a year or two, although their effects lingered far longer. Tourism recovered and has grown steadily since 2010, spurred by an expanding middle class, growing prosperity in developing countries, low-cost airlines and the continued expansion of internet-mediated, low-cost accommodations.

But this growth has come at a cost. Beginning in 2016, residents in Venice, Barcelona and other European cities marched to protest tourist crowds, drunken behavior and rising housing costs they blamed partially on the explosion in short-term vacation rentals.

The United Nations proclaimed 2017 the International Year of Sustainable Tourism for Development. Its goal was to recognize that well-managed tourism can contribute to sustainable development.

CURRENT SITUATION

Hotel Workers Strike

The global tourism industry is facing a host of challenges, ranging from labor strikes to climate change.

Guests at 21 Marriott International hotels in six cities across Massachusetts, California and Hawaii have to cross picket lines as more than 7,000 hotel employees strike at the world's largest hotel chain. Strikers at two hotels, in Oakland, Calif., and Detroit, reached an agreement with Marriott early this month.[64]

The walkout began in early October, after months of fruitless negotiations between Marriott and Unite Here, which represents approximately 20,000 of the hotel's workers, over the terms of new labor contracts. It is the largest multicity hotel worker strike in U.S. history, according to the union.[65]

Housekeepers, front-desk attendants, restaurant employees and other non-management workers have joined the strike and are seeking higher pay, employee participation in decisions about automation and improvements in worker safety. "We are encouraged by the progress achieved in resolving the strikes in Oakland and Detroit with strong, fair contracts, and are hopeful that similar progress can be achieved in the other six cities still on strike," said D. Taylor, international president of Unite Here. The union said it will release contract details once all strikes end.[66]

The average hourly wage for workers in food preparation in the hotel industry is $11.80, according to the U.S. Bureau of Labor Statistics. For maintenance and cleaning workers, it is $11.07.[67]

"We're starting with the biggest and the richest hotel company and after that we are absolutely going to ensure that all the other hotel companies are giving workers enough pay so they're able to work with dignity," said Unite Here spokeswoman Rachel Gumpert.[68]

Travelers are taking notice of the strike and registering their complaints on TripAdvisor. One October guest who stayed at the Westin Boston Waterfront wrote, "We witnessed 2 bar employees FIST FIGHTING. We were and are absolutely horrified!!! When we spoke to the front desk about it at a later time, we were told they were 'just the replacement bar staff' due to the strike."[69]

In a statement issued before the recent settlements, Marriott said it is "disappointed that Unite Here has chosen to resort to a strike instead of attempting to resolve these disputes at the bargaining table."[70]

National Park Funding

Bills to fund long-neglected repairs on National Park Service lands are gaining public support as they move through Congress. The Restore Our Parks Act in the Senate and a similar measure in the House would provide $6.5 billion over five years to reduce $11.6 billion in deferred maintenance. The money would come from existing, unallocated revenues the government receives from energy development.[71]

The legislation has garnered the support of congressional Democrats and Republicans, Interior Secretary Ryan Zinke and an array of travel and business groups.

"It is critical to preserve and protect our national parks to benefit generations to come," said Tori Barnes, senior vice president of government relations for the U.S. Travel Association in Washington, a membership organization that lobbies on behalf of the travel industry. "In 2017 alone, visitors to national parks spent $18 billion in gateway communities, which supported

Is volunteer tourism a good way to help the poor?

YES   Konstantinos Tomazos
Associate Business School Dean, Senior Lecturer in International Tourism Management, University of Strathclyde, U.K.

Written for *CQ Researcher*, November 2018

Volunteer tourism is a meaningful form of travel whose purpose is to contribute to a cause or alleviate a need.

It is not purely tourism, given its underlying mission, and it is not purely international aid or volunteering, given that you cannot separate the volunteer from the tourist. In its current state, volunteer tourism may not be the best way to help the poor. Nevertheless, it is an excellent way to make a difference in the lives of some poor people.

Volunteer tourism has become, to no small extent, a victim of its own success. When you offer entrepreneurs the opportunity to make simultaneous demands on people's time, effort and money, and when minimal barriers of entry into the market exist, the inevitable result is a vast network of projects, stakeholders and beneficiaries who are all pursuing their own interests. The volunteers pay for their flights, their placement, their food, their insurance, their entertainment—everything really—and all the entrepreneur/project broker or nongovernmental organization (NGO) has to supply are the placements. This signals an opportunity to many and leads to proliferation and ambiguity.

While the intentions are good, volunteer tourism falls into the same traps as international aid. This trap fosters relationships and patronage that limit the benefits of volunteer tourism to the same recipients, similar to an automated garden sprinkler that waters at a set time and place.

However, it would be disastrous to dismiss volunteer tourism as harmful to the poor. In most parts of the world where volunteer tourists operate, there is a clear need for help in a variety of areas and projects. The truth is, there will never be a magic bullet that will solve all problems with one stroke. No one contribution could take children out of orphanages, bring water to villages or provide relief to areas hit by catastrophes, and the volunteers themselves are fully conscious of this fact. Volunteers are probably getting more out of the experience than what they are putting in.

But we can find solace and hope in knowing that others will follow who can build on what their predecessors have left behind. It is this cycle that gives meaning and purpose to the volunteer tourism phenomenon. In the long run, and as locals seize the increased economic opportunities, volunteer tourism will meet its potential.

NO   Elisa Burrai
Senior Lecturer, School of Events, Tourism and Hospitality Management, Leeds Beckett University, U.K.

Written for *CQ Researcher*, November 2018

Numerous studies and industry debates have focused on the potential of volunteer tourism to alleviate poverty, particularly in the global south.

Volunteer tourism is often regarded as an alternative, responsible form of tourism. It developed in response to significant social, environmental and economic challenges experienced by our modern societies. Volunteer tourists usually travel from "developed" to "developing" countries with the purpose of helping those in need. So, "need," "help" and "development" are central to volunteer tourism discourses and often are used to justify the roles and practices of those involved.

The way that volunteer tourists, sending organizations, local stakeholders and beneficiaries interpret and engage with the concept of poverty is complex. Yet, the ability of volunteer tourism to alleviate poverty is controversial. There are three main reasons for this.

First, need in volunteer tourism is communicated as poverty and is powerfully marketed to attract volunteers. Western representations romanticize poverty in order to meet the expectations of volunteer tourists. Poverty, in other words, becomes a commodity—an object to be experienced and consumed by tourists.

Current debates on the commercialization of poverty highlight the voyeuristic and exploitative nature of volunteer tourism, whose supporters insist it can help the poor across the globe.

Second, poverty is constructed and marketed following an oversimplified Western view of what poverty is. Under such a construct, volunteer tourists can help alleviate poverty. Yet, these tourists often are young, unskilled and have not experienced poverty or participated in development projects before.

Third, volunteer tourism fosters dependency on charity. Destinations and communities that receive volunteer tourists become financially reliant on foreign help. So, volunteer tourism reinforces dependence on foreign "expert" knowledge instead of helping communities learn how to break out of the poverty cycle.

Volunteer tourism, in short, is a contested form of traveling. Although it often has been flagged as a way out of poverty, particularly in the global south, its aspirations are, in some cases, unachievable.

This is because volunteer tourism emphasizes stereotyped views of poverty. It enables inexperienced volunteers to work in development, and it enhances financial dependency on foreign charitable help. A reformed, more critical engagement with the concepts of poverty and development can make volunteer tourism and its practices more meaningful.

Tourists pack a street in Dubrovnik, Croatia, on Aug. 6, 2018. The coastal city, a World Heritage Site, began limiting the number of visitors to its historic old town in 2017 because of the crowds. Popular tourist locations are looking for ways to protect residents' quality of life while keeping visits enjoyable for tourists.

thousands of local jobs and fueled nearby businesses, like restaurants, hotels and retail shops."[72]

Conservationists also praised the bill but said Congress should do far more.

"America's public lands and wildlife are inextricably linked—and require dedicated funding to conserve and protect them," said Collin O'Mara, president and CEO of the National Wildlife Federation, an environmental advocacy organization in Reston, Va. O'Mara called on Congress to find a similar bipartisan solution to increase funding for wildlife habitat.[73]

The deterioration in many of the National Park Service's 417 units—national parks, battlefields, national monuments and other lands—is significant and sometimes dangerous, said Marcia Argust and Tom Wathen, who head conservation efforts at the Pew Charitable Trusts, a global research and public policy organization in Philadelphia, and support the bills' passage. "Now, deteriorating historic buildings, eroding trails, outdated water and electrical systems, unsafe roads, disintegrating monuments and timeworn campgrounds, waterfronts and visitor centers need repairs," they wrote in a September op-ed.[74]

Both bills have been reported out of committee to the full chambers for action. The number of co-sponsors is growing: As of early November, 17 Democrats, 15 Republicans and one independent are co-sponsors of the Senate version. In the House, 128 Democrats and 84 Republicans are co-sponsors. Supporters are hoping that Congress will turn its attention to the bills by year-end.[75]

Climate Change and Tourism

Ferrara, Italy, is known among tourists for its architecture dating to the Middle Ages and the Renaissance and for its bicycle-riding citizens.

It also is one of 37 World Heritage Sites around the Mediterranean at risk of being inundated by water in a 100-year flood because of rising seas, according to a study published last month in the journal *Nature Communications.*[76]

The researchers analyzed 49 cultural World Heritage Sites—places that illustrate a significant stage in human history—in low-lying coastal areas of the Mediterranean, many of them popular tourist draws. Rising seas also are causing coastal erosion, and the researchers determined that 42 of the sites are at risk.

Historic sites in the Northern Adriatic are most in danger from rising seas, from the Palladian buildings in Vicenza just east of Venice to several ancient cities across the water in Croatia. And the risk will only grow as sea levels continue to rise. "Until 2100, flood risk may increase by 50 percent and erosion risk by 13 percent across the region, with considerably higher increases at individual World Heritage Sites," the researchers said.

Each country is responsible for managing its World Heritage Sites, but management plans rarely consider how to adapt to sea level rise, according to the study.

"We cannot put a value on what we will lose," said Lena Reimann, a researcher at Kiel University in Germany and the study's lead author. "It's our heritage—things that are signs of our civilization. . . . It's more an ethical question, a moral question. We will not be able to replace them once they are lost."[77]

While climate change hurts the tourism industry, tourism also contributes to global warming, according to the UNWTO.[78]

The tourism industry generates four times more CO2, a greenhouse gas and driver of global warming, than thought, according to a study published in the journal *Nature Climate Change* in June. The industry accounts for 8 percent of greenhouse gas emissions, it said, and "the majority of this footprint is exerted by and in high-income countries."[79]

The UNWTO urges tourists around the world to plan trips closer to home and to rely more on public transportation and less on flying. It also urges tourism operators to reduce energy use and to switch to alternative forms of energy. "Our findings provide proof that so far these mitigation strategies have yielded limited success," the researchers said.[80]

OUTLOOK

Overtourism's Threat

In the years ahead, overtourism will remain a problem in the United States and abroad, many experts say.

Fretwell of the Property and Environment Research Center says she doubts that U.S. national parks will be less crowded 10 years from now.

"After working on these issues for 20 years, I think we're going to have similar problems as we do right now," says Fretwell. "And my guess is we're not likely to see congestion pricing" in which visitors would pay higher prices during peak times. But she says she hopes some pilot projects "can demonstrate how congestion fees . . . can benefit both us, as the recreationists that are out there using these areas, and society as a whole because we're taking care of the landscapes overall."

Recreation ecologist Marion predicts that within a decade, a few parks will experiment with reservations systems to control visitation, and he urges park administrators to invest in research and adjust the systems as they are implemented.

"I'm a believer in adaptive management, where you try new tools from the toolbox," he says, "and you evaluate them as you try them and make corrections as you evaluate them and learn new things." This kind of research was not done when Zion began its shuttle system 18 years ago, says Marion.

Marion says he is placing hope in the work of the 7-year-old Interagency Visitor Use Management Council, which is developing science-based best practices for visitor use on federally managed lands and waters. The council consists of six federal agencies, including the National Park Service, the Bureau of Land Management and the Forest Service.

"I'm not sure [the council will] make a difference in five years. That's a fairly short time horizon," he says. "But over 10 years and longer, I think it will."

Sustainable-tourism expert Tourtellot says he is pessimistic about the ability of tourist destinations in the United States and abroad to rein in overcrowding over the next decade.

"Absent a major kind of a paradigm shift in how we travel and how we do tourism, I expect it to be worse and particularly exacerbated by the day-trippers," he says. "Cruise lines, tour bus people, taxi drivers make a lot of money, and they all pressure the government to keep it going. And not until it gets to the breaking point, as it has in Barcelona, does that start to change."

Travel operator Francis shares this bearish outlook. "Some overcrowded places will escape the overtourism trap," says Francis. "Many others won't, residents will leave, and they will become 'sacrifice destinations'— theme parks that absorb large numbers of tourists and protect other places from overtourism. In doing so, they will lose every sense of their true value and identity."

Epler Wood of Harvard says she is unsure about the ability and the will of Europe's major cities to create the necessary master plans to manage tourism within a decade's time. "It's too early to say," she says. "I think we're at a really tipping-point moment, and I can't say I'm either hopeful or pessimistic, honestly."

But Turner of the World Travel & Tourism Council is optimistic. "In a decade from now, I think we'll see a lot more management plans," she says. "It might mean that we have to book further in advance, that we might need to be prepared to pay timed ticketing or that businesses will have to think more about the value that they create in destinations than they do at the moment."

NOTES

1. "Trevi Fountain fight, Rome: Women throw punches over selfies as authorities try to deal with overcrowding," *Traveller*, Aug. 15, 2018, https://tinyurl.com/y79rzzvd.

2. "International Tourism 2017—Market share by region of tourist arrivals and tourism receipts," World Tourism Organization (UNWTO), https://tinyurl.com/ybv9olde.

3. Will Coldwell, "First Venice and Barcelona: now anti-tourism marches spread across Europe," *The Guardian*, Aug. 10, 2017, https://tinyurl.com/ya8swn2o; Rafat Ali, "The Genesis of Overtourism: Why We Came Up With the Term and What's Happened Since," *Skift*, Aug. 14, 2018, https://tinyurl.com/ycplyt6t.

4. Shannon Jones, "Top 5 Industries in Hawaii: Which Parts of the Economy are the Strongest?" *Newsmax*, March 3, 2015, https://tinyurl.com/y98dewye.

5. Andrew Sheivachman, "Proposing Solutions to Overtourism in Popular Destinations: A Skift Framework," *Skift*, Oct. 23, 2017, https://tinyurl.com/ybckx7tc.

6. Freya Higgins-Desbiolles, "Sustainable tourism: Sustaining tourism or something more?" *Tourism Management Perspectives*, January 2018, https://tinyurl.com/y7ly4gmk.

7. John Steinhorst, "Leaders look for solutions to avoid overtourism," *The Garden Island*, March 4, 2018, https://tinyurl.com/yc7jhroh.

8. "UNWTO World Tourism Barometer and Statistical Annex," UNWTO, October 2018, https://tinyurl.com/yaco45fl; "International Tourism 2017—Market share by region of tourist arrivals and tourism receipts," *op. cit.*

9. Elizabeth Becker, "Tourism takeover: Chinese travelers changing the industry," *Travel Weekly*, Aug. 1, 2018, https://tinyurl.com/ya4dzqb9.

10. *Ibid.*

11. "Homi Kharas, "The Unprecedented Expansion of the Global Middle Class: An Update," Brookings Institution, February 2017, p. 2, https://tinyurl.com/yd2f4smb.

12. "Coping With Success: Managing Overcrowding in Tourism Destinations," McKinsey & Co., December 2017, p. 15, https://tinyurl.com/ycbwz2xg.

13. *Ibid.*

14. "Travel & Tourism: Economic Impact 2018, World," World Travel & Tourism Council, March 2018, the foreword and p. 1, https://tinyurl.com/y93lynfj.

15. Manfred Lenzen *et al.*, "The carbon footprint of global tourism," *Nature Climate Change*, June 2018, p. 522, https://tinyurl.com/y8b8jyrh.

16. Lauren McMah, "Tourists will not be banned from Thai beach, officials say," news.com.au, Feb. 22, 2018, https://tinyurl.com/y9tx5mqw; "Dubrovnik Set to Lower Daily Tourist Limit in Old Town to 4,000?" *Croatia Week*, Aug 12, 2017, https://tinyurl.com/yb2b587f; "Barcelona approves new tourist accommodation cap," *The Local*, Jan. 27, 2017, https://tinyurl.com/yc3rwo9g; and Costas Paris, "A Greek Island Paradise Tries to Be a Little Less Welcoming," *The Wall Street Journal*, Sept. 1, 2018, https://tinyurl.com/ya4pv9ln.

17. Katherine LaGrave, "Barcelona Approves New Law to Limit Tourist Numbers," *Condé Nast Traveler*, Jan. 27, 2017, https://tinyurl.com/yc8rx9fk.

18. Janine Puhak, "Amsterdam officials crack down on excessive, 'naughty Disneyland' style partying," Fox News, Oct. 17, 2018, https://tinyurl.com/y9x5wbbn; "Detourism: travel Venice like a local," Office of Sustainable Tourism of the City of Venice, https://tinyurl.com/y945w3pd.

19. "Corfu Garbage: Travel Agents, Hoteliers and Local Community Demand Solution Now!" *Keep Talking Greece*, June 21, 2018, https://tinyurl.com/y7k62l7s.

20. "How can destinations reduce overcrowding?" World Travel & Tourism Council, Aug. 13, 2018, https://tinyurl.com/yca576f4; "13 ways to Do London like a Londoner," Visit London Official Visitor Guide, https://tinyurl.com/yay8yxqd.

21. Gene Sloan, "Sneak peek: Inside Royal Caribbean's Symphony of the Seas, largest cruise ship ever," *USA Today*, Feb. 14, 2018, https://tinyurl.com/ybffs4nr.

22. John Hutchinson, "Barcelona bans large tourist groups from entering city's famous La Boqueria food market . . . so locals can do their weekly shop," *Daily Mail*, April 9, 2015, https://tinyurl.com/y9ps98eu.

23. "Challenges Facing the Galápagos Islands," International Galapagos Tour Operators Association, https://tinyurl.com/y7nfrzej.

24. Courtney Tanner, "One Utah national park is looking into limiting the number of visitors each day and requiring permits for certain trails," *Salt Lake Tribune*, June 1, 2018, https://tinyurl.com/ybsgfhfl.

25. "Recreation Visitors by Month," Zion National Park, https://tinyurl.com/yda2t5kc; "Annual Park

Ranking Report for Recreation Visits in: 2017," *Annual Park Ranking Report,* https://tinyurl.com/lvj4tpl; and "Preliminary Alternative Concepts Newsletter," Zion National Park, Summer 2017, https://tinyurl.com/y8jyhvon.

26. Tanner, *op. cit.*

27. "National Parks System, Recreation Visits by Year," National Park Service, https://tinyurl.com/yab8olrm; "Quick History of the National Park Service," National Park Service, May 14, 2018, https://tinyurl.com/ycy65w9q.

28. Jim Robbins, "How a Surge in Visitors Is Overwhelming America's National Parks," *Yale Environment 360,* July 31, 2017, https://tinyurl.com/y9cx6gp3.

29. "National Park Service Comprehensive Survey of the American Public, 2008–2009: Racial and Ethnic Diversity of National Park System Visitors and Non-Visitors," National Park Service, July 2011, p. 10, https://tinyurl.com/yc7u3n3d.

30. "National Parks Punt on Overcrowding," Public Employees for Environmental Responsibility, July 14, 2016, https://tinyurl.com/yd84gkuw.

31. "About Airbnb: Advancing home sharing as a solution," Airbnb, https://tinyurl.com/yc3xomzc.

32. "Healthy Travel and Healthy Destinations," Airbnb, May 29, 2018, pp. 16, 19, 34, https://tinyurl.com/ydz89dxu; Daniel Guttentag *et al.,* "Why Tourists Choose Airbnb: A Motivation-Based Segmentation Study," *Journal of Travel Research,* April 27, 2017, p. 354, https://tinyurl.com/yba6cuh5.

33. Sadie Whitelocks, "'We're nearly full!' Visit Cornwall boss blames Airbnb for gridlocked roads and packed beaches as the number of rental properties spikes to 9,000—from just SEVENTEEN two years ago," *Daily Mail,* Sept. 28, 2018, https://tinyurl.com/yazg5le7.

34. Casey Newton, "Airbnb opens up a complaint center for neighbors to report problem guests," *The Verge,* May 31, 2016, https://tinyurl.com/yakrwart.

35. "My Neighbors Killed My Airbnb Unit," Learnairbnb.com, https://tinyurl.com/y8hgn75f.

36. "Airbnb, New York and Housing," Airbnb Citizen, May 3, 2018, https://tinyurl.com/y86hhkvo; "The Impact of Airbnb on NYC Rents," Office of the New York City Comptroller, May 3, 2018, https://tinyurl.com/ybej26ng.

37. Daniel Guttentag, "Regulating Innovation in the Collaborative Economy: An Examination of Airbnb's Early Legal Issues," Collaborative Economy and Tourism, May 31, 2017, p. 107, https://tinyurl.com/ycydo8wy.

38. Daniel Guttentag, "What Airbnb really does to a neighborhood," BBC, Aug. 30, 2018, https://tinyurl.com/yd94asrw.

39. Dara Kerr, "Airbnb purges thousands of San Francisco listings overnight," CNET, Jan. 18, 2018, https://tinyurl.com/ybmkalkj.

40. Maxine Feifer, *Tourism in History: From Imperial Rome to the Present* (1985), pp. 8-10, 15.

41. *Ibid.,* pp. 27-28.

42. "Crusades," The History Channel, https://tinyurl.com/yd2vofh5; *ibid.,* pp. 28-29.

43. Feifer, *ibid.,* pp. 29-31, 41, 64-65, 68-69.

44. Eric G.E. Zuelow, *A History of Modern Tourism* (2016), pp. 9, 21, 25-26.

45. *Ibid.,* pp. 50-51.

46. "The Pullman Company," Pullman Museum, https://tinyurl.com/yaqh358m.

47. Zuelow, *op. cit.,* pp. 55-59.

48. "Thomas Cook History," Thomas Cook, https://tinyurl.com/ydhrmpor.

49. Ethan Carr, "Olmsted and Scenic Preservation," PBS, https://tinyurl.com/y9dkfvap.

50. Barbara Mantel, "Managing Western Lands," *CQ Researcher,* April 22, 2016, pp. 361-84.

51. Zuelow, *op. cit.,* p. 109.

52. "A Brief History of AAA," AAA, https://tinyurl.com/ybtsuvxq.

53. Zuelow, *op. cit.,* pp. 115, 121, 123-24.

54. Amy Harris, "The History of Airline Industry," *USA Today,* https://tinyurl.com/ychbf23v.

55. Feifer, *op. cit.*, p. 221.

56. "Disneyland opens," The History Channel, Aug. 21, 2018, https://tinyurl.com/ycmn9n2x.

57. Zuelow, *op. cit.*, pp. 168, 170, 171.

58. Erin Blakemore, "A Black American's Guide to Travel in the Jim Crow Era," Smithsonian.com, Nov. 3, 2015, https://tinyurl.com/y8olx8hd.

59. Feifer, *op. cit.*, p. 223.

60. Bonnie Gringer, "Average Gas Prices in the U.S. Through History," TitleMax, https://tinyurl.com/yd6eqg5n.

61. Zuelow, *op. cit.*, p. 159.

62. Madhu Unnikrishnan, "A Law That Changed the Airline Industry Beyond Recognition (1978)," *Aviation Week*, June 4, 2015, https://tinyurl.com/yalbx6ya; Derek Thompson, "How Airline Ticket Prices Fell 50% in 30 Years (and Why Nobody Noticed)," *The Atlantic*, Feb. 28, 2013, https://tinyurl.com/ya8rw536.

63. "History of Budget Carriers," Eurocheapo, https://tinyurl.com/yd96hryz.

64. "Hotel Workers Reach Settlements With Marriott in Oakland, Detroit; Marriott Strikes Continue in 6 Other Cities," Marriott Travel Alert, Nov. 4, 2018, https://tinyurl.com/y94ewloj.

65. "Marriott Strike Escalates With Largest Yet Actions in National Day of Mass Action," Unite Here, Oct. 19, 2018, https://tinyurl.com/yddpo9fo.

66. "Hotel Workers Reach Settlements With Marriott in Oakland, Detroit; Marriott Strikes Continue in 6 Other Cities," *op. cit.*

67. "May 2017 National Industry-Specific Occupational Employment and Wage Estimates: NAICS 721100—Traveler Accommodation," U.S. Bureau of Labor Statistics, March 30, 2018, https://tinyurl.com/y888pdxt.

68. Ting, *op. cit.*

69. "The Westin Boston Waterfront," Trip Advisor, https://tinyurl.com/y8bbzr6a.

70. Nancy Trejos, "Marriott workers on strike in eight US cities," *USA Today*, Oct. 8, 2018, https://tinyurl.com/y8oltede.

71. Marcia Argust, "Restore America's Parks," Pew Charitable Trusts, https://tinyurl.com/y8uk5wn5.

72. "Bishop, Grijalva Introduce Bill to Establish a Fund Addressing National Park Maintenance Backlog," House Committee on Natural Resources, July 25, 2018, https://tinyurl.com/yazx4q7q.

73. Kellie Lunney, "Rare bipartisan cheer for rollout of 'fix our parks' bill," E&E News, July 25, 2018, https://tinyurl.com/yanbwe5s.

74. Marcia Argust and Tom Wathen, "Restoring our national parks would be a bipartisan win for Congress," *The Hill*, Sept. 5, 2018, https://tinyurl.com/y9tmavwm.

75. S.3172: Restore Our Parks Act, GovTrack, https://tinyurl.com/ycng559l; S.3172—Restore Our Parks Act, congress.gov, https://tinyurl.com/y9ctre9n; H.R.6510—Restore Our Parks and Public Lands Act, https://tinyurl.com/y7gdtury.

76. Lena Reimann *et al.*, "Mediterranean UNESCO World Heritage at risk from coastal flooding and erosion due to sea-level rise," *Nature Communications*, Oct. 16, 2018, https://tinyurl.com/yacxw22y.

77. Chris Mooney and Brady Dennis, "The latest thing climate change is threatening is our history," *The Washington Post*, Oct. 16, 2018, https://tinyurl.com/y9xlpx8s.

78. "FAQ—Climate Change and Tourism," World Tourism Organization, http://tinyurl.com/h9ufug8.

79. Lenzen *et al.*, *op. cit.*

80. *Ibid.*, p. 526.

BIBLIOGRAPHY
Selected Sources
Books

Becker, Elizabeth, *Overbooked: The Exploding Business of Travel and Tourism,* **Simon & Schuster, 2013.**
A journalist examines the tourism industry and its huge effect on the global economy, environment and culture.

Feifer, Maxine, *Tourism in History: From Imperial Rome to the Present,* **Stein and Day, 1986.**
A researcher traces the evolution of tourism, currently

one of the world's largest economic sectors, across nearly 2,000 years.

Zuelow, Eric G.E., *A History of Modern Tourism,* **Palgrave, 2016.**
A historian examines tourism's political and cultural impacts from earliest times to the present.

Articles

Becker, Elizabeth, "Tourism takeover: Chinese travelers changing the industry," *Travel Weekly,* **Aug. 1, 2018, https://tinyurl.com/ya4dzqb9.**
Chinese tourists outnumber and outspend international tourists from other countries.

Coldwell, Will, "First Venice and Barcelona: now anti-tourism marches spread across Europe," *The Guardian,* **Aug. 10, 2017, https://tinyurl.com/ya8swn2o.**
Protesters in several European cities have decried tourism congestion and day-trippers disembarking from cruise ships.

Paris, Costas, "A Greek Island Paradise Tries to Be a Little Less Welcoming," *The Wall Street Journal,* **Sept. 1, 2018, https://tinyurl.com/ya4pv9ln.**
Santorini limits the number of cruise ship passengers arriving on the Greek island, as garbage and crowds overwhelm residents.

Steinhorst, John, "Leaders look for solutions to avoid overtourism," *The Garden Island,* **March 4, 2018, https://tinyurl.com/yc7jhroh.**
Officials in Kauai are looking for ways to manage growing tourism on the Hawaiian island, including negotiating with federal authorities about the number of incoming airline flights.

Tanner, Courtney, "One Utah national park is looking into limiting the number of visitors each day and requiring permits for certain trails," *Salt Lake Tribune,* **June 1, 2018, https://tinyurl.com/ycjg3vaw.**
Zion National Park is considering requiring reservations to limit record numbers of visitors, but critics say the proposal is unfair.

Reports and Studies

"Coping With Success: Managing Overcrowding in Tourism Destinations," McKinsey & Co., December 2017, https://tinyurl.com/ycbwz2xg.
A management consultant says limiting tourist numbers should be a last resort.

"Healthy Travel and Healthy Destinations," Airbnb, May 29, 2018, https://tinyurl.com/ydz89dxu.
The leading home-sharing company examines the impact of short-term vacation rentals in eight tourist destinations.

"Travel & Tourism: Economic Impact 2018 World," World Travel & Tourism Council, 2018, https://tinyurl.com/y93lynfj.
The travel and tourism sector accounted for 313 million jobs and 10.4 percent of global gross domestic product in 2017, according to an industry trade group.

Guttentag, Daniel, "Regulating Innovation in the Collaborative Economy: An Examination of Airbnb's Early Legal Issues," *Collaborative Economy and Tourism,* **May 31, 2017, https://tinyurl.com/ycydo8wy.**
Cities are increasingly imposing regulations on Airbnb, including limiting the number of days per year that an owner can rent an accommodation.

Higgins-Desbiolles, Freya, "Sustainable tourism: Sustaining tourism or something more?" *Tourism Management Perspectives,* **January 2018, https://tinyurl.com/y7ly4gmk.**
The tourism industry is promoting growth despite finite natural resources and should embrace measures to make tourism more sustainable, argues a researcher from the University of South Australia.

Kharas, Homi, "The Unprecedented Expansion of the Global Middle Class: An Update," Brookings Institution, February 2017, https://tinyurl.com/yd2f4smb.
Within a few years, most of the world's population, for the first time ever, might live in middle-class or wealthy households.

Sheivachman, Andrew, "Proposing Solutions to Overtourism in Popular Destinations: A Skift Framework," *Skift,* **Oct. 23, 2017, https://tinyurl.com/ybckx7tc.**
A tourism industry research firm suggests destinations adopt several strategies to solve overtourism, including making travel more expensive.

For More Information

Center for Responsible Travel, 1225 I St., N.W., Suite 600, Washington, DC 20005; 202-347-9203; https://responsibletravel.org. Research organization that helps policymakers, the tourist industry, nonprofits and international agencies find solutions to critical tourism issues, such as overcrowding and environmental degradation.

Cruise Lines International Association, 1201 F St., N.W., Suite 250, Washington, DC 20004; 202-759-9370; www.cruising.org. The world's largest cruise industry trade association, representing more than 50 cruise lines.

The International Ecotourism Society, 427 N. Tatnall St., Wilmington, DE 19801; www.ecotourism.org. Association of ecotourism professionals, industry experts and ecotourism operators in more than 190 countries that sets standards for the industry.

National Park Service, 1849 C St., N.W., Washington, DC 20240; 202-208-6843; www.nps.gov. Bureau of the U.S. Department of the Interior that is charged with preserving national parks for public use.

Public Employees for Environmental Responsibility, 962 Wayne Ave., Suite 610, Silver Spring, MD 20910; 202-265-7337; www.peer.org. Advocacy group that promotes responsible management of public natural resources and investigates claims from public employees about environmental misconduct by the government.

United Nations Educational, Scientific and Cultural Organization (UNESCO), 7 Place de Fontenoy, 75007 Paris, France; www.unesco.org. U.N. agency that promotes cultural heritage, including by designating World Heritage Sites.

World Tourism Organization, Calle Poeta Joan Maragall, 42, 28020 Madrid, Spain; +34 91 567 81 00; www2.unwto.org. U.N. agency that promotes tourism as a driver of economic growth, inclusive development and environmental sustainability.

World Travel & Tourism Council, 65 Southwark St., London SE1 0HR United Kingdom; +44 (0)20 7481 8007; www.wttc.org. Membership organization of more than 150 travel and tourism companies around the world.

12

Global Population Pressures

Susan Straight

AFP/Getty Images/Boureima Hama

Women wait with their children for a consultation at a health clinic in Madarounfa, Niger, on Sept. 9, 2015. Niger has the world's highest fertility rate—more than seven children per woman of childbearing age on average—and one of Africa's worst infant mortality rates, at 127 deaths per 1,000 births. As the global population grows, resources are being stretched thin.

From *CQ Researcher*,
June 22, 2018

Roukaya Hamani, the second wife to a man twice her age, lives in rural Niger, a desert-covered West African country with the world's highest fertility rate of more than seven children per woman. Married at age 10, Hamani never went to school and had her first baby when she was 11. By 18 she had given birth four times.

Hamani wants to take a break from having children but fears disappointing her husband and in-laws. In Niger, the best way for a woman to protect her status in the family is to have many children.

"If they want me to have another pregnancy, I can do it just for them to feel happy," Hamani said.[1]

Her situation is emblematic of why the world's population—currently 7.6 billion—continues to rise. The biggest increases are occurring mostly in rapidly growing developing countries like Niger, Chad, and Somalia, while populations in wealthy countries such as Japan and Germany are shrinking. Regardless of the precise numbers, population specialists and some policymakers vigorously disagree over whether population growth is a problem and what, if anything, should be done about it.

Some experts say the Earth will reach a breaking point in terms of how many people it can support, with burgeoning populations exacerbating climate-change-related droughts and floods and creating catastrophic shortages of food, energy, water, and arable land. Conflicts over natural resources and massive cross-border migrations could result, they say, triggering deep divisions in the receiving countries, as Europe's ongoing migration crisis has shown.[2]

Growth in Africa, Decline in Europe

Africa will experience the world's biggest leap in population by 2050, with the continent's total population more than doubling, according to U.N. Population Division projections. But some African countries and regions will expand faster than others. Niger and Angola will grow the most, while North Africa and Southern Africa will see the continent's slowest growth. Europe is expected to see a 3 percent population decline, with countries such as Germany and Italy experiencing double-digit decreases.

Change in Global Population 2015-2050 by Region

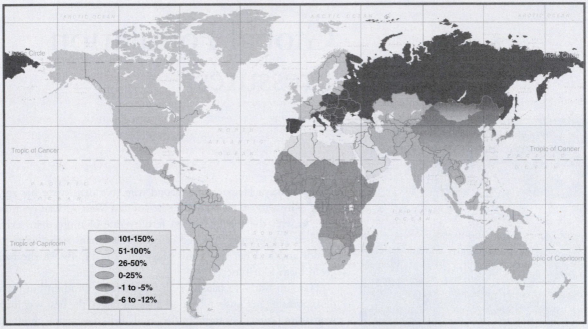

Legend:
- 101-150%
- 51-100%
- 26-50%
- 0-25%
- -1 to -5%
- -6 to -12%

How Today's Most Populous Countries Will Change

Countries	2015 Population	2050 Population	Percentage change	Countries	2015 Population	2050 Population	Percentage change
China	1.4 billion	1.36 billion	−2%	Pakistan	189 million	307 million	62%
India	1.3 billion	1.66 billion	27%	Nigeria	181 million	411 million	127%
U.S.	320 million	390 million	22%	Russian Fed.	144 million	133 million	−8%
Indonesia	258 million	322 million	25%	Japan	128 million	109 million	−15%
Brazil	206 million	233 million	13%	Mexico	126 million	164 million	30%

Source: "World Population Prospects 2017," Population Division, Department of Economic and Social Affairs, United Nations, June 2017, https://tinyurl.com/y7vwc27k

"It's increasingly hard to imagine any scenario other than a horrifying ecological collapse in our future," given the difficulties of reducing consumption, wrote Erik Assadourian, a senior fellow with the Worldwatch Institute, an independent environmental research organization in Washington.[3]

But others say fears of overpopulation are overblown and that long-term population projections are tricky. "There's no reliable method for calculating how many babies will be born," says Nicholas Eberstadt, a political economist at the American Enterprise Institute (AEI), a conservative think tank in Washington. "We can see out pretty well for about 20 years. Once we start talking about babies of the unborn, we go into science fiction."

"Alarmist projections regarding the myth of global overpopulation continue to be promoted by some—and they are wrong," says Theresa Notare, assistant director of the Natural Family Planning Program for the Secretariat of Laity, Marriage, Family Life and Youth at the U.S. Conference of Catholic Bishops. "People are not the problem. The imbalance of resources, [such as] access to education, a living wage, nutritional and medical help, are among the problems."

Many experts contend that increased access to contraception would help stem population growth and improve the lives of women in developing countries.

Substantial evidence shows that women and societies are healthier and better off economically when they use family planning, according to the United Nations Population Fund (UNFPA). For example, "contraception helped spark a trend towards later marriage, helping women and men to find stable, economically attractive matches," according to the UNFPA.[4]

But Pope Francis, in a 2015 encyclical, criticized those who "can only propose a reduction in the birth rate" to solve resource scarcity problems and who blame population growth "instead of extreme and selective consumerism on the part of some."[5]

Ironically, even as population continues to rise, the worldwide fertility rate—the average number of births per woman of childbearing age—peaked in 1950 at about five children and has since fallen to about half that.[6] Demographers say rising population during declining fertility is the result of "population momentum"—the several-generation lag time between declining fertility and smaller subsequent generations as the babies born during peak birth periods grow up and have children and grandchildren—albeit fewer than their forebears.[7]

Projections on when the global population will peak and start to decline differ according to certain variables. United Nations demographers say the global population could peak at anywhere from 9.4 billion by midcentury to 13.2 billion by 2100, with a medium-range projection of 11.2 billion by then.[8]

The difference in those projections is a single child per woman, says John Seager, president of Population Connection, a nongovernmental organization in Washington that advocates for reducing population growth.

Other key aspects of the global population outlook, according to U.N. population experts, include:[9]

• China and India, with more than 1 billion people each, make up 37 percent of the world's population. In about 2024, India is expected to overtake China as the world's most populous country.

• Of the 2.2 billion babies born between 2017 and 2050, more than half will be African.

• By 2050, 51 countries will see population declines, but by 2100, 33 other countries could triple in size. Six African countries—Angola, Burundi, Niger, Somalia, Tanzania, and Zambia—are projected to grow fivefold by then.

• Through midcentury, much of the migration from high-growth developing countries to lower-growth developed ones likely will come from five Asian countries: India, Bangladesh, China, Pakistan, and Indonesia. They will send more than 100,000 migrants annually to countries such as the United States, Germany, Canada, the United Kingdom, Australia, and the Russian Federation.

• Before 2100, the global population should shift from mostly young to elderly, straining national health and social program budgets as fewer young people are available to support those programs.

Within just a few decades, for example, Americans ages 65 years or older "are projected to outnumber children for the first time in U.S. history," said Jonathan Vespa, a demographer with the U.S. Census Bureau.[10] Worldwide, "national health services, and even economies, are predicted to collapse" under demands for health care and pensions, writes Sarah Harper, professor of gerontology and director of the Oxford Institute of Population Aging at the University of Oxford in Britain.[11]

While population growth may not be a serious problem right now in developed countries, it should be addressed as a global problem because it will have worldwide implications, Seager says. "We were pretty insulated from the world by vast oceans 100 years ago," he says. "It doesn't work that way anymore."

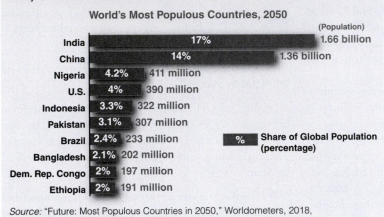

India Projected Most Populous

Projections show that by 2050 India will account for 17 percent of the global population, closely followed by China at 14 percent, according to Worldometers, a digital platform that tracks changes in global statistics in real time. The site projects that by midcentury, India will have nearly 1.7 billion inhabitants, compared to nearly 1.4 billion in China.

World's Most Populous Countries, 2050

(Population)

Country	Share	Population
India	17%	1.66 billion
China	14%	1.36 billion
Nigeria	4.2%	411 million
U.S.	4%	390 million
Indonesia	3.3%	322 million
Pakistan	3.1%	307 million
Brazil	2.4%	233 million
Bangladesh	2.1%	202 million
Dem. Rep. Congo	2%	197 million
Ethiopia	2%	191 million

% Share of Global Population (percentage)

Source: "Future: Most Populous Countries in 2050," Worldometers, 2018, https://tinyurl.com/yb9cfjop

For example, Seager says, if billions more people begin producing greenhouse gases, and "global systems—ocean, climate—begin to really degrade, it's going to have a huge impact," with cross-border implications. "Desperate people either starve, move, or steal."

Population projections in a particular region can change, however, if the rates of contraception use go up or down. Based on current trends, contraceptive use will grow, especially in sub-Saharan Africa where it has previously been low. For example, in East Africa, the unmet need for contraceptives is expected to fall from 24 percent to 18 percent between 2015 and 2030, say U.N. population experts.[12]

"The rate of future population growth is primarily dependent on family planning," contends Meaghan Parker, founding editor of *New Security Beat*, an online publication focusing on environmental change and global sustainability at the Woodrow Wilson International Center for Scholars, a centrist think tank in Washington. "If women are given access to modern contraception, [it creates] a huge change," she says.

Yet, some 214 million women who want access to modern contraceptives cannot obtain them, says

Kristen P. Patterson, program director of People, Health, Planet in International Programs at the Population Reference Bureau, an organization in Washington that conducts research on population, health, and the environment. "The real crisis is that it's 2018 and everyone in the world should have the ability to decide whether and when to have children, space births, complete their education, get jobs," she says.

But many people oppose contraception for cultural or religious reasons. For example, in patrilineal societies such as Nigeria, men often determine familial fertility and contraceptive decisions, and many rural societies regard large families as necessary to work the land.[13] Contraceptives have also been controversial from a religious viewpoint, and not just among Catholics. Leaders in many Muslim countries, such as Egypt, have endorsed family planning, which is not forbidden by the Quran. But in some countries where ultraconservative strains of Islam have risen to prominence, clerics have condemned contraceptives as infanticide, which is forbidden by the Quran, or as a Western plot to stop Muslims from multiplying.[14]

Meanwhile, some academics see Western nongovernmental organizations' family planning programs in the developing world as racist or paternalistic. "Racist and patriarchal ideas" underpin such family planning initiatives, denying women in poor countries "real control over their bodies," argued Kalpana Wilson, an instructor at the London School of Economics' Gender Institute. "The appropriation of the notion of 'women's right to choose' for neoliberal population control must be challenged."[15]

Many Catholics and evangelical Christians who oppose abortion have long opposed using U.S. funds for international programs that provide abortion services or discuss the option. The Trump administration, following through on a campaign promise, has reinstated and expanded a long-standing Republican policy to ban U.S. funding for international groups that provide abortion services or discuss abortion as a family planning option.

Trump also banned U.S. funding for a U.N. family planning program that he said cooperated with a Chinese population-control agency overseeing coercive abortions, a charge the program denies.[16]

Educating girls can reduce population growth without government involvement in family planning, according to Wolfgang Lutz, founding director of the Wittgenstein Centre for Demography and Global Human Capital, a research organization in Vienna, Austria, that provides demographic data to policymakers. "Women with more education have fewer children, both because they want fewer and because they find better ways to pursue their goals," Lutz wrote.[17]

Some environmentalists say using renewable energy and other technologies that address rising carbon dioxide emissions and global warming can alleviate population pressures. The world's top carbon emitters—China, India, and the United States—also are the world's most populous countries.[18]

Yet, while many experts worry about rising population, others are more concerned about what will happen after a country's population peaks and starts to decline, leading to an aging populace. Joel Kotkin, a fellow in urban studies at Chapman University in Orange, Calif., and author of *The Next Hundred Million: America in 2050*, argues that migration can solve many of the resultant challenges.

Adding another 100 million people to the nation's 328 million by 2050, fueled by large numbers of immigrants, will give the United States a competitive advantage over its rivals due to innovation and economic strength powered by diversity, he said.[19]

As population experts, policymakers and social policy advocates discuss the challenges posed by population growth, here are some of the questions being debated:

Is a global population crisis impending?

Many demographers take a more nuanced approach than the doomsday language of the 1960s, when Stanford University biologist Paul R. Ehrlich and his wife, Anne, authors of the 1968 best-seller *The Population Bomb*, predicted mass starvation and societal upheavals in the 1970s and '80s due to overpopulation.

An official from the Pakistan Bureau of Statistics collects information from a resident in Karachi during a census in March 2017 as an army soldier looks on. The country's population is expected to increase by more than 100 million between 2015 and 2050.

The Population Reference Bureau "would never use the term 'population crisis,'" said the organization's Patterson. "People don't really know what the maximum population of the world will be." She contends that "a lot depends on meeting the unmet need for contraception." If all women could plan the timing and spacing of their pregnancies, she says, it would "greatly affect what the total world population will end up being."

Seager, of the Population Connection, says rather than being a global crisis, population pressures are "regional, local and even personal." For instance, he says, of the hundreds of millions of people facing population crises right now, most live in developing countries and are poor. On a personal level, he adds, a woman who has had a baby every year for the last six years and whose body cannot survive another pregnancy will probably die if she gets pregnant again, leaving "her children without a mother."

Moreover, he says, the true toll often goes unmeasured: Children dying because their governments cannot afford to provide basic health care or because of conflicts triggered by population pressures are not counted as victims of a population crisis. "The families of the 29,000 children who die every day due to preventable causes are affected by population crises, even though no death certificates are likely to cite population growth as a cause of death," he says. "Wars and civil strife in some of the most

A woman walks past houses in Yubari, Japan, a former coal-mining town known as Japan's "oldest" city because many of its residents have moved away, leaving an aging population behind. Japan's declining birth rate means that as the country's population ages, fewer young people are available to support the elderly or keep the economy strong.

rapidly growing places on Earth are consequences of population crises."

Assadourian, of the Worldwatch Institute, wrote that ignoring what he sees as a coming crisis "is like looking out the window of a plane and realizing you're about to crash but refusing to tell the other passengers about the impending crash." He continued, "Stabilizing population is urgent. The goal should not simply be to nudge along a little less growth so population stabilizes at 9 billion rather than 9.5 or 10 billion. Instead, we need to make a long-term plan to get population back to a manageable range."[20]

To reduce environmental pressures due to growing populations, he advocates drastic changes in lifestyle and consumption patterns in wealthier countries.

However, AEI's Eberstadt says he does not see an impending population crisis. "I always thought this talk of the population explosion in 1970s was a little silly and overblown," he says. "Humans within the last century have recast their child-bearing habits."

He adds, "The reason the planetary income level is six times higher today than it was in 1900 is that we've accumulated knowledge, pushed new frontiers for knowledge and have applied that knowledge in a way that allows us to do more with less."

Many anti-abortion groups, such as the Population Research Institute, based in Front Royal, Va., also reject evidence-based projections that population growth represents an impending crisis. The group's mission, says its website, is to "debunk the myth of overpopulation, which cheapens human life and paves the way for abusive population control programs."[21] The group strongly supports Trump's decision to cut off U.S. funding for U.N. contraception programs.

Others, such as environmental writer Fred Pearce, says he is more worried about what he calls the coming population "crash"—when declining birth rates lead to aging and dying populations with fewer young people to build the economy, such as is occurring in Japan. Reversing declining birth rates by getting people to have more children will be more difficult than reducing fertility, he wrote in *The Coming Population Crash and Our Planet's Surprising Future*. "Once the trend [of reduced fertility] has set in, it will be very hard to break. As well as having ever fewer potential mothers, societies may get out of the habit of having babies."[22]

Seager says migration from high-population countries to low-growth regions can solve problems caused by declining populations. The immigrants can then produce more total goods and services, boosting a country's output, he argued in *The Good Crisis: How Population Stabilization Can Foster a Healthy U.S. Economy*. In other words, he wrote, overall population growth "is not essential for per capita economic growth, which is the common economic measure of individual well-being."[23]

But migration has its challenges, as Europe and Africa have seen in recent years. "Tensions surrounding migratory flows through West Africa—including . . . competition over land, resources and employment—have contributed to violence and conflict across the sub-region," wrote World Bank specialists on international conflict and violence.[24]

Can technology relieve the pressures of population growth on food, energy, and other resources?

As population growth exacerbates shortages of food, water, and energy and worsens climate change, some experts believe technology can overcome such problems.

For instance, to help feed the world's growing population, rice production will need to rise as much as an estimated 40 percent by 2050, even as arable farmland shrinks because of new commercial and residential development, said James E. Hill, associate dean for international programs in the College of Agricultural and Environmental Sciences at the University of California, Davis.[25] Agricultural experts say new technologies can help, such as by allowing farmers to grow rice varieties that use less fertilizer and water than standard varieties.[26]

Scientists across the globe—part of the C4 Rice Consortium funded largely by the Bill & Melinda Gates Foundation—are trying to engineer a more efficient rice plant.[27] "The scope and audacity of the project are hard to overstate," wrote science journalist Charles M. Mann. "Rice is the world's most important foodstuff, the staple crop for more than half the global population."[28]

Some officials, nonprofit groups, and population experts are pushing for greater use of renewable-energy technologies, such as solar panels and wind farms. For example, Nigeria, Africa's most populous nation, is growing so fast it cannot provide electricity to all of its 190 million citizens, even though it has the world's 11th-largest proven oil reserves.[29] One in four rural Nigerians and many urban residents lack electricity. And the country's population is expected to double within 30 years.

To address the problem, the Nigerian government plans to provide solar-generated electricity to 75 percent of Nigerians by 2020 and obtain 30 percent of the country's energy needs from renewable sources by 2030.[30]

But some population experts say that while technology can help mitigate the effects of climate change and resource scarcity, it is not the sole solution to population pressures. Focusing too much on new technology can be a distraction from what they consider more important approaches, such as changing personal consumption patterns or improving access to contraceptives, they say.

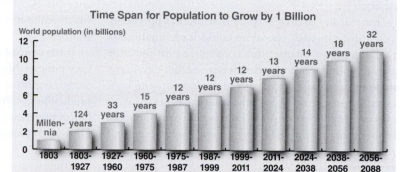

Global Count Rising Fast

The world's population has increased rapidly since the early 20th century, when it took some 33 years to grow by 1 billion people. Since 1975, the population has grown by roughly a billion people every 12 or so years. The pace is expected to ease somewhat in coming decades.

Time Span for Population to Grow by 1 Billion

World population (in billions)

Period	Time Span
1803	Millennia
1803–1927	124 years
1927–1960	33 years
1960–1975	15 years
1975–1987	12 years
1987–1999	12 years
1999–2011	12 years
2011–2024	13 years
2024–2038	14 years
2038–2056	18 years
2056–2088	32 years

Source: Max Roser and Esteban Ortiz-Ospina, "World Population Growth," Our World in Data, updated April 2017, https://tinyurl.com/yc5x5hhb

"The most dangerous thing we could do is to think technology is going to save us, so that we don't have to become much more aware of ourselves and our impact and be willing to change," says Joan Diamond, executive director of the Millennium Alliance for Humanity and the Biosphere at Stanford University, which focuses on educating people about the dangers of population growth, consumption, and environmental degradation. "The only salvation is through individual consciousness, commitment, action and behavior."

The problem requires a multipronged solution that addresses "population, consumption and technology," she continues. "No one factor in that equation is sufficient to save us from the collapse of civilization. We're definitely headed toward that and need to be working on all three fronts."

For the moment, say some population experts, population growth in developing countries with low individual consumption rates is not contributing much to environmental problems. For example, "in Nigeria, 100,000 more people won't change carbon emissions that much," says Parker, at the Wilson Center.

Currently, "more than half the world's population lives at or below a fair Earth-share," meaning their lifestyles are within ecologically sustainable limits, according to Jennie Moore, associate dean at the British Columbia

Institute of Technology's School of Construction and the Environment, and William E. Rees, a professor emeritus in the School of Community and Regional Planning at the University of British Columbia. "These people are mostly in Latin America, Asia and Africa."[31]

But Moore and Rees warn that increasing energy availability in such countries could lead inhabitants there to adopt unsustainable consumption patterns similar to those in the United States or other developed nations. Such patterns, they said, include driving cars, traveling in airplanes, and building large homes with central air and heating. "If everybody consumed like residents of [developed] countries, we would need more than four Earths" to provide resources for them all, they wrote.

The Worldwatch Institute's Assadourian takes an equally pessimistic view. "Reducing the global population is essential in addressing humanity's impact on the planet" by drastically cutting consumption and the use of unsustainable technologies, he wrote. For example, if everyone lived within the planet's sustainable limits, "gone would be the days of driving personal vehicles, flying, eating meat, living in large homes, and essentially the entire consumer society that we know today."[32]

Some population experts consider contraceptives effective technologies that could improve the quality of life when widely available in all forms. Based on data in developing countries, says Parker, "when everyone has access to information about contraception . . . they will choose to have fewer children." But providing family planning depends on funding and political will, she says.

Should the United States provide more money for international family planning?

Three days after his inauguration in January 2017, President Trump issued an executive order to reinstate—and greatly expand—the so-called Mexico City Policy that Republican administrations since 1984 have adopted and Democratic administrations have suspended.

Initiated by the Reagan administration during a 1984 U.N. population conference in Mexico City, the policy prohibits the distribution of U.S. family planning funds to any group that provides abortion services or discusses abortion as a family planning option—even if those activities are not financed with U.S. money. The policy is an extension of the Helms Amendment, passed shortly after the Supreme Court legalized abortion in 1973, which prohibited the use of U.S. foreign aid for abortion services.

Birth control advocates derisively call the Mexico City policy a "global gag rule" because it restricts how foreign organizations can use their non-U.S. government funds, limits conversations between patients and their health providers, and prevents groups that receive U.S. funds from pressing for legalizing abortion in their own countries.

Trump's action substantially expanded the impact of the Mexico City policy by applying it not just to health programs that receive U.S. family planning funds but to all other U.S. funded global health programs, such as those that provide vaccines or that fight malaria, tuberculosis, or HIV, if those programs partner with or receive money from any organization that provides abortion or abortion counseling.[33]

"I direct the Secretary of State . . . to extend the requirements of the reinstated [policy] to global health assistance furnished by all departments or agencies," Trump's executive order said. "I further direct the Secretary of State to take all necessary actions, . . . to ensure that U.S. taxpayer dollars do not fund organizations or programs that support or participate in the management of a program of coercive abortion or involuntary sterilization."[34]

"This marks a significant expansion" of the scope of previous Mexico City policies, potentially affecting $7.4 billion in funds for health programs in fiscal 2018, of which $600 million is used for family planning, according to the Henry J. Kaiser Family Foundation, a nonprofit that focuses on national and international health issues.[35]

Shortly after announcing his Mexico City policy, Trump notified Congress on April 3, 2017—and again in the spring of 2018—that he was blocking all U.S. funding for the U.N. Population Fund (UNFPA), saying the organization was in violation of the 1985 Kemp-Kasten Amendment, which forbids U.S. funding of organizations that support or participate in forced sterilizations and abortions.[36]

The decision was criticized by family planning advocates and praised by anti-abortion groups and critics of China's controversial one-child-per-family population-control policy, instituted in the 1970s and often enforced with state-mandated abortions.

The decision meant that $32.5 million earmarked for the UNFPA in fiscal 2017 may be redirected to similar programs administered by the U.S. Agency for International Development (USAID). The United States has been the third-largest contributor to the UNFPA, which provides family planning services in 150 countries.[37]

"Defunding UNFPA is a great victory for the women of China and everyone who respects the inherent dignity of each and every human life," wrote Population Review Institute President Steven Mosher. The institute contends that the UNFPA has cooperated with the Chinese agency that has overseen more than 364 million abortions since the 1970s, citing China's own population control agency and a 2016 U.S. State Department report on human rights practices.[38]

Reggie Littlejohn, founder of Women's Rights Without Frontiers, which lobbied for defunding UNFPA, said the needs of women and girls in countries affected by the U.S. cuts will be met by other organizations "that are not walking hand in hand with a regime that is continuing" to force women to abort fetuses.[39]

The UNFPA vigorously denies that it has been complicit in coerced abortions. Trump's decision "is based on the erroneous claim that UNFPA 'supports, or participates in the management of a programme of coercive abortion or involuntary sterilization' in China," the UNFPA said, adding its work "promotes the human rights of individuals and couples to make their own decisions, free of coercion or discrimination."[40]

A lengthy State Department memo, obtained by the Associated Press, said there was no evidence that UNFPA funds were used to support forced abortions or sterilization in China.[41]

UNFPA "goes where few others do—into war zones and countries wracked by natural disasters—to try to make sure that pregnant women and girls get health care, can deliver babies safely and are protected from gender-based violence," wrote Amanda Klasing, a senior researcher in the Women's Rights Division at Human Rights Watch, an international nongovernmental advocacy group based in New York that researches and promotes human rights. "Blocking this money will hurt its core functions of addressing gender-based violence, child marriage and female genital mutilations."[42]

Rep. Eliot L. Engel of New York, the ranking Democrat on the House Foreign Affairs Committee, called the UNFPA cuts a "grave error," saying the agency is "a lifeline for the world's most vulnerable women and girls, many of whom have nowhere else to turn." Latanya Mapp Frett, executive director of Planned Parenthood Global, the international arm of Planned Parenthood Federation of America, which partners with local providers and advocates for reproductive health care for all women, said, withdrawing U.S. support for UNFPA "will have a devastating impact" on the agency and "hurts the lives of the women, men and young people they serve."[43]

Parker, of the Wilson Center, says family planning funds represent only a sliver of the federal budget but they deliver "a huge bang for the buck" because population growth contributes to climate change and resource scarcity.

The cutoff of UNFPA funding also means some 214 million women who want access to modern contraceptives do not have them, says Seema Jalan, executive director of the Universal Access Project and Policy, Women and Population, which advocates for increasing access to family planning under the auspices of the United Nations Foundation. The foundation creates partnerships with nongovernmental organizations, corporations, and foundations to support U.N. work.

"There is an absolutely high need for women who want to use modern contraceptives but aren't able," she says.

BACKGROUND
Exponential Growth

For millennia, the Earth's population grew relatively slowly, not reaching 1 billion until the early 1800s. Then, as health care and sanitation improved in the late

19th century and life expectancies rose, the Earth quickly added another billion people by the late 1920s.[44]

Before cities became cleaner and the food supply more abundant, many theorists worried population growth was unsustainable. Famines, they warned, were constants in history, including one in 1315-17 that killed millions of Europeans after a succession of failed harvests.

In 1798, Thomas Malthus, a Cambridge-educated British pastor, published his famous "An Essay on the Principle of Population." According to him, "the progress of mankind toward happiness" had been impeded by a "constant tendency in all animated life to increase beyond the nourishment prepared for it."[45]

Malthus, who was born into a prosperous family, believed famine and disease were necessary checks on population growth and should be allowed to claim lives in order to reduce numbers so that others would have enough to eat. With the world population approaching 1 billion when Malthus wrote his essay, cities were more crowded and filthier than ever.

Because demand for food would always outstrip supply, Malthus said, charity would only encourage the poor to reproduce. His theory of population control, known as Malthusianism, influenced British policy governing treatment of the poor. By 1834, British "poor laws" that provided assistance to those earning below subsistence wages were replaced by the Poor Law Amendment Act, which considered poverty a moral failing and sent violators to workhouses as punishment.[46]

When the Irish potato famine of 1845-49 struck, the government in London authorized the importation of corn from the United States in an attempt to alleviate hunger, but it did little else. With a blight having destroyed their primary food source, more than a million people in Ireland starved.[47]

The Industrial Revolution, meanwhile, was bringing sweeping changes to Europe and the United States, as rural inhabitants began moving to cities in search of factory work. Urban populations soared in the 19th century, even as families were getting smaller. One reason for the change was that parents no longer needed large numbers of children to work the fields.

And as wealth increased because of industrialization, a growing middle class came to value smaller families and opted to have fewer children. People began to live longer in the 19th century because of the invention of vaccines, improved medical care, and agricultural gains that led to a more secure food supply. England's population, for example, nearly tripled from less than 7 million in 1750 to almost 21 million in 1850.

Birth Control Emerges

In 1839, American inventor Charles Goodyear discovered how to vulcanize natural rubber so that it had a higher tensile strength and elasticity. This new rubber had immediate appeal as a replacement for the then-current version of condoms made from animal intestines.[48]

But information on contraceptives was hard to obtain, at least in England and the United States because of laws banning the printing of "obscene" materials. In 1877, Charles Bradlaugh and Annie Besant were put on trial in London on obscenity charges for publishing Charles Knowlton's *Fruits of Philosophy*, describing contraceptive methods. Knowlton, an American physician whose book had first been published in the United States and who also had been tried on obscenity charges (though not convicted), is often credited with introducing the concept of birth control to the masses.[49]

With contraceptive methods improving and industrialization spreading, the fertility rates of 10 Northern European countries peaked by 1880 and have been declining ever since. Southern and Eastern Europe followed suit.[50]

In 1878, the fledging field of demography held its first international conference in Paris. The conference for the first time defined demography as a "new discipline, aimed at providing an exclusive space for the discussion of all subjects related to the 'mathematics of population.'"[51]

As population studies gained momentum, the legacy of Malthusianism lived on in the 1880s and '90s. Francis Galton, a cousin of scientist Charles Darwin, became interested in applying Darwin's principles of natural selection to humans. A medical school dropout who had a mental breakdown in his 20s, Galton dabbled in genetics after he inherited a family fortune. That led him to eugenics, the belief that human genes can be improved through careful breeding, and a commitment to

CHRONOLOGY

1800s-1940s *Population growth accelerates rapidly; Industrial Revolution leads to overcrowded cities and a desire by some for smaller families, but new birth control methods stir controversy.*

1804 Global population reaches 1 billion.

1832 American physician Charles Knowlton introduces methods for controlling conception to the general public in his book, *Fruits of Philosophy: Or the Private Companion of Young Married People.*

1839 Charles Goodyear begins manufacturing rubber condoms and other contraceptives.

1914 American obstetrical nurse and social crusader Margaret Sanger coins the term *birth control*; two years later she opens the nation's first birth control clinic in Brooklyn, N.Y.

1946 U.N. Population Commission begins to research demographics and advise the United Nations on population trends and policies.

1960s-1970s *Annual global population growth rate peaks at more than 2 percent in the early 1960s; some international groups promoting birth control in developing countries are accused of funding abortions and sterilizations.*

1960 Thirty U.S. states restrict or prohibit sales or advertising of birth control products. . . . U.S. Food and Drug Administration approves the first oral contraceptive, Enovid (later known as "the pill").

1968 Pope Paul VI affirms the Roman Catholic Church's ban on artificial birth control. . . . Stanford University biologist Paul R. Ehrlich's best-seller, *The Population Bomb*, predicts mass starvation and major societal upheavals due to overpopulation, but birth rates start to decline slowly.

1973 U.S. Supreme Court legalizes abortion. . . . Congress passes the Helms Amendment, barring use of U.S. foreign aid for abortions or abortion counseling.

1979 China announces a one-child-per-family policy to limit population, which leads to coerced abortions and sterilizations.

1980s-1990s *World leaders debate links between population growth and development.*

1981 Economist Julian Simon's *The Ultimate Resource* challenges the idea that poverty and high population growth rates are linked. . . . Republican President Ronald Reagan institutes Mexico City Policy barring federal funding for international nongovernmental organizations that provide abortion counseling or referrals. Subsequent Democratic administrations rescind the policy; Republicans reinstate it.

1988 Global population increases by almost 93 million, the largest annual increase ever.

1994 A total of 179 countries adopt a 20-year action plan to meet women's and girls' educational and health needs.

2000-Present *Population growth rate continues to decline; politicians seek to curtail funds for family planning.*

2011 Global population reaches 7 billion.

2012 U.N. Population Division declares family planning a human right.

2015 China eases its one-child policy, allowing couples to have two children.

2017 President Trump reinstates and expands Mexico City policy by prohibiting foreign organizations from receiving U.S. funds for any health services if the groups accept funds from a non-U.S. donor to perform or provide information on abortions. . . . Trump blocks U.S. funding for the U.N. Population Fund (UNFPA), claiming it supports a Chinese coercive abortion program, which the agency strongly denies.

2018 World population reaches 7.6 billion. . . . Trump again blocks U.S. funding for the UNFPA. China is considering scrapping its limits on family size by the end of the year, according to news reports.

Scientists Seek Novel Ways to Boost Food Supplies

U.N. warns food production must rise 50 percent by 2050.

In a greenhouse, a researcher sprays radishes with a fertilizer created from a "bionic leaf," which performs photosynthesis 10 times more efficiently than normal. The fertilizer produces vegetables more than twice normal size.[1]

Another agricultural innovation, known as C4 photosynthesis, could create plants that increase crop yields by roughly 50 percent or use less water and fertilizer than normal crops, according to researchers working with a consortium of scientists from 12 institutions in eight countries that is seeking ways to increase rice yields.[2]

Such technologies could become common farming techniques in the future, used to help feed the world's growing population. According to the United Nations Food and Agriculture Organization, which leads international efforts to end hunger, about 815 million people do not have enough to eat. The group says food production must increase by 50 percent by 2050 to satisfy global needs.[3]

Against that backdrop, scientists are searching for ways to significantly increase agricultural yields.

One way could be through the bionic leaf, which boosts photosynthesis, the process by which plants use sunlight to convert carbon dioxide into carbohydrates to fuel the plants' cellular activities. Scientists hope such biofertilizers will someday increase crop production in developing countries that lack easy access to chemical fertilizers.

The bionic leaf was developed in 2016 by Harvard University professors Daniel Nocera (chemistry) and Pamela Silver (biology).[4] The leaf uses bacteria that take nitrogen from the air to produce the fertilizers ammonia and phosphorus.

"Quite surprisingly, it's a fairly potent [fertilizer]," said Kelsey Sakimoto, a Ziff Environmental Fellow at Harvard who is helping Nocera and Silver expand the technology for use by subsistence farmers. "It's grown very simply and applied very simply," he said.[5]

Another technology aims to create bioengineered plants named C4 for a four-carbon molecule that captures carbon dioxide. The plants suppress photorespiration, a process that wastes some of the chemical compounds produced by photosynthesis. Some fast-growing plants, such as corn and sugar cane, have developed that process naturally.

C4 technology could someday significantly increase crop yields for widely used grains such as rice, according to the C4 Project, a rice research consortium overseen by the International Rice Research Institute, based in the Philippines.[6]

"Rice yields need to increase by 50 percent over the next 35 years," according to the consortium's website, which calls C4 technology "one of the most plausible approaches to enhancing crop yield and increasing resilience in the face of reduced land area, decreased use of fertilizers and less predictable supplies of water."[7]

---

discouraging or preventing what he considered inferior people from having children.[52]

To Galton, anyone who was not white and wealthy was less than desirable. Those he labeled inferior should be prevented from reproducing so their weaker traits would not be perpetuated in the human race. In the United States in the late 19th and early 20th centuries, Galton's theories contributed to bans on interracial marriage and to the forced sterilizations of 60 million Americans. Eugenics in the

United States helped inspire similar programs in Nazi Germany and elsewhere, as governments sought to make sure that "humanity shall be represented by the fittest races."[53]

A leader in the birth control movement was American obstetrical nurse and social crusader Margaret Sanger, who advocated on behalf of women who wanted to be able to decide when and whether to have children. Her mother's experience of 18 pregnancies in 22 years, plus Sanger's nursing work attending

Other experts promote the use of conservation agriculture and agroforestry to boost crop yields. Conservation agriculture leaves soil undisturbed—rather than turning it over mechanically—to preserve the soil's microbial life and prevent erosion. Agroforestry returns to an earlier practice of integrating trees and shrubs into crop and animal farming to conserve and restore soil and natural water supplies.

Some contend that the best way to feed the world's growing population and protect the environment is to better manage existing food supplies, 25 percent of which are lost or wasted, according to Mercy Corps, a global humanitarian organization in Washington. "If all the world's food were evenly distributed, there would be enough for everyone to get 2,700 calories per day, even more than the minimum 2,100 requirment for proper health," the group said.[8]

In 2016 France began requiring grocery stores to donate leftover edibles to a food bank network that distributes it among some 5,000 charities. In the United States, California, Connecticut, Massachusetts, Rhode Island, and Vermont prohibit businesses from sending uneaten food to landfills. The laws differ, but they are designed to reduce the amount of food waste dumped in landfills, where it creates harmful greenhouse gases, and to encourage businesses to donate usable leftover food to the hungry or to recycle it by creating compost or biomass energy.[9]

In Connecticut, for instance, businesses must donate or recycle leftover food. And Vermont's Universal Recycling Law increased donations to the state's food bank by 40 percent in 2016.[10]

"The law encourages Vermonters to stop wasting food that instead can help families in need, feed animals to produce local eggs and meat, or create rich soil and renewable energy products," according to the Natural Resources Defense Council, an environmental advocacy group in Washington.[11]

— *Susan Straight*

[1] Amy L. Jia and Sanjana L. Narayanan, "Harvard Researchers Pioneer Photosynthetic Bionic Leaf," *The Harvard Crimson*, Feb. 16, 2018, https://tinyurl.com/ycc5tqfg.

[2] Kevin Bullis, "Supercharged Photosynthesis: Advanced Genetic Tools Could Help Boost Crop Yields and Feed Billions More People," *MIT Technology Review*, 2016, https://tinyurl.com/ybbuyefy; Charles C. Mann, "Can Planet Earth Feed 10 Billion People?" *The Atlantic*, March 2018, https://tinyurl.com/y7twfqnj.

[3] "End Rural Poverty: A Path towards Hunger-Free, Peaceful and Inclusive Societies," U.N. Food and Agriculture Organization, Oct. 10, 2017, https://tinyurl.com/yd3s37r2.

[4] Powell, *op. cit.*

[5] *Ibid.*

[6] Bullis, *op. cit.* Also see "About the C4 Rice Center," International Rice Research Institute, undated, https://tinyurl.com/yczj8ruy.

[7] "Goals of the C4 Rice Project," The C4 Rice Project, undated, https://tinyurl.com/hef9bre.

[8] "Quick Facts: What You Need to Know about Global Hunger," Mercy Corps, April 28, 2018, https://tinyurl.com/ppswlkn.

[9] Eleanor Beardsley, "French Food Waste Law Changing How Grocery Stores Approach Excess Food," NPR, Feb. 24, 2018, https://tinyurl.com/yav59oeq; Amy Leibrock, "Are Food Waste Bans Working?" Sustainable America, Jan. 11, 2017, https://tinyurl.com/ycgya3x9.

[10] Leibrock, ibid.

[11] Yerina Mugica, "Food to the Rescue: Vermont's Universal Recycling Law," Natural Resources Defense Council, Oct. 24, 2017, https://tinyurl.com/y7x5pwlp.

unwanted births and complications from unsafe abortions, animated her.[54] In 1914 Sanger coined the term *birth control* and two years later opened the first birth control clinic in Brooklyn, N.Y., advocating various types of methods and procedures.[55]

In 1946, the newly created United Nations established a U.N. Population Commission to research demographics and advise the organization on population trends and policies.[56] The first U.N. World Population Conference was held in Rome in 1954 and participants agreed to promote local training and data collection to develop ways to deal with population issues in developing countries.[57]

Population and the Environment

The U.S. Food and Drug Administration approved the birth control pill as an oral contraceptive in 1960, amid considerable controversy over who should have access to it. Thirty states had laws restricting or prohibiting the sale or advertising of birth control.[58]

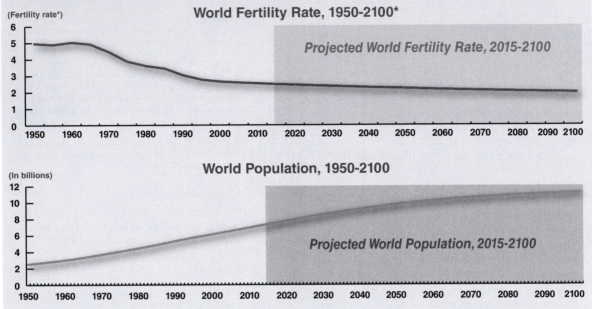

U.N.: Population Growth to Slow

The world's population nearly tripled between 1950 and 2015, even though the fertility rate fell by half during that period, from about 5 live births per woman of childbearing age to 2.5. Demographers call this phenomenon "population momentum"—the several-generation lag time between declining fertility and smaller subsequent generations as babies born during periods of high birth rates grow up and have children and grandchildren.

World Fertility Rate, 1950-2100*

(Fertility rate*)

Projected World Fertility Rate, 2015-2100

World Population, 1950-2100

(In billions)

Projected World Population, 2015-2100

* Live births per woman of childbearing age

Source: "World Population Prospects 2017," Population Division, Department of Economic and Social Affairs, United Nations, June 2017, https://tinyurl.com/y7vwc27k

The Roman Catholic Church reacted forcefully to the pill. In 1968, Pope Paul VI issued an encyclical, *Humanae Vitae* (On Human Life), reaffirming that the church forbade all modern birth control methods. Millions of Catholics—including an inventor of the pill who was a devout Catholic—disagreed with the church. Many continued to use the pill or other forms of contraception.

That same year, the controversial *The Population Bomb* was published by Paul Ehrlich and his wife, Anne. The biologists asserted that in the 1970s, hundreds of millions of people would starve to death due to unmanageable population growth. "At this late date nothing can prevent a substantial increase in the world death rate," they wrote.[59]

But the global population growth rate had peaked in the 1960s at just over 2 percent and has declined steadily ever since.[60] Still, total population continued to grow—by 2.1 percent in 1968, adding about 73 million people to the global count.[61]

In the late 1960s, USAID began distributing contraceptives in developing countries. Republican President Richard M. Nixon supported the effort, calling population growth "one of the most serious challenges to human destiny in the last third of this century."[62] But aid groups were sometimes accused of racism and infringement on women's rights by trying to control the populations of developing countries. By the 1990s, USAID began stressing that family planning was about "quality of life" issues for women and stepped up its efforts to encourage men to be involved in helping to plan their family size.[63]

The debate in the United States over women's reproductive rights resulted in the Supreme Court's landmark *Roe v. Wade* decision in 1973, which legalized abortion and gave women the right to terminate unwanted pregnancies.

The decision caused a fierce backlash among social conservatives. In 1973, Congress passed the Helms Amendment barring U.S. foreign aid for abortion services. The law said that "no foreign assistance funds may be used to pay for the performance of abortion as a method of family planning or to motivate or coerce any person to practice abortions." Anti-abortion activists and the Catholic Church praised it for protecting the lives of fetuses, and for shielding doctors and clinics from being forced to provide abortions.[64]

Abortion opponents won another victory in 1984 when Reagan announced the Mexico City policy barring federal funding for nongovernmental organizations that performed abortions or mentioned it as an option. Since the Reagan administration, this policy has been lifted by Democratic presidents (in 1993 by Bill Clinton and in 2009 by Barack Obama) and reinstated by Republican presidents (in 2001 by George W. Bush and in 2017 by Donald Trump).[65]

Global Developments

In 1979 China announced a one-child-per-family policy as a way to control the communist nation's burgeoning population. Violators could be fined, harassed, imprisoned, or even forced to get abortions or sterilizations.[66] The policy, which remained in effect until 2015, reduced China's fertility rate from about 2.8 children per woman in 1979 to 1.2 by the 2010 census.[67]

The Chinese government claims the one-child policy successfully avoided 400 million births, but critics of the policy point out that the nation's fertility dropped more before the policy took effect than after—from more than five children in the 1960s.[68]

China began allowing married couples to have two children, in part because of concerns about the nation's rapidly aging population and shortage of young workers. At a December 2015 congressional hearing on China's population policies, Mosher of the Population Research Institute, who claimed he sent investigators to China to verify allegations of coercive family planning practices, testified that such activities were continuing.[69]

China is considering ending all limits on reproduction later this year, according to recent press reports.[70]

In 1988 the Earth recorded another milestone: It added more people—some 93 million—than in any year before or since.[71]

In 1994 representatives from 179 countries met in Cairo to adopt a 20-year action plan on meeting the educational and health needs of women and girls, a move considered crucial for stabilizing populations.[72] Since then, according to the U.N., the percentage of girls in developing countries who attend school has increased, and global contraception use rose from 55 percent to 63 percent between 1990 and 2010. The change was most drastic in Africa, where there was a 14-point rise.[73]

In 2011, when the world population reached 7 billion, *National Geographic* depicted the face of the most typical person alive: a 28-year-old Han Chinese man.[74] But by 2030, the most typical face will be that of a resident of India, after that country's population eclipses China's.

Fertility is hard to predict, especially as more and more girls are educated and women have increasing access to contraception. In addition, the U.N. Population Division declared in 2012 that family planning is a human right. To reinforce this position, 193 U.N. member countries in 2015 promised to promote gender equality, empowerment of women, and improvement of maternal health among their long-term "sustainable development" goals.[75]

Under Obama, the United States increased its family planning funding: His last budget proposal, submitted to the Congress in early 2016 for fiscal 2017, pledged $32.5 million to the U.N. Population Fund—part of $607.5 million in bilateral and multilateral funding for global family planning and reproductive health.[76]

Then President Trump began reversing Obama's family planning policies. He not only reinstated the Mexico City policy on Jan. 23, 2017, but expanded on it by prohibiting foreign nongovernmental organizations from receiving U.S. funds for any health services—not just family planning services—if the organization receives funds from a non-U.S. donor to perform or provide information on abortions.

Getty Images/NurPhoto/Mehedi Hasan

Bangladeshi women collect drinking water in Dhaka on June 5, 2018. With a population of more than 15 million, Dhaka shares many of the water-management problems common to other major cities in developing countries. Some experts say burgeoning populations will create catastrophic shortages of water, food, energy, and arable land in high-growth regions of the world.

According to the Kaiser Foundation, had the expanded policy been in effect during the fiscal 2013-15 period, at least 1,275 foreign nongovernmental organizations would have been subject to it.[77]

In April 2017, Trump ordered that no U.S. funds could go to the U.N. Population Fund, saying it had cooperated with the Chinese agency that oversees forced sterilizations and abortions.

In March 2018, Trump again notified Congress that it could not send U.S. funds to the UNFPA because, he said, it had cooperated with the Chinese agency that coerced abortions.[78]

However, Congress designated $32.5 million for the UNFPA in 2018 anyway, but because of Trump's executive order, the money must be redirected to other international agencies that provide health and family planning services.

"Congress essentially rebuked the administration and still provided funding to UNFPA in the federal budget," says Jalan, of the U.N. Foundation.

At present, the 2017 and 2018 UNFPA money is still under the administration's jurisdiction, but family planning advocates are trying to convince Trump officials to use it to support USAID's family planning efforts. As of April 2018, "neither FY 2017 nor FY 2018 funds for UNFPA had been allocated for other family planning,

reproductive health or maternal health programs," according to the Guttmacher Institute.[79]

"It remains to be seen what will happen," says Jalan, noting that when previous Republican administrations defunded U.N. family planning, "the funds have sat around and not been appropriated or have been used for women's health like breast cancer screening."

CURRENT SITUATION
Population Trends

The U.S. birth rate fell for the 10th straight year, to a new low of 60.2 live births per 1,000 women, the U.S. National Center for Health Statistics announced in May. But immigration has more than offset the decline: As of this month, the U.S. population is about 329 million, up from 325.7 million in July 2017.[80]

The falling native-born U.S. population puzzles demographers. "Lots of people have lots of different theories on what moves fertility levels," says the American Enterprise Institute's Eberstadt. Whether the cause is postponement of births to later ages, economic pressures causing couples to decide not to have children or something else, he says, "mapping it out is hard to do because we don't have the detailed data. These are all factors that seem to have some influence but no one has done the deep-dive work to nail this beyond generalizations."

Some blame the continued drop on "the rise of the nones," or the religiously unaffiliated. About 36 percent of American adults under age 30 claim no religious affiliation.[81]

Changing marital mores are seen as another major factor. "No longer is family defined as a male husband and a female wife, much less involving children," wrote pastor and author James Emery White in his 2017 bestselling book, *Meet Generation Z: Understanding and Reaching the New Post-Christian World.*[82]

To combat its declining birth rates, Japan has introduced such measures as cash incentives for having children, greater access to child care, and paternity leave. The goal is to increase the number of births per woman to 1.8 by 2025. But, says Seager of the Population Connection, "there has never been a successful effort to get people to have more children. Incentives can work in the short term," but not long term.

Is population growth a major concern?

YES
Roger-Mark De Souza
President and CEO, Sister Cities International

Written for *CQ Researcher*, June 2018

Population is a powerful variable. Some believe that a larger population conveys status, power, and wealth. Yet, the relationship between population and a country's priorities, such as general well-being and economic vitality, is not a simple linear equation.

Scratch the surface and you discover a complex system of interrelationships. Rapid population growth tends to affect local resource scarcity first (e.g., deforestation, water and land use, fisheries depletion), while consumption drives many other types of environmental issues, such as pollution.

It is also important to remember that in parts of the world that are still growing rapidly, people are generally more reliant on their local natural resources than are people elsewhere. These resources may be easily depleted with a growing population.

Ultimately, however, it's not just about population and numbers, it's about the power of allowing people to choose how many children they would like. History has shown that when women are given the opportunity and means to control their fertility, they tend to have fewer children.

Population is also about possibility. Countries with large youth populations will face increasing demands for education, health care, and employment. If these countries are able to meet the demands of their youth, they might reap what's called the "demographic dividend" as they leverage these young populations to increase economic productivity.

Without these investments, some countries may be more vulnerable to instability. Researchers have found that 80 percent of all new civil conflicts from 1970 to 2007 occurred in countries with youthful age structures (where 60 percent of the population is under age 30). Meeting unmet demand for family planning in countries with high numbers of young people could therefore help indirectly reduce the potential for conflict.

Population dynamics is mostly about plausibility. Demography is by no means destiny. However, fragile and impoverished states have very little resilience to adapt to the pressures created by young age structures and urbanizing populations. Context matters, and with tremendous complexity within social, economic, political, and environmental factors, there is no single formula to guarantee successful economic development or conflict prevention.

Ultimately, responses require coordinated interventions from a variety of sectors. What is clear, however, is that when states pay attention to demographic variables and combine them with the empowerment of women, they increase their chances for sustained development and the well-being of their populace.

NO
Anne Hendrixson
Director, Population and Development Program, Hampshire College

Written for *CQ Researcher*, June 2018

The population picture today is very different from even 50 years ago. Since the 1960s, birth rates have declined more quickly than anticipated, and while the overall global population is still growing, it is growing at a slower rate.

Differences in birth rates among countries have contributed to a youthful Global South and an aging North. These age dynamics mean that most population growth will be in Africa, while countries including Japan, Italy, and Germany will likely experience population declines because of aging. Over time, all countries will experience aging populations, where the majority of people are over 60. Current age dynamics mean that population will have varied impacts in different places.

Now, as ever, it is important to put population in perspective. This means challenging the notion that growth is the primary issue in population studies and policy. Population growth has historically been positioned as the key driver of global problems such as poverty, environmental degradation, hunger, and even war. This mindset too often over-determines the role of the number of people and detracts from a serious conversation about the complex interplay of political, economic, and social factors that propel problems. Population numbers do not predetermine how people affect the world around them or automatically worsen problems.

Consider the relationship of people to the environment: Attributing environmental degradation to population growth assumes each person has an equal and negative "footprint." Not so. The rich have a greater impact than the poor, toxic industries generate more than their share of carbon emissions, and unregulated development contributes to degradation. Dominant patterns of production, consumption, and distribution are unsustainable, regardless of the number of people.

A focus on population growth has gender implications for policy. A primary response to population growth is curtailing fertility, specifically women's, as the point of intervention. This makes women responsible for family planning and too often sidelines men's role. It pits women's sexual and reproductive health decisions against larger and sometimes conflicting agendas, often to the detriment of comprehensive care.

Population is an important issue. Nuanced analyses of population trends are needed to create policies that support the environment and people of all ages. This is particularly true in the context of climate change, which disproportionately affects those least responsible for greenhouse gas emissions, while potentially deepening existing economic and other inequalities.

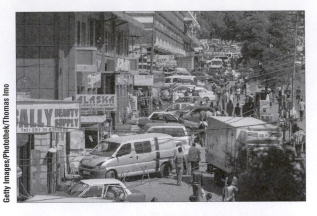

A street in Addis Ababa, Ethiopia, bustles with activity in October 2015. Ethiopia is expected to be the world's 10th-most-populous country by 2050, with more than 190 million citizens. Sub-Saharan Africa is a hotspot for rapid population growth.

High growth rates in some regions are leading to instability, such as conflict, migration, or food scarcity. The 48 countries in sub-Saharan Africa have the highest overall population growth rate on the planet, causing millions to move to other African countries or to flee to Europe.[83] In Nigeria, Africa's most populous country, about 3.7 million people do not consistently have enough to eat.[84]

But population growth is also a problem in North Africa. The Egyptian government is worried that its population growth will hinder economic reforms, so in May it began a new five-year, $19 million program with USAID to improve contraceptive use and reduce fertility.[85]

Technological Solutions

Also in May, researchers led by the International Institute for Applied Systems Analysis announced that if the average global temperature rises 2 degrees Celsius, 29 percent of the global population—double the current percentage—would be affected by rising seas, crop failure, or water scarcity. Depending on which growth estimate is used, climate change could affect roughly 2.7 billion people in 2050.[86]

As a result, 143 million people in the high-growth, developing countries in sub-Saharan Africa, South Asia, and Latin America would become "climate migrants," according to a new World Bank report. And that trend "will accelerate unless there are significant cuts in greenhouse gas emissions and robust development action."[87]

"The number of environmental refugees every year is increasing due to climate chaos," says Seager, of Population Connection.

Experts say technological innovation will be needed to provide environmental, energy, and food stability for billions more people over the coming years. And densely crowded and growing populations make countries more vulnerable to climate change, experts say. For example, heavily populated Bangladesh is highly susceptible to tiny changes in sea level, which can cause flooding, contaminate water, destroy crops, and displace already-struggling farmers and fishers.

Last winter, the ice cover in the Bering Sea was the lowest on record, and in June, a group of 80 scientists revealed that Antarctica's ice sheet is melting three times faster than a decade ago.[88] Melting sea ice raises ocean levels around the world, threatening low-lying farmland and displacing those living along the coasts.

Scientists say reducing the amount of carbon released into the atmosphere is key to checking the rise of ocean levels, and innovators are researching carbon-reduction methods.

One of the most promising, according to scientists, is to reduce the use of hydrofluorocarbon (HFC) gases, used as refrigerants. In 2017, then-appeals court judge Brett Kavanaugh ruled that the U.S. Environmental Protection Agency's plan to curb HFCs exceeded its authority. In October 2018, during Kavanaugh's first week as Supreme Court justice, the court declined to revisit his earlier decision.[89]

In other actions, Nigeria, which has a fertility rate of 5.5 children per woman and a population expected to more than double within 30 years, has invested more than $20 billion in solar power in the past year, using a World Bank loan to build 10,000 solar mini-grids in rural areas. It also has received money from China to build the Mambilla hydropower station in central Nigeria.[90]

Some development aid projects are taking a holistic approach to solving local issues such as food scarcity by addressing population growth along with health and environmental degradation. Proponents of such integrated population, health, and environment programs point out that they provide contraceptives on request, arguing that women have a right to plan whether and when they have children.

China, on the other hand, is actively trying to convince women to have more than one child. Some provinces are offering longer maternity and paternity leaves and other incentives. In August 2018, the *New York Times* reported that the Chinese travel company Ctrip will help defray costs of freezing eggs for managers. The company currently provides incentives to new parents such as taxi rides for pregnant employees and bonuses when employees' offspring are old enough to start school.[91]

OUTLOOK

Fertility and Immigration

A decade from now, two-thirds of Earth's population will live in countries where women will have an average of fewer than 2.1 children.[92] Kenneth Johnson, senior demographer at the University of New Hampshire, says future world population hinges on two variables—fertility trends and immigration.

"Because immigrants are usually young adults, they bring not just themselves but the potential for children in the near future," says Johnson. "And the converse is also true: When people emigrate, due to climate change, economic opportunities, violence, etc., they also take [away] with them the potential for adding children to their home country."

Some population experts see no cause for alarm. "Population will keep rising but at a slower pace than in the past. Africa is a huge unknown. But leave out sub-Saharan Africa and the world is at or below replacement" of its current population, says AEI's Eberstadt. "I don't believe population decline dooms societies to poverty and misery any more than population explosions do. The devil is all in how you respond to it."

But some experts see dire consequences from the planet's overall increase in population. "We are on the path toward global contraction which will force a simplification of lifestyles and consumption," says Diamond of the Millennium Alliance for Humanity and the Biosphere. "The planet has so much potential to come back, but we can't keep pushing it further and further and keep expecting it to come back. Something major will need to trigger the opportunity for the planet to come back. On dark days I think it will be pandemics or famines or some combination."

"Projections suggest that by 2028 we'll add another 770 million people to the world's population—bringing us to 8.4 billion," says the Worldwatch Institute's Assadourian. "Add to that hundreds of millions more livestock and dogs and cats, as the consumer culture spreads around the globe," he adds. That adds up to big trouble in terms of consumption of resources, he says.

But some trust in humanity's ability to adjust, either by good governance or ingenuity. "I don't think anyone is seriously suggesting the world can't produce enough food for 10 billion people," says Eberstadt. "I don't know what the carrying capacity of the world is, and I don't think anyone else does. So far, all of the apocalyptic predictions have been wrong."

NOTES

1. Jill Filipovic, "Why have four children when you could have seven? Family planning in Niger," *The Guardian*, March 15, 2017, https://tinyurl.com/huoqkm4.

2. For background, see Sarah Glazer, "European Migration Crisis," *CQ Researcher*, July 31, 2015, pp. 649-672.

3. Erik Assadourian, "Why We Must Talk About Population," Worldwatch, Oct. 2, 2017, https://tinyurl.com/y9uhd6v9.

4. "New Study Shows Benefits of Family Planning to the Well-Being of Women, Families and Economies," United Nations Population Fund, March 21, 2013, https://tinyurl.com/y9gkgocz.

5. Pope Francis, "Encyclical Letter Laudato Si' Of The Holy Father Francis On Care For Our Common Home," https://tinyurl.com/o6sowft.

6. Max Roser, "Fertility Rate," Our World in Data, Dec. 2, 2017, https://tinyurl.com/ycqsb4v3.

7. G. Nargund, "Declining Birth Rate in Developed Countries: A Radical Policy Re-Think is Required," *Facts Views & Vision*, National Institutes of Health, 2009, https://tinyurl.com/zj3u683.

8. "World Population Prospects: The 2017 Revision, Key Findings and Advance Tables," Department of Economic and Social Affairs, Population Division,

United Nations (2017), p. 3, https://tinyurl.com/ydhrcnn4.

9. *Ibid.*

10. "Older People Projected to Outnumber Children for First Time in U.S. History," U.S. Census Bureau, March 13, 2018, https://tinyurl.com/yd4nmvdd.

11. Sarah Harper, "As the World Ages: When Older Populations Become the Majority," Pew Charitable Trusts, Trend, Winter 2018, https://tinyurl.com/ya4dlxy2.

12. "Trends in Contraceptive Use Worldwide," Department of Economic and Social Affairs, Population Division, United Nations (2015), p. 1, https://tinyurl.com/y7at7rhu; "Trends in Contraceptive Use Worldwide," 2015, Population Division, Department of Economic and Social Affairs, United Nations, https://tinyurl.com/y7at7rhu.

13. Mustapha C. Duze and Ismaila Z. Mohammed, "Male Knowledge, Attitudes, and Family Planning Practices in Northern Nigeria," *African Journal of Reproductive Health*, December 2006, https://tinyurl.com/y8lbtn8f.

14. "The problems of family planning in Nigeria," *The Economist*, April 29, 2017, https://tinyurl.com/yac4obd9; and Samreen Shahbaz, "Islam and family planning in Pakistan," *The Nation*, March 6, 2017, https://tinyurl.com/ybjjscpy.

15. Kalpana Wilson, "Challenging neoliberal population control," Open Democracy, 50.50, July 11, 2013, https://tinyurl.com/y7bt55l5.

16. Nurith Aizenman, "Citing Abortions in China, Trump Cuts Funds for U.N. Family Planning Agency," National Public Radio, April 4, 2017, https://tinyurl.com/ybfk56qw.

17. Wolfgang Lutz, William P. Butz, Samir KC, *Executive Summary: World Population & Human Capital in the Twenty-First Century* (2017), p. 6, https://tinyurl.com/ybb7hp93.

18. "Most Populous Countries in the World," Worldometers, https://tinyurl.com/ybqhbkp5; "Each Country's Share of CO2 Emissions," Union of Concerned Scientists, Nov. 20, 2017, https://tinyurl.com/y7nf3m58.

19. Joel Kotkin, *The Next Hundred Million: America in 2050* (2010); U.S. and World Population Clock, June 15, 2018, https://tinyurl.com/pf8vpc8.

20. Assadourian, *op. cit.*

21. "Our Mission," Population Research Institute, https://tinyurl.com/ya23jmcf.

22. Fred Pearce, *The Coming Population Crash and Our Planet's Surprising Future* (2010), p. 248.

23. John Seager and Lee S. Polansky, eds., *The Good Crisis: How Population Stabilization Can Foster a Healthy U.S. Economy* (2016), p. viii.

24. Alexandre Marc, Neelam Verjee and Stephen Mogaka, *The Challenge of Stability and Security in West Africa* (2015), p. 60, https://tinyurl.com/ybk5dmln.

25. Harry Cline, "California research playing key role in rice production increase," *Western FarmPress*, Sept. 6, 2012, https://tinyurl.com/y7eb55er.

26. Gaia Vince, "Power Plants to Boost Our Crops," BBC, July 25, 2013, https://tinyurl.com/y9sgl8hg.

27. Charles C. Mann, "How Will We Feed the New Global Middle Class?" *The Atlantic*, March 2018, https://tinyurl.com/y7twfqnj.

28. *Ibid.*

29. "The World's Largest Oil Reserves By Country," World Atlas, 2018, https://tinyurl.com/ybsdxcor.

30. *Ibid.*

31. Jennie Moore and William E. Rees, "Is Sustainability Still Possible?" The Worldwatch Institute, p. 42, https://tinyurl.com/oarhffd.

32. Assadourian, *op. cit.*

33. "The Mexico City Policy: An Explainer," Henry J. Kaiser Foundation, May 15, 2018, https://tinyurl.com/y9dwdmo2.

34. Donald J. Trump, "Presidential Memorandum Regarding the Mexico City Policy," Jan. 23, 2017, https://tinyurl.com/y72rnk5v.

35. The Mexico City Policy, *op. cit.* Also see "Trump's 'Mexico City Policy' or 'Global Gag Rule'— Questions and Answers," Human Rights Watch, Feb. 8, 2018, https://tinyurl.com/y9r88brp.

36. The U.N. Population Fund was formerly called the U.N. Fund for Population Activities. Carol Morello, "Trump administration to eliminate its funding for U.N. Population Fund over abortion," *The Washington Post*, April 4, 2017, https://tinyurl.com/yco99bzx.

37. Morello, *ibid.*

38. Jonathan Abbamonte, "President Trump Ends Funding for United Nations Population Fund," Population Research Institute Review, May-June 2017, https://tinyurl.com/y89em28k.

39. Morello, *op. cit.*

40. "Statement by UNFPA on U.S. Decision to Withhold Funding," United Nations Population Fund, April 4, 2017, https://tinyurl.com/ychaz88a.

41. *Ibid.*; Josh Lederman, "U.S. cites abortion provision in cutting off UN agency funding," The Associated Press, PBS Newshour, April 4, 2017, https://tinyurl.com/yatd4lbr; "UNFPA Funding & Kemp-Kasten: An Explainer," Henry J. Kaiser Foundation, May 4, 2018, https://tinyurl.com/yaawqdrt.

42. Amanda Klasing, "US Blocks Funds to UN Population Fund—Again; Baseless Claims Made That Fund Supports Coercive Abortion, Sterilization," Human Rights Watch, March 16, 2018, https://tinyurl.com/y7hmmedk.

43. Morello, *op. cit.*

44. "Max Roser and Esteban Ortiz-Ospina, "World Population Growth," Our World in Data, April 2017, https://tinyurl.com/yc5x5hhb.

45. "Thomas Malthus: English Economist and Demographer," *Encyclopedia Britannica*, https://tinyurl.com/y9b6hxby; Thomas Malthus, *An Essay on the Principal of Population* (1798), p. 14, https://tinyurl.com/ycl3me83.

46. Lauren F. Landsburg, "Thomas Robert Malthus," Library of Economics and Liberty, https://tinyurl.com/3naguyg; "Poor Law: British Legislation," *Encyclopedia Britannica*, https://tinyurl.com/y7boct3t.

47. "Great Famine" *Encyclopedia Britannica*, https://tinyurl.com/z7ntujp.

48. "Birth control," *Encyclopedia Britannica*, 2018, https://tinyurl.com/y8nvtl2y.

49. Vern L. Bullough, ed., *Encyclopedia of Birth Control* (2001), p. 162, https://tinyurl.com/ych82plu; "Charles Knowlton," *Encyclopedia Britannica*, 2018, https://tinyurl.com/y8au2zuh.

50. Ansley J. Coale and Susan Watkins, *The Decline of Fertility in Europe* (1986), p. 39, pp. 183-189.

51. Graziella Caselli, Jacques Vallin, Guillaume J. Wunsch, *Demography: Analysis and Synthesis* (2006), p. 854, https://tinyurl.com/ybn8pywf.

52. Pearce, *op. cit.*, p. 20.

53. Francis Galton, "Eugenics: Its Definition, Scope, and Aims," *The American Journal of Sociology*, July 1904, https://tinyurl.com/y7gj6rkk.

54. "Margaret Sanger," VCU Libraries Social Welfare History Project, https://tinyurl.com/y6vrst8z; "Margaret Sanger (1879-1966)," PBS, American Experience, https://tinyurl.com/y73ev2yp.

55. "Margaret Sanger," *Encyclopedia Britannica*, https://tinyurl.com/y889e3nz.

56. "Background Document on the Population Programme of the UN," U.N. Population Division, United Nations Population Information Network, March 24, 1994, https://tinyurl.com/y8lbu2xb.

57. "Outcomes On Population," United Nations, https://tinyurl.com/3kvzvmt.

58. "Anthony Comstock's 'Chastity' Laws," "American Experience," WGBH/Public Broadcasting Service, https://tinyurl.com/y9ecf26p.

59. Paul and Anne Erlich, *The Population Bomb* (1968), p. xi.

60. Max Roser and Esteban Ortiz-Ospina, *op. cit.*

61. Wolfgang Fengler, "The Rapid Slowdown of Population Growth," The World Bank, Sept. 9, 2014, https://tinyurl.com/o5rv9ej.

62. "Family Planning Timeline," U.S. Agency for International Development, https://tinyurl.com/yc2m4z9g.

63. *Ibid.*

64. "Global Health Legislative and Policy Requirements," U.S. Agency for International Development, https://tinyurl.com/y7gsuq9v.

65. "The Mexico City Policy: An Explainer,"*op. cit.*

66. "China's one-child policy itself leads to forced abortions," Population Research Institute, Dec. 12, 2012, https://tinyurl.com/yajs76mn.

67. Baochang Gu, "Fertility Trends and Population Growth in China," China Policy Institute, May 10, 2016, https://tinyurl.com/y9d8aj8g.

68. *Ibid.*

69. "China's New 'Two-Child Policy' and the Continuation of Massive Crimes Against Women and Children," Congressional-Executive Commission on China, https://tinyurl.com/yd5d6lcd.

70. "China's Two-Child Policy," Bloomberg News, June 6, 2018, https://tinyurl.com/y7fve4vd.

71. Fengler, *op. cit.*

72. "Outcomes On Population," United Nations, undated, https://tinyurl.com/3kvzvmt.

73. "Global Levels of Contraceptive Use by Married Women Have Risen, Especially in Developing Countries," Guttmacher Institute, July 9, 2013, https://tinyurl.com/y7ed4qul.

74. Robert Kunzig, "Population 7 Billion," *National Geographic*, January 2011, https://tinyurl.com/y9vt9x32; "Seven Billion: Are You Typical?" *National Geographic*, https://tinyurl.com/y9l6wp9d.

75. "U.N. Sustainable Development Goals," United Nations Development Programme, https://tinyurl.com/hepclrn.

76. "Just the Numbers: The Impact of U.S. International Family Planning Assistance, 2017," Guttmacher Institute, May 5, 2017, https://tinyurl.com/ycmbzue8.

77. "The Mexico City Policy: An Explainer," *op. cit.*

78. "Just the Numbers: The Impact of U.S. International Family Planning Assistance, 2018," Guttmacher Institute, April 2018, https://tinyurl.com/yd8pxfqs.

79. *Ibid.*

80. "U.S. Population Clock," https://www.census.gov; "Quick Facts," https://tinyurl.com/ybpzlne7.

81. James Emery White, *Meet Generation Z* (2017), https://tinyurl.com/ycsm7wyd.

82. *Ibid.*, "America's Changing Religious Landscape: Christians Decline Sharply as Share of Population; Unaffiliated and Other Faiths Continue to Grow," Pew Research Center, May 12, 2015, https://tinyurl.com/ydeymm5m.

83. "End the 'harmful narrative'; migration is a net-gain for Africa, finds UN report," *UN News*, United Nations, May 31, 2018, https://tinyurl.com/y7ppuhqh; "World Population Prospects: The 2017 Revision, Key Findings and Advance Tables," Department of Economic and Social Affairs, Population Division, United Nations (2017), p. 3, https://tinyurl.com/ydhrcnn4.

84. "Cadre Harmonisé? for Identification of Risk Areas and Vulnerable Populations in Sixteen (16) States and the Federal Capital Territory (FCT) of Nigeria," Food and Agriculture Organization, March 15, 2018, https://tinyurl.com/y7vfca9v.

85. Mirit Agaiby, "Population Increase is Eating up Economic Reforms: MP," *Egypt Today*, May 25, 2018, https://tinyurl.com/yc6doasm.

86. "Global temperature rise of 2°C doubles the population exposed to multiple climate risks compared to a 1.5°C rise," International Institute for Applied Systems Analysis, May 16, 2018, https://tinyurl.com/yblxygld.

87. Kanta Kumari Rigaud *et al.*, *Groundswell: Preparing for Internal Climate Migration* (2018), p. xix, https://tinyurl.com/y9dfsvsn.

88. Andrea Thompson, "Shock and Thaw—Alaskan Sea Ice Just Took a Steep, Unprecedented Dive," *Scientific American*, May 2, 2018, https://tinyurl.com/y98cxglh; Chris Mooney, "Antarctic ice loss has tripled in a decade. If that continues, we are in serious trouble," *The Washington Post*, June 13, 2018, https://tinyurl.com/y8z338kn.

89. Sharon Lerner, "One Way to Stay Cool," *New York Times*, Oct 15, 2018, https://search-proquest-com.library.access.arlingtonva.us/docview/2119996857/41DAB6E97FF144E5PQ/1?accountid=57895.

90. "Nigeria total fertility rate," U.N. Population Fund, https://tinyurl.com/yceyhysa; Sunita Chikkatur Dubey, "Solar Mini Grids Put Nigeria on Path to Energy for All by 2030," The World Bank, Jan. 25, 2018, https://tinyurl.com/y74f2ave.

91. Steven Lee Myers, Olivia Mitchell Ryan, "Burying 'One Child' Limits, China Pushes Women to Have More Babies," *New York Times*, Aug. 11, 2018, https://search-proquest-com.library.access.arlingtonva.us/docview/2091858562/3D23/2E166844/A8PQ/4?accountid=57895.

92. "The end of high fertility is near," *Population Facts*, Department of Economic and Social Affairs, United Nations, October 2017, https://tinyurl.com/y83esr2y.

BIBLIOGRAPHY
Selected Sources
Books

Graffin, Greg, *Population Wars: A New Perspective on Competition and Coexistence*, Thomas Dunne Books, 2015.
A zoologist challenges the notion that competition is central to progress among species and says humans have more to gain through cooperation than competition.

Hawken, Paul, *Drawdown: The Most Comprehensive Plan Ever Proposed to Reverse Global Warming*, Penguin Books, 2017.
Family planning ranks among the 10 most effective ways to reverse global warming, according to an international coalition of researchers, scientists, and policymakers.

Last, Jonathan V., *What to Expect When No One's Expecting: America's Coming Demographic Disaster*, Encounter Books, 2013.
A senior writer at the conservative *Weekly Standard* magazine warns of economic and social consequences unless Americans begin having more children.

Pearce, Fred, *The Coming Population Crash and Our Planet's Surprising Future*, Beacon Press, 2010.
An environmentalist argues that a declining world population will lead to surprisingly positive outcomes.

Articles

Kaneda, Toshiko, and Carl Haub, "How Many People Have Ever Lived on Earth?" Population Reference Bureau, March 9, 2018, https://tinyurl.com/yatw9hrn.
A research associate with a Washington organization that studies population (Kaneda) and a former senior demographer with the group (Haub) explain past population trends and growth projections.

Mann, Charles C., "Can Planet Earth Feed 10 Billion People?" *The Atlantic*, March 2018, https://tinyurl.com/y7twfqnj.
A journalist who specializes in science issues looks at modern fertilizer's detrimental environmental effects on rivers, lakes, and streams and at innovative agricultural solutions for feeding billions more humans.

Murphy, Stacie, "So Far, 2018 Looks Like More of the Same," *Population Connection*, March 2018, https://tinyurl.com/y6vbyjzt.
The policy director of an organization that advocates for greater access to family planning examines recent U.S. legislative developments on contraception and health care.

Parker, Meaghan, "Story of the Decade: Population Dynamics (and Women and Water) Top List of Our Most Popular Posts," *New Security Beat*, Jan. 16, 2018, https://tinyurl.com/yc3fnnw7.
The founding editor of the Washington-based Wilson Center's Environmental Change and Security Program blog summarizes the program's articles on global population trends and related issues.

Tavernise, Sabrina, "Fertility Rate Again Falls to a Record Low, Confounding Demographers," *New York Times*, May 17, 2018, https://tinyurl.com/ydgh7thw.
Demographers puzzle over the possible reasons behind America's longest fertility decline since the 1960s.

Reports and Studies

"Just the Numbers: The Impact of U.S. International Family Planning Assistance, 2018," Guttmacher Institute, April 11, 2018, https://tinyurl.com/ycpxqqus.
A think tank that provides information, research, and analysis on family planning explains the state of U.S. funding for international family planning in developing countries.

"Trump's Mexico City Policy or Global Gag Rule," Human Rights Watch, Feb. 14, 2018, https://tinyurl.com/y9r88brp.
A global human-rights research group analyzes the Trump administration's decision to reinstate a policy barring federal aid to nongovernmental organizations that provide or promote abortion as a family planning method.

"World Population Prospects: The 2017 Revision," Department of Economic and Social Affairs, Population Division, United Nations, 2017, https://tinyurl.com/ydhrcnn4.

The latest U.N. estimates on global, regional, and national population trends indicate that by 2050, 26 African countries are expected at least to double in population while 51 other countries across the globe will lose population.

Rigaud, Kanta Kumari, *et al.*, **"Groundswell: Preparing for Internal Climate Migration" World Bank, 2018, https://tinyurl.com/y9dfsvsn.**

Environmental experts say that without serious efforts to reduce greenhouse gas emissions, sub-Saharan Africa, South Asia and Latin America will experience massive population shifts as a result of climate change.

Multimedia

World Population: An Interactive Experience, world-populationhistory.org, undated, https://tinyurl.com/yasxhmv7.

An interactive map and timeline show global population growth from prehistory to the present.

For More Information

Environmental Change and Security Program, Woodrow Wilson Center, Ronald Reagan Building and International Trade Center, 1 Woodrow Wilson Plaza, 1300 Pennsylvania Ave., N.W., Washington, DC 20004-3027; 202-691-4000; www.wilsoncenter.org/program/global-sustainability-and-resilience-program. Researches the connections between the environment, health, population, development, conflict, and security.

Millennium Alliance for Humanity and the Biosphere, https://mahb.stanford.edu. A network of activists, research teams, private citizens, and others based at Stanford University that advocates for greater social and environmental sustainability and works to educate the public about threats to global ecosystems.

National Right to Life Committee, 512 10th St., N.W., Washington, DC 20004; 202-626-8800; www.nrlc.org. Advocacy group that opposes abortion.

Population and Development Program (Popdev), Hampshire College, 893 West St., Amherst, MA 01002; 413-549-4600; www.popdev.hampshire.edu. Advocacy and education group that challenges the view that overpopulation and immigration are the primary causes of environmental degradation.

Population Connection, 2120 L St., N.W. #500, Washington, DC 20037; 202-332-2200; www.population connection.org. Advocacy organization focused on reducing population growth.

Population Reference Bureau, 1875 Connecticut Ave., N.W., Suite 520, Washington, DC 20009; 800-877-9881; www.prb.org. Organization that analyzes, translates, and disseminates information and researches population, health, and the environment.

Universal Access Project and Policy, Women and Population, United Nations Foundation, 1750 Pennsylvania Ave., N.W., Suite 300, Washington, D.C. 20006; 202-862-6314; www.unfoundation.org. International aid organization that works to improve women's access to reproductive health and family planning services.

13

Algorithms and Artificial Intelligence

Patrick Marshall

A U.S. Customs and Border Protection officer uses facial-recognition technology at a security checkpoint at Miami International Airport on Feb. 27, 2018. Advocates see facial recognition, which relies on algorithms to make identifications, as a powerful tool, but critics say the technology is unreliable.

From *CQ Researcher,*
July 6, 2018

When Jason Doss lost his job as an autoworker several years ago, his problems were just beginning.

The state of Michigan improperly seized more than $14,000 from his paychecks between 2015 and 2017, claiming that Doss had fraudulently collected unemployment in 2011. Worse, the state's Unemployment Insurance Agency said he owed a $62,000 penalty. Doss insisted he was innocent.[1]

Turns out he was not alone.

In early January, Michigan conceded that Doss and some 34,000 other residents had been improperly accused of fraud because of a faulty algorithm the state had installed to monitor unemployment claims. The state Legislature created a fund to compensate the victims. Michigan also halted all collection activities against those who could show they had been wrongfully accused.[2]

For critics, the incident is a dramatic example of all that can go wrong when computers, and not people, are making decisions. The state began using the algorithm a year after Michigan's unemployment agency laid off one-third of its workforce. An internal state review discovered a 93 percent computer error rate.

"Government by spreadsheet does not work," said Jennifer Lord, a Michigan attorney who represented the workers at no charge.[3]

But some experts argue that such incidents are exceptions and that as algorithm-driven artificial intelligence (AI) improves, and as the public comes to understand it better, everyone will benefit.

"Artificial intelligence is one of the hottest, least understood and most debated technological breakthroughs in modern times,"

313

Americans Hold Mixed Views of Automation

Most American adults are more worried than optimistic about the effects of artificial intelligence and automation on employment, transportation and other aspects of everyday life.

Percentage of U.S. Adults Worried or Not Worried About Automation

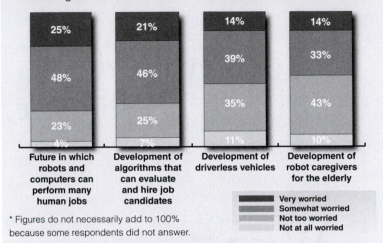

Future in which robots and computers can perform many human jobs	Development of algorithms that can evaluate and hire job candidates	Development of driverless vehicles	Development of robot caregivers for the elderly
25%	21%	14%	14%
48%	46%	39%	33%
23%	25%	35%	43%
4%	7%	11%	10%

Very worried
Somewhat worried
Not too worried
Not at all worried

* Figures do not necessarily add to 100% because some respondents did not answer.

Source: Aaron Smith and Monica Anderson, "Automation in Everyday Life," Pew Research Center, Oct. 4, 2017, https://tinyurl.com/y9tfmjf6

wrote Lili Cheng, vice president of Microsoft AI & Research, in January. "AI can truly help solve some of the world's most vexing problems, from improving day-to-day communication to energy, climate, health care, transportation and more. The real magic of AI, in the end, won't be magic at all. It will be technology that adapts to people. This will be profoundly transformational for humans and for humanity."[4]

At their simplest, algorithms are a sequence of mathematical instructions for solving a problem. In Michigan, the algorithm flagged discrepancies in unemployment filings. At human resource departments, algorithms evaluate résumés to weed out unqualified applicants. In the retail industry, they enable online stores to offer personalized recommendations based on a consumer's shopping history. Algorithms also are the tool that helps make AI possible: Computers use algorithms to process data on their own, in a way that can mimic human decision-making.

AI enthusiasts say the technology is showing tremendous promise. By 2035, AI-powered technologies will increase labor productivity by 40 percent, according to business consulting company Accenture, and could double the U.S. economy's rate of growth.[5]

"AI is just the latest in technologies that allow us to produce a lot more goods and services with less labor," Microsoft co-founder Bill Gates said recently. "And overwhelmingly, over the last several hundred years, that has been great for society."[6]

But critics say the ubiquity of algorithms and the spread of AI are raising numerous ethical questions about fairness and bias, power and accountability. Algorithms, they warn, too often make mistakes similar to what happened in Michigan or perpetuate societal biases on gender and race.

Algorithms are "sorting winners and losers in the standard, old-fashioned way that we've been trying to get over, that we've been trying to transcend—through class, through gender, through race," warned mathematician Cathy O'Neil, author of *Weapons of Math Destruction: How Big Data Increases Inequality and Threatens Democracy.*[7]

Critics also say the list of potential problems is growing, as artificial intelligence advances and machines improve their ability to "learn" on their own—a process known as machine, or deep, learning. Deep learning enables AI to modify underlying algorithms as it finds patterns and gains experience.

Because of their growing prowess, "algorithms are likely to be capable of inflicting unusually grave harm," wrote former Justice Department lawyer Andrew Tutt last year. "When a machine-learning algorithm is responsible for keeping the power grid operational, assisting in a surgery or driving a car, it can pose an immediate and severe threat to human health and welfare in a way many other products simply do not."[8]

A number of experts say algorithms remain error-prone and contain hidden biases.

"Algorithmic bias, like human bias, results in unfairness," said Joy Buolamwini, founder of the Algorithmic

Justice League, an advocacy group focused on eliminating bias in programs. "Algorithms, like viruses, can spread bias on a massive scale."[9]

Buolamwini, an African-American, was an undergraduate at the Georgia Institute of Technology when she noticed that facial-recognition programs she was working with would perform accurately with her white friends but could not recognize her face. In subsequent work at MIT's Media Lab, she researched bias in facial-recognition algorithms and found software from Microsoft, IBM and Face++ were more likely to misidentify the gender of black women than white men. For example, the algorithms' error rates identifying the gender of darker-skinned females in a set of 271 photos was 35 percent.[10]

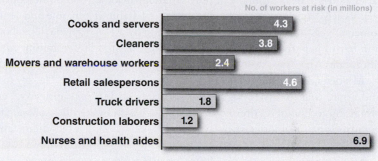

Robots Could Soon Replace Millions of Jobs

Cooks, servers and other restaurant workers are most at risk of being replaced by automation, according to CB Insights, which studies machine intelligence trends. The organization estimates that nearly 11 million service and warehouse jobs in the United States are at high risk of replacement by machines within the next decade.

Occupations Most at Risk From Automation Within 10 Years

No. of workers at risk (in millions)

Occupation	No. of workers at risk (in millions)
Cooks and servers	4.3
Cleaners	3.8
Movers and warehouse workers	2.4
Retail salespersons	4.6
Truck drivers	1.8
Construction laborers	1.2
Nurses and health aides	6.9

Source: "AI Will Put 10 Million Jobs At High Risk—More Than Were Eliminated By The Great Recession," CB Insights, Oct. 6, 2017, https://tinyurl.com/y76jecb2

High risk
Medium risk
Low risk

Similar problems in other settings, critics say, can lead to discriminatory mortgage lending and to racial profiling in law enforcement.

"The algorithms that dominate policymaking—particularly in public services such as law enforcement, welfare and child protection—act less like data sifters and more like gatekeepers, mediating access to public resources, assessing risks and sorting groups of people into 'deserving' and 'undeserving' and 'suspicious' and 'unsuspicious' categories," wrote Virginia Eubanks, a fellow at New America, a Washington public policy think tank.[11]

AI also may be keeping some people in prison longer than warranted, according to a recent study by researchers at Dartmouth College. A program that courts use to predict the likelihood of recidivism is no more accurate than nonexpert humans, the study found.

"It is troubling that untrained [humans] can perform as well as a computer program used to make life-altering decisions about criminal defendants," said Hany Farid, a Dartmouth professor of computer science and a research team leader.[12]

Polls show that AI worries the public, too: 67 percent of respondents were concerned about algorithms making hiring decisions, according to a 2017 Pew Research Center survey, while 73 percent worried that AI will steal jobs from humans.[13]

A 2016 White House report said that over the next two decades, AI could threaten between 9 and 47 percent of jobs and increase income inequality between educated and less-educated workers.[14]

AI's risks derive from two major features, experts say. First, AI programs arrive at decisions based on algorithms that are often inscrutable to humans. Due to this lack of transparency, people may not even know AI was involved when they applied for, say, a mortgage, much less what "reasoning" resulted in that decision.

"The big piece we are missing is the ability to know when a piece of AI is doing something it shouldn't," says Finale Doshi-Velez, an assistant professor of computer science at Harvard University's John A. Paulson School of Engineering and Applied Sciences. "These algorithms can screw up in ways that even the makers did not intend."

In addition, machine learning can lead an algorithm to do things its human creators did not envision. "The behavior of a learning AI system depends in part on its post-design experience, and even the most careful designers, programmers and manufacturers will not be able to control or predict what an AI system will experience after it leaves their care," wrote Matthew U. Scherer, a lawyer in Portland, Ore., who specializes in artificial intelligence-related issues.[15]

The possibility of machines becoming autonomous raises a host of fears for many in the technology field, as well as legal questions about who would be liable if someone gets hurt because of mistakes made by AI. A number of experts call for tighter regulation of algorithms and AI.

AI's defenders, however, say such fears are overblown and argue that excessive regulation will only stifle a promising technology. Already, the technology is showing surprising capabilities, they say:

- A program pioneered by Mount Sinai Hospital in New York City uses AI-powered speech analysis to predict psychosis in at-risk patients with 83 percent accuracy, a recent study said.[16]

- Between October 2017 and April 2018, a Facebook AI program that scans feeds for signs that users might harm themselves or others has alerted public safety agencies on more than 1,000 occasions, according to a Facebook spokesperson.

- A team from Purdue Polytechnic Institute, a college at Purdue University, developed an AI tool—the Chat Analysis Triage Tool—to help law enforcement officials spot sex offenders in online chat rooms.[17]

The late famed physicist Stephen Hawking, while worried AI could become too powerful, said in 2016, "The potential benefits of creating intelligence are huge. We cannot predict what we might achieve when our own minds are amplified by AI."[18]

As researchers and policymakers consider the challenges of artificial intelligence and the algorithms that inform them, here are some questions they are asking:

Will algorithms perpetuate discrimination?

Many experts warn that shortcomings in algorithms are inevitable, difficult to detect and in numerous cases discriminatory.

Rachel Goodman, a staff attorney in the American Civil Liberty Union's (ACLU) racial justice program, said, "We are increasingly aware that AI-related issues impact virtually every civil rights and civil liberties issue that the ACLU works on."[19] The ACLU is focusing on three areas where government and the private sector are deploying AI: criminal justice, lending and credit and surveillance.

Some courts are using algorithms and AI to make parole and sentencing decisions. These programs make predictions about the likelihood of a defendant or prisoner committing future crimes, but neither the software nor its creators reveal the factors that go into those predictions.

"The key to our product is the algorithms, and they're proprietary," an executive of Northpointe, which provides software to the courts, told a reporter. "We've created them, and we don't release them, because it's certainly a core piece of our business."[20]

"Governments are really being pushed to do more with less money and AI tools are, at least on a surface level, appealing ways to do that and make decisions efficiently," Goodman said. "We want to see if there are appropriate roles [for AI] and to ensure tools are fair and free of racial biases. Those are hard questions and hard math problems."[21]

Due to this lack of transparency, detecting shortcomings in an algorithm can be difficult, experts say. Houston teachers, for instance, complained that the use of an algorithm to assess their performances based on students' test scores violated the teachers' civil rights. The software company that designed the system, the SAS Institute, refused to reveal the workings of the algorithms powering its Educational Value-Added Assessment System, saying they were trade secrets. U.S. Magistrate Judge Stephen Smith ruled the teachers have the right to sue over the use of algorithms. "Algorithms are human creations, and subject to error like any other human endeavor," he wrote in his 2017 opinion.[22]

As the analytic capabilities of AI increase, some experts say the potential for abuse grows as well.

For example, "digital phenotyping" assesses individuals' health through their interactions with their devices, such as social media posts and internet searches.

"Our interactions with the digital world could actually unlock secrets of disease," said Dr. Sachin H. Jain, chief executive of CareMore Health, a company that uses software to analyze Twitter posts for indications of sleep problems.[23]

But other experts question digital phenotyping's usefulness. While an individual who suddenly stops text messaging to friends might be depressed, it also might mean "that somebody's just going on a camping trip and has changed their normal behavior," said Dr. Steve Steinhubl, director of digital medicine at the Scripps Translational Science Institute in San Diego, a medical reform group. Digital phenotyping, he said, presents "new potential for snake oil."[24]

The latest generation of AI, a number of analysts say, is bringing unprecedented capabilities for businesses and others to monitor and analyze people. Insurance companies can use AI to mine consumer and demographic data to determine which consumers are unlikely to shop around for lower prices. They then charge those consumers more, according to mathematician O'Neil.[25]

But insurance companies say algorithms give them the ability to customize insurance options and to provide faster and better service. Algorithms also help insurers "better understand the data so we could make predictions about what's happening in the insurance marketplace," said Pavan Divakarla, data and analytics business leader at the Progressive Casualty Insurance Co.[26]

A team from Stanford University recently developed a neural network—a program designed to process data in a manner similar to how the human brain works—that uses images to detect individuals' sexual orientation. With a single image, the program could correctly distinguish between gay and heterosexual men 81 percent of the time. Humans got it right only 61 percent of the time. If the program used five images, its accuracy rate increased to 91 percent.

"Given that companies and governments are increasingly using computer vision algorithms to detect people's intimate traits, our findings expose a threat to the privacy and safety of gay men and women," the study authors wrote.[27]

While aware of the potential for algorithmic abuse—intentional or otherwise—AI's defenders say the technology can also protect against abuse.

"There is a hopeful note in this," says Martin Ford, a software developer and futurist. "To the extent that human beings are biased, fixing that is really hard. But fixing it in an algorithm is possible. If it does get fixed, then a world in which algorithms have more control is actually less biased."

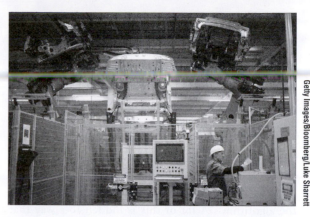

Robots weld car-body parts at the BMW assembly plant in Greer, S.C., on May 10, 2018. Sales of industrial robots have soared in recent years, and as AI-driven automation spreads, some experts estimate it could replace millions of restaurant, cleaning and warehouse jobs.

Getty Images/Bloomberg/Luke Sharrett

In fact, in most if not all cases, the bias that results from an AI application originates in the data it is fed. "Bias never comes from the way the algorithm is written," says Jack Clark, director of strategy and communications at OpenAI, an industry-funded nonprofit focused on developing safe and beneficial AI. "The algorithm will reflect that which is in the data."

Ford and Clark agree that programmers can design an algorithm to detect bias, a process some researchers call "input-output" analysis. The program feeds a screened set of data into the AI application and then analyzes the output, detecting patterns of bias without actually having to examine the inner workings of the application. If the algorithm's output demonstrates a pattern of discrimination—say, a lender rejecting minorities for loans—it can be taken out of service regardless of its reasoning.

And some experts argue that, at least for current levels of AI, existing laws in principle offer protection against most cases of discriminatory or intrusive AI applications.

"The good news is that we do have laws that apply in some of these situations," says Goodman. "The civil rights laws, the Fair Housing Act, the Equal Credit Opportunity Act and other laws continue to regulate those areas even when those transactions are taking place mediated by artificial intelligence."

An AI-driven screening tool used in employment applications, for example, can be challenged in court "if that tool is having a disparate impact on women or people of color," she says.

Should government regulate algorithms and AI?

Algorithms' opacity has led some analysts to argue that they need to be tested for problems, including bias, before they are used.

Victims of a poorly designed algorithm cannot challenge the results if they are unaware of the role played by the algorithm. "A lot of this is hidden in a way that sometimes an applicant or user doesn't even know," the ACLU's Goodman says. "That's why we're going to need more aggressive regulation."

Even some executives in technology companies are urging regulation not only of algorithms but more broadly of AI. Calling AI an "existential threat," Elon Musk, a founder of SpaceX and Tesla, told a 2017 meeting of governors that government must intervene, and fast, because of rapid technological advances: "Until people see robots going down the street killing people, they don't know how to react because it seems so ethereal," he said. "AI is a rare case where I think we need to be proactive in regulation instead of reactive. Because I think by the time we are reactive in AI regulation, it's too late."[28]

Other experts, primarily within private-sector companies, warn against regulation, saying it will stifle innovation.

"We encourage governments to evaluate existing policy tools and use caution before adopting new laws, regulations or taxes that may inadvertently or unnecessarily impede the responsible development and use of AI," said the Information Technology Industry Council, an industry lobbying group based in Washington. "As applications of AI technologies vary widely, overregulating can inadvertently reduce the number of technologies created and offered in the marketplace, particularly by startups and smaller businesses."[29] The council declined several requests for an interview.

"Governments should focus their attention now on enabling the development of AI," Amir Khosrowshahi, chief technology officer for Intel Corp., told a congressional subcommittee in February. "We are in the early days of an innovation of a technology that can do tremendous good. Governments should make certain to encourage this innovation, and they should be wary of regulation that will stifle its growth."[30]

Sara Jordan, an assistant professor in the School of Public and International Affairs at Virginia Tech who studies the ethics of AI, says, however, that regulation would not stifle AI's development.

"It's a normal argument trotted out by those who want the opportunity to build without consequences, then deal with it later," Jordan says. She points to similarly complex technologies that were developed successfully despite federal regulation. "We dealt with recombinant DNA, which had the same hype around it back in the 1980s and 1990s, and the same with genome sequencing," she says. "We have done this. We know how to do it."

Still some representatives of AI-related industries argue that regulation, at least at this point, is unnecessary because companies are aware of the technology's risks and will take appropriate steps to guard against them.

"The companies I have talked with know that it's in their interest to ensure that their algorithms are thoroughly tested," says Michael Hayes, a senior manager for government affairs at the Consumer Technology Association, a trade organization in Arlington, Va. Hayes says companies are very aware that "the success of AI products depends on public trust."

In any case, sufficient laws and regulations are already in place, according to Adam Thierer, senior research fellow at the Technology Policy Program at George Mason University's Mercatus Center. Algorithms and other "AI applications already are regulated by a host of existing legal policies," he said. "If someone does something stupid or dangerous with AI systems, the Federal Trade Commission has the power to address unfair and deceptive practices. State attorneys general and consumer-protection agencies also routinely address unfair practices and advance their own privacy and data-security policies."[31]

But other experts say existing regulations are far from sufficient, especially in light of the technology's lack of transparency.

"The rise of AI has so far occurred in a regulatory vacuum," wrote lawyer Scherer. "With the exception of a few states' legislation regarding autonomous vehicles and drones, very few laws or regulations exist that specifically address the unique challenges raised by AI, and virtually no courts appear to have developed standards specifically addressing who should be held legally responsible if an AI causes harm."[32]

Former Justice Department lawyer Tutt, who follows artificial intelligence issues closely, has called for creating "an FDA for algorithms."

"As algorithms get more advanced and more complex, they actually are all going to tend to converge technologically," he says. "You're going to see solutions in governing autonomous vehicles that could just as easily apply in the privacy sphere. So having those pockets of expertise at different agencies might not make sense."

Tutt envisions the new agency as a place where the government can concentrate its expertise on algorithms and AI across all sectors. "It is going to have to be an agency that is a resource for existing regulators because they are going to understand their specific problem sets," he says.

Thierer says that when additional regulation is truly needed, the government should rely on existing agencies rather than creating a new one devoted to algorithms and AI.

"We should exhaust whatever solutions are already on the books before we look to new ones that may stifle new forms of life-enriching innovation," he says. "We don't need to rush to regulate before we exhaust all the possibilities for determining whether or not there is an actual problem or harm to be addressed preemptively at all."

Will AI be good for the economy?

At a time when the unemployment rate is below 4 percent, more and more companies are turning to AI-driven automation to overcome a labor shortage and increase productivity.

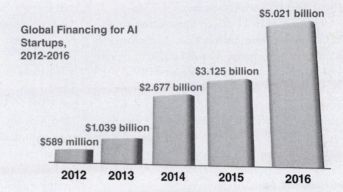

Investment in AI Is Soaring

Startup companies developing artificial intelligence raised a record $5 billion in funding from private investors and other sources in 2016—more than an eightfold increase from 2012, according to CB Insights, which analyzes data on technology trends.

Global Financing for AI Startups, 2012-2016

$589 million — 2012
$1.039 billion — 2013
$2.677 billion — 2014
$3.125 billion — 2015
$5.021 billion — 2016

Source: "The 2016 AI Recap: Startups See Record High In Deals And Funding," CB Insights, Jan. 19, 2017, https://tinyurl.com/yb5zn3ro

Large corporations invested $18 billion to $27 billion in AI-related technologies in 2016, according to the global management company McKinsey, and technology companies are racing to develop AI applications in a wide range of industries, from retailing to marketing and human resources. Globally, more than 550 startups with AI as a core part of their products raised $5 billion in funding from private investors and others in 2016—more than eight times the amount startups raised in 2012, according to CB Insights, which studies machine intelligence trends.[33]

Small businesses and manufacturers see AI-powered automation as a way to remain competitive with foreign competitors who have a deep pool of cheap labor to draw on. "If we don't get things automated and we don't start moving things forward, we're going to be the ones who get left behind," said David Maletto, who runs a small packaging company in Eau Claire, Wis.[34]

But AI is no panacea for workers, says OpenAI's Clark.

"Why is wage growth unbelievably low even though we have a really tight labor market right now?" Clark asks. "The economy may display symptoms of being fine, but we know that there are big epochal changes happening under the hood. We just don't know how to respond to it."

Software developer Ford agrees. "The first impacts [of AI] are showing up in terms of stagnant wages rather than outright unemployment," he says.

Some experts expect AI-driven automation to cost more jobs as it moves from factory floors to the broader economy. By some estimates, AI will be able to replace sales people within 20 years, be able to write a best-selling book within 31 years and be capable of replacing surgeons within 35 years.[35]

A landmark 2013 study estimated that 47 percent of jobs are at high risk for automation over the next decade or two, although the authors stressed that they were estimating how many jobs *could be* replaced by AI and not how many jobs *will be* replaced by AI.[36]

Other researchers project lower rates of job losses from AI. A 2016 study of AI's impact on the 35 member countries of the Paris-based Organisation for Economic Co-operation and Development (OECD), whose constituent economies are similar to that of the United States, found only 9 percent of jobs to be at high risk.[37]

A number of experts say AI will actually generate employment.

"Automation does not simply destroy jobs, it creates them," Charles Isbell, professor in the School of Interactive Computing at the Georgia Institute of Technology, told Congress last February. "In this particular case, it creates jobs that require technological sophistication and understanding," such as computer scientists and programmers.[38]

Gary Shapiro, president and CEO of the Consumer Technology Association, an industry association in Arlington, Va., said, "AI is predicted to create millions of new jobs unheard of today." To stay employed, he said, many workers will need to develop new skills. "While the full impact of AI on jobs is not yet fully known, in terms of both jobs created and displaced, an ability to adapt to rapid technological change is critical," he told Congress. "People entering the workforce in nearly all sectors of our economy will need to have skill sets necessary to work alongside technology and adapt to the new job opportunities that it will bring."[39]

Those who minimize AI's impact on employment point to another factor: Machines lack the human touch and do not interact well with people, thus limiting the types of jobs they can do. For example, a digital financial adviser cannot provide the personalized service that human wealth managers do. "A robot has no consciousness, no ethics," said Vasant Dhar, a professor of information systems at New York University.[40]

The worst-case scenario—the loss of virtually all human jobs—is "highly unlikely," according to participants at a 2016 conference at Stanford University called "Artificial Intelligence and Life in 2030." In the short term, education, retraining and inventing new goods and services can mitigate the impact of job losses, the conference attendees agreed.[41]

But the conference report said job losses could be great enough that "the current social safety net may need to evolve into better social services for everyone, such as health care and education, or a guaranteed basic income."[42]

The 2016 White House report said AI's effects on workers will likely be unevenly distributed throughout the economy.

"Research consistently finds that the jobs that are threatened by automation are highly concentrated among lower-paid, lower-skilled and less-educated workers," the analysts said. "This means that automation will continue to put downward pressure on demand for this group, putting downward pressure on wages and upward pressure on inequality."[43]

Clark says AI's effects on employment will be "extremely severe."

"Anyone who tells you that it's going to be fine is lying to you," Clark says. In addition to outright job losses, he says, AI will cause other problems for many workers.

"We are going to automate increasingly large chunks of jobs, which will mean that the part of the job a human does is more sort of boxed in, allowing for less and less independent thought and action on the part of the human," he says. "That will compress wages since there will be less stuff you will be able to show that you're doing, and it's going to make it harder to switch shops and change careers."

BACKGROUND

Algorithms' Beginnings

Ancient peoples used algorithms to keep track of their grain stocks and cattle, and Greek mathematicians in the days of Euclid and Archimedes began devising complex algorithmic formulas. In the ninth century, a Persian astronomer and mathematician named Abu Abdullah Muhammad ibn Musa Al-Khwarizmi came up with a name for this mathematical wizardry; in Latin, the word was *algorismus*.[44]

Advances in math, including the invention of binary algebra in 1847, laid the groundwork for the development of computing logic and more-sophisticated algorithms. By 1950, computers and algorithms were far enough along that British mathematician Alan Turing began wondering when "machines will eventually compete with men in all purely intellectual fields." That year, Turing first publicly posed the question: "Can machines think?" Historians date the field of artificial intelligence to that question.[45]

Turing himself was a pioneer in the computer field. In 1936, he invented the Turing machine, a device that employed instructions to manipulate symbols on a strip of tape. The Turing machine, which was never built, provided a blueprint for the development of the first electronic digital computers.[46]

That feat was achieved in 1939 when an Iowa State College physics professor, John Atanasoff, and his assistant, Clifford Berry, built the first electronic digital binary computer, which performed its operations using a binary numeral system.[47] The device, however, was not programmable. Konrad Zuse, a German engineer, succeeded in building a programmable computer in 1941, although his work went mostly unnoticed in the United States because of World War II.[48]

The first general purpose electronic computer—and the first computer to attract broad public attention—was ENIAC (Electronic Numerical Integrator and Computer), a room-sized device consisting of nearly 18,000 vacuum tubes. Funded by the military and completed in 1946, ENIAC was put to work on calculations for the development of the hydrogen bomb.[49]

In 1951, Marvin Minsky, then at Princeton University, and fellow graduate student Dean Edmonds built the first simple neural network machine—a machine capable of learning—that simulated a rat finding its way through a maze.[50]

A 1956 conference at Dartmouth College gave a further boost to artificial intelligence with the primary attendees—computer scientists Minsky, John McCarthy, Allen Newell and Herbert Simon—becoming the field's research leaders for several decades.

The conference proposed a two-month study of the conjecture that "every aspect of learning or any other feature of intelligence can in principle be so precisely described that a machine can be made to simulate it." The conference highlighted two issues for study: "automatic computers" (machines that can carry out a special set of operations without human intervention) and ways to teach computers to use language, form abstractions and become creative.[51]

In 1966, MIT computer scientist Joseph Weizenbaum published a report on his creation of ELIZA, the earliest program that used natural language processing to interact with humans. He designed Eliza to conduct a psychotherapy session with humans via keyboard-entered text.[52]

Interestingly, Weizenbaum's experience with Eliza—specifically, with the willingness of humans to take the program seriously—caused him to become a critic of computers and artificial intelligence. "The dependence on computers is merely the most recent—and the most extreme—example of how man relies on technology in order to escape the burden of acting as an independent agent," Weizenbaum told a reporter in 1985. "It helps him avoid the task of giving meaning to his life, of deciding and pursuing what is truly valuable."[53]

In 1969, researchers at the Stanford Research Institute (now SRI International) first integrated artificial intelligence and robotics in the form of "Shakey." To maneuver, the robot used a TV camera, a laser range finder and bump sensors to collect data, which was processed by an onboard program called STRIPS.[54]

When recession struck in the early 1970s, funding for AI research—including critical support from the Department of Defense—largely disappeared, and scientists lamented the arrival of an "AI winter," with the field suffering from a lack of financial support.

Beyond the Theoretical

The Japanese helped end the AI winter, according to Nick Bostrom, director of the Oxford Martin Programme on the Impacts of Future Technology at Oxford University.

"A new springtime arrived in the early 1980s," he wrote, "when Japan launched its Fifth-Generation Computer Systems Project, a well-funded public-private partnership that aimed to leapfrog the state of the art by developing a massively parallel computing architecture that would serve as a platform for artificial intelligence."[55]

AI research also received a boost in the United States in the early 1980s with the development of "expert systems," problem-solving software designed to simulate the analytical capabilities of experts in a variety of fields, including accounting, finance and medicine.[56]

A surge in funding from the Pentagon's Defense Advanced Research Projects Agency (DARPA) helped expand the field. Intent on matching and surpassing Japan's Fifth-Generation Project, DARPA undertook a Strategic Computing Initiative in 1983. For the next decade, DARPA focused on, among other things, chip design and AI software.[57]

Computing power, meanwhile, was growing rapidly and software was steadily improving. The field of artificial intelligence started booming in the late 1990s, especially in the areas of data mining, language and logistics.

Another "magic moment" occurred in 1995, according to Peter Singer, a senior fellow at New America, when unmanned aircraft—which the United States and Germany had invented during World War II—began using GPS data from satellites, thus greatly improving drones' navigational skills.[58] That year the U.S. military also introduced two advanced unmanned aerial vehicles, the attack Predator drone and the surveillance Global Hawk drone.

Challenging Humans

On May 11, 1997, newspapers trumpeted the surprising news that a computer had bested the world chess champion in a six-game match. "In brisk and brutal fashion," reported *The New York Times*, "the IBM computer Deep Blue unseated humanity, at least temporarily, as the finest chess-playing entity on the

planet yesterday, when Garry Kasparov, the world chess champion, resigned the sixth and final game of the match after just 19 moves, saying, 'I lost my fighting spirit.'"[59]

Over the next decade and a half, the most visible progress in artificial intelligence was in robotics.

In 1999, Sony introduced AIBO (Artificial Intelligence Bot), a canine robot that changes its behavior in response to cues from its owners and surroundings. Sony did not intend to sell AIBO to the public when it began research in 1993. But the company soon recognized AIBO's commercial potential and put 5,000 on sale in Japan and the United States in 1999, with 3,000 robots selling in Japan in the first 20 minutes and 2,000 selling in four days in the United States.[60]

In 2002, iRobot introduced the Roomba, a robot that autonomously maneuvers through rooms while vacuuming and then returns to its charging station when its batteries need charging. The robot adjusts to a variety of surfaces, including wood, carpet, tile and linoleum. Touch-sensitive and infrared sensors prevent it from getting stuck under furniture or harming pets or small children.[61]

In January 2004, NASA landed two autonomous rovers, Spirit and Opportunity, on opposite sides of Mars. "With far greater mobility than the 1997 Mars Pathfinder rover, these robotic explorers have trekked for miles across the Martian surface, conducting field geology and making atmospheric observations," according to NASA's website.[62]

That same year, to encourage the development of autonomous vehicles, DARPA began its Grand Challenge in which 15 self-driving cars attempted to traverse 142 miles of the Mojave Desert in California and Nevada. None made it.[63]

As the technology advanced, DARPA held the Urban Challenge in 2007, requiring contestants "to build an autonomous vehicle capable of driving in traffic, performing complex maneuvers such as merging, passing, parking and negotiating intersections."[64]

In 2011, the public became aware of dramatic improvements in machine intelligence when, on Feb. 16, IBM's Watson supercomputer thrashed the top two all-time champions in the final edition of a special three-episode trivia competition on the TV show "Jeopardy."

CHRONOLOGY

1930s-1950s *Early computers lay the groundwork for artificial intelligence.*

1936 British mathematician Alan Turing submits an article describing the "Turing machine," a thought experiment that served as the blueprint for the first electronic digital computers.

1946 ENIAC, the first general purpose electronic computer, is completed and put to work on calculations for development of the hydrogen bomb.

1950 In a seminal article, Turing raises the question of whether machines can think; his question is credited with giving birth to the field of artificial intelligence.

1951 Princeton University graduate students Marvin Minsky and Dean Edmonds construct the first simple neural network machine, which simulated a rat finding its way through a maze.

1955 John McCarthy, an assistant professor of computer science at Dartmouth, coins the term "artificial intelligence."

1956 Dartmouth College hosts a conference that lays out the primary directions for research on artificial intelligence.

1960s-1970s *Researchers seek to advance artificial intelligence.*

1967 MIT programmer Richard Greenblatt develops MacHack, which performs at the level of a good high school chess player.

1969 SRI International demonstrates the first robot, named Shakey, that employs artificial intelligence.

1979 The Stanford Cart—the first computer-controlled, autonomous vehicle—successfully circumnavigates the Stanford University AI laboratory.

1980s-1990s *AI begins to have commercial applications.*

1980 First expert systems—programs that emulate human decision-makers—are introduced. A variety of programs appear through the decade for analyzing data.

1985 Inventor Danny Hillis designs the Connection Machine, which uses parallel computing—in which several processors execute multiple applications or computations simultaneously—to bring new power to AI.

1997 IBM's Deep Blue supercomputer defeats chess champion Garry Kasparov in a match.

2000-Present *AI appears in consumer products.*

2002 iRobot introduces the Roomba, a robotic vacuum that autonomously maneuvers through rooms.

2009 Google begins testing self-driving cars.

2011 IBM's Watson supercomputer beats two former "Jeopardy" champions in a three-day televised tournament. . . . Apple launches speech-recognition and language-processing software called Siri; Google follows in 2012 with Google Now and Microsoft in 2013 with Cortana.

2012 WorkFusion, a platform that assigns work to humans and evaluates their work, hits the market.

2014 Facebook announces that its AI-powered DeepFace facial recognition program has achieved 97.25 percent accuracy, virtually matching that of humans.

2017 The Defense Advanced Research Projects Agency undertakes a program that seeks to track and explain how AI arrives at decisions.

2018 Facebook CEO Mark Zuckerberg testifies before Congress about the theft of personal data (April). . . . Europe's new privacy law—the General Data Protection Regulation—takes effect (May). It requires that companies doing business in Europe provide European Union citizens with "meaningful information about the logic" of automated decision-making processes. . . . An IBM computer debates humans in a San Francisco competition; it won on knowledge but the humans had better delivery (June).

Assigning Blame When Algorithms Do Harm

AI will raise "incredibly complicated questions."

On a March night in Tempe, Ariz., 49-year-old Elaine Herzberg stepped out of the shadows to walk her bicycle across the street. An autonomous Uber vehicle with a backup human driver struck and killed her. Her death, legal analysts say, raises difficult questions as to who should be legally liable for the tragedy: the maker of the software that controlled the car? Uber? The human who was supposed to intervene if trouble arose?

Experts say the law on artificial intelligence (AI) liability remains unclear because no major cases have come before the courts. And the Tempe case will provide no opportunity for judges to weigh in: Uber quickly paid an undisclosed amount to Herzberg's family, apparently before a lawsuit was filed.[1]

When the courts do take up the liability question, analysts say, judges will likely have their hands full trying to determine culpability because humans find it difficult to understand how AI operates.

"AI decision-making rules . . . are completely different from how the human brain processes information," wrote Finale Doshi-Velez, an assistant professor of computer science at Harvard University, and Mason Kortz, a clinical instructional fellow at the Harvard Law School cyberlaw clinic. "If a self-driving car could spit out a raw record of what it was 'thinking' at the time of a crash, it would probably be meaningless to a human."[2]

And because multiple programmers in different locations or companies often are responsible for writing complex AI programs, authorities will find it hard to assign blame for a specific action. More challenging still, if an AI program includes machine learning—the ability of algorithms to "learn" using data it has gathered—it may change its behavior in ways unforeseen by its creators, further muddying the legal waters.

"It is not clear to me who should be held responsible," says lawyer Matthew U. Scherer, who specializes in artificial intelligence-related issues. "The people who designed [AI] to a certain degree have an obligation to build in safeguards to ensure that their products are not misused. But it is difficult to know how feasible that will be as a form of control for machine learning."

Oren Etzioni, CEO of the Allen Institute for Artificial Intelligence, a research group seeking to build advanced AI capabilities, says a company or individual that puts an autonomous vehicle on the market "absolutely" is liable for

---

In fact, Watson earned three times as much money as its human competitors.

Watson's performance was especially impressive because—as any fan of "Jeopardy" knows—the show's questions involve double entendres and other tricks in phrasing.[65]

Algorithms and AI Spread

In the mid-2010s, artificial intelligence and the algorithms that underlay it began to show up in public and in workplaces.

Although Google had been testing its self-driving cars at private locations in California since 2009, the internet giant did not begin road tests on public streets until 2015 when its cars ventured onto Austin, Texas, streets without human drivers.[66]

Lionbridge, a British company, achieved a major step forward in computers' ability to process human speech with its introduction in April 2011 of GeoFluent, a cloud-based service that instantly translates speech or written text for users, and that can translate text into multiple languages for workgroups that do not share a common language.[67]

Siri, Apple's speech recognition and language processing software, was introduced in 2011, initiating a flood of AI-powered, voice-interactive consumer products. Google's Google Now debuted in 2012 and Microsoft's Cortana in 2013. Amazon's Alexa arrived a year later.[68]

AI also made striking inroads into white-collar workplaces in 2012 when WorkFusion, a platform developed at MIT's Computer Science and Artificial Intelligence

any damage that vehicle causes, even when machine learning played the key role in the accident. "We are responsible for our AI . . . even if the car is on cruise control," he says.

Other experts argue that holding creators of AI directly responsible for damages is unrealistic. "Is it really my fault if I have a product that I deploy into an environment and the environment has a couple of traits that the program processes and that causes the program to do something bad?" says Jack Clark, strategy and communications director at OpenAI, an industry-funded nonprofit focused on developing safe AI. "It's very hard to think of everything that can go wrong and protect against everything that can go wrong."

While AI presents clear challenges in civil litigation, the situation in criminal cases is even more daunting.

Criminal law in the United States "attaches great importance to the concept of *mens rea*—the intending mind," wrote the standing committee of Stanford University's One Hundred Year Study of Artificial Intelligence project. Can an artificial intelligence "intend" to commit a crime? "As AI applications engage in behavior that, were it done by a human, would constitute a crime, courts and other legal actors will have to puzzle through whom to hold accountable and on what theory," the committee said.[3]

The uncertainties of AI liability have led some experts to suggest adopting a legal framework similar to the one on vaccines. Because vaccines offer obvious benefits to public health but can cause bad reactions in some individuals, Congress established a federally funded no-fault system to compensate those injured by mandated vaccines. Rebecca J. Krystosek, managing editor of the *Minnesota Law Review*, supports the strategy but only for medical algorithms and driverless cars, both of which offer what she called "a clear and compelling public safety benefit." In other cases, she said, "the law should not afford any special 'out' for algorithmic harms."[4]

Whatever approach is taken, AI is going to raise "incredibly complicated questions," says lawyer Andrew Tutt, who studies artificial intelligence issues. The courts, he says, were barely able to understand cars when they replaced horse-drawn carriages at the beginning of the 20th century. "Imagine them trying to figure out whether the data [used to teach AI] was really what was responsible for the vehicle that crashed."

— *Patrick Marshall*

[1] "Uber appears to have reached settlement with family of woman who died in Arizona accident," The Associated Press, *Los Angeles Times*, March 29, 2018, https://tinyurl.com/yaw9g9mh.

[2] Finale Doshi-Velez and Mason Kortz, "A.I. is more powerful than ever. How do we hold it accountable?" *The Washington Post*, March 20, 2018, https://tinyurl.com/ya5xcu4m.

[3] "Artificial Intelligence and Life in 2030," Report of the 2015 Study Panel, Stanford University, September 2016, p. 49, https://tinyurl.com/znl2ep4.

[4] Rebecca J. Krystosek, "The Algorithm Made Me Do It and Other Bad Excuses," *Minnesota Law Review*, May 17, 2017, https://tinyurl.com/yatfe9jj.

Lab, went on the market. WorkFusion is essentially an automated project manager that selectively assigns work to humans—even posting the assignments on social media, such as Craigslist—and then evaluates the research and writing produced by the human, and reassigns it if it is not up to standards.

"As the workers complete their assigned tasks, WorkFusion's machine-learning algorithms continuously look for opportunities to further automate the process," wrote software developer and futurist Ford. "In other words, even as the freelancers work under the direction of the system, they are simultaneously generating the training data that will gradually lead to their replacement with full automation."[69]

As robots' motor skills improve, more prosaic jobs are increasingly being turned over to machines.

Momentum Machines, for example, in 2014 introduced a robot that can grill a hamburger, place it on a bun, layer it with lettuce, tomatoes, pickles and onions and wrap it in paper. The company says the machine can take the place of two to three full-time workers, turning out 360 burgers per hour. Our "device isn't meant to make employees more efficient," said co-founder Alexandros Vardakostas. "It's meant to completely obviate them."[70]

Sales of industrial robots more than doubled between 1995 and 2013, according to the International Federation of Robots, an industry trade group, with more than 178,000 sold in 2013.[71] In 2014, sales climbed 27 percent—to about 225,000 units—with automotive and electronics industries, especially those in China and South Korea, accounting for the lion's share of the increase.[72]

No Small Task: Ensuring Humanity's Survival

Some argue AI poses terrible risks, but others aren't worried.

They are fodder for countless dystopian sci-fi books and films: rogue robots that turn against humankind.

Some experts say the threat from artificial intelligence is real.

Interviewed in a 2018 documentary about AI's dangers, Tesla founder Elon Musk warned: "We are rapidly headed towards digital super intelligence that far exceeds any human," adding that these machines have the potential to become "an immortal dictator from which we would never escape."[1]

Stuart Armstrong, a fellow at the Future of Humanity Institute, a research group at Oxford University that studies risk, agrees the threat to humanity posed by autonomous machines is great. "Humans steer the future not because we're the strongest or the fastest, but because we're the smartest," he told a reporter in 2015. "When machines become smarter than humans, we'll be handing them the steering wheel."[2]

But others say talk of AI's threat to the human race is way overblown.

"I am not terribly worried," says Mark MacCarthy, senior vice president of public policy for the Software and Information Industry Association, an industry group.

No research is yet aimed at developing "general AI"—AI that is smart enough to adapt to different environments and activities, he says. "Almost all real computer science research at the university level and [in] research operations of businesses is focused on narrow AI—it's just a tool trying to accomplish a particular purpose."

Oren Etzioni, CEO of the Allen Institute for Artificial Intelligence, an AI research group, also says he is not worried—at least not yet. "I believe that we have canaries in the coal mine—that is, identifiable points that, if reached, could lead us to be more alarmed," he says. "One example is a physical robot capable of replicating itself. We don't have any such robot or machine today."

Nevertheless, experts who say talk of an AI apocalypse is overblown note that humanity should still develop ways to ensure the safety of AI before it is capable of modifying or replicating itself.

The core problem, says Jack Clark, strategy and communications director at OpenAI, an industry-funded group that conducts research on developing advanced AI, is: "How do you ensure that increasingly autonomous systems that have some self-modification behavior cannot go haywire? It's an extremely unpleasant problem."

"I think it is fair to say we have barely scratched the surface of the important safety and basic security research that can be done in AI," Ben Buchanan, a fellow at the Belfer Center's Cybersecurity Project at Harvard University, told Congress in April.[3]

The Robotic Industries Association, another industry trade group, reported that North American companies ordered 27,685 robots valued at $1.6 billion in 2014, an increase of 28 percent in units and 19 percent in value over the previous year.[73]

Also in 2014, Facebook announced that its AI-powered DeepFace facial-recognition program had achieved an accuracy rate of 97.25 percent; humans by comparison can recognize faces 97.5 percent of the time.[74]

And in July 2014, Google released details about Sibyl, the company's machine-learning platform that tracks massive amounts of data to allow Google to make predictions about user behavior. Sibyl, for example, enables YouTube to guess which videos a website visitor would want to see.[75]

As AI and their algorithms grow increasingly powerful and inscrutable, researchers want the machines to be able to explain their thinking so humans will know whether to trust AI's findings. DARPA in March 2017 announced that it had chosen 13 projects from academia and industry to participate in its new Explainable Artificial Intelligence program, which seeks to pull back the curtain on AI's decision-making.

"It's often the nature of these machine-learning systems that they produce a lot of false alarms," said David Gunning, the program's manager at DARPA. "So an

One strategy for ensuring safe artificial intelligence is to create an abort system that would allow a human to interrupt any algorithm that is misbehaving or becoming threatening.[4] At the same time, researchers are aware that AI might eventually develop the ability to take defensive action. AI experts at DeepMind, a London-based AI research firm recently bought by Google, and the University of Oxford are seeking ways to prevent that from happening.[5]

Bas Steunebrink, a researcher at IDSIA, an AI laboratory in Switzerland, is working on a different strategy—teaching AI to be safe and monitoring it until humans are convinced it poses no danger. With Steunebrink's approach—called EXPAI (experience-based artificial intelligence)—the emphasis shifts from searching for ways to control AI to developing ways to "grow" AI that has human-like ethical values.

Still, some experts are concerned that even if developers can ensure the safety of artificial intelligence, problems can result if humans misuse AI tools.

One such area is nuclear warfare. AI's advances "could spur arms races or increase the likelihood of states escalating to nuclear use" as their military capabilities improve, according to a recent paper by RAND, a California think tank that conducts research under government contracts. For example, improved sensor technologies could tempt nations to launch a nuclear strike because AI increases their chances of destroying an enemy's nuclear missiles aboard submarines or on mobile launchers.[6]

In a fast-moving crisis, militaries also would be relying on AI to make split-second decisions.

"Some experts fear that an increased reliance on artificial intelligence can lead to new types of catastrophic mistakes," said Andrew Lohn, co-author of the paper and an associate engineer at RAND. "There may be pressure to use AI before it is technologically mature, or it may be susceptible to adversarial subversion. Therefore, maintaining strategic stability in coming decades may prove extremely difficult and all nuclear powers must participate in the cultivation of institutions to help limit nuclear risk."[7]

— *Patrick Marshall*

[1] Peter Holley, "Elon Musk's nightmarish warning: AI could become 'an immortal dictator from which we could never escape,' " *The Washington Post*, April 6, 2018, https://tinyurl.com/y8jr4m5u.

[2] Patrick Sawer, "Threat from Artificial Intelligence not just Hollywood fantasy," *The Telegraph*, June 27, 2015, https://tinyurl.com/y94k7way.

[3] Testimony of Ben Buchanan, House Oversight Committee Subcommittee on IT, April 18, 2018, https://tinyurl.com/yb8ee9rx.

[4] Sam Shead, "Google has developed a 'big red button' that can be used to interrupt artificial intelligence and stop it from causing harm," *Business Insider*, June 3, 2016, https://tinyurl.com/ycxdgbn8.

[5] Laurent Orseau and Stuart Armstrong, "Safely Interruptible Agents," Association for Uncertainty in Artificial Intelligence, 2016, https://tinyurl.com/ycv3avdf.

[6] Edward Geist and Andrew J. Lohn, "How Might Artificial Intelligence Affect the Risk of Nuclear War?" RAND Corp., 2018, pp. 1, 11, https://tinyurl.com/ydc4lacb.

[7] "By 2040, artificial intelligence could upend nuclear stability," press release, RAND, April 24, 2018, https://tinyurl.com/y7exd2uh.

intel analyst really needs extra help to understand why a recommendation was made."[76]

CURRENT SITUATION
Russian Hacking

Russian hackers and others use AI to manipulate the views of Americans by mining data and disseminating fake news on social media sites, according to computer experts.

"Where there were once a couple dozen human operators stitching together a few divisive messages during working hours in Moscow to pick at the digital halls of our democracy," wrote Dipayan Ghosh, a fellow at New America and a former technology adviser to the Obama White House, "there will soon be countless AI systems testing and probing a plethora of content on a vast field of social media user audiences that are highly segmented by race, ethnicity, gender, location, socioeconomic class and political leaning."[77]

To counter AI-generated misinformation campaigns, Ghosh urges improving algorithms.

"Given the scale of platforms like Google and Facebook—with billions of people using the platforms—you cannot have just humans checking the veracity of certain content," he told *CQ Researcher*. "You need AI to be checking content and essentially checking its veracity continuously and flagging possible fake information for human review."

Although current technology is not up to the task, he says, "as the AI gets better and better and as these companies hire more and more people, I think they have a good chance of [making] sure this does not become a broader problem going forward. It will be a big challenge."

The controversy over Cambridge Analytica, a consulting firm that worked with the Trump campaign in the 2016 presidential campaign, shows how big that challenge could be. University of Cambridge psychology professor Aleksandr Kogan developed an app that gathered data on up to 87 million Facebook users. The data were then analyzed for user personality traits, and that analysis was sold to Cambridge Analytica.[78]

The company, in turn, used the data to identify potential Trump supporters and tailor pitches to them, a strategy known in politics as microtargeting. Kogan said the software he used to generate psychological profiles was ineffective. "In fact, from our subsequent research on the topic," he wrote, "we found out that the predictions we gave [Cambridge Analytica] were 6 times more likely to get all 5 of a person's personality traits wrong as it was to get them all correct. In short, even if the data was used by a campaign for microtargeting, it could realistically only hurt their efforts."[79]

Still, the situation sufficiently alarmed Congress that Facebook founder and CEO Mark Zuckerberg was called in to testify before Congress in early April.

Zuckerberg told senators that Facebook would be "investigating many apps, tens of thousands of apps, and if we find any suspicious activity, we're going to conduct a full audit of those apps to understand how they're using their data and if they're doing anything improper. If we find that they're doing anything improper, we'll ban them from Facebook, and we will tell everyone affected."[80]

Zuckerberg also said his company had recently deployed AI tools that could detect malicious activity aimed at influencing elections.

Sen. Richard Blumenthal, D-Conn., said Facebook could not regulate itself and that Congress must act. "The old saying: 'There ought to be a law.' There has to be a law," he said. "Unless there's a law, their business model is going to continue to maximize profit over privacy."

Sen. John Thune, R-S.D., echoed Blumenthal when he said that "in the past, many of my colleagues on both sides of the aisle have been willing to defer to tech companies' efforts to regulate themselves. But this may be changing."[81]

Congress Stirs

In addition to the Senate hearing on the misuse of Facebook data, the House Subcommittee on Information Technology held a hearing in February on artificial intelligence, looking at ways public policy can help the United States remain a world leader in the technology.

Intel's Khosrowshahi told the panel that the federal government "can play an important role in enabling the further development of AI technology. Since data is fuel for AI, the U.S. government should embrace open data policies." He also urged the government to increase funding for scientific research and for programs to teach workers the skills needed to develop AI.[82]

Two bills under consideration also will have a bearing on the safety of artificial intelligence.

The Self Drive Act, which passed the House last year and is now being considered by the Senate Committee on Commerce, Science and Transportation, encourages the testing and deployment of autonomous vehicles; requires developers to certify that the technology is safe; and requires manufacturers to develop written cybersecurity and privacy plans for self-driving vehicles.

The bill also pre-empts states from enacting their own laws regarding the design, construction or performance of autonomous vehicles, a controversial provision.

In a letter to Congress, the National Governors Association complained that the bill encroaches on safety regulations that remain under the states' purview. The governors also expressed concern about a lack of state representation on the councils and advisory groups proposed in the legislation.

"Especially with respect to the cybersecurity advisory council, the sharing of threat information with state government will be a critical component of preventing and mitigating security threats in autonomous vehicles," the association wrote.[83]

The other major legislation—the Future of Artificial Intelligence Act of 2017—is a bipartisan bill that would create a committee of experts from within and outside government to advise the secretary of Commerce on artificial intelligence, its economic effects and the legal and ethical issues, such as algorithmic bias.[84]

The bill has not cleared committee and its future is uncertain, although Rep. Ted Lieu, D-Calif., one of the bill's co-sponsors, says he hopes the legislation's bipartisan sponsorship will help it gain passage.

"Nothing is going to have a greater impact on American competitiveness and innovation than developments in machine learning and AI," says Lieu. "As members of Congress, we need to make sure these powerful tools are deployed safely and responsibly—and that the right people are talking to each other about how to prepare for what's coming. My bill will help bring together policymakers and industry experts to sketch out roles and relationships that will become crucial as this technology proliferates."

The Trump administration is calling for light and perhaps even reduced regulation of AI. The day after a May 10 meeting with industry representative, a White House statement said, "Overly burdensome regulations do not stop innovation—they just move it overseas."[85]

Pressure to Act

Despite the reluctance of Congress and the White House to push for comprehensive regulation of algorithms and AI, pressure from outside the federal government is increasing.

Europe's new privacy law—the General Data Protection Regulation, or GDPR—which went into effect in May, requires U.S. companies doing business in Europe to provide to EU citizens "meaningful information about the logic" of automated decision-making processes. "In many cases, global companies that do business in Europe will need to disclose what factors go into the algorithms they use," said Mark MacCarthy, senior vice president of public policy for the Software and Information Industry Association, a trade industry group in Washington.[86]

Similarly, the New York City Council unanimously passed legislation in December to establish a task force to examine the city's automated decision systems—which are used to allocate city resources on everything from firehouses to food stamps—to reduce bias and make them more open to examination.[87]

"I don't know what [an algorithm] is. I don't know how it works. I don't know what factors go into it," said Bronx City Council Rep. James Vacca, sponsor of the legislation. "As we advance into the 21st century, we

Facebook Chairman and CEO Mark Zuckerberg arrives to testify before the House Energy and Commerce Committee in Washington on April 11, 2018. Zuckerberg responded to reports that Cambridge Analytica, a British political consulting firm linked to the Trump campaign, used Facebook data during the 2016 presidential campaign to identify potential Trump supporters.

Getty Images/Chip Somodevilla

must ensure our government is not 'black-boxed.' I have proposed this legislation not to prevent city agencies from taking advantage of cutting-edge tools, but to ensure that when they do, they remain accountable to the public."[88]

Even as other jurisdictions try to fill in the regulatory gaps, critics say the federal government still needs to act.

"The industry has done an incredibly good job of making sure that it stays in an environment that is essentially unregulated," says Ghosh. "What we need is to defeat political gridlock to offer more transparency into how these technologies work, because I don't see any other way of holding industry accountable."

Lieu agrees, saying greater congressional oversight is necessary. "I think there's a happy medium between overbearing regulation that stifles innovation and a completely hands-off approach to such a powerful set of tools," he says. "We've tried that, and it hasn't worked."

OUTLOOK
Outperforming Humans

As algorithms improve, so will machine learning and AI. Futurist and inventor Ray Kurzweil famously predicts that by 2029, an AI program will pass the Turing test, devised to measure whether a computer has reached human levels of intelligence. Kurzweil, who since 2012 has been Google's engineering director, also predicts that

Does AI require a new federal regulatory structure?

YES Matthew U. Scherer
*Attorney in Employment Law and
AI issues, Littler Mendelson*

Written for *CQ Researcher*, July 2018

NO Adam Thierer
*Senior Research Fellow, Mercatus Center,
George Mason University*

Written for *CQ Researcher*, July 2018

Artificial intelligence (AI) represents a departure from previous generations of human technology in many ways. In law and policy, the most radical feature of AI is that for the first time in human history, consequential decisions are being made by something other than a human being. From a legal perspective, this is problematic for many reasons, but two in particular stick out.

First, our system of laws assumes that humans will make all legally significant decisions. True, corporations and other legal "persons" are not themselves human beings. But dig down even a little, and it quickly becomes obvious that the law always assumes that humans will retain ultimate control. This assumption is so obvious and fundamental that it rarely is spelled out in legal codes. As a result, as AI systems start making more decisions that carry legal consequences, many of their decisions and acts may fall into a legal gray area.

The second major reason for concern is that people have a worrying tendency to blindly trust machines that are marketed as being designed to perform a particular task. People will often follow the directions provided by a GPS even if they know exactly where they are going, and even if they know that the GPS' suggested route is incorrect. This means that even decisions that are not supposed to be delegated to machines under the law may nevertheless be delegated to machines in practice—particularly if the machine is marketed as having the necessary capabilities.

These two factors point to the need for legal reform and, where necessary, public oversight of how AI systems are marketed and operated. Unfortunately, traditional centralized forms of government regulation may prove particularly ill-suited for managing the risks associated with AI. Those risks—unlike previous large-scale ones made by humans, such as environmental threats, nuclear technology and mass-produced consumer products—do not require a large physical footprint or a centralized production facility.

Indeed, AI researchers may work together on projects at different times and from different places (or even different countries) without any conscious coordination. That too represents a unique challenge for regulators, who are used to having large, highly visible targets for regulation. AI thus may not require "regulation" in the traditional sense, but it will require fundamentally rethinking how we manage the risks associated with new technologies.

Artificial intelligence (AI) is already all around us and is helping make our lives better. It holds the promise of further helping improve our economy and even saving lives. But some worry about the dangers of autonomous systems and machine learning and wonder whether more regulation is needed.

The question of whether we need a new federal regulatory structure for AI and robotics implies an absence of any law or oversight for them. In reality, these technologies already are governed by a wide variety of policies and agencies.

The Federal Trade Commission, National Highway Traffic Safety Administration, Federal Aviation Administration, National Telecommunications and Information Administration, Department of Homeland Security and the White House itself already have looked into various facets of AI policy and issued reports on it. Moreover, plenty of policies and procedures already govern AI: civil rights law, product defects law, the law of torts, contract law, property law, class-action lawsuits and a wide variety of consumer protection policies aimed at addressing "unfair and deceptive practices."

Thus, when people ask whether we need a new federal regulatory structure for AI, what they mean to suggest is that we need a new, technocratic approach to regulating autonomous systems, machine learning and robotics. This means a dedicated law (or set of laws) and likely a new federal bureaucracy to preemptively regulate this rapidly evolving set of technologies.

That would be a mistake. While it's always worth thinking about the dangers new technologies might pose and whether new policies are needed, we shouldn't let fears about worst-case scenarios lead us to create another huge federal bureaucracy until we have exhausted other policy solutions.

Top-down, technocratic laws and bureaucracies tend to focus on preemptive remedies that aim to predict the future and on hypothetical problems that may never come about. Although such laws and agencies are well-intentioned, they pose many trade-offs. Heavy-handed preemptive restraints on innovation can discourage new entry into emerging technological fields, increase compliance costs and create more risk and uncertainty for entrepreneurs and investors. For a nation, this can seriously threaten economic growth, competitive advantage and long-run prosperity.

To the maximum extent possible, then, policymakers should work to make "permissionless innovation" the lodestar of AI policy and avoid letting Chicken Little thinking lead to the creation of a new, innovation-limiting federal regulatory regime.

by 2045 AI will attain "the singularity"—the point at which artificial intelligence will be so advanced, "we will multiply our effective intelligence a billionfold."[89]

While some AI programs already can outperform humans in certain tasks, such as performing rapid mathematical operations, some experts believe Kurzweil's prediction is off by decades or more.

"I think the singularity could happen, but my sense is it could be a lot further off than what Kurzweil is suggesting," says futurist Ford. Ford also believes Kurzweil is overly optimistic about how soon AI can pass the Turing test. "AI will eventually build a machine that can think at a human level, but I don't think it's going to happen 11 years from now," he says. "It's a lot further in the future. I would say at least 50 years and maybe 100 years. But these are just wild guesses."

Last summer, the Future of Humanity Institute at the University of Oxford asked 1,634 experts in algorithms and artificial intelligence when they expected machines to be outperforming humans at a variety of tasks. The institute reported the following predictions by the 352 who responded:

- By 2024 AI will outperform translators of foreign languages.
- By 2031 AI will outperform retail salespersons.
- By 2049 AI will write a best-selling book.
- By 2053 AI will be capable of working as a surgeon.[90]

Some experts say AI's very nature points to the likelihood that once the next major advance comes, it will advance at an exponential rate.

"The day that the first self-driving car company goes commercial, I would imagine that one year from that day, there's going to be four other companies with self-driving cars on the road," says former Justice Department attorney Tutt. What's more, advances in one AI sector are expected to bring rapid advances in other areas, he says.

"When you have software that is able to do something as sophisticated as drive a car, its adaptability to other solution spaces is going to be quite high," Tutt says.

At the same time, AI's opaque nature—and especially the ability of machine learning to change its own code without human help—means regulating AI will remain difficult.

"It's a problem that is going to require a lot of trial and error," Tutt says.

According to other experts, however, advocates of comprehensive regulation of AI are responding to baseless fears. "Their thinking has been conditioned by years upon years of popular culture narrative about AI and robotics that are dripping with dystopian dread," says Thierer of the Mercatus Center. "There are no plots about AI and robotics that end with a good-news story."

If those fears win out, says Thierer, humans will inevitably forgo a brighter future. "The problem with that thinking is that it means we need to foreclose almost all AI-based innovation," he says. "Only by allowing a certain amount of experimentation with new technologies can we find new life-enriching or even lifesaving applications."

NOTES

1. Ted Roelofs, "Broken: The human toll of Michigan's unemployment fraud saga," *Bridge*, Feb. 7, 2017, https://tinyurl.com/yd5okhnd.

2. Robert N. Charette, "Michigan's MiDAS Unemployment System: Algorithm Alchemy Created Lead, Not Gold," *IEEE Spectrum*, Jan. 24, 2018, https://tinyurl.com/yc7glpw2; David Eggert, "State of Michigan apologizes for unemployment fiasco, wants to reduce penalties," The Associated Press, Lenconnect.com, Jan. 30, 2017, https://tinyurl.com/yau3ekcq.

3. Roelofs, *op. cit.*; Jack Lessenberry, "State unemployment computer had anything but the golden touch," *Traverse City Record Eagle*, Dec. 31, 2017, https://tinyurl.com/y7qqkbm3.

4. Lili Cheng, "Why You Shouldn't Be Afraid of Artificial Intelligence," *Time*, Jan. 4, 2018, https://tinyurl.com/y9ekv9ww.

5. "Artificial Intelligence Poised to Double Annual Economic Growth Rate in 12 Developed Economies and Boost Labor Productivity by up to 40 Percent by 2035, According to New Research by Accenture," press release, Accenture, Sept. 28, 2016, https://tinyurl.com/lff276d.

6. Catherine Clifford, "Bill Gates: 'A.I. can be our friend,' " CNBC, Feb. 16, 2018, https://tinyurl.com/yc5p2r88.

7. "Cathy O'Neil: Do Algorithms Perpetuate Human Bias?" TED Radio Hour, NPR, Jan. 26, 2018, https://tinyurl.com/ybj4mlv7.

8. Andrew Tutt, "An FDA for Algorithms," *Administrative Law Review*, 2017, p. 117, https://tinyurl.com/y9cet9ax.

9. "Joy Buolamwini, How Does Facial Recognition Software See Skin Color?" TED Talks, NPR, Jan. 26, 2018, https://tinyurl.com/ycjr3koa.

10. Steve Lohr, "Facial Recognition Is Accurate, if You're a White Guy," *The New York Times*, Feb. 9, 2018, https://tinyurl.com/ybewlyjh.

11. Aaron Glantz and Emmanuel Martinez, "Detroit-area blacks twice as likely to be denied home loans," *Detroit News*, Feb. 15, 2018, https://tinyurl.com/ydc4enb6; Virginia Eubanks, "The dangers of letting algorithms make decisions in law enforcement, welfare, and child protection," *Slate*, April 30, 2015, https://tinyurl.com/y88qwexr.

12. "Court software may be no more accurate than web survey takers in predicting criminal risk," press release, Eurekalert, Jan. 17, 2018, https://tinyurl.com/y99xg5wc.

13. Aaron Smith and Monica Anderson, "Automation in Everyday Life," Pew Research Center, Oct. 4, 2017, https://tinyurl.com/y78f5jq3.

14. "Artificial Intelligence, Automation, and the Economy," The White House, Dec. 20, 2016, https://tinyurl.com/zou9urd.

15. Matthew U. Scherer, "Regulating Artificial Intelligence Systems: Risks, Challenges, Competencies and Strategies," *Harvard Journal of Law & Technology*, Spring 2016, p. 365, https://tinyurl.com/y8jngt8o.

16. "Speech analysis software predicted psychosis in at-risk patients with up to 83 percent accuracy," press release, Mount Sinai Hospital, Jan. 22, 2018, https://tinyurl.com/yc6vy7ag.

17. "Algorithm tool works to silence online chatroom sex predators," press release, Purdue University, April 17, 2018, https://tinyurl.com/y9c5ckbe.

18. Alex Hern, "Stephen Hawking: AI will be 'either best thing or worst thing' for humanity," *The Guardian*, Oct. 19, 2016, https://tinyurl.com/jk84lns.

19. Diana Budds, "Biased AI Is A Threat To Civil Liberties," Co.Design, July 25, 2017, https://tinyurl.com/y9c9qgoj.

20. Adam Liptak, "Sent to Prison by a Software Program's Secret Algorithms," *The New York Times*, May 1, 2017, https://tinyurl.com/lzwshya.

21. Budds, *op. cit.*

22. Cameron Langford, "Houston Schools Must Face Teacher Evaluation Lawsuit," Courthouse News Service, May 8, 2017, http://tinyurl.com/y73j3zrm.

23. Natasha Singer, "How Companies Scour or Digital Lives for Clues to Our Health," *The New York Times*, Feb. 25, 2018, https://tinyurl.com/y7yfoy8r.

24. *Ibid.*

25. Cathy O'Neil, *Weapons of Math Destruction: How Big Data Increases Inequality and Threatens Democracy* (2016).

26. Kumba Sennaar, "How America's Top Four Insurance Companies are Using Machine Learning," *Tech Emergence*, June 18, 2018, https://tinyurl.com/yb82knwj.

27. Michal Kosinski and Yilun Wang, "Deep Neural Networks Are More Accurate Than Humans at Detecting Sexual Orientation From Facial Images," *Journal of Personality and Social Psychology*, American Psychological Association, 2018, https://tinyurl.com/ydcxta4f.

28. Samuel Gibbs, "Elon Musk: regulate AI to combat 'existential threat' before it's too late," *The Guardian*, July 17, 2017, https://tinyurl.com/ybpyczvt; Kurt Wagner, "Elon Musk just told a group of America's governors that we need to regulate AI before it's too late," *Recode*, July 15, 2017, https://tinyurl.com/y9ov7ann.

29. "ITI AI Policy Principles," Information Technology Industry Council, Oct. 24, 2017, https://tinyurl.com/y7r4zea3.

30. Testimony of Amir Khosrowshahi before the House Committee on Oversight and Government Reform, Subcommittee on Information Technology, Feb. 14, 2018, https://tinyurl.com/y7a5sleu.

31. Heidi Vogt, "Should the Government Regulate Artificial Intelligence?" *The Wall Street Journal*, April 30, 2018, https://tinyurl.com/y7t4vovl.

32. Scherer, *op. cit.*, p. 356.

33. Jacques Bughin *et al.*, "Artificial Intelligence: The Next Digital Frontier?" McKinsey & Company, June 2017, pp. 9-10, http://tinyurl.com/yapjawqd; "The 2016 AI Recap: Startups See Record High In Deals And Funding," CB Insights, Jan. 19, 2017, https://tinyurl.com/yb5zn3ro.

34. Ben Casselman, "Robots? Training? Factories Tackle the Productivity Puzzle," *San Francisco Chronicle*, June 28, 2018, https://tinyurl.com/y7s9bfcy.

35. "Experts Predict When Artificial Intelligence Will Exceed Human Performance," Emerging Tech from the arXiv, *MIT Technology Review*, May 31, 2017, https://tinyurl.com/y8emjzzs.

36. Carl Benedikt Frey and Michael A. Osborne, "The Future of Employment: How Susceptible are Jobs to Computerization?" Oxford Martin, Sept. 17, 2013, https://tinyurl.com/y9mcxlep.

37. Melanie Arntz, Terry Gregory and Ulrich Zierahn, "The Risk of Automation for Jobs in OECD Countries: A Comparative Analysis," Organisation for Economic Co-operation and Development, June 16, 2016, https://tinyurl.com/y9la2ovz.

38. Testimony of Charles Isbell before the House Committee on Oversight and Government Reform, Subcommittee on Information Technology, Feb. 14, 2018, https://tinyurl.com/y97e2f8s.

39. Testimony of Gary Shapiro before the House Committee on Oversight and Government Reform Subcommittee on Information Technology, Feb. 14, 2018, https://tinyurl.com/y9eq7f66.

40. Lisa Beilfuss, "The Future Robo Adviser: Smart and Ethical?" *The Wall Street Journal*, June 19, 2018, https://tinyurl.com/yacgglau.

41. "Artificial Intelligence and Life in 2030," One Hundred Year Study on Artificial Intelligence, Stanford University, September 2016, https://tinyurl.com/znl2ep4.

42. *Ibid.* For background, see Sarah Glazer, "Universal Basic Income," *CQ Researcher*, Sept. 8, 2017, pp. 725-48.

43. "Artificial Intelligence, Automation and the Economy," *op. cit.*, p. 2.

44. Souvik Das, "The Origin and Evolution of Algorithms," *Digit*, May 3, 2016, https://tinyurl.com/yahz5o54.

45. *Ibid.*; A.M. Turing, "Computing Machinery and Intelligence," *Mind*, pp. 433-460, https://tinyurl.com/hrkzejk.

46. "Turing Machine," *Encyclopedia Britannica*, https://tinyurl.com/yc87x9xf.

47. "Atanasoff-Berry Computer," Computer History Museum, https://tinyurl.com/yaonhk8t.

48. "Konrad Zuse," Computer History Museum, https://tinyurl.com/ybk2cmuz.

49. Michael R. Swaine and Paul A. Freiberger, "Eniac," *Encyclopedia Britannica*, https://tinyurl.com/y842zk3c.

50. "1951—SNARC Maze Solver—Minsky/Edmonds (American)," Cyberneticzoo.com, https://tinyurl.com/y99vs33w.

51. J. McCarthy *et al.*, "A Proposal for the Dartmouth Summer Research Project on Artificial Intelligence," Aug. 31, 1955, https://tinyurl.com/yacnlzh.

52. Joseph Weizenbaum, "ELIZA—A Computer Program For the Study of Natural Language Communication Between Man and Machine," Communications of the ACM, January 1966, https://tinyurl.com/y8p7h4ou.

53. "Joseph Weizenbaum, professor emeritus of computer science, 85," *MIT News*, March 10, 2008, https://tinyurl.com/y73wybbz.

54. "Shakey," Artificial Intelligence Center, https://tinyurl.com/y7lcp558.

55. Nick Bostrom, *Superintelligence: Paths, Dangers, Strategies* (2014), p. 7.

56. Avron Barr and Shirley Tessler, "Expert Systems: A Technology Before Its Time," Stanford University, undated, https://tinyurl.com/ydy3xoes.

57. Alex Roland and Philip Shiman, *Strategic Computing: DARPA and the Quest for Machine Intelligence, 1983-1993* (2002).

58. P.W. Singer, *Wired for War: The Robotics Revolution and Conflict in the 21st Century* (2010), p. 58.

59. Bruce Weber, "Swift and Slashing, Computer Topples Kasparov," *The New York Times*, May 12, 1997, https://tinyurl.com/yckh6xko.

60. "Aibos History," Aibos, https://tinyurl.com/y9ykotvy.

61. "Tired of Chasing Dustballs? Let a Robot Do the Job," *The New York Times*, Sept. 26, 2002, https://tinyurl.com/yc9ya4uh.

62. "Spirit and Opportunity," *Program & Missions*, NASA, https://tinyurl.com/y9w87lc6.

63. Alex Davies, "An Oral History of the Darpa Grand Challenge, the Grueling Robot Race That Launched the Self-Driving Car," *Wired*, Aug. 3, 2017, https://tinyurl.com/y8bo79f9.

64. "Urban Challenge," Defense Advanced Research Projects Agency, https://tinyurl.com/d6m9mrq.

65. Anahad O'Connor, "Watson Dominates 'Jeopardy' but Stumbles Over Geography," *The New York Times*, Feb. 15, 2011, https://tinyurl.com/ybjsl6vv.

66. Kirsten Korosec, "Google self-driving cars arrive in Austin," *Fortune*, July 7, 2015, https://tinyurl.com/qcr93o4.

67. Donald A. DePalma, "Lionbridge Announces Availability of GeoFluent Machine Translation," Common Sense Advisory, April 12, 2011, https://tinyurl.com/ychqlna6.

68. Ava Mutchler, "Voice Assistant Timeline: A Short History of the Voice Revolution," Voicebot.ai, July 14, 2017, https://tinyurl.com/y8xtbdtp.

69. Martin Ford, *Rise of the Robots: Technology and the Threat of a Jobless Future* (2015), p. 95.

70. Dylan Love, "Here's the burger-flipping robot that could put fast-food workers out of a job," *Business Insider*, Aug. 11, 2014, https://tinyurl.com/klx53px.

71. "Industrial robot sales increase worldwide by 29 percent," International Federation of Robotics, https://tinyurl.com/owpfjv8.

72. "Global industrial robot sales rose 27 pct in 2014," Reuters, March 22, 2015, https://tinyurl.com/yc84fco8.

73. "North American Robotics Market has Strongest Year Ever in 2014," Robotic Industries Association, Feb. 4, 2015, https://tinyurl.com/y86tpp5h.

74. Amit Chowdhry, "Facebook's DeepFace Software Can Match Faces With 97.25% Accuracy," *Forbes*, March 18, 2014, https://tinyurl.com/yalz87a9.

75. Alex Woodie, "Inside Sibyl, Google's Massively Parallel Machine Learning Platform," *Datanami*, July 17, 2014, https://tinyurl.com/ycxv2yhk.

76. Will Knight, "The Dark Secret at the Heart of AI," *Technology Review*, April 11, 2017, https://tinyurl.com/k2j8y9k; David Gunning, "Explainable Artificial Intelligence (XAI)," Defense Advanced Research Projects Agency, https://tinyurl.com/yayu9wtx.

77. Dipayan Ghosh, "Beware of A.I. in Social Media Advertising," *The New York Times*, March 26, 2018, https://tinyurl.com/y9hvka5n.

78. Sheera Frenkel, "Scholars Have Data on Millions of Facebook Users. Who's Guarding It?" *The New York Times*, May 6, 2018, https://tinyurl.com/y9r5bxbk.

79. Lauren Etter and Sarah Frier, "Facebook App Developer Kogan Defends His Actions With User Data," Bloomberg, March 21, 2018, https://tinyurl.com/yddpkpqp.

80. "Mark Zuckerberg Testimony: Senators Question Facebook's Commitment to Privacy," *The New York Times*, April 10, 2018, https://tinyurl.com/y782wlm7.

81. *Ibid.*

82. "Game Changers: Artificial Intelligence Part I, Artificial Intelligence and Public Policy," Subcommittee on Information Technology, Feb. 14, 2018, https://tinyurl.com/yakts4k4.

83. "Self Drive Act," National Governors Association, July 27, 2017, https://tinyurl.com/ybbc2k6l.

84. "US Politicians Call for 'Future of AI Act', May Shape Legal Factors," *Artificial Lawyer*, Dec. 18, 2017, https://tinyurl.com/ycypsb24.

85. "White House Creates AI Committee, Favors Light Regs, Education," *MeriTalk*, May 11, 2018, https://tinyurl.com/y9qgteh4.

86. Mark MacCarthy, "EU privacy law says companies need to explain the algorithms they use," CIO, Oct. 19, 2017, https://tinyurl.com/yam3az5f.

87. Julia Powles, "New York City's Bold, Flawed Attempt to Make Algorithms Accountable," *The New Yorker*, Dec. 20, 2017, https://tinyurl.com/ybe7pyb2.

88. Elizabeth Zima, "Could New York City's AI Transparency Bill Be a Model for the Country?" *Government Technology*, Jan. 4, 2018, https://tinyurl.com/yckpolpk.

89. Dom Galeon and Christianna Reedy, "Kurzweil Claims That the Singularity Will Happen by 2045," *Futurism*, Oct. 5, 2017, https://tinyurl.com/l4t74sz.

90. "Experts Predict When Artificial Intelligence Will Exceed Human Performance," *op. cit.*

BIBLIOGRAPHY

Selected Sources

Books

Agrawal, Ajay, Joshua Gans and Avi Goldfarb, *Prediction Machines: The Simple Economics of Artificial Intelligence*, Harvard Business Review Press, 2018.
Three professors of management and marketing explain what artificial intelligence (AI) will mean for jobs, business and the economy.

Noble, Safiya Umoja, *Algorithms of Oppression: How Search Engines Reinforce Racism*, New York University Press, 2018.
An assistant professor of information studies at the University of California, Los Angeles, argues that algorithms that power search engines promote bias against women and people of color.

O'Neil, Cathy, *Weapons of Math Destruction: How Big Data Increases Inequality and Threatens Democracy*, Broadway Books, 2016.
A mathematician and data scientist explains how algorithms used by banks, police departments and companies discriminate against groups of people, primarily due to bias in the underlying data that the algorithms analyze.

Articles

Scherer, Matthew U., "Regulating Artificial Intelligence Systems: Risks, Challenges, Competencies and Strategies," *Harvard Journal of Law & Technology*, Spring 2016, https://tinyurl.com/y8jngt8o.
A lawyer who specializes in artificial intelligence-related issues proposes creating a federal agency to oversee AI.

Townsend, Tess, "The Right and Wrong Way to Regulate Artificial Intelligence," *Inc.*, May 3, 2016, https://tinyurl.com/yb3vavfe.
The founder of Singularity University, a Silicon Valley think tank, does not want to see advances in artificial intelligence stifled by governmental rules, a journalist reports.

Tutt, Andrew, "An FDA for Algorithms," *Administrative Law Review*, 2017, https://tinyurl.com/yam58jsn.
As with pharmaceuticals, harms traceable to algorithms may be difficult to detect, argues a lawyer who focuses on AI issues. He calls for establishing a federal agency with powers similar to those of the Food and Drug Administration to regulate AI.

Wang, Yilun, and Michal Kosinski, "Deep Neural Networks Are More Accurate Than Humans at Detecting Sexual Orientation From Facial Images," *Journal of Personality and Social Psychology*, 2018, https://tinyurl.com/ydcxta4f.
Two Stanford University researchers found that neural networks—programs designed to process data in a manner similar to how the human brain works—accurately detected the sexual orientation of males from photographs 81 percent of the time. Such an ability, they say, could raise privacy concerns.

Vogt, Heidi, "Should the Government Regulate Artificial Intelligence?" *The Wall Street Journal*, April 30, 2018, https://tinyurl.com/y7t4vovl.
Three experts in technology and public policy debate the pros and cons of regulating AI.

Reports and Studies

"Artificial Intelligence, Automation, and the Economy," The White House, Dec. 20, 2016, https://tinyurl.com/zou9urd.
The Obama administration reported that while AI-driven automation would continue to boost the U.S. economy,

workers would need to adapt their skills to automation, and policy changes would be required to help workers deal with structural changes in the economy.

"The Malicious Use of Artificial Intelligence: Forecasting, Prevention, and Mitigation," Future of Humanity Institute, Oxford University, February 2018, https://tinyurl.com/y9cvemk7.
This report—which was produced with the help of the Centre for the Study of Existential Risk, the University of Cambridge, the Center for a New American Security, the Electronic Frontier Foundation and OpenAI—surveys potential security threats from malicious uses of artificial intelligence and proposes ways to better forecast, prevent or mitigate the harm.

Brynjolfsson, Erik, Daniel Rock and Chad Syverson, "Artificial Intelligence and the Modern Productivity Problem: A Clash of Expectations and Statistics," National Bureau of Economic Research, November 2017, https://tinyurl.com/ya3fp3wr.
Three management professors explore why artificial intelligence has not yet increased worker productivity as much as many expected, and conclude that it is simply taking longer than expected for the technologies to be implemented.

Osoba, Osande, and William Welser IV, "An Intelligence in Our Image: The Risks of Bias and Errors in Artificial Intelligence," RAND Corp., 2017, https://tinyurl.com/y9y3kupr.
Two Pardee RAND Graduate School professors analyze the potential effects of unintended flaws in algorithms in such areas as criminal justice, public works and welfare administration.

For More Information

American Civil Liberties Union, 125 Broad St., New York, NY 10004; 212-284-7387; www.aclu.org. Civil rights group that is studying algorithms' impact on criminal justice, surveillance and credit and lending.

Association for the Advancement of Artificial Intelligence, 445 Burgess Drive, Suite 100, Menlo Park, CA 94025; 650-328-3123; www.aaai.org. Organization that focuses on advancing the scientific understanding of the mechanisms underlying thought and intelligent behavior and their embodiment in machines.

Carnegie Mellon University Robotics Institute, 5000 Forbes Ave., Pittsburgh, PA 15213; 412-268-3818; www.ri.cmu.edu. Institute established in 1979 to conduct basic and applied research on robotics technologies relevant to industrial and societal tasks.

Consumer Technology Association, 1919 S. Eads St., Arlington, VA 22202; 703-907-7600; www.cta.tech. Advocacy group for entrepreneurs and technology developers.

Defense Advanced Research Projects Agency, 3701 N. Fairfax Drive, Arlington, VA 22203; 703-526-6630; www.darpa.mil. Defense Department agency whose mission is to maintain the technological superiority of the U.S. military by sponsoring research that bridges fundamental discoveries and their military use.

Information Technology Industry Council, 1101 K St., N.W., Suite 610, Washington, DC 20005; 202-737-8888; www.itic.org. Advocacy group for technology companies.

Machine Intelligence Research Institute, 2030 Addison St., #300, Berkeley, CA 94704; intelligence.org/research. Organization that seeks to ensure that artificial intelligence has a positive impact on humankind.

OpenAI, San Francisco, CA; openai.com. Research company focused on developing safe AI; sponsored by Microsoft, Amazon, Tesla founder Elon Musk and venture capitalist Peter Thiel, among others.

Software & Information Industry Association, 1090 Vermont Ave., N.W., Sixth Floor, Washington, DC 20005-4905; 202-289-7442; www.siia.net. Trade association for software companies, including those developing AI products.

14

Climate Change and National Security

William Wanlund

Getty Images/UN Ocha/Giles Clarke

Fourteen-year-old Achwaq and her family fled warfare in western Yemen to seek shelter in Khamir in May. The civil uprisings that began in 2011 in Yemen and other countries in the Middle East, known as the Arab Spring, can be blamed in part on drought and heavy rains caused by climate change, many analysts say.

From *CQ Researcher*,
September 22, 2017

The deadly six-year civil war in Syria has many causes, including brutal government repression, economic mismanagement and ethnic and religious tensions. But a less obvious force may have helped fuel what has become one of the most violent conflagrations in recent history: climate change.

Environmental scientists, military officials and others say an unprecedented drought in Syria from 2006 to 2009 and torrid temperatures led to soaring food prices and mass migration, which in turn sparked civil unrest, a government crackdown and, finally, a war that has killed nearly a half-million people, displaced millions more and unleashed new waves of terrorism.[1]

"First, brutally hot temperatures and drought in western Russia fed fires which reduced the wheat crop," causing Russia—a major supplier of wheat to Syria—to stop exporting the grain, says retired U.S. Marine Brig. Gen. Stephen Cheney. "Then, a four-year drought in Syria caused crop failures there, leading to massive internal migration and social unrest." The chaos and instability that followed made Syria fertile ground for terrorists, he says.

Cheney, now head of the American Security Project (ASP), a defense policy think tank in Washington, says the Syrian crisis arose out of a series of 2011 civil uprisings in the Middle East known as the Arab Spring. Nonetheless, he says, "climate change was a contributor. . . . Syria's civil war is a poster child for climate change as a national security threat."

Many other analysts trace some of the impetus for other Arab Spring uprisings—in Egypt, Tunisia, Yemen and Libya—to soaring global food prices resulting from drought in some

Coastal Bases Vulnerable to Climate Change

A three-foot sea level rise could damage 128 U.S. coastal military installations, nearly half of them naval bases, according to the Union of Concerned Scientists. Eighteen installations along the East and Gulf coasts are at highest risk of flooding that could damage roads and other infrastructure. Even under conservative climate change estimates, nine installations would lose at least one-fourth of their land area by the end of the century.

Key Military Bases on East and Gulf Coasts

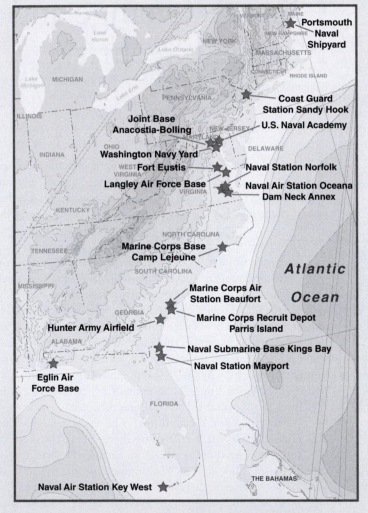

Source: "The US Military on the Front Lines of Rising Seas," Union of Concerned Scientists, July 2016, https://tinyurl.com/hq9u2zd

agricultural exporting regions and to ruinously heavy rains in others.[2]

"No one would say that climate change caused the Arab Spring or the conflicts in those countries," says Francesco Femia, president of the Center for Climate and Security, a Washington think tank. "You can't distinguish it in isolation from other threats and risks." Still, Femia says, climate change "exacerbated conditions in those countries and helped precipitate those conflicts."

Not everyone is ready to accept the link between climate change and the Syrian conflict. In September, a multidisciplinary group of researchers led by Jan Selby, an international relations professor at the University of Sussex in England, cast doubt on the theory that Syria's drought caused large-scale internal migration and that the migrants were a major cause of the unrest that sparked the civil war.[3]

But researchers and military officials generally agree that climate change represents an international security concern. The U.S. Department of Defense (DOD) considers climate change a "threat multiplier"— a factor that can aggravate other conditions, such as poverty and political or social instability, and create security or geopolitical risks for the United States or its allies.[4]

"By increasing the intensity, frequency and severity of extreme weather events, climate change can make states more unstable, which can lead to increased power of terrorist organizations," Femia says. "It can affect the geostrategic environment in areas that are important to the United States, like the Arctic, Asia and the Middle East."

Drought is not the only potential manifestation of climate change that concerns Pentagon leaders. Another is sea-level rise, stemming largely from the melting of glaciers in Greenland and Antarctica.

In addition, melting Arctic sea ice has unlocked ice-bound areas, opening them to shipping, oil and gas drilling, mining and even tourism and leading to intensified economic competition for access rights. Russia has increased its military presence in the region, a buildup that Russian officials say is intended to strengthen homeland defense and protect commercial interests. Some U.S. military observers, however, worry that Russia's actions may signal future aggression, such as efforts to take control of shipping lanes at the top of the globe.

Military planners also fear that rising coastal waters could harm the readiness of U.S. forces. A report by the Union of Concerned Scientists said a "roughly three-foot increase in sea level would threaten 128 coastal DOD installations in the United States."[5]

Global warming is expected to raise sea levels between 0.3 meters (1 foot) and 2.5 meters (8.2 feet) by 2100, according to a January report from the National Oceanic and Atmospheric Administration.[6] The report identifies a rise of 1 meter as an "intermediate" projected increase. That, say Navy veterans, could result in troop-deployment delays and reduced access to docking and repair facilities.

Naval Station Norfolk in Virginia, the world's largest naval base and the headquarters of the Navy's Atlantic Fleet, is among the threatened facilities. Parts of the base already flood 10 times a year during extreme high tides.[7] "If you can't get ships underway with a crew intact out of Norfolk, you're going to delay the application of military force or humanitarian assistance somewhere else where they are called upon to go," says retired Navy Vice Adm. Dennis McGinn, president of the American Council on Renewable Energy.

But Dakota Wood, a former Marine officer who is a senior research fellow for defense programs at the Heritage Foundation, a conservative think tank in Washington, says the military's options are limited. "If you accept that sea levels are rising and you expect more localized flooding of coastal areas with major naval bases like San Diego or Norfolk, what is the military supposed to do?" he asks. "Preemptively move a major naval base 50 miles upriver? Where's the funding for that?"

The Navy is already taking steps to fortify its facilities against the effects of climate change, for example by strengthening piers and erecting structures on higher ground, according to Todd Lyman, a spokesman for the Navy Facilities Engineering Command for the mid-Atlantic region.[8]

Former President Barack Obama believed climate change constituted an economic and security threat to the nation. In 2015 he signed the Paris climate agreement, which pledged its nearly 200 participants to work to stem global warming. Without such a worldwide effort, Obama said, "we are going to have to devote more and more and more of our economic and military resources not to growing opportunity for our people, but to adapting to the various consequences of a changing planet."[9]

On Sept. 21, 2016, he instructed federal agencies to consider climate change when drawing up their national security plans.[10] The same day, the National Intelligence Council (NIC), which performs analytical work for the 16 U.S. intelligence agencies, backed Obama with a report saying climate change is "almost certain to have significant direct and indirect social, economic, political, and security implications [and] pose significant national security challenges for the United States over the next two decades."[11]

But President Trump, who succeeded Obama in January, once tweeted that climate change was "a total, and very expensive, hoax."[12] He later said he was keeping an "open mind" on the subject.[13] Nevertheless, on March 28, he declared the costs of complying with government regulations designed to limit climate change pose a greater threat to national security than do the changes themselves, and he rescinded Obama's 2016 national security memorandum and many of Obama's other climate-related directives. Trump said his aim was to end "regulatory burdens that unnecessarily encumber energy production, constrain economic growth and prevent job creation."[14] On June 1, he made similar comments in announcing the United States would withdraw from the Paris agreement.[15]

Natural Disasters Force Millions from Homes

From 2008 to 2016, 227.6 million people were displaced worldwide, most of them within their own country's borders, by weather-related or geophysical disasters, such as earthquakes. Weather-related disasters were responsible for 86 percent of the displacements. In the first half of 2017, disasters in 76 countries and territories uprooted another 4.5 million people.

Displacements by Weather or Geophysical Disasters, 2008-16

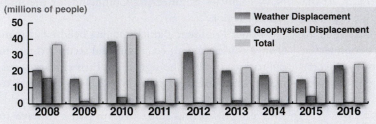

Sources: "Global Report on Internal Displacement," May 22, 2017, https://tinyurl.com/y8dvj789; "Provisional Mid-year Figures, Internal Displacement in 2017," Aug. 16, 2017, https://tinyurl.com/ybhc676k, Norwegian Refugee Council and Internal Displacement Monitoring Centre

James Taylor, a senior fellow for environment and energy policy at the Heartland Institute, a libertarian think tank in Arlington Heights, Ill., agrees with Trump. "Climate change certainly isn't a national security threat the way the Obama administration said it was, whereby global warming is causing catastrophes and migrations of people and scarce resources and food and water shortages, which they said would be threat multipliers," Taylor says. "You're not seeing any of these. The greater threat to national security would be forcing our economy onto an expensive renewable-power trajectory."

However, Trump's Defense secretary, James Mattis, said in written responses to questions at his Senate confirmation hearing in January that "climate change is impacting stability in areas of the world where our troops are operating today. It is appropriate for [military commanders] to incorporate drivers of instability that impact the security environment in their areas into their planning."[16]

Some observers see signs that the political split over climate change may be narrowing. The House of Representatives has established a bipartisan Climate Solutions Caucus to explore approaches to dealing with a changing climate. The caucus was instrumental in the House's July passage of legislation declaring climate change to be "a direct threat" to U.S. national security and requiring the Pentagon to report on how climate change affects military operations and readiness. (The legislation has not yet reached the Senate floor.)[17]

In late summer, back-to-back hurricanes caused devastating flooding in Texas and Louisiana and widespread destruction in Florida and other Southeastern states, raising new worries about potential links between climate change and extreme weather. Scientists did not attribute the hurricanes to climate change, but a number said warming ocean temperatures increase the intensity and frequency of such storms. At the same time, the hurricanes tested the military's ability to both protect its assets and contribute to relief efforts.

As Americans debate possible effects of global climate change on national security, here are some key questions they are asking:

Does a weakened commitment to slowing climate change make the United States less secure?

President Trump's announcement on June 1 that the United States would withdraw from the Paris agreement on climate change pleased some members of his administration and GOP lawmakers but dismayed many world leaders who had counted on participation by the planet's second-largest polluter.[18]

The agreement, adopted in 2015 and signed by 196 nations, aims to limit global temperature increases and encourages adoption of renewable-energy resources.[19] British Prime Minister Theresa May called it "the right global framework for protecting the prosperity and security of future generations."[20]

Trump's critics say withdrawing from the accord will isolate the United States and diminish its global influence. But others say the decision will help the country negotiate better trade and other international deals.

"Both the diplomatic costs of leaving and the benefits of staying have been exaggerated," said Nicolas Loris, an economist with the Heritage Foundation.[21] Withdrawing from the accord could help the United States negotiate future agreements by showing other governments "the U.S. is willing and able to resist diplomatic pressure in order to protect American interests," he said.[22]

Peter Engelke, a senior fellow with the Strategic Foresight Initiative at the Atlantic Council think tank in Washington, says Trump's decision will have the opposite effect and will make it "a real challenge . . . to craft complex international agreements in the future."

"There's a real risk that we could have harmed our position as the world's foremost power," says Engelke, whose group works to help international decision-makers by identifying global trends.

In addition to withdrawing from the Paris agreement, Trump appointed a climate change skeptic, former Oklahoma Attorney General Scott Pruitt, to head the Environmental Protection Agency (EPA). Trump has reversed Obama administration policies aimed at addressing climate change and recently disbanded the federal advisory panel for the National Climate Assessment, which helps policymakers and private-sector officials incorporate the government's climate analysis into long-term planning.[23]

Nigel Purvis, who participated in climate change negotiations as a State Department official in the Clinton and George W. Bush administrations, says most other countries view climate change as their biggest threat. The U.S. withdrawal from the Paris agreement means "foreign leaders will think twice about whether to cooperate with President Trump in trade, security and other foreign policy areas," says Purvis, now president of Climate Advisers, a Washington consulting firm that advocates for a low-carbon economy.

Roger Pielke, a political scientist and environmental studies professor at the University of Colorado, says withdrawing from the agreement made little sense, because its goals are voluntary. Trump's decision, he says, "is not a meaningful action unless you want to stick your finger in someone's eye."

Opponents of the Paris agreement say the United States plays too important a role in the world for Trump's decision to jeopardize national security.

"Other countries have a multitude of security, economic, and diplomatic reasons to work with America to address issues of mutual concern," Loris wrote. "Withdrawal from the agreement will not change that."

Under the terms of the Paris agreement, no country can withdraw from it before Nov. 4, 2020—by chance, the day after the next U.S. presidential election.[24]

Much of the debate over U.S. security and action on climate change focuses on China, the world's biggest polluter, and whether Beijing wants to use the Trump administration's skepticism of climate change to gain political and economic leverage.

"China is stepping up to say, 'We are going to be a leader' in green technology innovation and development while the U.S. is appearing to retreat," Engelke says. "This is an important geopolitical question, because it speaks to who can develop the technology and be a step ahead of the other in seizing the commercial high ground for trade, for seizing military advantages, for having the best technology, etc."

Five of the world's top six solar panel manufacturers and five of the top 10 wind turbine makers are in China. The country invested $88 billion in renewable energy in 2016, more than any other country.[25] In January, China's National Energy Administration announced plans to invest another $360 billion in renewable-power generation by 2020.[26]

Kelly Sims Gallagher, a China specialist and energy and environmental policy professor at the Fletcher School of Law and Diplomacy at Tufts University in Medford, Mass., says Chinese officials see green-energy investments as "key to their own economic development during the 21st century"—and a chance to gain a competitive advantage over the United States. "That's what's at risk: technological leadership and the socioeconomic consequences of ceding this market to the Chinese," she says.

Yale University researchers Angel Hsu and Carlin Rosengarten doubt China will assume the climate change leadership mantle. "Despite China's massive investments in renewable energy, the country is still investing in coal and exporting it," they wrote. China cannot develop as quickly as it wants to "while simultaneously filling a climate leadership vacuum," they said.[27]

But even if that is true, China still stands to gain diplomatically from Trump's decision to leave the Paris climate deal, says David Livingston, an associate fellow in the Energy and Climate Program at the Carnegie Endowment for International Peace. "Headlines like, 'China steps in to help climate adaptation in Africa because the U.S. will no longer fund the Green Climate

Getty Images/TASS

Russia has established a military base on Alexandra Land island in the Arctic. Russia says it has increased its military presence in the region to strengthen homeland defense and protect commercial interests. Some U.S. military observers, however, worry that Russia's actions may signal future aggression.

fund'—this is partially reality, partially rhetoric, but it's a powerful source of leverage for China," he says.

Does climate change affect U.S. military preparedness?

Naval Station Norfolk occupies about 3,400 acres on the Atlantic Coast of southeastern Virginia. The base is home to 75 ships, 134 aircraft and about 70,000 military and civilian employees.[28]

It also is highly vulnerable to the effects of climate change. Ocean levels around Norfolk could rise 4.5 to 6.9 feet by the end of the century, largely because of melting polar ice, according to the Union of Concerned Scientists, a research and advocacy group in Cambridge, Mass. The group says that at the upper end of its estimate, about 20 percent of the base would flood every day by the year 2100, with storm surges creating even more severe problems.[29]

Flooding already is disrupting operations at the base. At least 10 times a year, personnel cut power to the piers that service ships because strong winds or unusually high tides threaten to submerge electrical cables. "It's more than an inconvenience," said retired Navy Capt. Joseph Bouchard, the base's former commander and an expert on the national security aspects of climate change policy. "A ship is on a tight timeline to do all the training and maintenance that's required to be combat ready for

deployment. If you interrupt that . . . they have a hard time being ready for deployment."[30]

Climate change raises the possibility that U.S. military assets may not always be available when needed, says retired Vice Adm. McGinn, of the American Council on Renewable Energy. "If you can't get ships underway with a crew intact out of [Norfolk], you're going to delay the application of military force or humanitarian assistance somewhere else," he says.

Fifty-six naval installations around the country could be affected by a sea-level rise of at least 3.3 feet. Such a rise would damage piers and repair facilities, electrical and communications equipment and sewage treatment facilities, according to a 2011 book published by the National Academy of Sciences.[31]

U.S. military bases overseas also are facing climate change challenges, according to a report by the American Security Project. It rated the naval facility on the Indian Ocean island of Diego Garcia as the military's most climate change-vulnerable installation—the island, with a mean elevation of four feet above sea level, is at risk from coastal erosion and flooding, the report said, noting "A sea-level rise of . . . several feet would force the U.S. military to undertake a costly and difficult military relocation process."[32]

Another American Security Project study noted that the U.S. base on the Pacific island of Guam, while not unusually threatened by rising sea levels, could suffer diminished combat readiness. "Because of a changing climate, the joint military base on Guam could lose access to essentials like food and water and will be increasingly threated by extreme weather events" such as extreme storms and erosion, senior fellow for energy and climate Andrew Holland wrote in August.[33]

Michael Werz, a senior fellow at the Center for American Progress, a liberal think tank in Washington, says that in times of global emergency, the U.S. Navy "becomes the 911 number."

Adds Werz, whose work focuses on the intersection of climate change, migration and security, "If friendly neighbors or partners have a climate-related crisis and need a tent city and medical supplies for 40,000 refugees, only the Navy has the capacity to provide it quickly. It would be impossible just to say, 'Sorry, you're on your own.'"

Langley Air Force Base, about 21 miles from Norfolk, is home to nearly 12,000 military and civilian personnel.

Retired Gen. Ronald Keys, former commander of the Air Force's Air Combat Command, headquartered at Langley, said the base is only 7 feet above sea level. In about 15 years, he said, the base could experience 100 days of tidal flooding a year due to climate change, meaning "we [would] lose access to certain parts of our base" at high tide.[34]

Sea-level rise is not the military's only climate concern. Prolonged droughts have disrupted artillery practice because of wildfire risks, and flash flooding in the Southwestern desert forced the closure of an emergency runway for training and testing aircraft for about eight months, according to the Government Accountability Office (GAO), the investigative arm of Congress. The GAO also said rising temperatures at one Army installation halted training for three weeks because the thawed ground was too soft to traverse and made airborne training areas unsafe.[35]

But a 2015 report by the libertarian Heartland Institute challenged the GAO's findings, concluding that reports of climate change's negative effects on military infrastructure are overblown and unsupported by scientific evidence. "Requiring DOD to invest in mitigation or adaptation to address phantom risks could divert resources from other more urgent needs, reducing military preparedness," the think tank said.[36]

In 2014, the Pentagon said climate change will create conditions that make terrorist activity and humanitarian crises more likely—for example by causing or exacerbating food and water shortages and degrading the environment. Such stressors aggravate social tensions and political and social instability—while making U.S. military intervention more difficult.[37]

But the Heritage Foundation's Wood says typhoons and other major storms are nothing new and occur every year. "Are we proposing then that the U.S.

Navy or Marine Corps should push more forces into the Western Pacific, and be poised in the event that some major series of storms comes through the region?" he asks. "That's deploy time, it's increased manpower costs, you're tying your ships up on a 'be prepared to' mission rather than being off doing other sorts of things."

Femia of the Center for Climate and Security says the U.S. military already understands the challenge posed by climate change. "It's part of the culture of security institutions, the U.S. military in particular, to plan for long-term risks," he says. "It has to take into account a lot of scenarios, and in a lot of cases plan for the worst."

Does climate change pose a global economic threat?

The World Bank says climate change threatens its "core mission" of supporting economic growth and reducing poverty around the globe.

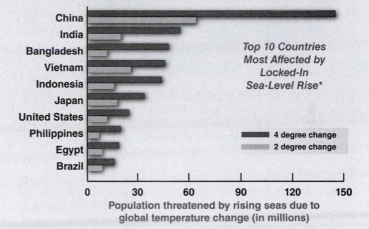

Asia at Highest Risk of Rising Seas

If the planet warms by 4 degrees Celsius, which scientists expect to happen unless nations act aggressively to stem greenhouse gas emissions, seas would eventually submerge land that currently is home to 145 million Chinese, 55 million Indians and millions of others worldwide, according to Climate Central. If warming rises a less drastic 2 degrees Celsius, the current goal of the Paris climate agreement, the number of people threatened in China and India by rising seas would drop by more than half.

Top 10 Countries Most Affected by Locked-In Sea-Level Rise*

■ 4 degree change
■ 2 degree change

Population threatened by rising seas due to global temperature change (in millions)

* Figures based on 2015 projections of 2010 population data.

Source: "Mapping Choices, Carbon Climate, and Rising Seas, Our Global Legacy," Climate Central, November 2015, https://tinyurl.com/yd9u7p2p

AFP/Getty Images/Emily Kask

The Texas National Guard helps rescue people in Orange, Texas, on Aug. 31 from floods caused by Hurricane Harvey. The havoc caused by that disaster and Hurricane Irma raised new concerns about potential links between climate change and extreme weather.

"Current weather extremes already affect millions of people, putting food and water security at risk and threatening agricultural supply chains and many coastal cities," the bank reported in 2016. "Without further action to reduce extreme poverty, provide access to basic services and strengthen resilience, climate impacts could push an additional 100 million people into poverty by 2030."[38]

Many parts of the business world also see climate change as a compelling danger. Mars, the U.S. candy company, remains committed to achieving "the carbon reduction targets the planet needs," said CEO Grant Reid. Mars is among dozens of firms that recently announced they will submit a plan to the United Nations for meeting U.S. emissions targets under the Paris agreement, even though Trump has pulled the country out of the accord.[39]

The World Economic Forum (WEF)—a Swiss nonprofit that promotes business involvement in global economic, political and social issues—ranks climate change along with cultural polarization and wealth and income disparities as "one of the truly existential risks to our world."[40]

Others who have studied climate change, however, say accurately predicting its economic effects is virtually impossible. Such forecasts fall into a range, and at the low end of that range "are some fairly benign outcomes with which we could probably muddle along without

terrible consequence," says the University of Colorado's Pielke. "It's a risk-management problem, like buying insurance," he says. "How much do you need to be covered, and how much is too much?"

Scientists at Stanford University and the University of California, Berkeley, said in 2015 that if climate change is not mitigated, the global economy could be more than 20 percent smaller by 2100.[41] That does not mean the world will be poorer in 2100 than it is today, however, because other factors will cause economies to grow, said the study's lead author, Marshall Burke, an assistant professor in Stanford's Department of Earth System Science.

"Instead, it means that the world will be substantially less rich than it would have been had temperatures not warmed," Burke said.[42]

The study also concluded that not all countries will suffer equally from global warming. About 20 percent—including countries in cooler climates such as Northern Europe and much of Russia—may benefit from rising temperatures, thanks largely to a longer growing season. Warmer countries, including those in Africa and South America, will suffer lower crop yields and drops in labor productivity, the study said. This will result in "a huge redistribution of wealth from the global poor to the wealthy," said study co-author Solomon Hsiang, a professor in the Goldman School of Public Policy at UC-Berkeley.[43]

Poor people also will suffer if countries curtail the use of fossil fuels in response to global warming, said Iain Murray, vice president for strategy at the libertarian Competitive Enterprise Institute, a think tank in Washington.[44]

Pielke says that while climate change threatens the economy over the long term, "there's an ignorance factor, too. We just don't know how things are going to turn out. We're not good at predicting the future 100 years from now."

William Nordhaus, an economics professor at Yale University, agrees, saying human ingenuity and advances in technology add to the uncertainty surrounding the economic impact of climate change. "We don't actually have a good handle on when the impacts will become dangerous," he said. "We're taking something that might happen 50 years from now and addressing aspects of economy and human life that will change in unknown ways."[45]

Some believe a warming climate can, at least in the near term, be beneficial. Matthew Ridley, a Conservative Party member in the British House of Lords, cites a study that indicates adding carbon dioxide, a primary culprit in global warming, to the atmosphere has actually contributed to a greener planet. In the last three decades, he wrote, data showed that worldwide plant growth has increased dramatically thanks to the increasing presence of atmospheric carbon dioxide. Another study noted by Ridley found that global economic output has been rising, thanks to climate change, and will continue to do so until around 2080.

Ridley said the real problem stems from government policies designed to fight climate change. These, he said, "have had negligible effects on carbon dioxide emissions" but they have caused food and fuel prices to go up, made industries uncompetitive, hastened destruction of forestland, killed rare birds of prey and divided communities. Strategies to mitigate climate change, he said, are [impeding] "a change that will produce net benefits for 70 years."[46]

BACKGROUND

Weaponizing the Weather

In 1824, French physicist Joseph Fourier theorized that gases in the Earth's atmosphere keep the planet warm by trapping heat from the sun—a phenomenon now known as the greenhouse effect.[47]

Swedish scientist Svante Arrhenius advanced the theory in 1896 by demonstrating that the heat trapped by carbon dioxide (CO_2) increases as concentrations of the gas increase in the atmosphere. Eight years later, he concluded that human use of fossil fuels was causing carbon dioxide to build up in the atmosphere, but he considered this a benefit, reasoning that a warming atmosphere would help the world grow crops and feed its growing population.[48]

Most scientists dismissed or ignored Arrhenius' work, but in 1938 British engineer Guy S. Callendar confirmed that historically, higher concentrations of CO_2 in the atmosphere raised global temperatures.[49]

Beginning in the late 1940s, scientists started studying the possibility of changing the weather to gain a military advantage, by creating a drought that would ruin an enemy's agricultural harvest, or producing other catastrophic weather events.

By the 1950s, Pentagon planners were investigating whether "seeding" clouds with silver iodide crystals would produce rain. That led to Operation Popeye, a 1967 project (motto: "Make mud, not war") designed to create heavy rainfall over enemy communication lines during the Vietnam War "to interdict or at least interfere with truck traffic between North and South Vietnam."[50]

Public opinion turned against Operation Popeye after *The New York Times* disclosed details of the program in July 1972. It was quickly shut down—after 2,602 cloud-seeding flights over North and South Vietnam, Laos and Cambodia—without its having achieved evidence of success.[51]

The following year, the Senate approved a resolution calling for an international treaty to ban "environmental or geophysical modification activity as a weapon of war," and in 1976 the U.N. General Assembly approved a treaty banning environmental modification techniques for hostile purposes.[52]

CIA officials had begun studying climate change by 1974, when the agency's Office of Political Research said that climate change's potential effect on global food supplies "could have an enormous impact, not only on the food-population balance, but also on the world balance of power."[53]

The 1974 CIA report said wealthier countries, including the United States, probably would escape the worst effects of a cooling climate, while U.S. foes such as the Soviet Union and China likely would suffer. It also said, however, that if climate change caused severe food shortages, potential risks to the United States would rise as other, militarily powerful nations made "increasingly desperate attempts" to get food. "Massive migration backed by force would become a very live issue," the report said. "Nuclear blackmail is not inconceivable."[54]

Fears Gain Momentum

Public awareness of climate change's dangers began increasing in the 1980s. The topic first made the front page of *The New York Times* on Aug. 22, 1981, in a story about a NASA report tracing evidence of a global warming trend back to 1880 and predicting global warming of "almost unprecedented magnitude" in the next century.[55]

In 1989, Al Gore, then a Democratic senator from Tennessee, said in a *Washington Post* op-ed that "America's future is inextricably tied to the fate of the globe."

"In effect, the environment is becoming a matter of national security—an issue that directly and imminently menaces the interests of the state or the welfare of the people," wrote Gore, who became President Bill Clinton's vice president in 1993 and shared the 2007 Nobel Peace Prize with the Intergovernmental Panel on Climate Change (IPCC) for his efforts to raise awareness of global warming.[56]

Meanwhile, scientists were becoming increasingly convinced that human activity was causing climate change. In 1990, the IPCC, established by the United Nations to study climate change and develop strategies to counter it, asserted in its first report that the greenhouse effect was real, human activity contributed to it, and global temperatures and sea levels would continue to rise.[57]

Republican President George H.W. Bush acknowledged in a 1990 speech that "human activities are changing the atmosphere in unexpected and in unprecedented ways," but stopped short of committing the United States to strong measures to curb greenhouse gas emissions.[58]

His secretary of State, James Baker, however, told an IPCC conference the world needed to address climate change immediately rather than waiting "until all the uncertainties have been resolved."[59] In 1990, Baker linked environmental protection to national security, saying, "Traditional concepts of what constitutes a threat to national and global security need to be updated and extended to such divergent concerns as environmental degradation, narcotics trafficking, and terrorism."[60]

In 1997, President Bill Clinton signed the Kyoto Protocol, a U.N. treaty requiring developed countries to reduce greenhouse gas emissions to below-1990 levels by 2012. However, U.S. auto and steel manufacturers, oil and gas companies and other industries lobbied against the treaty, saying it would drive up fuel prices and destroy jobs.[61] In addition, the Senate unanimously passed a resolution saying no climate treaty was acceptable that did not require developing countries to reduce their emissions as well. Clinton never submitted the Kyoto Protocol to the Senate for ratification.[62]

Many experts regard the Kyoto debate as the point when U.S. attitudes regarding climate change began to form along partisan lines. Edward Maibach, director of the Center for Climate Change Communication at George Mason University in Virginia, notes that congressional Republicans deeply disliked Clinton, "and when he asked Congress to ratify the Kyoto Protocol . . . they essentially said, 'Screw you,' and that really started the differential trajectory of public understanding of climate change."

In a 1997 Gallup Poll, 46 percent of Democrats and 47 percent of Republicans said they believed "the effects of global warming have already begun." Ten years later, 76 percent of Democrats told Gallup they held that view, but only 41 percent of Republicans said the same.[63]

In 2001, Republican President George W. Bush announced the United States would not adhere to the Kyoto Protocol, saying the treaty's emission reduction targets "were arbitrary and not based upon science." He also noted that China and India, the world's No. 2 and No. 3 polluters, were exempt from Kyoto's mandates.[64]

Security Concerns

After the Sept. 11, 2001, terrorist attacks on the United States, U.S. defense officials began paying more attention to the effects of climate change on military operations. In 2003, a report prepared for the Pentagon predicted that abrupt climate change could "destabilize the geopolitical environment, leading to skirmishes, battles, and even war" due to food and water shortages and disrupted access to energy. The report recommended elevating the possibility of abrupt climate change "beyond a scientific debate to a U.S. national security concern."[65]

In 2008, the Pentagon said in its "National Defense Strategy" report that climate change would affect "existing security concerns such as international terrorism and weapons proliferation," marking defense officials' first major public statement that they would factor climate change into planning.[66]

Two years later, the Pentagon warned that "climate change will shape the operating environment, roles and missions that we undertake." It noted that rising sea levels would threaten coastal military bases, saying defense officials "will need to adjust to the impacts of climate change on our facilities and military capabilities."[67]

C H R O N O L O G Y

1940s–1970s *Climate becomes a tool of war.*

1946 American scientist Bernard Vonnegut discovers that seeding clouds with silver iodide crystals can produce rain.

1967 U.S. military's Operation Popeye seeds clouds over Southeast Asia to interfere with enemy logistics during the Vietnam War. . . . National Oceanic and Atmospheric Administration scientists Syukuro Manabe and Richard T. Wetherald publish a paper widely considered the first to accurately model climate change.

1972 In response to public pressure, U.S. military officials end Operation Popeye without evidence of success. . . . U.N. Environmental Program is founded to promote sound global environmental practices.

1974 CIA report warns that climate change could alter "the world balance of power" by affecting food supplies.

1980s–1990s *World confronts climate change.*

1981 NASA scientists predict global warming "of almost unprecedented magnitude" over the next century.

1988 United Nations Intergovernmental Panel on Climate Change (IPCC) is formed to monitor the effects of climate change and develop strategies to cope with them.

1990 IPCC says human activity contributes to climate change and the resulting rise in global temperatures.

1992 U.N.'s Framework Convention on Climate Change is signed by the U.S. and 191 other nations seeking to stabilize greenhouse gas emissions.

1997 Kyoto Protocol commits participating countries to establishing targets for reducing greenhouse gas emissions; Democratic President Bill Clinton signs the agreement, but opposition from industry groups and Republican senators keeps it from being ratified.

1998 Gallup Poll finds Republicans and Democrats share similar views on the effects of climate change, with roughly half of respondents saying those effects are already evident.

2000s *Climate change becomes a security issue.*

2003 Defense Department report says abrupt climate change could "destabilize the geopolitical environment" and recommends elevating the issue "beyond a scientific debate to a U.S. national security concern."

2006 Former Democratic Vice President Al Gore releases "An Inconvenient Truth," a documentary about the dangers of global warming.

2007 Gore and the IPCC share the Nobel Peace Prize for their efforts to educate the public about human-caused climate change.

2008 Pentagon calls climate change a "national security challenge." . . . Gallup Poll shows partisan divide on climate change, with 76 percent of Democrats saying the effects "have already begun" and 41 percent of Republicans agreeing.

2011 Climate change-related drought from 2006 to 2009 is cited as one cause of Syria's civil war.

2014 Defense Department says the effects of climate change could "enable terrorist activity and other forms of violence." . . . United States and China agree to reduce greenhouse gas emissions.

2015 Obama administration calls climate change a national security priority. . . . President Obama signs Paris climate change agreement, a global pact signed by more than 190 countries to reduce carbon emissions.

2016 Obama directs federal agencies to take climate change into account in national security plans.

2017 President Trump signs executive order reversing Obama administration actions on climate change, including the directive on climate change and national security. . . . Trump announces United States will withdraw from Paris climate change agreement. . . . Hurricane Harvey slams Houston with record-breaking rainfall and flooding, and Hurricane Irma causes widespread devastation in the Caribbean and Florida, raising new concerns about potential links between climate change and extreme weather.

Climate Change Stoking Fear of Migration, Conflict

Weather events could result in up to 1 billion refugees.

It's only a tiny island amid the vast Louisiana bayous, but it could foreshadow what is ahead for tens of millions of people living in small island countries and coastal communities around the world.

Isle de Jean Charles, located in the Gulf of Mexico about 80 miles from New Orleans, has lost 98 percent of its land since 1955 to coastal erosion and rising sea levels attributed to climate change. The Department of Housing and Urban Development (HUD) and the Rockefeller Foundation, a private philanthropy, have provided $48 million in grant money to relocate people living on the island's remaining 320 acres, making them the country's first official climate refugees.[1] By some estimates, the island will disappear completely by 2055.[2]

Around the world, rising sea levels, droughts, intense storms, floods and other extreme conditions caused by climate change could lead to mass migrations to higher ground, competition for scarce resources, political instability and conflict, experts say. "The impacts of climate change combine to make it a clear threat to collective security and global order in the first half of the 21st Century," the International Institute for Strategic Studies, a London security policy think tank, said in a 2011 report.[3]

The report said that "in areas with weak or brittle states, climate change will increase the risks of resource shortages, mass migrations, and civil conflict. These could lead to failed states, which threaten global stability and security."[4]

As climate change worsens, seas could rise one meter—3.3 feet—by 2100, displacing up to 2 billion people.[5]

According to regional studies, 5 million to 10 million people in the Philippines and 10 million in Vietnam would be displaced. Seventy percent of the Nigerian coast would be swamped, displacing 4 million people, and 5 million people would be forced to leave areas in the South Pacific. In the United States, a sea level rise of 2.95 feet could inundate the homes of 4.2 million people.[6]

By 2050, between 25 million and 1 billion "environmental migrants" will move within their own countries or across borders, with 200 million being the most widely cited estimate, according to the International Organization for Migration in Switzerland, which works for international cooperation on migration issues. "It is evident that gradual and sudden environmental changes are already resulting in substantial population movements," the group said.[7]

Koko Warner at the United Nations University in Bonn, Germany, wrote in a blog post that people displaced by climate change will move to areas "they hope will provide safe and sustainable livelihoods."

"All countries and governments will be affected by people on the move whether those countries are areas of origin, transit or destination," wrote Warner, who runs the university's Environmental Migration, Social Vulnerability and Adaptation section.[8]

Environmental migration on such a large scale is frequently cited as a major security threat. The Pentagon's 2014 "Climate Change Adaptation Roadmap" said it could affect the deployment of U.S forces and test the Defense Department's "capability to provide logistical material and security assistance on a massive scale or in rapid fashion."[9]

Climate change gained new attention during Obama's second term. "We will respond to the threat of climate change," Obama said in his 2013 inaugural address. "Some may still deny the overwhelming judgment of science, but none can avoid the devastating impact of raging fires and crippling drought and more powerful storms."[68]

In 2014, defense officials described the effects of climate change as potential "threat multipliers that will aggravate stressors abroad such as poverty, environmental

Some experts say climate-driven migration is a factor behind the vicious ethnic conflict that has been underway in Darfur in western Sudan since 2003. "[A] decade of drought in the 1970s and 1980s . . . prompted large movements of people within the region of Darfur as well as into it from neighboring areas seeking more fertile land," said a report by the Woodrow Wilson International Center for Scholars, a think tank in Washington. "The new arrivals' need for land—both for agriculture and grazing—caused tension, which slowly escalated into outright hostility and eventually the explosive violence."[10] The conflict had killed as many as 300,000 people as of 2008, when the U.N. released its last estimate of casualty figures.[11]

Some experts attribute the Darfur migration mainly to forces other than climate change. Most migrants into Darfur's pastoral areas were "Arab nomadic groups who had been squeezed out of Chad" by a civil war there and competed with "pastoral groups whose animals were dying and needed land to cultivate," says Alex de Waal, executive director of the World Peace Foundation at the Fletcher School of Law and Diplomacy at Tufts University. "You can see a little climatic factor in there, but it wasn't a big one," he says.

Experts acknowledge that it is difficult to gauge the effects of climate change, migration and other factors in causing conflict or instability, but they say climate change is an increasingly important factor to consider.

"Climate change and large movements of people clearly present major societal and governance challenges," the Woodrow Wilson center report said. "Governments, international organizations and civil society are being asked to respond, whether they are prepared or not."[12]

In a 2016 report, the National Intelligence Council, composed of intelligence experts from government, academia, and the private sector who aid the U.S. director of national intelligence, said that "even if climate-induced environmental stresses do not lead to conflict,

they are likely to contribute to migrations that exacerbate social and political tensions, some of which could overwhelm host governments and populations."

— William Wanlund

[1] Laura Small, "Government Awards $48 Million to Help Climate Change-Impacted Tribe Relocate," Environmental and Energy Study Institute, Feb. 24, 2016, https://tinyurl.com/yacvvezr.

[2] Katy Reckdahl, "Losing Louisiana," Weather.com, undated, https://tinyurl.com/moufhny.

[3] "The IISS Transatlantic Dialogue on Climate Change and Security," International Institute for Strategic Studies, January 2011, https://tinyurl.com/y9j3wu3f.

[4] *Ibid.*

[5] Ariel Scotti, "Two billion people may become refugees from climate change by the end of the century," *New York Daily News*, June 27, 2017, https://tinyurl.com/yauqr3fx.

[6] "Living with the oceans.—A report on the state of the world's oceans," *World Ocean Review*, undated, https://tinyurl.com/jgogzjr; Don Hinrichsen, "The Oceans Are Coming Ashore," *World Watch*, November/December 2000, https://tinyurl.com/ya2uckmf; and Matthew E. Hauer, Jason M. Evans and Deepak R. Mishra, "Millions projected to be at risk from sea-level rise in the continental United States," *Nature Climate Change*, March 14, 2016, https://tinyurl.com/ya8xcfr7.

[7] "Migration, Climate Change and the Environment," International Organization for Migration, undated, https://tinyurl.com/y88vzstl.

[8] Koko Warner, "Climate Change and Migration: The World Must Be Prepared," *The Huffington Post*, Dec. 1, 2015, https://tinyurl.com/y7bospoo; updated Nov. 20, 2016.

[9] "2014 Climate Change Adaptation Roadmap," U.S. Department of Defense, June 2014, https://tinyurl.com/y9kxrm9o.

[10] Schuyler Null and Heather Herzer Risi, "Navigating Complexity: Climate, Migration, and Conflict in a Changing World," Woodrow Wilson International Center for Scholars, Nov. 22, 2016, https://tinyurl.com/yd8arm5q.

[11] "Darfur death toll could be as high as 300,000: UN official," CBC News, April 22, 2008, https://tinyurl.com/yah2tjao.

[12] Null and Risi, *op. cit.*

degradation, political instability, and social tensions—conditions that can enable terrorist activity and other forms of violence."[69] Later that year, the Defense Department released a "Climate Change Adaptation Roadmap" outlining the steps it would take to confront

such conditions, such as upgrading construction standards to provide better protection from severe storms and reviewing weapons systems to ensure they can operate under extreme weather conditions such as excessive heat or rainfall.[70]

Rising Sea Levels Threaten a Nation's Future

Climate change could displace millions of Bangladeshis.

Countries around the world view climate change as a national security threat, but for some, the threat is potentially existential.

Bangladesh, an impoverished nation of 158 million on the Bay of Bengal, is among them.

Global warming is expected to raise sea levels between 0.3 meters (1 foot) and 2.5 meters (8.2 feet) by 2100, according to a January report from the National Oceanic and Atmospheric Administration.[1] An "intermediate" increase of 1 meter (3.3 feet) could cost Bangladesh 20 percent of its land mass and force 30 million people to move elsewhere inside the country, says ANM Muniruzzaman, founder and president of the Bangladesh Institute of Peace and Security Studies, a research group focused on South and Southeast Asia.

"My country is on the front lines of the climate change crisis," says Muniruzzaman, who is a retired major general in the Bangladeshi army. "In Bangladesh, climate change is not a theory or a concept—it is a way of life."

Bangladesh is emblematic of nations with limited resources confronting potentially catastrophic climate change challenges. Rising sea levels also threaten to permanently inundate low-lying island states in the Pacific Ocean (the Marshall Islands, Kiribati, Tuvalu, Tonga, the Federated States of Micronesia and the Cook Islands), the Caribbean Sea (Antigua and Nevis) and the Indian Ocean (the Maldives).[2]

Worldwide, rising ocean water will increase the potential for violent conflict by wiping out supplies of fresh water

and creating "economic turmoil, migration, and social instability," said Aubrey Paris, a senior fellow at the Institute on Science for Global Policy, a science and technology think tank in Tucson, Ariz.[3]

"The impact of rising seas . . . is severe enough to threaten the national security of the United States and nearly all other countries," Paris said.[4]

In 2010, the United Nations established the Green Climate Fund, financed by industrialized nations, to help poorer countries limit their greenhouse gas emissions and take other steps to mitigate and adapt to climate change. The fund aims to raise $100 billion a year by 2020. So far, it has collected $10.3 billion in pledges.[5]

In Bangladesh, the fund has approved $40 million—to be matched by contributions from Bangladesh and Germany—for a six-year project to build cyclone shelters, protect access to critical roads and make urban infrastructure more climate-resistant.[6]

"Bangladesh is one of the worst victims of climate change," Prime Minister Sheikh Hasina said. "We need the developed countries to keep their promise and help us."[7]

Other South Asian countries also face severe climate-change threats, with potentially serious consequences for security, according to the Global Military Advisory Council on Climate Change, a network of active and retired military officers concerned about the potential security implications of climate change. The council describes the region as

In November 2014, Obama and Chinese President Xi Jinping agreed to cooperate on climate change abatement and reduce their countries' greenhouse gas emissions, which account for an estimated 38 percent of emissions worldwide. They also said they would work to persuade other countries to limit their emissions.[71]

The United States and 195 other countries on Dec. 12, 2015, signed the Paris Agreement on climate

change, which aims to limit global temperature increases through use of renewable energy resources. It also calls on developed countries to contribute $100 billion a year to a fund created to help developing countries switch to renewable energy sources.[72]

The Obama administration's 2015 National Security Strategy identified climate change as a major national security priority, drawing ridicule from some Republicans. Then-GOP presidential candidate Jeb

"already politically unstable and particularly vulnerable to further impacts."[8]

Pakistan, for example, has a weak government, terrorist groups operating inside its borders and a black market in nuclear weapons, says Francesco Femia, co-founder and president of the Center for Climate and Security, a policy group in Washington. Global warming is melting Pakistan's glaciers, leading to flooding and shrinking water supplies for drinking and farming.[9] "Climate change can exacerbate Pakistan's political instability, with global repercussions," Femia says.

In Bangladesh, people displaced by rising sea levels will have few options to leave the country. The country is bordered by India on three sides (except for a 169-mile border with Myanmar), and India protects that border with fencing and armed guards, Muniruzzaman says. "If large numbers of climate migrants try to cross over into India, it will certainly result in a human catastrophe of unknown proportion," he says.

Bangladesh has developed a climate change action plan that addresses food security, public health, national infrastructure and other issues.[10] Muniruzzaman says the plan includes "technical" steps such as planting grains that can tolerate higher salinity, raising the foundations of houses and building cyclone shelters. "Beyond that, I don't think there's much that can be done," he says. "The government hasn't been able to implement the adaptation strategies for lack of funds."

Benjamin Strauss, a vice president at Climate Central, a New Jersey organization composed of scientists who study climate change, said Bangladesh's future beyond 2100 depends on whether global greenhouse gas emissions drop. "It is very plausible that the amount of carbon we put in the atmosphere between today and 2050 will determine whether Bangladesh can even exist in the far future," he said."[11]

— *William Wanlund*

[1] "Global And Regional Sea Level Rise Scenarios For The United States," National Oceanic and Atmospheric Administration, January 2017, p. 23, https://tinyurl.com/zvn25ua.

[2] "Working Group II: Impacts, Adaptation and Vulnerability," Intergovernmental Panel on Climate Change, undated, https://tinyurl.com/yd8h7n47.

[3] Aubrey Paris, "Sea Level Rise: Sink or Swim," War Room, U.S. Army War College, July 21, 2017, https://tinyurl.com/y7tkrda5.

[4] *Ibid.*

[5] "Resource Mobilization," Green Climate Fund, undated, https://tinyurl.com/yd5fecrp.

[6] "Project FP004—Climate-Resilient Infrastructure Mainstreaming in Bangladesh," Green Climate Fund, June 14, 2017, https://tinyurl.com/ybju8j9f.

[7] Anup Kaphle, "An interview with Bangladeshi Prime Minister Sheikh Hasina," *The Washington Post*, Oct. 11, 2011, https://tinyurl.com/yaoxxycx.

[8] Tariq Waseem Ghazi, A.N.M. Muniruzzaman and A.K. Singh, "Climate Change and Security in South Asia," Global Military Advisory Council on Climate Change, May 2016, https://tinyurl.com/z856o2s.

[9] "Pakistan seeks to track flood risk from melting glaciers," Climate Himalaya, Sept. 20, 2011, https://tinyurl.com/yd9gnwvj.

[10] "Bangladesh Climate Change Strategy and Action Plan 2009," Bangladesh Ministry of Environment and Forests, September 2009, https://tinyurl.com/ybl5pfhy.

[11] Megan Darby, "What will become of Bangladesh's climate migrants?" *Climate Change News*, Aug. 14, 2017, https://tinyurl.com/yb8vddpa.

Bush told Fox News that "perhaps the most ludicrous comment I've ever heard [is] that climate change is a bigger threat to our country than radical Islamic terrorism. It's baffling to me that the leader of the free world, the commander-in-chief of the greatest armed forces ever created, would state that."[73]

Obama was undeterred. In a 2016 interview with *The Atlantic*, he said climate change represented a more serious threat than the jihadist Islamic State.

"Climate change is a potential existential threat to the entire world if we don't do something about it," he said. "It involves every single country, and it is a comparatively slow-moving emergency, so there is always something seemingly more urgent on the agenda."[74]

On Sept. 21 last year, Obama directed federal agencies to identify climate change-related risks that affect national security objectives and develop plans to address them.[75]

Trump issued an executive order in March rescinding the Sept. 21 directive and other Obama administration energy-and climate-related regulatory actions, including the recommendations for action in the military's 2014 "Climate Change Adaptation Roadmap."[76] Trump's order said the move was "in the national interest, to promote clean and safe development of our Nation's vast energy resources, while . . . avoiding regulatory burdens that unnecessarily encumber energy production, constrain economic growth, and prevent job creation."[77]

The White House later announced the United States would withdraw from the Paris Agreement, saying the accord worked against U.S. economic interests.[78] He added, however, that the country would continue to participate in international climate change negotiations and meetings "to protect U.S. interests and ensure all future policy options remain open to the administration."[79]

A Pew Research Center survey conducted in 37 countries before Trump announced his decision on the Paris accord found 71 percent disapproval for withdrawal, with 19 percent voicing approval.[80] In a U.S. poll taken the week after Trump's announcement by The Associated Press and University of Chicago, 46 percent of those surveyed said they opposed the withdrawal, with 29 percent saying they supported it. In that poll, 51 percent of Republicans supported the withdrawal and 69 percent of Democrats opposed it.[81]

CURRENT SITUATION

Military Leaders See Risks

Although President Trump has made clear he wants to roll back many Obama-era environmental initiatives, Pentagon leaders apparently plan to continue factoring climate change into their strategic and operational planning.[82]

Air Force Gen. Paul Selva, vice chairman of the Joint Chiefs of Staff, told the Senate Armed Services Committee on July 18 that "the dynamics that are happening in our climate will drive uncertainty and will drive conflict."

"If we see tidal rises, if we see increasing weather patterns of drought and flood and forest fires and other natural events . . . then we're gonna have to be prepared for what that means in terms of the potential for instability," Selva said.[83]

Geoffrey Dabelko, director of environmental studies at the George V. Voinovich School of Leadership and Public Affairs at Ohio University, believes the military needs to stay above the partisan fray over climate change.

"The military is rightly agnostic in terms of threats and opportunities," he says. "They can't afford to ignore any of them just because they may be out of fashion with whoever's in power. Environment and climate change are among the appropriate issues to track."

Other experts are skeptical that the military needs to deal with climate change now. "There's a temporal component here—how urgent is the issue?" says Wood of the Heritage Foundation. "If it's urgent, then funding should go along with that—so where's the funding? If it's not going to happen for 40 or 50 years, well, the nation has problems we need to deal with today."

A Worrisome Arctic

"Arctic amplification" is the top climate-related concern for David Titley, director of the Center for Solutions to Weather and Climate Risk at Pennsylvania State University. The term refers to the process that causes temperatures to increase faster at the poles than elsewhere. That causes the Arctic ice cap to melt, warming the surrounding water and leading to still more melting.

Diminished sea ice enables more human activity, including "energy and mineral exploitation, fishing, tourism, even celebrity cruises," says Titley, a retired rear admiral who established the Navy's climate change task force in 2009.

That means a bigger job for the Navy, he says. "One of the duties of the Navy is to protect the sea lines of communication"—the maritime routes between ports, which are becoming more extensive as Arctic sea ice melts. "We want to be able to do that, especially when the U.S. has sovereign territory—Alaska—in that Arctic region," Titley says.

Fran Ulmer, chair of the U.S. Arctic Research Commission, an independent federal agency that advises the president and Congress on Arctic policy, says Arctic temperatures are increasing two to three times faster than temperatures around the world. Since the 1970s, she says, the volume of sea ice has declined 75 percent and the area it covers has declined 50 percent.

"That is a very dramatic change for a place that has been covered with ice for a very, very long time," Ulmer says.

This year, the area covered by Arctic winter ice reached a record low, continuing a decades-long trend toward diminished ice coverage.[84] The melting polar ice cap, along with rising ocean temperatures and thawing glaciers, has contributed to an average sea-level rise of 3 inches since 1992, according to satellite data. Seas could rise between 1 and 3 feet by the end of the century, NASA has reported.[85]

The Arctic warming trend has made Russian officials "particularly enthusiastic about their northern sea routes that connect eastern Russia and Europe across the Arctic," Ulmer says. "Russia has a lot of oil and gas resources, and they are developing them in the Yamal region [in northern Siberia]," she says. "Less ice means easier access in and out of their northern ports."

In late August, the *Christophe de Margerie*, a modified 984-foot Russian tanker, became the first merchant vessel without an icebreaker escort to pass through the Northern Sea Route, which runs through the Arctic waters connecting the Atlantic and Pacific oceans along the Siberian coast. The ship, carrying liquefied natural gas from Norway to South Korea, made the trip via the Arctic Ocean in 19 days, about 30 percent faster than the conventional route through the Suez Canal, according to the ship's owner, Sovcomflot. The ship, which is designed to break through ice 7 feet thick, is the first of a reported 15 ships constructed by Russia to take advantage of diminishing Arctic sea ice and allow faster and cheaper shipment of goods between European and Asian ports.[86]

Sherri Goodman, a public policy fellow at the Woodrow Wilson International Center for Scholars, says the United States should not underestimate the economic significance of climate change's effects on the Arctic. "With economic opportunity comes political influence," she says. "That's why U.S. global leadership in [the Arctic] is so important, and we

The Chinese aircraft carrier Liaoning steams past a wind turbine as it approaches Hong Kong on July 7, 2017. Much of the debate over U.S. security and action on climate change focuses on China, and whether Beijing wants to use the Trump administration's skepticism of climate change to gain political and economic leverage, in part by embracing green technology.

ignore the Arctic at our peril. We'd wake up to find this great land mass right off Canada that isn't too far from the U.S., [and] is no longer under friendly leadership."

The melting ice also has military implications. Reuters has reported that Russia also plans to open or reopen six Arctic military facilities "as it pushes ahead with a claim to almost half a million square miles" there. Some of the facilities are equipped with air defense and anti-ship missiles, and possibly military fighters and bombers, the news agency said.[87]

A 2015 Russian military exercise involved 45,000 personnel, 15 submarines and 41 warships, and "practiced full combat readiness," according to a report by the Center for Strategic and International Studies, a Washington think tank.[88] Russian military incursions into other countries' airspace also have picked up, according to the Henry Jackson Society, a conservative British think tank, which said that in 2016, the Norwegian air force intercepted 74 Russian warplanes patrolling its coast, up from 58 in 2015.

Nikolay Lakhonin, press secretary at the Russian Embassy in Washington, says Russia's Arctic policy is "very transparent and predictable." He cites a Russian policy document that says the country's Arctic interests include tapping oil, gas and other strategic raw

AFP/Getty Images/Tengku Bahar

materials, maintaining a military force to protect Russia's borders and conducting environmental and scientific research.[89]

But Penn State's Titley says Russia's intentions in the Arctic aren't clear. "They talk about having search-and-rescue bases, but these bases have missiles on them," he says. "It's more than search-and-rescue, it's more than constabulary—it's real military capability."

U.S. military officials have taken notice. "What concerns me about Russia is . . . the offensive military capability that they are adding to their force that's Arctic-capable," said Air Force Lt. Gen. Kenneth Wilsbach, the senior U.S. military officer in Alaska. "If you really want to keep the Arctic a peaceful place . . . then why are you building offensive capabilities?"[90]

The two massive storms that struck the United States in late summer—Hurricane Harvey wreaking havoc mainly in Texas and Louisiana, and Hurricane Irma in Florida—showed how weather can affect military operations, causing some military bases to curtail or suspend operations.

The military moved aircraft, ships and thousands of civilian and military workers ahead of the storms from Army, Navy and Air Force bases in Texas and Florida.[91] "Local training and work schedules were affected by the storms, but it did not impact military readiness," DOD spokesperson Heather Babb told *CQ Researcher* in an email.

The storms also highlighted the military's humanitarian responsibilities: Thousands of state and U.S. military personnel were deployed to help with law enforcement and rescue efforts. Republican Texas Gov. Greg Abbott mobilized all 12,000 members of the Texas National Guard, and Republican Florida Gov. Rick Scott called up nearly 8,000 of his state's Guard to help with law enforcement and search and rescue efforts. Guard units from other states also contributed equipment and personnel.[92]

Some climate scientists believe climate change affected the severity of the storm. Michael Mann, a professor of atmospheric science at Pennsylvania State University, said rising sea levels caused by global warming made Hurricane Harvey's storm surge—the sea water driven inland by the hurricane's winds—considerably higher than would have occurred a few decades ago, causing "far more flooding and destruction."[93]

Mann also said warmer water temperatures brought on by global warming put more moisture into the atmosphere, causing greater rainfalls and coastal flooding. Over six days, Harvey dumped an estimated 27 trillion gallons of rain over Texas and Louisiana, according to meteorologist Ryan Maue of WeatherBELL, a meteorology consulting firm.[94]

But Clifford Mass, a University of Washington professor of atmospheric sciences, said climate change can't be blamed for the enormity of Harvey. "You really can't pin global warming on something this extreme. It has to be natural variability. It may juice it up slightly but not create this phenomenal anomaly."[95]

A 2014 government national climate assessment said North Atlantic hurricanes have all increased in intensity, frequency and duration since the 1980s. "Hurricane-associated storm intensity and rainfall rates are projected to increase as the climate continues to warm," it said.[96]

Emerging Bipartisanship?

In July, the House approved an amendment to the fiscal 2018 defense authorization bill calling climate change "a direct threat to the national security of the United States." The amendment, sponsored by Rep. Jim Langevin, D-R.I., would require the secretary of Defense to submit to Congress within one year "a report on vulnerabilities to military installations and combatant commander requirements resulting from climate change over the next 20 years."[97] Forty-six Republicans joined 188 Democrats in voting for the amendment. All 185 "no" votes came from Republicans.

Femia, of the Center for Climate Change and Security, calls the vote "the most significant climate security action in many years."

"Most of those 46 Republicans belong to the Climate Solutions Caucus, and a lot of them are in coastal districts and/or in districts that have been affected by climate and/or have military bases that are vulnerable," he says.

As of mid-September, the Senate had not acted on the defense authorization legislation.

The Climate Solutions Caucus was set up in 2016 by two House members from Florida "to educate members on economically viable options to reduce climate risk and protect our nation's economy, security, infrastructure, agriculture, water supply and public safety." Caucus

Should climate change be a national security priority?

YES Rep. Jim Langevin, D-R.I.
*Member, House Committee on
Armed Services*

Written for *CQ Researcher*, September 2017

There is widespread consensus that the effects of climate change threaten not only our environment and our economy, but also our national security. In fact, the Pentagon's top military and civilian officials have repeatedly stated that climate change poses a direct threat to the national security of the United States, an assessment echoed and amplified by leaders in the intelligence community. Defense Secretary James Mattis understands the risks, as evidenced by testimony given at his confirmation hearing: "The effects of a changing climate—such as increased maritime access to the Arctic, rising sea levels, desertification, among others—will impact our security situation."

We are already feeling those effects. Mission-critical assets like Naval Station Norfolk, home of the Atlantic Fleet, are experiencing "nuisance flooding," and the storm surges are only expected to get worse. Warmer temperatures and more volatile weather could affect training operations at inland bases, reducing readiness capabilities. Moreover, the changing global climate is expected to lead to increased instability due to migration, competition over resources and possibly more failed states, which we know to be breeding grounds for extremism and terrorism.

Policymakers cannot turn a blind eye to the changing environment, because doing so places our troops at risk. Unfortunately, President Trump and his administration seem to be doing just that, withdrawing the United States from the Paris climate accord and rescinding executive actions supporting climate research.

Congress must support our servicemen and women and address the concerns raised by our military leaders about global warming, which is why I amended the fiscal 2018 National Defense Authorization Act to ensure that climate change is properly incorporated into our national security strategy. Specifically, the provision acknowledges that climate change is a direct threat to the national security of the United States and requires the secretary of Defense to provide an assessment of—and recommendations to mitigate vulnerabilities to—the top 10 most threatened military installations in each service branch. It also requires the Department of Defense to address how combatant commander requirements will change as a result of this threat.

Climate change is real, and the threat it poses to our national security is imminent. Congress is listening to the warnings of our military and intelligence leaders. It's time the president does the same.

NO Marlo Lewis
*Senior Fellow, Competitive
Enterprise Institute*

Written for *CQ Researcher*, September 2017

Climate change should not be a national security priority. Directing the Pentagon to focus on it will actually make America less secure. Generals know how to fight and win wars. They know little about nation building and even less about "sustainable development." Compelling the Department of Defense (DOD) to incorporate climate assessments and strategies in scores of programs, as the Obama administration did, can only promote groupthink, wasteful mission creep and inattention to bona fide security threats.

Climate change would indeed be a security issue if, as is often claimed, it were an existential threat. However, the latest U.N. climate report poured cold water on global warming doomsday scenarios. In the 21st century, Atlantic Ocean circulation collapse is "very unlikely," ice sheet crackup is "exceptionally unlikely" and catastrophic release of methane from melting permafrost is "very unlikely."

The Obama DOD defined climate change as a "threat multiplier," exacerbating conditions like poverty and political stability that "enable" terrorism and violence. However, the research linking climate change to conflict is highly dubious. For example, warming will supposedly exacerbate drought, leading to "water wars." However, studies repeatedly find that water scarcity promotes cooperation rather than conflict.

Climate campaigners have long sought military leaders as spokespersons, hoping to split conservatives on energy policy. But preaching climate peril and carbon taxes would ill-serve both DOD and U.S. national security.

President Trump seeks to secure an era of U.S. "energy dominance" as part of a strategy to achieve 3 percent annual GDP growth. A return to carbon-suppression policies would chill growth, forcing painful tradeoffs between guns and butter.

As an analysis by the Institute for 21st Century Energy shows, if we assume the validity of "consensus" climatology, the world cannot achieve the Paris agreement's goal of limiting global warming to 2 degrees Celsius unless developing countries dramatically reduce their current consumption of fossil fuels. Yet more than 1 billion people in those countries have no access to electricity, and billions more have too little to support development.

Putting energy-poor people on an energy diet would be a cure worse than the alleged disease. It would not promote stability or peace.

membership is equally divided between the parties, currently with 28 Republicans and 28 Democrats.[98]

Mark Reynolds, executive director of the Citizens' Climate Lobby, a nonprofit in California that advocates for national policies to address climate change, said it is only a matter of time before caucus members take steps to produce "meaningful legislation to combat climate change."

"At a time when the Trump administration has turned its back on the Paris agreement and partisanship plagues Washington, a bipartisan effort of this size shows the tide is turning on the climate issue," he said.[99]

Some climate change experts say the vote on Langevin's amendment could signal that partisanship on climate change is moderating.

"We have to wait and see, but it's certainly a positive step," says Dabelko of Ohio University. "The true test of whether a reemerging bipartisan approach to climate change is actually taking hold in Congress will be when it comes to budgets and allocating money."

OUTLOOK

More People, Higher Temperatures

In January, the National Intelligence Council predicted that "more extreme weather, water and soil stress, and food insecurity will disrupt societies. Sea-level rise, ocean acidification, glacial melt and pollution will change living patterns." The threat "will require collective action to address—even as cooperation becomes harder," the council said.[100]

But whether climate change is accepted by Americans as a national security concern that must be addressed is another question.

Some experts believe that evidence that the climate is changing is too distant in time and space for many Americans to fully absorb its significance.

Veteran environmental journalist Andrew Revkin of the nonprofit investigative news organization ProPublica says environmental policies implemented today won't show any effect for many years. "Our vulnerability to floods and wildfire and agricultural destruction will get worse, and nothing we do right now will have any effect for decades to come," he says. "Global population is heading for 9 billion by 2050 or 2060, and that vulnerability is built in until at least then."

Engelke of the Atlantic Council says there is no question climate change is a national security concern but that more Americans need to understand "it's not just happening to people living in low-lying island states or in the Sahel [in Africa]. And not only is it going to happen to us, it already is."

In June, 13 federal agencies released a report saying average annual temperatures in the United States have risen 1.5 degrees Fahrenheit since 1901 and will increase another 5 to 7.5 degrees by the end of the century. It is "extremely likely" that human activity has caused most of the global temperature increase since 1951, it said.[101]

Engelke believes such evidence will help end the rancorous partisan debate over climate change within 20 years. "There will no longer be a debate about whether climate change is occurring, but rather about how to mitigate it and how to adapt to its effects," he says.

Femia at the Center for Climate and Security says dealing with climate change as a national security issue "will take more than just technical solutions like putting more money into drought-resistant crops or building a seawall—it's going to take a large-scale national and international approach."

He also says technology will allow researchers to be increasingly accurate in predicting the effects of a warming climate. "Climate change is an unprecedented security risk," Femia says. "But we also have unprecedented foresight."

NOTES

1. "Syrian war monitor says 465,000 killed in six years of fighting," Reuters, March 13, 2017, https://tinyurl.com/y7qktus3.

2. Caitlin E. Werrell and Francesco Femia, eds., "The Arab Spring and Climate Change," Center for American Progress, February 2013, https://tinyurl.com/ovlsq4j.

3. Jan Selby et al., "Climate change and the Syrian civil war revisited," *Political Geography*, September 2017, https://tinyurl.com/ybr3ppe6.

4. "Quadrennial Defense Review 2014," U.S. Department of Defense, March 4, 2014, https://tinyurl.com/j9yf7l3.

5. Spanger-Siegfried et al., "The US Military on the Front Lines of Rising Seas," Union of Concerned Scientists, 2016, https://tinyurl.com/hq9u2zd.

6. "Global And Regional Sea Level Rise Scenarios For The United States," National Oceanic and Atmospheric Administration, January 2017, p. 23, https://tinyurl.com/zvn25ua.

7. Laura Parker, "Who's Still Fighting Climate Change? The U.S. Military," *National Geographic*, Feb. 7, 2017, https://tinyurl.com/jppz85j.

8. Tara Copp, "Pentagon is still preparing for global warming even though Trump said to stop," *Military Times*, Sept. 12, 2017, https://tinyurl.com/y7dz6mrz.

9. "Press Conference by President Obama," The White House, Dec. 1, 2015, https://tinyurl.com/yd3l6fc9.

10. "Presidential Memorandum—Climate Change and National Security," The White House, Sept. 21, 2016, https://tinyurl.com/ychwqf36.

11. "Implications for US National Security of Anticipated Climate Change," National Intelligence Council, Sept. 21, 2016, https://tinyurl.com/hp9arwj.

12. Donald J. Trump, Twitter post, Dec. 6, 2013, https://tinyurl.com/jaelpj7.

13. Transcript, Donald J. Trump interview with *The New York Times*, Nov. 23, 2016, https://tinyurl.com/juymes5.

14. "Presidential Executive Order on Promoting Energy Independence and Economic Growth," The White House, March 28, 2017, https://tinyurl.com/ny2k4wt.

15. "Statement by President Trump on the Paris Climate Accord," The White House, June 1, 2017, https://tinyurl.com/ydaz28yb.

16. "Secretary of Defense James Mattis's Views on Climate, Energy and More," document obtained by *Pro Publica* journalist Andrew Revkin, March 14, 2017, https://tinyurl.com/yd9obggm.

17. Mark Hand, "46 Republicans buck party to help Democrats take down anti-climate action amendment," *Think Progress Blog*, July 14, 2017, https://tinyurl.com/yc8bynvp.

18. Michael D. Shear, "Trump Will Withdraw U.S. From Paris Climate Agreement," *The New York Times*, June 1, 2017, https://tinyurl.com/y7hj9x7k.

19. "Paris Agreement," United Nations, 2015, https://tinyurl.com/y75g5pqb.

20. Anushka Asthana, "No 10 defends May not signing letter opposing US on Paris climate deal," *The Guardian*, June 2, 2017, https://tinyurl.com/ya47xdp4.

21. Nicolas Loris, "Trump's Decision to Ditch the Climate Agreement Will Help America Negotiate Better Deals," Heritage Foundation, June 7, 2017, https://tinyurl.com/yahurm5w.

22. Loris, *op. cit.*

23. Juliet Eilperin, "The Trump administration just disbanded a federal advisory committee on climate change," *The Washington Post*, Aug. 20, 2017, https://tinyurl.com/ydbtvup4.

24. Brad Plumer, "The U.S. Won't Actually Leave the Paris Deal Anytime Soon," *The New York Times*, June 7, 2017, https://tinyurl.com/yb4bcagv.

25. Nicholas Stern, "China is shaping up to be a world leader on climate change," *Financial Times*, Jan. 20, 2017, https://tinyurl.com/y8amfz24.

26. "Here's How Much Money China Is Throwing at Renewable Energy," *Fortune*, Jan. 5, 2017, https://tinyurl.com/jxcne9q.

27. Angel Hsu and Carlin Rosengarten, "The leadership void on climate change," *China Dialogue*, April 21, 2017, https://tinyurl.com/y8jfqumn.

28. "Naval Station Norfolk: Welcome to the World's Largest Naval Station," Military.com, https://tinyurl.com/y9hgn8cq.

29. "On the Front Lines of Rising Seas: Naval Station Norfolk, Virginia," Union of Concerned Scientists, July 27, 2016, https://tinyurl.com/y9fspcnv.

30. Evan Lehmann, "Inside one naval base's battle with sea-level rise," *E&E News*, Oct. 27, 2016, https://tinyurl.com/je482eq.

31. *National Security Implications of Climate Change for U.S. Naval Forces* (2011), National Academies Press, https://tinyurl.com/y9c3wezn.

32. Catherine Foley, "Military Basing and Climate Change," American Security Project, November 2012, https://tinyurl.com/y99p5p5y.

33. Andrew Holland, "North Korea Threatens Guam Today; Climate Change Threatens it in the Long Term," American Security Project, Aug. 10, 2017, https://tinyurl.com/y8ndq4x5.

34. Caitlin Werrell and Francesco Femia, "General Keys: The military thinks climate change is serious," Center for Climate and Security, June 2016, https://tinyurl.com/y8na8dgy.

35. "Climate Change Adaptation: DOD Can Improve Infrastructure Planning and Processes to Better Account for Potential Impacts," U.S. Government Accountability Office, May 2014, https://tinyurl.com/ya6x8obk.

36. Taylor Smith, "Critique of 'Climate Change Adaptation: DOD Can Improve Infrastructure Planning and Processes to Better Account for Potential Impacts,'" Heartland Institute, Feb. 5, 2015, https://tinyurl.com/ya97c3u8.

37. "Quadrennial Defense Review 2014," U.S. Department of Defense, March 4, 2014, https://tinyurl.com/j9yf7l3.

38. "Climate Change Action Plan 2016–2020," World Bank Group, 2016, https://tinyurl.com/yc7kveo3.

39. Hiroko Tabuchi and Henry Fountain, "Bucking Trump, These Cities, States and Companies Commit to Paris Accord," *The New York Times*, June 1, 2017, https://tinyurl.com/y9wkrawd.

40. Cecilia Reyes, "Four key areas for global risks in 2017," World Economic Forum, Jan. 11, 2017, http://tinyurl.com/y889qp8r.

41. Marshall Burke, Solomon M. Hsiang and Edward Miguel, "Global non-linear effect of temperature on economic production," stanford.edu, Oct. 21, 2015, https://tinyurl.com/y9n3ytqk. Originally published in *Nature*, Nov. 12, 2013, pp. 235–239.

42. Marshall Burke, "The global economic costs from climate change may be worse than expected," Brookings Institution, Dec. 9, 2015, https://tinyurl.com/ycg7phd5.

43. David Rotman, "Hotter Days Will Drive Global Inequality," *MIT Technology Review*, Dec. 20, 2016, https://tinyurl.com/jxshnb5.

44. Iain Murray, "An Issue of Science and Economics," Competitive Enterprise Institute, 2008, https://tinyurl.com/y73hrwts.

45. "The Economics of Climate Change: Cocktails and Conversation with William Nordhaus," Becker Friedman Institute for Research in Economics, University of Chicago, April 16, 2014, https://tinyurl.com/yby4eham.

46. Matt Ridley, "Why climate change is good for the world," *The Spectator*, Oct. 19, 2013, https://tinyurl.com/yanh9vvm.

47. David Wogan, "Why we know about the greenhouse gas effect," *Scientific American*, May 16, 2013, https://tinyurl.com/y8fehazt.

48. Steve Graham, "Svante Arrhenius (1859–1927)," NASA, Jan. 18, 2000, https://tinyurl.com/y9vhbo6d.

49. "The Carbon Dioxide Greenhouse Effect," American Institute of Physics, January 2017, https://tinyurl.com/yaqnh5l9.

50. Edward C. Keefer, ed., "Foreign Relations of the United States, 1964–1968, Vol. XXVIII, Laos," Office of the Historian, U.S. State Department, https://tinyurl.com/y7laoxa7.

51. "Memorandum From the Deputy Under Secretary of State for Political Affairs (Kohler) to Secretary of State Rusk," Office of the Historian, U.S. Department of State, http://tinyurl.com/yccsgu49.

52. "Convention on the Prohibition of Military or Any Other Hostile Use of Environmental Modification Techniques," U.S. State Department, undated, https://tinyurl.com/ydxoqsnt.

53. "Potential Implications of Trends in World Population, Food Production, and Climate," CIA, made available through The Black Vault, August 1974, https://tinyurl.com/yc36rosb.

54. "Potential Implications of Trends in World Population, Food Production, and Climate," *op. cit.*

55. Walter Sullivan, "Study Finds Warming Trend That Could Raise Sea Levels," *The New York Times*, Aug. 22, 1981, https://tinyurl.com/ycc88cp2.

56. Al Gore, "Earth's Fate Is the No. 1 National Security Issue," *The Washington Post*, Oct. 12, 2007, https://tinyurl.com/y6vqzou8.

57. J.T. Houghton, G.J. Jenkins and J.J. Ephraums, eds., "Climate Change: The IPCC Scientific Assessment," U.N. International Panel on Climate Change, Cambridge University Press, 1990, https://tinyurl.com/n7r4iyj.

58. President George H.W. Bush, "Remarks to the Intergovernmental Panel on Climate Change," American Presidency Project, Feb. 5, 1990, https://tinyurl.com/yakl8acu.

59. John H. Goshko, "Baker Urges Steps on Global Warming," *The Washington Post*, Jan. 31, 1989, https://tinyurl.com/yd5ewl3n.

60. "U.S. Foreign Policy Priorities and FY 1991 Budget Request," Secretary of State James Baker's statement to the Senate Foreign Relations Committee, Feb. 1, 1990, https://tinyurl.com/y8k2uo6l.

61. John H. Cushman Jr., "Intense Lobbying Against Global Warming Treaty," *The New York Times*, Dec. 7, 1997, https://tinyurl.com/ybbkjpoy.

62. Amy Royden, "U.S. Climate Change Policy Under President Clinton: A Look Back," *Golden Gate University Law Review*, January 2002, https://tinyurl.com/yapzyucf.

63. Riley E. Dunlap, "Partisan Gap on Global Warming Grows," Gallup, May 29, 2008, https://tinyurl.com/y7toqhw8.

64. "President Bush Discusses Global Climate Change," The White House, June 11, 2001, https://tinyurl.com/y6tvzksb.

65. Peter Schwartz and Doug Randall, "An Abrupt Climate Change Scenario and Its Implications for United States National Security," report for the Department of Defense, October 2003, https://tinyurl.com/ybd2bzss.

66. "National Defense Strategy," Department of Defense, June 2008, https://tinyurl.com/jcvrjnk.

67. "Quadrennial Defense Review Report," Department of Defense, February 2010, https://tinyurl.com/yd5enopn.

68. "Inaugural Address by President Barack Obama," The White House, Jan. 21, 2013, https://tinyurl.com/y9lhewr7.

69. "Quadrennial Defense Review 2014," *op. cit.*

70. "2014 Climate Change Adaptation Roadmap," *op. cit.*

71. "U.S.-China Joint Announcement on Climate Change," The White House, Nov. 11, 2014, https://tinyurl.com/yd6kxfj6.

72. "Paris Agreement," United Nations, 2015, https://tinyurl.com/y75g5pqb.

73. "National Security Strategy," The White House, February 2015, https://tinyurl.com/y9nj6jx3; Colin Campbell, "Jeb Bush is spitting fire at Obama for touting climate-change efforts after Paris attacks," *Business Insider*, Nov. 25, 2015, https://tinyurl.com/y7l6oswp.

74. Jeffrey Goldberg, "The Obama Doctrine," *The Atlantic*, April 2016, https://tinyurl.com/zfzlg5g.

75. "Presidential Memorandum—Climate Change and National Security," The White House, Sept. 21, 2016, https://tinyurl.com/hj6c6fw.

76. Copp, *op. cit.*

77. "Presidential Executive Order on Promoting Energy Independence and Economic Growth," The White House, March 28, 2017, https://tinyurl.com/ny2k4wt.

78. "Statement by President Trump on the Paris Climate Accord," The White House, June 1, 2017, https://tinyurl.com/ydaz28yb.

79. "Communication Regarding Intent To Withdraw From Paris Agreement," Office of the Spokesperson, State Department, Aug. 4, 2017, https://tinyurl.com/ybyk5ury.

80. Richard Wike et al., "U.S. Image Suffers as Publics Around World Question Trump's Leadership," Pew Research Center, June 26, 2017, https://tinyurl.com/ya65l6js.

81. "Views on the Paris Climate Agreement," AP-NORC poll, June 2017, https://tinyurl.com/y9os6hqy.

82. "Secretary of Defense James Mattis's Views on Climate, Energy and More," *op. cit.*

83. "Vice Chairman of the Joint Chiefs on Climate Instability and Political Instability," Center for Climate and Security, July 25, 2017, https://tinyurl.com/y7x63jsg.

84. "Sea Ice Extent Sinks to Record Lows at Both Poles," NASA, March 22, 2017, https://tinyurl.com/k96bsdo.

85. "NASA Science Zeros in on Ocean Rise: How Much? How Soon?" press release, NASA, Aug. 26, 2015, https://tinyurl.com/yd87goqh.

86. Patrick Barkham, "Russian tanker sails through Arctic without icebreaker for first time," *The Guardian*, Aug. 24, 2017, https://tinyurl.com/ybqgo9ru; "Sovcomflot's unique LNG carrier sets new record with Northern Sea Route transit of just 6.5 days," press release, Sovcomflot, Aug. 23, 2017, https://tinyurl.com/ybyfyrh7.

87. Andrew Osborn, "Putin's Russia in biggest Arctic military push since Soviet fall," Reuters, Jan. 30, 2017, https://tinyurl.com/jpheshv.

88. Heather A. Conley and Caroline Rohloff, "The New Ice Curtain," Center for Strategic & International Studies, August 2015, https://tinyurl.com/ycuyqevt.

89. "Russian Federation Policy for the Arctic to 2020," Arctis Knowledge Hub, undated, https://tinyurl.com/y7wcxjct.

90. "U.S. General Concerned About Russia's Arctic Military Buildup," Radio Free Europe/Radio Liberty, May 26, 2017, https://tinyurl.com/ya6zkbom.

91. Ellen Mitchell, "Governor activates entire Texas National Guard in response to Harvey," *The Hill*, Aug. 28, 2017, https://tinyurl.com/yaac5llw; Melissa Nelson Gabriel, "Military bases in Hurricane Irma's path assess storm damage," *Pensacola News Journal*, Sept. 11, 2017, https://tinyurl.com/y7f8tu4z.

92. *Ibid.*

93. Michael E. Mann, "It's a fact: climate change made Hurricane Harvey more deadly," *The Guardian*, Aug. 28, 2017, https://tinyurl.com/ycamv4bl.

94. *Ibid.*, Ellen Mitchell, http://tinyurl.com/yaac5llw.

95. Seth Borenstein, "Is there a connection between Harvey and global warming?" The Associated Press, Aug. 28, 2017, https://tinyurl.com/y7x2bjkk.

96. "Climate Change Impacts in the United States," U.S. Global Change Research Program, October 2014, https://tinyurl.com/jfruuux.

97. "Amendment to H.R. 2810 Offered by Mr. Langevin of Rhode Island," House.gov, June 21, 2017, https://tinyurl.com/ybrjqedy.

98. "What is the Climate Solutions Caucus?" Citizens' Climate Lobby, https://tinyurl.com/yd26bc4v.

99. Steve Valk, "25 Republicans And 25 Democrats Now Belong To The Climate Solutions Caucus," Ecosystem Marketplace, July 29, 2017, https://tinyurl.com/ycnd9w2k.

100. "Paradox of Progress: Trends Transforming the Global Landscape," National Intelligence Council, Jan. 9, 2017, https://tinyurl.com/yagksyqa.

101. "U.S. Global Change Research Program Climate Science Special Report (CSSR)," DocumentCloud.org, June 28, 2017, https://tinyurl.com/y9fvnjs2.

BIBLIOGRAPHY
Selected Sources
Books

Campbell, Kurt M., ed., *Climatic Cataclysm: The Foreign Policy and National Security Implications of Climate Change*, Brookings Institution Press, 2008.
Experts discuss climate-change scenarios and their effects on science, politics, foreign policy and national security.

Miller, Todd, *Storming the Wall: Climate Change, Migration, and Homeland Security*, City Lights Books, 2017.
A journalist predicts border battles as more climate change-displaced migrants seek refuge in developed countries; he chronicles examples of recent climate-induced struggles and forecasts where future clashes might occur.

Moran, Daniel, ed., *Climate Change and National Security: A Country-Level Analysis*, Georgetown University Press, 2011.
An international collection of scholars analyzes the security risks posed by climate change in 19 countries and regions.

Articles

Bromund, Theodore R., "Climate change is not a national security threat," Heritage Foundation Commentary, June 4, 2015, https://tinyurl.com/y7rdm3jk.

A senior research fellow at a conservative think tank argues that ideology, not climate, endangers national security.

Busby, Joshua W., "Climate and Security," *Duck of Minerva* **(blog), Oct. 17, 2014, https://tinyurl.com/ y8gcn6vf.**
An associate professor of public affairs wonders if the climate change-security link might be "a finding in need of a theory" and questions framing the climate change debate in national security terms.

Epstein, Richard A., "Containing Climate Change Hysteria," Hoover Institution, June 5, 2017, https:// tinyurl.com/y7sotxj4.
A law professor says American withdrawal from the Paris climate agreement isn't the threat to U.S. security and economic prosperity that President Trump's critics claim.

Lehmann, Evan, "Inside one naval base's battle with sea-level rise," Climatewire, E&E News, Oct. 27, 2016, https://tinyurl.com/je482eq.
A journalist examines the threat that rising sea levels pose to Naval Station Norfolk in Virginia.

Werrell, Caitlin, and Francesco Femia, "Climate Change and Security," *Crisis-Response,* **April 2017, https://tinyurl.com/ycwwdbqh.**
The co-presidents of the Center for Climate Change and Security, a Washington think tank, discuss how and why the U.S. military views climate change as a "threat multiplier."

Reports and Studies

"Implications for US National Security of Anticipated Climate Change," National Intelligence Council, Sept. 21, 2016, https://tinyurl.com/hp9arwj.
The 16 agencies of the National Intelligence Community look at how climate change could affect global social, economic, political and security conditions in the next 20 years.

"National Security Implications of Climate-Related Risks and a Changing Climate," U.S. Department of Defense, July 23, 2015, https://tinyurl.com/ p5qlyz9.

A Pentagon report to the Senate Appropriations Committee outlines the climate-related security risks for each geographic military command and how the commands intend to mitigate those risks.

"Quarterly Defense Review 2014," U.S. Department of Defense, March 14, 2014, https://tinyurl.com/ j9yf7l3.
The most recent edition of the Defense Department's quadrennial outline of security issues and strategies identifies climate change as a "threat multiplier" and a "significant challenge for the U.S. and the world at large."

Dellink, Rob and Elisa Lanzi, "The Economic Consequences of Climate Change," Organisation for Economic Co-operation and Development, Nov. 3, 2015, https://tinyurl.com/y7dwmrse.
An intergovernmental organization predicts the possible geographic and sectoral consequences of climate change.

Idso, Craig D., Robert M. Carter and S. Fred Singer, "Why Scientists Disagree About Global Warming: The NIPCC Report on Scientific Consensus, (Second Ed.)," The Heartland Institute, 2016, https://tinyurl. com/y8jhjcaa.
The Nongovernmental International Panel on Climate Change argues against the claim that scientists are virtually unanimous in acknowledging the dangers of climate change.

Pezard, Stephanie, *et al.,* **"Maintaining Arctic Cooperation With Russia: Planning for Regional Change in the Far North," RAND Corp., March 7, 2017, https://tinyurl.com/ybpnqgmk.**
Researchers consider the effects of climate change, along with a host of geopolitical issues, in analyzing Russian-U.S. tensions in the Arctic.

Selby, Jan, *et al.,* **"Climate Change and the Syrian civil war revisited,"** *Political Geography,* **September 2017, https://tinyurl.com/ybr3ppe6.**
Researchers from the United Kingdom, United States and Germany conclude that, so far, there is "no convincing evidence" linking climate change to the Syrian civil war, and further investigation is required.

For More Information

American Security Project, 1100 New York Ave., N.W., Suite 710W, Washington, DC 20005; 202-347-4267; www .americansecurityproject.org. Public policy organization focused on national security issues, including climate change.

Center for American Progress, 1333 H St., N.W., Washington, DC 20005; 202-682-1611; www.american progress.org. Progressive think tank that addresses a range of social, economic and political issues, including climate change and security.

Center for Climate and Security, 1025 Connecticut Ave., N.W., Suite 1000, Washington, DC 20036; 202-246–8612; climateandsecurity.org. Organization that researches and disseminates information about the impact of climate.

Competitive Enterprise Institute, 1310 L St., N.W., 7th Floor, Washington, DC 20005; 202-331-1010; https:// cei.org/. Libertarian think tank that questions concerns

about global warming and advocates access to affordable energy.

Heritage Foundation, 214 Massachusetts Ave., N.E., Washington DC 20002-4999; 202-546-4400; www.heritage .org. Conservative think tank that researches and disseminates information about climate change, national security and other issues.

Intergovernmental Panel on Climate Change, c/o World Meteorological Organization, 7bis Avenue de la Paix, C.P. 2300, CH- 1211 Geneva 2, Switzerland; +41-22-730- 8208/54/84; www.ipcc.ch. Group set up under the United Nations that regularly updates policymakers on the scientific evidence of climate change.

NASA Global Climate Change, 300 E St., S.W., Washington, DC 20546; 202-358-0000; climate.nasa.gov. Provides information on the effects of global warming.

Fishermen in pirogues head to sea in Dakar, Senegal, in April. The Senegalese say fish have been scarcer and harder to catch in recent years because of illegal fishing by foreign trawlers.

15

Global Fishing Controversies

Does overfishing threaten the survival of ocean species?

By Charles P. Wallace

Along the Senegalese coast of West Africa, many local fishermen take to the sea in pirogues—brightly painted, canoe-like boats powered by outboard engines. As generations of fishers did before them, they range into the Atlantic in search of white grouper and other catch. Increasingly, they return home all but empty-handed. "The fish just vanished," said Mor Ndiaye, a Senegalese fisherman. "We used to catch enough fish in a day or two. Now we need to go out to sea for weeks to catch the same amount."[1]

The fishers, marine scientists and others blame the poor catches on both illegal fishing and overfishing by large foreign fleets operating in what was once one of the world's richest fishing grounds.

Over two months in 2017, for example, authorities from Guinea, Sierra Leone and Guinea-Bissau detained eight Chinese fishing vessels off West Africa, alleging they were either fishing illegally by encroaching on territorial waters or using prohibited fishing gear. The vessels were among an estimated 500 Chinese ships working West African waters.[2]

The foreign competition costs the region an estimated $1.3 billion annually in fishing revenue, according to the Africa Progress Panel, a Swiss-based research group. Senegal alone loses $300 million a year, or about 2 percent of its gross domestic product.

From *CQ Researcher*, May 31, 2019

"Trawlers catch all the fish available regardless of protected species or safety standards," said Abdou Karim Sall, president of the Platform of Senegalese Artisanal Fishermen, an advocacy group. "These big vessels hold heavy nets that destroy the ocean and the marine habitat but especially nurseries for juveniles, which prevents the fish from reproducing."[3]

Globally, overfishing is at record highs, according to scientists. Along with widespread illegal fishing, it is placing severe pressure on fish stocks and the fishermen whose livelihoods depend on them. Climate change—which scientists say is causing ocean temperatures to rise and acidity to increase—poses another significant threat to marine life and fishers. The warmer temperatures, scientists have found, force some species to migrate to cooler waters, significantly altering marine habitats.[4]

"We're catching more fish, but we are extracting them from stocks that have been reduced," says Daniel Pauly, a professor of biology at the Institute for the Oceans and Fisheries at the University of British Columbia in Vancouver.

As global fishing stocks fall, aquaculture—the cultivation of oysters, clams, shrimp and fish on so-called fish farms—is helping to replace the losses, but some experts worry that such farming will not be enough to satisfy demand as global population rises, nor will aquaculture compensate for the loss of livelihoods in poor countries that depend on commercial fishing.

The stakes are high, according to marine scientists and other experts. Fishing, both wild capture and aquaculture, accounted for 17 percent of animal protein consumed by the global population in 2015.[5]

"We've doubled per capita fish consumption, even though the population moved from a few billion to 7.5 billion," says Manuel Barange, director of the fisheries and aquaculture policy and resources division at the U.N. Food and Agriculture

Organization, which collects global data about fishing. Aquaculture has greatly helped, he adds. "Fish is fundamentally food for the poor, much more than for the rich."

In its efforts to satisfy global demand, the fishing industry has become increasingly efficient and high-tech. Drones and sonar, for example, can help fishers locate big schools of fish. Industrial fishing fleets, composed of large factory ships with refrigerated holds and the latest technology, operate far from home for months at a time.

"Fishing has a 50,000-year-old history, but now we're doing it with robots, drones, helicopters and satellites," says Douglas McCauley, an associate professor in the ecology, evolution and marine biology department at the University of California, Santa Barbara. "It's a little unfair, not only to fish but to future generations of fishermen."

The fishing fleets of just five countries—China, Taiwan, Japan, South Korea and Spain—account for 86 percent of the catch on the high seas, according to a 2018 study by McCauley and six other marine scientists. Across the globe, government subsidies totaling $35 billion a year—mainly for fuel and gear—help fishing fleets operate.[6]

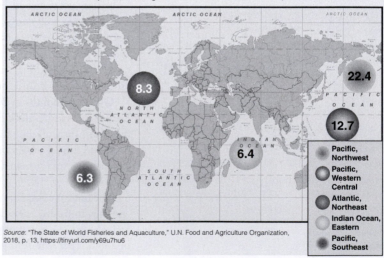

Pacific Richest in Fishing Grounds

The Pacific Ocean contained three of the world's five most productive fishing grounds, yielding about 41 million metric tons of seafood in 2016, according to the latest U.N. data. The northeast Atlantic Ocean produced 8.3 million metric tons, followed by the eastern Indian Ocean, at 6.4 million.

Top Ocean Fishing Grounds in Millions of Metric Tons, 2016

Pacific, Northwest
Pacific, Western Central
Atlantic, Northeast
Indian Ocean, Eastern
Pacific, Southeast

Source: "The State of World Fisheries and Aquaculture," U.N. Food and Agriculture Organization, 2018, p. 13, https://tinyurl.com/y69u7hu6

China has the world's largest fleet, with an estimated 2,500 distant-water fishing vessels, followed by Taiwan with 2,000.[7] While much of China's catch is for domestic consumption, either as food for humans or fishmeal for animals, the country is the world's largest exporter of fish and fish products. It is followed by Norway, Vietnam and Thailand. The European Union (EU), the United States and Japan are the biggest importers.[8]

With the leading fishers becoming more efficient and dominant, the pressure on fish stocks is growing: One-third of all species are overfished, up from 10 percent in 1974. And 93 percent of marine fisheries, or fishing grounds, worldwide are fished at or beyond sustainable catch levels. The pressure from overfishing is especially acute in the South China and Mediterranean seas, experts say.[9]

Some types of fish have experienced drastic declines due to overfishing. Pacific bluefin tuna, which commands astronomical prices in Japan, have fallen to just 3 percent of their former population, scientists found. Overfishing also has drastically reduced stocks of scad, herring and mackerel in the South China Sea, prompting Chinese vessels to venture thousands of miles from home.[10]

In addition to overfishing, illegal fishing poses a growing problem, according to marine scientists. In 1982, the United Nations adopted the Law of the Sea Convention, which granted each nation an exclusive economic zone extending 200 nautical miles (230 miles) into the sea from its territorial sea base and gives it sovereignty over fish in those waters.[11]

Foreign vessels that fish in another country's exclusive economic zone without gaining permission or paying for access are fishing illegally. Estimates of catches derived from illegal fishing range from 11 million metric tons to as high as 26 million metric tons a year.[12]

International efforts are seeking to curb overfishing and illegal fishing by pursuing two different, yet complementary, measures to prevent damage to fish species.

The United Nations is trying to create protected areas outside national jurisdictions that would allow overfished species to regenerate. In these zones on the high seas, fishing would be limited or prohibited. Satellite and radar monitoring and other techniques would be used to monitor the zones, but who would enforce the restrictions remains undecided.[13] The Convention on Biological Diversity has set a goal of establishing protected areas in more than 10 percent of the oceans by 2020.[14]

China Dominates Global Fishing

China hauled in 15.2 million metric tons of fish from the world's oceans in 2016, according to the latest U.N. data. Indonesia was a distant second at 6.1 million metric tons, while the United States was third at nearly 4.9 million.

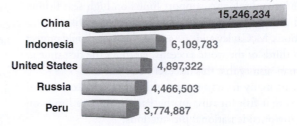

Top Ocean Fish Harvests by Nation, 2016
Harvest (metric tons)

Nation	Harvest (metric tons)
China	15,246,234
Indonesia	6,109,783
United States	4,897,322
Russia	4,466,503
Peru	3,774,887

Source: "The State of World Fisheries and Aquaculture," U.N. Food and Agriculture Organization, 2018, p. 9, https://tinyurl.com/y779rs5w

A worker at an aquaculture farm near Kuleshovka, Russia, weighs a sturgeon in 2017. As fishing stocks fall, the cultivation of oysters, clams, shrimp and fish on fish farms is helping to replace the losses, according to scientists.

Getty Images/TASS/Valery Matytsin

At the same time, the World Trade Organization (WTO) is debating whether to limit the subsidies governments can give their fishing fleets. Some scientists believe that fishing far from home would be unprofitable if these fleets did not receive subsidies for fuel and gear.

Marine biologists support limits on high seas fishing and praise international efforts to replenish fish stocks. Nations, McCauley said, are asking "how we should protect two-thirds of the world's oceans, [and] it's the first time in human history that this has ever been asked."[15]

But many fishermen, including the U.S. owners of ships that fish for tuna in the Pacific, oppose limits on fishing outside national jurisdictions.

Eric Kingma, executive director of the Hawaii Longline Association, which represents the state's commercial fishermen, says any effort to close the high seas would devastate Hawaii's 145-boat tuna and swordfish fleet. "Because of existing restrictions and protected areas, only 17 percent of U.S. territorial waters around Hawaii are open to commercial fishing," he says. That, he says, forces vessels to fish in the high seas.

Christopher Brown, a Rhode Island fisherman who is president of the Seafood Harvesters of America, an umbrella organization for commercial fishermen, defends federal fuel subsidies. Fishermen exist on extremely narrow profit margins, he says, and would find it hard to survive without cheap fuel. He notes that farmers also receive much help from the government.

In the United States, fishing is a historic but diminishing part of the local economy. New Bedford, Mass., for example, started out as the center of the American whaling fleet in the 1800s. When demand for whale oil fell, New Bedford turned to fishing. But fishing has declined over the past century due to foreign competition and other factors, and the city now survives on its catch of scallops, which brings in $379 million, making it the largest U.S. fishing port by revenue.[16]

"Just about every port city in Massachusetts and Rhode Island had major fishing infrastructure," says Scott Lang, a former mayor of New Bedford. "It's all gone now."

European fishers face many of the same challenges as their American cousins, as well as a different one: Continental and British fishermen are clashing over fishing rights in U.K. waters. If the United Kingdom exits the EU in the fall as scheduled, British fishermen want member states to negotiate bilateral agreements on access to their fishing grounds. But the EU wants its other members to keep access to British waters.

Climate change is another significant threat to commercial fishing. Scientists say ocean temperatures are rising because of carbon emissions in the atmosphere, causing some marine species to migrate toward the northern and southern poles in search of colder water. The problem threatens the availability of fish in tropical zones, where much of the population depends on fishing for food and income.[17]

The U.N. released a report in early May that said up to 1 million plant, animal and marine species are on the verge of extinction because of climate change. A warming planet is harming ocean ecosystems, including coral reefs, the report said, and the damage could lead to a collapse of commercial and indigenous fishing.[18]

Christopher Free, a postdoctoral researcher at Rutgers University, published a study in February estimating that 4 percent of the globe's fish supply has already been lost due to climate change.[19]

"A 4 percent change might sound small, but it is large, and it means a 4 percent reduction in the fish available to feed people and the fish available for fishermen whose livelihoods depend on the availability of this resource," Free says.

As marine biologists, governments, fishermen and others debate the state of global fishing, here are some of the questions they are asking:

Should the high seas be closed to fishing?

As overfishing grows, an international effort is underway to close parts of the high seas to commercial fishing in the belief that restrictions would allow stocks to regenerate. But fishers disagree with such a strategy, saying the number of fish caught on the high seas remains small and species' migratory habits make a ban of little use.

Negotiators met in April at the United Nations in New York for a second round of talks on a conservation agreement to establish sustainable fish stocks. The talks are expected to resume later this year.[20]

Negotiators are exploring whether the U.N. should close parts of the high seas to fishing, and if so, how much. Under the U.N. Convention on the Law of the Sea, 64 percent of the oceans' surface is in international waters. The United States never signed the U.N. convention because of Republican opposition but observes most of its rules.[21]

Crow White, an assistant professor of biology at the Center for Coastal Marine Sciences at California Polytechnic State University, San Luis Obispo, likens high seas fishing to the "tragedy of the commons," a concept outlined by biologist Garrett Hardin in 1968. Hardin gave the example of herders grazing their cattle on a common pasture: Individual herders seek to maximize their personal gain, but are unconcerned with overgrazing and the depletion of common resources; by putting their individual interests first, they end up hurting everyone.[22]

"Closing the high seas removes the open-access fishing conditions, which are leading to a tragedy of the commons—disastrous both economically and for conservation," White says. If the high seas were closed to commercial fishing, he argues, fish stocks would rejuvenate and spill into territorial waters—the 200-nautical-mile exclusive economic zones that individual countries control—where they could be responsibly harvested.

On balance, restricting high seas fishing will help, says Pauly of the University of British Columbia. Although the high seas account for only about 4 percent of the annual global fish catch, the five big powers—China, Taiwan, Japan, South Korea and Spain—are aggressively fishing in the open seas and reaping most of the profits there.[23]

"If we ban high seas fishing, in the course of migration tuna will cross the [exclusive economic zones] of countries," Pauly says. "Instead of being caught by a few countries,

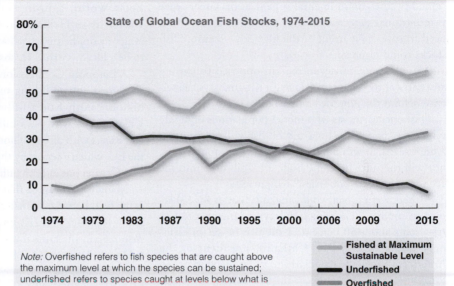

Overfishing Threatens Third of Ocean Species

One-third of fish species in the world's oceans are overfished—up from 10 percent in 1974, according to a U.N. agency. The proportion of underfished species has fallen from 39 percent in 1974 to 7 percent in 2015.

State of Global Ocean Fish Stocks, 1974-2015

Note: Overfished refers to fish species that are caught above the maximum level at which the species can be sustained; underfished refers to species caught at levels below what is necessary to maintain maximum sustainability.

Source: "The State of World Fisheries and Aquaculture," U.N. Food and Agriculture Organization, 2018, https://tinyurl.com/y3yu42wy

Fished at Maximum Sustainable Level
Underfished
Overfished

there would now be 50 to 70 countries that have tuna in their waters. It would be a more equitable situation."

Pauly says advances in satellite monitoring—every deep-water fishing boat is required to have a transponder—would make enforcement of the ban on high seas fishing relatively easy.

But critics contend the small size of the high seas catch means a ban would have little effect on fish stocks. "If you close the high seas, you protect a very large area, but actually reduce a very small volume of the catch overall, so it would have little impact," says Barange of the U.N.'s Food and Agriculture Organization.

Barange also says reaching agreement at the U.N. on a fishing ban in international waters would be difficult. "The Law of the Sea Convention says all countries have a right to access the high seas and any change would require them to agree to close the high seas. That might be politically complicated."

A compromise under discussion would establish sanctuaries in 30 percent to 50 percent of the entire ocean in order to protect the spawning grounds of selected fish.[24]

Using mapping software that details where people are fishing and the value of their catch, a study commissioned by the environmental organization Greenpeace International determined that protected areas would need to cover 37 percent of the high seas to ensure fish stocks could regenerate.[25]

Many fishers, however, remain opposed to closing any parts of the high seas. Hawaii's Kingma says the science behind the proposed ban is faulty.

"Fisheries scientists who model populations of highly migratory species like tuna and billfish will tell you that a high seas ban will have no effect on the stock status, nor will the tuna from the high seas spill over into the economic zones of countries," Kingma says.

Others warn a ban would make it harder for fishermen to survive. "The tuna industry in American Samoa represents about 80 percent of the private-sector economy there," says Stuart Chikami, president of the American Tunaboat Association, a membership group for owners of U.S. vessels. "Closure of high seas areas would jeopardize the ability of the U.S. fleet to remain viable."

Should nations subsidize their fishing fleets?

To cut down on overfishing, since 2005 the WTO has been trying, without success, to limit subsidies offered by governments to their fishing industries. The talks are so politically contentious that they were suspended from 2011 until late 2016 and have been inconclusive since 2017.[26]

For fishers, especially in poorer countries, government subsidies enable them to keep working. For marine biologists, the subsidies help drive overfishing because they enable industrial fishing fleets to roam thousands of miles from home.

A National Geographic-led study concluded that fishing in 54 percent of the ocean would be unprofitable were it not for government help, especially for fuel. It estimated the total value of the high seas catch in 2014, the last year for which statistics were available, at $7.6 billion and total profit at up to $1.4 billion. But government subsidies, according to the study, totaled about $4.2 billion that year, meaning the fishing fleets would have lost $2.8 billion without the help.[27]

"High seas fishing from an economic standpoint is probably not even profitable if it wasn't for the subsidies that are being given to a lot of high sea fishing companies from the nations that harbor those companies," says Boris Worm, a professor of biology at Dalhousie University in Halifax, Nova Scotia. "You have to go a long way on the high seas, where the density of fish tends to be a lot lower than in coastal waters."

A European Commission study found that China had the largest annual fishing subsidies, at $4 billion to $6.7 billion. South Korea followed with $1.7 billion, the United States with $1.5 billion, Japan with $1.3 billion and Russia with $308 million.[28] The study did not include the EU, which a report by the nongovernmental organization Oceana put at $3.3 billion, second only to China.[29]

Many experts agree that the most important subsidy is for fuel, because it makes long-distance fishing financially feasible. A 2012 paper in the journal *Fisheries Research* put the annual value of global fuel subsidies for fishing at between $4.2 billion and $8.5 billion. In the United States, fuel subsidies in the form of tax relief for fishers was $300 million a year.[30]

"Our results show that [a subsidy] tends to increase fishing effort, and support based on fuel is the worst of them all," says Roger Martini, an economist at the International Centre for Trade and Sustainable Development, a nonprofit in Paris that advocates for sustainable development.

In addition to fuel, other types of subsidies are for fishing gear, ice to preserve catches, crew salaries and vessel construction costs.

An Organisation for Economic Co-operation and Development (OECD) study concluded that subsidies for industrial fleets harm small-scale fishers. "Support based on the use of fuel can make smaller fishers worse off than they would be without them, as they are displaced by more fuel-intensive fishing operations," the study said.[31]

In 2015, U.N. members voted to adopt a 2030 Agenda for Sustainable Development, which included 17 goals. No. 14 would prohibit by 2020 "certain forms of fisheries subsidies which contribute to overcapacity and overfishing, eliminate subsidies that contribute to illegal, unreported and unregulated fishing and refrain from introducing new ones." The goals are voluntary.[32]

A vendor prepares fish at a market in Izmir, Turkey, in April. The fishing industry is an important part of local economies throughout the world, particularly in developing countries.

But fishing communities defend subsidies. They argue that their industry operates on thin profit margins and that removing the fuel and other benefits would simply raise the cost of fish to consumers. The subsidies, they say, benefit not only long-distance fleets but struggling small-scale commercial fishermen who work closer to home. And they say that because agriculture is heavily subsidized, so should be fishing.

"The minimal subsidies that the fishing industry gets are not the kinds of things that you would toy with thinking that they really don't need them," says New Bedford's Lang, who is on the board of directors of the Center For Sustainable Fisheries, a nonprofit that supports the economic health of fishing communities.

Developing countries, including China, which provide much larger subsidies in the form of crew and gear costs and even fund the construction of fishing boats, seek exemptions from any bans on subsidies.

India nearly caused the WTO talks to break down in 2017 because it wanted its small fishing fleet exempted from the proposed subsidy ban. It said its fishers were so poor they could not survive without help.[33] While countries generally agree on the need to limit subsidies that contribute to illegal fishing, China and Indonesia want to continue subsidies for fishermen operating in their exclusive economic zones.[34]

In an effort to resolve the dispute, the United States and Australia in March 2019 proposed three tiers of subsidy caps. The first would subject nations with annual catches over 0.7 percent of the "total marine capture"—their share of the global fish catch—to the smallest subsidies. They include the United States, China, the European Union, Indonesia, India, Russia, Mexico, Canada and Japan. Countries with more than 0.05 percent of the global catch would be subject to a cap of $5 million in subsidies, and those below 0.05 percent would have no subsidy cap.[35]

The proposed changes' impact on fuel subsidies, especially tax breaks on diesel such as exist in the United States, is unclear. But fishers oppose any changes.

"It doesn't make a lot of sense to tax agriculture or where your food comes from because the citizens end up paying it anyway," says Rhode Island fisherman Brown. "No, I wouldn't support that at all."

Should EU fishing vessels have access to British waters after Brexit?

The political crisis over the United Kingdom leaving the EU has reignited a four-decade-old dispute over continental fishing rights. British fishermen, who say their government betrayed their interests when the United Kingdom joined the European Economic Community—the EU's predecessor—in 1973, want the U.K. to take back control of the country's fishing grounds as a way to help their industry. The other EU members, however, remain determined to maintain access to British waters for their fleets.

A British government background paper shows why the fishermen are angry: In 2015, fishing vessels from other EU countries caught 683,000 metric tons of seafood worth $660 million in U.K. waters. But U.K. vessels caught only 111,000 metric tons worth $156 million in other EU member waters.[36]

Under a withdrawal agreement, the U.K. is now scheduled to officially leave the EU on Oct. 31, 2019, after Brexit was twice postponed from the original date of March 29. The agreement, negotiated by British Prime Minister Theresa May but not yet approved by the British Parliament, provides for a transition period until December 2020 to give the two sides time to negotiate trade details, including the terms for fishing rights. (Because of her failure to win parliamentary backing for her Brexit deal, May said she will resign as prime minister over the summer after the Conservative Party selects a successor.)[37]

Barrie Deas, chief executive of Britain's National Federation of Fishermen's Organisations, says that if Brexit happens, the U.K. will become an independent country in control of its own waters and fishing grounds. "If we leave the EU, we become an independent coastal state under the U.N. Law of the Sea," Deas says. "That gives us a number of rights and responsibilities, in particular to manage resources out to 200 [nautical] miles."

In 1973, British fishermen caught around 1 million metric tons of fish a year. By 2016, the catch had fallen in half, to about 500,000 metric tons of cod, mackerel and other fish. The number of fishermen employed in the industry also has fallen sharply, from 21,443 in 1970 to 12,405 in 2011.[38]

The competition from EU rivals is not the only problem facing British fishermen. Because of climate change, mackerel are migrating from British waters toward Iceland. This has severely affected the annual catch by Britain's fishermen, especially those based in Scotland.[39]

British fishermen want to scrap an agreement reached by the European Economic Community in January 1983 known as the Common Fisheries Policy, which set quotas for each country's fishing fleet in member states' territorial waters. The quotas were based on the historical catch records for 1973-78, the years before the 1982 adoption of exclusive economic zones.[40]

For example, the quotas gave French fishermen 90 percent of the cod in the English Channel and British fishermen just 10 percent.[41]

Other EU fishing interests argue that the 1983 quotas were fair and should remain in place after Brexit. "We see no rationale in changing the system currently in place, as it provided the basis for the sustainable management of the many shared stocks as well as stability and continuity for both the EU and U.K. industries," said the European Fisheries Alliance, a coalition of continental fishing fleets.[42]

With the Mediterranean Sea overfished, the waters off Britain are the richest fishing ground in Europe and much sought after by the continent's top fishing fleets. Spain has Europe's largest, followed by Britain, France and Italy.[43]

Fishing for Leave, a group of British fishermen who campaigned for Brexit, have denounced the government for agreeing to a transition period in which the old quota system would remain but the U.K. would have no say in formulating the Common Fisheries Policy. "Under this dire deal Britain will re-obey all EU law for the transition period of up to four years," the group said in a statement. "However, we will have no say or veto, meaning Britain will be a gagged EU satellite."[44]

Instead of their country being part of the Common Fisheries Policy, British fishermen want a status similar to that of Norway, which is not a member of the EU but negotiates bilaterally with Brussels—considered the EU's capital—over fishing quotas in the North Sea. Deas says that because the two nations' respective economic zones overlap, the U.K. should be able to enter into trilateral negotiations with Norway and the EU to determine what share of the catch each party is entitled.

The EU says the current arrangements benefit everyone. Michel Barnier, the top EU official in the Brexit negotiations, warned the British fishing industry that their ability to sell their products in Europe would be affected if other European fishermen are denied access to U.K. waters. "The two things are clearly linked," Barnier said.[45]

Daniel Fasquelle, a member of France's parliament, agreed. "You could ask whether it's fair that the city of London gets access to all of Europe," he said. "The U.K. doesn't consume anywhere close to all the fish that's taken in its waters. They need access to our markets."[46]

French President Emmanuel Macron said the U.K. should be required to stay in a customs union with the European Union after the transition unless it grants European fishermen full access to U.K. waters.

"We as 27 [member states] have a clear position on fair competition, on fish, on the subject of the EU's regulatory autonomy, and that forms part of our lines for the future relationship talks," Macron said.[47]

BACKGROUND
Early Fishing Riches

Fish have always been a prime source of food for humans.

For the most part, early fishers worked in coastal waters, where fish were plentiful and relatively easy to catch with spears or a crude net. Aquaculture made an early appearance as well: It began in China around 1500 B.C. and remained relatively unchanged until the Middle Ages. The Chinese bred carp in ponds, while a few centuries later the Romans farmed crustaceans and fish in lagoons. Mussel farming was developed in the 13th century and remained virtually unchanged until the 1960s.[48]

In 1497, the Italian explorer Giovanni Caboto, better known in English as John Cabot, set sail from Bristol, England, in search of a Northwest Passage to Asia. But instead of finding exotic spices, Cabot's expedition stumbled upon waters rich in cod off the coast of what is now Newfoundland. "They declare that the sea there is full of fish that can be taken not only with nets but with fishing-baskets, a stone being placed in the basket to sink it in the water," said Raimondo di Soncino, an Italian in London who spoke with the crew.[49]

Soon after news of Cabot's discovery reached Europe, fishing ships from England, France, Spain and Portugal began arriving off Newfoundland in an area called the Grand Banks and found an abundance of cod. The fish were salted on board and brought to Europe, where they were dried and taken to market.[50] The Grand Banks was one of the first places that attracted fishermen from thousands of miles away who harvested their catch, preserved it and transported it home. The area became the focus of international fishing in the 19th and 20th centuries.

Globally, the size of the catch to a large extent depended on the evolution of fishing technology. In the 15th century, fishing was done in boats called doggers with crews of 10 to 12 who typically fished with rod and line. Larger wooden ships crossed the Atlantic, sending out small boats to catch cod, which were so abundant they could be hauled in by the basket-load. England's development of trawlers with sails, which dragged huge nets and were more efficient than fishing with line, changed the fishing industry globally. The advent of steam engines in the late 19th century allowed fishing boats to venture farther from home and remain at sea longer.[51]

Post-World War II Developments

Ocean fishing began to change radically after World War II, because of advances in fishing technology, including new types of nets and oceangoing freezers, which enabled fishermen to reap greater harvests. Other forms of transport, such as trains and airplanes, made it possible to get fish to market faster.

In the Pacific, Japanese fishermen expanded industrial fishing, sending out more than 100 ships in the waters around Micronesia. Initially, the fishermen used longline gear, which are fishing lines up to 30 miles long with thousands of hooks that are pulled through the ocean and that can indiscriminately snag fish along the way. But in competition with American tuna boats, the Japanese developed so-called purse-seine fishing for tuna—the use of vertical nets that surround large groups of fish and then capture them as the bottom of the nets are tightened, as with a drawstring purse.[52]

In addition, fishermen began deploying technology developed in World War II, such as sonar, which uses sound waves that reflect off of fish and other underwater objects.

International political developments after the war began to change commercial fishing. Since the 17th century, fishermen had roamed the oceans under a doctrine called "freedom of the seas," which limited a nation's maritime jurisdiction to a narrow strip off its coast. Everywhere else in the ocean was fair game for fishers.[53]

But in 1945, President Harry Truman declared that the continental shelf off the U.S. coast was henceforth under American jurisdiction. Truman did not mention fish in his proclamation but instead focused on the seabed where oil was located. Later he issued a separate proclamation to preserve fishing rights.[54]

Truman's extension of U.S. territory prompted other nations to follow suit. In 1947, Chile and Peru claimed the seas extending 200 nautical miles off their coasts, as did Ecuador three years later, in hopes of limiting access by foreign fishing fleets.[55]

Similar concerns led Iceland in 1952 to protect its fishing grounds from the fleets of British fishermen that ventured farther afield as cod stocks near the U.K. declined from overfishing. That year, Iceland made its offshore territory a 4-mile zone, which prompted Britain to ban imports of Icelandic fish. In 1958, Iceland expanded the zone to 12 miles.[56]

Iceland's actions led to the first of three "Cod Wars" between Iceland and Britain. During the first conflict, Iceland's coast guard threatened to open fire on British trawlers when the vessels tried to ram them. The U.K. responded by sending naval ships to protect its fishing fleets. Iceland extended its territorial waters to 50 miles in 1972 and 200 nautical miles in 1975, prompting the

CHRONOLOGY

1400s-1800s *Ships fish far from home waters.*

1497 Italian explorer John Cabot discovers abundant sea life off Newfoundland, Canada.

1500s In wake of Cabot's discovery, England, France, Spain and Portugal send ships across the Atlantic to bring back cod from Canada's Grand Banks.

1609 Dutch jurist Hugo Grotius argues that the sea is international territory, giving rise to a "freedom of the seas" doctrine limiting a nation's ocean rights to three miles offshore.

1800s Grand Banks becomes the world's most heavily fished area.

1920s-1970s *Industrial fishing, in which bigger vessels with high-tech gear travel farther for larger catches, gains momentum.*

1929 Japan, granted control over Micronesia by the League of Nations after World War I, funds a fishing fleet to catch tuna near more than 600 Pacific islands.

1945 To protect U.S. natural resources, President Harry Truman expands the nation's territorial waters to include the continental shelf. Other nations follow suit.

1952 The Japanese government helps finance the construction of a longline tuna fleet—vessels deploying extremely long fishing lines containing hundreds of hooks—to replace fishing vessels destroyed in World War II.

1950s In response to Japanese competition, U.S. vessels using purse-seine nets—vertical "curtains" that surround and capture schools of fish—begin fishing in the Pacific.

1965 South Korea and Taiwan open large-scale tuna fisheries.

1970s Facing stiffer competition from Korea and Taiwan, Japanese fishing companies invent flash-freezing to better preserve catches.

1973 Third United Nations Conference on the Law of the Sea opens in New York to determine jurisdiction of coastal areas and freedom of navigation.

1976 Congress approves a conservation act to govern U.S. fishing grounds and extends U.S. jurisdiction to 200 nautical miles from shore.

1980s-Present *Governments move to restrict fishing.*

1980s European purse-seine fishing boats begin operating in the Indian Ocean, and South American fishing boats move into the eastern Pacific.

1982 The United Nations' landmark Convention on the Law of the Sea, which allows countries to establish exclusive economic zones extending 200 nautical miles from their territorial waters, is signed; the convention takes effect in 1994 after getting the requisite number of signatories.

1992 Canada declares a moratorium on fishing for Grand Banks northern cod after stocks fall to less than 1 percent of previous levels.

2001 A U.N. conservation agreement enters into force, setting out principles for the management of fish stocks.

2005 World Trade Organization opens talks on reducing government subsidies for the fishing industry; the negotiations continue to this day.

2010 U.N. members adopt the Convention on Biological Diversity, pledging the signatories to protect 10 percent of marine areas from overfishing by 2020.

2015 U.N. votes to adopt the 2030 Agenda for Sustainable Development, which includes a provision to prohibit certain forms of fishing subsidies by 2020. . . . Lobster catch in Long Island Sound falls to 30,000 pounds, down from nearly 7 million pounds in 1998. Scientists say warmer waters from climate change cause lobsters to migrate northward to cooler areas.

2017 President Trump withdraws the United States from the Paris Agreement on climate change; scientists say the pact is vital to protecting marine life.

2018 A scientific panel reports that the biomass of bluefin tuna—the total available stock of the species—is only 3 percent of former levels.

2019 U.N. holds talks on whether to ban fishing in parts of the high seas to permit fish stocks to regenerate. . . . The U.K. and European Union (EU) seek to work out fishing rights as the U.K. prepares to withdraw from the EU in October.

second and third Cod Wars, which resulted in a British naval ship and an Icelandic coast guard vessel colliding. Because of Iceland's strategic location—NATO forces were located on the island to monitor Soviet military movements—the alliance intervened to end the conflict. Under an agreement reached in 1976, Iceland allowed 30 British vessels to fish in its waters for six months at a time.[57]

Law of the Sea Convention

The Cod Wars and growing concerns about protecting national interests in coastal seabeds for minerals, oil and other natural resources prompted the United Nations to begin negotiations on a comprehensive treaty covering the law of the sea. It convened a conference in New York City in 1972, and a Convention on the Law of the Sea was adopted after nine years of negotiations at a meeting in Jamaica in December 1982. The agreement, which replaced four treaties from 1958, came into force in 1994 after it received the requisite number of signatories.[58]

For the first time, the Law of the Sea Convention created exclusive economic zones extending 200 nautical miles from territorial waters. The agreement stipulated that adjoining countries, such as the United States and Canada, would share the 200-mile zone. The treaty also included a provision to protect each country's fish resources: "The coastal state shall determine the allowable catch of the living resources in its exclusive economic zone," the convention said.[59]

The United States never ratified the Law of the Sea Convention because of Republican opposition in the Senate. Conservatives said the treaty was an unacceptable encroachment on U.S. sovereignty.[60] Nevertheless, the nation has abided by its terms, according to a State Department spokesman.

Congress was so worried about declining fish stocks along U.S. coasts that in 1976 it passed the Magnuson-Stevens Fishery Conservation and Management Act, named after the bill's sponsors, U.S. Sens. Warren Magnuson, D-Wash., and Ted Stevens, R-Alaska. It took effect on March 1, 1977.[61]

Nearly two decades before the Law of the Sea entered force, the Magnuson-Stevens Act created a 200-nautical-mile "fishery conservation zone" to protect fish from foreign fishers. It also created eight

Regional Fishery Management Councils, composed of federal officials from the National Marine Fisheries Service and local representatives appointed by state governors. The councils are charged with developing fishery management plans based on scientific advice to achieve optimal fishing yields while at the same time conserving stocks.[62]

A number of other countries, including Canada, also did not wait for the ratification of the Law of the Sea Convention to protect their fish stocks. Alarmed at the decline of the Atlantic cod by foreign fishing trawlers, Canada extended its territory 200 nautical miles into the ocean in 1977.

When foreign fishermen were banned from Canadian coastal waters, local fishers were encouraged to take their place, and they developed "rock hopper dredges"—large wheels on the bottom of nets that allowed the fishermen to drag the nets safely on the sea bottom without becoming snagged.[63]

The cod catch in 1968 reached 1.9 million metric tons. By 1992, overfishing had reduced cod stocks to just 1 percent of their former population. The Canadian minister of fisheries and oceans, John C. Crosbie, declared a moratorium on cod fishing, which resulted in 40,000 people in Newfoundland—fishers and fish processing plant workers—losing their jobs.[64] The moratorium remains in effect.

The collapse of the Grand Banks cod fishery led nations to take steps to conserve their fisheries. In 1993, the United Nations began negotiations on an agreement to conserve and manage fish stocks that range over wide areas. A pact was achieved two years later.[65]

This international cooperation resulted in the creation of 17 Regional Fishery Management Organizations that are composed of nations, including the United States, with a common interest in preserving specific species in areas where no single government has control.[66] Six of the organizations deal exclusively with preserving tuna stocks, and the others regulate fishing for a particular species on the high seas.

President Barack Obama vastly enlarged protected areas of the Pacific under U.S. control. In 2014, he expanded the Pacific Remote Islands Marine National Monument to cover 490,000 square miles of the southern Pacific, including three wildlife refuges: Wake Atoll National Wildlife

Ocean Warming Leads to Confusion, Conflict for Fishermen

Shifts in fish populations help some areas while hurting others.

In 2015, fishermen plucked about 30,000 pounds of lobster out of Long Island Sound. A mere 17 years earlier, the catch was 6.9 million pounds—230 times as much.[1]

The decline has been "devastating," Mike Craig, a 57-year-old lobsterman in Long Island, N.Y., said last year. "Here you are making a living, living a lifestyle—and then it's gone."[2]

The primary culprit has been a massive migration of lobsters to colder waters caused by climate change, which has warmed ocean temperatures around Long Island, said Richard A. Wahle, director of the University of Maine's Lobster Institute. Wahle said lobsters might not survive in Long Island Sound beyond 2050.

"The temperatures are excessive during the summers, and if projections for warming hold true, the waters will be increasingly worse for lobsters as decades pass," he said.[3]

Fishing boats sit idle in Taizhou, China, during the country's annual fishing moratorium, which began May 1 and ended Aug. 16. China imposed the ban as a conservation measure in parts of the South China Sea, but critics say China is a major culprit in overfishing.

Oceans have absorbed about 90 percent of the atmosphere's excess heat, and scientists say they are warming even faster than originally thought. The trend is causing many fish and other marine life to migrate to colder waters nearer the poles and making reproduction harder for fish that do not migrate.[4]

Migration also is creating winners and losers among fishermen. In the case of the lobster, Long Island's loss has been Canada's gain. The lobster catch in Nova Scotia increased from 22,000 metric tons in 1990 to almost 50,000 metric tons in 2017, according to Canadian fisheries officials.[5]

Maine lobstermen also have seen big increases in their catches over the past two decades, but now they worry the lobsters are moving even farther north. After reaching a record 60,154 metric tons in 2016, the Maine lobster haul was 54,268 metric tons in 2018, a decline of almost 10 percent.[6]

"Climate change really helped us for the last 20 years," said Dave Cousens, a former president of the Maine Lobstermen's Association. But he said climate change "is going to kill us, in probably the next 30."[7]

Other species also are turning up in new places. Flounder and black sea bass, once plentiful off the North Carolina coast, are more abundant off New Jersey.[8]

Fishermen in Iceland, who caught almost no Atlantic mackerel in 2000, now catch so many that the species is the country's third most valuable fish, bringing in more than $100 million a year. "This mackerel story is maybe one of the most marked ones . . . demonstrating the changes taking place in the fish stock in the North Atlantic in recent years," said Ólafur S. Ástþórsson, a scientist at Reykjavik's Marine and Freshwater Research Institute.[9]

As mackerel catches have increased in Iceland, they have decreased in the waters around Scotland and Ireland, triggering a conflict over fishing quotas among the European Union, Norway, the Faroe Islands and Iceland.[10]

Fishing regulators are beginning to incorporate climate change into their quota policies. In 2014, U.S. officials began using water temperature data to set catch limits for butterfish. But in some cases, implementation lags behind rising seawater temperatures. Fishermen in North Carolina, for example, still have the highest state quota for black sea bass, even though the fishing ground has shifted to New England.[11]

Scientists say warming ocean temperatures pose a particularly severe threat to fishermen close to the equator, including those in tropical regions such as Indonesia and southeast Asia where fishing has been a way of life for thousands of years.[12]

"The tropics are the areas where we expect the overall capacity of the oceans . . . to be reduced the most," says Manuel Barange, director of the Fisheries and Aquaculture Policy and Resources Division of the U.N. Food and Agriculture Organization.

Tropical areas also include many countries where people depend heavily on fish as a source of protein, says Douglas McCauley, an associate professor in the ecology, evolution and marine biology department at the University of California, Santa Barbara. "These are poor nations that are developing and are less food-secure."

Excess carbon dioxide in the atmosphere not only is warming the oceans, it also is making them more acidic, posing a threat to fish that eat plankton to survive, scientists say. Zooplankton need calcium carbonate to build their tiny shells and skeletons, and increasing acidity could make that process more difficult, or could cause plankton's shells and skeletons to dissolve, they say.[13]

"An important element in the marine food web which serves as the first food for many fish larvae is in danger of being lost," *Eurofish Magazine*, a leading European fisheries journal, said in a 2017 article. "Fishes, particularly during earlier development stages, can also be damaged directly by acidification which can, for example, cause tissue damage in cod larvae."[14]

— *Charles P. Wallace*

[1] "Status & Trends: LISS Environmental Indicators," Long Island Sound Study, 2019, https://tinyurl.com/y3tl7gpc.

[2] Craig Schneider, "One man's tale of lobstering 50 years in Long Island Sound—and simply loving it," *Newsday*, July 15, 2018, https://tinyurl.com/y4fzf9rp.

[3] Nishanth Krishnan, "Consider the Lobstermen: Climate Change Threatens Connecticut Lobsters," *The Politic*, Dec. 30, 2018, https://tinyurl.com/y2h9urgc.

[4] Hilary Brueck, "Earth's oceans may be way hotter than scientists realized—here's how worried you should be," *Business Insider*, Nov. 1, 2018, https://tinyurl.com/y3gphsk4; Cheryl Katz, "How Long Can Oceans Continue To Absorb Earth's Excess Heat?" Yale Environment 360, March 30, 2015, https://tinyurl.com/y3vsppan; and Sarah Gibbens, "Climate change is depleting our essential fisheries," *National Geographic*, Feb. 28, 2019, https://tinyurl.com/y5tu58w4.

[5] "1990 Volume of Atlantic & Pacific Coasts Commercial Landings, By Province (metric tonnes, live weight)," Fisheries and Oceans Canada, Oct. 6, 2016, https://tinyurl.com/y43nrxz6; "2017 Atlantic & Pacific Coasts Commercial Landings, By Province (metric tonnes, live weight)," Fisheries and Oceans Canada, Jan. 30, 2019, https://tinyurl.com/yynr3jhn.

[6] "Historical Maine Lobster Landings," Maine.gov, Feb. 19, 2019, https://tinyurl.com/y2qmfult.

[7] Livia Albeck-Ripka, "Climate Change Brought a Lobster Boom. Now It Could Cause a Bust," *The New York Times*, June 21, 2018, https://tinyurl.com/yag49ulp; "Richard A. Wahle," Lobster Institute, University of Maine, undated, https://tinyurl.com/y64bbhvy.

[8] Ken Branson, "Climate Change Pushing Some Fish to Cooler Waters," *Rutgers Today*, Dec. 16, 2014, https://tinyurl.com/yyk4shlm; Ben Goldfarb, "Feeling the Heat: How Fish Are Migrating from Warming Waters," Yale Environment 360, June 15, 2017, https://tinyurl.com/yau99cvm.

[9] Thin Lei Win, "Feature: Iceland reaps riches from warming oceans as fish swim north," Reuters, Sept. 20, 2017, https://tinyurl.com/yy2yqw4f.

[10] Jessica Spijkers and Wiebren J. Boonstra, "Environmental change and social conflict: the northeast Atlantic mackerel dispute," Regional Environmental Change, August 2017, https://tinyurl.com/y2jux4qw.

[11] Goldfarb, *op. cit.*

[12] Alex Kirby, "Climate Change Threatens Fish Living Near the Equator," Climate Central, Feb. 15, 2014, https://tinyurl.com/yypwrm5y.

[13] "Ocean Acidification," Woods Hole Oceanographic Institution, undated, https://tinyurl.com/yxwq652a.

[14] "Climate change threatens fisheries with immense losses," *Eurofish Magazine*, January/February 2017, https://tinyurl.com/y6s3jm4v.

Seafood Contamination Poses Risks, Scientists Say

Mercury, microplastics are among the threats to the food chain.

Toxic chemicals. Microscopic particles of plastic. Garbage from ships and other sources. It's all adrift in the world's oceans, and fish are ingesting it.

To what degree the pollution poses a serious risk to human health is a matter of growing debate among scientists. But many warn that pregnant women and young children, in particular, should limit their consumption of certain types of seafood, especially fish with the highest known levels of toxic chemicals.

Potential problems run the gamut, experts say:

• Heavy metals, namely lead and cadmium, can accumulate in shrimp and lobster, and some Pacific oysters have elevated levels of cadmium.[1]

• Shrimp harvested in Southeast Asian "farms"—where shellfish and fish are cultivated under controlled conditions—often contain antibiotics, according to Larry Olmsted, author of *Real Food, Fake Food*, a book about food safety.[2]

• Microplastics—tiny beads of plastic so small that they pass through most water treatment plants and are carried into the oceans—are entering the marine food chain and pose a threat to human health.[3]

• Methylmercury, an industrial pollutant that becomes airborne and settles in the ocean, also is entering the food chain, according to scientists.[4]

Mercury is among the more potentially significant threats, experts say. "Exposure to mercury—even small amounts—may cause serious health problems, and is a threat to the development of the child in utero and early in life," the World Health Organization (WHO) said in 2017.[5]

In 2004, the U.S. Food and Drug Administration (FDA) said that for most people, the mercury in fish was "not a health concern," but it cautioned that pregnant women and young children should not consume fish because high levels of mercury "may harm an unborn baby or young child's developing nervous system." The FDA issued updated advice in March 2018 that removed the wording about the possible neurological effects of mercury, but the agency still recommended eating types of fish that contain lower mercury levels.[6] The bigger the fish, the higher the level of mercury it is likely to contain because it feeds on smaller fish that also have mercury present.

The FDA's change reflected the debate that is ongoing in the scientific community. For example, a 27-year study by the University of Rochester in New York of populations in such places as the Seychelles, Samoa and Peru, where people consume a lot of fish, said it "has not identified any adverse associations between [methylmercury] exposure from fish consumption and clinical symptoms or signs."[7]

But the WHO said in its 2017 assessment that human fetuses may suffer developmental defects resulting from a mother's consumption of fish, particularly in poorer nations where fishing is a way of life. Among certain subsistence fishing populations, between 1.5 and 17 per 1,000 children "showed cognitive impairment caused by the consumption of fish containing mercury," the WHO said. "These

Refuge, Johnston Atoll National Wildlife Refuge and Jarvis Island National Wildlife Refuge.[67] Two years later he expanded the Papahānaumokuākea Marine National Monument to encompass 582,578 square miles, the largest marine reserve in the world.[68] The moves angered commercial fishermen, who said the monuments severely hurt their livelihoods.

To clamp down on what is known as illegal, unreported and unregulated fishing, the U.N. in 2016 adopted the Agreement on Port State Measures, which is aimed at preventing fishing vessels engaged in illegal fishing activities from landing their catch. The treaty requires fishers to ask permission to dock and to tell the port the details of their fishing operations.[69]

included populations in Brazil, Canada, China, Colombia and Greenland."[8]

The Environmental Defense Fund, an advocacy group based in New York City, said the species of most concern to consumers are bluefin tuna, walleye, king mackerel and marlin, which contain the highest mercury levels.[9]

But debates about seafood's safety have not affected Americans' appetite for fish. Per capita consumption of fish and other seafood in 2017 was 16 pounds, up 1.1 pounds from the previous year. U.S. commercial fishermen caught 4.5 million metric tons of fish valued at $5.4 billion in 2017, an increase of $110 million, or 2 percent, from the previous year. In addition, the United States imported $38.4 billion worth of fish.[10]

Recently, scientists and environmentalists have raised alarms about the huge amount of plastic being ingested by fish and marine mammals, including whales. One study found that up to 8 million metric tons of plastic pollute the ocean each year.[11]

Research is beginning to focus on microplastics, which are used in cosmetics, cleaners and toothpaste.[12]

"Microplastics are likely the most numerically abundant items of plastic debris in the ocean today, and quantities will inevitably increase, in part because large, single plastic items ultimately degrade into millions of microplastic pieces," said marine scientists Karen Lavender Law and Richard Thompson in the journal *Science*.[13]

Concern over microplastics in the oceans is so great that in December 2015, President Barack Obama signed the Microbead-Free Waters Act, banning plastic microbeads in cosmetics and personal care products.[14]

The Marine Debris Program at the National Oceanic and Atmospheric Administration is supporting several research projects exploring the impact of microplastics on seafood in American Samoa, black sea bass in North Carolina and oysters in the Long Island Sound.[15]

"We still are just beginning to learn the impacts of the widespread use of plastic on human health, but early indications are certainly troubling," said John Hocevar, oceans campaign director for Greenpeace USA. "In the environment, plastic has become a problem throughout the food chain."[16]

— *Charles P. Wallace*

[1] Markham Heid, "Is Shellfish Healthy? Here's What the Experts Say," *Time*, July 18, 2018, https://tinyurl.com/y549rlpe.

[2] *Ibid.*

[3] Jane Fullerton Lemons, "Plastic Pollution," *CQ Researcher*, Dec. 7, 2018, https://tinyurl.com/yy6upmja.

[4] "How Does Mercury Get Into Fish?" *Scientific American*, https://tinyurl.com/zgu4bog.

[5] "Mercury and Health," World Health Organization, March 31, 2017, https://tinyurl.com/y9ppgyf6.

[6] "What You Need to Know About Mercury in Fish and Shellfish," U.S. Food and Drug Administration, March 2004, https://tinyurl.com/y6f3n8qo; "Eating Fish: What Pregnant Women and Parents Should Know," U.S. Food and Drug Administration, March 27, 2018, https://tinyurl.com/yyxebegh.

[7] G.J. Myers *et al.*, "Twenty-seven years studying the human neurotoxicity of methylmercury exposure," *Environmental Research*, December 1999, https://tinyurl.com/y2aro2kk.

[8] "Mercury and Health," *op. cit.*

[9] "PCBs in fish and shellfish," Environmental Defense Fund, https://tinyurl.com/yd9skwlo.

[10] "Fisheries of the United States, 2017 Report," National Oceanic and Atmospheric Administration, Dec. 12, 2018, https://tinyurl.com/y5e8sjy6.

[11] John Schwartz, "Study Finds Rising Levels of Plastics in Oceans," *The New York Times*, Feb. 12, 2015, https://tinyurl.com/y27y74rp.

[12] "What are microplastics?" National Oceanic and Atmospheric Administration, June 25, 2018, https://tinyurl.com/y8za6na8.

[13] Steve Connor, "Microplastic waste: This massive (tiny) threat to sea life is now in every ocean," *The Independent*, July 14, 2014, https://tinyurl.com/y5uhgfqq.

[14] "Statement by the Press Secretary on H.R. 1321, S. 2425," The White House, Dec. 28, 2015, https://tinyurl.com/y6lwk3qt.

[15] "Research," Marine Debris Program, National Oceanic and Atmospheric Administration, https://tinyurl.com/yahnan7y.

[16] Lemons, *op. cit.*

Climate Change's Growing Impact

In addition to being concerned about overfishing, marine scientists in the final decades of the 20th century became increasingly worried about climate change's effects on the world's oceans and their marine life. Studies found that carbon dioxide released into the atmosphere since the dawn of the industrial age in the 19th century was leading to both warming and acidification of the oceans.[70]

Since 1970, global surface temperatures in the oceans have warmed about 1.8 degrees Celsius, the largest increase since recordings began in 1880. One result is that fish stocks have diminished in warm waters and spawning grounds have been damaged. In addition, carbon dioxide absorbed into the ocean has caused a reduction in pH levels, which decreases coral growth and causes bleaching, threatening their viability.[71]

"Ocean warming is driving changes in ocean circulation and stratification, losses in oxygen concentration, and shifts in primary productivity," said a research paper by Rutgers scientist Free. "As a result, marine fish populations are experiencing large-scale redistributions, increased physiological stress, and altered food availability."[72]

In 2015, a U.N. conference negotiated the Paris Agreement on climate change. The agreement set a goal of limiting global temperature increases to below 2 degrees Celsius above pre-industrial levels, while pursuing efforts to limit the increase to 1.5 degrees. Some 185 parties have ratified the agreement, including the United States.[73]

But on June 1, 2017, President Trump announced that the United States would "cease all implementation of the nonbinding Paris Accord and the draconian financial and economic burdens the agreement imposes on our country." Under the pact's rules, the U.S. withdrawal will become effective in November 2020. Experts say a Democratic administration could reverse Trump's decision if the Republicans lose the 2020 election.[74]

The Trump administration also hoped to increase U.S. seafood exports. It declared a National Ocean Month in June 2017, declaring: "We must recognize the importance of our offshore areas to our security and economic independence, all while protecting the marine environment for present and future generations." Trump urged development of the nation's fishery resources to help reduce what he called the nation's $13 billion seafood trade deficit.[75]

CURRENT SITUATION
Fishing Moratoriums

Global efforts to protect and replenish fish stocks in the seas continue, experts say. Recent major initiatives include:

- A moratorium on all fishing in the Arctic for the next 16 years while scientists assess the effects of climate change there. Nine nations—the United States, Russia, Canada, Norway, Denmark, Iceland, Japan, South Korea and China—as well as the European Union agreed to the moratorium.[76]

- A moratorium on shrimp harvesting in a large area known as the Flemish Cap in the North Atlantic, says Dayna Bell MacCallum, a scientific information administrator at the Northwest Atlantic Fisheries Organization, a group of 12 nations that includes the United States, Canada, Russia and the EU.

- A three-month ban on the use of so-called fish aggregating devices (FADs) in Asia. These devices are platforms, typically made of bamboo, that fishing fleets leave in the ocean. Similar to piers, the FADs attract small fish, which then attract larger fish that feed on the smaller fish. Fishers monitor the FADs by satellite and return when sufficient numbers of large fish have gathered. The Western and Central Fisheries Commission, an organization established to preserve tuna and other migratory fish, imposed the ban after it determined that tuna stocks in the Pacific had fallen to one-third of their pre-industrial-fishing levels.[77]

- A fishing ban imposed by China in areas it controls in the South China Sea from May 1 until Aug. 16. The ban has been a yearly fixture since 1999.[78]

Greg Poling, director of the Asia Maritime Transparency Initiative at the Center for Strategic and International Studies, a centrist think tank in Washington, said fish stocks in the South China Sea, which accounts for about 12 percent of the global fish catch, "are on the verge of collapse."[79]

Overfishing in China's coastal waters has prompted the government to trim the size of the country's fishing fleet, the world's largest, by about 3 percent, according to China National Radio. Agriculture minister Han Changfu told the radio network that fishing in the world's oceans must proceed under tighter regulations and supervision. Nations should gradually get "rid of the outdated ways of production that are destructive to the environment," Han said.[80]

But skeptics note that China's practices contribute to overfishing. It provides the largest financial subsidy to its fishing fleet of any country. Its construction of islands atop coral reefs in the South China Sea for military installations has destroyed thousands of acres of the reefs, according to scientists. And its territorial claims in the strategic South China Sea are spurring an intense contest with rival Asian nations to capture the most fish in the area—a contest that is devastating fish stocks, Poling said.[81]

Aquaculture's Rise

While international attention is focused on protecting fishing grounds, aquaculture is continuing to grow. The Food and Agriculture Organization said aquaculture produced 80 million metric tons of fish in 2017, nearly as much as the 81.2 million metric tons caught in the wild. Thirty-seven countries now harvest more fish from aquaculture than from wild catches.[82]

About half of aquaculture takes place in freshwater ponds and lakes, with the remainder in saltwater, says the U.N.'s Barange. Yields include clams and mussels, as well as farmed fish like salmon.

"Aquaculture has been an incredible success in the world over the last five, six decades to a level that completely surprised me over the last 10 years," Barange says. "It has been the fastest-growing food production system in the world in the last 50 years."

Lobsterman Tom Tomkiewcz leaps from his boat in Fairhaven, Mass., in November 2017. Maine has seen record lobster catches in recent years as climate change warms ocean waters, causing lobsters to migrate north from Long Island Sound.

Trump Administration

The Trump administration's trade war with China is affecting U.S. fishermen, according to economists. China doubled tariffs on live U.S. seafood last year in retaliation for U.S. levies on Chinese imports. The Chinese tariffs have hurt exports of Maine lobsters and other seafood, economists said.[83]

To help the industry thrive and reverse what Trump calls a large seafood trade deficit, the administration is considering easing fishing restrictions in U.S. coastal waters and marine monuments.

"There's some potential that some of the constraints we had on fresh catch here maybe need to be relaxed a little bit," said Commerce Secretary Wilbur Ross, who oversees the National Oceanic and Atmospheric Administration (NOAA), which sets fishing quotas. "I think it's easy to be a little bit overzealous and therefore hold down the production of fish."[84]

In July, NOAA's acting administrator, Rear Adm. Timothy Gallaudet, suggested opening the country's 13 national marine sanctuaries and marine national monuments covering 600,000 square miles of ocean and lakes to commercial fishermen as part of an effort to produce more U.S. seafood.[85]

Marine biologists and NOAA scientists say U.S. conservation efforts since the Magnuson-Stevens Conservation Act went into effect in 1977 have achieved great success.

"As of 2017, 91 percent of the stocks that we've done stock assessments for are not subject to overfishing, so we see that as a real plus, and 85 percent of the stocks are not overfished," says Jenni Wallace, deputy director of the NOAA's Office of Sustainable Fisheries. "We feel like we've made really good progress in implementing the law and creating sustainable fisheries."

A recent success is the rejuvenation of the haddock population on the Georges Bank, between Cape Cod and Canada. Although the haddock had been severely overfished, the implementation of quotas and other restrictions caused the "spawning stock biomass," a key measure of a species health, to increase fivefold since 2009 to a level greater than recorded in the 1930s, according to NOAA.[86]

Experts say a recent U.S. conservation innovation called "the catch-share" program also is helping. To head off ruinous competitions to catch the most fish, the program reserves a share of fish to individual fishermen or cooperatives in 16 areas of the country.[87]

Rhode Island's Brown says the catch-share system allows him to catch his quota whenever it is convenient to do so, rather than racing against other fishermen to catch as many fish as possible in a short period of time. "The past system was terrible," Brown says. "With the

Should the high seas be closed to fishing?

YES   Crow White
Assistant Professor, Center for Coastal Marine Sciences, California Polytechnic State University

Written for *CQ Researcher*, May 2019

Protecting the high seas is a long overdue conservation measure. Doing so also could generate higher fishery yields and profits. Because access to the high seas is unrestricted, current governance encourages exploitation by nations racing against each other to harvest fish stocks. This behavior erodes long-term yields and profits, and leads to the tragedy-of-the-commons scenario we are experiencing, in which individual countries acting in their own interest collectively deplete shared stocks.

Closing the high seas to fishing could solve this problem. Furthermore, building up stocks of protected fish in the high seas would boost stocks of migratory fish such as tuna in adjacent territorial waters, where catch regulations are better enforced and fishermen have fewer incentives to overfish. That, in turn, could increase yields and profits for fisheries that target these migratory species.

Thus, closing the high seas could better support both conservation and sustainable fishery goals. Of course, there are many details to work out, such as accounting for the uneven spillover of migratory fish from the high seas into territorial waters and the similarly uneven distribution of gains to each maritime nation.

Other issues include providing landlocked nations with access to ocean fishing, eliminating massive government subsidies that high seas fisheries depend on and managing nonmigratory species that would become inaccessible in the high seas under a complete closure.

But facing and overcoming these challenges is worth it, given the current disgraceful state we are in and the benefits that could be attained by changing international policy.

It is worth noting that a United Nations decision to negotiate closing only a small- or medium-sized proportion of the high seas could exacerbate the current problem by intensifying overfishing in those areas that remain open.

Maintaining a tragedy of the commons in even just part of the high seas could have broad negative global effects. For migratory stocks, it could eliminate the benefits of conserving fish in closed areas. Reduced buildup of stocks in those areas would in turn diminish the spillover into territorial waters, limiting yields and profits there.

To avoid this outcome, the United Nations needs to push hard for closing a substantial proportion—if not all—of the high seas. In any international waters left open to fishing, regulations and incentives need to be developed to prevent a tragedy of the commons.

NO   Eric Kingma
Executive Director, Hawaii Longline Association

Written for *CQ Researcher*, May 2019

The emerging United Nations convention on conserving biological diversity on the high seas is highly concerning to responsibly managed fishing fleets. A major component of the new convention is establishing protected areas, which likely means closing those areas to fishing.

The Hawaiian longline fishery, which targets highly migratory tuna and billfish, is sustainably managed, highly monitored and comprehensively regulated. However, due to a combination of factors, the fleet fishes mostly in international waters adjacent to the Hawaii archipelago. In fact, only 17 percent of U.S. territorial waters around the archipelago are open to the 145-vessel fleet, which catches fish primarily for local consumption and the U.S. mainland.

President Barack Obama's expansion of the Pacific Remote Islands and Papahānaumokuākea marine national monuments in 2014 and 2016, respectively, closed important fishing grounds to the Hawaiian fleet, which already was subject to much lower bigeye tuna quotas than foreign fleets. Hawaiian longline vessels now must compete on the high seas with foreign vessels flagged to China, Taiwan, South Korea and Japan. They also face unfair price competition with imports from countries that often provide significant subsidies for fuel, labor and fish transportation.

Closing the high seas to fishing under the U.N. convention, on top of the restrictions that came with Obama's monument expansions, would leave the Hawaiian fleet with few areas to fish. This is a recipe for disaster, as the Hawaiian longline fishery is the largest producer of food in the state.

Environmental organizations that support new restrictions on high seas fishing cite the need to protect the oceans from pollution and overfishing. While such concerns may be relevant in some parts of the world, well-managed and intensely monitored fisheries targeting highly migratory species should be exempt from the new U.N. convention.

Indeed, international fisheries that target tuna already are subject to substantial international management through regional fisheries management groups. And there is little to no empirical evidence that establishing protected areas for highly migratory species such as tuna and billfish helps conserve those species. In fact, such policies can shift fishing pressure to areas with higher levels of endangered species.

The U.N. negotiations should focus on problem areas—such as fishing activities that cause environmental damage—and should stay away from fisheries that target highly migratory fish and are already subject to comprehensive international and domestic management.

catch-share program, you're not acting in a counterproductive way."

Europe's record of protecting fish species is more mixed than that of the United States, according to experts. One study concluded that species in Europe's protected areas fared worse than those in its unprotected areas because, as one analysis explained, "bottom-trawling fishing fleets are more likely to target those areas, like hungry diners scooping up the most sumptuous offerings at an all-you-can-eat buffet."[88]

Although the Europe Union imposes fishing quotas, a recent analysis of the catch limits set by Brussels in December 2018 found that they could lead to overfishing. The reason, according to the Pew Charitable Trusts, is that the limits are too generous and "continue to exceed scientific advice and permit overfishing."[89]

"It was one of the big iconic policy failures of the EU that the commission themselves recognized that they were failing to get to grips with overfishing," says Pew's Andrew Clayton, project director for ending overfishing in northwestern Europe. "This was primarily because of the way decisions are made. It's highly politicized," adding that fishing communities in many EU states have powerful political influence in Brussels.

International experts, meanwhile, are monitoring the size of the tuna catch, which an industry newsletter called *Fish 2.0* put at $10 billion annually, or about 8 percent of the overall seafood trade.[90] The annual supply, at 4.6 million metric tons in 2013, is growing by 100,000 metric tons a year.

Skipjack tuna makes up 58 percent of the annual catch and is used mostly for canned tuna. Experts say bluefin tuna, despite representing just 1 percent of the catch, is the most threatened tuna: A study found that the bluefin species is now at just 3 percent of earlier levels.[91]

Changing tastes might be affecting the tuna catch. According to a study of consumer tastes by the Forum Fisheries Agency, a grouping of Pacific fishing nations, 80 percent of tuna for the sashimi market is sold to Japan, with the U.S. second at about 8 percent. Sashimi is thinly sliced raw fish that the Japanese consider a delicacy.[92]

But the study noted that consumption of sashimi in Japan peaked in 2002 at 650,000 metric tons and declined to about 308,000 metric tons seven years later.

The decline was ascribed to Japan's economic crisis, with more people eating cheaper cuts of tuna at home than expensive bluefin in restaurants, as well as to concern about radioactivity from fish after a tsunami hit the Fukushima nuclear power plant in 2011.

OUTLOOK
Inflection Point

With record overfishing, the commercial fishing industry is at an inflection point, according to scientists. On one hand, if the problem continues at its current rate, many species of fish that the world depends on for nutrition might disappear. Alternatively, if sound management programs are put in place, fish stocks could regenerate and provide sufficient food for many generations.

According to the United Nations, the world population, now around 7.6 billion, is expected to reach 9.8 billion in 2050 and 11.2 billion in 2100. But the U.N.'s Food and Agricultural Organization also expects global fish production to expand, from 171 metric tons to 201 million metric tons by 2030, an increase of 18 percent.[93]

Pauly, of the University of British Columbia who heads a research initiative called the Sea Around Us, predicts that the current industrial methods for commercial fishing could lead to what he terms "Aquacalypse Now."

"The truth is that governments are the only entities that can prevent the end of fish," Pauly wrote. "There is no need for an end to fish, or to fishing for that matter. But there is an urgent need for governments to free themselves from the fishing-industrial complex and its Ponzi scheme, to stop subsidizing the fishing-industrial complex and awarding it fishing rights, when it should in fact pay for the privilege to fish. If we can do this, then we will have fish forever."[94] By Ponzi scheme, Pauly meant taking fish now without concern for raising the next generation of fish.

Other experts are more optimistic than Pauly. Callum Roberts, a marine conservation biologist in the department of environment and geography at the University of York in Britain, says high-tech fishing gear has helped commercial fleets find and catch more fish than ever before. At the same time, Roberts says, satellite monitoring of fishing vessels' transponders, which is being done by a Google-affiliated organization called Global Fishing

Watch, is giving scientists a much clearer picture of commercial fishing and its effects.

"We now have much more nuanced sense of what people are doing, what they're catching, how much it's worth, how much they're getting subsidized by their governments to go out and use the high seas," Roberts says. "Taking all this information together, we can come up with a much better view of how to protect the high seas and their wildlife."

Despite the great stresses marine species are under, some fish are thriving and making a comeback, says McCauley of UC Santa Barbara. He says careful management has brought back the so-called groundfish—fish that live on or near the ocean floor—on the U.S. West Coast, including rock fish and red snapper.

"There are some good examples of how resilient stocks can be if you actually use information, data and technology to help make smart management decisions," says McCauley. "The problem in some less wealthy places, you're getting all the technology to harvest more, but you're not actually using the data to help manage [catches]."

Experts agree the biggest long-term threat to fish is climate change. With the discharge of carbon into the atmosphere, not only are the oceans getting warmer, but they also are becoming more acidic and contain less oxygen, damaging stocks of fish.

Many marine scientists believe the best option is to implement the Paris climate accord.[95]

Free, of Rutgers University, says nations must begin to reduce carbon emissions because of the damage they are doing to the ocean and its marine life. But he adds that protecting the environment and fishing grounds go hand in hand.

"Well-managed fisheries have been more resilient to climate change," Free says, because good management helps marine spawning grounds, enabling fish to survive. "So actions to prevent overfishing and to rebuild overfished populations are really important for making ocean fisheries more resilient to climate change."

NOTES

1. " 'Fish are vanishing'—Senegal's devastated coastline," BBC, Nov. 1, 2018, https://tinyurl.com/ydat-w8cj; Meaghan Beatley and Sam Edwards, "Overfished: In Senegal, empty nets lead to hunger and violence," *Medium*, May 30, 2018, https://tinyurl.com/y4o4qz6n.

2. Emma Farge, "Eight Chinese vessels detained off West Africa for illegal fishing," Reuters, May 3, 2017, https://tinyurl.com/y3joqp7y; Lily Kuo, "A glimpse of life onboard the Chinese fishing boats dominating West Africa's seas," *Quartz Africa*, Nov. 23, 2016, https://tinyurl.com/y6abosm4.

3. Kieron Monks, "The great fish robbery that costs Africa billions," CNN, Jan. 2, 2018, https://tinyurl.com/y22jeqe4.

4. J.-P. Gattuso *et al.*, "Contrasting futures for ocean and society from different anthropogenic CO2 emissions scenarios," *Science*, July 3, 2015, https://tinyurl.com/y2sp8x55.

5. *Ibid.*

6. "Relative effects of fisheries support policies," policy brief, Organisation for Economic Co-operation and Development, February 2019, https://tinyurl.com/y38kmtz5; Douglas McCauley *et al.*, "Wealthy Countries Dominate Industrial Fishing," *Science Advances*, Aug. 1, 2018, https://tinyurl.com/y27exvjw.

7. Nick Aspinwall, "The high seas danger to workers in Taiwan's fishing fleet," *The Interpreter*, Lowy Institute, 2019, https://tinyurl.com/y5nk44px; David Brewster, "Chinese fishing fleet a security issue for Australia," *The Interpreter*, Lowy Institute, Nov. 7, 2018, https://tinyurl.com/ybwst7d3.

8. "The State of World Fisheries and Aquaculture 2018," Food and Agriculture Organization, 2018, https://tinyurl.com/y3yu42wy.

9. *Ibid.*; "State of World Fisheries and Aquaculture 2018 Released," press release, Sustainable Fisheries, July 10, 2018, https://tinyurl.com/yybja9vo; Christopher Bodeen, "Recent developments surrounding the South China Sea," *The Washington Post*, May 20, 2019, https://tinyurl.com/y3sces8c; and "Overfishing Leaves Much of Mediterranean a Dead Sea, Study Finds," *National Geographic*, March 2, 2012, https://tinyurl.com/y4sqyy85.

10. Amanda Nickson, "Pacific Bluefin Tuna Stock Remains Highly Depleted, New Science Shows,"

Pew Charitable Trusts, May 21, 2018, https://tinyurl.com/yysexps9; "An investigation report into China's marine trash fish fisheries," Greenpeace, https://tinyurl.com/y36kyjg8.

11 "United Nations Convention on the Law of the Sea," United Nations, 1994, https://tinyurl.com/yxqrpysu.

12 "Illegal fishing," *World Ocean Review*, 2013, https://tinyurl.com/y4nxegj5.

13. "Delegates Discuss Creating Mechanism for Storing, Exchanging Information, as Intergovernmental Negotiations on New High Seas Treaty Continues," U.N. Media Center, April 4, 2019, https://tinyurl.com/y5lmwgoh.

14. "Global marine protected area target of 10% to be achieved by 2020," U.N. Environment Program, June 5, 2017, https://tinyurl.com/yyjld3zu.

15. Alex Fox, "First ever high-seas conservation treaty would protect life in international waters," *Science*, April 3, 2019, https://tinyurl.com/y684v4cg.

16. "New Bedford, MA," NOAA Fisheries, https://tinyurl.com/y5ujovhb.

17. Goldfarb, *op. cit.*; Gattuso *et al.*, *op. cit.*

18. Darryl Fears, "One million species face extinction, U.N. report says. And humans will suffer as a result," *The Washington Post*, May 6, 2019, https://tinyurl.com/y3y7zyro.

19. Christopher Free *et al.*, "Impacts of historical warming on marine fisheries production," *Science*, March 1, 2019, https://tinyurl.com/y5zogco6.

20. "Delegates Discuss Creating Mechanism for Storing, Exchanging Information, as Intergovernmental Negotiations on New High Seas Treaty Continues," *op. cit.*

21. Enric Sala *et al.*, "The economics of fishing the high seas," *Science Advances*, June 6, 2018, https://tinyurl.com/y2wo9wgm; William Gallo, "Why Hasn't the US Signed the Law of the Sea Treaty?" Voice of America, June 6, 2016, https://tinyurl.com/y25rj398.

22. Garrett Hardin, "The Tragedy of the Commons," *Science*, Dec. 13, 1968, https://tinyurl.com/y6jt56w8.

23. Sala *et al.*, *op. cit.*

24. Fox, *op. cit.*

25. "30x30: A Blueprint for Ocean Protection," Greenpeace International, April 4, 2019, https://tinyurl.com/y5bu4jpb.

26. "Introduction to fisheries subsidies in the WTO," World Trade Organization, 2018, https://tinyurl.com/y2qdgcem.

27. Sala *et al.*, *op. cit.*

28. "Study on the subsidies to the fisheries, aquaculture and marketing and processing subsectors in major fishing nations beyond the EU," European Commission, 2011, https://tinyurl.com/y2qf8o6o.

29. Anne Schroeer *et al.*, "The European Union and Fishing Subsidies," Oceana, September 2011, https://tinyurl.com/yxtnvyc9.

30. Sarah Harper *et al.*, "Fuelling the fisheries subsidy debate: Agreements, loopholes and implications," *Fisheries Research*, 2012, https://tinyurl.com/yyzgzjs5.

31. Roger Martini and James Innes, "Relative Effects of Fisheries Support Policies," Organisation for Economic Co-operation and Development, 2018, https://tinyurl.com/yysnt2f7.

32. "Sustainable Development Goals," U.N. Department of Public Information, accessed April 30, 2019, https://tinyurl.com/ph4ntgn; "Goal 14: Conserve and sustainably use the oceans, seas and marine resources," United Nations, accessed April 29, 2019, https://tinyurl.com/yd4p6oor.

33. Todd Woody, "Go Fish: International Talks to Ban Harmful Fishery Subsidies Collapse," *Oceans Deeply*, Dec. 17, 2017, https://tinyurl.com/y75twhq3.

34. "Proposed disciplines on prohibitions and special and differential treatment for fisheries subsidies," World Trade Organization, July 12, 2017, https://tinyurl.com/y5e6unk7.

35. "A cap-based approach to addressing certain fisheries subsidies," World Trade Organization, March 22, 2019, https://tinyurl.com/yyryvczf.

36. "The Queen's Speech 2017," U.K. Government Publishing Service, June 21, 2017, https://tinyurl.com/yxlpm25u.

37. Jessica Elgot, "What are the key dates between now and the new Brexit deadline?" *The Guardian*, April 12, 2019, https://tinyurl.com/y3gytgb5; "Brexit and Ireland," European Commission, March 5, 2019, https://tinyurl.com/y2qf52rs; and Karla Adam and William Booth, "Theresa May to resign, make way for new prime minister, after Brexit failures," *The Washington Post*, May 24, 2019, https://tinyurl.com/yxbtxgtk.

38. Gregory Viscusi, "European fishermen brace for Brexit," Bloomberg, Feb. 6, 2019, https://tinyurl.com/y9rnydss; "UK Sea Fisheries Statistics 2011," U.K. National Archives, 2011, https://tinyurl.com/y2byu3z8.

39. "Q&A: Mackerel Wars Explained," BBC, Jan. 14, 2011, https://tinyurl.com/y47ouy25.

40. "Council Regulation (EEC) No 170/83," Official Journal of the European Commission, Jan. 27, 1983, https://tinyurl.com/y6tfoc7c; "Each their fair share: quotas distribution," European Fisheries Alliance, 2017, https://tinyurl.com/yykk86qo.

41. Dan Roberts, "Britain's fishing fleet and Brexit promises—key questions answered," *The Guardian*, March 23, 2018, https://tinyurl.com/ycr36hj3.

42. "Each their fair share: quotas distribution," *op. cit.*

43. "Overfishing Leaves Much of Mediterranean a Dead Sea, Study Finds," *op. cit.*; "Spain: largest fishing fleet capacity in the EU in 2016," Eurostat, 2016, https://tinyurl.com/yxlqvxah.

44. "Why the withdrawal agreement is disastrous for British fishing and why fishermen must join the march to leave," Fishing for Leave, March 23, 2019, https://tinyurl.com/yy9o8kte.

45. Jenny Hjul, "Barnier urged to get tough with UK on fish," *Fish Farmer*, March 6, 2018, https://tinyurl.com/y26opnl4.

46. Viscusi, *op. cit.*

47. Daniel Boffey and Jennifer Rankin, "UK will stay in customs union without fishing deal, says Macron," *The Guardian*, Nov. 25, 2018, https://tinyurl.com/yczdtlcz.

48. "The history of aquaculture," Alimentarium, https://tinyurl.com/y24kqwps.

49. Heather Pringle, "Cabot, Cod and the Colonists," *Canadian Geographic*, July/August 1997, https://tinyurl.com/y3tusb84.

50. Shannon Ryan, "History of Newfoundland Cod fishery," Memorial University of Newfoundland, March 26, 1990, https://tinyurl.com/y4lozmks.

51. John C. Sainsbury *et al.*, "Commercial Fishing," Encyclopedia Britannica, March 25, 2019, https://tinyurl.com/yyjlwxvy.

52. Robert Gillett, "A short history of industrial fishing in the Pacific Islands," Asia-Pacific Fishery Commission, 2007, https://tinyurl.com/y23xanzh; "Long line fishing," Fishcount.org.uk, https://tinyurl.com/y5uc4w8e; and "Purse Seine," Marine Stewardship Council, accessed April 7, 2019, https://tinyurl.com/y3bpz6ax.

53. "The United Nations Convention on the Law of the Sea (A historical perspective)," U.N. Division for Oceans Affairs and the Law of the Sea, 2012, https://tinyurl.com/yxmg53m5.

54. "Truman Proclamation on the Seabed," University of Oregon, September 1945, https://tinyurl.com/y43y6xsv.

55. "The United Nations Convention on the Law of the Sea (A historical perspective)," *op. cit.*

56. Andy Forse, Ben Drakeford and Jonathan Potts, "Fish Fights: Britain has a long history of trading away access to coastal waters," *The Conversation*, March 26, 2019, https://tinyurl.com/y24ex7jr.

57. *Ibid.*

58. "United Nations Convention on the Law of the Sea," *op. cit.*

59. *Ibid.*

60. Thomas Wright, "Outlaw of the Sea: the Senate Republicans' UNCLOS Blunder," Brookings Institution, Aug. 7, 2012, https://tinyurl.com/y2wrtw87.

61. "Public Law 94-265," U.S. Government Publishing Office, April 13, 1976, https://tinyurl.com/y5pvohmd.

62. "Conserving and managing the Fisheries of the United States," U.S. Regional Fisheries Management Councils, 2019, https://tinyurl.com/88t6xp6.

63. Orrin H. Pilkey and Linda Pilkey-Jarvis, *Useless Arithmetic: Why Environmental Scientists Can't Predict the Future* (2009).

64. "Crosbie Announces First steps in Northern Cod Recovery Plan," press release, Government of Canada, July 2, 1992, https://tinyurl.com/y2evnzyg; A. Holly Dolan *et al.*, "Restructuring and Health in Canadian Coastal Communities," *EcoHealth*, 2005, https://tinyurl.com/y63msdxy.

65. "United Nations Conference on Straddling Fish Stocks and Highly Migratory Fish Stocks," U.N. Division for Ocean Affairs and the Law of the Sea, 2012, https://tinyurl.com/yy2j7ltq.

66. "FAQ: What is a Regional Fishery Management Organization?" Pew Charitable Trusts, Feb. 23, 2012, https://tinyurl.com/y27ffjql.

67. "Refuge Association Praises Expansion of Pacific Remote Islands Marine National Monument," National Wildlife Refuge Association, Sept. 25, 2014, https://tinyurl.com/y5fdn953.

68. "About Papahānaumokuākea," Papahānaumokuākea Marine National Monument, https://tinyurl.com/yxbfxnox.

69. "Agreement on Port State Measures to Prevent, Deter and Eliminate Illegal, Unreported and Unregulated Fishing," Food and Agriculture Organization, Feb. 21, 2019, https://tinyurl.com/y2aswh88.

70. Gattuso *et al.*, *op. cit.*

71. Goldfarb, *op. cit.*; "Climate Change A Major Threat to Coral Reefs," National Ocean Service, July 11, 2018, https://tinyurl.com/yas28qod.

72. Free *et al.*, *op. cit.*

73. "What is the Paris Agreement?" United Nations, October 2018, https://tinyurl.com/yd4d3j7x; "Paris Agreement—Status of Ratification," United Nations, https://tinyurl.com/yblunp23.

74. "Statement by President Trump on the Paris Climate Accord," The White House, June 1, 2017, https://tinyurl.com/yazkrs3d.

75. "President Donald J. Trump Proclaims June 2017 as National Ocean Month," The White House, May 31, 2017, https://tinyurl.com/y3whx9gs.

76. Fiona Harvey, "Commercial fishing banned across much of the Arctic," *The Guardian*, Oct. 3, 2018, https://tinyurl.com/ydd34xh9.

77. Kevin McQuillan, "Bans on tuna fishing devices in the Pacific to continue," Business Advantage PNG, Feb. 4, 2019, https://tinyurl.com/y6evyouv.

78. "Annual fishing ban begins in South China Sea," Fish and Information Services, https://tinyurl.com/y4juhp46.

79. Bodeen, *op. cit.*

80. Stephen Chen, "China pledges to cut size of its massive fishing fleet due to serious threat to nation's fish stocks," *South China Morning Post*, Aug. 15, 2016, https://tinyurl.com/y8afmxh3.

81. "Study on the subsidies to the fisheries, aquaculture and marketing and processing subsectors in major fishing nations beyond the EU," *op. cit.*

82. "The State of World Fisheries and Aquaculture 2018," *op. cit.*

83. Ana Radelat, "China trade war threatens CT companies," *CT Post*, May 13, 2019, https://tinyurl.com/y3tgaer6; Willy Blackmore, "Consider the Lobster Tariffs," *The Nation*, Nov. 5, 2018, https://tinyurl.com/yct2l29g.

84. Steve Bittenbender, "US Commerce Secretary Wilbur Ross questions safety of seafood imports," *Seafood Source*, March 22, 2018, https://tinyurl.com/y7hsakkh.

85. Chris D'Angelo, "Ocean Agency Suggests Opening Marine Monuments To Commercial Fishing," *HuffPost*, July 5, 2018, https://tinyurl.com/y3mryedp.

86. Liz Brooks, "Georges Bank haddock," Groundfish Operational Assessments 2017, National Oceanic and Atmospheric Administration, https://tinyurl.com/y5nd86g2.

87. "Catch Shares," NOAA Fisheries, April 17, 2019, https://tinyurl.com/yxlz6drk.

88. Ivan Semeniuk, "Protected waters exploited by industrial fishing even more than unprotected areas, scientists find," *The Globe and Mail*, Dec. 20, 2018, https://tinyurl.com/y43r8aps.

89. "Analysis of Fisheries Council agreement on fishing opportunities in the north-east Atlantic for 2019,"

Pew Charitable Trusts, March 14, 2019, https://tinyurl.com/y5g9brfm.

90. "Fish 2.0 Market Report: Tuna An Investor Update on Sustainable Seafood," Fish20.org, April 20, 2015, https://tinyurl.com/y34lslvt.

91. Nickson, *op. cit.*

92. Amanda Hamilton *et al.*, "Market and Industry Dynamics in the Global Tuna Supply Chain," Forum Fisheries Agency, June 2011, https://tinyurl.com/pvtk9sb.

93. "World population projected to reach 9.8 billion in 2050, and 11.2 billion in 2100—says UN," U.N. Department of Public Information, June 21, 2017, https://tinyurl.com/y3etkoxf; "Is the planet approaching 'peak fish'? Not so fast, study says," U.N. Food and Agriculture Organization, July 9, 2018, https://tinyurl.com/y3nxwax5.

94. Dave Cohen, "Aquacalypse—The End Of Fish," *Decline of the Empire* blog, Sept. 1, 2013, https://tinyurl.com/y56kk3b8.

95. William W.L. Cheung, Gabriel Reygondeau and Thomas L. Frölicher, "Large benefits to marine fisheries of meeting the 1.5°C global warming target," *Science*, Dec. 23, 2016, https://tinyurl.com/y5jjzb3u.

BIBLIOGRAPHY

Books

Greenberg, Paul, *Four Fish: The Future of the Last Wild Food*, Penguin Press, 2010.
A seafood expert argues for the sustainable farming of tuna, salmon, bass and cod to feed a growing world population.

Hilborn, Ray, and Ulrike Hilborn, *Overfishing: What Everyone Needs to Know*, Oxford University Press, 2012.
A marine biologist and his writer wife examine overfishing, including how scientists estimate sustainable yields and whether depleted fish stocks can recover.

Petrossian, Gohar A., *The Last Fish Swimming: The Global Crime of Illegal Fishing*, Praeger, 2019.
An assistant professor of criminal justice at the City University of New York who specializes in the environment details the global and local factors that facilitate illegal fishing.

Articles

Dillon, Tom, "How Fishing Subsidies Hurt the Ocean—and Us, Too," Pew Charitable Trusts, April 4, 2019, https://tinyurl.com/y6c43m9p.
The head of environmental issues at a Philadelphia research organization explains how government subsidies contribute to overfishing.

Leape, Jim, "We have the tools to tackle illegal fishing. It's time to use them," World Economic Forum, June 18, 2019, https://tinyurl.com/y3sxplqa.
A noted marine scientist says the technology exists to track down and prevent illegal fishing everywhere in the world.

Leschin-Hoar, Clare, "Seafood Without The Sea: Will Lab-Grown Fish Hook Consumers?" NPR, May 5, 2019, https://tinyurl.com/y58h594y.
A startup in San Diego is growing seafood in a lab to help meet demand for fish that cannot be easily farmed.

Monks, Kieron, "The great fish robbery that costs Africa billions," CNN, Jan. 2, 2018, https://tinyurl.com/y22jeqe4.
A journalist describes how foreign fishing fleets are exploiting Africa's coastal waters, causing local fishing economies to collapse.

Rahadiana, Rieka, "Indonesia Sinks 13 Vietnamese Boats in War on Illegal Fishing," Bloomberg, May 5, 2019, https://tinyurl.com/y579vqnc.
Indonesia is sinking foreign vessels as part of a campaign to end illegal fishing in the world's largest archipelago.

Viscusi, Gregory, "European fishermen brace for Brexit," Bloomberg, Feb. 7, 2019, https://tinyurl.com/y9rnydss.
A reporter looks at how Britain's decision to leave the European Union (EU) will affect fishermen in the United Kingdom and Europe.

Reports and Studies

"Netting Billions: A Global Valuation of Tuna," Pew Charitable Trusts, May 2, 2016, https://tinyurl.com/y6fjwze9.
A Philadelphia research group gives a comprehensive review of tuna stocks around the world and the pressures they face from overfishing.

"The State of World Fisheries and Aquaculture," U.N. Food and Agriculture Organization, 2018, https://tinyurl.com/y3kmuswa.
This annual study from a U.N. agency provides in-depth statistics on overfishing and global fish consumption.

"Status of Stocks 2017," National Oceanic and Atmospheric Administration, May 14, 2018, https://tinyurl.com/y2ojzub9.
A U.S. government agency says the number of domestic fish stocks identified as overfished was at an all-time low at the end of 2017.

McCauley, Douglas J., *et al.*, "Wealthy countries dominate industrial fishing," *Science*, Aug. 1, 2018, https://tinyurl.com/y5m2ojbu.
Researchers at the University of California, Santa Barbara, say wealthy countries account for the vast majority of industrial fishing on the high seas and in the national waters of lower-income countries.

Sumaila, U. Rashid, *et al.*, "Benefits of the Paris Agreement to ocean life, economies, and people," *Science*, Feb. 27, 2019, https://tinyurl.com/y3smbby5.
Researchers at the University of British Columbia say implementing the Paris Agreement on Climate Change would protect millions of metric tons of annual fish catches and billions of dollars in annual fishing revenue.

White, Crow, and Christopher Costello, "Close the High Seas to Fishing?" *PLOS Biology*, March 25, 2014, https://tinyurl.com/yxd2pxqf.
Two marine biologists say closing the high seas to fishing would allow endangered species to regenerate and increase fish populations in territorial areas where countries claim exclusive fishing rights.

Videos

Adams, Paul, "Is China's Fishing Fleet Taking All of West Africa's Fish?" BBC, March 26, 2019, https://tinyurl.com/y3msjzxn.
A journalist gives a detailed look at the destructive impact of foreign fishing off Africa's west coast.

THE NEXT STEP

At-Risk Species

Heaver, Stuart, "Tilapia, a fish to feed the world, and the deadly virus that may destroy it," *South China Morning Post*, May 6, 2019, https://tinyurl.com/y5bsznk8.
The second most widely farmed fish in the world, tilapia, is popular because it is cheap to grow and was disease resistant, but it is now susceptible to a virus with an extremely high morbidity rate.

Neslen, Arthur, "Plans to expand Iceland's fish farms risk decimating wild salmon populations," *The Guardian*, April 19, 2019, https://tinyurl.com/y5rgco2r.
Proposed legislation to open more fish farms in Iceland would create massive pollution and risk harming that country's wild salmon population, scientists say.

Solly, Meilan, "Ocean-Dwelling Species Are Disappearing Twice as Quickly as Land Animals," *Smithsonian*, April 25, 2019, https://tinyurl.com/yy4mu673.
Several marine species, including many types of fish, are far more at risk from climate change than land animals, with some coral reef dwellers already disappearing, according to a recently published study in the journal *Nature*.

Climate Change

Arnold, Carrie, "Shipwrecks may help tropical fish adapt to climate change," *National Geographic*, May 10, 2019, https://tinyurl.com/y5b36eoa.
Reefs of artificial detritus such as sunken ships could provide refuge for tropical fish as waters warm in coming years, according to a study by two marine ecologists.

Loctier, Denis, "New risks and opportunities for fishing industry with climate change," Euronews, May 10, 2019, https://tinyurl.com/y6mvoloh.
Researchers studying the effects of climate change at fishing sites across Europe have found that warming temperatures are forcing fish to migrate north.

McGrath, Kaitlyn, "Warming Oceans Changing the Game for Connecticut Fishermen," NBC Connecticut, May 9, 2019, https://tinyurl.com/y3so4zgc.
Waters off the U.S. northeastern coast have been warming faster than in the rest of the world, diminishing fish and lobster populations.

Fishing Bans

"Pulse fishing ban off East Anglian coast extended," BBC, Feb. 3, 2019, https://tinyurl.com/ya6gk5bt.

Dutch fishermen, who use electrical pulses to stun and catch fish, agreed not to use the technique off the Suffolk coast of the United Kingdom.

"Super trawlers threaten Australian fisheries, conservationists warn," Australian Associated Press, *The Guardian*, May 6, 2019, https://tinyurl.com/yyysevas.

Marine experts are urging the Australian government to extend its ban on supersized industrial fishing trawlers to cover more than six of the 76 types in operation worldwide.

Inveen, Cooper, "Sierra Leone's fishing ban to replenish stocks yields little," Reuters, April 26, 2019, https://tinyurl.com/yxtg5r8k.

Sierra Leone's ban on industrial fishing was too short to replenish fish stocks, environmental groups say, and they worry that Chinese and South Korean trawlers will continue to overfish in the region.

Technology

"Calysta and Thai Union Offer World First Taste of Commercial Shrimp Fed FeedKind Protein," *Business Wire*, The Associated Press, May 8, 2019, https://tinyurl.com/y4j8b3ws.

A major seafood producer has begun using a protein produced from natural gas to feed its shrimp in an effort to increase production without putting extra pressure on environmental resources.

Cimons, Marlene, "Meet the 'Oyster Wench'—a single mom fighting pollution with the power of clams and kelp," *Popular Science*, May 14, 2019, https://tinyurl.com/yygr6z6v.

To help oceans and their marine life, a Rhode Island woman is trying "3D farming" in which seaweed and shellfish are grown in underwater vertical columns.

Kaufman, Rachel, "How Scientists Are Using Real-Time Data to Help Fishermen Avoid Bycatch," *Smithsonian*, April 12, 2019, https://tinyurl.com/y2hqethx.

Scientists are using satellite data to locate schools of fish and follow their movements; the information helps trawlers find the best fishing grounds and avoid catching other species.

For More Information

Division for Ocean Affairs and the Law of the Sea, Office of Legal Affairs, United Nations, 2 United Nations Plaza, New York, NY 10017; 212-963-6430; www.un.org/Depts/los/index.htm. U.N. agency responsible for applying the provisions of the U.N. Convention on the Law of the Sea, which governs how individual countries use the world's oceans.

European Fisheries Control Agency, Edificio Odriozola, Avenida García Barbón 4, E–36201, Vigo, Spain; 34 986 12 06 10; www.efca.europa.eu/en. European Union (EU) agency that assists member countries in implementing EU fishing policies.

Fisheries Directorate, National Oceanic and Atmospheric Administration, 1315 East-West Highway, 14th Floor, Silver Spring, MD 20910; 301-427-8000; www.fisheries.noaa.gov. U.S. government agency that collects statistics on fishing and monitors fish stocks to help set catch quotas.

Fisheries and Oceans Canada, 200 Kent St., Ottawa, ON K1A 0E6; 613-993-0999; www.dfo-mpo.gc.ca/index-eng.htm. Canadian government agency that maintains statistics on fishing in Canadian waters.

Pew Charitable Trusts, One Commerce Square, 2005 Market St., Suite 2800, Philadelphia, PA 19103-7077; 215-575-9050; www.pewtrusts.org. Research organization that conducts studies and recommends policy changes in ocean conservation, illegal fishing and overfishing.

Sea Around Us, Global Fisheries Cluster, University of British Columbia, 2202 Main Mall, Vancouver, BC V6T 1Z4; 604-822-2731; www.seaaroundus.org. Canadian research initiative that assesses how fisheries affect marine ecosystems.

World Trade Organization, Centre William Rappard, Rue de Lausanne, 154, Case Postale, 1211, Genève 2, Switzerland; +41 (0)22 739 51 11; www.wto.org. Global agency responsible for establishing and enforcing trade agreements; it currently is debating capping fishing subsidies.

16

Extreme Weather

Will global warming produce more disasters?

By Stephen Ornes

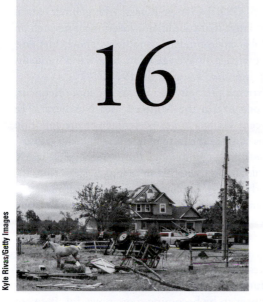

Kyle Rivas/Getty Images

Farm equipment and debris lie scattered near a damaged home after a tornado passed through Linwood, Kan., on May 29, 2019. The month of May brought one of the most active streaks of tornado activity in U.S. history.

From *CQ Researcher,*
September 20, 2019

At first, people living on Ocracoke Island in North Carolina thought they had been spared the worst of Hurricane Dorian's fury.

"We were all on social media laughing about how we'd done well and there was really no flooding at all, just rain, typical rain," recalled Steve Harris, one of hundreds of people who defied orders to evacuate Ocracoke as Dorian approached on Sept. 6.[1]

The sense of relief was short-lived. A storm surge from the hurricane sent what Harris described as a "wall of water" cascading down local roads as people scrambled to get into their attics. "I've been through every storm," said Ocracoke resident Dan Garrish, 66. "I've never seen water come in like this."[2]

The hurricane, which flattened communities in the Bahamas as a Category 5 storm on its way to the U.S. East Coast, was just one example of the extreme weather the country and much of the world have experienced this year.

New national records for total rainfall in a 12-month period in the United States have been set three times since Jan. 1, with torrential downpours causing massive flooding along the Missouri River and ruining crops. Record cold hit the Midwest in January. A 13-day period in May brought one of the most active streaks of tornado activity in the country's history, with at least eight twisters per day. Worldwide, July was the hottest month on record. The temperature in Paris reached 108.7 degrees Fahrenheit on July 25, and Germany, Belgium and the Netherlands also broke heat records.[3]

Scientists are increasingly convinced that some extreme weather events are becoming more frequent and more intense as a result of global warming caused by greenhouse gas emissions.

"Scientists have long predicted we would eventually reach a point where human-caused climate change altered Earth's system to such a degree that we would begin to see weather and climate events that would not have been possible without human contributions," said Stephanie Herring, a climate scientist with the Center for Weather and Climate at the National Oceanic and Atmospheric Administration (NOAA).[4]

Outside the scientific community, arguments that extreme weather events are tied to carbon emissions are politically divisive, with many conservatives and other skeptics disputing any connection. They say Democrats and environmentalists are using worst-case theories about extreme weather to feed alarmism over climate change and that, in any case, communities will adapt to whatever weather-related changes the country experiences.

Recent extreme weather events also have heightened the debate about whether the federal government should continue subsidizing the post-disaster rebuilding of homes and businesses in areas particularly vulnerable to weather-related disasters, such as coastal flooding. Repeated rebuilding in disaster-prone regions wastes taxpayer dollars and puts lives at risk, say critics of the subsidy programs. They note that, as of July 9, the United States had experienced six extreme weather-related events this year (two floods and four severe storms) with losses exceeding $1 billion each. Hurricane Dorian is certain to bring the number to seven.[5]

Supporters of the subsidies counter that many people living in areas affected by extreme weather cannot afford to leave, and that damaged communities can rebuild in ways that protect them from disastrous damage in future events. "You can't just pick up people and say, 'You have to go somewhere else,'" former New Orleans Mayor Mitch Landrieu said. "The world doesn't work that way."[6]

Scientists define extreme weather events as those that fall into the most unusual 10 percent of a particular region's meteorological history, often causing extensive damage or deaths. They include unusually severe heat waves, droughts, tornadoes, wildfires, flooding, blizzards, freezes and hurricanes.[7]

Such events have occurred throughout history and can result from natural variability in the weather. But scientists say some trends are becoming more apparent:

- Heat waves are happening more often. The average heat wave season across 50 major U.S. cities is 47 days longer than in the 1960s, according to the U.S. Global Change Research Program, a federal initiative that coordinates government research on global environmental conditions. Those cities now experience an average of six heat waves annually, up from two a year in the 1960s.[8]
- Extreme precipitation events are more frequent, especially in the Midwest and Northeast. "In recent years, a larger percentage of precipitation has come in the form of intense single-day events," the U.S. Environmental Protection Agency said.[9]
- Wildfires in California are getting bigger. "Since the early 1970s, California's annual wildfire extent increased fivefold, punctuated by extremely large and destructive wildfires in 2017 and 2018," university researchers said in a study published in July. Scientists say rising temperatures are drying out soil, leaving trees and vegetation parched and primed to fuel fires.[10]
- Hurricanes are not occurring more often, but they appear to be becoming more powerful. Between 1988 and 2017, the average power of major hurricanes around the world, as measured by wind speed and duration, increased 41 percent compared to the previous 30-year period, according to an Associated Press analysis. "There's no question that the storms are stronger than they were 30 years ago," said James Kossin, an atmospheric research scientist at NOAA.[11]

Hurricanes also are moving more slowly than they used to because climate change is decreasing the speed of winds high in the atmosphere that propel the storms along, researchers say. They cite Hurricane Dorian, which remained parked over the Bahamas for 40 hours this past Labor Day weekend. "This is yet another example of the kind of slow-moving tropical systems that we expect to see more often as a response to climate change," Jennifer Francis, a scientist with the Woods Hole Research Center in Falmouth, Mass., said of Dorian.[12]

Slower hurricanes produce more rain. Hurricane Harvey, which slammed Texas as a Category 4 storm in 2017, dropped more than 60 inches of rain on an area northeast of Houston, breaking the U.S. total storm rainfall record of 52 inches set in 1950.[13]

As extreme weather events become more frequent, long-term trends show they also are becoming deadlier and more costly, experts say. The 14 most destructive weather and climate disasters in the United States in 2018 killed at least 247 people and cost the government an estimated $91 billion. The toll in 2017 was even worse, with 16 billion-dollar disasters that killed 362 and caused a record-setting $306 billion in damage.[14]

"We know that the costs of extreme events are rising," says Noah Diffenbaugh, a climate scientist at Stanford University.

As recently as 15 years ago, scientists were reluctant to link specific extreme weather events to climate change, but advances in computer modeling and data collection have made it possible to measure that connection. Researchers who are part of a new scientific field called climate attribution now feel comfortable saying global warming increases the likelihood and severity of certain events—such as heat waves, thunderstorms and coastal flooding from rising sea levels. Higher temperatures, they say, are melting glaciers and putting more moisture into the air through evaporation, which increases rainfall.[15]

Even periods of bitter cold, such as the record low temperatures parts of the United States experienced in January, are tied to global warming, climate experts say. They say climate change is destabilizing an area of atmospheric low pressure over the Arctic known as the polar vortex and bringing cold air southward. Overall, however, scientists say such freezes are becoming less common with climate change.[16]

Linking climate change to some weather events is complicated and uncertain, scientists acknowledge. Data on tornadoes, for example, does not go back far enough for researchers to detect clear patterns in frequency and severity. But tornadoes do appear to be more clustered than in the past, with outbreaks of multiple twisters occurring more often, and they seem to be forming more often in unexpected locations, researchers say.[17]

Climate experts warn that global warming caused primarily by the burning of fossil fuels will lead to an increase in extreme weather events around the world. In the United States, the Northeast and Midwest will

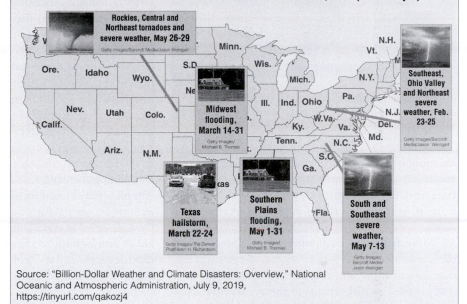

Billion-Dollar Disasters on the Rise

Six of the weather-related disasters the United States experienced during the first half of 2019 each caused damages exceeding $1 billion. Hurricane Dorian is expected to be this year's seventh billion-dollar disaster. The average annual number of such disasters between 2016 and 2018 was more than double the long-term average. Government scientists attribute that to increased development in vulnerable areas, which heightens damage costs, and to climate change.

Billion-Dollar U.S. Weather and Climate Disasters, 2019 (as of July 9)

Source: "Billion-Dollar Weather and Climate Disasters: Overview," National Oceanic and Atmospheric Administration, July 9, 2019, https://tinyurl.com/qakozj4

Parisians try to cool off in a fountain near the Eiffel Tower during a July 2019 heat wave in which the temperature hit a record-setting 108.7 degrees Fahrenheit.

see more heat waves and heavy downpours, while the Southeast and Northwest will experience more wildfires and insect outbreaks threatening crops and human health, according to the Global Change Research Program.[18]

"More frequent and intense extreme weather and climate-related events . . . are expected to continue to damage infrastructure, ecosystems, and social systems that provide essential benefits to communities," the program said in its "Fourth National Climate Assessment" released last year.[19]

Climate change skeptics, including President Trump, dismiss such concerns, arguing that weather patterns fluctuate constantly due to factors unrelated to greenhouse gas emissions. They say activists use the term "extreme weather" to stoke fear about climate change as part of a political agenda. "It used to be called global warming. That wasn't working," the president said in a June interview on a British television program. "Then it was called climate change. Now it's actually called extreme weather because with extreme weather you can't miss."[20]

Politics largely determines how individual Americans view extreme weather in context with climate change, surveys show. "Partisan affiliation . . . powerfully shapes individual perceptions of extreme weather events," said Wanyun Shao, an assistant professor of geography at the University of Alabama. "Where Democrats perceive rising air temperatures and an increasing number of hurricanes, droughts and floods, Republicans are less

likely to agree that climate conditions are changing or that extreme weather is increasing."[21]

Extreme weather affects Americans from all socioeconomic and ethnic backgrounds, but research shows it can be particularly devastating for low-income and minority Americans. A 2013 study by researchers at the University of California, Berkeley, found that blacks were 52 percent more likely than whites to live in the hottest parts of U.S. cities, with the least tree cover. And a 2018 study by sociology professors at the University of Pittsburgh and Rice University in Houston found that, because of how disaster aid is distributed, black victims of extreme weather events tend to lose wealth after a disaster while white victims tend to gain wealth. The researchers cited evidence from prior studies showing that blacks had lower access to government aid and were more likely to experience housing and income losses due to an extreme weather event.[22]

Building standards also are improving in areas repeatedly hit by severe weather. Since 2008, when an insurance industry research group created a set of construction standards designed to make homes hurricane-proof, the number of homes built to those standards in "a handful of hurricane-prone states" has increased from 1,122 to more than 12,500, according to *Insurance Journal*, an online industry publication.[23]

As climatologists, policymakers and researchers weigh the significance of recent trends in extreme weather, here are some of the questions they are asking:

Will extreme weather events become more frequent?

Climate experts have warned for decades that unless greenhouse gas emissions fall drastically, certain extreme weather events—especially heat waves, droughts and torrential downpours—will increase around the world. Such events will occur more frequently, they say, even if countries meet their commitments under the 2015 Paris Agreement on climate change.

"Many areas are still likely to experience substantial increases in the probability of unprecedented [weather] events," researchers at Stanford University, Columbia University and Washington State University said in a study published in February 2018.[24]

North America, Europe and East Asia, for example, should expect to see more "record-setting hot, wet, and/

or dry events," the study said. A special report issued in October 2018 by the Intergovernmental Panel on Climate Change (IPCC), a United Nations group that assesses the science related to global warming, reached similar conclusions.[25]

Officials in California say extreme weather caused by climate change is taking an increasing toll there, noting that the state's six worst wildfire years since 1950 (in total acres burned) have all occurred since 2006.[26]

"There's no debate about whether climate change is or isn't impacting extremes," says climate scientist Stephanie Herring at NOAA's Center for Weather and Climate.

But the difficulties involved in separating natural climate cycles from aberrant weather patterns have led climate change skeptics to challenge the consensus view that severe weather will happen more often as the planet warms.

"Researchers from many different subject areas study extreme events," university researchers said in one 2018 study. "However . . . researchers from different backgrounds may use very different words to communicate about these events and different ways of deciding what makes an extreme event 'extreme.'"[27]

Some political conservatives say there is little or no evidence that severe weather will get more frequent. They cite language in the IPCC's fifth report, finalized in 2014, noting a lack of "robust trends" in the annual number of tropical storms and hurricanes over the past 100 years in the North Atlantic. The IPCC also said last year it had only "medium confidence" that a temperature increase of 1.5 degrees Celsius (2.7 degrees Fahrenheit) would bring more intense, more frequent droughts.[28]

"Overall, we are not seeing more floods, droughts, tornadoes or hurricanes in spite of the steady rise in the small amount of carbon dioxide, and in spite of the mild warming of the planet," said David W. Kreutzer, an economist and former senior research fellow at the Heritage Foundation, a conservative think tank in Washington, "The data show that there is no significant upward trend in any of these weather events."[29]

Even within the climate science community, a small minority of experts say the computer models that the vast majority of climatologists use to predict future extreme weather trends grossly exaggerate the amount of global warming and, by extension, the likelihood of future extreme weather events.

"Climate models are overwhelming the system," says John Christy, a climate scientist at the University of Alabama in Huntsville who also serves as the state's climatologist. "They are not trustworthy in determining what is going to happen in the future."

The vast majority of climate experts defend the computer models as scientifically sound, but they acknowledge that the models have limitations. "For some event types, we have a much higher degree of confidence in our understanding of how those events are changing than for other types," Herring says.

The Paris Agreement's top goal is to limit increases in the average global surface temperature to "well below" 2 degrees Celsius (3.6 degrees Fahrenheit) above levels predating the start of the Industrial Revolution in the late 1700s, and to "strive for" an increase of no more than 1.5 degrees Celsius. Already, the Earth has warmed by 1 degree Celsius (1.8 degrees Fahrenheit) since the 1800s.[30]

Many experts doubt that the 1.5 degree Celsius goal is achievable. "Stabilizing global warming at 1.5C will be extremely difficult if not impossible at this point," said Michael Mann, a climatologist who runs the Earth System Science Center at Pennsylvania State University.[31]

The Washington Post reported on Sept. 11 that its analysis of temperature data from around the world shows that many locations already have warmed by at least 2 degrees Celsius over the past century.[32]

Many climate scientists expect the world to warm by at least 3 degrees Celsius over pre-industrial levels by 2100. That would increase the risk of extreme hot, wet and dry events between threefold and fivefold in much of the world, according to the February 2018 study report by university researchers.[33]

Predictions regarding trends in extreme weather vary depending on the type of event. NOAA predicts "more frequent and intense droughts," as well as increases in flooding events. It also says future hurricanes will likely dump more rainfall than they do now, and it has "medium confidence" that hurricanes will become more intense, with higher wind speeds.[34]

Dorian, for example, was the strongest storm ever to hit the Bahamas and one of the most powerful to occur in the Atlantic, with sustained winds of 185 mph when it made landfall in the Abaco Islands on Sept. 1.[35]

Predicting future tornado activity is more difficult, scientists say, due to a lack of reliable, long-term historical data. Recent research has found that, although the number of tornadoes each year has remained relatively constant, tornado patterns are shifting, with more in the Midwest and Southeast and fewer in portions of the central and southern Great Plains that are traditionally considered part of Tornado Alley. Researchers could not explain the reasons for the shift.[36]

"Both tornado reports and tornado environments indicate an increasing trend in portions of Mississippi, Alabama, Arkansas, Missouri, Illinois, Indiana, Tennessee and Kentucky," the National Weather Service says on its website.[37]

Will extreme weather events become more destructive?

Last year was remarkable for weather-related havoc around the world. Wildfires killed more than 80 people in Greece. A heat wave killed 65 in a single week in Japan, which also experienced record rainfall and flooding. Extreme heat was blamed for up to 70 deaths in Quebec in July.[38]

In the United States, 14 weather-related disasters, each of which did at least $1 billion in damage, killed 247 people and cost about $91 billion. Those disasters included two devastating Atlantic hurricanes—Florence and Michael—and California wildfires that burned 1.8 million acres. One wildfire alone, the Camp Fire, killed at least 85 people and destroyed an entire town. The country fared even worse in 2017, with 16 billion-dollar disasters—including floods, hurricanes, droughts and wildfires—that killed more than 300 people and cost $306 billion.[39]

The long-term trend in billion-dollar disasters is especially alarming, experts say. The annual average number of such disasters in 2016, 2017 and 2018 was more than double the long-term average, according to NOAA.[40]

"The number of billion-dollar weather disasters has been increasing, and the total cost associated with those disasters has been increasing," says Diffenbaugh at Stanford University.

But experts disagree about the role that climate change plays in the rising cost of extreme weather events—in both damage to infrastructure and loss of life—and about the best ways to respond. Most scientists say there is clear evidence that climate change caused by greenhouse gas emissions from cars, power plants and other sources is creating hotter, dryer conditions that have made heat waves more intense, expanded the acreage burned in wildfires and increased the amount of rainfall from hurricanes.[41]

"Climate change is adding to what's going on naturally, and it's that extra stress that causes things to break," said Kevin Trenberth, a scientist at the National Center for Atmospheric Research in Boulder, Colo. "It takes the experience well outside anything that's been experienced before. . . . As a result, things break, people die, and things burn."[42]

Other experts say that a variety of other factors unrelated to climate change influence the potential impact of severe weather. They note, for example, that an increasing number of people live in areas vulnerable to hurricanes, flooding and wildfires. Forty percent of the nation's population lives on a coast, and one in 12 homes in California is at high risk from wildfires.[43]

In addition, building codes in many locations have not been updated to require that homes and other structures withstand a severe weather event. A 2018 report by

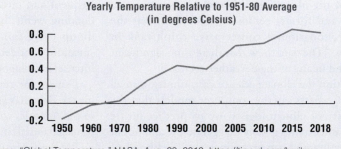

Global Temperatures Heating Up

The global average surface temperature last year was 0.82 degrees Celsius (1.5 degrees Fahrenheit) higher than the 1951-80 average, according to data from NASA. Eighteen of the 19 warmest years have occurred since 2001, with 1998 being the 19th. The warmest year on record was 2016.

Yearly Temperature Relative to 1951-80 Average (in degrees Celsius)

Source: "Global Temperature," NASA, Aug. 28, 2019, https://tinyurl.com/hsrjbmr

the Insurance Institute for Business & Home Safety, an organization in South Carolina and Florida that works to minimize insurance losses from severe weather, cited a "concerning lack of progress in the adoption and enforcement of updated residential building code systems" in some coastal states.[44]

Climate change skeptics say some global warming studies make wild predictions about the destructiveness of future weather-related disasters as a way to justify proposals such as a tax on carbon emissions or the Green New Deal proposed by progressive Democrats in Congress that would require dramatic actions by the federal government and the private sector to reduce carbon emissions.[45]

"Investing in . . . preparation for extreme weather events can be worthwhile," said Nicolas Loris, an economist and research fellow at the Heritage Foundation. "However, the combination of fearmongering and offering solutions that would require a takeover of the global economy are unrealistic and counterproductive."[46]

Jeff Berardelli, a meteorologist and extreme-weather expert in New York City, said warmer ocean water caused by climate change clearly is fueling stronger storms, which he cited as the reason Dorian was the fifth Category 5 storm to form in the Atlantic over the past four years.[47]

"The more heat that there is in the ocean, especially near the surface of the ocean, the stronger these systems tend to get," he said.[48]

Public opinion on connections between climate change and the destructive power of extreme weather events can depend largely on personal experience. Studies show that people who have lived through an event are more likely to believe that climate change played a role. That is especially true when extreme weather severely damages whole communities, according to a study published in May by researchers at Duke University and the University of Colorado, Denver.[49]

"How our community or neighborhood fares—the damages it suffers—may have a stronger and more lasting effect on our climate beliefs than individual impacts do," said Elizabeth A. Albright, assistant professor of the practice of environmental science and policy methods at Duke's Nicholas School of the Environment. "We found that damage at the zip code level . . . was positively associated with stronger climate change beliefs even three or four years after the extreme flooding event our study examined."[50]

At the same time, however, people who experienced extreme temperatures repeatedly over an extended period—generally between two and eight years—came to view it as normal, according to a study published in February by government and academic researchers.

"The definition of 'normal weather' shifts rapidly over time in a changing climate," the researchers said. And people who no longer consider extreme weather to be unusual may also be less likely to consider climate change a pressing issue, they said.[51]

Should government subsidize rebuilding in vulnerable areas?

After Hurricane Harvey left one-third of Houston underwater in 2017, a familiar pattern played out. Area residents whose home or business had flooded filed a claim with the National Flood Insurance Program (NFIP), waited for their checks to arrive, then financed repairs with the money. The program eventually paid out about $9 billion on more than 90,000 Harvey-related claims.[52]

Many of the homes in the storm's path had flooded multiple times before. An investigation by the *Houston Chronicle* found that Houston is home to seven of 10 homes throughout the country that experience substantial flooding most frequently. One home in Kingwood, Texas, has received more than $2.5 million in flood insurance payouts on 22 claims since 1979, the investigation found.[53]

Wildfire victims also can count on government help. In the wake of California's devastating 2018 wildfire season, the Federal Emergency Management Agency (FEMA) and the Small Business Administration (SBA) approved grants and loans totaling $500 million to help victims rebuild, including in areas at high risk for future wildfires. And new homes continue to go up in those same areas. University researchers predicted in 2014 that an estimated 1 million new homes will be built in fire-prone zones in California by 2050.[54]

With scientists predicting that climate change will make weather-related calamities more frequent and more intense, many disaster management experts say it makes no sense for taxpayers to continue absorbing the cost of letting homeowners rebuild in vulnerable areas.

"If you want to rebuild in an area where there's a good chance your home is going to burn down again, go for it," said Ian Adams, a policy analyst at the R Street

Institute, a free-market think tank in Washington. "But I don't want to be subsidizing you."[55]

Many environmentalists say planning efforts should focus on discouraging people from moving into disaster-prone areas and either building new homes or buying those of people already there. This allows the vacated property to be turned into parks or, in the case of areas prone to flooding, wetlands.[56]

"We can begin by shifting development away from areas that are or will soon be subject to frequent flooding," the Environmental Defense Fund, an advocacy group in Washington, says on its website. "Immediately after a flood event is a good time to make this shift with property buyouts, but before the next flood is even better."[57]

Many people living or working in disaster-prone areas, however, have developed strong personal or financial ties to their communities and cannot imagine moving. Robert and Janice Jucker, owners of Three Brothers Bakery in Houston, have seen their business flood at least five times since 2001, including after Hurricane Harvey. They rebuilt using SBA loan money and said last year they had no plans to move. "We've become really good at disasters," Robert Jucker said. "How do we survive without our customers? We can't."[58]

Policymakers, moreover, often are reluctant to tell individual homeowners they cannot rebuild in areas susceptible to a weather-related disaster.

"One could make the argument that people were not meant to live in those environments," said Susan Gorin, a member of the Board of Supervisors in Sonoma County, Calif. But, she added, "it is very difficult for governments or anyone to tell another person, another property owner, that they could not, should not, rebuild."[59]

Joseph T. Edmiston, executive director of the Santa Monica Mountains Conservancy, which works to protect open space and wildlife in Southern California, disagrees. He has suggested that people whose houses have been destroyed twice by wildfire should be ineligible to receive additional federal rebuilding money. "I think two strikes is enough and they ought to be bought out," he said.[60]

Some disaster experts see buyouts in flood-prone areas as a way to minimize further losses for the National Flood Insurance Program, which is $20.5 billion in debt. "Rebuilding out of harm's way can help avoid future devastation in a way that flood insurance cannot," said David Maurstad, who heads the program as FEMA's deputy associate administrator for insurance and mitigation.[61]

But critics say buyout programs can leave communities pockmarked with blighted properties and are hampered by delays and other problems. In flood-prone areas, such programs "are extremely expensive, extremely disruptive, and many of the attempts have not gone well," said former FEMA Administrator Craig Fugate.[62]

Over the past 30 years, federal and local government officials have spent more than $5 billion buying vulnerable properties across the country from homeowners who volunteer to sell, according to an Associated Press analysis of data from FEMA and the Department of Housing and Urban Development. In most cases, local and state governments take over ownership of the properties.[63]

Other options aimed at minimizing repeated rebuilding in disaster-prone areas include charging people fees to build homes in those areas, and using federal money to buy land before people move there to maintain it as open space.[64]

"It's a wicked dilemma, for sure," Donald Falk, fire specialist with the University of Arizona's School of Natural Resources and the Environment, said of the debate over whether to continue subsidizing rebuilding in disaster-prone areas. "We at least like to think that we take care of people who have been exposed to disaster. Does that compassion lead us to simply do the same dance over and over again?"[65]

Some experts say congressional disaster aid packages should require that communities repeatedly victimized by weather-related disasters adopt tougher building codes. And homeowners are increasingly asking architects to design houses that can survive floods, wildfires and other disasters.[66]

Sean Jennings, for example, built his house in Lake County, Calif., out of polystyrene foam, steel and concrete. He said that explains how the building survived a 2015 wildfire that destroyed everything else in the area. "I wanted something that was fireproof, earthquake proof, flood proof," Jennings said. "Future proof, basically."[67]

BACKGROUND

Ancient Disasters

The extreme weather events that countries around the world are experiencing today are mild compared to the changes in climate that occurred millions of years ago as a result of volcanic activity, widespread cooling with the formation of glaciers, fluctuating sea levels and asteroid collisions. Those events drastically elevated carbon levels in the atmosphere—the same process that climate scientists say is occurring today with the release of greenhouse gases—and some killed most life on the planet.[68]

"Major mass extinctions of species closely coincided with abrupt rises of atmospheric carbon dioxide and ocean acidity," said Andrew Glikson, a climate scientist at Australian National University in Canberra, Australia. "These increases took place at rates to which many species could not adapt."[69]

Some researchers also have theorized that certain mass extinction events, including the one that wiped out dinosaurs 66 million years ago, could have started with an asteroid impact that then produced hypercanes, giant hurricanes with winds of 675 miles per hour that would have suffocated animals and plants by drastically lowering air pressure. The storms would have been caused by superheated ocean water, possibly due to underwater volcanic eruptions.[70]

Such eruptions were a major cause of extreme weather in the ancient world. One of the world's oldest known weather reports, written 3,500 years ago on a stone block in Egypt, describes torrential rain and refers to "the sky being in storm without cessation, louder than the cries of the masses." Scholars believe those conditions could have been caused by a volcanic eruption on an island in the Mediterranean Sea.[71]

Extreme weather also may have played a role in the collapse of entire civilizations. Some studies blame a prolonged drought for wiping out the Mayan Empire around A.D. 900 in what is now Guatemala. Researchers at the University of California, Davis, said such a drought "likely corresponded with crop failures, death, famine [and] migration." And environmental historians believe the ancient Khmer empire of Angkor in Cambodia collapsed in the early 15th century due to a severe drought followed by unusually intense monsoon rains that caused massive flooding and destroyed the city's infrastructure.[72]

A period known as the Little Ice Age began around 1300 and lasted until about 1850, possibly caused by a series of volcanic eruptions in the tropics that ejected clouds of sulphate particles into the upper atmosphere. The particles reflected heat from the sun back into space, lowering temperatures on Earth enough to expand ice sheets. The period brought bitterly cold winters to North America and Europe, leading to crop failure and famine.[73]

Centuries ago, people were less able to prepare for extreme weather, resulting in huge loss of life. The Great Hurricane in October 1780, for example, killed more than 20,000 people in the Caribbean and sank British and French warships fighting in the American Revolutionary War.[74]

Links to Pollution

In the 1820s, Jean Fourier, a French mathematician, became the first scholar to explain that the Earth's atmosphere retains heat radiation. Decades later, John Tyndall, a natural historian in Britain, discovered that water vapor and carbon dioxide (CO_2) are effective at trapping heat.[75]

Tyndall's research led Svante Arrhenius, a Swedish chemist, to perform experiments establishing that carbon dioxide, not water vapor, is the key to regulating the Earth's temperature. In 1896, Arrhenius said burning fossil fuels could eventually double CO_2 levels in the atmosphere, raising average global temperatures up to 4 degrees Celsius. Other scientists dismissed his findings as implausible.[76]

In the United States, extreme weather killed hundreds of people during the 1800s. A fast-moving Arctic cold front created the so-called Children's Blizzard that killed 235 people, including many children walking home from school, across the Great Plains on Jan. 12, 1888. Another blizzard in March that year killed more than 400 people in the Northeast, the nation's highest death toll from a winter storm. In October 1871, following an unusually dry summer, the most destructive forest fire in the country's history—the Peshtigo Fire—raged through parts of Wisconsin, killing at least 1,200 people.[77]

In 1849, the Smithsonian Institution, established to expand scientific and other knowledge, began supplying weather instruments to telegraph companies. By the end of the year, volunteers were reporting on weather conditions across the country.[78]

The next century brought new record-setting weather events. The Great Galveston Hurricane of 1900 on the Gulf Coast of Texas killed more than 6,000 people and still stands as the deadliest hurricane in U.S. history. The country's most lethal tornado killed almost 700 people in 1925, destroying entire towns in the Midwest with 300-mile-per-hour winds. A series of droughts crippled large parts of the United States during the 1930s, causing cropland to dry up and inspiring the term "Dust Bowl" to describe the south-central part of the country.[79]

Around the world, meanwhile, temperatures set new records in 1937, a development that climate scientists say would have been virtually impossible without rising levels of carbon in the atmosphere due to greenhouse gas emissions.[80]

In 1938, Guy Callendar, a steam engineer in Britain, said his research on the atmosphere and global weather patterns showed that burning fossil fuels had raised global temperatures by increasing carbon dioxide in the atmosphere. Callendar saw this as a benefit, saying the warming effect would help prevent the return of "deadly glaciers." As with Arrhenius before him, his contributions were considered improbable by other scientists at the time.[81]

After rising rapidly during the early decades of the 20th century, average global temperatures began dropping after 1940 and remained low until 1970. Many scientists attributed the cooler period to aerosols that had entered the atmosphere due to volcanic eruptions and increased industrial activity after World War II. They said sulfates in the aerosols reflected solar energy back into space, lowering surface temperatures on Earth. Temperatures began rising quickly again after new anti-pollution laws around the world reduced aerosol emissions.[82]

In 1981, scientists at Columbia University announced findings that they said confirmed the warming effect of carbon dioxide pollution entering the atmosphere. Their report followed another by scientists at NASA noting increases in global temperatures since 1880.[83]

New Research

In response to such discoveries, the United Nations and the World Meteorological Organization, located in Geneva, created the IPCC in 1988 "to provide a comprehensive summary of what is known about the drivers of climate change, its impacts and future risks, and how adaptation and mitigation can reduce those risks."[84]

A year later, Republican President George H.W. Bush established the U.S. Global Change Research Program. Congress codified the program the following year to help the nation and the world "understand, assess, predict and respond to" climate change from human and natural causes.[85]

In its first climate assessment report, issued in 2000, the program said that "Climate change is likely to decrease the number of some types of weather extremes, while increasing others," and predicted that rising temperatures likely would lead to "greater frequency of both very wet and very dry conditions."[86]

Five years later, Hurricane Katrina became the costliest hurricane to hit the United States. Damage from Katrina, which overwhelmed levees in New Orleans and caused massive flooding, totaled $161 billion. In 2012, Hurricane Sandy, also known as Superstorm Sandy, hit the U.S. East Coast, affecting 24 states. It set records for storm surge and caused about $71 billion in damage.[87]

The Global Change Research Program's first report was tentative in describing links between greenhouse gas emissions and extreme weather, but by 2014, the group was expressing greater confidence that the two were connected.[88]

"Changes in extreme weather and climate events, such as heat waves and droughts, are the primary way that most people experience climate change," the 2014 report said. "Human-induced climate change has already increased the number and strength of some of these extreme events. Over the last 50 years, much of the U.S. has seen increases in prolonged periods of excessively high temperatures, heavy downpours, and in some regions, severe floods and droughts."[89]

CHRONOLOGY

1800s *The U.S. government makes its first efforts to monitor and predict extreme weather.*

1849 Smithsonian Institution establishes a national weather-monitoring network.

1870 President Ulysses S. Grant signs a bill establishing a national weather warning service under the federal Department of War.

1871 The Peshtigo Fire in Wisconsin kills 1,200 people, making it the deadliest wildfire in U.S. history.

1890 The national weather warning service is named the U.S. Weather Bureau and is transferred to the Department of Agriculture.

1900-1940s *Scientists see early signs of global warming.*

1900 Hurricane strikes Galveston, Texas, and kills at least 6,000 people, becoming the deadliest extreme weather event in U.S. history.

1920 Meteorologist Charles Franklin Brooks founds the American Meteorological Society in Massachusetts to advance the study of weather.

1925 The Tri-State Tornado, the deadliest in U.S. history, kills nearly 700 people in Missouri, Illinois and Indiana. Some observers estimate it at a mile wide.

1935 Congress approves money to improve hurricane warning services, including new forecast centers in Jacksonville, Fla., New Orleans, Puerto Rico and Boston.

1938 Guy Callendar, a British engineer and inventor, links carbon dioxide emissions to rising global temperatures, but his work goes largely unnoticed.

1940 U.S. Weather Bureau is moved to the Department of Commerce.

1950s-1990s *Satellites make weather monitoring more accurate as scientists warn of global warming.*

1950 U.S. Weather Bureau begins issuing tornado alerts.

1960 NASA launches TIROS-1, the first successful weather satellite, which takes pictures of Earth's cloud cover for 78 days and paves the way for an orbiting weather-monitoring network used worldwide.

1968 Congress establishes the National Flood Insurance Program, which offers insurance to people living in areas at high risk for flooding.

1970 U.S. Weather Bureau, now part of the National Oceanic and Atmospheric Administration, is renamed the National Weather Service.

1975 NASA launches the first Geostationary Operational Environmental Satellite (GOES), a "hurricane hunter" that tracks tropical cyclones.

1981 Scientists report a warming in global temperatures since 1880 and attribute the trend to carbon emissions entering the atmosphere.

1990 The Intergovernmental Panel on Climate Change (IPCC) issues its first assessment, laying the groundwork for international efforts to predict the effects of global warming.

2000-Present *As billion-dollar disasters occur more often, scientists and policymakers seek ways to predict and prepare for extreme weather.*

2004 In one of the first studies linking climate change to a specific weather event, British scientists say a 2003 record-setting heat wave in Europe that killed 35,000 people was made twice as likely by climate change.

2005 Hurricane Katrina overwhelms levees in New Orleans and causes about $161 billion in damage, becoming the most expensive weather disaster in U.S. history.

2011 *The Bulletin of the American Meteorological Society* begins publishing a special issue highlighting studies on links between climate change and extreme weather events.

2017 Sixteen weather-related disasters costing at least $1 billion each in the U.S. kill 362 people and cause $306 billion in damage.

2018 The Camp Fire in California kills 85 people, burns more than 150,000 acres and destroys more than 18,000 buildings, becoming the deadliest and most destructive fire in the state's history—and the deadliest in the country since 1918.

2019 U.S. experiences six billion-dollar weather disasters by July 9 with a combined death toll of 15. . . . Hurricane Dorian hits the Bahamas as a Category 5 storm and stalls over the islands for two days, killing dozens of people and causing massive destruction.

Farmers Face Difficult Odds as Extreme Weather Grows

"Dry areas will get even dryer, and wet areas will get even wetter."

Kate Glastetter, a 25-year-old Missouri farmer, likened her fields this past spring to lakefront property. "The fields are washing away," she said.[1]

A combination of heavy rains and melting snow led to historic flooding throughout much of the United States last spring, especially in areas that drain into the Missouri or Mississippi Rivers. By March, some regions had received more than twice their yearly rainfall average, according to the National Oceanic and Atmospheric Administration.[2]

The floods forced farmers such as Glastetter's neighbors to delay planting, and by mid-May, for the first time in recorded U.S. history, less than half the nation's corn fields had been planted, according to the U.S. Department of Agriculture (USDA).

David L. Ryan/The Boston Globe via Getty Images

Sam Gray, who manages a farm in North Easton, Mass., drives along a flooded road on May 14. Climate scientists say rising global temperatures will bring increasing episodes of both intense rain and severe droughts, threatening crops around the world.

The Farm Bureau, an organization that represents agricultural interests, estimated spring flooding damage to stored crops, livestock, fields, farm buildings and equipment in Nebraska and Iowa, among the most affected states, at more than $3 billion.[3]

And flooding damage in the central part of the country was only the beginning. Although the effects of high water had begun to abate by late June, with most fields planted by then, according to the USDA, a new peril loomed. In late July a heat wave threatened to stunt root development and further decrease crop yields.[4]

Climate scientists have long predicted that climate change would spur increases in severe droughts and floods like those that have occurred this year. Computer models still cannot accurately predict when or where such events will occur, but the models do suggest that the future will see an increase in drastic weather swings.

"Dry areas will get even dryer, and wet areas will get even wetter," says climate scientist Jhordanne Jones, a doctoral student at Colorado State University in Fort Collins who focuses on predicting tropical cyclones.

Farmers cannot plant in fields that are too saturated or too dry, and massive flooding can spoil stored crops before they are sold. Excessive rain or heat also promotes the growth of destructive pests, weeds and fungi.

A drought in 2012 sent corn yields nationwide more than 26 percent below predictions, and farm income decreased by nearly $5 billion nationwide. The drought also drove the Mississippi River to record low levels, making it impossible for grain-carrying barges to deliver their cargo. Animals that feed on grain also were affected.[5]

A July report by the USDA's Economic Research Service predicted that U.S. corn and soybean yields could fall by as much as 80 percent in the next 60 years due to weather extremes driven by climate change.[6]

In a June 2018 study published in the *Proceedings of the National Academy of Sciences*, researchers estimated that corn production by the top four corn-producing countries—the United States, China, Brazil and Argentina—will drop significantly if the average global temperature rises by 4 degrees Celsius (7 degrees Fahrenheit).[7]

Agricultural production in tropical regions will be hit hardest, according to other studies.[8] "That's where you have the weakest institutions in terms of helping farmers," says Dan Blaustein-Rejto, senior food and agriculture analyst at the Breakthrough Institute, an environmental research center in San Francisco.

The USDA report predicted that declining yields will sharply drive up the cost of wheat, corn and soybeans as well as the cost of crop insurance. As of July 15, the department had spent about $300 million on insurance on 2019 crops; the report predicted that in six decades that will climb to more than $10 billion.[9] As much as 85 percent of a farmer's land is protected against natural disasters or market fluctuations by crop insurance subsidized by the federal government, which covers an average of 62 percent of the insurance premiums.[10]

Experts also predict that extreme weather events will lead to periods of food scarcity. After studying five decades of data on crops, livestock, aquaculture and fisheries, an international team of researchers in January reported that food-scarcity episodes have been increasing in recent years, especially in developing countries, because of extreme weather.[11]

As researchers look for ways to deal with the effects of extreme weather on agriculture, information from the USDA has become harder for them to find, according to an investigation by *Politico*, an online news publication. It found that the Trump administration has "refused to publicize dozens of government-funded studies that carry warnings about the effects of climate change, defying a longstanding practice of touting such findings by the Agriculture Department's acclaimed in-house scientists."[12]

Many researchers and policymakers see some hope in biotechnology. Scientists have been developing crop seeds genetically modified to resist pests, drought and floods, but Blaustein-Retjo says funding for crop research in the United States has fallen in the last 20 years. In addition, a complicated approval process and public mistrust of genetically modified organisms—including seeds and livestock—have slowed research.

— *Stephen Ornes*

[1] Emily Moon, "'The Fields are Washing Away': Midwest Flooding is Wreaking Havoc on Farmers," *Pacific Standard*, June 6, 2019, https://tinyurl.com/y3maxvlz.

[2] "January-May Precipitation," National Climate Report, National Oceanic and Atmospheric Administration, May 2019, https://tinyurl.com/y4p2qxnl.

[3] Jessie Higgins, "Midwestern farmers devastated by uninsured flood losses," UPI, March 29, 2019, https://tinyurl.com/y6973lhz; Matthew Schwartz, "Nebraska Faces over $1.3 Billion in Flood Losses," *NPR*, March 21, 2019, https://tinyurl.com/y22gm5nb.

[4] Mark Weinraub, "U.S. corn plantings top expectations despite floods; prices sink," *Reuters*, June 28, 2019, https://tinyurl.com/y6ax4bk6; Emma Newburger, "'It never stops': US farmers now face extreme heat wave after floods and trade war," *CNBC*, July 20, 2019, https://tinyurl.com/yy9ffb6w.

[5] Ben Foster, "Drought and the Mighty Mississippi," *Property and Environment Research Center Magazine*, Vol. 35, No. 2, 2016, https://tinyurl.com/yyzz4m33.

[6] Andrew Crane-Droesch *et al.*, "Climate Change and Agricultural Risk Management into the 21st Century," U.S. Department of Agriculture, July 2019, https://tinyurl.com/y2zlwtdz.

[7] Michelle Tigchelaar *et al.*, "Future warming increases probability of globally synchronized maize production shocks," *Proceedings of the National Academy of Sciences*, Vol. 115, No. 26, pp. 6644-6649, June 11, 2018, https://tinyurl.com/y4dqnftn.

[8] *Ibid.*

[9] Crane-Droesch, *op. cit.*; Kirk Maltais, "USDA Report Sees Dire Climate-Change Impact on U.S. Crops," *The Wall Street Journal*, July 23, 2019, https://tinyurl.com/y42r9cx3.

[10] Maltais, *ibid.*

[11] Cottrell Richard *et al.*, "Food production shocks across land and sea," *Nature Sustainability*, Vol. 2, pp. 130-137, Jan. 28, 2019, https://tinyurl.com/y2mz6nvv.

[12] Helena Bottemiller Evich, "Agriculture Department buries studies showing dangers of climate change," *Politico*, June 23, 2019, https://tinyurl.com/yxbzqhnq.

Insurers React as Extreme Weather Boosts Claims

Many raise rates and reassess risk in response to changing climate.

As extreme weather events become more frequent and powerful, insurance companies are changing how they price homeowner policies and determine what to cover.

The change has occurred largely because recent extreme weather has led to record annual payouts by insurers to cover losses. Insured losses from disasters around the world in 2017 totaled $140 billion, higher than ever before, according to German reinsurance company Munich Re Group. Those losses included at least one event not tied to the weather, a severe earthquake in Mexico. Munich Re said losses in the United States dominated the statistics.[1]

Insured losses worldwide dropped to $80 billion in 2018, which Munich Re noted was still "substantially higher than the long-term average." Again, earthquakes accounted for some of those losses. Claims in 2017 were driven up by the costliest Atlantic hurricane season on record. The single most expensive event in 2018 was a wildfire, the Camp Fire in California, Munich Re said.[2]

A Nationwide Mutual Insurance Co. survey of 100,000 claims in 2017 found that the number and amount of claims have climbed significantly in recent years. Between 2014 and 2016, a period of unusually warm winters and other unexpected weather events, including massive flooding, the average claim amount was 26 percent higher than in the seven-year period between 2007 and 2013.[3]

Many insurers have raised rates in recent years in response to extreme weather events.[4] Others have stopped insuring homeowners in certain high-risk areas, or raised premiums in those locations. At least one carrier, USAA, offers discounts to homeowners who live in communities that are at risk of fire but have taken precautions, such as consulting with fire experts and clearing flammable debris and vegetation near buildings.[5]

"Few sectors of the economy play a role as intense in catastrophe recovery as insurance," said Anna Maria D'Hulster, then-secretary general of the Geneva Association, an international insurance think tank in Geneva.[6]

The availability—or lack—of insurance coverage can induce homeowners to make better decisions about preparation and even about where to live, experts say. Pricing premiums according to weather risk, for example, can help shape the real estate market.

"If it's expensive to insure a house on the coast, individuals will have an incentive to live elsewhere," three University of Southern California economists wrote in an article for *Harvard Business Review.* "If insurers offer a discount for climate-proofing homes, homeowners will likewise have an incentive to make that investment."[7]

JOSH EDELSON/AFP/Getty Images

Cars and homes burn as the Camp Fire roars through Paradise, Calif., in November 2018. Experts say the number of acres burned by wildfires in California has increased fivefold since the early 1970s, one of many events driving up insurance losses.

The economists said insurers increasingly use tools that more precisely assess the risk of damage to individual houses. In coastal communities, for example, houses built closer to the shore or at lower elevations typically are at greater risk than those on hills or further inland.

Insurance companies also have developed new modeling and pricing tools that explicitly take into consideration the latest scientific findings and predictions about weather. In particular, they are exploring ways to account for extremes due to climate change.

Catastrophic-loss models have traditionally been defined by long-term climate data, averaged over time. They have treated the climate as a stationary, or unchanging, influence. But a 2014 report by Lloyd's of London, the British insurance firm, said Atlantic hurricane risk varies dramatically over time, due to natural variation and also due to human activities. Lloyds concluded that new models need to reflect a changing climate to better predict future losses.[8]

Extreme weather is an issue for crop insurance, which farmers use to recover from disasters. Insurance can shield farmers against low yields of crops such as wheat, soybeans and corn and unexpected drops in market prices. If extreme weather events become more severe and common, insurance will become increasingly important in protecting farmers' livelihoods, experts say.

However, crop insurance raises questions of responsibility. The U.S. government pays 60 percent of farmers' premiums.[9] Critics argue that the Federal Crop Insurance Program favors large farms and rewards farmers for using practices known to diminish land resiliency, such as planting a single crop rather than rotating crops.

"The current U.S. crop insurance program encourages farmers to adopt production practices that will not be sustainable in the face of climate change, and in the short term contribute to greenhouse gas emissions," said Montana State University agricultural economist Vincent Smith. "Crop insurance encourages people to adopt production practices that are riskier, and by definition, reduce resiliency."[10]

That is similar to arguments made against other government-subsidized insurance programs, such as the National Flood Insurance Program (NFIP) and Florida's Citizens Property Insurance Corp., a nonprofit insurance company created in 2002 by the Florida Legislature that offers property insurance to people unable to get a policy from a private insurer. These government-subsidized programs insure people living in high-risk areas, but they may distort a homeowner's perception of the danger, some researchers say.

"Once the government subsidizes the risk, then people view it as less costly than it is to live in a risky area," says Omri Ben-Shahar, a law professor at the University of Chicago who has studied the effects of government subsidies in relation to extreme weather. He says programs such as the NFIP encourage people to build and live in places known to be at high risk of damage from extreme weather.

"Sometimes the answer isn't to build a wall two feet higher, but not to live somewhere at all," he says.

— *Stephen Ornes*

[1] "Natural catastrophe review: Series of hurricanes makes 2017 year of highest insured losses ever," Munich Re, Jan. 4, 2018, https://tinyurl.com/y7y9jhc6; "Extreme storms, wildfires and droughts cause heavy nat cat losses in 2018," Munich Re, Jan. 8, 2019, https://tinyurl.com/yakmgnpd.

[2] "Natural catastrophe review," *ibid.*

[3] "Nationwide Warns of Widening Gap Between Disaster Risks and Business Preparedness," press release, Nationwide, Feb. 28, 2017, https://tinyurl.com/y259efox; Don Jergler, "Nationwide Says Extreme Weather Brings Bigger Claims, Need for Disaster Plans," *Insurance Journal*, March 2, 2017, https://tinyurl.com/y6ztwrun.

[4] Jeff Blyskal, "How Climate Change Could Affect Your Homeowners Insurance Coverage," *Consumer Reports*, Sept. 20, 2017, https://tinyurl.com/y3bgx4ob.

[5] "Firewise USA," National Fire Protection Association, accessed Sept. 5, 2019, https://tinyurl.com/y5v4hfef.

[6] "Managing Physical Climate Risk: Leveraging Innovations in Catastrophe Risk Modeling," The Geneva Association, November 2018, https://tinyurl.com/y4ny64vw.

[7] Matthew Kahn, Brian Casey and Nolan Jones, "How the Insurance Industry Can Push us to Prepare for Climate Change," *Harvard Business Review*, Aug. 28, 2017, https://tinyurl.com/yblbjhgg.

[8] "Catastrophe Modelling and Climate Change," Lloyd's of London, 2014, https://tinyurl.com/yywur4gn.

[9] "Reduce Subsidies in the Crop Insurance Program," Option for Reducing the Deficit, Congressional Budget Office, Dec. 13, 2018, https://tinyurl.com/y3yspdvw.

[10] Georgina Gustin, "U.S. Taxpayers on the Hook for Insuring Farmers Against Growing Climate Risks," *Inside Climate News*, Dec. 31, 2018, https://tinyurl.com/y863tvos.

The report also said that:

- Climate change from human activity "has generally increased the probability of heat waves" and "prolonged (multimonth) extreme heat has been unprecedented since the start of reliable instrumental records in 1895."
- The amount of rain falling in the United States in very heavy precipitation events has been significantly above average since 1991.
- The intensity, frequency and duration of Atlantic hurricane activity has significantly increased since the early 1980s. "Quantifying the relative contributions of natural and human-caused factors is an active focus of research," the report said.

In December the following year, the United States and 194 other countries signed the Paris Agreement on climate change as part of a global effort to reduce carbon emissions and limit the temperature increases that scientists blamed for the increasing frequency and severity of some types of extreme weather.[90]

Disaster Costs Grow

Improvements in computer climate models allowed scientists to increasingly link specific extreme weather events to climate change. Research published in the *Bulletin of the American Meteorological Society* last December, for example, found that three extreme weather-related events that took place in 2017: droughts in the U.S. northern Plains and East Africa, floods in South America, China and Bangladesh, and heat waves in China and the Mediterranean—were all made more likely because of greenhouse gas emissions.[91]

The report also said that certain ocean heat events, including severe marine heat waves in the Tasman Sea, were "virtually impossible" without climate change caused by human activity.

The year 2017 was notable in the United States for a record number of billion-dollar weather-related disasters. The 16 events included hurricanes (Harvey, Irma and Maria), eight severe storms and two inland floods. In June that same year, President Trump announced that the United States would withdraw from the Paris Agreement in November 2020, citing "the draconian

financial and economic burdens the agreement imposes on our country."[92]

The president's critics, however, cite reports showing the federal government has spent more than $430 billion since 2005 on humanitarian assistance following weather-related disasters in the country. A report from the Government Accountability Office (GAO), the investigative arm of Congress, predicts such costs will grow.

"The costliness of disasters is projected to increase as extreme weather events become more frequent and intense due to climate change," the GAO said in March. It also noted that government officials since 2017 have rolled back policies designed to deal with climate change.[93]

The Center for Climate Security, which advocates for action on climate change to protect national security, said the GAO report "makes a strong case that the U.S. is moving backwards in that effort, despite the regular warnings coming from the defense, intelligence and science agencies of our government, and the broader national security community."[94]

CURRENT SITUATION
Flood Insurance Future

This year's wet-weather extremes—including storm surge and heavy downpours in North Carolina as a result of Hurricane Dorian and torrential rain and flooding in the Midwest and Southeast—focused new attention on attempts to reform the National Flood Insurance Program. The program is set to expire—and run out of money—on Sept. 30 unless Congress acts to reauthorize it.[95]

Critics of the program, which provides about $1.3 trillion in coverage for about 5 million homes across the country, say it charges premiums that are too low for some homeowners and too high for others, produces shoddy flood maps and encourages rebuilding in areas that are sure to flood repeatedly.[96]

"Here you have a program that is subsidizing people to live and develop in harm's way," said Steve Ellis, vice president of Taxpayers for Common Sense, a budget watchdog group in Washington.[97]

Completely overhauling the program would require congressional approval. In the meantime, FEMA, which oversees the NFIP, has proposed changing how the program calculates premiums to make sure they accurately reflect an individual home's flood risks.[98]

Congress last reauthorized the program in May, the 12th reauthorization since the fall of 2017. Without new legislation extending it, FEMA will stop issuing new flood insurance policies for millions of homes across the country, potentially threatening 40,000 home-sale closings each month.[99]

"NFIP reauthorization is an opportunity for Congress to take bold steps to reduce the complexity of the program and strengthen the NFIP's financial framework," FEMA said in a statement.[100]

Reform proposals include a measure introduced by Sen. Bob Menendez, D-N.J., in July that would reauthorize the flood insurance program for five years. It would cap annual premium increases at 9 percent, boost funding for flood maps and for grants to homeowners who want to relocate or elevate their homes, and close loopholes that the NFIP has used in the past to deny reimbursement to flood victims. At least four Republicans have signed on as co-sponsors. Menendez is a member of the Senate Banking Committee that oversees the NFIP and sits on a Senate task force formed in 2015 to improve FEMA's handling of flood claims related to Hurricane Sandy, which caused extensive damage to his state.[101]

A rival bill introduced by Rep. Maxine Waters, D-Calif., chairwoman of the House Financial Services Committee, also would reauthorize the NFIP for five years but does not include other provisions Menendez is pushing.[102]

Administration Actions

The Trump administration, meanwhile, continues acting to minimize the role of climate change science in government policy:

- In May, James Reilly, director of the U.S. Geological Survey, ordered his office to use computer-generated climate models that project conditions only through 2040 instead of the end of the century. Scientists see that as a move to ignore the time period when they say the effect of climate change on weather conditions will be most apparent.[103]
- Administration officials have decided that the next national climate assessment from the Global Change Research Program will not include worst-case scenarios such as a temperature increase of 8 degrees Fahrenheit that would result in a drastic rise in sea levels and a sharp increase in devastating storms and droughts.[104] "The previous use of inaccurate modeling that focuses on worst-case emissions scenarios, that does not reflect real-world conditions, needs to be thoroughly re-examined and tested if such information is going to serve as the scientific foundation of nationwide decision-making now and in the future," said James Hewitt, a spokesman for the Environmental Protection Agency.
- William Happer, a physicist and a member of the White House National Security Council, is working to create a new panel inside the White House that would challenge the science behind global warming, including evidence that climate change is causing more incidents of extreme weather.[105]
- Last year, FEMA removed references to climate change from its four-year strategic plan, and a section in the plan titled "Emerging Threats" includes no references to extreme weather. The agency's public affairs director said the plan "fully incorporates future risks from all hazards regardless of cause."[106]
- The administration has abandoned its former practice of announcing the result of studies by scientists at the Agriculture Department warning of the effects of climate change, including severe weather events.[107]

"The intent is to try to suppress a message—in this case, the increasing danger of human-caused climate change," said Mann at Penn State. "Who loses out? The people, who are already suffering the impacts of sea level rise and unprecedented super storms, droughts, wildfires and heat waves."[108]

Climate scientists also castigated the administration recently for what they view as actions intended to politicize government weather forecasting. On Sept. 8, NOAA's acting chief scientist, Craig McLean, said he will investigate whether the agency violated its own ethical policies when it defended the president's inaccurate

AT ISSUE:

Should the federal government subsidize rebuilding in areas vulnerable to extreme weather?

YES
Alan Rubin
Principal, Blank Rome Government Relations LLC

Written for *CQ Researcher*, September 2019

The question of where development can take place in the United States has always been a controversial one. Cities, municipalities, counties and states have looked to property taxes and other taxes to support their growth and pay for social programs. Environmentalists, social scientists and green advocates have always advocated for a minimalist approach to development to prevent what they view as the destruction of ecosystems and natural resources.

As the country has grown and population densities have increased, these priorities have not been kept in balance. However, people in areas where natural disasters have occurred have attempted to rebuild with the intention of "building back better." Because 60 percent of the population lives along or near the coast, intelligent recovery and the use of zoning laws and unique construction designs must be implemented. In the recovery and resiliency process, we must recognize the potential for repetitive natural and man-made disasters.

With that as a premise, federal programs should allow for rebuilding in areas that are prone to extreme weather events. The key is making sure the redevelopment utilizes all of the innovative concepts and latest strategies in the legislative toolkit.

Examples include reauthorizing the National Flood Insurance Program for five to 10 years as opposed to the current practice of reauthorizing the program after it runs out of money following a natural disaster. As a part of this reauthorization, there should be an annual limit on premium increases that would exclude catastrophic-loss years. Additionally, a formula for increased rates would apply to the most expensive properties. And of course, there would need to be a means test for affordability and low income in setting rates.

Multiple programs at the local, state and federal levels can be used to facilitate rebuilding in areas devastated by natural disasters. These include:

- Mold mitigation assistance grants.
- Hazard mitigation grants.
- Elevation requirements for commercial and residential buildings.
- Mapping modernization and implementation.

NO
Josiah Neeley
Senior Fellow and Energy Policy Director, R Street Institute

Written for *CQ Researcher*, September 2019

When it comes to practicing medicine, doctors try to follow a simple rule set forth in the Hippocratic Oath: First, do no harm. Government should follow the same rule, but it often doesn't.

A clear example of this is the way government subsidizes building in storm-prone areas.

We've all seen the damage that storms like Hurricanes Harvey and Sandy can cause. And such storms are expected to become more dangerous in the future. A recent study by the Risky Business Project, which assesses the economic risks to the United States from climate change, concluded that in the Southeast alone, between $48.2 billion and $68.7 billion worth of existing coastal property will be below sea level by 2050. By the end of the century, some parts of Louisiana may be at least 4.3 feet below sea level. Yet even as the danger from flooding and storms grows, the number of people moving to flood-prone areas is increasing.

Why are people moving into the path of future storms? Part of the answer is that the government encourages them to do so. Take, for example, the National Flood Insurance Program (NFIP). The NFIP was founded in 1968 as a means of providing flood insurance to properties that simply couldn't qualify for flood insurance from the private insurance market. The rates the NFIP charges, however, are far below what are necessary to pay out expected claims. Unsurprisingly, this has led the NFIP to incur chronic financial difficulties. The NFIP is currently more than $20 billion in debt, and that's after Congress canceled $16 billion in debt in 2017.

Beyond these financial problems, the NFIP's artificially low rates create perverse incentives for developers. Prices convey information. If the cost to insure property in a given area is prohibitively high, that is a signal that the risks of building in that area are similarly high. By subsidizing rates, the NFIP sends a false signal that building in flood-prone areas is far less risky than it really is, leading to overdevelopment. The NFIP is one of many such programs that subsidize risky development.

People should be free to live where they want, of course. But the rest of us shouldn't have to pay for it. Ending government

- Revolving loan funds for affected areas.
- Mandatory business interruption insurance.
- Mold damage identification.

subsidies for building in disaster-prone areas won't eliminate risk, but it will give people a better sense of the true costs and help us all be better prepared for when the rains come.

Many of these items are being addressed. Certainly, improved zoning laws, buffer zones and architectural designs that prevent repetitive damage are all important weapons in legislating new and successful rules to help rebuilding in areas that have been or could be affected by extreme weather.

It is possible to successfully recover and prevent additional damage. This is required in order to coexist in a period of climate change and massively destructive storms.

claim on Sept. 1 that Alabama was in the path of Hurricane Dorian.[109]

Many national security experts also fear that political motivations are increasingly driving the government's reaction to extreme weather caused by climate change.

"When extreme weather hits the United States, it degrades the fighting force," 58 former military and national security leaders wrote to President Trump in March. "We support the science-driven patriots in our national security community who have rightly seen addressing climate change as a threat reduction issue, not a political one."[110]

In January, then-Director of National Intelligence Dan Coats warned in a report about national security dangers across the globe that heat waves, droughts and floods are a growing threat to food and water supplies, "increasing the risk of social unrest, migration and interstate tension in countries such as Egypt, Ethiopia, Iraq and Jordan."[111]

"Extreme weather events, many worsened by accelerating sea level rise, will particularly affect urban coastal areas in South Asia, Southeast Asia and the Western Hemisphere," Coats' report said. "Damage to communication, energy and transportation infrastructure could affect low-lying military bases, inflict economic costs, and cause human displacement and loss of life."[112]

On Sept. 12, the Internal Displacement Monitoring Centre, an agency in Geneva that estimates the number of people displaced around the world by disasters, conflict and other causes, reported that weather disasters displaced a record 7 million people during the first half of 2019.[113]

"In today's changing climate, mass displacement triggered by extreme weather events is becoming the norm," the report said.[114]

A poll conducted in July and August this year by *The Washington Post* and the Kaiser Family Foundation, a private research group located in San Francisco and Washington, found that about eight in 10 Americans—and 60 percent of Republicans—believe human activity fuels climate change. Nearly 40 percent of Americans said climate change has reached "crisis" levels, up from less than 25 percent five years ago. And 67 percent of

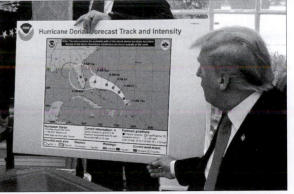

President Trump displays a map of Hurricane Dorian's predicted path that appears to have been altered to validate his earlier, incorrect statement that Dorian was expected to hit Alabama. Scientists say some of Trump's actions have politicized government weather forecasting.

those surveyed said they are unhappy with how President Trump has handled climate change.[115]

Campaign Issue

Extreme weather and its link to climate change caused by carbon emissions is a key issue for candidates vying for the Democratic presidential nomination in 2020.

Most of the candidates—20 were still in the race as of mid-September—have strategies, costing trillions of dollars, to reduce greenhouse gas emissions. A number, for example, have expressed support for a tax on emissions. That includes the three candidates who were leading in the polls at the time—former Vice President Joseph Biden, Sen. Elizabeth Warren of Massachusetts and Sen. Bernie Sanders of Vermont, an independent who caucuses with Democrats.[116]

Sen. Kamala Harris of California supports a "progressively increasing fee" targeting companies that pollute. Julián Castro of Texas, former Housing and Urban Development secretary, argues for an emissions fee for the "biggest . . . industrial scale polluters." Former Rep. Beto O'Rourke, also of Texas, supports a cap-and-trade plan that would impose a limit on carbon pollution and let polluters buy and sell allowances for emissions within that limit.[117]

Virtually all of the 10 Democratic candidates who spoke at a *CNN* town hall on climate change issues on Sept. 4 said the United States should remain committed to the Paris Agreement.[118]

The Green New Deal, or something similar to it, is widely supported by the Democratic field. The sweeping proposal, which is pending in Congress, aims to cut U.S. greenhouse gas emissions in half by 2030. It would dramatically increase reliance on renewable energy sources to address climate change while providing jobs and economic security for low-income Americans. Biden has offered qualified support but says the plan lacks specifics about its goals.[119]

Republican critics of the plan say it would result in soaring energy costs, and even some moderate Democrats say its goals are too ambitious.[120]

Mental Health

New research finds that people whose homes are damaged by extreme weather are more likely to experience serious mental health issues such as depression. A study published in September by researchers in Britain, for example, found that people who had experienced storm and flood damage were about 50 percent more likely to suffer poorer mental health.

"This is reflective of the huge impact storms and flooding have on people's lives, as alongside the physical damage to homes and businesses, there is the emotional damage to the sense of security that many people derive from their home," said Hilary Graham, a professor at the Department of Health Sciences at the University of York and the study's lead author.[121]

Researchers said in a study published in August that recent Atlantic hurricanes—Harvey, Irma and Maria in 2017, and Florence and Michael in 2018—led to increased rates of common mental disorders such as depression and post-traumatic stress disorder among storm victims. "As hurricanes become increasingly severe, health care systems may expect to see more mental illness related to these extreme storms," the authors said.[122]

Tools used to forecast extreme weather, meanwhile, continue to improve. In June, NOAA announced a significant upgrade to its Global Forecast System software used by meteorologists around the world. The agency says the upgrade should allow forecasters to more accurately predict the track and intensity of hurricanes, as well as rainfall amounts.[123]

Experts warn that the damaging impact of extreme heat on mental health around the world will become an increasing problem as the world continues to warm. They anticipate higher rates of violent conflict, suicide, depression and cognitive impairment.[124]

"By 2050 there may be between 9,000 to 40,000 additional suicides in the U.S. and Mexico," the *Psychiatric Times* reported in July. "These rates are comparable to the effects on suicide incidence due to economic recessions and unemployment and offset gains in suicide prevention programs and gun control policies."[125]

OUTLOOK
Worsening Trends

Climate scientists expect some forms of extreme weather to worsen later this century. Floods so severe they would normally occur just 1 percent of the time will take place every year in New England and every 1 to 30 years along the southeast Atlantic and Gulf of Mexico coastlines, according to a study published in August by researchers from the Stevens Institute of Technology in Hoboken, N.J., Princeton University and the Massachusetts Institute of Technology. The researchers based their prediction on an analysis of how hurricanes and rising sea levels combine to produce coastal flooding.[126]

"Current flood risk mapping from the U.S. Federal Emergency Management Agency (FEMA) has not accounted for the effects of climate change," the authors said.[127]

Other researchers predict that within 60 years, the climate in 540 urban areas in North America—with a combined population of 250 million—will shift to essentially duplicate the climate of cities much farther to the south. In 2080, for example, living in Washington, D.C., could feel as hot as living near Greenwood, Miss., feels now, according to researchers at the University of Maryland and North Carolina State University. That would mean an increase of 8 degrees Fahrenheit in average temperature.[128]

"Cities in the northeast will tend to feel more like the humid subtropical climates typical of parts of the Midwest or southeastern U.S. today . . . whereas the climates of western cities are expected to become more like those of the desert Southwest or southern California," the researchers said.[129]

NOTES

1. Jack Healy, "They Rode Out Dorian in the Outer Banks. Now Comes the Hard Part," *The New York Times*, Sept. 8, 2019, https://tinyurl.com/yxut5k7a.

2. *Ibid.*

3. Max Golembo, "US sets rain record for 3rd time this year as Gulf prepares for tropical system," *ABC News*, July 9, 2019, https://tinyurl.com/yxh93npc; Allison Mollenkamp, "Floods That Hit The Midwest In March Continue To Affect The Farm Economy," *NPR*, May 21, 2019, https://tinyurl.com/yx9fpdzl; "Global Climate Report—July 2019," National Oceanic and Atmospheric Administration, August 2019, https://tinyurl.com/y3ggxd3z; Jonathan Watts, "Holiday heat headlines not focusing enough on climate crisis reality—experts," *The Guardian*, Aug. 27, 2019, https://tinyurl.com/y366fets; Amanda Schmidt, "May 2019 could be historic month for tornadoes after unprecedented twister streak finally ends at 13 days," AccuWeather, July 12, 2019, https://tinyurl.com/y6p2rols; and Doyle Rice, "Paris sets new temperature record at 108 as Europe heat wave continues to sizzle," *USA Today*, July 25, 2019, https://tinyurl.com/yxhnwl53.

4. James Rainey, "Global warming can make extreme weather worse. Now scientists can say by how much," *NBC News*, Aug. 19, 2018, https://tinyurl.com/ybdu6obc.

5. "Billion-Dollar Weather and Climate Disasters: Overview," National Oceanic and Atmospheric Administration, July 9, 2019, https://tinyurl.com/qakozj4; Jeff Dahdah, "Dorian set to be the seventh billion dollar hurricane for U.S. in four years," *Spectrum News1*, Sept. 10, 2019, https://tinyurl.com/y4735rl2.

6. John Schwartz, "After a Natural Disaster, Is It Better to Rebuild or Retreat?" *The New York Times*, Dec. 13, 2018, https://tinyurl.com/yauxhdmv.

7. Kimberly Amadeo, "Extreme Weather, Its Effect on the Economy and You," *the balance*, June 25, 2019, https://tinyurl.com/y2pmohzp; "Extreme Events," National Oceanic and Atmospheric Administration, undated, https://tinyurl.com/y6zymaqz.

8. "U.S. heat wave frequency and length are increasing," U.S. Global Change Research Program, 2018, https://tinyurl.com/yxf4kg86.

9. "Extreme Precipitation and Climate Change," Center for Climate and Energy Solutions, undated, https://tinyurl.com/y6hsgpzn; "Climate Change Indicators: Heavy Precipitation," U.S. Environmental Protection Agency, undated, https://tinyurl.com/yyywbum4.

10. A. Park Williams *et al.*, "Observed Impacts of Anthropogenic Climate Change on Wildfire in California," *Earth's Future*, Vol. 7, No. 8, July 15, 2019, https://tinyurl.com/yxucv5h6; Robinson Meyer, "California's Wildfires Are 500 Percent

Larger Due to Climate Change," *The Atlantic*, July 16, 2019, https://tinyurl.com/y4lln8qz.

11. Seth Borenstein, "Science Says: Era of Monster Hurricanes Roiling the Atlantic," The Associated Press/WeatherBug, Sept. 10, 2019, https://tinyurl.com/yy7ahmeu.

12. Emma Newburger, "A signal of climate change: Hurricane Dorian stalls over Bahamas, causing massive destruction," *CNBC*, Sept. 3, 2019, https://tinyurl.com/y6fh74jy; Jason Samenow and Andrew Freedman, "Hurricane Dorian poised to slam the Carolinas after scraping the coasts of Florida and Georgia," *The Washington Post*, Sept. 4, 2019, https://tinyurl.com/y26gz2fa; and John Schwartz, "How Has Climate Change Affected Hurricane Dorian?" *The New York Times*, Sept. 3, 2019, https://tinyurl.com/yxvh6yvf.

13. Giorgia Guglielmi, "Hurricanes slow their roll around the world," *Nature*, June 6, 2018, https://tinyurl.com/y6pgnsx3; Merrit Kennedy, "Harvey The 'Most Significant Tropical Cyclone Rainfall Event In U.S. History,' " *NPR*, Jan. 25, 2018, https://tinyurl.com/yyc3qzub.

14. Brady Dennis and Chris Mooney, "Wildfires, hurricanes and other extreme weather cost the nation 247 lives, nearly $100 billion in damage during 2018," *The Washington Post*, Feb. 6, 2019, https://tinyurl.com/y89avatx; Doyle Rice, "Natural disasters caused record $306 billion in damage to U.S. in 2017," *USA Today*, Jan. 8, 2018, https://tinyurl.com/yatrtw3h.

15. Nicola Jones, "Wild Weather and Climate Change: Scientists Are Unraveling the Links," *YaleEnvironment360*, May 9, 2017, https://tinyurl.com/y2ldlq2g; Rainey, *op. cit.*; "The Science Connecting Extreme Weather to Climate Change," Union of Concerned Scientists, undated, https://tinyurl.com/yyafc9ly; Justin Fox, "Climate Change Definitely Probably Caused This Heat Wave," *Bloomberg*, July 26, 2019, https://tinyurl.com/y6kuu4rg; and "Hurricanes and Climate Change," Union of Concerned Scientists, June 25, 2019, https://tinyurl.com/ybo2282m.

16. Ethan Siegel, "This Is Why Global Warming Is Responsible For Freezing Temperatures Across The U.S.," *Forbes*, Jan. 30, 2019, https://tinyurl.com/y5wjotj5; "Future Days Below Freezing," *Climate Central*, Jan. 23, 2019, https://tinyurl.com/y2dbswzt.

17. Zeke Hausfather, "Tornadoes and climate change: what does the science say?" *CarbonBrief*, May 31, 2019, https://tinyurl.com/yyeyoh57; Kevin Williams and Alan Blinder, "Kansas City-Area Tornadoes Add to 12 Straight Days of Destruction," *The New York Times*, May 28, 2019, https://tinyurl.com/yxtuhgve; and Nsikan Akpan, "Is climate change making U.S. tornadoes worse?" *WETA*, March 5, 2019, https://tinyurl.com/y6lo3pt5.

18. "Overview and Report Findings," Global Change Research Program, 2014, https://tinyurl.com/y6rdpkbv.

19. "Fourth National Climate Assessment," Global Change Research Program, 2018, https://tinyurl.com/ybw3k3rr.

20. "Trump says 'climate change goes both ways,' " *BBC News*, June 5, 2019, https://tinyurl.com/y4grp2cj.

21. Wanyun Shao, "Can 2018's extreme weather convince skeptics that the climate is changing?" *The Washington Post*, Dec. 7, 2018, https://tinyurl.com/yxotlvk8.

22. Bill M. Jesdale, Rachel Morello-Frosch and Lara Cushing, "The Racial/Ethnic Distribution of Heat Risk—Related Land Cover in Relation to Residential Segregation," *Environmental Health Perspectives*, July 1, 2013, https://tinyurl.com/y5hh3nzz; Rachel Leven, "Natural Disasters Are Getting Worse. People With The Least Power Are More At Risk," The Center for Public Integrity, April 25, 2019, https://tinyurl.com/yxmogb62; and Junia Howell and James R. Elliott, "As Disaster Costs Rise, So Does Inequality," *Socius*, 2018, https://tinyurl.com/y6sahsqz.

23. Jim Efstathiou Jr. and Prashant Gopal, "How Homes Are Being Built, Raised to Withstand Extreme Weather," *Insurance Journal*, May 13, 2019, https://tinyurl.com/y5e997gt.

24. Noah S. Diffenbaugh, Deepti Singh and Justin S. Mankin, "Unprecedented climate events: Historical changes, aspirational targets, and national commitments," *Science Advances*, Feb. 14, 2018, https://tinyurl.com/y25we8rd.

25. *Ibid.*; "Summary for Policymakers," Intergovernmental Panel on Climate Change, Oct. 8, 2018, https://tinyurl.com/y4wh6cka.

26. Alex Barnum and Sam Delson, "Impacts of climate change in California significant and increasingly stark, new report says," California Environmental Protection Agency, May 9, 2018, https://tinyurl.com/y6sf56jm.

27. Lauren E. McPhillips *et al.*, "Defining Extreme Events: A Cross-Disciplinary Review," *Earth's Future*, Vol. 6, No. 3, Feb. 22, 2018, https://tinyurl.com/y5bpwgwc.

28. David W. Kreutzer, "Hurricane Florence Is Not an Omen About Climate Change," The Heritage Foundation, Sept. 13, 2018, https://tinyurl.com/yxvot24b; "Observations: Atmosphere and Surface," Intergovernmental Panel on Climate Change, 2014, https://tinyurl.com/l4lhs8f; and "Global Warming of 1.5° C," Intergovernmental Panel on Climate Change, Oct. 8, 2018, https://tinyurl.com/ydxvgtdl.

29. Kreutzer, *ibid.*

30. "Global Warming of 1.5° C," *op. cit.*; Brad Plumer and Nadja Popovich, "Why Half a Degree of Global Warming Is a Big Deal," *The New York Times*, Oct. 7, 2018, https://tinyurl.com/yad3lzj7.

31. Stephen Leahy, "Climate change impacts worse than expected, global report warns," *National Geographic*, Oct. 7, 2018, https://tinyurl.com/y97cm5aq.

32. Chris Mooney and John Muyskens, "Dangerous new hot zones are spreading around the world," *The Washington Post*, Sept. 11, 2019, https://tinyurl.com/y26ctye5.

33. Diffenbaugh, Singh and Mankin, *op. cit.*

34. "Future Drought," National Oceanic and Atmospheric Administration, August 2019, https://tinyurl.com/y34r437l; "Global Warming and Hurricanes," Geophysical Fluid Dynamics Laboratory, National Oceanic and Atmospheric Administration, Aug. 15, 2019, https://tinyurl.com/yxerocox.

35. Ian Livingston, "Hurricane Dorian has smashed all sorts of intensity records in the Atlantic Ocean," *The Washington Post*, Sept. 1, 2019, https://tinyurl.com/y5qjhcj3.

36. Kate Wheeling, "Is Climate Change Creating More Tornadoes?" *Pacific Standard*, March 5, 2019, https://tinyurl.com/y2g9mecq; Vittorio A. Gensini and Harold E. Brooks, "Spatial trends in United States tornado frequency," Climate and Atmospheric Science, 2018, https://tinyurl.com/y5obtdmt; and "US tornado frequency shifting eastward from Great Plains," *Science Daily*, Oct. 17, 2018, https://tinyurl.com/yazee2fz.

37. "Is tornado frequency increasing in parts of the U.S.?" National Weather Service, undated, https://tinyurl.com/y5f9qtkt.

38. Joel Achenbach and Angela Fritz, "Climate change is supercharging a hot and dangerous summer," *The Washington Post*, July 26, 2018, https://tinyurl.com/ycywsq88.

39. Charles Duncan, "Hurricane Florence was among the costliest disasters on record. Here's NOAA's tally," *The News & Observer*, Feb. 8, 2019, https://tinyurl.com/y3jcxz6b; "Billion-Dollar Weather and Climate Disasters: Overview," *op. cit.*; Dennis Romero, "California had nation's worst fire season in 2018," *NBC News*, March 9, 2019, https://tinyurl.com/y5rhpm9s; Angela Fritz, "The cost of natural disasters this year: $155 billion," *The Washington Post*, Dec. 26, 2018, https://tinyurl.com/y56urlqz; Laura Santhanam, "2017 is on track to be a record-setting year for massive natural disasters in the U.S.," *WETA*, Oct. 13, 2017, https://tinyurl.com/y87gqfq5; and Adam B. Smith, "2017 U.S. billion-dollar weather and climate disasters: a historic year in context," National Oceanic and Atmospheric Administration, Jan. 8, 2018, https://tinyurl.com/ybkume5y.

40. Adam B. Smith, "2018's Billion Dollar Disasters in Context," National Oceanic and Atmospheric Administration, Feb. 7, 2019, https://tinyurl.com/y6mnyk5o.

41. "Billion-Dollar Disasters Trending Up," *Climate Central*, Dec. 5, 2018, https://tinyurl.com/yyzcefzn.

42. Joel Achenbach, "Extreme weather in 2018 was a raging, howling signal of climate change," *The Washington Post*, Dec. 31, 2018, https://tinyurl.com/yd2eaj52.

43. "Areas At Severe Risk of California Wildfires Are Home to 2.7 Million People, Analysis Finds," The Associated Press and The Weather Channel, April 11, 2019, https://tinyurl.com/y2o7gr4l; "Economics and Demographics," Office for Coastal Management, National Oceanic and Atmospheric Administration, undated, https://tinyurl.com/y4vepfln.

44. "Rating the States," Insurance Institute for Business and Home Safety, March 2018, https://tinyurl.com/y6gdgbsb.

45. Nicolas Loris, "4 Problems With the New Climate Change Report," The Heritage Foundation, Nov. 27, 2018, https://tinyurl.com/yyp4emfo.

46. Nicolas Loris, "Climate Alarmists Admit They Want to Dismantle Our Free-Enterprise System," The Heritage Foundation, Oct. 11, 2018, https://tinyurl.com/yxw8pnuj.

47. Samenow and Freedman, *op. cit.*; Ailsa Chang, "When It Comes To Recent Powerful Storms, Hurricane Dorian Is 1 Of Many," *NPR*, Sept. 2, 2019, https://tinyurl.com/yyff54uv.

48. Chang, *ibid.*

49. "Community impacts from extreme weather shape climate beliefs," *Science Daily*, May 31, 2019, https://tinyurl.com/yxb5p66k.

50. *Ibid.*

51. Frances C. Moore *et al.*, "Rapidly declining remarkability of temperature anomalies may obscure public perception of climate change," *PNAS*, Feb. 25, 2019, https://tinyurl.com/y67sr8ar; Kendra Pierre-Louis, "Extreme Weather Can Feel 'Normal' After Just a Few Years, Study Finds," *The New York Times*, Feb. 26, 2019, https://tinyurl.com/y5lcotbr.

52. "NFIP Proof of Loss claim deadline is just weeks away," Federal Emergency Management Agency, July 24, 2018, https://tinyurl.com/y4ewxn6m.

53. Mark Collette, "Flood Games," *Houston Chronicle*, undated, https://tinyurl.com/y33frbes.

54. "Whom to Call, Where to Go When FEMA Can't Help," Federal Emergency Management Agency, July 29, 2019, https://tinyurl.com/y5b6cw2y; Michael L. Mann *et al.*, "Modeling residential development in California from 2000 to 2050: Integrating wildfire risk, wildland and agricultural encroachment," *Science Direct*, November 2014, https://tinyurl.com/y6nnrwd9.

55. Christopher Flavelle, "Why Is California Rebuilding in Fire Country? Because You're Paying for It," *Bloomberg Businessweek*, March 1, 2018, https://tinyurl.com/yamyoca8.

56. Stephen Paulsen, "Flood the market," *grist*, Aug. 27, 2019, https://tinyurl.com/y4rok79a.

57. "4 ways to strengthen coastal communities' resilience before the next storm," Environmental Defense Fund, April 12, 2019, https://tinyurl.com/y3g9ltup.

58. Sahil Chinoy, "The Places in the U.S. Where Disaster Strikes Again and Again," *The New York Times*, May 24, 2018, https://tinyurl.com/ybc4zd45; Greg Morago, "The 'King and Queen of Disaster' look back at Harvey flooding," *Houston Chronicle*, Aug. 27, 2018, https://tinyurl.com/y32gk5h6.

59. Flavelle, *op. cit.*

60. Doug Smith, "After California's most destructive fire season, a debate over where to rebuild homes," *Los Angeles Times*, Dec. 16, 2017, https://tinyurl.com/y56tc7gq.

61. John Schwartz, "As Floods Keep Coming, Cities Pay Residents to Move," *The New York Times*, July 6, 2019, https://tinyurl.com/y4alwa75.

62. Jen Schwartz, "Surrendering to Rising Seas," *Scientific American*, Aug. 1, 2018, https://tinyurl.com/y9hodsj5.

63. David A. Lieb, "AP: Flood Buyout Costs Rise as Storms Intensify, Seas Surge," *U.S. News & World Report*, May 28, 2019, https://tinyurl.com/yy5kgo3w.

64. "A Brief Introduction to the National Flood Insurance Program," Congressional Research

Service, Aug. 14, 2019, https://tinyurl.com/y6rulye2; Doug Smith, *op. cit.*

65. Doug Smith, *ibid.*

66. Cathleen Kelly, Kristina Costa and Sarah Edelman, "Safe, Strong, and Just Rebuilding after Hurricanes Harvey, Irma and Maria," Center for American Progress, Oct. 3, 2017, https://tinyurl.com/ya2ectbp.

67. Anna Bahney, "These homes can withstand hurricanes, earthquakes and fires," *CNN Business*, Oct. 8, 2018, https://tinyurl.com/ycgvbz5u.

68. Mishana Khot, "The Five Deadly Extinctions In Earth's History," The Weather Channel, July 13, 2018, https://tinyurl.com/y4s3jxfw.

69. Andrew Glikson, "Another link between CO2 and mass extinctions of species," *The Conversation*, March 21, 2013, https://tinyurl.com/y3uly4hp.

70. "675 m.p.h. 'Hypercanes' May Be Cause Of Ancient Mass Extinctions," *Chicago Tribune*, Sept. 10, 1995, https://tinyurl.com/y2dzg4c4; Kerry A. Emanuel *et al.*, "Hypercanes: A possible link in global extinction scenarios," *Journal of Geophysical Research: Atmospheres*, July 20, 1995, https://tinyurl.com/y2mnefpw.

71. "Ancient stormy weather: World's oldest weather report could revise bronze age chronology," University of Chicago and *Science Daily*, April 1, 2014, https://tinyurl.com/y3ahf2vn.

72. Stefan Lovgren, "Angkor Wat's Collapse From Climate Change Has Lessons for Today," *National Geographic*, April 5, 2017, https://tinyurl.com/y2xfzp9x; "Extreme weather preceded collapse of ancient Maya civilization," University of California-Davis and *Science Daily*, Nov. 8, 2012, https://tinyurl.com/y6nfgfus; and Catie Leary, "5 ancient civilizations that were destroyed by climate change," *MNN*, May 12, 2016, https://tinyurl.com/y6lumeza.

73. K. Jan Oosthoek, "Little Ice Age," Environmental History Resources, June 5, 2015, https://tinyurl.com/yawyxwf7; Richard Black, "Volcanic origin for Little Ice Age," *BBC News*, Jan. 30, 2012, https://tinyurl.com/yynx2dxu.

74. "Great Hurricane of 1780," *History*, April 12, 2019, https://tinyurl.com/yx9rkd9n.

75. Hans Kaper, "The Discovery of Global Warming," Rutgers University and American Institute of Physics, undated, https://tinyurl.com/y4sxulg2; "1820-1930: Fourier to Arrhenius," CO2.earth, undated, https://tinyurl.com/y3gj22yq.

76. Elisabeth Crawford, "Svante Arrhenius," Encyclopaedia Britannica, undated, https://tinyurl.com/y4sbe4mz; "Svante Arrhenius," *Famous Scientists*, undated, https://tinyurl.com/y49kcjpc.

77. "Blizzard brings tragedy to Northwest Plains," *History*, Nov. 13, 2009, https://tinyurl.com/y5b9h53j; Becky Oskin, "The 10 Worst Blizzards in US History," LiveScience, Feb. 8, 2013, https://tinyurl.com/y5a9j8rn; and Kim Estep, "The Peshtigo Fire," *Green Bay Press-Gazette* and National Weather Service, undated, https://tinyurl.com/y4mkstjb.

78. "History of the National Weather Service," National Weather Service, undated, https://tinyurl.com/yxunvecn.

79. Adam Augustyn, "Tri-State Tornado of 1925," Encyclopaedia Britannica, undated, https://tinyurl.com/y9bpzycr; "The Dust Bowl," National Drought Mitigation Center, University of Nebraska, undated, https://tinyurl.com/yylowsng.

80. John Upton, "Scientists Trace Climate-Heat Link Back to 1930s," *Climate Central*, March 9, 2016, https://tinyurl.com/y9k269t8.

81. Charles C. Mann, "Meet the Amateur Scientist Who Discovered Climate Change," *Wired*, Jan. 23, 2010, https://tinyurl.com/y98t5etp; James Rodger Fleming, "The Callendar Effect," American Meteorological Society, 2007, https://tinyurl.com/y4j99qek.

82. "From A Dimmer Past to a Brighter Future?" NASA, Nov. 5, 2007, https://tinyurl.com/y9q2alsy; Catherine Brahic, "Climate myths: The cooling after 1940 shows CO2 does not cause warming," *New Scientist*, May 16, 2007, https://tinyurl.com/jfbg79a.

83. Robert Reinhold, "Evidence is Found of Warming Trend," *The New York Times*, Oct. 19, 1981, https://tinyurl.com/y36fm27e.

84. "About the IPCC," Intergovernmental Panel on Climate Change, undated, https://tinyurl.com/y328s33m.

85. "Legal Mandate," U.S. Global Change Research Program, Nov. 16, 1990, https://tinyurl.com/y4ytzqsr.

86. U.S. Global Change Research Program, *Climate Change Impacts on the United States: The Potential Consequences of Climate Variability and Change* (2000), https://tinyurl.com/hc349th.

87. "Hurricane Costs," National Oceanic and Atmospheric Administration, July 10, 2019, https://tinyurl.com/y6ouof2s; "Hurricane Sandy Fast Facts," *CNN*, Oct. 29, 2018, https://tinyurl.com/ybd7unn8.

88. *Climate Change Impacts on the United States, op. cit.*

89. "Extreme Weather," U.S. Global Change Research Program, 2014, https://tinyurl.com/y93s6fkm.

90. "Historic Paris Agreement on Climate Change: 195 Nations Set Path to Keep Temperature Rise Well Below 2 Degrees Celsius," United Nations, Dec. 13, 2015, https://tinyurl.com/yy5jlmq7.

91. "Explaining Extreme Events from a Climate Perspective," American Meteorological Society, December 2018, https://tinyurl.com/hdktbd4.

92. Adam Smith, *op. cit.*; Robinson Meyer, "The Indoor Man in the White House," *The Atlantic*, Jan. 13, 2019, https://tinyurl.com/yxcqcwy6.

93. "High-Risk Series: Substantial Efforts Needed to Achieve Greater Progress on High-Risk Areas," Government Accountability Office, March 2019, https://tinyurl.com/y5qbs2fq.

94. Caitlin Werrell and Francesco Femia, "GAO Report: U.S. Government Has Regressed on Managing Climate Change Risks," The Center for Climate and Security, March 8, 2019, https://tinyurl.com/y54nvvmh.

95. Umair Irfan, "The severe floods soaking the Midwest and Southeast are not letting up," *Vox*, June 11, 2019, https://tinyurl.com/y52a5kqy; Richard Fausset, Nicholas Bogel-Burroughs and Patricia Mazzei, "Carolinas Hit by Winds, Floods and Tornadoes," *The New York Times*, Sept. 6, 2019, https://tinyurl.com/y2tacrj2; and "National Flood Insurance Program: Reauthorization," Federal Emergency Management Agency, June 11, 2019, https://tinyurl.com/y4dazchr.

96. "The National Flood Insurance Program: Critical Issues and Needed Reforms," Environmental and Energy Study Institute, undated, https://tinyurl.com/y6bcwawu; Michelle Cottle, "Can Congress Bring the National Flood Insurance Program Above Water?" *The Atlantic*, Aug. 5, 2017, https://tinyurl.com/yayynsyn; and "Menendez Co-Leads Bipartisan Push for Comprehensive Flood Insurance Reforms," press release, Office of Sen. Bob Menendez, May 23, 2019, https://tinyurl.com/y284fco4.

97. Cottle, *ibid.*

98. "NFIP Transformation and Risk Rating 2.0," Federal Emergency Management Agency, May 22, 2019, https://tinyurl.com/y56jrf72.

99. Kathleen Howley, "Congress approves a 4-month rescue of flood insurance program," *Housing Wire*, June 4, 2019, https://tinyurl.com/yy8ryojl.

100. "National Flood Insurance Program: Reauthorization," *op. cit.*

101. David Levinsky, "Menendez unveils bill to reform federal flood insurance program, cap premium hikes," *Burlington County Times*, July 17, 2019, https://tinyurl.com/y2jtna8a; "S.2187—National Flood Insurance Program Reauthorization and Reform Act of 2019," Congress.gov, undated, https://tinyurl.com/yyezebcv; and "NJ, NY Senators Convene Sandy Task Force," press release, Office of Sen. Bob Menendez, April 28, 2015, https://tinyurl.com/y6ejntaw.

102. Levinsky, *ibid.*

103. Coral Davenport and Mark Landler, "Trump Administration Hardens Its Attack on Climate Science," *The New York Times*, May 27, 2019, https://tinyurl.com/y2v5s9ff.

104. *Ibid.*

105. *Ibid.*

106. Richard Gonzales, "FEMA Drops 'Climate Change' From Its Strategic Plan," *NPR*, March 15, 2018, https://tinyurl.com/y8tkdhg4.

107. Helena Bottemiller Evich, "Agriculture Department buries studies showing dangers of climate change," *Politico*, June 23, 2019, https://tinyurl.com/yxbzqhnq.

108. *Ibid.*

109. Kayla Epstein *et al.*, "NOAA's chief scientist will investigate why agency backed Trump over its experts on Dorian, email shows," *The Washington Post*, Sept. 9, 2019, https://tinyurl.com/y296hv6u.

110. "Letter to the President of the United States: 58 Senior Military and National Security Leaders Denounce NSC Climate Panel," The Center for Climate and Security, March 5, 2019, https://tinyurl.com/yx8vzv67.

111. "Worldwide Threat Assessment of the U.S. Intelligence Community," Daniel R. Coats, Director of National Intelligence, Jan. 29, 2019, https://tinyurl.com/y9r6kkhu.

112. *Ibid.*

113. "Internal Displacement From January To June 2019," Internal Displacement Monitoring Center, Sept. 12, 2019, https://tinyurl.com/y4h5bk75.

114. *Ibid.*

115. Brady Dennis, Steven Mufson and Scott Clement, "Americans increasingly see climate change as a crisis, poll shows," *The Washington Post*, Sept. 13, 2019, https://tinyurl.com/yyvcrnv8.

116. Aylin Woodward, "What the 10 Democrats running for president each think the US should do about climate change," *Business Insider*, Sept. 7, 2019, https://tinyurl.com/yykejxey.

117. "How cap and trade works," Environmental Defense Fund, undated, https://tinyurl.com/p9dp6qy.

118. Woodward, *op. cit.*

119. *Ibid.*; Matt Mossman, "Renewable Energy Debate," *CQ Researcher*, March 15, 2019, https://tinyurl.com/yywe9rhy.

120. *Ibid.*

121. "Extreme weather events linked to poor mental health," *Science Daily*, Sept. 5, 2019, https://tinyurl.com/y3rglofr.

122. Zelde Espinel *et al.*, "Forecast: Increasing Mental Health Consequences From Atlantic Hurricanes Throughout the 21st Century," *Psychiatric Services*, Aug. 12, 2019, https://tinyurl.com/y5eomgpr.

123. Henry Fountain, "A Software Upgrade (After 40 Years) Aims to Improve U.S. Weather Forecasts," *The New York Times*, June 12, 2019, https://tinyurl.com/y2go7sl3.

124. Robin Cooper, "The Impacts of Extreme Heat on Mental Health," *Psychiatric Times*, July 30, 2019, https://tinyurl.com/y3eeahgr.

125. *Ibid.*

126. Jen A. Miller, " '100-year' floods will happen every one to 30 years, according to new coastal flood prediction maps," Princeton University, Aug. 27, 2019, https://tinyurl.com/y5kac9yc; Reza Marsooli *et al.*, "Climate change exacerbates hurricane flood hazards along US Atlantic and Gulf Coasts in spatially varying patterns," *Nature Communications*, Aug. 22, 2019, https://tinyurl.com/y4hatwjm.

127. *Ibid.*

128. Matthew C. Fitzpatrick, "Contemporary climatic analogs for 540 North American urban areas in the late 21st century," *Nature Communications*, Feb. 12, 2019, https://tinyurl.com/y97ks2v9, "U.S. climate data," usclimatedata.com, 2019, https://tinyurl.com/y5uuvp48.

129. Fitzpatrick, *ibid.*

BIBLIOGRAPHY
Books

Blum, Andrew, *The Weather Machine: A Journey Inside the Forecast*, Ecco, 2019.
A science journalist shows how weather observation and meteorological theory merged to produce the contemporary approach to weather forecasting.

Brannen, Peter, *The Ends of the World: Volcanic Apocalypses, Lethal Oceans, and Our Quest to Understand Earth's Past Mass Extinctions*, Ecco, 2017.
A science journalist offers a lively telling of how ancient climate and weather conditions led to the five mass extinctions in Earth's history.

Kolbert, Elizabeth, *Field Notes from a Catastrophe: Man, Nature, and Climate Change*, Bloomsbury USA, 2006.
This modern environmental classic by an award-winning writer at The New Yorker reports on the frontiers of climate change, from rapidly changing Inuit villages to policymaking circles in Washington, D.C.

Wallace-Wells, David, *The Uninhabitable Earth: Life After Warming*, Tim Duggan Books, 2019.
A deputy editor at *New York* magazine offers a vivid and alarming narrative about how climate change can bring about future weather catastrophes, as well as transform global and human progress.

Articles

"Climate Change Is Sinking the National Flood Insurance Program," **Natural Resources Defense Council**, 2017, https://tinyurl.com/y3rd7xh2.
An environmental advocacy group highlights ongoing problems with a national program that subsidizes flood insurance premiums for people who live in areas at high risk of extreme weather.

Campbell, SueEllen, "Farm Bureau shows little concern about climate change ag effects," **Yale Climate Connections**, April 16, 2019, https://tinyurl.com/y3xhca5m.
An environmental writer and retired English professor says that despite recent droughts and excess rainfall that have imperiled crops, the American Farm Bureau Federation, the most influential agricultural organization in the nation, remains unconvinced that human-caused climate change is real "and disapproves of nearly all proposed means of lessening its impacts."

Comen, Evan, "Here are 20 places where weather is getting worse because of climate change," *24/7 Wall Street and USA Today*, Aug. 4, 2019, https://tinyurl.com/y2uodpmh.

Researchers interview climate scientists and examine evidence connecting recent extreme weather events to climate change.

Robinson, Meyer, "How Climate Change Could Trigger the Next Global Financial Crisis," *The Atlantic*, Aug. 1, 2019, https://tinyurl.com/y2huu3qd.
In an interview, Adam Tooze, an author and economic historian at Columbia University, describes potential financial pitfalls of climate change.

Simon, Ruth, "One House, 22 Floods: Repeated Claims Drain Federal Insurance Program," *The Wall Street Journal*, Sept. 15, 2017, https://tinyurl.com/yd7atzoa.
A reporter focuses on a Texas homeowner who received more than $1.8 million from the National Flood Insurance Program to repeatedly rebuild his $800,000 home in the wake of hurricanes.

Reports and Studies

"Attribution of Extreme Weather Events in the Context of Climate Change," **National Academies of Sciences, Engineering and Medicine**, 2016, https://tinyurl.com/y6q3kh2r.
Experts provide an overview of how scientists are connecting climate change to extreme weather events.

"Extreme Weather and Climate Change," **Center for Climate and Energy Solutions**, 2019, https://tinyurl.com/y8gpmt9u.
This interactive infographic shows major weather disasters and how scientists believe those events are linked to climate change.

"Fourth National Climate Assessment Volume II: Impacts, Risks, and Adaptation in the United States," **U.S. Global Change Research Program**, 2018, https://tinyurl.com/ybw3k3rr.
This federally mandated report summarizes recent research in the wake of destructive hurricanes, wildfires and other events and suggests that extreme weather could worsen.

"Special Report on climate change, desertification, land degradation, sustainable land management, food security, and greenhouse gas fluxes in terrestrial ecosystems," Intergovernmental Panel on Climate Change, Aug. 8, 2019, https://tinyurl.com/y6dlmvog.

A report from a United Nations group that assesses the science related to global warming includes contributions from more than 100 scientists in 52 countries and focuses on how land systems will be affected by climate change and extreme weather.

Herring, Stephanie, *et al.*, "Explaining Extreme Events of 2017 from a Climate Perspective," *Bulletin of the American Meteorological Society*, Feb. 15, 2019, https://tinyurl.com/hdktbd4.

The most recent issue of the society's annual report on extreme weather includes studies that quantify the impact of climate change on droughts, floods and hurricanes worldwide.

THE NEXT STEP

Climate Change

Mann, Michael, and Andrew E. Dessler, "Global heating made Hurricane Dorian bigger, wetter—and more deadly," *The Guardian*, Sept. 4, 2019, https://tinyurl.com/yxlxhyl9.

Two climate experts explain how warmer ocean waters may have strengthened Hurricane Dorian.

Minchin, Rod, and Phoebe Weston, "Harsh winters are not triggered by loss of Artic sea ice, study finds," *The Independent*, Aug. 12, 2019, https://tinyurl.com/y4urbsab.

Weather experts in Europe determined that random fluctuations in atmospheric circulation, not the loss of Arctic sea ice, likely caused unusually cold winters in more moderate latitudes.

Myers, Chad, "I am a CNN meteorologist. I used to be a climate crisis skeptic," *CNN*, Sept. 4, 2019, https://tinyurl.com/y249ojwb.

A CNN meteorologist explains how he became convinced that greenhouse gas emissions affect the climate and lead to extreme weather events.

Climate Modeling

"New climate model for the IPCC," Alfred Wegener Institute and Phys.org, Sept. 6, 2019, https://tinyurl.com/yxdl7ysv.

A German research institute explains how its global climate model works and announces plans to make its data part of the next global climate assessment issued by an international panel on climate change.

Snowden, Scott, "Greenland's Massive Ice Melt Wasn't Supposed to Happen Until 2070," *Forbes*, Aug. 16, 2019, https://tinyurl.com/y26euwrm.

Greenland's ice sheet is melting at a rate that was not supposed to happen until 2070, according to many climate models.

Temple, James, "Climate change or just crazy weather? How improving tools make it easier to tell," *MIT Technology Review*, Aug. 15, 2019, https://tinyurl.com/yyfxsud2.

Climate models have improved enough in just the past few years to give scientists a better understanding of the relationship between global warming and extreme weather.

Disaster-Proof Homes

Barlyn, Suzanne, "How Insurers Help Design High-End Homes That Mitigate Disaster Risk," *Insurance Journal*, Aug. 30, 2019, https://tinyurl.com/y452227f.

Some insurers offer to help design luxury properties to withstand disasters, a service that will become more popular if extreme weather events become more frequent.

Lazarus, Eli, and Evan B. Goldstein, "Why are Atlantic and Gulf coast property owners building back bigger after hurricanes?" *The Conversation*, July 23, 2019, https://tinyurl.com/y62o7mpf.

Two climate experts say building codes that require storm-proofing send mixed signals about which areas are safe for development.

Peters, Adele, "This hurricane-proof home is made from 600,000 plastic bottles," *Fast Company*, July 2, 2019, https://tinyurl.com/yyvacmfa.

A Canadian startup company recently unveiled a prototype of a house in Nova Scotia that is environmentally friendly and can withstand extreme weather.

National Flood Insurance Program

"Editorial: People keep building and waters keep rising," *The* (Fredericksburg, Va.) *Free Lance-Star*, Sept. 4, 2019, https://tinyurl.com/y5j9ejfk.

Editors at a Virginia newspaper say state and federal officials should provide subsidies to local governments to help them absorb tax revenue losses they incur by discouraging development in flood-prone areas.

Brodsky, Robert, "How 2020 revamp of federal flood insurance rates could affect you," *Newsday,* **April 6, 2019, https://tinyurl.com/y6zaz8sd.**
The Federal Emergency Management Agency's planned revamp of flood insurance assessments is expected to increase premiums for expensive waterfront homes and decrease premiums for less expensive homes farther inland.

Lucas, Dave, "Schumer Seeks Changes to National Flood Insurance Program," WAMC, Sept. 6, 2019, https://tinyurl.com/y2l48a8g.
Sen. Chuck Schumer, D-N.Y., stood with homeowners in flood zones to promote his proposal to limit premium increases under the National Flood Insurance Program.

For More Information

350.org, 20 Jay St., Suite 732, Brooklyn, NY 11201; 802-448-0839; 350.org. Organization that advocates for ways to decrease fossil fuel use and address climate change.

California Department of Forestry & Fire Protection, 1416 Ninth St., P.O. Box 944246, Sacramento, CA 94244-2460; 916-653-5123; fire.ca.gov. State agency that monitors wildfires and provides real-time updates on them.

American Farm Bureau Federation, 600 Maryland Ave., S.W., Suite 1000 W, Washington DC 20024; 202-406-3600; fb.org. Organization that advocates on behalf of agricultural interests.

Intergovernmental Panel on Climate Change, World Meteorological Organization, 7 bis Avenue de la Paix, C.P. 2300, CH-1211 Geneva 2, Switzerland; +41 22 730 8208/54/84; ipcc.ch. International organization of scientists that focuses on climate change.

National Flood Insurance Program, c/o FEMA, 500 C St., S.W., Washington, DC 20472; 800-621-FEMA; floodsmart.gov. Government program that provides flood insurance for homes in high-risk areas.

National Oceanic and Atmospheric Administration, 1401 Constitution Ave., N.W., Room 5128, Washington, DC 20230; 301-427-9855; noaa.gov. Scientific agency within the Commerce Department that monitors weather and climate.

National Weather Service, 1325 East West Highway, Silver Spring, MD 20910; 828-271-4800; weather.gov. Federal agency that supports weather research, monitors weather conditions and issues warnings for extreme weather events.